CODES
CHE

WINTER 2009 EDITION

Prima Games
An Imprint of Random House, Inc.
3000 Lava Ridge Court, Suite 100
Roseville, CA 95661
www.primagames.com

Code Compiler: Nasson Boroumand
Product Manager: Jason Wigle
Design & Layout: Winter Graphics North
Manufacturing: Suzanne Goodwin

ISBN: 978-07615-5948-1
Library of Congress Catalog Card Number: 2008930548
Printed in the United States of America

08 09 10 11 HH 10 9 8 7 6 5 4 3 2 1

Table of Contents - DS

Alex Rider: Stormbreaker

Enter the password screen from the main menu and input the following.

Password	Effect
JESSICA PARKER	Allows you to purchase black belt
6943059	Allows you to purchase disk 6 after completing game
VICTORIA PARR	Allows you to purchase M16 badge
RENATO CELANI	Allows you to purchase the fugu
SARYL HIRSCH	Allows you to purchase the sunglasses
9785711	Allows you to select level HARD
4298359	Everything at shop is at half price!
9603717	Gallery is added to Secret mode
5204025	Get 10,000 spy points
6894098	Outfit change is added to Secret mode

Animaniacs: Lights, Camera, Action!

To activate a cheat, pause the game and enter the code, then un-pause the game.

Cheat Codes

Code	Effect
L, R, ←, ←, ↑, ↑	Disable Time
→, →, →, ←, ←, ←, R, L	Kingsize Pickups
L, L, R, R, ↓, ↓	Skip Level
Wakko, Wakko, Wakko, Wakko, Wakko	Level 1
Dot, Yakko, Brain, Wakko, Pinky	Level 2
Yakko, Dot, Wakko, Wakko, Brain	Level 3
Pinky, Yakko, Yakko, Dot, Brain	Level 4
Pinky, Pinky, Yakko, Wakko, Wakko	Level 5
Brain, Dot, Brain, Pinky, Yakko	Level 6
Brain, Pinky, Wakko, Pinky, Brain	Level 7
Brain Pinky, Pinky, Wakko, Wakko	Level 8
Dot, Dot, Yakko, Pinky, Wakko	Level 9
Brain, Dot, Brain, Yakko, Wakko	Level 10
Akko, Yakko, Pinky, Dot, Dot	Level 11
Pinky, Pinky, Brain, Dot, Wakko	Level 12
Yakko, Wakko, Pinky, Wakko, Brain	Level 13
Pinky, Wakko, Brain, Wakko, Yakko	Level 14
Dot, Pinky, Wakko, Wakko, Yakko	Level 15

Bust a Move DS

Enter this code at the Main menu.

Unlockable	Code
Sound Test	[SELECT], Ⓐ, Ⓑ, ←, →, Ⓐ, [SELECT], →

The Chronicles of Narnia: The Lion, The Witch, and The Wardrobe

Enter these codes at the Main menu.

Unlockable	Code
Acquire Armor	Ⓐ, Ⓧ, Ⓨ, Ⓑ, ↑, ↑, ↑, ↓
All Blessings	←, ↑, Ⓐ, Ⓑ, →, ↓, Ⓧ, Ⓨ
All Skills at Maximum	Ⓐ, ←, →, Ⓑ, ↓, ↑, Ⓧ, Ⓧ
Extra Money	↑, Ⓧ, ↑, Ⓧ, ↓, Ⓑ, ↓, Ⓑ
Invincibility	Ⓐ, Ⓨ, Ⓧ, Ⓑ, ↑, ↑, ↓, ↓
Maximum Attributes	←, Ⓑ, ↑, Ⓨ, ↓, Ⓧ, →, Ⓐ
Restore Health	←, →, ↑, ↓, Ⓐ, Ⓐ, Ⓐ, Ⓐ
Stronger Attacks	Ⓐ, ↑, Ⓑ, ↓, Ⓧ, Ⓧ, Ⓨ, Ⓨ

Disney's Kim Possible Kimmunicator

Enter these codes while playing—do not pause. You must hold down [L]+[R] to enter these codes.

Unlockable	Code
9,999 parts	Ⓨ, Ⓨ, Ⓧ, Ⓑ, Ⓐ, Ⓨ
99 lives	Ⓐ, Ⓐ, Ⓐ, Ⓨ, Ⓧ, Ⓨ, Ⓑ, Ⓐ
Don't lose lives	Ⓨ, Ⓨ, Ⓨ, Ⓧ
Extra Life	Ⓐ, Ⓐ, Ⓐ, Ⓨ, Ⓧ, Ⓨ
Full Health	Ⓐ, Ⓐ, Ⓐ, Ⓨ
Invincibility	Ⓨ, Ⓨ, Ⓨ, Ⓧ, Ⓐ, Ⓑ
Unlock all gadgets	Ⓨ, Ⓨ, Ⓧ, Ⓑ, Ⓐ, Ⓨ, Ⓨ, Ⓐ
Unlock all missions	Ⓧ, Ⓨ, Ⓧ, Ⓐ, Ⓧ, Ⓑ
Unlock all outfits	Ⓑ, Ⓐ, Ⓧ, Ⓨ, Ⓐ, Ⓑ

Dragon Booster

At the Main menu, select Password to enter these cheats.

Unlockable	Password
999,999 Dracles	8, 9, 7, 10, 5, 13
Blue Energy Bolt Gear Obtained	9, 2, 13, 8, 1, 12
Draculim Bars are replaced by sushi in All City Race/Free Run	7, 8, 13, 12, 10, 10
Dragon Booster and Legendary Beau are unlocked	12, 6, 12, 10, 13, 3
Dragon-Human Duel vs. Reepyr	1, 9, 3, 6, 5, 2
Green Charging Gear Obtained	5, 12, 13, 5, 8, 11
Shadow Booster and Shadow Dragon are unlocked	2, 5, 4, 11, 6, 2
Skills Competition vs. Wulph	13, 9, 8, 12, 10, 1
Sprint Meter can't be recharged	1, 7, 5, 3, 2, 11
Take Super Damage from obstacles and opponents in All City Race/Free Run	11, 11, 11, 11, 11, 11
Unlimited sprint meter	9, 13, 6, 5, 5, 12

DS | PSP | PS2 | PS3 | Wii | Xbox | Xbox 360 | Index

Dragon Quest Monsters: Joker

Monsters

Unlockable	How to Unlock
Empyrea	Obtain ALL monsters.
Grandpa Slime	Obtain 200 monsters.
Leopold	Obtain ALL skills.
Liquid Metal Slime	Obtain 100 monsters.
Metal Kaiser Slime	Obtain 150 skills.
Metal King Slime	Obtain 100 skills.
Robbin' Hood	Complete both monster and skill libraries.
Trode	Complete both monster and skill libraries and speak to the skill library NPC.

Elements of Destruction

Codes

Pause the game and hold the following four buttons simultaneously.

Unlockable	How to Unlock
Unlimited Energy	Y, L, →, SELECT
Unlimited Time	X, R, ↓, SELECT

All Levels

Hold down the following buttons during the first cutscene to unlock all levels for the current profile.

Unlockable	How to Unlock
Unlock All Levels	B, L, SELECT

Juiced 2: Hot Import Nights

Codes

Enter the codes in the cheat menu.

Unlockable	How to Unlock
$5,000 Added to Balance	HSAC
All Cars Unlocked	SRAC
All Races Unlocked	EDOM
All Tracks Unlocked	KART

LEGO Batman

Codes

Enter the following codes at the main menu. If you enter them correctly you will hear a sound.

Effect	Code
Add 1 Million Studs	X, Y, B, B, Y, X, L, L, R, R, ↑, ↓, ←, →, START, SELECT
All Characters	X, ↑, B, ↓, Y, ←, START, →, R, R, L, R, R, ↓, ↓, ↑, Y, Y, Y, START, SELECT
All Episodes and Free Play mode	→, ↑, R, L, X, Y, →, ←, B, L, R, L, ↓, ↓, ↑, ^, Y, X, X, B, B, ↑, ↑, L, R, START, SELECT
All Extras	↑, ↓, L, R, L, R, ←, →, X, X, Y, Y, B, B, L, ↑, ↓, L, R, L, R, ↑, ↑, ↓, START, SELECT

LEGO Indiana Jones: The Original Adventures

Codes

Effect	Code
All Characters Unlocked	Ⓧ, Up, Ⓑ, Down, Ⓨ, Left, START, Right, R, R, L, R, R, Down, Down, Up, Ⓨ, Ⓨ, Ⓨ, START, SELECT
All Episodes Unlocked + Free Play	Right, Up, R, L, Ⓧ, Ⓨ, Right, Left, 4, L, R, L, Down, Down, Up, Ⓨ, Ⓨ, Ⓧ, Ⓧ, 4, 4, Up, Up, L, R, START, SELECT
All Extras Unlocked	Up, Down, L, R, L, R, L, Left, Right, Ⓧ, Ⓧ, Ⓨ, Ⓨ, 4, 4, L, Up, Down, L, R, L, R, Up, Up, Down, &, SELECT
Start with 1,000,000 Studs	Ⓧ, Ⓨ, 4, 4, Ⓨ, Ⓧ, L, L, R, R, Up, Down, Left, Right, START, SELECT
Start with 3,000,000 Studs	Up, Up, 4, Down, Down, Ⓧ, Left, Left, Ⓨ, L, R, L, R, 4, Ⓨ, Ⓧ, START, SELECT

LEGO Star Wars II: The Original Trilogy

Enter this password in the Cantina.

Unlockable	Password
10 extra studs	4PR28U

Luminous Arc

Unlockables

Completion bonuses are available after you finish the game by hitting Ⓧ when "Fin" is on the screen after the credits. Save the game, and then replay with all of your attained levels and items, as well as being able to access "Mysteria Ruins" (north of the starting location), and extras such as music, sound effects, and character profiles.

Madden NFL 2005

Codes

Touch the small spot in the middle of the main menu to display the cheat entry box. Then enter one of the following codes to activate the corresponding cheat function:

Code	Effect
SMASHMOUTH	Harder hits
SUPERSLICK	More fumbles
BADPASS	More interceptions
SAD SACK	More sacks
SHORTTIME	Opponent gets 3 downs
LONGTIME	You get 5 downs

Mega Man Battle Network 5: Double Team

Codes

Highlight the corresponding program from the list and hold down the right button. Then push the following buttons to compress them by one block. To uncompress them, just repeat the above process again.

Code	Effect
BLBABLBBAA	Air Shoes
RBBARBRARB	Anti-Damage
LLLRRBARBL	Attack MAX
RLRLRBBRAB	Auto Recover
AABRABRLLR	Battery
ABBRAABRBR	Beat
BARABRLRRA	Body Pack
BABLABRLRB	Bug Stop
LLRARLBLAR	Buster Pack
ALAARBRBAR	Charge MAX
RRBBRBRBAA	Chivalry
BRALARBAAB	Collect

Mega Man Battle Network 5: Double Team (continued)

Code	Effect	Code	Effect
AARLBABALB	Custom+1	AABLARBLAA	Mega Virus
BARLLRALBR	Custom+2	RLRARRLLLR	Millions
RLABBARALR	First Barrier	LBRARLABLB	Oil Body
BABALRARAA	Fish	LLRBLLAALB	Reflect
ALLBRLAAAL	Float Shoes	RBLRBRLLRL	Rush
RRLBLLARBL	Giga Folder +1	ABARALRBBA	Shield
BBRALBLARR	Giga Virus	RLLALLBABB	Sneak Run
ALRABLRALR	Hub Batch	RARLLRRABA	Speed MAX
ABLARABLRL	Humor	RABRALLRBA	Super Armor
LRLABLBBLA	Jungle	LBLABLABAL	Tango
LABBLBAALL	Mega Folder +2	ARBBRLRALA	Undershirt
BBABBRRLAR	Mega Folder+1		

Prize Codes

Go to the numberman machine in Higsby's shop when it is placed there, and enter the passwords to get your prize. These codes can only be used for the DS version, they won't work on the GBA versions.

Code	Effect	Code	Effect
99428938	Area Steal	76820385	P.Attack+3
91182599	Dark Recovery	48582829	P.Chip+50
78234329	DoroTsunamiBall	28475692	P.HP+100
01285874	Leaders Raid L	53891756	P.HP+50
39285712	Lord of Chaos X	29486933	Super Kitakaze
29387483	MagmaSeed	12495783	Sword
64836563	NumberBall	85375720	TP Chip
22323856	P. Battle Pack 1	19283746	Tsunami Hole
66426428	P. Battle Pack 2	15733751	Unlocker

Numberman Navi Customizer Program Codes

Enter these codes in the Numberman Lotto Number to get a Navi customizer program

Password	Effect	Password	Effect
25465278	Anti Aqua*	68799876	Dark Invis*
35607360	Anti Elec*	52052687	Death Match 3 V
73877466	Anti Fire*	91098051	DjangoSP D
05068930	Anti Navi V	83143652	Fast Gauge*
44213168	Anti Recovery P	12118790	Full Energy
10386794	Anti Sword R	90914896	Full Energy
10133670	Anti Wood*	68942679	Grab Revenge P
63231870	Attack MAX (Yellow NCP)	35321321	Gun Del Sol 3 O
79877132	BeatSupport NCP	90630807	HP +200 (Pink NCP)
30112002	BodyPack (Green)	48785625	HP+300 (Pink NCP)
50364410	Bug Fix*	13926561	HP+300 (White NCP)
80246758	BusterPack NCP	03419893	HP+400 (Pink NCP)
87412146	Charge MAX (White NCP)	45654128	HP+400 (Yellow)
15595587	Custom 2	31084443	HP+50 NCP
07765623	Custom Bolt 3 G	50906652	HP+500 (Pink)

Mega Man Battle Network 5: Double Team (continued)

Password	Effect	Password	Effect
72846472	HP+500 (White NCP)	78987728	Spin Green
29789661	Lock Enemy	30356451	Spin Red
97513648	Mega Folder 2 NCP	48958798	Static S
18746897	Recovery 300 Y	54288793	Tango (Green)
09609807	Rush (Yellow)	73978713	Unlocker
64892292	Sneakrun	28706568	Unlocker
28256341	SoulT+1 (Yellow)	64664560	Unlocker
36695497	Speed MAX (Pink NCP)	00798216	Untrap
12541883	Spin Blue		

Unlockable prizes

Every time a Liberation Mission is completed, you get a prize depending on the number of phases you completed it in.

Unlockable	How to Unlock
AntiNavi M	Beat Liberation 4 in 9–10
Anubis A	Beat Liberation 9 in 14 or less
BlackWing W	Beat Liberation 7 in 10 or less
BlizzardMan B	Beat Liberation 1 in 6–7
BlizzardManSP B	Beat Liberation 1 in 5 or less
CloudMan C	Beat Liberation 3 in 8–9
CloudManDS B	Beat Liberation 8 in 13–14
CloudManSP C	Beat Liberation 3 in 7 or less
Colonel C	Beat Liberation 6 in 9–10 (Colonel version only)
CosmoMan C	Beat Liberation 5 in 8–9
CosmoManDS	Beat Liberation 9 in 15–16
CosmoManSP C	Beat Liberation 5 in 7 or less
FullCust *	Beat Liberation 4 in 8 or less
Muramasa M	Beat Liberation 8 in 12 or less
ProtoMan B	Beat Liberation 6 in 9–10 (ProtoMan version only)
ShadeMan S	Beat Liberation 2 in 8–9
ShadeManDS S	Beat Liberation 7 in 11–12
ShadeManSP S	Beat Liberation 2 in 7 or less
Z-Saber Z	Beat Liberation 6 in 8 or less

Mega Man Star Force: Dragon

Passwords

Compose a mail by pressing "X" in the mail screen, and send it to yourself. Type "Cipher" in the subject, then type the code in the body of the email. Send the email, and exit back to the main screen (Map screen). If you entered it correctly, it should give you a card.

Password	Effect	Password	Effect
Let's combine our strength!	Brave Sword 3 Card	SIXGAME-O	D.Energy SubCard
Dec. 17, 1986	ChainBubble3	CENCARLEBBUB	D.Eye Mega Weapon
ISNBDUBO	Cloaker	KNIGSPIAREM	FlickrKck3
ILABCLERSAS	D. Energy	NGYNGIWCUS	GhostPulse2 B. Card

DS PSP PS2 PS3 Wii Xbox Xbox 360 Index

Mega Man Star Force: Dragon (continued)

Password	Effect
Legendary SP Card Master Shin	Grants DragonSky
ROHNATPE	Heatball3
Star Force, the ultimate power!	LeoKingdm SP
KMALEETZCP	M. Breath (Mega Weapon) 1/2/1 Charge may Freeze or Bubble target
Ride On the Wave Road!	MopLance3
Go On Air battle card to trade info with friends.	PegasusMagic SP
Wave Change!	Porcupine Needle Mega Weapon, AT1|SP3|CH1 Geo Stellar, On The Air!!
Brother Action RPG	QnOphiucaSP Card
AURIEFRUTS	Recovery 50 B. Card
PREOBCOPB	SearchEye SubCard
LAREBARAON	TimeBomb1 B. Card
Let's form a BrotherBand!	TimeBomb3
ALPTUNZLA	Unlocker
NROSIMAMSTU	Unlocker SubCard
DWOWOOLFS	Unlocks Cloaker Subcard
Fly away for skies unknown!	Unlocks CygnusWingSP
NGAMEMA RESCAFROT	Unlocks D. Energy
Transers are really useful!	Unlocks FireBazooka3
How many more until you have all the cards?	Unlocks Freezenukle
Pegasus, Leo, Dragon - which is for you?	Unlocks Gatling3
Check out the Mega Man website!	Unlocks GhstPulse3
Get stronger through BrotherBands!	Unlocks GrndWave3
Only you can protect the Wave Road!	Unlocks JetAttack3
Win big with a Star Force Big Bang!	Unlocks PlasmaGun3
Mega Man 20th Anniversary Game	Unlocks Stikyrain3
I love Battle Network!	Unlocks SyncHook1
IPHAUEOEUNQC	Unlocks TailBurner3
Store info in your Transer!	Unlocks TaurusFireSP
Time to bust some EM viruses!	Unlocks WideWave3
OSLEGRATE	You get Heavy Cannon

Puyo Pop Fever

To enter this code, go into Options, then Gallery, then highlight Cutscene Viewer.

Unlockable	Code
Unlock all characters and cutscenes	Hold ⓧ and press ↑, ↓, ←, →

N+

Codes

Hold Ⓛ and Ⓡ and insert the following code at the Unlockables menu.

Effect	Code
Unlocks Atari Bonus Levels	Ⓐ,Ⓑ,Ⓐ,Ⓑ,Ⓐ,Ⓐ,Ⓑ

SimCity DS

Passwords

At the main menu, go to "Museum" then select "Landmark Collection," and finally "Password," then enter the following codes.

Unlockable	Code
Anglican Cathedral (UK)	kipling
Arc de Triomphe (France)	gaugin
Atomic Dome (Japan)	kawabata
Big Ben (UK)	orwell
Bowser Castle (Nintendo)	hanafuda
Brandenburg Gate (Germany)	gropius
Coit Tower (USA)	kerouac
Conciergerie (France)	rodin
Daibutsu (Japan)	mishima
Edo Castle (Japan)	shonagon
Eiffel Tower (France)	camus
Gateway Arch (USA)	twain
Grand Central Station (USA)	f.scott
Great Pyramids (Egypt)	mahfouz
Hagia Sofia (Turkey)	ataturk
Helsinki Cathedral (Finland)	kivi
Himeji Castle (Japan)	hokusai
Holstentor (Germany)	durer
Independence Hall (USA)	mlkingjr
Jefferson Memorial (USA)	thompson
Kokkai (Japan)	soseki
LA Landmark (USA)	hemingway
Lincoln Memorial (USA)	melville
Liver Building (UK)	dickens
Melbourne Cricket Ground (Australia)	damemelba
Metropolitan Cathedral (UK)	austen
Moai (Chile)	allende
Mt. Fuji (Japan)	hiroshige
National Museum (Taiwan)	yuantlee
Neuschwanstein Castle (Germany)	beethoven
Notre Dame (France)	hugo
Palace of Fine Arts (USA)	bunche
Palacio Real (Spain)	cervantes
Paris Opera (France)	daumier
Parthenon (Greece)	callas
Pharos of Alexandria (Egypt)	zewail
Rama IX Royal Park (Thailand)	phu
Reichstag (Germany)	goethe
Sagrada Famillia (Spain)	dali
Shuri Castle (Japan)	basho
Smithsonian Castle (USA)	pauling

SimCity DS (continued)

Sphinx (Egypt)	haykal
St. Paul's Cathedral (UK)	defoe
St. Basil's Cathedral (Russia)	tolstoy
St. Stephen's Cathedral (Austria)	mozart
Statue of Liberty (USA)	pollack
Stockholm Palace (Sweden)	bergman
Sydney Opera House Landmark # 12 (Australia)	bradman
Taj Mahal (India)	tagore
Tower of London (UK)	maugham
Trafalgar Square (UK)	joyce
United Nations (USA)	amnesty
United States Capitol (USA)	poe
Washington Monument (USA)	capote
Westminster Abbey (UK)	greene
White House (USA)	steinbeck

Unlockable Buildings from Population Growth

When your city reaches a certain number of people, Dr. Simtown unlocks buildings that help your city.

Unlockable	How to Unlock
Center for the Arts	Reach a population of 100,000.
Court House	Reach a population of 25,000.
Mayor's House	Reach a population of 5,000.
Medical Research Lab	Have a population of 80,000 when you reach year 1999.
Museum	Reach a population of 3,000.
Post Office	Reach a population of 100.

Sonic Rush Adventure

Unlockables

Unlockable	How to Unlock
Blaze the Cat	Defeat the Kraken boss in Coral Cave to unlock Blaze as a playable character.
Deep Core: Final extra boss stage	Collect all Sol Emeralds and Chaos Emeralds.

Star Wars: The Force Unleashed

Codes

From the main menu select "Extras," then "Unleashed Codes," and then enter the codes.

Effect	Code
Uber Lightsaber	lightsaber
Rahm Kota's costume	mandalore
Sith Robes	holocron
Starkiller's Father's Robes	wookiee

Tom Clancy's Splinter Cell Chaos Theory

Unlockables

Unlockable	How to Unlock
Argus Mercenary Costume	In Machi Akko, go to the bar and use the microphone. Look behind you for a keycard. Go back to the hallway with three doors, and use it on the closet.
Camouflage Sam Costume	In the Lighthouse level, snipe the man on the roof, but don't rappel down. On the high right corner is the costume.
Displace Mercenary Costume in Display Level	Go to floor three. Use the optic cable to see which room has the green package. Enter the room, and use keypad code 5800
Displace Suit	Room next to the room where you have a last chance to save, code is 5800.
Masked Sam Costume	In the Penthouse level, go to Zherkezhi's apartment, and go to the first room on the top floor. Go down the long, dark hall and type 5698 in the pad.
National Guard Costume	In the Manhattan Streets level, go to the open area before the penthouse. Climb the pipe, jump left, and go down to the next platform, in the corner.
Shadownet Agent Costume	In Kokubo Sosho, go down the elevator, where lasers are at the bottom. Find a ladder to climb back up. The room will have lasers and the costume.
Short Sleeved Sam Costume in Bank Level	Go to the small vault left of the computer and use the lockpick.
Snow Guard Costume in Battery Level	Get the wrench, and go to the U-shaped room. Enter the keycard room, take out the guard, climb on the crate, and bash next crate.
Thermal Suit Costume in Hokkaido Level	Find the wrench, and find the man who is shooting on the roof, get to him and fall through the vent, exiting the room, and bash the door.
Full Equipment Mode (infinite ammo etc.)	Beat the game at least once.

Tony Hawk's American Sk8land

Unlockables

Unlockable	How to Unlock
Always Special	Beat Classic mode 9 times
Crate-a-Skater	Beat Classic mode once
First Person Camera	Beat Classic mode 6 times
Giant Mode	Beat Classic mode 4 times
Hoverboard	Beat Classic mode 11 times
Lip Balance	Beat Classic mode twice
Manual Balance	Beat Classic mode twice
Matrix Mode	Beat Classic mode 5 times
Nearly Always Ribbon	Beat Classic mode 12 times
Ninja Skater	Beat Classic mode with all characters (13 times)
Paper Tony	Beat Classic mode 10 times
Rail Balance	Beat Classic mode twice
Replay Cam	Beat Classic mode 7 times
Tiny Mode	Beat Classic mode 3 times
Turbo Mode	Beat Classic mode 8 times

DS
PSP
PS2
PS3
Wii
Xbox
Xbox 360
Index

Tony Hawk's Proving Ground

Cheats

Enter the codes in the Options menu of the main menu.

Unlockable	How to Unlock
100% Branch Completion (NTT)	FOREVERNAILED
Invisible Man	THEMISSING
Mini Skater	TINYTATER
No Bails	ANDAINTFALLIN
No Board	MAGICMAN
Perfect Manual	STILLAINTFALLIN
Perfect Rail	AINTFALLIN
Super Check	BOOYAH
Unlimited Focus	MYOPIC
Unlimited Slash Grind	SUPERSLASHIN
Unlock Judy Nails	LOVEROCKNROLL

Items

Unlockable	How to Unlock
50 Extra Skill Points	NEEDSHELP
All CAS Items	GIVEMESTUFF
All Decks	LETSGOSKATE
All Fun Items	OVERTHETOP
All Game Movies	WATCHTHIS
All Lounge Bling Items	SWEETSTUFF
All Lounge Themes	LAIDBACKLOUNGE
All Rigger Pieces	IMGONNABUILD
All Special Tricks Available	LOTSOFTRICKS
All Video Editor Effects	TRIPPY
All Video Editor Overlays	PUTEMONTOP
Full Stats	BEEFEDUP

Levels

Unlockable	How to Unlock
Unlock Air & Space Museum	THEINDOORPARK
Unlock FDR	THEPREZPARK
Unlock Lansdowne	THELOCALPARK

Skaters

Unlockable	How to Unlock
Boneman	CRAZYBONEMAN
Bosco	MOREMILK
Cam	NOTACAMERA
Cooper	THECOOP
Eddie X	SKETCHY
El Patinador	PILEDRIVER
Eric	FLYAWAY
Mad Dog	RABBIES
MCA	INTERGALACTIC

Tony Hawk's Proving Ground (continued)

Unlockable	How to Unlock
Mel	NOTADUDE
Rube	LOOKSSMELLY
Shayne	MOVERS
Spence	DAPPER
TV Producer	SHAKER

Touch the Dead

Codes

Enter the following code at the main menu. A zombie will moan if you enter the code successfully and the Logo Screen will turn red. After that you will have access to all missions, all modes, and all bonuses. You will also be able to use the L and R shoulder buttons to switch to the next/previous camera.

Effect	Code
Unlocks everything, allows camera switching	ⓧ,Ⓨ,✚(Right),✚(Left),ⓧ

Yu-Gi-Oh! GX: Spirit Caller

Card Passwords

Enter the card passwords into the password machine to be able to purchase the card. You can only get cards you already have, or have a pack list with the card in it.

Password	Effect
83994646	4-Starred Ladybug of Doom
23771716	7 Colored Fish
24140059	A Cat of Ill Omen
06850209	A Deal with Dark Ruler
49140998	A Feather of the Phoenix
68170903	A Feint Plan
21597117	A Hero Emerges
00295517	A Legendary Ocean
51351302	A Man with Wdjat
05728014	A Rival Appears!
28596933	A Wingbeat of Giant Dragon
13026402	A-Team: Trap Disposal Unit
89718302	Abare Ushioni
27744077	Absolute End
49771608	Absorbing Kid from the Sky
18318842	Abyss Soldier
89801755	Abyssal Designator
21323861	Acid Rain
41356845	Acid Trap Hole
47372349	Acrobat Monkey
62325062	Adhesion Trap Hole
53828396	Adhesive Explosive
25345186	After the Struggle
16135253	Agido
18036057	Airknight Parshath
48202661	Aitsu
06150044	Alkana Knight Joker

Password	Effect
99785935	Alpha the Magnet Warrior
21070956	Altar for Tribute
91869203	Amazon Archer
67987611	Amazoness Archers
67987611	Amazoness Archers
73574678	Amazoness Bowpiper
29654737	Amazoness Chain Master
47480070	Amazoness Paladin
94004268	Amazoness Swords Woman
10979723	Amazoness Tiger
95174353	Amoeba
67371383	Amphibian Beast
64342551	Amphibious Bugroth MK-3
00303660	Amplifier
23927567	An Owl of Luck
93221206	Ancient Elf
31557782	Ancient Gear
10509340	Ancient Gear Beast
80045583	Ancient Gear Cannon
92001300	Ancient Gear Castle
67829249	Ancient Gear Drill
83104731	Ancient Gear Golem
56094445	Ancient Gear Soldier
54912977	Ancient Lamp
43230671	Ancient Lizard Warrior
17092736	Ancient Telescope
15013468	Andro Sphinx

Yu-Gi-Oh! GX: Spirit Caller (continued)

Password	Effect
02204140	Ante
13250922	Anteatereatingant
65064143	Anti-Aircraft Flower
53112492	Anti-Spell
09156135	Apprentice Magician
09156135	Apprentice Magician
48539234	Appropriate
85639257	Aqua Madoor
40916023	Aqua Spirit
55001420	Arcane Archer of the Forest
50287060	Archfiend of Gilfer
18378582	Archlord Zerato
53153481	Armaill
90374791	Armed Changer
00980973	Armed Dragon LV 3
46384672	Armed Dragon LV 5
73879377	Armed Dragon LV 7
59464593	Armed Dragon LV 10
09076207	Armed Ninja
84430950	Armed Samurai—Ben Kei
07180418	Armor Axe
79649195	Armor Break
36868108	Armored Glass
15480588	Armored Lizard
17535588	Armored Starfish
20277860	Armored Zombie
69296555	Array of Revealing Light
42364374	Arsenal Bug
55348096	Arsenal Robber
85489096	Arsenal Summoner
62633180	Assault on GHQ
37053871	Astral Barrier
02134346	Asura Priest
88236094	Aswan Apparition
87340664	Atomic Firefly
63689843	Attack and Receive
91989718	Attack Reflector Unit
37970940	Aussa the Earth Charmer
71453557	Autonomous Action Unit
99284890	Avatar of the Pot
84914462	Axe Dragonute
40619825	Axe of Despair
48305365	Axe Raider
11901678	B. Skull Dragon
15317640	B.E.S. Covered Core
22790789	B.E.S. Crystal Core
44954628	B.E.S. Tetran
88819587	Baby Dragon

Password	Effect
47453433	Back to Square One
82705573	Backfire
36280194	Backup Soldier
40633297	Bad Reaction to Simochi
07165085	Bait Doll
00242146	Ballista of Rampart Smashing
61528025	Banisher of the Light
41925941	Bark of Dark Ruler
81480460	Barrel Dragon
10963799	Barrier Statue of the Torrent
46145256	Barrier Statue of the Heavens
89091579	Basic Insect
61181383	Battery Charger
63142001	Batteryman AA
19733961	Batteryman C
48094997	Battle Footballer
05053103	Battle Ox
18246479	Battle Steer
55550921	Battle Warrior
94463200	Battle-Scarred
40133511	Bazoo the Soul-Eater
46009906	Beast Fangs
35149085	Beast Soul Swap
99426834	Beastking of the Swamps
16899564	Beautiful Headhuntress
32452818	Beaver Warrior
16255442	Beckoning Light
49522489	Beelze Frog
20374520	Begone, Knave
22996376	Behemoth the King of All Animals
33731070	Beiige, Vanguard of Dark World
85605684	Berserk Dragon
39168895	Berserk Gorilla
39256679	Beta the Magnet Warrior
25655502	Bickuribox
61127349	Big Bang Shot
95472621	Big Burn
14148099	Big Core
16768387	Big Eye
53606874	Big Insect
42129512	Big Koala
65240384	Big Shield Gardna
51562916	Big Wave Small Wave
59380081	Big-Tusked Mammoth
58696829	Bio-Mage
45547649	Birdface
41426869	Black Illusion Ritual

Yu-Gi-Oh! GX: Spirit Caller (continued)

Password	Effect
55761792	Black Luster Ritual
72989439	Black Luster Soldier—Envoy of the Beginning
65169794	Black Pendant
38670435	Black Tyranno
87564352	Blackland Fire Dragon
39507162	Blade Knight
58268433	Blade Rabbit
97023549	Blade Skater
28470714	Bladefly
89041555	Blast Held By a Tribute
21051146	Blast Magician
98239899	Blast with Chain
21466326	Blasting the Ruins
05464695	Blazing Inpachi
30653113	Blessings of the Nile
32015116	Blind Destruction
25880422	Block Attack
23995346	Blue Eyes Ultimate Dragon
20871001	Blue Medicine
80906030	Blue-Eyes White Dragon
89631139	Blue-Eyes White Dragon
89631139	Blue-Eyes White Dragon (SDK-001 Version)
02204140	Book of Life
14087893	Book of Moon
91595718	Book of Secret Arts
76532077	Bottomless Shifting Sand
16507828	Bracchio-raidus
87910978	Brain Control
20101223	Breath of Light
82878489	Bright Castle
24294108	Burning Land
18937875	Burning Spear
80163754	Burst Breath
27191436	Burst Return
17655904	Burst Stream of Destruction
78193831	Buster Blader
04861205	Call of the Mummy
11384280	Cannon Soldier
72892473	Card Destruction
57953380	Card of Safe Return
00062121	Castle of Dark Illusions
44209392	Castle Walls
95727991	Catapult Turtle
36468556	Ceasefire
90101050	Celtic Guardian
01248895	Chain Destruction
51449743	Chain Detonation
79323590	Chain Energy

Password	Effect
25050038	Chain Healing
64599569	Chimeratech Overdragon
81380218	Chorus of Sanctuary
21888494	Chosen One
22479888	Clay Charge
06967870	Cliff the Trap Remover
92667214	Clown Zombie
40240595	Cocoon of Evolution
60682203	Cold Wave
07565547	Collected Power
10375182	Command Knight
93889755	Crass Clown
67494157	Crawling Dragon
38289717	Crawling Dragon #2
46696593	Crimson Sunbird
57728570	Crush Card Virus
66742250	Curse of Anubis
28279543	Curse of Dragon
12470447	Curse of Fiend
02926176	Curse of Royal
94377247	Curse of the Masked Beast
70095154	Cyber Dragon
80316585	Cyber Harpie Lady
63224564	Cyber Shield
48766543	Cyber-Tech Alligator
40418351	Cyberdark Dragon
77625948	Cyberdark Edge
41230939	Cyberdark Horn
03019642	Cyberdark Keel
05494820	Cyclon Laser
81866673	D Hero—Dasher
40591390	D Hero—Dreadmaster
70074904	D. D. Assailant
37043180	D.D. Warrior
28378427	Damage Condenser
72520073	Dark Artist
32344688	Dark Chimera
01804528	Dark Coffin
70231910	Dark Core
04614116	Dark Energy
90980792	Dark Jeroid
99789342	Dark Magic Curtain
40609080	Dark Magician
40737112	Dark Magician of Chaos
99261403	Dark Rabbit
92377303	Dark Sage
40933924	Dark Scorpion Burglars
20858318	Dark Scorpion Combination
93599951	Dark Spirit of the Silent

DS PSP PS2 PS3 Wii Xbox Xbox 360 Index

Yu-Gi-Oh! GX: Spirit Caller (continued)

Password	Effect
45895206	Dark-Piercing Light
80168720	Darkness Approaches
95286165	De-Fusion
19159413	De-Spell
69122763	Deal of Phantom
39719977	Delta Attacker
93747864	Desert Sunlight
94212438	Destiny Board
05616412	Destruction Punch
84257639	Dian Keto the Cure Master
22959079	Dimensionhole
74701381	DNA Surgery
76922029	Don Zaloog
67464807	Dora of Fate
50045299	Dragon Capture Jar
01435851	Dragon Treasure
66672569	Dragon Zombie
55991637	Dragon's Gunfire
54178050	Dragon's Rage
32437102	Dragonic Attack
13215230	Dream Clown
00473469	Driving Snow
12493482	Dunames Dark Witch
51228280	Dungeon Worm
31476755	Dust Barrier
59820352	Earth Chant
42578427	Eatgaboon
97342942	Ectoplasmer
69954399	Ekibyo Drakmord
37820550	Electro-Whip
90219263	Elegant Egotist
30314994	Element Dragon
21844576	Elemental Hero Avian
79979666	Elemental Hero Bubbleman
84327329	Elemental Hero Burstinatrix
84327329	Elemental Hero Clayman
35809262	Elemental Hero Flame Wingman
47737087	Elemental Hero Rampart Blaster
25366484	Elemental Hero Shining Flare Wingman
20721928	Elemental Hero Sparkman
40044918	Elemental Hero Stratos
61204971	Elemental Hero Thunder Giant
39897277	Elf's Light
28649820	Embodiment of Apophis
30531525	Enchanting Fitting Room
98045062	Enemy Controller

Password	Effect
94716515	Eradicating Aerosol
56606928	Eternal Draught
95051344	Eternal Rest
63749102	Exarion Universe
26725158	Exile of the Wicked
74131780	Exiled Force
33396948	Exodia the Forbidden One
21598948	Fairy Box
97687912	Fairy Meteor Crush
17653779	Fairy's Hand Mirror
19394153	Feather Shot
71060915	Feather Wind
41392891	Feral Imp
77456781	Fiend Kraken
18591904	Final Destiny
73134081	Final Flame
66788016	Fissure
60862676	Flame Cerebrus
34460851	Flame Manipulator
40502030	Flame Swordsman
98252586	Follow Wind
81439173	Foolish Burial
74923978	Forced Requisition
87430998	Forest
24094653	Fusion Gate
26902560	Fusion Sage
56594520	Gaia Power
66889139	Gaia the Dragon Champion
06368038	Gaia the Fierce Knight
37313786	Gamble
14977074	Garoozis
25833572	Gate Guardian
30190809	Gear Golem the Moving Fortress
69140098	Gemini Elf
24668830	Germ Infection
41762634	Giant Flea
13039848	Giant Soldier of Stone
42703248	Giant Trunade
36354007	Gilford the Lightning
04149689	Goblin Fan
11868825	Goblin's Secret Remedy
67959180	Goddess of Whim
53493204	Goddess with the Third Eye
15367030	Gokibore
27408609	Golden Homunculus
52648457	Gorgon's Eye
79571449	Graceful Charity
74137509	Graceful Dice

Yu-Gi-Oh! GX: Spirit Caller (continued)

Password	Effect
02906250	Grappler
82542267	Gravedigger Ghoul
25262697	Gravekeeper's Assailant
16762927	Gravekeeper's Servant
63695531	Gravekeeper's Spear Soldier
33737664	Graverobber's Retribution
85742772	Gravity Bind
14141448	Great Moth
13429800	Great White
41172955	Green Gadget
53829412	Griffore
90502999	Ground Collapse
40659562	Guardian Sphinx
73079365	Gust
55321970	Gust Fan
31122090	Gyakutenno Megami
88789641	Hallowed Life Barrier
76812113	Harpie Lady
91932350	Harpie Lady 1
27927359	Harpie Lady 2
54415063	Harpie Lady 3
12206212	Harpie Lady Sisters
18144506	Harpie's Feather Duster
52040216	Harpie's Pet Dragon
35762283	Heart of the Underdog
19613556	Heavy Storm
54493213	Helios—the Primordal Sun
80887952	Helios Duo Megistus
17286057	Helios Tris Megiste
76052811	Helpoemer
52584282	Hercules Beetle
22020907	Hero Signal
81167171	Hero Spirit
46130346	Hinotama
76184692	Hitotsu-Me Giant
69669405	Horn Imp
38552107	Horn of Light
64047146	Horn of the Unicorn
75830094	Horus the Black Flame Dragon Lv. 4
11224103	Horus the Black Flame Dragon Lv. 6
48229808	Horus the Black Flame Dragon Lv. 8
15083728	House of Adhesive Tape
30353551	Human-Wave Tactics
22587018	Hydrogeddon
28546905	Illusionist Faceless Mage
61740673	Imperial Order

Password	Effect
52684508	Inferno Fire Blast
12247206	Inferno Reckless Summon
94163677	Infinite Cards
54109233	Infinite Dismissal
79575620	Injection Fairy Lily
03492538	Insect Armor with Laser Cannon
23615409	Insect Barrier
96965364	Insect Imitation
16227556	Inspection
36261276	Interdimensional Matter Transporter
98374133	Invigoration
21770260	Jam Breeding Machine
21558682	Jam Defender
83968380	Jar of Greed
14851496	Jellyfish
77585513	Jinzo #7
15401633	Jirai Gumo
30113682	Judge Man
55256016	Judgment of Anubis
24068492	Just Desserts
76634149	Kairyu-Shin
12829151	Kanan the Swordmistress
62340868	Kazejin
88979991	Killer Needle
79853073	Kinetic Soldier
69455834	King of Yamimakai
60519422	Kishido Spirit
01184620	Kojikocy
67724379	Koumori Dragon
76512652	Krokodilus
37390589	Kunai with Chain
97590747	La Jinn the Mystical Genie of the Lamp
66526672	Labyrinth of Nightmare
99551425	Labyrinth Tank
67284908	Labyrinth Wall
87756343	Larvae Moth
77007920	Laser Cannon Armor
90330453	Last Day of Witch
85602018	Last Will
87322377	Launcher Spider
20394040	Lava Battleguard
00102380	Lava Golem
07902349	Left Arm of the Forbidden One
44519536	Left Leg of the Forbidden One
61854111	Legendary Sword
03136426	Level Limit—Area B
62867251	Light of Intervention

Yu-Gi-Oh! GX: Spirit Caller (continued)

Password	Effect
55226821	Lightning Blade
23171610	Limiter Removal
81777047	Luminous Spark
17658803	Luster Dragon #2
25769732	Machine Conversion Factory
46700124	Machine King
30241314	Macro Cosmos
83746708	Mage Power
62279055	Magic Cylinder
59344077	Magic Drain
77414722	Magic Jammer
53119267	Magic Thorn
96008713	Magic-Arm Shield
81210420	Magical Hats
31560081	Magician of Faith
93013676	Maha Vailo
09074847	Major Riot
99597615	Malevolent Nuzzler
40374923	Mammoth Graveyard
54652250	Man-Eater Bug
44287299	Masaki the Legendary Swordsman
82432018	Mask of Brutality
28933734	Mask of Darkness
20765952	Mask of Dispel
29549364	Mask of Restrict
56948373	Mask of the Accursed
57882509	Mask of Weakness
10189126	Masked Sorcerer
22046459	Megamorph
48642904	Mesmeric Control
44656491	Messenger of Peace
75646520	Metal Detector
68339286	Metal Guardian
68540058	Metalmorph
50705071	Metalzoa
90660762	Meteor Black Dragon
64271667	Meteor Dragon
33767325	Meteor of Destruction
64274292	Meteorain
37580756	Michizure
32012841	Millennium Shield
07489323	Milus Radiant
37520316	Mind Control
01918087	Minor Goblin Official
44095762	Mirror Force
93108433	Monster Recovery
74848038	Monster Reincarnation
97612389	Monster Tamer
58074572	Mooyan Curry
33508719	Morphing Jar
50913601	Mountain
70307656	Mucus Yolk
46657337	Muka Muka
22493811	Multiplication of Ants
40703222	Multiply
14181608	Mushroom Man
68191243	Mustering of the Dark Scorpions
54098121	Mysterious Puppeteer
68516705	Mystic Horseman
18161786	Mystic Plasma Zone
49251811	Mystic Probe
15025844	Mystical Elf
36607978	Mystical Moon
05318639	Mystical Space Typhoon
63516460	Mystical Wind Typhoon
14315573	Negate Attack
17955766	Neo-Spacian Aqua Dolphin
58775978	Nightmare's Steelcage
19230407	Offerings to the Doomed
79335209	Ojama Black
12482652	Ojama Green
90140980	Ojama King
42941100	Ojama Yellow
19523799	Ookazi
63120904	Orca Mega-Fortress of Darkness
39537362	Ordeal of a Traveler
78986941	Order to Charge
39019325	Order to Smash
74191942	Painful Choice
42035044	Panther Warrior
50152549	Paralyzing Potion
62762898	Parrot Dragon
24433920	Pendulum Machine
36039163	Penguin Knight
93920745	Penguin Soldier
48579379	Perfectly Ultimate Great Moth
58192742	Petit Moth
90669991	Pineapple Blast
24094653	Polymerization
70828912	Premature Burial
00549481	Prevent Rat
51371017	Princess of Tsurugi
43711255	Prohibition
29155212	Pumpking the King of Ghosts

Yu-Gi-Oh! GX: Spirit Caller (continued)

Password	Effect
76754619	Pyramid Energy
77044671	Pyramid Turtle
94905343	Rabid Horseman
12580477	Raigeki
56260110	Raimei
66719324	Rain of Mercy
51267887	Raise Body Heat
07625614	Raregold Armor
33066139	Reaper of the Cards
86445415	Red Gadget
38199696	Red Medicine
36262024	Red-Eyes B. Chick
74677422	Red-Eyes Black Dragon
64335804	Red-Eyes Black Metal Dragon
32807846	Reinforcement of the Army
17814387	Reinforcements
51482758	Remove Trap
08951260	Respect Play
99518961	Restructer Revolution
27174286	Return from the Different Dimension
77622396	Reverse Trap
70903634	Right Arm of the Forbidden One
08124921	Right Leg of the Forbidden One
83555666	Ring of Destruction
20436034	Ring of Magnetism
70344351	Riryoku Field
88279736	Robbin' Goblin
68846917	Rock Ogre Grotto #1
91939608	Rogue Doll
93382620	Rope of Life
51452091	Royal Decree
26378150	Rude Kaiser
70046172	Rush Recklessly
15303296	Ryu-Kishin
24611934	Ryu-Kishin Powered
66602787	Saggi the Dark Clown
32268901	Salamandra
25955164	Sanga of the Thunder
26202165	Sangan
11760174	Sasuke Samurai #2
50400231	Satellite Cannon
02792265	Servant of Catabolism
03819470	Seven Tools of the Bandit
30778711	Shadow Ghoul
58621589	Shadow of Eyes
56830749	Share the Pain

Password	Effect
52097679	Shield & Sword
59560625	Shift
73665146	Silent Magician LV 4
72443568	Silent Magician LV 8
01557499	Silver Bow and Arrow
90357090	Silver Fang
08131171	Sinister Serpent
73752131	Skilled Dark Magician
00126218	Skull Dice
98139712	Skull Invitation
06733059	Skull Lair
63035430	Skyscraper
78636495	Slate Warrior
00596051	Snake Fang
86318356	Sogen
41420027	Solemn Judgment
35346968	Solemn Wishes
47852924	Soul of the Pure
05758500	Soul Release
92924317	Soul Resurrection
97362768	Spark Blaster
76103675	Sparks
31553716	Spear Dragon
42598242	Special Hurricane
38275183	Spell Shield Type-8
18807108	Spellbinding Circle
49328340	Spiral Spear Strike
94772232	Spirit Message "A"
31893528	Spirit Message "I"
30170981	Spirit Message "L"
67287532	Spirit Message "N"
92394653	Spirit's Invitation
15866454	Spiritualism
94425169	Spring of Rebirth
81385346	Stamping Destruction
65810489	Statue of the Wicked
13599884	Steel Scorpion
02370081	Steel Shell
83225447	Stim-Pack
63102017	Stop Defense
98434877	Suijin
70781052	Summoned Skull
85520851	Super Conductor Tyranno
27770341	Super Rejuvenation
40453765	Swamp Battleguard
13069066	Sword Arm of Dragon
37120512	Sword of Dark Destruction
98495314	Sword of the Deep-Seated
05372656	Sword of the Soul-Eater

DS PSP PS2 PS3 Wii Xbox Xbox 360 Index

Yu-Gi-Oh! GX: Spirit Caller (continued)

Password	Effect
72302403	Swords of Revealing Light
50005633	Swordstalker
18895832	System Down
43641473	Tailor of the Fickle
41142615	The Cheerful Coffin
30606547	The Dark Door
92408984	The Dragon's Bead
68400115	The Emperor's Holiday
42829885	The Forceful Sentry
84136000	The Grave of the Enkindling
81820689	The Inexperienced Spy
66926224	The Law of the Normal
25109950	The Little Swordsman of Aile
49064413	The Masked Beast
16430187	The Reliable Guardian
43434803	The Shallow Grave
29491031	The Snake Hair
06285791	The Wicked Worm Beast
41462083	Thousand Dragon
05703682	Thousand Energy
63519819	Thousand-Eyes Restrict
91781589	Thunder of Ruler
40907090	Tiger Axe
80987696	Time Machine
71625222	Time Wizard
82003859	Toll
59383041	Toon Alligator
42386471	Toon Gemini Elf
89997728	Toon table of contents
80813021	Torike
53582587	Torrential Tribute
35686187	Tragedy
64697231	Trap Dustshoot
04206964	Trap Hole
46461247	Trap Master
46918794	Tremendous Fire
02903036	Tribute Doll
79759861	Tribute to the Doomed
03149764	Tutan Mask
94119974	Two-Headed King Rex
83887306	Two-Pronged Attack
72842870	Tyhone
21237481	Type Zero Magic Crusher

Password	Effect
94568601	Tyrant Dragon
80604091	Ultimate Offering
15894048	Ultimate Tyranno
22702055	Umi
82999629	Umiiruka
70368879	Upstart Goblin
01784619	Uraby
06007213	Uria, Lord of Searing Flames
22056710	Vampire Genesis
53839837	Vampire Lord
95220856	Vengeful Bog Spirit
50259460	Versago the Destroyer
39774685	Vile Germ
15052462	Violet Crystal
14898066	Vorse Raider
12607053	Waboku
63162310	Wall Shadow
90873992	Warrior Elimination
23424603	Wasteland
85066822	Water Dragon
38992735	Wave Motion Cannon
15150365	White Magical Hat
77754944	Widespread Ruin
87796900	Winged Dragon, Guardian of the Forest #1
57116033	Winged Kuriboh
98585345	Winged Kuriboh LV 10
49417509	Wolf
12253117	World Suppression
62651957	X-Head Cannon
02111707	XY-Dragon Cannon
91998119	XYZ-Dragon Cannon
99724761	XZ-Tank Cannon
65622692	Y-Dragon Head
25119460	YZ-Tank Dragon
59197169	Yami
13834120	Yellow Gadget
04542651	Yellow Luster Shield
64500000	Z-Metal Tank
30090452	Zanki
69123138	Zera the Mant
24311372	Zoa
31339260	Zombie Warrior

Yu-Gi-Oh! GX: Spirit Caller (continued)

Unlockables

Unlockable	How to Unlock
Acrobat Monkey	Defeat Kagemaru
Adhesive Explosive	Starter at well
Babycerasaurus	After finalists are decided in tournament
Batteryman C	Finish game
Batteryman D	Finish game
Beelze Frog	After finalists are decided in tournament
Blast Asmodian	After finalists are decided in tournament
Dragon Capture Jar	Finish game
Ebon Magician Curran	After abandoned dorm events
Hane-Hane	Defeat Bastion for the second time
Jerry Beans Man	Starter at well
Oscillo Hero #2	Starter at well
Skelengel	Defeat Kagemaru
Soitsu	After abandoned dorm events
Star Boy	Defeat Bastion for the second time
White Magician Pikeru	Finish game
Alchemy Disk	Defeat Prof. Banner until he gives it to you
Amazonness Disk	Defeat Tania until she gives it to you
Cheap Duel Disk	Get from linking with Nightmare Troubadour
Gorgeous Disk	Defeat Admiral until he gives it to you
Kaibaman Disk	Deafeat Kaibaman until he gives it to you
Pharaoh Disk	Defeat Abidos until he gives it to you
Vampire Disk	Defeat Camula until she gives it to you
Academy Jersey	Defeat Fonda until she gives it to you
Black Uniform	Defeat Chazz until he gives it to you
Blue Uniform	Defeat Dark Zane until he gives it to you
Duel Coat	Defeat Crowler until he gives it to you
Hawaiian Shirt	Defeat Atticus until he gives it to you
Kaibaman Coat	Defeat Kaibaman until he gives it to you
North Academy Uniform	Defeat Chazz until he gives it to you
Stuffy Collared Shirt	Get from linking with Nightmare Troubadour
Suit	Duel Chumley until he gives it to you
Titan Coat	Defeat Titan until he gives it to you
Yellow Uniform	Defeat Professor Sartyr until he gives it to you

Table of Contents - PSP

300: March to Glory

Enter this code while the game is paused.

Unlockable	Code
25,000 Kleos	⇩, ⇦, ⇩, ⇦, ⇧, ⇦

Armored Core: Formula Front

Manual Controlled Tricks

Use during a manually controlled battle.

Code	Effect
✣ and ✤ Simultaneously	Drop Extensions
✣ and ● Simultaneously	Drop Left Arm Weapon
✣ and ■ Simultaneously	Drop Right Arm Weapon
Boost Forward on the ground and press ●	Fire Energy Wave

Unlockable Features

For *Armored Core: Formula Front International* version only.

Unlockable	How to Unlock
50 Exhibition Matches	Beat Formula Regular League
Ending Credits (movie attachment)	Beat all 50 Exhibition Matches

ATV Offroad Fury Blazin Trails

To enter these passwords go to the Options menu, select the Player Profile menu, and then enter the Cheat menu.

Unlockable	Code
1,500 Credits	$MONEYBAGS$
All Music Videos	BILLBOARDS
All Rider Gear	DUDS
Unlock Everything (except the Fury Bike)	ALL ACCESS
Unlock Rims	DUBS

Ben 10: Protector of Earth

Codes

Press Start at the Map screen to bring up the Option menu, select the "Enter Secret Code" menu, and enter the following codes to get the corresponding effects.

Unlockable	How to Unlock
Dark Heroes	Cannonbolt, Cannonbolt, Fourarms, Heatblast
DNA Force	Wildvine, Fourarms, Heatblast, Cannonbolt
Invincibility	XLR8, Heatblast, Wildvine, Fourarms
Master Control	Cannonbolt, Heatblast, Wildvine, Fourarms
Unlock Alien Forms	Wildvine, Fourarms, Heatblast, Wildvine
Unlock ALL Combos	Cannonbolt, Heatblast, Fourarms, Heatblast
Unlock All Locations on Map	Heatblast, XLR8, XLR8, Cannonbolt

Blitz: Overtime

Password

In the main menu in the "extras" option, input these codes to unlock the following.

Password	Effect
ONFIRE	Ball trails always on. Only affects Quick Play mode.
BOUNCY	Beach Ball. Only affects Quick Play mode.
PIPPED	Double unleash icons. Only affects Quick Play mode.
CHAMPS	In Campaign mode, highlight a team but do not select it. Stay on the menu and press ■,■,▲, Triangle to instantly win against the selected team.
NOTTIRED	Stamina disabled. Only affects Quick Play mode.
CLASHY	Super Clash mode. Only affects Quick Play mode.
BIGDOGS	Super Unleash Clash mode. Only affects Quick Play mode.
CHUWAY	Two player co-op mode.

Capcom Classic Collection Remixed

Enter this code at the Press Start screen.

Unlockable	Code
Arts, Tips, and Sound Tests for Every Game	Press ⇦, ⇨ on D-pad, ⇦, ⇨ on Analog stick, ■, ●, ⇧, ⇩

Death Jr.

To enter these codes, pause the game and hold L+R.

Unlockable	Code
All Weapons and Weapon Upgrades	↑, ↑, ↓, ↓, ←, →, ←, →, ×, ●
Ammo Refilled	▲, ▲, ×, ×, ■, ●, ■, ●, ↓, →
Assist Extender	↑, ↑, ↓, ↓, ▲, ▲, ×, ×, ▲, ▲
Attacks Have Different Names	↑, ↑, ↓, ←, ▲, ▲, ■, ×, ●, ■
Big Heads	▲, ●, ×, ■, ▲, ↑, →, ↓, ←, ↑
Big Scythe	▲, ■, ×, ●, ▲, ↑, ←, ↓, →, ↑
Bullet Holes Become Pictures	↑, →, ↓, ←, ↑, ▲, ●, ×, ■, ▲
Eyedoors Don't Require Souls to Open	↑, ←, ↓, →, ←, ▲, ■, ×, ●, ■
Fill Pandora's Assist Meter	↑, ↑, ↓, ↓, ↑, →, ↓, ←, ×, ×
Free All Characters and Unlock All Levels (Must be entered in the stage and re-entered in the museum)	↑, ↑, ↑, ↑, ↓, ↓, ↓, ↓, ×, ×
Free Seep	←, ←, →, →, ←, →, ←, →, ×, ×
Increased Health and Stamina	↑, ↑, ↓, ↓, ×, ●, ▲, ■, ×, ×
Invincibility	↑, ↑, ↓, ↓, ←, ←, →, →, ■, ▲
Monsters Are Different Colors and Scythe Has Trails	↓, ×, ↓, ×, ↓, ×, ↓, ×, ↓, ×
Odd Monsters and Scythe Has Trails	▲, ↑, ●, →, ×, ↓, ■, ←, ▲, ↑
Unlimited Ammo	▲, ▲, ×, ×, ■, ●, ■, ●, →, ↓
Warp to Advanced Training Stage	↓, ×, ↓, ×, ↓, ×, ↓, ×, ↓, ■
Warp to Basic Training Stage	↑, ▲, ↑, ×, ↓, ×, ↓, ×, ↓, ×
Warp to Big Trouble in Little Downtown Stage	↑, ▲, ↓, ×, ↓, ×, ↓, ×, ↓, ×
Warp to Bottom of the Bell Curve Stage	↓, ×, ↓, ×, ↓, ×, ↓, ×, ↓, ▲
Warp to Burn it Down Stage	↓, ×, ↑, ▲, ↓, ×, ↓, ×, ↓, ×
Warp to Final Battle Stage	↓, ×, ↓, ×, ↓, ×, ↓, ▲, ↑, ×
Warp to Growth Spurt Stage	↓, ×, ↓, ×, ↓, ×, ↓, ×, ↑, ×
Warp to Happy Trails Insanitarium Stage	↓, ×, ↓, ▲, ↑, ×, ↓, ×, ↓, ×
Warp to Higher Learning Stage	↓, ×, ↓, ×, ↓, ×, ↓, ▲, ↓, ×
Warp to How a Cow Becomes a Steak Stage	↓, ×, ↓, ×, ↓, ▲, ↓, ×, ↓, ×
Warp to Inner Madness Stage	↓, ×, ↓, ×, ↑, ▲, ↓, ×, ↓, ×
Warp to Into the Box Stage	↓, ×, ↓, ×, ↓, ×, ↑, ▲, ↓, ×
Warp to Moving on Up Stage	↓, ▲, ↑, ×, ↓, ×, ↓, ×, ↓, ×
Warp to My House Stage	↓, ×, ↓, ▲, ↓, ×, ↓, ×, ↓, ×
Warp to Seep's Hood Stage	↓, ▲, ↓, ×, ↓, ×, ↓, ×, ↓, ×
Warp to Shock Treatment Stage	↓, ×, ↓, ×, ↓, ▲, ↑, ×, ↓, ×
Warp to The Basement Stage	↓, ×, ↓, ×, ↓, ×, ↓, ×, ↑, ▲
Warp to The Burger Tram Stage	↓, ×, ↓, ×, ↓, ×, ↑, ×, ↓, ×
Warp to The Corner Store Stage	↓, ×, ↑, ×, ↓, ×, ↓, ×, ↓, ×
Warp to The Museum	↑, ×, ↓, ×, ↓, ×, ↓, ×, ↓, ×
Warp to Udder Madness Stage	↓, ×, ↓, ×, ↑, ×, ↓, ×, ↓, ×
Weapons Have Different Names	↓, ↓, ↑, ↑, ←, →, ←, →, ■, ▲
Widget	→, ↑, ↓, ↑, ▲, ↑, ←, ■, ▲, →

Death Jr. II: Root of Evil

Enter these codes while the game is paused.

Unlockable	Code
All Weapon Upgrades	Hold L2 and press ⇧, ⇧, ⇩, ⇩, ⇦, ⇨, ⇦, ⇨, ×, ●
Invincibility	Hold L2 and press ⇧, ⇧, ⇩, ⇩, ⇦, ⇦, ⇨, ⇨, ■, ▲
Refill Ammunition	Hold L2 and press ▲, ▲, ×, ×, ■, ●, ■, ●, ⇩, ⇨
Unlimited Ammunition	Hold L2 and press ▲, ▲, ×, ×, ■, ●, ■, ●, ⇨, ⇩

Def Jam: Fight for NY–The Takeover

Enter these passwords in the Cheats menu under extras.

Unlockable	Password
After Hours by Nyne	LOYALTY
Anything Goes by C-N-N	MILITAIN
Blindside by Baxter	CHOPPER
Bust by Outkast	BIGBOI
Comp by Comp	CHOCOCITY
Dragon House by Masa Mix	AKIRA
Get It Now by Bless	PLATINUMB
Koto by Chiang's Mix	GHOSTSHELL
Lil Bro by Ric-A-Che	GONBETRUBL
Man Up by Sticky Fingaz	KIRKJONES
Move! by Public Enemy	RESPECT
Original Gangster by Ice-T	POWER
Poppa Large by Ultramagnetic MC's	ULTRAMAG

Unlockable	Password
Seize the Day by Bless	SIEZE
Take a Look at my Life by Fat Joe	CARTAGENA
Walk with Me by Joe Budden	PUMP
Add 100 reward points	REALSTUFF
Add 100 reward points	GOUNDRGRND
Add 100 reward points	THEEMCEE
Add 100 reward points	BULLETPROOF
Add 100 reward points	DASTREETS
Add 200 reward points	REAL STYLE
Add 200 reward points	SUPER FREAK
Add 200 reward points	DRAGONHOUSE
Add 300 reward points	NEWYORKCIT

Disgaea: Afternoon of Darkness

Etna Mode

Disgaea contains a hidden mode called Etna mode. Normally you have to get this mode by going through the game and reading Etna's diary every chapter, but you can unlock it instantly by entering the following code during the title screen, with the pointer on "New Game." If you're successful, you'll hear Etna's voice.

Effect	Code
Unlock Etna Mode (US)	▲, ■, ●, ▲, ■, ●, ×

Extra Classes

Unlockable	How to Unlock
Angel	Female Cleric, Knight, and Archer all at level 100 or higher.
Archer	Level 3 or higher in Bow Weapon Mastery.
EDF Soldier	Level 30 or higher Gun Weapon Mastery.
Galaxy Mage	Level a Prism Mage to Level 50.
Galaxy Skull	Level a Prism Skull to Level 50.
Knight	Female Warrior and Female Mage each at level 10 or higher.
Majin	Male Warrior, Brawler, Ninja, Rogue, and Scout all at level 200 or higher.
Ninja	Male Fighter and Male Warrior with a total level of 10 or higher.
Prism Mage	Level a Star Mage to Level 35.
Prism Skull	Level a Star Skull to Level 35.
Rogue	Both Fighter and Warrior, Males or Females, each at level 5 or higher.
Ronin	Female Warrior and Female Fighter with a total level of 10 or higher.
Scout	Two Fighters/Warriors, Males or Females, each at level 5 or higher.
Star Mage	Get one Fire, Ice, and Wind Mage and level all three of them to level 5.
Star Skull	Get one Fire, Ice, and Wind Skull and level all three of them to level 5.

Dragon Ball Z: Shin Budokai

Unlockables

You must complete every fight quickly and with most of your health.

Card Sheet	How to Unlock
No. 10	Finish all fights in Chapter 5
No. 13	Z rank on all fights for Chapter 1
No. 14	Z rank on all fights for Chapter 2
No. 15	Z rank on all fights for Chapter 3
No. 16	Z rank on all fights for Chapter 4
No. 17	Z rank on all fights for Chapter 5
No. 24	Z rank on all fights for Dragon Road

Unlockable Characters

Defeat the specified characters in Dragon Road mode.

Unlockable	How to Unlock
Adult Gohan—Mystic Form	Defeat Vegeta in Chapter 4-A-B 5.
Adult Gohan—Super Saiyan 2 Form	Defeat Broly in Chapter 2-6
Adult Gohan—Super Saiyan Form	Defeat Frieza in Chapter 1-8
Broly—Legendary Super Saiyan Form	Defeat Frieza in Chapter 4-A-B 6
Cell—Super Perfect Form	Defeat Cell in Chapter 2-5
Cooler—Final Form	Defeat Pikkon in Chapter 4-B-A 5
Frieza—100% Full Power Form	Defeat Frieza in Chapter 3-2
Future Trunks—Super Saiyan Form	Defeat Gotenks in Chapter 4-2
Goku—Kaioken Form	Defeat Krillin in Chapter 1-2
Goku—Super Saiyan 2 Form	Defeat Fake Goku in Chapter 2-2
Goku—Super Saiyan 3 Form	Defeat Vegeta in Chapter 3-7
Goku—Super Saiyan Form	Defeat Janemba in Chapter 1-9
Goku SS3	Beat Majin Vegeta in Chapter 3
Gotenks	Defeat Gotenks in Chapter 1-4
Gotenks—Super Saiyan 3 Form	Defeat Cell in Chapter 3-A-4
Gotenks—Super Saiyan Form	Defeat Gotenks in Chapter 1-5
Janemba	Beat Story Mode
Krillin—Unlock Potential Form	Defeat Goku in Chapter 5-1
Piccolo—Fuse with Kami Form	Defeat Cell in Chapter 2-1
Pikkon	Defeat Janemba in Chapter 2- 9
Teen Gohan—Super Saiyan 2 Form	Defeat Teen Gohan in Chapter 3-9
Teen Gohan—Super Saiyan Form	Defeat Cell in Chapter 3-8
Vegeta—Majin Form	Defeat Vegeta in Chapter 4-7
Vegeta—Super Saiyan 2 Form	Defeat Janemba in Chapter 2-7
Vegeta—Super Saiyan Form	Defeat #18 in Chapter 2-3
Vegetto and Gogeta	Beat the last chapter choosing either path
Vegetto—Super Saiyan Form	Defeat Kid Buu in Chapter 5–B-9

Exit

In order to use these codes, you must complete the first situation level.

Unlockable	Code
Unlocks Situation 8	L, R, ←, →, ■, ●, ×, ▲
Unlocks Situation 9	▲, ↓, ●, ←, ×, ↑, ■, →
Unlocks Situation 10	→, ↓, ↑, ←, ●, ×, R, L

FlatOut: Head On

Codes

At main screen, go to Extras, then to Enter Code.

Effect	Code
All Cars and 1 Million Credits	GIEVEPIX
All Tracks	GIVEALL
Big Rig	ELPUEBLO
Big Rig Truck	RAIDERS
Flatmobile Car	WOTKINS
Mob Car	BIGTRUCK
Pimpster Car	RUTTO
Rocket Car	KALJAKOPPA
School Bus	GIEVCARPLZ

Full Auto 2: Battlelines

Enter these codes in the codes section under features.

Unlockable	Code
All Cars	⇧, ⇧, ⇧, ⇧, ⇦, ⇩, ⇧, ⇨, ⇩, ⇩, ⇩, ⇩
All Events	START, ⇦, SELECT, ⇨, ⇨, ▲, ×, ■, START, R, ⇩, SELECT

Gradius Collection

Codes

Unlockable	How to Unlock
All Power-ups and Weapons	Pause the game and then insert the famous "Konami Code": ↑,↑,↓,↓,←,→,←,→,←,→

Grand Theft Auto: Liberty City Stories

Enter these codes during gameplay. Do not pause the game.

Unlockable	Code
$250,000	L, R, ▲, L, R, ●, L, R
Aggressive Drivers	■, ■, R, ×, ×, L, ●, ●
All Green Lights	▲, ▲, R, ■, ■, L, ×, ×
All Vehicles Chrome Plated	▲, R, L, ⇩, ⇩, R, R, ▲
Black Cars	●, ●, R, ▲, ▲, L, ■, ■
Bobble Head World	⇩, ⇩, ⇩, ●, ●, ×, L, R
Cars Drive On Water	●, ×, ⇩, ●, ×, ⇧, L, L
Change Bike Tire Size	●, ⇨, ×, ⇧, ⇨, ×, L, ■
Clear Weather	⇧, ⇩, ●, ⇧, ⇩, ■, L, R
Commit Suicide	L, ⇩, ⇦, R, ×, ●, ⇧, ▲
Destroy All Cars	L, L, ⇦, L, L, ⇨, ×, ■
Display Game Credits	L, R, L, R, ⇧, ⇩, L, R
Faster Clock	L, L, ⇦, L, L, ⇨, ●, ×
Faster Gameplay	R, R, L, R, R, L, ⇩, ×
Foggy Weather	⇧, ⇩, ▲, ⇧, ⇩, ×, L, R
Full Armor	L, R, ●, L, R, ×, L, R
Full Health	L, R, ×, L, R, ■, L, R
Have Girls Follow You	⇩, ⇩, ⇩, ▲, ▲, ●, L, R
Never Wanted	L, L, ▲, R, R, ×, ■, ●
Overcast Weather	⇧, ⇩, ×, ⇧, ⇩, ▲, L, R
Pedestrians Attack You	L, L, R, L, L, R, ⇧, ▲
Pedestrians Have Weapons	R, R, L, R, R, L, ⇨, ●

Grand Theft Auto: Liberty City Stories (continued)

Unlockable	Code
Pedestrians Riot	L, L, R, L, L, R, ⇦, ■
Perfect Traction	L, ⇧, ⇦, R, ▲, ●, ⇩, ×
Rainy Weather	⇧, ⇩, ■, ⇧, ⇩, ●, L, R
Raise Media Attention	L, ⇧, ⇨, R, ▲, ■, ⇩, ×
Raise Wanted Level	L, R, ■, L, R, ▲, L, R
Random Pedestrian Outfit	L, L, ⇦, L, L, ⇨, ■, ▲
Slower Gameplay	R, ▲, ×, R, ■, ●, ⇦, ⇨
Spawn Rhino	L, L, ⇦, L, L, ⇨, ▲, ●
Spawn Trashmaster	▲, ●, ⇩, ▲, ●, ⇧, L, L
Sunny Weather	L, L, ●, R, R, ■, ▲, ×
Upside Down Gameplay	⇩, ⇩, ⇩, ×, ×, ■, R, L
Upside Up	▲, ▲, ▲, ⇧, ⇧, ⇨, L, R
Weapon Set 1	⇧, ■, ■, ⇩, ⇦, ■, ■, ⇨
Weapon Set 2	⇧, ●, ●, ⇩, ⇦, ●, ●, ⇨
Weapon Set 3	⇧, ×, ×, ⇩, ⇦, ×, ×, ⇨
White Cars	×, ×, R, ●, ●, L, ▲, ▲

Grand Theft Auto: Vice City Stories

Enter any of these codes while playing.

Unlockable	Code
25% of MP Content	⇧, ⇧, ⇧, ■, ■, ▲, R, L
50% of MP Content	⇧, ⇧, ⇧, ●, ●, ×, L, R
75% of MP Content	⇧, ⇧, ⇧, ⇧, ×, ×, ■, R, L
100% of MP Content	⇧, ⇧, ▲, ▲, ●, L, R
All Cars Are Black	L, R, L, R, ⇦, ●, ⇧, ×
Armor	⇧, ⇩, ⇦, ⇨, ■, ■, L, R
Cars Avoid You	⇧, ⇧, ⇨, ⇦, ▲, ●, ●, ■
Chrome Cars	⇨, ⇧, ⇦, ⇩, ▲, ▲, L, R
Clear Weather	⇦, ⇩, R, L, ⇨, ⇧, ⇦, ×
Commit Suicide	⇨, ⇨, ●, ●, L, R, ⇩, ×
Destroy All Cars	L, R, R, ⇦, ⇨, ■, ⇩, R
Faster Clock	R, L, L, ⇩, ⇧, ×, ⇩, L
Faster Gameplay	⇦, ⇦, R, R, ⇧, ▲, ⇩, ×
Foggy Weather	⇦, ⇩, ▲, ×, ⇨, ⇧, ⇦, L
$250,000	⇧, ⇩, ⇦, ⇨, ×, ×, L, R
Guys Follow You	⇨, L, ⇩, L, ●, ⇧, L, ■
Health	⇧, ⇩, ⇦, ⇨, ●, ●, L, R
Lower Wanted Level	⇧, ⇨, ▲, ▲, ⇩, ⇦, ×, ×
Nearest Ped Gets in Your Vehicle (Must Be in a Car)	⇩, ⇧, ⇨, L, L, ■, ⇧, L
Overcast Weather	⇦, ⇩, L, R, ⇨, ⇧, ⇦, ■
Peds Attack You	⇩, ▲, ⇧, ×, L, R, L, R
Peds Have Weapons	⇧, L, ⇩, R, ⇦, ●, ⇨, ▲
Peds Riot	R, L, L, ⇩, ⇦, ●, ⇩, L
Perfect Traction	⇩, ⇦, ⇧, L, R, ▲, ●, ×
Rainy Weather	⇦, ⇩, L, R, ⇨, ⇧, ⇦, ▲
Raise Wanted Level	⇧, ⇨, ■, ■, ⇩, ⇦, ●, ●
Slower Gameplay	⇦, ⇦, ●, ●, ⇩, ⇧, ▲, ×
Spawn Rhino	⇧, L, ⇩, R, ⇦, L, ⇨, R

Grand Theft Auto: Vice City Stories (continued)

Unlockable	Code
Spawn Trashmaster	↓, ↑, →, ▲, L, ▲, L, ▲
Sunny Weather	←, ↓, R, L, →, ↑, ←, ●
Upside Down Mode 1	■, ■, ■, L, L, R, ←, →
Upside Down Mode 2	←, ←, ←, R, R, L, →, ←
Weapon Set 1	←, →, ✕, ↑, ↓, ■, ←, →
Weapon Set 2	←, →, ■, ↑, ↓, ▲, ←, →
Weapon Set 3	←, →, ▲, ↑, ↓, ●, ←, →

Gretzky NHL

At the Gretzky Challenge Unlockables screen, press START to bring up the cheat entry.

Unlockable	Password
Get One Gretzky Point	CANADIAN DOLLAR
RoboEnforcer Model-44	ROBO CHECKS
Unlock 1910 Montreal Canadians Uniform	THE HABS
Unlock 1924 Montreal Canadians Uniform	LE HABITANT
Unlock 1927 Detroit Red Wings Uniform	BEEP BEEP
Unlock 1928 Boston Bruins Uniform	WICKED HAAAAAHD
Unlock 1929 Ottawa Senators Uniform	THE SENANATOR
Unlock 1930 Toronto Maple Leafs Uniform	NORTH OF THE BORDER
Unlock 1967 Pittsburgh Penguins Away Uniform	POPPIN TALK
Unlock 1970 Minnesota North Stars Uniform	TWIN STARS
Unlock 1975 Kansas City Scouts Uniform	YOU LITTLE DEVIL
Unlock 1976 New York Rangers Away Uniform	NEW YORK NEW YORK
Unlock 1977 Calgary Flames Away Uniform	FLAME ON
Unlock 1977 Colorado Rockies Uniform	DEVIL MADE ME DO IT
Unlock 1977 Vancouver Canucks Home Uniform	GREAT WHITE NORTH
Unlock 1977 Washington Capitals Away Uniform	CONGRESSIONAL WISDOM
Unlock 1978 New York Islanders Away Uniform	ORDWAY MADE ME DO IT
Unlock 1979 Edmonton Oilers Away Uniform	A SCARY SIGHT TO THE HOME CROWD
Unlock 1979 Edmonton Oilers Home Uniform	THREADS OF CHAMPS
Unlock 1979 St. Louis Blues Away Uniform	A BLUE NOTE
Unlock 1979 St. Louis Blues Home Uniform	MARDI GRAS
Unlock 1980 Quebec Nordiques Uniform	FRENCH FOR CANADIAN
Unlock 1983 Edmonton Oilers Away Uniform	ALL HAIL WAYNE
Unlock 1988 Pittsburgh Penguins Away Uniform	STEEL TOWN
Unlock 1989 Los Angeles Kings Away Uniform	KING GRETZKY
Unlock 1989 Los Angeles Kings Home Uniform	KING WAYNE
Unlock 1990 Winnipeg Jets Away Uniform	PORTAGE AND MAIN
Unlock 1990 Winnipeg Jets Home Uniform	MIDDLE OF CANADA
Unlock 1993 San Jose Sharks Away Uniform	SHARK BAIT
Unlock 1995 St. Louis Blues Away Uniform	VINTAGE BLUES
Unlock 1999 New York Rangers Home Uniform	UPPER WEST SIDE
Unlock Alternate Anaheim Mighty Ducks Uniform	FLYING VEE
Unlock Alternate Atlanta Thrashers Uniform	THRASHED TO THE MAX
Unlock Alternate Boston Bruins Uniform	NOMAR STILL RULES
Unlock Alternate Buffalo Sabers Uniform	IN THE SNOW BELT
Unlock Alternate Calgary Flames Uniform	THREE ALARM BLAZE
Unlock Alternate Chicago Blackhawks Uniform	WINDY CITY
Unlock Alternate Colorado Avalanche Uniform	SNOW DRIFTS

Gretzky NHL (continued)

Unlockable	Password
Unlock Alternate Columbus Blue Jackets Uniform	BLUE SHOES
Unlock Alternate Dallas Stars Uniform	HOCKEY IN TEXAS
Unlock Alternate Edmonton Oilers Uniform	PUMPIN OIL
Unlock Alternate Florida Panthers Uniform	SOUTH BEACH
Unlock Alternate Los Angeles Kings Uniform	IT IS GOOD TO BE THE KING
Unlock Alternate Minnesota Wild Uniform	COLD AS HECK
Unlock Alternate Nashville Predators Uniform	ALIEN VS NASHVILLE
Unlock Alternate New York Islanders Uniform	LAWNG ISLAND
Unlock Alternate New York Rangers Uniform	GREAT WHITE WAY
Unlock Alternate Ottawa Senators Uniform	MAJORITY RULE
Unlock Alternate Philadelphia Flyers Uniform	FANATICAL
Unlock Alternate San Jose Sharks Uniform	GET A BIGGER BOAT
Unlock Alternate Toronto Maple Leafs Uniform	HEY TERRANCE
Unlock Alternate Vancouver Canucks Uniform	WEST COAST EH
Unlock Big Boards Checking Option	ALL ABOARD
Unlock Everything	SHOENLOC
Unlock No Skate Fatigue Option	CAFFEINATED
Unlock Perfect Aim Option	THREAD THE NEEDLE
Unlock Perfect Slap Shots Option	SLAP THAT PUCK
Wayne Gretzky 1979	UNSTOPPABLE GREATNESS
Wayne Gretzky 1987	GLORY DAZE
Wayne Gretzky 1994	WEST COAST WAYNE
Wayne Gretzky 1999	A LEGEND ON ICE

Gretzky NHL 06

At the Main menu, select Features. Next, select "Gretzky Challenge" and unlockables. At the unlockables screen, press START to bring up the Password Entry menu.

Unlockable	Password
Earn one Gretzky point	CULKY NETC
Unlock all alternate uniforms	NNIADOUAMFM
Unlock all vintage uniforms	DLEONG ARE
Unlock all Wayne Gretzkys	TEH ESATGRTE NOES
Unlock big boards checking	LAL ABRAOD
Unlock bigger players	ARGLE NI RAGECH
Unlock everything	CONHEOSL
Unlock no skater fatigue	EFDTAFEACIN
Unlock perfect aim mode	TADHRE TEH EDNELE
Unlock perfect slap shots	SAPL TATH CUKP
Unlock RoboEnforcer Model-44	OBOR SKHECC
Unlock smaller players	IGHTMY UOSEM
Unlock Stanley Cup Championship video	VINIOS FO LYRGO

Harry Potter and the Goblet of Fire

Unlockable Levels

Unlockable	How to Unlock
Defense Against the Dark Arts (Lesson 1)	Finish the opening level
Moody's Challenges	Complete the "Forbidden Forest" level

Harry Potter and the Goblet of Fire (continued)

Unlockable Minigames

Unlockable	How to Unlock
Dugbog Bulb Raid	Get 5 Tri-wizard Shields
Exploding Snap	Get 2 Tri-wizard Shields
Niffler Time Challenge	Get 8 Tri-wizard Shields
Wizard Pairs	Beat the first level of the game

Hot Shots Golf Open Tee

Unlockable	Code
Easy Loyalty	To gain loyalty much quicker than playing an entire round of golf, start a match play game under challenge mode. Give up on the first three holes by pressing Select then Start to forfeit. After the match you will still gain loyalty for your character.

Juiced 2: Hot Import Nights

Driver DNA Car Unlockables

Enter the passwords in the DNA lab to unlock the special challenges. If you win the challenges, you unlock a custom version of the following cars.

Unlockable	How to Unlock
Audi TT 1.8L Quattro	YTHZ
BMW Z4 Roadster	GVDL
Frito-Lay Infiniti G35	MNCH
Holden Monaro	RBSG
Hyundai Coupe 2.7L V6	BSLU
Infiniti G35	MRHC
Koenigsegg CCX	KDTR
Mitsubishi Prototype X	DOPX
Nissan 350Z	PRGN
Nissan Skyline R34 GT-R	JWRS
Saleen S7	WIKF
Seat Leon Cupra R	FAMQ

LEGO Batman

Codes

Enter the codes on the second level of the Batcave at the computer above the outfit changer.

Effect	Code
Alfred	ZAQ637
Bat-Tank	KNTT4B
Batgirl	JKR331
Bruce Wayne	BDJ327
Bruce Wayne's Private Jet	LEA664
Catwoman (Classic)	M1AAWW
Catwoman's Motorcycle	HPL826
Clown Goon	HJK327
Commissioner Gordon	DDP967
Fishmonger	HGY748
Freeze Girl	XVK541
Garbage Truck	DUS483
Glideslam	BBD7BY
Goon Helicopter	GCH328
Harbor Helicopter	CHP735
Harley Quinn's Hammer Truck	RDT637
Joker Goon	UTF782
Joker Henchman	YUN924
Mad Hatter	JCA283
Mad Hatter's Glider	HS000W
Mad Hatter's Steamboat	M4DM4N
Man-Bat	NYU942
Military Policeman	MKL382
Mr. Freeze's Iceberg	ICYICE
Mr. Freeze's Kart	BCT229
Nightwing	MVY759
Penguin Goon	NKA238
Penguin Goon Submarine	BTN248
Penguin Henchman	BJH782
Penguin Minion	KJP748
Poison Ivy Goon	GTB899
Police Bike	LJP234
Police Boat	PLC999
Police Car	KJL832
Police Helicopter	CWR732
Police Marksman	HKG984

LEGO Batman (continued)

Effect	Code	Effect	Code
Police Officer	JRY983	Sailor	NAV592
Police Van	MAC788	Scientist	JFL786
Police Watercraft	VJD328	Security Guard	PLB946
Riddler Goon	CRY928	The Joker (Tropical)	CCB199
Riddler Henchman	XEU824	The Joker's Van	JUK657
Riddler's Jet	HAHAHA	Two-Face's Armored Truck	EFE933
Robin's Submarine	TTF453	Yeti	NJL412
S.W.A.T.	HTF114	Zoo Sweeper	DWR243

Extra Codes

Effect	Code	Effect	Code
Always Score Multiply	9LRGNB	Ice Rink	KLKL4G
Area Effect	TL3EKT	Immune to Freeze	JXUDY6
Armor Plating	N8JZEK	Invincible	WYD5CP
Bats	XFP4E2	Minikit Detector	ZXGH9J
Beep Beep	RAFTU8	More Batarang Targets	XWP645
Character Studs	DY13BD	More Detonators	TNTN6B
Decoy	TQ09K3	Piece Detector	KHJ544
Disguise	GEC3MD	Power Brick Detector	MMN786
Extra Toggle	EWAW7W	Regenerate Hearts	HJH7HJ
Extra Hearts	ML3KHP	Score x2	N4NR3E
Fast Batarangs	JRBDCB	Score x4	CX9MAT
Fast Build	GHJ2DY	Score x6	MLVNF2
Fast Grapple	RM4PR8	Score x8	WCCDB9
Fast Walk	ZOLM6N	Score x10	18HW07
Faster Pieces	EVG26J	Silhouettes	YK4TPH
Flaming Batarangs (Used with heat batman)	D8NYWH	Slam	BBD7BY
		Sonic Pain	THTL4X
Freeze Batarang	XPN4NG	Stud Magnet	LK2DY4

LEGO Indiana Jones: The Original Adventures

Character Codes

Enter the codes on the blackboard in the math classroom of Barnett College(the 2nd door on the left in the main hallway).

Effect	Code	Effect	Code
Bandit	12N68W	British Troop Commander	B73EUA
Bandit Swordsman	1MK4RT	British Troop Soldier	DJ5I2W
Barranca	04EM94	Captain Katanga	VJ3TT3
Bazooka Trooper (Crusade)	MK83R7	Chatter Lal	ENW936
Bazooka Trooper (Raiders)	S93Y5R	Chatter Lal (Thuggee)	CNH4RY
Belloq	CHN3YU	Chen	3NK48T
Belloq (Jungle)	TDR197	Colonel Dietrich	2K9RKS
Belloq (Robes)	VEO29L	Colonel Vogel	8EAL4H
British Officer	VJ5TI9	Dancing Girl	C7EJ21

LEGO Indiana Jones: The Original Adventures (continued)

Effect	Code	Effect	Code
Donovan	3NFTU8	Kazim (Desert)	3M29TJ
Elsa (Desert)	JSNRT9	Lao Che	2NK479
Elsa (Officer)	VMJ5US	Maharaja	NFK5N2
Enemy Boxer	8246RB	Major Toht	13NS01
Enemy Butler	VJ48W3	Masked Bandit	N48SF0
Enemy Guard	VJ7R51	Mola Ram	FJUR31
Enemy Guard (Mountains)	YR47WM	Monkey Man	3RF6YJ
Enemy Officer	572 E61	Pankot Assassin	2NKT72
Enemy Officer (Desert)	2MK450	Pankot Guard	VN28RH
Enemy Pilot	B84ELP	Sherpa Brawler	VJ37WJ
Enemy Radio Operator	1MF94R	Sherpa Gunner	ND762W
Enemy Soldier (Desert)	4NSU7Q	Slave Child	0E3ENW
Fedora	V75YSP	Thuggee	VM683E
First Mate	0GIN24	Thuggee Acolyte	T2R3F9
Grail Knight	NE6THI	Thuggee Slavedriver	VBS7GW
Hovitos Tribesman	H0V1SS	Village Dignitary	KD48TN
Indiana Jones (Desert Disguise)	4J8S4M	Village Elder	4682 E1
Indiana Jones (Officer)	VJ850S	Willie (Dinner Suit)	VK93R7
Jungle Guide	24PF34	Willie (Pajamas)	MEN4IP
Kao Kan	WM046L	Wu Han	3NSLT8
Kazim	NRH23J		

Item Codes

Enter the codes on the blackboard in the math classroom of Barnett College(the 2nd door on the left in the main hallway).

Effect	Code	Effect	Code
Artifact Detector	VIKED7	Regenerate Hearts	MDLP69
Beep Beep	VNF59Q	Secret Characters	3X44AA
Character Treasure	VIES2R	Silhouettes	3HE85H
Disarm Enemies	VKRNS9	Super Scream	VN3R7S
Disguises	4ID1N6	Super Slap	0P1TA5
Fast Build	V83SL0	Treasure Magnet	H86LA2
Fast Dig	378RS6	Treasure x2	VM4TS9
Fast Fix	FJ59WS	Treasure x4	VLWEN3
Fertilizer	B1GW1F	Treasure x6	V84RYS
Ice Rink	33GM7J	Treasure x8	A72E1M
Parcel Detector	VUT673	Treasure x10	VI3PS8
Poo Treasure	WWQ1SA		

Invincibility

Enter the code on the blackboard of the math classroom.

Effect	Code
Invincibility	B83EA1

DS PSP PS2 PS3 Wii Xbox Xbox 360 Index

LEGO Indiana Jones: The Original Adventures (continued)

Secret Levels

Unlockable	How to Unlock
Ancient City	Collect all of the artifacts in Temple of Doom.
Warehouse Level	Collect all of the artifacts in The Last Crusade.
Young Indy level	Collect all of the artifacts in Raiders of the Lost Ark.

LEGO Star Wars II: The Original Trilogy

Passwords

Enter the following codes at the Mos Eisley Cantina to unlock the character for purchase in Free Play mode.

Unlockable	How to Unlock	Unlockable	How to Unlock
Beach Trooper	UCK868	Imperial Spy	CVT125
Ben Kenobi's Ghost	BEN917	Lobot	UUB319
Bespin Guard	VHY832	Palace Guard	SGE549
Bib Fortuna	WTY721	Rebel Pilot	CYG336
Boba Fett	HLP221	Rebel Trooper from Hoth	EKU849
Death Star Trooper	BNC332	Red Noses on All Characters	NBP398
Emperor	HHY382	Santa Hat and Red Clothes	CL4U5H
Ewok	TTT289	Skiff Guard	GBU888
Gamorean Guard	YZF999	Snow Trooper	NYU989
Gonk Droid	NFX582	Stormtrooper	PTR345
Grand Moff Tarkin	SMG219	TIE Fighter	HDY739
Han Solo with Hood	YWM840	TIE Fighter Pilot	NNZ316
IG-88	NXL973	TIE Interceptor	QYA828
Imperial Guard	MMM111	Ugnaught	UGN694
Imperial Officer	BBV889	White Beard Extra	TYH319
Imperial Shuttle Pilot	VAP66		

Unlockable Characters

Complete challenge by collecting 10 Blue Minikits within the time limit allowed per level.

Unlockable	How to Unlock
R4-P17, PK Droid	Episode 4, Chapter 2
Battle Droid, B. D. (Security), B. D. (Geonosis), B. D. (Commander)	Episode 4, Chapter 4
Chancellor Palpatine, General Grievous, Grievous' Bodyguard	Episode 6, Chapter 5
Clone (Episode III, Pilot)	Episode 4, Chapter 6
Clone (Episode III, Swamp)	Episode 5, Chapter 4
Clone, Clone (Episode III), Commander Cody, Clone (Episode III Walker)	Episode 6, Chapter 3
Disguised Clone, Boba Fett (Boy)	Episode 6, Chapter 1
Droideka	Episode 4, Chapter 5
Geonosian	Episode 5, Chapter 3
Jango Fett	Episode 6, Chapter 2
Luminara, Ki-Adi-Mundi, Kit Fisto, Shaak Ti	Episode 5, Chapter 1
Mace Windu, Mace Windu (Episode 3)	Episode 6, Chapter 6
Padmé (Battle), Padmé (Clawed), Padmé (Geonosis)	Episode 5, Chapter 2
Padmé, Anakin Skywalker (boy)	Episode 4, Chapter 3
Queen Amidala, Royal Guard, Captain Panaka	Episode 5, Chapter 6

Star Wars II: The Original Trilogy (continued)

Unlockable	How to Unlock
Super Battle Droid	Episode 5, Chapter 5
TC-14	Episode 4, Chapter 1
Wookiee, Jar Jar Binks	Episode 6, Chapter 4

Madden NFL 07

Passwords

Enter these names in the password section to get the Madden cards.

Password	Effect
B57QLU	1958 Colts Gold card
1PL1FL	1966 Packers Gold card
MIE6WO	1968 Jets Gold card
CL2TOE	1970 Browns Gold card
NOEB7U	1972 Dolphins Gold card
YOOFLA	1974 Steelers Gold card
MOA11I	1976 Raiders Gold card
C8UM7U	1977 Broncos Gold card
VIU007	1978 Dolphins Gold card
NLAPH3	1980 Raiders Gold card
COAGI4	1981 Chargers Gold card
WL8BRI	1982 Redskins Gold card
H0EW7I	1983 Raiders Gold card
M1AM1E	1984 Dolphins Gold card
QOETO8	1985 Bears Gold card
ZI8S2L	1986 Giants Gold card
SP2A8H	1988 49ers Gold card
2L4TRO	1990 Eagles Gold card
J1ETRI	1991 Lions Gold card
W9UVI9	1992 Cowboys Gold card
DLA3I7	1993 Bills Gold card
DR7EST	1994 49ers Gold card
F8LUST	1996 Packers Gold card
FIES95	1998 Broncos Gold card
S9OUSW	1999 Rams Gold card
YI8P8U	Aloha Stadium Gold card
5LAWO0	Lame Duck card
XL7SP1	Mistake Free card
XL7SP1	Mistake Free card, effective for one half
WROA0R	QB on Target card
WROA0R	Quarterback 100% Accuracy for one half
RLA9R7	Super Bowl XLI Gold card
WRLUF8	Super Bowl XLII Gold card
NIEV4A	Super Bowl XLIII Gold card
M5AB7L	Super Bowl XLIV Gold card
5LAQ00	Your opponent will have to throw Lob Passes for one half

MediEvil Resurrection

To enter this code, pause the game.

Unlockable	Code
Invincibility and All Weapons	Hold R, then press ⇩, ⇧, ■, ▲, ▲, ●, ⇩, ⇧, ■, ▲

Metal Gear Acid

Enter the following in the Passwords menu through the Main menu.

Card	Password
Gives Card No. 173 - Viper	Viper
Gives Card No. 178 - Mika Slayton	Mika
Gives Card No. 182 - Karen Houjou	Karen
Gives Card No. 184 - Jehuty	Jehuty
Gives Card No. 199 - XM8	Xmeight
Gives Card No. 200 - Kosaka Yuka	Kobe
Gives Card No. 201 - Asaki Yoshida	umeda
Gives Card No. 202 - Yu Saito	YEBISU
Gives Card No. 203 - Shibuya Eri	Roppongi

DS
PSP
PS2
PS3
Wii
Xbox
Xbox 360
Index

Metal Gear Acid 2

Enter these passwords at the password screen. You'll obtain them as you load your saved games.

Password	Effect
Ronaldsiu	Banana Peel Card
Dcy	Card No. 203—Decoy Octopus
SONOFSULLY	Card No. 291—Jack
Vrs	Card No. 046—Strain (JP Version only)
Cct	Card No. 099—Gijin-san (JP Version only)
Konami	Card No. 119—Reaction Block
Viper	Card No. 161—Viper
Mika	Card No. 166—Mika Slayton
Karen	Card No. 170—Karen Houjou
Jehuty	Card No. 172—Jehuty
Xmeight	Card No. 187—XM8
Signt	Card No. 188—Mr. Sigint
Sgnt	Card No. 188—SIGINT (JP Version only)
Hrrr	Card No. 197—Sea Harrier (JP Version only)
Dcyctps	Card No. 203—Decoy Octopus (JP Version only)
Rgr	Card No. 212—Roger McCoy (JP Version only)
Xx	Card No. 281—Hinomoto Reiko (JP Version only)
Kinoshitaa	Card No. 285—Kinoshita Ayumi (JP Version only)
Shiimeg	Card No. 286—Ishii Meguru (JP Version only)
Nonat	Card No. 287—Sano Natsume (JP Version only)
No Place	Card No. 288—MGS4 (JP Version only)
Snake	Card No. 294—Solid Snake (MGS4)
Otacon	Card No. 295—Otacon (MGS4)
shrrr	Card No. 197 Sea Harrier (US version)
Ginormousj	Emma's Parrot Card
Gekko	Gekko (US Version)
NEXTGEN	Get MGS4 card
shinta	Gives you card Gijin-san
nojiri	Gives you card Strand
mgr	Ishii Meguru
aym	Kinoshita Ayumi
mk2	Metal Gear MK. II (MGS4) Card unlocked
smoking	No Smoking card (US Version)
thespaniard	Possessed Arm card
gcl	Reaction Block 119 (Japanese version only)
tobidacid	Solid Eye card (US/UK Version)
ntm	Unlocks Natsume Sano Card an Solid Eye Video
Hnmt	Unlocks Reiko Hinomoto card
Mccy	Unlocks the Roger McCoy card

Card Pack Upgrades

Complete the game once. Load your finished game save and play through the game again. At the points where you received the card packs, they will be upgraded into newer versions.

Metal Gear Acid 2 (continued)

Unlockable	How to Unlock
Chronicle Unlimited Pack	Upgrade Chronicle Pack
MGS1 Integral Pack	Upgrade MGS1 Pack
MGS2 Substance Pack	Upgrade MGS2 Pack
MGS3 Subsistence Pack	Upgrade MGS3 Pack

Unlockable Cards

Complete the game on any difficulty and get a certain rare card.

Unlockable	How to Unlock
"E-Z Gun" Card	Beat 6 levels in Arena mode on Easy setting
"G36C" Card	Beat 6 levels in Arena mode on Extreme setting
"Stealth Camo" Card	Beat 6 levels in Arena mode on Normal setting
Metal Gear RAY	Beat Campaign mode twice
Metal Gear Rex	Complete game on Normal
MGS4	Complete game on Easy
Running Man Card	Complete 6 rounds in the Arena on Hard setting

Midnight Club Racing 3: Dub Edition

Go into the Options menu, then into the Cheats menu to enter these passwords.

Unlockable	Password
Max Nitro	fillmeup
Unlock All Cities in Arcade Mode	crosscountry
Unlocks Atlanta & Detroit	roadtrip
Vehicles Take No Damage	ontheroad

MLB 07: The Show

Codes

Code	Effect
All Pitches Have Max Break	Pause during a game and enter: ⇨, ×, □, △, ×, ○, ○, △
All Pitches Have Max Speed	Pause during a game and enter: ⇧, ○, △, ×, ○, □, ○, △
Silver Era Team and Gold Era Team Unlocked	At the main menu: ⇦, ×, □, △, △, ○, ×, △

MVP Baseball

Under the "My MVP" menu, create a player named "Dan Carter." Once you do this, there will be a message indicating that the code was successful.

N+

Codes

Hold Ⓛ and Ⓡ and insert the following code at the Unlockables menu.

Effect	Code
Unlocks Atari Bonus Levels	×,●,×,●,×,×,●

NBA Ballers Rebound

Enter these passwords in the Phrase-ology under Inside Stuff.

Unlockable	Password
All Alternate Gear, Players, and Movies	NBA Ballers True Playa
Allen Iverson's Recording Studio	The Answer
Alonzo Mourning Alternate Gear	Zo
Ben Gordon's Yacht	Nice Yacht
Chris Weber's Alternate Gear	24 Seconds
Clyde Drexler's Alternate Gear	Clyde The Glide
Dikembe Mutumbo's Alternate Gear	In The Paint
Emanuel Ginobli Alternate Gear	Manu
Jerry Stackhouse Alternate Gear	Stop Drop And Roll
Julius Irving Alternate Gear	One On One
Kevin McHale Alternate Gear	Holla Back
Lebron James' Alternate Gear	King James
Magic Johnson Alternate Gear	Laker Legends
Nene's Hilarios Alternate Gear	Rags To Riches
Pete Maravich's Alternate Gear	Pistol Pete
Rasheed Wallace Alternate Gear	Bring Down The House
Rick Hamilton's Alternate Gear	Rip
Stephon Marbury's Alternate Gear	Platinum Playa
Steve Francis Alternate Gear	Ankle Breaker
Steve Francis' Alternate Gear	Rising Star
Tim Duncan Alternate Gear	Make It Take It
Wilt Chamberlain's Alternate Gear	Wilt The Stilt

Need for Speed Carbon: Own the City

Unlockable Cars

Beat the following bosses to unlock these cars:

Unlockable	How to Unlock
911 Carrera S	Beat MK
Aston Martin DB9	Beat Jenna
Carrera GT and Lamborghini Gallardo	Beat Clutch
Chevy Cobalt SS and VW Golf GTI	Beat Marcus
Chrysler 300 and Pontiac GTO	Beat Layla 1
Firebird, Toyota MR2, and '67 Mustang	Beat Poorboy
Lotus Elise and Mustang GT	Beat Steve
Mercedes SL65, Corvette, and Ford GT	Beat Scotty
Mitsubishi Eclipse	Beat Sly
Nissan 350Z	Beat Daemon
Pontiac Solstice	Beat Striker
RX-7, Skyline GTR, and WRX STI	Beat Buddy
RX-8, Toyota Supra, and Audi TT	Beat Layla 3

DS
PSP
PS2
PS3
Wii
Xbox
Xbox 360
Index

NFL Street 2 Unleashed

Enter the following in the Cheats menu.

Unlockable	Codes
AFC East All Stars	EAASFSCT
AFC North All Stars	NAOFRCTH
AFC South All Stars	SAOFUCTH
AFC West All Stars	WAEFSCT
EA Field	EAField
Fumble Mode (Other team fumbles)	GreasedPig
Gargantuan Players	BIGSmash
Max Catch	MagnetHands
NFC East All Stars	NNOFRCTH
NFC North All-Stars	NNAS66784
NFC South All Stars	SNOFUCTH
NFC West All Stars	ENASFSCT
No Fumble Mode	GlueHands
Reebok Team	Reebok
Unlimited Turbo	NozBoost

Pac-Man World 3

Enter this code at the main menu.

Unlockable	Code
Unlock levels and mazes	⇦, ⇨, ⇦, ⇨, ●, ⇧

Pinball Hall of Fame

Enter these passwords on the Password screen.

Unlockable	Password
999 Credits	JAT
Freeplay on Big Shot	UJP
Freeplay on Black Hole	LIS
Freeplay on Goin' Nuts	PHF
Freeplay on Love Meter	HOT
Freeplay on Tee'd Off	PGA
Freeplay on Xolten	BIG
Unlocks Payout mode	WGR
Unlocks Aces High for freeplay	UNO
Unlocks Central Park for freeplay	NYC
Unlocks custom balls in Options	CKF
Unlocks freeplay on Strikes 'N Spares	PBA
Unlocks optional tilt in Options	BZZ
Unlocks Play Boy table for freeplay	HEF

DS
PSP
PS2
PS3
Wii
Xbox
Xbox 360
Index

Ratatouille

Codes

Select "Options" at the main menu, then "Extras," and finally "Cheats." Enter one of the following codes to activate the corresponding cheat function. A sound confirms correct code entry. Make sure you enter the codes in lowercase.

Code	Effect
saycheese	9,999 Cheese
anyonecancook	All recipes
gusteauvid	All videos
itscake	Any health restored to full
boingspawn	Bouncy cheese
skycan	Can all blue cheese
pieceocake	Easy enemies
myhero	Enemies cause no damage
deepfryer	Hard enemies

The Simpsons Game

Codes

Go into the "Extras" section of the main menu and insert the following codes. If your code is accepted, you hear a sound effect.

Unlockable	How to Unlock
All Movies	⇦,■,⇨,▲,⇨,[L]
All Clichés	■,⇦,■,⇨,▲,[R]
Unlimited Power for All Characters	▲,⇦,⇨,▲,■,[L]

Spider-Man 2

Go to Options, Special, and Cheats on the Main menu, and then type in the following passwords.

Unlockable	Password
All Levels Unlocked	WARPULON
All Moves Purchased	MYHERO
All Movies Unlocked	POPPYCORN
Enemies Have Big Heads and Feet	BAHLOONIE
Infinite Health	NERGETS
Infinite Webbing	FILLMEUP
Spidey Has Big Head and Feet	HEAVYHEAD
Tiny Spider-Man	SPIDEYMAN
Unlock All Production Art	SHUTT
Unlock Storyboard Viewer	FRZFRAME

Star Wars: The Force Unleashed

Codes

From the "Extras" menu inside the Rogue Shadow, select "Cheat Codes" and enter the following codes. Specific skin codes are not necessary after you enter the "Unlock All Costumes" code.

Effect	Code
1,000,000 Force Points	SPEEDER
All Combos at Maximum Level	COUNTDOOKU
All Force Powers	TYRANUS

Star Wars: The Force Unleashed (continued)

Effect	Code
All Force Powers at Maximum Level	KATARN
Amplified Lightsaber Damage	LIGHTSABER
Immunity to All Damage	CORTOSIS
Unlimited Force Power	VERGENCE
Unlock All Costumes	GRANDMOFF

Skin Codes

Effect	Code	Effect	Code
501st Legion	LEGION	Juno Eclipse	ECLIPSE
Aayla Secura	AAYLA	Kento's Robe	WOOKIEE
Admiral Ackbar	ITSATWAP	Kleef	KLEEF
Anakin Skywalker	CHOSENONE	Lando Calrissian	SCOUNDREL
Asajj Ventress	ACOLYTE	Luke Skywalker	T16WOMPRAT
Ceremonial Jedi Robes	DANTOOINE	Mace Windu	JEDIMASTER
Chop'aa Notimo	NOTIMO	Mara Jade	MARAJADE
Classic Stormtrooper	TK421	Maris Brood	MARISBROOD
Count Dooku	SERENNO	Navy Commando	STORMTROOP
Darth Desolous	PAUAN	Obi-Wan Kenobi	BENKENOBI
Darth Maul	ZABRAK	PROXY	HOLOGRAM
Darth Phobos	HIDDENFEAR	Qui-Gon Jinn	MAVERICK
Darth Vader	SITHLORD	Shaak Ti	TOGRUTA
Drexl Roosh	DREXLROOSH	Shadowtrooper	INTHEDARK
Emperor Palpatine	PALPATINE	Sith Robes	HOLOCRON
General Rahm Kota	MANDALORE	Sith Stalker Armor	KORRIBAN
Han Solo	NERFHERDER	Twi'lek	SECURA
Heavy Trooper	SHOCKTROOP	Yavin Luke	YELLOWJCKT

Star Wars Battlefront 2

Pause the game and enter this code.

Unlockable	Code
Invincibility	↑, ↑, ↑, ←, ↓, ↓, ↓, ←, ↑, ↑, ↑, ←, →

Syphon Filter: Logan's Shadow

Bonus Abilities and Upgrades

Earn the Career Ratings to unlock these abilities and upgrades.

Unlockable	How to Unlock
Dual Wield	Earn Combat Sharp Shooter Rating 3
Increased Health	Earn Survival Specialist Rating 2
Max Darts x 5 (MB150)	Earn Elite Weapons Expert 1
Max Darts x 8 (MB150)	Earn Elite Weapons Expert 2
Max Darts x 10 (MB150)	Earn Elite Weapons Expert 3

Bonus Missions

Unlockable	How to Unlock
Behind the Scenes Bonus Mission	Beat Story Mode on Normal Difficulty
Bonus Lian Mission	Complete all 5 training missions
Killing Time	Earn Combat Knife Specialist Rating 4

Syphon Filter: Logan's Shadow (continued)

Unlockable	How to Unlock
Left Behind	Earn Elite Weapons Expert Rating 4
Shadowed Bonus Mission	Beat Story Mode on Hard Difficulty

Bonus Weapons

Unlockable	How to Unlock
C11	Earn Combat Knife Specialist 2
Calico HE	Earn Survival Specialist Rating 4
Chinese Type 56	Earn Combat Knife Specialist Rating 3
EPDD	Earn Stealth Combat Specialist Rating 4
FAMAS	Complete Training 2 in less than 3 minutes
Flashbang Grenade	Earn Combat Knife Specialist Rating 1
Jackhammer HE	Earn Tactical Combat Specialist Rating 4
Jerico-41	Earn Tactical Combat Specialist Rating 2
M4 Silenced	Earn Survival Specialist Rating 3
M67 Grenade	Earn Tactical Specialist Rating 3
M82 BFG	Earn Combat Sharp Shooter Rating 4
MDS A4 Silenced	Earn Stealth Combat Specialist Rating 2
Over Under	Earn Combat Sharp Shooter Rating 2
Sawed-Off Pistol	Earn Survival Specialist Rating 1
Silenced .44	Earn Stealth Combat Specialist Rating 3
SP - 57	Complete Training 1 in less than 1 minute and 30 seconds
SSP 90	Earn Combat Sharp Shooter Rating 1
TK-9 Silenced	Earn Stealth Combat Specialist Rating 1
UNP .45	Complete Training 3 without wasting a shoot
USAS - 12	Earn Tactical Combat Specialist Rating 1

Tony Hawk's Underground 2 Remix

Go to Game Options, then Cheat Codes and enter the following codes.

Unlockable	Code
Perfect Rail Balance	Tightrope
Unlock Tony Hawk from Tony Hawk Pro Skater 1	Birdman

Teenage Mutant Ninja Turtles

Codes

Enter this in the Mission Briefing screens.

Code	Effect
→, ←, →, ←, ↓, ↑, ↓, ↑, ×	Unlocks a Fantasy Costume

Thrillville

Codes

Enter these while in a park. You hear a chime if it worked.

Unlockable	How to Unlock
Add $50,000	■, ●, ▲, ■, ●, ▲, ×
Mission Complete	■, ●, ▲, ■, ●, ▲, ●
Unlock All Parks	■, ●, ▲, ■, ●, ▲, ■
Unlock All Rides in Park	■, ●, ▲, ■, ●, ▲, ▲

DS PSP PS2 PS3 Wii Xbox Xbox 360 Index

Tom Clancy's Splinter Cell Essentials

Bonus Mission Codes

Enter the following at the bonus mission screen (you have to enter the code each time you want to play the mission).

Unlockable	How to Unlock
Unlock the Heroin Refinery Mission	Hold Select and press L+R three more times
Unlock the Paris-Nice Mission	Hold Select and press L+R 12 more times
Unlock the Television Free Indonesia Mission	Hold Select and press L+R three times

Tomb Raider: Legend

Codes

Enter these codes while playing a level, but they only work once you have unlocked them.

Code	Effect
Bulletproof	Hold L, then: ×, R, ▲, R, ■, R
Draw Enemy Health	Hold L, then: ■, ●, ×, R, R, ▲
Infinite Assault Rifle Ammo	Hold L, then: ×, ●, ×, R, ■, ▲
Infinite Grenade Launcher	Hold L, then: R, ▲, R, ●, R, ■
Infinite Shotgun Ammo	Hold L, then: b, ●, ■, R, ■, ×
Infinite SMG Ammo	Hold L, then: ●, ▲, R, R, ×, ●
One Shot Kill	Hold L, then: ▲, ×, ▲, ■, R, ●
Wield Excalibur	Hold L, then: ▲, ×, ●, R, ▲, R
Wield Soul Reaver	Hold L, then: ×, R, ●, R, R, ■

Unlockable Cheats

These cheats are only unlocked when you clear the game or meet the following criteria.

Unlockable	How to Unlock
Bulletproof Lara	Clear England under 27:00 in Time Trials
Infinite Grenade Launcher Ammo	Clear Kazakhstan under 27:10 in Time Trials
Infinite MG415 Ammo	Clear Peru under 21:30 in Time Trials
Infinite RC650 Ammo	Clear Japan under 12:15 in Time Trials
Infinite shotgun Ammo	Clear Ghana under 20:00 in Time Trials
One Hit Deaths	Clear Bolivia (stage 8) under 4:15 in Time Trials
Show Enemy Health	Clear Bolivia under 12:30 in Time Trials
Textureless Mode	Clear the game on any difficulty
Unlock Excalibur	Clear Nepal under 13:40 in Time Trials
Unlock the Soul Reaver	Clear the game and complete all time trials

Unlockables

Unlockable	How to Unlock
Alister Fletcher	Collect 90% of all bronze rewards
Amanda Evert	Collect 70% of all bronze rewards
Anaya Imanu	Collect 30% of all bronze rewards
Biker, Brown Jacket Outfit	Complete Bolivia on the Medium setting in Treasure Hunt mode
Bolivia Redux—100% of all object models	Collect all silver rewards in Bolivia (level 8)
Bolivia	Collect all bronze rewards from Bolivia
Bolivia—100% of all object models	Collect all silver rewards in Bolivia

Tomb Raider: Legend (continued)

Unlockable	How to Unlock
Bronze Gallery	In Tomb trials, finish all levels in Treasure Hunt mode on Easy difficulty
Croft Manor—100% of all object models	Collect all silver rewards in Croft Manor
England	Collect all bronze rewards from England
England—100% of all object models	Collect all silver rewards in England
Ghana	Collect all bronze rewards from Ghana
Ghana—100% of all object models	Collect all silver rewards in Ghana
Gold Gallery	In Tomb trials, finish all levels in Treasure Hunt mode on Hard difficulty
Increased Accuracy	50% of silver and bronze rewards
Increased Damage	75% of silver and bronze rewards
Increased Magazine Capacity	25% of silver and bronze rewards
James Rutland	Collect 50% of all bronze rewards
Japan	Collect all bronze rewards from Japan
Japan—100% of all object models	Collect all silver rewards in Japan
Kazakhstan	Collect all bronze rewards from Kazakhstan
Kazakhstan—100% of all object models	Collect all silver rewards in Kazakhstan
Lara Croft	Collect 10% of all bronze rewards
Legend, Camo Shorts	Beat Bolivia on the Hard setting in Treasure Hunter mode
Nepal	Collect all bronze rewards from Nepal
Nepal—100% of all object models	Collect all silver rewards in Nepal
Peru	Collect all bronze rewards from Peru
Peru—100% of all object models	Collect all silver rewards in Peru
Shogo Takamoto	Collect 60% of all bronze rewards
Silver Gallery	Complete Bolivia, Croft Manor, and Fiery Maze on the Easy setting in Treasure Hunt mode
Silver Gallery	In Tomb trials, finish all levels in Treasure Hunt mode on Medium difficulty
Special	Collect all bronze rewards from Croft Manor
Toru Nishimura	Collect 40% of all bronze rewards
Unknown Entity	Collect 100% of all bronze rewards
Winston Smith	Collect 80% of all bronze rewards
Zip	Collect 20% of all bronze rewards

Twisted Metal Head On

Input these codes during gameplay.

Unlockable	Code
Invulnerability	→, ←, ↓, ↑ and finally press L1 + R1
Infinite Weapons	▲, ▲, ↓, ↓, L1 + R1

Virtua Tennis World Tour

Enter these codes at the Main menu while holding R3.

Unlockable	Code
All Racquets and Clothing Available in the Home Screen	⇨, ⇦, ⇨, ⇨, ⇧, ⇧, ⇧
Begin World Tour mode with $1,000,000	⇧, ⇩, ⇦, ⇩, ▲, ▲, ▲
Earn $2000 Every Week in World Tour mode	⇧, ⇩, ⇨, ⇩, ▲, ■, ▲
Unlock All Stadiums	⇧, ⇩, ⇦, ⇨, ■, ■, ■
Unlock the players King & Queen	⇧, ⇩, ⇧, ⇩, ■, ▲, ■

WALL-E

Cheats

Enter the following codes in the Cheats menu in the corresponding code slot.

Effect	Code
Code 1: Kills or Stuns Everything within Range	BOTOFWAR
Code 2: Can Move Undetected by any Enemy	STEALTHARMOR
Code 3: Laser Switches Color Continuously	RAINBOWLASER
Code 4: Every Cube Is a Explosive Cube	EXPLOSIVEWORLD
Code 5: Lights Dark Areas	GLOWINTHEDARK
Code 6: Wears Ski Goggles	BOTOFMYSTERY
Code 7: WALL-E has Golden Tracks	GOLDENTRACKS

WRC: FIA World Rally Championship

Enter these passwords as Profile names.

Unlockable	Password
Bird camera	dovecam
Enables Supercharger cheat	MAXPOWER
Extra avatars	UGLYMUGS
Ghost car	SPOOKY
Reverses controls	REVERSE
Time trial ghost cars	AITRIAL
Unlock everything	PADLOCK

X-Men Legends II: Rise of Apocalypse

These codes must be entered on the pause screen.

Unlockable	Code
1-Hit Kills with Punches	⇦, ⇦, ⇨, ⇦, ⇨, ⇧, START
God Mode	⇩, ⇧, ⇩, ⇧, ⇨, ⇩, ⇨, ⇦,
Super Speed	⇧, ⇧, ⇧, ⇩, ⇧, ⇩, START
Unlimited XTreme Power	⇦, ⇩, ⇨, ⇩, ⇧, ⇧, ⇩, ⇧, START

Enter these at Forge or Beast's equipment screen.

Unlockable	Code
100,000 techbits	⇧, ⇧, ⇧, ⇩, ⇨, ⇨, START

Enter these codes at the team management screen.

Unlockable	Code
All Characters	⇨, ⇦, ⇦, ⇨, ⇧, ⇧, ⇧, START
All Character Skins	⇩, ⇧, ⇦, ⇨, ⇧, ⇧, START
All Skills	⇦, ⇨, ⇦, ⇨, ⇩, ⇧, START
Level 99 Characters	⇧, ⇩, ⇧, ⇩, ⇦, ⇧, ⇦, ⇨, START

Enter these in the Review menu.

Unlockable	Code
All Comic Books	⇨, ⇦, ⇦, ⇨, ⇧, ⇧, ⇨, START
All Concept Art	⇦, ⇨, ⇦, ⇨, ⇧, ⇧, ⇩, START
All Game Cinematic	⇦, ⇨, ⇨, ⇦, ⇩, ⇩, ⇦, START

Enter this in the Danger Room.

Unlockable	Code
All Danger Room Courses	⇨, ⇨, ⇦, ⇦, ⇧, ⇩, ⇧, ⇩, START

DS
PSP
PS2
PS3
Wii
Xbox
Xbox 360
Index

Table of Contents - PS2

DS
PSP
PS2
PS3
Wii
Xbox
Xbox 360
Index

.hack//Part 2: Mutation

Unlockable	Code
DVD EASTER EGG	On the companion DVD, from the Title Menu—select Data, highlight Gallery, press ➔, then enter/confirm your selection.

.hack//Part 4: Quarantine

Unlockable	Objective
Parody Mode	Complete the game once.

007: Nightfire

For the following codes, select the "Codenames" option at the main menu. Select your character and enter one of the following codes at the Secret Unlocks screen. Save your Codename after entering the code. Then exit your Codename and begin gameplay.

Unlockable	Code
All Gadget Upgrades	Q LAB
All Multiplayer Options	GAMEROOM
Alpine Escape Level	POWDER
Camera Upgrade	SHUTTER
Chain Reaction Level	MELTDOWN
Bigger Clip for Sniper Rifle	MAGAZINE
Countdown Level	BLASTOFF
Decrypter Upgrade	SESAME
Deep Descent Level	AQUA
Double-Cross Level	BONSAI
Enemies Vanquished Level	TRACTION
Equinox Level	VACUUM
Golden P2K	AU P2K
Golden PP7	AU PP7
Grapple Upgrade	LIFTOFF
Island Infiltration Level	PARADISE
Laser Upgrade	PHOTON
Level Select	PASSPORT
Multiplayer Bond Spacesuit	ZERO G
Multiplayer Mode All Characters	PARTY
Multiplayer Mode Assassination Option	TARGET
Multiplayer Mode Baron Samedi	VOODOO
Multiplayer Mode Bond Tuxedo	BLACKTIE
Multiplayer Mode Christmas Jones	NUCLEAR
Multiplayer Mode Demolition Option	TNT
Multiplayer Mode Drake	NUMBER 1 (Note: Don't forget the space in the code.)
Multiplayer Mode Elektra King	SLICK
Multiplayer Mode Explosive Scenery Option	BOOM
Multiplayer Mode GoldenEye Strike Option	ORBIT
Multiplayer Mode Goldfinger	MIDAS
Multiplayer Mode Jaws	DENTAL
Multiplayer Mode Max Zorin	BLIMP
Multiplayer Mode Mayday	BADGIRL
Multiplayer Mode Nick Nack	BITESIZE
Multiplayer Mode Oddjob	BOWLER

007: Nightfire (continued)

Unlockable	Code
Multiplayer Mode Protection Option	GUARDIAN
Multiplayer Mode Pussy Galore	CIRCUS
Multiplayer Mode Renard	HEADCASE
Multiplayer Mode Scaramanga	ASSASSIN
Multiplayer Mode Team King of the Hill Option	TEAMWORK
Multiplayer Mode Uplink Option	TRANSMIT
Multiplayer Mode Wai Lin	MARTIAL
Multiplayer Mode Xenia Onatopp	JANUS
Night Shift Level	HIGHRISE
P2K Upgrade	P2000
Phoenix Fire Level	FLAME
Rifle Scope Upgrade	SCOPE
Stunner Upgrade	ZAP
Vanquish Car Missile Upgrade	LAUNCH
Tranquilizer Dart Upgrade	SLEEPY

The following codes can be entered during gameplay.

Unlockable	Code
Berserk Racing	While racing on the Paris Prelude, Enemies Vanquished, Island Infiltration, or Deep Descent levels, press START to pause gameplay, hold L1, press ■, ▲, ▲, ■, ▲, ●, then release L1.
Bonus Race in Alps	While racing on the Enemies Vanquished level, press START to pause gameplay, hold L1, press ●, ●, ■, ■, ▲, then release L1.
Double Armor during Racing	While racing on the Paris Prelude, Enemies Vanquished, Island Infiltration, or Deep Descent levels, press START to pause gameplay, hold L1, press ■, ▲, ●, ■, ■, then release L1.
Drive a Shelby Cobra	Begin gameplay on the Enemies Vanquished level. Press START to pause gameplay, hold L1, press →, →, ←, ←, ↑, then release L1. You can now use the Shelby Cobra from the Paris Prelude level in the race through the Alps.
Drive an SUV	While racing on the Enemies Vanquished level, press START to pause gameplay, hold L1, press ■, ●, ▲, ■, ▲, then release L1.
Frantic Racing	While racing on the Paris Prelude, Enemies Vanquished, Island Infiltration, or Deep Descent levels, press START to pause gameplay, hold L1, press ■, ▲, ●, ■, ▲, ●, then release L1.
Quadruple Armor during Racing	While racing on the Paris Prelude, Enemies Vanquished, Island Infiltration, or Deep Descent levels, press START to pause gameplay, hold L1, press ■, ▲, ●, ■, ■, ■, ■ then release L1.
Super Bullets during Racing	While racing on the Paris Prelude, Enemies Vanquished, Island Infiltration, or Deep Descent levels, press START to pause gameplay, hold L1, press ●, ●, ●, ● then release L1. (You can also do this when you fly the plane with Alura.)
Trails during Racing	While racing on the Paris Prelude, Enemies Vanquished, Island Infiltration, or Deep Descent levels, press START to pause gameplay, hold L1, press ■, ●, ●, ■, then release L1.
Triple Armor during Racing	While racing on the Paris Prelude, Enemies Vanquished, Island Infiltration, or Deep Descent levels, press START to pause gameplay, hold L1, press ■, ▲, ●, ■, ■, ■ then release L1.

18 Wheeler American Pro Trucker

Unlockable	Code
Extra Truck	At the Start screen, hold any button and press START.

50 Cent Bulletproof

To enter these passwords, pause the game. Go into Options, then enter the Cheat menu.

Unlockable	Password
Action 26	orangejuice
All Music Tracks	GrabAllThat50
All Music Videos	HookMeUp50
All Weapons	GotThemRachets
Bloodhound Counterkill	gunrunner
Bulletproof aka Invincible	ny'sfinestyo
Empty n' Clips Counterkill	workout
"G'd Up" Counterkill	GoodDieYoung
"Guillotine" Counterkill	GettingDropped
Infinite Ammo	GrizzSpecial
Mike Mode	the hub is broken
My Buddy video	sayhellotomylittlefriend
So Seductive video	yayoshome Tony Yayo
"Wanksta" Counter-Kill	AintGotNothin

Aeon Flux

Outfits

Enter these codes into the Cheat menu.

1. In the Extras menu (press ● when at the main menu) pick Cheats.
2. In game, pause the game, go to Cheats, and then enter.

You will see the in game Cheats in the Cheat menu.

Password	Effect
ALPHA ROMEO MIKE SIERRA	(Arms) Unlock Revelation OutFits (Extras)
BRAVO ALPHA GOLF MIKE ALPHA NOVEMBER	(Bagman) Action Movie (In Game)
BRAVO ALPHA YANKEE OSCAR UNIFORM	(Bayou) Unlock All Replay Episodes (Extras)
BRAVO LIMA UNIFORM ROMEO	(Blur) Unlock War OutFits (Extras)
BRAVO UNIFORM CHARLIE KILO FOXTROT SIERRA TANGO	(Buckfst) One Strike Kills (In Game)
CHARLIE LIMA OSCAR NOVEMBER ECHO	(Clone) Unlimited Health (In Game)
CHARLIE LIMA OSCAR TANGO HOTEL ECHO SIERRA	(Clothes) Unlock Monican Freya/Hostess Judy/Una/Fashion Una OutFits (Extras)
CHARLIE UNIFORM TANGO INDIA OSCAR NOVEMBER ECHO	(Cutione) Free Fatalities (In Game)
FOXTROT UNIFORM GOLF	(Fug) Unlimited Ammo (In Game)
GOLF ROMEO ALPHA YANKEE	(Gray) Unlock Fame OutFit (Extras)
HOTEL ECHO ALPHA LIMA MIKE ECHO	(Healme) Restore Health (In Game)
JULIET ALPHA CHARLIE KILO ECHO TANGO	(Jacket) Unlock Bomber Jacket OutFit (Extras)
LIMA CHARLIE VICTOR GOLF	(Lcvg) Unlimited Power Strikes (In Game)
MIKE OSCAR VICTOR INDIA ECHO	(Movie) Unlock Seed OutFits (Extras)
PAPA INDIA XRAY ECHO SIERRA	(Pixes) Unlock All Slideshows (Extras)

Aeon Flux (continued)

Password	Effect
TANGO ROMEO INDIA ROMEO OSCAR XRAY	(Trirox) God Mode (In Game)
UNIFORM KILO GOLF ALPHA MIKE ECHO ROMEO	(Ukgamer) Action Movie (In Game)
UNIFORM ROMEO BRAVO ALPHA NOVEMBER	(Urban) Unlock Seed OutFits (Extras)
WHISKEY HOTEL INDIA TANGO ECHO	(White) Unlock Mrs. Goodchild OutFits (Extras)

Agassi Tennis Generation

Unlockable	Code
All Players	In the Main menu, press R2, L2, L3, ●, ×, ●.

Age of Empires II: The Age of Kings

Passwords

Enter on password menu:

Password	Effect
CHEESE STEAK JIMMY'S	1,000 Food
ROBIN HOOD	1,000 Gold
ROCK ON	1,000 Stone
LUMBERJACK	1,000 Wood
NATURAL WONDERS	Control nature (lose control of men)
RESIGN	Defeat yourself
BLACK DEATH	Destroy all the enemies
WIMPYWIMPYWIMPY	Destroy yourself
FURIOUS THE MONKEY BOY	Get a Furious Monkey Boy
HOW DO YOU TURN THIS ON	Gives a "cobra" car
TO SMITHEREENS	Gives a saboteur
I LOVE THE MONKEY HEAD	Gives a VDML
AEGIS	Immediate building
TORPEDOx	Kills opponent x
POLO	Remove shadow
MARCO	Reveal map
WOOF WOOF	Turns birds into super dogs

Aggressive Inline

Enter the following codes at the Cheat screen.

Unlockable	Code
All Bonus Characters	↓, →, →, ↓, ←, ↓, ←, ↓, →, →, →
All Keys	S, K, E, L, E, T, O, N
Juice Bar Is Always Full (Your juice bar will remain full, even if you crash.)	B, A, K, A, B, A, K, A
Juice Regeneration	←, ←, →, →, ←, →, ↓, ↑, ↑, ↓, A, I
Level Select, All Park Editor Objects, Full Stats	↑, ↑, ↓, ↓, ←, →, ←, →, B, A, B, A
Low Gravity Wallride	↑, ↓, ↑, ↓, ←, →, ←, →, A, B, A, B, S
Master Code	P, L, Z, D, O, M, E
Never Die	K, H, U, F, U
Perfect Grinds	B, I, G, U, P, Y, A, S, E, L, F

Aggressive Inline (continued)

Perfect Handplants	J, U, S, T, I, N, Space, B, A, I, L, E, Y
Perfect Manuals	Q, U, E, Z, D, O, N, T, S, L, E, E, P
Super Spin	←, ←, ←, ←, →, →, →, →, ←, →, ←, →, ↑
FMV Sequences	Complete the normal challenges in a level to unlock its FMV sequence.

Alien Hominid

Use the following passwords to unlock additional hats. Sound confirms correct entry.

Hat Description	Code	Hat Description	Code
Flowers Hat	Grrl	Afro Hat	Superfly
Abe Lincoln Hat	Abe	Slick Hair Hat	Goodman
Hunting Hat	Cletus	Crazy Hair Hat	Tomfulp
Blonde Wig Hat	April	Tiara Hat	Princess

Alter Echo

Enter the following codes during gameplay.

Unlockable	Code
Restore Health	↑,↑,↓,↓,←,→,←,→,L3+→
Restore Time Dilation	↑,↑,↓,↓,←,→,←,→,L3+↑

Amplitude

Unlockable	Code
Blurry Mode	Press R3,R3,R3,R3, L3,L3,L3,L3,R3.
Scramble Gem Positions	Press ×, ×, ←, ←,R3,R3, →, →.
Tunnel Mode	Press L3, L3, L3, R3, R3, R3, L3, R3, L3. Repeat the code for a different view.
Turn Notes into Monkey Heads	Press L3, L3, L3, L3, R3, R3, R3, R3, L3.

Unlock Freq Parts and Prefabs: Beat the Boss Song of any level to unlock extra Freq pieces. In addition, you can finish the Bonus Song on each level to gain new Freq parts and Prefabs.

Arctic Thunder

Enter these codes at the Mode Select screen

Unlockable	Code
Start Invisible	■, ●, ■, R2, ●, ●, START
Atomic Snowballs	■, ■, ■, L1, ●, START
Boost Mode	●, R1, R1, ●, R2, START
Catch Up	●, ■, ●, ●, ■, START
Clone Mode	L1, L2, L2, ●, L1, ●, START
Grappling Hooks	●, ●, L2, ●, ●, L1, START
No Drones	■, ■, ●, ●, L1, R1, START
No Power Ups	■, ■, ●, ■, R2, ■, START
Random Power Up Locations	R1, R2, ■, ●, R1, R2, START
Rooster Mode	R1, R2, L2, L1, ■, START
Snow Bombs	●, ●, R1, R2, START
Super Boosts	●, L1, ■, R2, ■, L2, START

Armored Core 3

Unlockable	Code
Add Defeated AC Emblems	Press SELECT+START when viewing a defeated AC at the Victory screen to add the defeated AC's emblem to the list. A sound confirms correct code entry.
Drop Parts	Hold L1+L2+R1+R2+▲ to drop your R arm weapon, Back Unit, and Inside parts. Hold L1+L2+R1+R2+L3 to drop Extension parts. Hold L1+L2+R1+R2+● to drop L arm weapons.
First-Person View	Insert a memory card with saved game files from Armored Core 2 or Armored Core 2: Another Age. After saving and resuming in Armored Core 3 from that memory card, pause gameplay, then press L1+R2+✕+■+Dir for a first-person view of the current screen. The screen returns to normal when you resume the game.

Armored Core: Silent Line

Unlockable	Code
Get Bonus Parts	Get an A or S on any mission.
Get Defeated AC Emblems	Press START and SELECT when the victory slogan appears.

Army Men: Air Attack 2

Level	Password
Level 2	↑, ✕, ▲, →, ←, ■, ●, ✕
Level 3	▲, ●, ↓, ←, ■, ■, ↑, ↑
Level 4	✕, →, ←, ✕, ●, ■, ■, ▲
Level 5	↓, ↓, ●, ■, ●, ■, →, ✕
Level 6	▲, ✕, ↑, ←, →, ←, ●, ▲
Level 7	←, ■, →, ↓, ●, ✕, ✕, →
Level 8	▲, →, ■, ■, ●, ↓, ↓, ✕
Level 9	↑, ✕, ■, ←, →, ●, ←, ←
Level 10	▲, ↑, ●, ✕, ■, ↓, ↓, ↓
Level 11	●, ●, ↑, ←, →, ✕, ▲, ■
Level 13	←, ←, ▲, ●, ✕, ✕, ↓, →
Level 15	←, →, ●, ✕, ■, ↓, ↓, ●
Level 16	▲, ●, ✕, →, →, ●, ■, ↓
Level 18	●, ✕, →, ▲, ■, ↑, ✕, ✕
Level 20	↑, ✕, ●, ↑, ←, ■, ●, ✕

Army Men: Sarge's Heroes 2

To enter Passwords, go to the Levels selection at the main menu. At the Input Code screen, insert the following codes.

Unlockable	Code
All Levels	FREEPLAY
All Weapons	GIMME
Bed	COT
Boot Camp	BOOTCAMP
Bridge	OVERPASS
Cashier	EXPRESS
Castle	CITADEL
Desk	ESCRITOIRE

Army Men: Sarge's Heroes 2 (continued)

Unlockable	Code
Dinner Table	DINNER
Graveyard	NECROPOLIS
Immortal	NODIE
Invisible	NOSEEUM
Mini Mode	SHORTY
Pinball Machine	BLACKKNIGHT
Plasticville	BLUEBLUES
Pool Table	EIGHTBALL
Refrigerator	COOLER
Revenge	ESCAPE
Rocket Base	NUKEM
Super Sized	IMHUGE
Tan Base	MOUSE
Test Info	THDOTEST
Toy Shelf	BUYME
Toy Train Town	LITTLEPEOPLE

ATV Offroad Fury

To access the following unlockables, select Pro-Career mode and enter code. You will then return to the Main menu and begin gameplay.

Unlockable	Code
2 ATVs	CHACHING
All Tracks	WHATEXIT
Tougher A.I.	ALLOUTAI

ATV Offroad Fury 2

Go to Profile Editor, Unlock Items, Cheats, and enter the following:

Unlockable	Code
1,000 Profile Points	GIMMEPTS
Aggressive AI	EATDIRT—Re-enter the code to deactivate it.
All ATVs	SHOWROOM
All Mini-Games	GAMEON
All Equipment	THREADS
All Tracks	TRLBLAZR
All Championship Events	GOLDCUPS
Disable Wrecks	FLYPAPER Re-enter the code to deactivate it.
San Jacinto Isles	GABRIEL
Unlock Everything	IGIVEUP
Widescreen Mode	WIDESCRN

ATV Offroad Fury 3

At the Main menu, go to Options. Select Player Profile, then select Enter Cheat.

Unlockable	Code
Everything Except Fury Bike	!SLACKER!

ATV Quad Power Racing 2

Enter the following codes as your player name.

Unlockable	Code
All Riders	BUBBA
All Tracks	ROADKILL
All Vehicles	GENERALLEE
All Challenges	DOUBLEBARREL
All Tricks	FIDDLERSELBOW
Max Stats	GINGHAM
Champ	REDROOSTER

Auto Modellista

Unlockable	Objective
Tamiya Kagegawa Circuit (Remote controlled car racing level)	Complete all 7 mountain based tracks.

B-Boy

Passwords

Enter the codes to unlock hidden stuff.

Password	Effect
93665	Crazy legs
26939	Disable all codes
41549	Disable HUD in battles
15483	Have maxim hype anytime (your opponent as well)
56239	Hide beat markers
35535	Play as Host 1
61275	Play as Rack
83083	Red Bull king of the ring
20014	Unlock all clothes
85363	Unlock all Jam mode characters
92750	Unlock all Jam mode levels
34589	Unlock all Jam mode levels, characters, and music
85872	Unlock all Jam mode music
39572	Unlock all Livin' Da Life mode moves, music, and clothes
50361	Unlock all moves
43649	Unlock all moves for both Livin' Da Life and Jam mode
78727	Unlock all music
17345	Unlock Club level
11910	Unlock Pro level

Bad Boys: Miami Takedown

Unlockable	Code
Cheat Mode	At the Title screen, press ●,↑,■,▲,→,↓.

Baldur's Gate: Dark Alliance

Enter the following codes during gameplay, then press START.

Unlockable	Code
Invulnerability and Level Warp	L1+R2+▲+←
Level 20 Character	L1+R2+←

Baldur's Gate: Dark Alliance II

Unlockable	Code
Invulnerability and Level Warp	During gameplay, hold L1+R1+▲+■+●+X and press START.
Level 10	During gameplay, hold L1+R1+▲+■+●+X and press L2.
Level Warp and Infinite Health	During game play press and hold L1 + R1 + ▲ + ■ + ● + X then, while still holding these buttons, press START. A menu should appear.

The Bard's Tale

During gameplay, hold L1+R1 and press the following buttons:

Unlockable	Code
Can't Be Hurt	→,←,→,←,↑,↓,↑,↓
Can't Be Struck	←,→,←,→,↑,↓,↑,↓
Damage X100	↑,↓,↑,↓,←,→,←,→
Everything On	↑,↑,↓,↓,←,→,←,→
Full Health and Mana	←,←,→,→,↑,↓,↑,↓

Batman: Rise of Sin Tzu

At the "Press Start" screen, hold L1+L2+R1+R2 and enter the following codes.

Unlockable	Code
All Characters at 100%	↑, ↑, ←, ←, →, →, ↓, ↓
All Rewards	↓, ↑, ↓, ↑, ←, →, ←, →
All Upgrades	↑, ↑, ←, ←, →, →, →, ↓, ↓
Everything	↓, ↑, ↓, ↑, ←, →, ←, →
Infinite Combo Bar	←, →, ↑, ↓, →, ←, ↓, ↑
Infinite Health	↑, →, ↓, ←, ↑, ←, ↓, →

Batman Vengeance

At the Main menu, enter the following codes.

Unlockable	Code
All Cheats	L2, R2, L2, R2, ■, ■, ●, ●
Infinite Batcuffs	■, ●, ■, ●, L2, R2, R2, L2
Infinite Bat Launcher	●, ■, ●, ■, L1, R1, L2, R2
Infinite Electric Batarangs	L1, R1, L2, R2

Battle Engine Aquila

Use these passwords as name profiles. You must have a memory card or it will not prompt you to enter a Profile. (Note: case sensitive).

Unlockable	Password
All Bonuses	105770Y2
God Mode	B4K42
Level Select	!EVAH!

Battlestar Galactica

Enter in the Extras Menu. A sound will confirm successful code entry.

Unlockable	Code
Unlock Everything	↑, ↓, ↓, ←, ←, ←, ←, →, →, ←, ←, ↑, ↑, ←, ←, ↓, ←, →
Production Stills and Artwork	←, ↑, ←, ←, ↓, ←, ↑, ↓
Production Stills and Artwork	↑, ↑, ↓, ↓, →, ↑, →, ↓
Production Stills and Artwork	↑, ←, ↑, →, ↑, ←, ↑, →
Production Stills and Artwork	→, →, ↑, ↑, ←, ←, ↑, ↑
Production Stills and Artwork	↓, ↓, ↓, ↓, ←, ←, ←, ←
Production Stills and Artwork	↑, ↑, ↑, ↓, ↓, ↓, ←, →

Big Mutha Truckers

Enter the cheats in caps below on the Cheats screen of the Options menu.

Unlockable	Code
Automatic Nav	USETHEFORCE
Diplomatic Immunity	VICTORS
Everything	CHEATINGMUTHATRUCKER
Evil Truck	VARLEY
Fast Truck	GINGERBEER
Infinite Time	PUBLICTRANSPORT
Level Select	LAZYPLAYER
Small Pedestrians	DAISHI
Toggle Damage	6WL
Tons of Cash	LOTSAMONEY

Unlockable	Objective
Bottomless Cash Account (This only works in a new game.)	On the Main menu, press ●, ●, ■, ●, ●, SELECT.
Extra Rig	Play the 60 day version of "Trial By Truckin'" and win the race to Big Mutha Trucking HQ to unlock a new rig.

Big Mutha Truckers 2

To enter these passwords, highlight "Trial by Trucking" and press ●.

Unlockable	Password
$115,000	CASH
Add Lots of Bikers	BIKERS
Add Lots of Cops	COPS
Invincible	NODAMAGE
Opens All Bridges	BRIDGE
Pays Off the Next Juror	PJ
Removes All Cops	NOCOPS
Unlock All Gallery Images	GALLERY
Unlock All Missions	MISSIONS

Black and Bruised

Go into the Setup menu and select the Codes menu. Press START, enter the code, then press START again.

Unlockable	Code
Second Skin	×, R1, ●, ■
All Boxers	×, ●, ■, ■, R1, R1, ■, ●, ×
All Boxer's Life	×, ■, ●, R1, ×, ■, ●, R1
Constant Power-Ups	×, ●, ×, ●, ×, ●, ■, ■, ■
Conversation Mode	R1, ×, ●, ■, R1, R1, R1
Double Speed	R1 10 times
Invincible Mode	×, ×, ●, ●, R1, R1, ■, ■
Scrap Yard Arena	●, R1, ●, R1, ×, ×

Blade II

Go to the Main menu (Blade II Logo), hold L1, and press enter code.

Unlockable	Code
All Weapons	■,●,↓,←,●,●,▲
All Missions	↓,↑,←,←,●,→,↓,■
Daywalker Difficulty	←,●,↑,↓,■,●,×

Blade II (continued)

During gameplay, pause the game. Hold L1 and enter code.

Unlockable	Code
Invulnerability for Friendlies	■,●,▲,×,■,●,▲,×
Unlimited Ammo	←,●,→,■,↑,▲,↓,×
Unlimited Health	▲,■,▲,■,▲,●,▲,●
Unlimited Rage	←,↓,←,↓,→,↑,→,↑

Blitz: The League

From the Main menu, go to "Extras," then "Codes" and enter the following passwords.

Unlockable	Password
Ball Trail Always On	ONFIRE
Beach Ball	BOUNCY
Double Unleash Icons	PIPPED
Stamina Off	NOTTIRED
Super Clash	CLASHY
Super Unleash Clash	BIGDOGS
Two Player Co-op	CHUWAY

BloodRayne

Under "Options" on the Cheat menu, enter the following codes to unlock the corresponding cheat.

Unlockable	Code
Enemy Freeze	DONTFARTONOSCAR
Fill Bloodlust	ANGRYXXXINSANEHOOKER
God Mode	TRIASSASSINDONTDIE
Gratuitous Dismemberment Mode	INSANEGIBSMODEGOOD
Juggy Mode	JUGGYDANCESQUAD
Level Select	ONTHELEVEL
Restore Health	LAMEYANKEEDONTFEED
Show Weapons	SHOWMEMYWEAPONS
Time Factor Mode	NAKEDNASTYDISHWASHERDANCE

Bloody Roar 3

Unlockable	Code
Debug Mode (Import Version)	From the Main menu, enter the Options menu. After you're at the Options menu, press and hold L2 and hit the ● button.
High Speed Mode	Win 100 battles in Survival with a single character, then record your name in the records.
Hyper Beast Mode	Win 10 fights with a single character in Arcade mode and record your name.
Kohryu	Win four rounds in Arcade mode without continuing, then defeat Kohryu in round five.
No Blocking Mode	Gain first place in Arcade mode
One Fall Mode (The first to fall will lose, but he or she will be invincible to all other attacks.)	Win 20 rounds in Survival mode with a single character.
One Hit Knockdowns	Get first place in Sudden Death mode.
Sudden Death Survival	Survive through nine fights in Survival mode.
Super Difficulty	Complete Arcade mode once without continuing.
Uranus	Complete Arcade mode without continuing once, then Uranus appears. Defeat him to play as him.

DS
PSP
PS2
PS3
Wii
Xbox
Xbox 360
Index

Bloody Roar 4

Characters

Gain the corresponding number of points to unlock the character.

Unlockable	How to Unlock
Dragon Ryoho	100,000 DNA points in Career mode.
Kohryu	30,000 DNA points in Career mode.
Long	5,000 MAX DNA points in Career mode
Shina	10,000 MAX DNA points in Career mode.
Uranus	50,000 DNA points in Career mode.

Blow Out

During gameplay, pause the game and choose Cheats. Enter the following:

Unlockable	Code
All Weapons	CHARLIEHUSTLEOVERDRESSEDROMEO
Big Feet Mode	DEADREDPARTYSHOES
Big Head	BUTTCHEATCANSURPRISE
Clear Map	YESTERDAYYOURZEBRADIE
Frozen Enemies	CHARLIEOSCARLIMADELTA
God Mode	NOPAINNOCANE
Level Select	COOLLEVELCHEATCODE
Level Up Weapons	FRIENDLIESTGODINGALAXY
Restore Health	CANEREADYTOROCK
Time Factor	CHARLIEALPHANOVEMBERECHO
Unlimited Ammo	FISHINABARREL
Unlock Doors	ANYANDALLCODE

BMX XXX

TIP

Remove the game cover from the case to see a more revealing picture on the reverse side.

Enter the following codes at the Cheat menu.

Unlockable	Code
All Bikes	65 SWEET RIDES
All FMV Sequences	CHAMPAGNE ROOM
Amish Boy's Bikes	AMISHBOY1699
Bonus Movie 1 FMV Sequence	THISISBMXX
Bonus Movie 2 FMV Sequence	KEEPITDIRTY
Dam 1 FMV Sequence	BOING
Dam 2 FMV Sequence	THONG
Final Movie FMV Sequence	DDUULRRLDRSQUARE
Fire Bullets	BRONXCHEER—Begin a level, stop your rider, then move the right analog stick to First-Person mode. Press ✕ to shoot people and cars.
Ghost Control Mode (This mode allows you to steer ghost-ridden bikes.)	GHOSTCONTROL
Green Skin Mode (Now you can choose a green skin tone in the custom rider creator.)	MAKEMEANGRY
Happy Bunny Mode (This mode allows you to get more air.)	FLUFFYBUNNY

BMX XXX (continued)	
Unlockable	Code
Hellkitty's Bikes	HELLKITTY487
Itchi's Bikes	ITCHI594
Joyride's Bikes	JOYRIDE18
Karma's Bikes	KARMA311
La'tey's Bikes	LATEY411
Las Vegas 1 FMV Sequence	HIGHBEAMS
Las Vegas 2 FMV Sequence	TASSLE
Las Vegas Level	SHOWMETHEMONEY
Launch Pad 69 1 FMV Sequence	IFLINGPOO
Launch Pad 69 2 FMV Sequence	PEACH
Launch Pad 69 Level	SHOWMETHEMONKEY
Level Select	XXX RATED CHEAT
Manuel's Bikes	MANUEL415
Mika's Bikes	MIKA362436
More Speed	Z AXIS
Night Vision Mode (Objects appear greenish.)	3RD SOG
Nutter's Bikes	NUTTER290
Park Editor	BULLETPOINT—See Caution
Play as Amish Boy	ELECTRICITYBAD or I LOVE WOOD
Rampage Skatepark 2 FMV Sequence	BURLESQUE
Rampage Skatepark Level	IOWARULES
Random Introduction Sequence (Now the introduction sequence is various FMV sequences you already unlocked.)	XXXINTRO
Rave's Bikes	RAVE10
Roots Level	UNDERGROUND
Sheep FMV Sequence	ONEDOLLAR
Sheep Hills 2 FMV Sequence	69
Sheep Hills Level	BAABAA
Skeeter's Bikes	SKEETER666
Stage Select	MASS HYSTERIA
Super Crash Mode (This mode makes your character extra bouncy when you crash.)	HEAVYPETTING
Syracuse 1 FMV Sequence	FUZZYKITTY
Syracuse 2 FMV Sequence	MICHAELHUNT
Syracuse Level	BOYBANDSSUCK
The Bronx, NYC, 1 FMV Sequence	LAPDANCE
The Bronx, NYC, 2 FMV Sequence	STRIPTEASE
The Bronx, NYC, 3 FMV Sequence	FREESAMPLE
The Dam Level	THATDAMLEVEL
Tripledub's Bikes	TRIPLEDUB922
Twan's Bikes	TWAN18
UGP Roots Jam 2 FMV Sequence	BOOTYCALL
Visible Gap Mode	PARABOLIC

CAUTION

Park Editor Caution!

This crashes the game. It is not known at this time if you can correctly enable this feature.

DS
PSP
PS2
PS3
Wii
Xbox
Xbox 360
Index

Bratz: Rock Angelz

Passwords

Once you have access to the Bratz Office, go to the Cheat computer and input the following codes for special results.

Password	Effect	Password	Effect
STYLIN	Changes Camerron	WAYFAB	Gives you 3,000 Blingz
MEYGEN	Changes Dylan	HOTTIE	Gives you 6,000 Blingz
PRTPRN	Changes Koby	KOOLKT	Unlocks party jewelry
BLINGZ	Changes London Boy	MODELS	Unlocks party outfit
ROCKIN	Changes Paris Boy	BLAZIN	Unlocks ringtone 12
YASMIN	Gives you 1,000 Blingz	BNYBOO	Unlocks ringtone 14
PHOEBE	Gives you 2,000 Blingz	FIANNA	Unlocks ringtone 15
DANCIN	Gives you 2,100 Blingz	ANGELZ	Unlocks ringtone 16

Brian Lara International Cricket 2005

Enter these passwords in the Cheat menu.

Unlockable	Password
Unlock All Classic Matches	BOWLEDHIM
Unlock All Teams	GOODLENGTH
Unlock All the Classic Players	GONEFORADUCK
Unlock All Trophys	DOLLY
Unlock the Classic XI Challenge	STUMPED
Unlock the Picture Gallery	SLEDGING

Brothers in Arms: Road to Hill 30

Unlockable	Code
All levels and difficulties	Create a profile with the name BAKERSDOZEN

Bully

To enter these codes you must have a second controller. Enter these codes while playing. Do not pause on controller two.

Unlockable	Code
All Clothes	L1, L1, R1, L1, L1, L1, R1, R1
All Gym	Hold L1 and press ↑, ←, ↓, ↓, ▲, ■, ×, ×
All Hobo Fighting Moves	Hold L1 and press ↑, ←, ↓, →, ▲, ■, ×, ●
Full Health	Hold L1 and press R2, R2, R2
All Weapons	Hold L1 and press ↑, ↑, ↑, ↑
Infinite Ammo Toggle	Hold L1 and press ↑, ↓, ↑, ↓
Massive Money Gain	Hold L1 and press ▲, ■, ●, ×
Refill Ammo	Hold L1 and press ↑, ↑

Burnout: Revenge

Have a *Madden NFL 06* and *Burnout 3: Takedown* saved before starting a new game. You will unlock two special cars for Crash mode.

Unlockable	Code
Dominator Assassin	Burnout 3 Save
Madden Challenge Bus	Madden 06 Save

Call of Duty Big Red One

To enter this code, go into the Chapter Selection menu.

Unlockable	Code
Level Select	Hold L1+R1 and press ⇧, ⇧, ⇩, ⇩, ⇦, ⇦, ⇨, ⇨, ■, ⇨, ■, ⇨, ■

Call of Duty: Finest Hour

Unlockable	Code
All levels	Hold up on controller two at the level select and enter with Start, Select, Select, Square with controller one.

Call of Duty 3

Enter this code in the Chapter Select screen.

Unlockable	Code
Unlock All Levels	Hold SELECT and press ⇨, ⇨, ⇦, ⇦, ■, ■

Capcom Classic Collection

Enter this code at the title screen.

Unlockable	Code
Unlock Everything	L1, R1, Up Right Analog, Down Right Analog, L1, R1, Up Left Analog, Down Left Analog, L1, R1, ⇧, ⇩

Capcom Classic Collection Vol. 2

Enter this code at the Press Start screen.

Unlockable	Code
Cheats, Tips, Arts, and Sound Tests for Every Game	⇦, ⇨, ⇧, ⇩, L1, R1, L1, R1

Cars

To enter these passwords, select Options, then select Cheat Codes.

Unlockable	Password
All cars	YAYCARS
All character skins	R4MONE
All tracks and mini games	MATTL66
Fast start	IMSPEED
Infinite boost	VROOOOM
Unlock art	CONC3PT
Unlock Master's speedy circuit and Master's countdown cleanup	TRGTEXC
Unlocks movie clips	WATCHIT

CART Fury: Championship Racing

From the Main menu, go to Options, then Cheats and enter the following:

Unlockable	Code
All Cars	▲,×,▲,■,L2,▲—Go to the Driver Select screen and press L1 to access them.
All Movies	L1,●,R2,×,L2,▲—Go to the Danny Sullivan Theater to access them.
All Tracks	▲,×,×,R2,R1
Big Heads	▲,■,■,L2,L1,R2
Death Cars	L2,■,L1,R2,R2,×
Death Wall	×,■,R2,▲,R1,R2

CART Fury: Championship Racing (continued)

Unlockable	Code
Extra Drivers	Press R1 at the Driver Select screen.
Extra Vehicles	Press L1 at the Driver Select screen.
Infinite Turbo	×,×,■,■,L2,L2
Infinite Continues	L1,L2,L1,■,▲,●
Low Gravity	R2,R1,■,■,L1,L1
Night Drive	×,●,▲,L2,R2,L1
Playable Death Car	L1,■,R1,R2,L2,L1
Rocket Wheels	L1,R2,▲,■,■,▲
Thick Fog	R2,R1,×,■,■,●
Unlimited Time	■,L1,R2,●,▲,R1

Catwoman

Unlockable	Code
Hidden Galleries	In the Vault Code Screen, enter 1940.

Champions of Norrath

Enter this code during gameplay.

Unlockable	Code
Instant Level 20 Character	Start a new character, and as soon as you have control of him or her, press L1+R2+▲+R3.

Champions of Norrath: Realms of Everquest

Unlockable	Code
Level 20 Character	During gameplay, press and hold L1+R2+▲+R3. This allows your character to unlock 75,000 coins, 999 skill points, and Level 20.

Chicken Little

At the Main menu, select Extras. Then select Cheat Codes to enter these passwords.

Unlockable	Password
Big Comb Mode	Ball, Bat, Bat, Ball
Big Feet	Hat, Glove, Glove, Hat
Big Head	Hat, Helmet, Helmet, Hat
Feathers Fly Off When Running	Bat, Shirt, Shirt, Ball
Invincibility	Ball, Ball, Ball, Shirt
Paper Pants	Bat, Bat, Hat, Hat
Sunglasses	Glove, Glove, Helmet, Helmet
Underwear	Hat, Hat, Shirt, Shirt

The Chronicles of Narnia: The Lion, The Witch, and The Wardrobe

To enter these codes, you must be at the title screen. Hold both L1+R1 simultaneously and press ↓, ↓, →, ↑. The words "Please Press Start" should turn green. You will now be able to enter any of the following codes.

Unlockable	Code
Automatically Complete Level	While in-game hold L1 and press ↓, ←, ↓, ←, ↓, →, ↓, →, ↑
Fill Combo Meter	While in-game hold L1 and press ↑, ↑, →, ↑
Receive 10,000 Coins	While in-game hold L1 and press ↓, ←, →, ↓, ↓
Restore All Children's Health	While in-game hold L1 and press ↓, ←, ←, →
Unlock All Abilities in Inventory	While in-game hold L1 and press ↓, ←, →, ←, ↑

The Chronicles of Narnia: The Lion, The Witch, and The Wardrobe (continued)

Unlockable	Code
Open All Levels	While on the Wardrobe screen hold L1 and press ⇧, ⇧, ⇨, ⇨, ⇧, ⇨, ⇩
Unlock All Bonus Levels	While on the Bonus Drawer hold L1 and press ⇩, ⇩, ⇨, ⇨, ⇩, ⇨, ⇧

Conflict: Desert Storm—Back to Baghdad

In the Main menu, press L1, L1, R1, R1, ■, ■, ▲, ▲, ●, ●. During gameplay, pause the game, then go to Options to access Cheats.

Conflict: Global Terror

Enter this code at the Main menu.

Unlockable	Code
Cheat Menu is activated	L1, R1, L1, R1, ●, ●, ●, ●

Conflict: Vietnam

Unlockable	Code
Cheat Menu	In the Main menu, press L1, R1, L1, R1, ■, ▲, ●, ▲, ■, ●. Go to the Options screen to access the cheats.

Conflict Zone

Pause gameplay, then enter the following codes.

Unlockable	Code
100 Population	×, →, →, ←, ↑
Access to All Missions in Replay Mode	×, ↑, ↑, ←, →, ←
Faster Building	×, ↓, ↓, ↑, ←, →
Money Cheat	×, ←, →, ↑, ←

Constantine

Press SELECT to open your journal and enter these codes.

Unlockable	Codes
Big Headed Demons	R2, ⇦, ⇨, ⇦, ⇦, ⇨, ⇦, R2.

Contra: Shattered Soldier

Unlockable	Objective
Contra vs. Puppy	Complete the game with an "S" rank.
Database Option	Complete the game with a "B" or "C" rank under the Normal difficulty setting.
Final Boss Battle in Training Mode	Defeat the final boss under Normal difficulty setting.
Gallery Option	Complete the game with an "A" rank under the Normal difficulty setting.
In-Game Reset	Hold L1+L2+R1+R2+START+SELECT during gameplay.
Level 5 in Training Mode	Complete Level 5 during the game under Normal difficulty setting.
Level 6	Complete Level 5 with an "A" rank.
Level 6 in Training Mode	Complete Level 6 under Normal difficulty setting.
Level 7	Complete Level 6 with an "A" rank.

DS PSP PS2 PS3 Wii Xbox Xbox 360 Index

Contra: Shattered Soldier (continued)

Unlockable	Objective
Level 7 in Training Mode	Complete Level 7 under Normal difficulty setting.
Return	Complete Level 7 up to the credits with an "A" rank.
Satellite Weapon	Complete Level 5 with a "B" or "C" rank.
Theater Option	Complete the game under the Normal difficulty setting. Your rank determines how much of the theater unlocks.
Thirty Lives (Only affects your first credit)	Press ↑, ↑, ↓, ↓, L1, R1, L2, R2, L3, R3 on controller two at the title screen. A sound confirms correct code entry. See Note.
Triumphant Return	Complete Level 7, including after the credits, with an "A" rank.

Corvette

Unlockable	Code
All Cars and Courses	Go to Options, then Game Options and select "Change Name." Enter XOPENSEZ.

Crazy Taxi

Unlockable	Code
Another View	Begin a game. While the game is in progress, press and hold L1 and R1, then press ● to enter first-person driving mode. Press ▲ (while holding L1 and R1) to show things from a wider angle.
Expert Mode	Press and hold L1 and R1, then press START before you see the character selection screen. "Expert" appears onscreen if done properly.
Taxi Bike	At the character select screen, hit L1+R1 three times quickly. You can also gain access to the bike after you beat all Crazy Box challenges. Press ↑ at the select screen to get it.
Turn Off Arrow	Hold R1 and press START before you see the character selection screen. "No Arrows" appears on the screen if entered correctly.
Turn Off Destination Mark	Press and hold, then press START before you see the character selection screen. "No Destination" appears on screen if done correctly.
Unlock Another Day	Press and hold R1. Keep holding it until you choose a taxi driver. After you do, "Another Day" appears onscreen, indicating correct code entry.

Dave Mirra Freestyle BMX 2

Input the following codes at the Main menu.

Unlockable	Code
All Bikes	↑, ←, ↓, →, ↓, ↓, →, ↓, ↓, ←, ■
Amish Boy	↑, ←, ↓, →, →, ←. ←, ↓, ↑, ←, ■
Colin Mackay's Competition Outfit	↑, ↓, →, ↓, ↑, →, →, ↑, ■
Dave Mirra's Competition Outfit	↑, ↓, ↑, ↓, →, ←, ↑, ↑, ■
Joey Garcia's Competition Outfit	↑, ↓, ↑, ←, ↓, →, ↓, →, ■
Kenan Harkin's Competition Outfit	↑, ↓, ←, ↓, ←, ↑, ↓, ↑, ■
Leigh Ramsdell's Competition Outfit	↑, ↓, ↓, ←, ↓, ↓, ↓, ←, ■
Luc-E's Competition Outfit	↑, ↓, ←, ↓, ←, →, ←, ←, ■
Mike Dias	↑, ←, ↓, →, →, ←, ↑, ↓, ↑, →, ■
Mike Laird's Competition Outfit	↑, ↑, ↓, ↓, ←, →, →, ←, ■
Rick Moliterno's Competition Outfit	↑, ↓, ↑, ↑, ↑, ↑, ←, ↑, ■
Ryan Nyquist's Competition Outfit	↑, ↓, ↓, ←, ↓, ↑, ↑, ↓, ■

Dave Mirra Freestyle BMX 2 (continued)

Unlockable	Code
Scott Wirch's Competition Outfit	↑, ↓, →, ↓, ↑, →, →, ↑, ■
Tim Mirra's Competition Outfit	↑, ↓, →, ←, ←, ↑, ↓, ↑, ■
Todd Lyons' Competition Outfit	↑, ↓, ↓, →, ↑, ←, ←, ↓, ■
Troy McMurray's Competition Outfit	↑, ↓, ←, ↓, →, ←, ↑, ←, ■
Zack Shaw's Competition Outfit	↑, ↓, ←, →, ↓, ↓, →, ↓, ■

Dead or Alive 2: Hardcore (DOA2)

Unlockable	Objective
Bayman	Beat Story mode with every character on the Easy Difficulty setting. Bayman becomes unlocked in all modes except for Story mode.
Bonus Options	Pause the game. Press ▲+×.
CG Gallery	Beat Team mode with five characters.
Longer Credits	Beat the Story mode with all the characters on Very Hard Difficulty.
More Bounce	Go into the Options menu. Change your age between 13 and 99. The higher you set your age, the more bounce you will see from the female characters.

Dead to Rights

Enter the follwing codes at the New Game screen, just after "Press Start" appears. After entering the following codes listen for a message that confirms correct code entry.

Unlockable	Code
10,000 Bullets Mode (unlimited ammo)	Hold L1+L2+R1+R2 and press ↑,←,↓,→,●.
Bang Bang Mode	Hold L1+L2+R1+R2 and press ●,▲,■,●,→.
Boomstick Mode (unlimited shotguns)	Hold L1+L2+R1+R2 and press →,●,●,●,■.
Chow Yun Jack Mode (You receive a pair of double guns at the beginning of the level, even if you would normally have none.)	Hold L1+L2+R1+R2 and press ▲,●,↑,↑,↑.
Double Melee Attack Damage	Hold L1+L2+R1+R2 and press ●,●,↑,↑,■.
Enemies Disarmed	Hold L1+L2+R1+R2 and press →,■,←,●,▲.
Enemies More Accurate	Hold L1+L2+R1+R2 and press ▲,■,←,←,●.
Hard-Boiled Mode (increases the challenge level significantly)	Hold L1+L2+R1+R2 and press ▲,■,←,←,●.
Invisible Character (Enemies can still see you, but you can only see your own shadow.)	Hold L1+L2+R1+R2 and press ▲,▲,↑,↑,▲.
Lazy Mode (all levels, minigames, and FMV sequences)	Hold L1+L2+R1+R2 and press ↓,←,↓,▲,↓.
One-Hit Wonder Mode	Hold L1+L2+R1+R2 and press ▲,●,●,●,●,←.
Powered-up Punches and Kicks	Hold L1+L2+R1+R2 and press ↓,●,←,←,←.
Precursor Mode (turns off all targeting cursors)	Hold L1+L2+R1+R2 and press ↑,↑,↓,↓,↑.
Sharpshooter Mode	Hold L1+L2+R1+R2 and press ■,■,■,↓,→.
Super Cop Mode (harder difficulty)	Hold L1+L2+R1+R2 and press ■,▲,←,↑,→.
Time to Pay Mode (all disarms)	Hold L1+L2+R1+R2 and press ■,■,●,●,→.
Unlimited Adrenaline	Hold L1+L2+R1+R2 and press ←,→,←,●,■.
Unlimited Armor	Hold L1+L2+R1+R2 and press ↑,↑,↑,■,↓.

Dead to Rights (continued)

Unlockable	Code
Unlimited Dual Guncons	Hold L1+L2+R1+R2 and press ▲,●,↑,↑,↑.
Unlimited Human Shields	Hold L1+L2+R1+R2 and press ■,▲,●,▲,■.
Unlimited Shadow Stamina	Hold L1+L2+R1+R2 and press ●,■,▲,●,↓.
Wussy Mode (less accurate enemies)	Hold L1+L2+R1+R2 and press ■,←,▲,↑,↓.

Def Jam Vendetta

Enter the following codes on any non-Story mode character select screen.

Unlockable	Code
Arii	Hold L2 + L2 + R1 + R2 and press ×, ■, ▲, ●, ■.
Briggs	Hold L2 + L2 + R1 + R2 and press ×, ▲, ●, ■, ●.
Briggs (alternate costume)	Hold L2 + L2 + R1 + R2 and press ×, ▲, ■, ×, ●.
Carla	Hold L2 + L2 + R1 + R2 and press ×, ■, ×, ×, ×.
Chukklez	Hold L2 + L2 + R1 + R2 and press ■, ■, ▲, ×, ●.
Cruz	Hold L2 + L2 + R1 + R2 and press ●, ▲, ×, ×, ●.
D-Mob	Hold L2 + L2 + R1 + R2 and press ■, ▲, ●, ×, ●.
D-Mob (alternate costume)	Hold L2 + L2 + R1 + R2 and press ■, ■, ▲, ■, ■.
Dan G	Hold L2 + L2 + R1 + R2 and press ×, ●, ×, ●, ■.
Deebo	Hold L2 + L2 + R1 + R2 and press ●, ●, ×, ×, ▲.
Deja	Hold L2 + L2 + R1 + R2 and press ●, ■, ●, ●, ×.
DMX	Hold L2 + L2 + R1 + R2 and press ●, ×, ●, ▲, ■.
Drake	Hold L2 + L2 + R1 + R2 and press ▲, ■, ●, ×, ×.
Drake (alternate costume)	Hold L2 + L2 + R1 + R2 and press ×, ▲, ▲, ●, ●.
Funkmaster Flex	Hold L2 + L2 + R1 + R2 and press ●, ▲, ●, ●, ■.
Headache	Hold L2 + L2 + R1 + R2 and press ▲, ▲, ▲, ■, ●.
House	Hold L2 + L2 + R1 + R2 and press ▲, ×, ▲, ●, ×.
Iceberg	Hold L2 + L2 + R1 + R2 and press ■, ▲, ●, ■, ●.
Ludacris	Hold L2 + L2 + R1 + R2 and press ●, ●, ●, ■, ▲.
Manny (alternate costume)	Hold L2 + L2 + R1 + R2 and press ●, ■, ●, ■, ●.
Masa	Hold L2 + L2 + R1 + R2 and press ×, ●, ▲, ■, ■.
Method Man	Hold L2 + L2 + R1 + R2 and press ■, ●, ×, ▲, ●.
Moses	Hold L2 + L2 + R1 + R2 and press ▲, ▲, ■, ■, ×.
N.O.R.E.	Hold L2 + L2 + R1 + R2 and press ●, ■, ▲, ×, ●.
Nyne	Hold L2 + L2 + R1 + R2 and press ■, ●, ×, ×, ▲.
Omar	Hold L2 + L2 + R1 + R2 and press ●, ●, ■, ▲, ▲.
Opal	Hold L2 + L2 + R1 + R2 and press ●, ●, ■, ■, ▲.
Peewee	Hold L2 + L2 + R1 + R2 and press ×, ×, ■, ▲, ■.
Peewee (alternate costume)	Hold L2 + L2 + R1 + R2 and press ×, ▲, ▲, ■, ●.
Penny	Hold L2 + L2 + R1 + R2 and press ×, ×, ×, ▲, ●.
Pockets	Hold L2 + L2 + R1 + R2 and press ▲, ■, ●, ■, ×.
Proof (alternate costume)	Hold L2 + L2 + R1 + R2 and press ×, ■, ▲, ■, ●.
Razor	Hold L2 + L2 + R1 + R2 and press ▲, ■, ▲, ●, ×.
Razor (alternate costume)	Hold L2 + L2 + R1 + R2 and press ■, ●, ×, ▲, ▲.
Redman	Hold L2 + L2 + R1 + R2 and press ●, ●, ▲, ■, ×.
Ruffneck	Hold L2 + L2 + R1 + R2 and press ×, ■, ×, ▲, ●.
Ruffneck (alternate costume)	Hold L2 + L2 + R1 + R2 and press ■, ●, ▲, ×, ■.
Scarface	Hold L2 + L2 + R1 + R2 and press ●, ■, ×, ▲, ■.
Sketch	Hold L2 + L2 + R1 + R2 and press ▲, ▲, ●, ■, ×.
Snowman	Hold L2 + L2 + R1 + R2 and press ▲, ▲, ×, ×, ●.
Spider (alternate costume)	Hold L2 + L2 + R1 + R2 and press ■, ▲, ×, ■, ●.
Steel	Hold L2 + L2 + R1 + R2 and press ×, ▲, ●, ●, ▲.
T'ai	Hold L2 + L2 + R1 + R2 and press ●, ●, ■, ×, ●.
Zaheer	Hold L2 + L2 + R1 + R2 and press ▲, ▲, ■, ×, ×.

Destroy All Humans

To activate these codes, pause the game and hold L1, then enter the code and release L1.

Unlockable	Code
Ammo-A-Plenty	⇦, ●, R2, ⇨, R1, ■
Aware Like a Fox	⇨, ■, R2, R1, ⇨, R2
Bulletproof Crypto	■, ●, ⇦, ⇦, ⇦, ●, ■
Deep Thinker	R1, R2, ●, ⇨, R2, ●
Mmmm...Brains!	R1, R1, R2, R2, ⇦, ⇨, ⇦, ⇨, R2 This code increases DNA. (You must be on the Mothership.)
More Upgrades	■, ●, ⇦, ⇦, ●, ■ (You must be on the Mothership.)
Nobody Loves You	⇨, R2, R1, ■, ⇨

Deus Ex: Conspiracy Theory

Activate Cheats: Enter the Goals/Notes/Images screen. Press L2, R2, L1, R1, START(3) to display another tab on this screen with the following cheats that you can turn on and off: God, Full Health, Full Energy, Full Ammo, Full Mods, All Skills, Full Credits, and Tantalus.

Devil May Cry 2

Unlockable	Objective
Alternate Dante Costume	Complete the game with Dante at Normal difficulty.
Alternate Devil May Cry 1 Costume for Dante	Complete the game in Dante Must Die mode.
Alternate Costumes for Lucia	Complete the game with Lucia to unlock her alternate costume. Complete the game with Lucia under the Hard difficulty setting to unlock another costume.
Bloody Palace Mode	Complete the game with Dante and Lucia.
Dante Must Die Mode	Complete the game with Dante and Lucia under the Hard difficulty setting.
Dante's Diesel Bonus Level and Costume	Play Dante's Mission 1, then save the game. Reset the PlayStation2, and wait for the "Press Start button" message to reappear. Press L3, R3, L1, R1, L2, R2, L3, R3. A sound confirms correct code entry. Press START to return to the Main menu. Choose the "Load game" option, press L3 or R3 to access the new costume, and then load a game to play the bonus level.
Dante's Diesel Costume	Press R1, R1, ▲, ■, R2, R2 during gameplay.
Hard Difficulty Setting	Complete the game with Dante and Lucia.
In-Game Reset	Press START+SELECT during gameplay to return to the title screen.
Level Select	Complete the game as either character under any difficulty setting.
Lucia's Arius bod	Complete the game in Lucia Must Die mode.
Lucia Must Die Mode	Complete the game with Lucia under the Hard difficulty setting.
Lucia's Diesel Bonus Level and Costume	Play Lucia's Mission 1, then save the game. Reset the PlayStation2, and wait for the "Press Start button" message to reappear. Press L3, R3, L1, R1, L2, R2, L3, R3. A sound confirms correct code entry. Press START to return to the Main menu. Choose the "Load game" option, press L3 or R3 to access the new costume, and then load a game to play the bonus level.
Lucia's Diesel Costume	Press L1, L1, ▲, ■, L2, L2 during gameplay.
Play as Trish	Complete the game with Dante under the Hard difficulty setting. Trish has Dante's stats and items and starts with the Sparda.

Devil May Cry 2 (continued)

Unlockable	Objective

Completion Bonuses: Use the following to unlock the completion bonuses by only playing Dante's game. Switch from Disc 1 to 2 anytime during Dante's game. Complete the game to unlock Level Select mode, Hard mode, Bloody Palace mode, and the credits. If you change from Disc 1 to 2 before completing the game in Hard mode, you unlock Trish and other bonuses.

Devil May Cry 3

Enter at the Main menu.

Unlockable	Code
Unlock Everything	Hold down L1, L2, R1, R2 and rotate the left analog stick until you hear Devil May Cry.

Disney's Extreme Skate Adventure

Go to Options, select Cheat Codes, then enter the following codes.

Unlockable	Code
All Create-a-Skaters	sweetthreads
All Skaters	friendsofbob
All Levels	extremepassport
Filled Special Meter	supercharger
***Lion King* Video**	savannah
***Tarzan* Video**	nugget
***Toy Story* Video**	marin

Dog's Life

Unlockable	Code
Enable Cheat menu	■, ■, ■ hold ■ (till the dog growls), hold ■ (till the dog growls), hold ■ (till the dog growls), ←, →, ↓

Downhill Domination

During your run, you must use the unlock code (↑,▲,↓,×,←,●,→,■) first before trying any of the others.

Unlockable	Code
Adrenaline Boost	↓,←,←,→
Always Stoked	↓,■,■,←,●
Anti-Gravity	↓,▲,■,■,↑
Combat Upgrade	↑,↓,←,←,→
Energy Restore	↓,→,→,←,←
Extra Smack Time	←,→,↓,↓
Infinite Bottles	↑,×,←,←,●,●
Mega Flip	→,↑,↑,→,→,■
More $$$	→,↑,↑,●,●,■
No Combat	←,■,●,■,←
Speed Freak	↓,▲,→,→,■
Stoke Trick Meter	↓,←,←,→,→
Super Bounce	←,■,×,↑,▲
Super Bunny Hop	↑,×,←,■,↑
Upgrade to Bottle	↑,↓,←,←,→,→

Dr. Muto

Enter the following as codes.

Unlockable	Code
All Gadgets	TINKERTOY
Invincibility (This has no effect when you fall from high places.)	NECROSCI
All Morphs	EUREKA
Go Anywhere	BEAMMEUP
Never Take Damage	CHEATERBOY
Secret Morphs	LOGGLOGG
Super Ending	BUZZOFF
View FMV Sequences	HOTTICKET

Dragon Ball Z

Unlockable	Objective
Android #16	Complete the "Aim for Perfect Form" episode.
Cell, Android #17, and Teen Gohan	Play through "The Androids Saga" at any level.
Dodoria	Defeat Recoome with Vegeta.
Freiza, Ginyu, and Recoome	Play through "The Namek Saga" at any level.
Mr. Satan (Hercule)	Win a World Match Tournament at the Adept level.
Radditz, Vegeta, and Nappa	Play through "The Saiyan Saga" at any level
Saiyaman (Gohan's Alter Ego)	Win a World Match Tournament at the Advanced level.
Super Saiyan Ability (Goku Only)	Play through "The Namek Saga" at any level.
Super Saiyan Ability (Vegeta Only)	Play through "The Androids Saga" at any level.
Super Vegeta	Complete the "Vegeta's Confidence" episode.
Trunks	Complete the "Perfect Form Cell Complete" episode.
Yamcha	Complete the "Aim for Perfect Form" episode.
Zarbon	Complete the "Vegeta's Attack" episode.
Alternate Appearance	Press ■ or ● at the Character Selection screen. Your character may have different clothes or colors. See Tip.
View Alternate Costumes	Press R1 and R2 at the Capsule Change screen to view the character's alternate costumes. Press L1 and L2 to zoom in and out. Use the left analog stick to rotate the characters.

TIP

Alternate Appearance Tip!

Try this with Trunks and make him go Super Saiyan!

Dragon Ball Z: Sagas

Pause the game and go into the Controller screen, then enter these codes.

Unlockable	Code
All Upgrades	⇧, ⇦, ⇩, ⇨, SELECT, START, ■, ×, ●, ▲
Invincibility	⇩, ×, SELECT, START, ⇨, ■, ⇦, ●, ⇧, ▲

Drakengard

Unlockable	Objective
Fly on a Jet	Complete the Free Mission at Shinjuku and this will unlock the Jet. On any sky mission where you chose which Dragon to take, highlight Chaos Dragon. Select it and start your mission while riding a Jet.

Driv3r

In the Main menu, enter the following cheats. Go to the Options menu and select Cheats to enable or disable them.

Unlockable	Code
All Missions	L1, R1, L1, L2, ■, ■, ●
All Vehicles	L1, L1, ■, ●, L1, R1, ●
All Weapons	R1, L2, ■, ●, R1, R2, L2
Immunity	●, ●, L1, L2, R1, R2, ■
Invincibility (Take a Ride)	■, ■, L1, R1, L2, R2, R2
Unlimited Ammo	R1, R2, R1, R2, ■, ●, ■

DS
PSP
PS2
PS3
Wii
Xbox
Xbox 360
Index

Driver Parallel Lines

Enter these passwords in the Cheat menu.

Unlockable	Password
All Vehicles	CARSHOW
All Weapons in Your Time Zone	GUNRANGE
Indestructible Cars	ROLLBAR
Infinite Ammunition	GUNBELT
Infinite Nitro	ZOOMZOOM
Invincibility	IRONMAN
Weaker Cops	KEYSTONE
Zero Cost	TOOLEDUP

Duel Masters

Enter these codes while in a duel.

Unlockable	Code
Add One Shield to Player One	Hold R1 and press ×, ■, ▲
Add One Shield to Player Two	Hold R1 and press ×, ●, ▲
Break One of Player One's Shields	Hold R1 and press ▲, ■, ×
Break One of Player Two's Shields	Hold R1 and press ▲, ●, ×
Player One Wins Instantly	Hold R1 and press L1, R1, L1
Player Two Wins Instantly	Hold R1 and press R1, L1, R1

Dynasty Warriors 3

After inputting the following codes, listen for the cheer that confirms correct code entry.

Unlockable	Code
All FMV Sequences	Highlight the Free Mode icon at the main menu. Press ▲, L1, ▲, R1, ▲, ■, L2, ■, R2, ■.
All Generals	Highlight the Free Mode icon at the main menu. Press R2, R2, R2, L1, ▲, L2, L2, L2, R1, ■.
All Items	Go to the "Options" in the main menu and highlight "Open Screen." Press R1, ■, R1, ▲, R1, L1, ■, L1, ▲, L1.
All Shu Generals	Highlight the Free Mode icon at the main menu. Press L1, ■, ▲, R2, L1, L2, L2, R1, ■, L1.
All Wei Generals	Highlight the Free Mode icon at the main menu. Press ▲, ▲, L1, ■, R1, R2, L1, L2, L2, L2.
All Wu Generals	Highlight the Free Mode icon at the main menu. Press L2, L1, ■, ▲, L1, L2, R1, R2, L1, L2.
Bonus FMV Sequence	Highlight the "Replay" option at the Opening Edit screen, hold R1+L1+R2+L2, then press ×. Alternately, hold R1+L1+R2+L2 and press START. You see all the people from the gray army dancing.
Control Loading Screen	Press ● to increase the wind as the level name flutters on the loading screen before a battle. Press × to decrease the wind speed.
Free Mode Side Selection	Highlight the Free Mode icon at the main menu. Press R1, R2, L2, L1, ■, L1, L2, R2, R1, ▲.
In-game Reset	Press SELECT+START during gameplay.
Opening Edit Option	Highlight the Free Mode icon at the main menu. Press R1, ■, R1, ▲, R1, L1, ■, L1.

TIP

Start the game with a memory card with a saved game from Dynasty Warriors 2 and some characters unlocked in Dynasty Warriors 2 are available in your new game!

EndGame

Enter these codes at the Main menu. The numbers represent how many times you shoot the screen. One shot is the letter "A," two shots are "B," and so forth. In between each letter you reload.

For example: 3-15-4-5 ("code") means you shoot three times, reload, shoot 15 times, reload, shoot four times, reload, and then shoot five times.

Unlockable	Code
All Mighty Joe Jupiter Mode	13-9-7-8-20-9-5-18 ("MIGHTIER")
All Specials	13-5-2-9-7-3-8-5-1-20 ("MEBIGCHEAT")
Arcade Mode	2-12-1-13 ("BLAM")
Country Challenges	1-2-18-15-1-4 ("ABROAD")
Unlock the Jukebox	12-5-20-19-2-15-15-7-9 ("LETSBOOGIE")

Enter the Matrix

Enable Cheats: Enter the hacking system and enter cheat.exe from the A prompt. Then you can enter the codes below.

TIP

Warning! The game can crash with cheats enabled.

Unlockable	Code
All weapons	0034AFFF
Blind Enemies	FFFFFFF1
Bonus level	13D2C77F
Deaf Enemies	4516DF45
Faster Logos	7867F443
Faster Logos	7867F443
Infinite ammo	1DDF2556
Infinite focus	69E5D9E4
Infinite Health	7F4DF451
Invisibility	FFFFFFF1
Low gravity	BB013FFF
Multiplayer	D5C55D1E
Recover Focus Fast	FFF0020A
Taxi Driving	312MF451
Turbo mode	FF00001A

ESPN NFL 2K5

Change VIP Profile name to the following and access the specified unlockable.

Unlockable	VIP Pofile Name
1,000,000 Crib Credits	"PhatBank"
All Crib items	"CribMax"
All Milestones complete (full trophy room)	"MadSkilz"

ESPN NHL 2K5

Unlockable	Code
Everything in the Skybox	Create a profile with the name LuvLeafs.

ESPN NHL Hockey

Enter this code at the Game Modes screen.

Unlockable	Code
Unlock everything	R1, R1, L1, ←, ←, ↓, ●, R1, ●, L1, ↑, →, ●, ↓, ←, ←, ●, R1, ↓, ↑

Evolution Skateboarding

After entering the following codes, listen for the sound to confirm correct entry.

Unlockable	Code
All Characters and Alt skins	↑, ↓, ←, →, ↑, ↓, ←, →, ↑, ↓, ←, →, ●
All Stages	L2, R2, ←, →, ←, →, ←, →, ↓, ↓, ↑, ↑, ↓, ↑

Fantastic Four

Enter these codes quickly at the Main menu. You will hear a sound to confirm a correct entry.

Unlockable	Code
Barge Arena Level and Stan Lee Interview #1	■,●,■,↓,↓,●,↑
Bonus Level Hell	→,→,■,●,←,↑,↓
Infinite Cosmic Power	↑,■,■,■,←,→,●

FIFA Street

Unlockable	Codes
Mini Players	Pause the game and hold L1+▲ and press ↑,←,↓,↓,→,↓,↑,←.
Normal Size Players	Pause the game and hold L1+▲ and press →,→,↑,↓,↓,←,→,←.
All Apparel	At the main menu hold L1+▲ and press →,→,←,↑,↑,↑,↓,←.

FIFA Street 2

Enter this code at the Main menu while holding L1 + ▲.

Unlockable	Code
All stages unlocked	←, ↑, ↑, →, ↓, ↓, →, ↓

Fight Club

Unlockable	Code
Play as a skeleton	Create a fighter and name him Skeleton

Fight Night Round 2

Unlockable	Code
Mini Fighters	At the choose Venue screen hold ↑ until you hear a bell ring.
Unlock Fabulous	Create a character with the first name GETFAB then cancel out and Fabulous will be available for Play Now and Career mode.
All Venues Unlocked	At the game mode selection screen hold ← until you hear a bell.

Finding Nemo

Unlockable	Code
Credits	▲,■,●,▲,▲,■,●,▲,■,●,▲,■,■,●,▲,■,●,▲,■,●,●,▲,■,●
Invincibility	▲,■,■,●,●,●,▲,▲,■,■,■,●,●,●,●,■,▲,●,●,●,■,●,▲,●, ●,■,●,●,▲,●,■,●,●,●,▲
Level Select	▲,▲,▲,■,■,●,■,▲,●,■,▲,■,▲,■,▲,●,▲,▲
Secret Level	▲,■,●,●,■,▲,▲,■,●,●,■,▲,▲,●,■,▲,■,●,●,■,▲

FlatOut

Create a profile using these passwords.

Unlockable	Code
Lots of Cash	GIVECASH
Unlocks Everything	GIVEALL
Use the Shift Up Button to Launch the Driver	Ragdoll

FlatOut 2

Enter these passwords in the Cheats menu under extras.

Unlockable	Password
All Cars and 1 Million Credits	GIEVEPIX
All Tracks	GIVEALL
Big Rig	ELPUEBLO
Flatmobile Car	WOTKINS
Lots of Money	GIVECASH
Mob Car	BIGTRUCK
Pimpster Car	RUTTO
Rocket Car	KALJAKOPPA
School Bus	GIEVCARPLZ

Freedom Fighters

Enter these codes during gameplay.

Unlockable	Code
Blind AI	▲,×,■,●,●,←
Nail Gun	▲,×,■,●,×,←
Slow Motion	▲,×,■,●,●,→
Unlimited Ammo	▲,×,■,●,×,→

Frogger Ancient Shadow

These codes can be entered in the Code menu from the Main menu.

Unlockable	Code
Art 1	Frogger, Frogger, Frogger, Frogger
Art 2	Finnus, Finnus, Finnus, Finnus
Art 3	Berry, Berry, Berry, Berry
Bird Nest Wig	Lily, Lily, Lily, Lily
Dev Picture 1	Wani, Frogger, Wani, Frogger
Dev Picture 2	Berry, Berry, Berry, Wani
Lobster Wig	Finnius, Wani, Lumpy, Frogger
Programmer Art 1	Wani, Wani, Wani, Wani
Programmer Art 2	Lumpy, Frogger, Berry, Lily
Programmer Art 3	Wani, Frogger, Lily, Finnius
Sail Boat Wig	Lumpy, Lumpy, Lumpy, Lumpy
Skull Wig	Frogger, Lumpy, Lily, Frogger

Fugitive Hunter: War on Terror

Unlockable	Code
Cheat Menu	On the Title Screen, press ●,●,●,●,●,■,■,■,■. A chime will sound. Select Special Features to access the Cheat menu.
Some enemies as Bin Laden	In the Afghanistan-Pakistan Border mission, pause the game and press ●,●,●,■,■,■,R2.

Full Spectrum Warrior

Enter these codes in the Cheat menu under Options.

Unlockable	Code
All bonuses	LASVEGAS
All chapters	APANPAPANSNALE9
All enemies displayed on GPS	CANADIANVISION
Authentic mode	SWEDISHARMY

Full Spectrum Warrior (continued)

Unlockable	Code
Big Head Mode	NICKWEST
Cloak Stealth Mode	BULGARIANNINJA
Opfors will have no cover	NAKEDOP4
Unlimited Ammo	MERCENARIES
Unlimited Rockets & Grenades	ROCKETARENA

Futurama

Press and hold down L1 + L2 while playing and enter the following codes to jump to that level.

Level	Code
Bogad's Swamp	↓, ■, ▲, ↓, ■, ▲, ■, ▲, ←, ↑, SELECT
Canyon	↓, ■, ▲, ↓, ■, ▲, ■, ▲, →, ↑, SELECT
Inner Temple	↓, ■, ▲, ↓, ■, ▲, ■, ▲, ↓, ▲, SELECT
Junkyard 1	↓, ■, ▲, ↓, ■, ▲, ■, ▲, →, ←, SELECT
Junkyard 2	↓, ■, ▲, ↓, ■, ▲, ■, ▲, →, ▲, SELECT
Junkyard 3	↓, ■, ▲, ↓, ■, ▲, ■, ▲, →, ●, SELECT
Left Wing	↓, ■, ▲, ↓, ■, ▲, ■, ▲, ↓, →, SELECT
Market Square	↓, ■, ▲, ↓, ■, ▲, ■, ▲, ↓, ↑, SELECT
Mine	↓, ■, ▲, ↓, ■, ▲, ■, ▲, →, →, SELECT
Mine Tunnel	↓, ■, ▲, ↓, ■, ▲, ■, ▲, →, ↓, SELECT
Mom's HQ—Bender	↓, ■, ▲, ↓, ■, ▲, ■, ▲, ▲, ↑, SELECT
Mom's HQ—Fry	↓, ■, ▲, ↓, ■, ▲, ■, ▲, ▲, ↓, SELECT
Mom's HQ—Leela	↓, ■, ▲, ↓, ■, ▲, ■, ▲, ▲, →, SELECT
New New York	↓, ■, ▲, ↓, ■, ▲, ■, ▲, ↑, ×, SELECT
Old New York	↓, ■, ▲, ↓, ■, ▲, ■, ▲, ↑, ←, SELECT
Planet Express	↓, ■, ▲, ↓, ■, ▲, ■, ▲, ↑, ↑, SELECT
Red Light District	↓, ■, ▲, ↓, ■, ▲, ■, ▲, ↑, ▲, SELECT
Right Wing	↓, ■, ▲, ↓, ■, ▲, ■, ▲, ↓, ↓, SELECT
Sewers	↓, ■, ▲, ↓, ■, ▲, ■, ▲, ↑, →, SELECT
Subway	↓, ■, ▲, ↓, ■, ▲, ■, ▲, ↑, ↓, SELECT
Temple Courtyard	↓, ■, ▲, ↓, ■, ▲, ■, ▲, ↓, ←, SELECT
Uptown	↓, ■, ▲, ↓, ■, ▲, ■, ▲, ↑, ●, SELECT

Future Tactics: The Uprising

Codes

Code	Effect
⇧, ⇦, ⇩, ⇦, ⇩, ⇧, ⇧, ⇦	Big Heads
L1, ⇦, L1, ⇦, R1, ⇨, R1, ⇨	Disco Mode
⇧, ⇧, ⇧, ⇧, ⇧, ⇧, ⇩, ⇨, ⇧	Low Gravity

Unlockables

Unlockable	How to Unlock
Custom	Get two 100% head shot statuses in a row
Defeat Leader	Have all team members beat an episode with 100%
Humans and Creatures	In Single Player mode, have a character upgrade a weapon. Also, do not have any character miss during the level.
Level Select	Beat the game twice
Team Power	Get two head shots in a row

Gauntlet: Dark Legacy

Enter the codes in the spot where you name new characters. You can only utilize one special character or game mode at a time. Choose the character type (i.e. Dwarf, Valkyrie, etc.), as well as naming that character according to the code. Use special game modes (i.e., Unlimited Supershot, Unlimited Invulnerability) with any character type.

Unlockable	Code
$10,000 Gold per level	10000K
9 Keys and 9 Potions Per Level	ALLFUL
Battle General (Knight)	BAT900
Castle General (Warrior)	CAS400
Chainsaw Jester	KJH105
Cheerleader (Valkyrie)	CEL721
Created By Don (Knight)	ARV984
Desert General (Wizard)	DES700
Dwarf General	ICE600
Employee Stig (Knight)	STG333
Ex-Employee Chris (Knight)	CSS222
Football Dude (Knight)	RIZ721
Happy Face Jester	STX222
Karate Steve (Knight)	SJB964
Manager Mike (Knight)	DIB626
Mountain General (Warrior)	MTN200
Ninja (Knight)	TAK118
Punkrock Jester	PNK666
Rat Knight (Warrior)	RAT333

Unlockable	Code
Regular Garm (Wizard)	GARM99
S & M Dwarf	NUD069
School Girl (Valkyrie)	AYA555
Sickly Garm (Wizard)	GARM00
Sky General (Wizard)	SKY100
Sumner (Wizard)	SUM224
Town General (Valkyrie)	TWN300
Unlimited 3 Way Shot	MENAGE
Unlimited Extra Speed	XSPEED
Unlimited Full Turbo	Purple
Unlimited Halo and Levitate	1ANGLI
Unlimited Invisibility	000000
Unlimited Invulnerability	INVULN
Unlimited Play As Pojo	EGG911
Unlimited Rapid Fire	QCKSHT
Unlimited Reflective Shot	REFLEX
Unlimited Shrink Enemy and Growth	DELTA1
Unlimited Supershot	SSHOTS
Unlimited X-Ray Glasses	PEEKIN
Waitress (Knight)	KA0292

Genji: Dawn of the Samurai

Unlockables

Unlockable	How to Unlock
BGM Test	Beat the game on Normal
Continue Mode	Beat the game on Normal
Movie Gallery	Beat the game on Normal
Voice Test	Beat the game on Normal
Character Art	Beat Hard mode
Enemy Art	Beat Hard mode
Stage Art	Beat Hard mode

The Getaway

During the opening movie, press the following buttons to access these cheats:

Unlockable	Code
Armored Car Weapon	↑,↓,←,→,■,▲,●
Double Health	↑,↑,←,←,→,→,●,●,↓
Free Roam Mode and Credits	▲,▲,▲,←,■,▲,▲,▲,←,●
Unlimited Ammo	↑,↓,←,→,▲,↑,↓,←,→,■

Ghosthunter

Description	Code
Increase damage	Hold right on d-pad while pressing L3 for 5 seconds, then press ●
Laz never dies	Hold right on d-pad while pressing L3 for 5 seconds, then press ▲

Gladius

At school, pause the game and enter the following codes.

Unlockable	Code
Equip Anything	→, ↓, ←, ↑, ←, ←, ←, ←, ▲, ▲, ▲
More Experience	→, ↓, ←, ↑, ←, ←, ←, ←, ▲, →
More Money	→, ↓, ←, ↑, ←, ←, ←, ←, ▲, ←

Goblin Commander: Unleash the Horde

Press and hold L1 + R1 + ▲ + ↓ for three seconds, then enter the following codes.

100 Gold	L1, R1, R1, R1, R1, L1, ▲, L1, L1, L1
God Mode	R1, R1, R1, L1, L1, L1, R1, L1, ▲, R1
Souls	R1, L1, L1, L1, L1, R1, ▲, R1, R1, R1
Win Level	R1, R1, L1, L1, L1, R1, R1, ▲, ▲, ▲

The Godfather

These codes can be entered on the pause screen.

Unlockable	Code
$5,000	■, ●, ■, ■, ●, L3
Full Ammo	●, ⇦, ●, ⇨, ■, L3

Unlockable	Code
Full Health	⇦, ■, ⇨, ●, ⇨, L3

Enter this code on the Join Family menu.

Unlockable	Code
Unlock All Movies	●, ■, ●, ■, ■, L3

Golden Eye: Rogue Agent

Enter these codes while the games is paused.

Unlockable	Code
All Eye Powers	L1, L1, R2, R2, R1, R2, L1, L2
Full Health and Armor	R1, R1, R2, L2, R2, R1, L1, R2
Fully Charge Eye power	L1, R1, L1, L2, L2, R2, R1, L2

Enter these codes at the Extras Screen.

Unlockable	Code
No Eye powers in multiplayer mode	⇧, ⇧, ⇩, ⇦, ⇨, ⇨, ⇦, ⇩
One-Life mode	⇦, ⇩, ⇧, ⇨, ⇧, ⇨, ⇦, ⇩
Unlock all levels	⇩, ⇨, ⇩, ⇨, ⇧, ⇩, ⇧, ⇦

Grand Prix Challenge

Description	Code
Ace difficulty	REDJOCKS
All Grand Prix Challenges	IMHRACING

Description	Code
All tracks	TEAMPEEP

Grand Theft Auto 3

Enter all of the following codes during gameplay. After doing so, wait for the message to confirm correct code entry.

Description	Code
All Weapons	Press R2, R2, L1, R2, ←, ↓, →, ↑, ←, ↓, →, ↑. See Tip.
Better Driving Skills	Press R1, L1, R2, L1, ←, R1, R1, ▲. Press L3 or R3 to jump while driving.
Destroy All Cars	Press L2, R2, L1, R1, L2, R2, ▲, ■, ●, ▲, L2, L1.
Different Costume	Press →, ↓, ←, ↑, L1, L2, ↑, ←, ↓, →.
Faster Gameplay	Press ▲, ↑, →, ↓, ■, L1, L2. Repeat this code to increase its effect.
Flying Car (Low Gravity)	Press →, R2, ●, R1, L2, ↓, L1, R1. Accelerate and press ↑ to fly.
Fog	Press L1, L2, R1, R2, R2, R1, L2, ×.
Full Armor	Press R2, R2, L1, L2, ←, ↓, →, ↑, ←, ↓, →, ↑.
Full Health	Press R2, R2, L1, R1, ←, ↓, →, ↑, ←, ↓, →, ↑. See Note.
Invisible Cars	Press L1, L1, ■, R2, ▲, L1, ▲.
More Money	Press R2, R2, L1, L1, ←, ↓, →, ↑, ←, ↓, →, ↑.
Normal Weather	Press L1, L2, R1, R2, R2, R1, L2, ▲.
Overcast Skies	Press L1, L2, R1, R2, R2, R1, L2, ■.
Rain	Press L1, L2, R1, R2, R2, R1, L2, ●.
Slower Gameplay	Press ▲, ↑, →, ↓, ■, R1, R2 This cheat also continues the effect of an adrenaline pill.
Speed Up Time	Press ●, ●, ●, ■, ■, ■, ■, ■, L1, ▲, ●, ▲. Repeat this code to increase its effect.
Tank (Rhino)	Press ●, ●, ●, ●, ●, ●, R1, L2, L1, ▲, ●, ▲. This may be repeated as many times as needed.

NOTE

Better Driving Skills Note

Saving the game allows your car to never tip. Also, every car will have hydraulics that enable it to jump 15 feet in the air over other cars. After this code is enabled, any time you roll your car, press ■ + × to flip back over. This works as long as your car is not on its roof.

TIP

All Weapons Code Tip

Repeat this code for more ammunition. To get unlimited ammunition, enable the "All Weapons" code continuously until whatever you want is at 9999 shots. The next time your clip runs out, it will reload automatically, but the magazine (9999) will stay the same. Note: If you are busted, your weapons will disappear and this code will have to be repeated.

NOTE

Full Health Code Note

If this code is enabled during a mission where there is damage on your car, the meter will reset to zero. If your vehicle is on fire, enable the "Full Health" code to extinguish it. This code also repairs your car. You can't see the repairs, but it acts like a new car. If you're on a mission where you need a mint-condition car, sometimes enabling the "Full Health" code will fulfill the requirements.

Grand Theft Auto 3 (continued)

CAUTION

Warning!

*Saving the game after inputting the **following** codes will make them permanent.*

Description	Code
All Pedestrians Have Weapons	Press R2, R1, ▲, ×, L2, L1, ↑, ↓. See Caution Below.
Higher Wanted Level	Press R2, R2, L1, R2, ←, →, ←, →, ←.
Increased Gore	Press ■, L1, ●, ↓, L1, R1, ▲, →, L1, ×. No confirmation message will appear. See Note.
No Wanted Level	Press R2, R2, L1, R2, ↑, ↓, ↑, ↓, ↑, ↓.
Pedestrians Attack You	Press ↓, ↑, ←, ↑, ×, R1, R2, L1, L2.
Pedestrians Riot	Press ↓, ↑, ←, ↑, ×, R1, R2, L2, L1.

NOTE

With this code enabled, you can shoot off pedestrians' arms, legs, and heads with some weapons (sniper rifle, assault rifle,explosives) with an increase in the overall amount of blood left behind.

CAUTION

Be careful after entering this code, some pedestrians will throw bombs or shoot at you if you steal their car.

Grand Theft Auto Liberty City Stories

Enter these codes during game play—do not pause.

Unlockable	Code
$250,000	L1, R1, ▲, L1, R1, ●, L1, R1
Aggressive Drivers	■, ■, R1, ×, ×, L1, ●, ●
All Green Lights	▲, ▲, R1, ■, ■, L1, ×, ×
All Vehicles Chrome Plated	▲, R1, L1, ↓, ↓, R1, R1, ▲
Black Cars	●, ●, R1, ▲, ▲, L1, ■, ■
Big Heads	↓, ↓, ↓, ●, ●, ×, L1, R1
Cars Drive On Water	●, ×, ↓, ●, ×, ↑, L1, L1
Change Bike Tire Size	●, →, ×, ↑, →, ×, L1, ■
Clear Weather	↑, ↓, ●, ↑, ↓, ■, L1, R1
Commit Suicide	L1, ↓, ←, R1, ×, ●, ↑, ▲
Destroy All Cars	L1, L1, ←, L1, L1, →, ×, ■
Display Game Credits	L1, R1, L1, R1, ↑, ↓, L1, R1
Faster Clock	L1, L1, ←, L1, L1, →, ●, ×
Faster Gameplay	R1, R1, L1, R1, R1, L1, ↓, ×
Foggy Weather	↑, ↓, ▲, ↑, ↓, ×, L1, R1
Full Armor	L1, R1, ●, L1, R1, ×, L1, R1
Full Health	L1, R1, ×, L1, R1, ■, L1, R1
Never Wanted	L1, L1, ▲, R1, R1, ×, ■, ●
Overcast Weather	↑, ↓, ×, ↑, ↓, ▲, L1, R1
Peds Attack You	L1, L1, R1, L1, L1, R1, ↑, ▲
Peds Have Weapons	R1, R1, L1, R1, R1, L1, →, ●
Peds Riot	L1, L1, R1, L1, L1, R1, ←, ■

Grand Theft Auto Liberty City Stories (continued)

Unlockable	Code
People Follow You	⇩, ⇩, ⇩, ▲, ▲, ●, L1, R1
Perfect Traction	L1, ⇧, ⇦, R1, ▲, ●, ⇩, ✕
Rainy Weather	⇧, ⇩, ■, ⇧, ⇩, ●, L1, R1
Raise Media Attention	L1, ⇧, ⇨, R1, ▲, ■, ⇩, ✕
Raise Wanted Level	L1, R1, ■, L1, R1, ▲, L1, R1
Slower Gameplay	R1, ▲, ✕, R1, ■, ●, ⇦, ⇨
Spawn a Rhino	L1, L1, ⇦, L1, L1, ⇨, ▲, ●
Spawn a Trashmaster	▲, ●, ⇩, ▲, ●, ⇧, L1, L1
Sunny Weather	L1, L1, ●, R1, R1, ■, ▲, ✕
Upside Down Gameplay	⇩, ⇩, ⇩, ✕, ✕, ■, R1, L1
Upside Down Gameplay2	✕, ✕, ✕, ⇩, ⇩, ⇨, L1, R1
Upside Up	▲, ▲, ▲, ⇧, ⇧, ⇨, L1, R1
Weapon Set 1	⇧, ■, ■, ⇩, ⇦, ■, ■, ⇨
Weapon Set 2	⇧, ●, ●, ⇩, ⇦, ●, ●, ⇨
Weapon Set 3	⇧, ✕, ✕, ⇩, ⇦, ✕, ✕, ⇨
White Cars	✕, ✕, R1, ●, ●, L1, ▲, ▲

Grand Theft Auto: San Andreas

Description	Code
250,000 & full health and armor	R1, R2, L1 , ✕, ←, ↓, →, ↑, ←, ↓, →, ↑
4 star wanted level	R1, R1, ●, L1, ↑, ↓, ↑, ↓, ↑, ↓
Aggressive Traffic	R2, ●, R1, L2, ← R1, L1, R2, L2
All Traffic Lights Stay Green	→, R1, ↑, L2, L2, ←, R1, L1, R1, R1
All Vehicles Invisible (Except Motorcycles)	▲, L1, ▲, R2, ■, L1, L1
Attain 2 star wanted level	R1, R1, ●, ←, →, ←, →
Black Traffic	●, L2, ↑, R1, ←, ✕, R1, L1, ←, ●
Cars on Water	→, R2, ●, R1, L2, ■, R1, R2
Commit Suicide	→, L2, ↓, R1, ←, ←, R1, L1, L2, L1
Destroy Cars	R2, L2, R1, L1, L2, R2, ■, ▲, ●, ▲, L2, L1
Faster Cars	→, R1, ↑, L2, L2, ←, R1, L1, R1, R1
Faster Clock	●, ●, L1, ■, L1, ■, ■, ■, L1, ▲, ●, ▲
Faster Gameplay	▲, ↑, →, ↓, L2, L1, ■
Flying Boats	R2, ●, ↑, L1, →, R1, →, ↑, ■, ▲
Fog	R2, ✕, L1, L1, L2, L2, L2, ✕
Get a Bounty on your head	↓, ↑, ↑, ↑, ✕, R2, R1, L2, L2
Lower Wanted Level	R1, R1, ●, R2, ↑, ↓, ↑, ↓, ↑, ↓
Morning	R2, ✕, L1, L1, L2, L2, L2, ■
Night	R2, ✕, L1, L1, L2, L2, L2, ▲
Overcast	R2, ✕, L1, L1, L2, L2, L2, ■
Pedestrian Attack (can't be turned off)	↓, ↑, ↑, ↑, ✕, R2, R1, L2, L2
Pedestrian Riot (can't be turned off)	↓, ←, ↑, ←, ✕, R2, R1, L2, L1
Pedestrians have weapons	R2, R1, ✕, ▲, ✕, ▲, ↑, ↓
Perfect Handling	▲, R1, R1, ←, R1, L1, R2, L1
Pink Traffic	●, L1, ↓, L2, ←, ✕, R1, L1, →, ●
Play as Wuzi	L2, R2, R2, L2, L2, L2, L1, L1, L1, L1, ▲, ▲, ●, ●, ■, L2, L2, L2, L2, L2, L2
Raise Wanted Level	R1, R1, ●, R2, →, ←, →, ←, →, ←
Romero	↓, R2, ↓, R1, L2, ←, R1, L1, ←, →

Grand Theft Auto: San Andreas (continued)

Description	Code
Slower Gameplay	▲, ↑, →, ↓, ■, R2, R1
Spawn a Ranger	↑, →, →, L1, →, ↑, ■, L2
Spawn A Rhino	●, ●, L1, ●, ●, ●, L1, L2, R1, ▲, ●, ▲
Spawn a Stretch	R2, ↑, L2, ←, ←, R1, L1, ●, →
Spawn Bloodring Banger	↓, R1, ●, L2, L2, ×, R1, L1, ←, ←
Spawn Caddy	●, L1, ↑, R1, L2, ×, R1, L1, ●, ×
Spawn Hotring Racer #1	R1, ●, R2, →, L1, L2, ×, ×, ■, R1
Spawn Hotring Racer #2	R2, L1, ●, →, L1, R1, →, ↑, ●, R2
Spawn Rancher	↑, →, →, L1, →, ↑, ■, L2
Spawns jetpack	L1, L2, R1, R2, ↑, ↓, ←, →, L1, L2, R1, R2, ↑, ↓, ←, →
Storm	R2, ×, L1, L1, L2, L2, L2, ●
Trashmaster	●, R1, ●, R1, ←, ←, R1, L1, ●, →
Weapons 1	R1, R2, L1, R2, ←, ↓, →, ↑, ←, ↓, →, ↑
Weapons 2	R1, R2, L1, R2, ←, ↓, →, ↑, ←, ↓, ↓, ←
Weapons 3	R1, R2, L1, R2, ←, ↓, →, ↑, ←, ↓, ↓, ↓

Grand Theft Auto: Vice City

Enter all of the following codes during gameplay. After doing so, wait for the message to confirm correct code entry.

Description	Code
Aggressive Traffic	Press R2, ●, R1, L2, ←, R1, L1, R2, L2
Armor	Press R1, R2, L1, ×, ←, ↓, →, ↑, ←, ↓, →, ↑
Better Driving Skills	Press ▲, R1, R1, ←, R1, L1, R2, L1. Press L3 or R3 to jump while driving.
Bikini Women with Guns (The women drop guns when they die.)	Press →, L1, ●, L2, ←, ×, R1, L1, L1, ×
Black Traffic	Press ●, L2, ↑, R1, ←, ×, R1, L1, ←, ●
Bloodring Banger (Style 1)	Press ↑, →, →, L1, →, ↑, ■, L2.
Bloodring Banger (Style 2)	Press ↓, R1, ●, L2, L2, ×, R1, L1, ←, ←
Caddy	Press ●, L1, ↑, R1, L2, ×, R1, L1, ●, ×
Candy Suxxx Costume	Press ●, R2, ↓, R1, ←, →, R1, L1, ×, L2.
Car Floats on Water	Press →, R2, ●, R1, L2, ■, R1, R2. See Note.
Change Wheel Size (The wheels of some vehicles become larger, while others become smaller.)	Press R1, ×, ▲, →, R2, ■, ↑, ↓, ■. Repeat this code to increase its effect.
Destroy Cars	Press R2, L2, R1, L1, L2, R2, ■, ▲, ●, ▲, L2, L1
Dodo Car (Flying)	Press →, R2, ●, R1, L2, ↓, L1, R1. Accelerate and press the analog stick back to glide.
Extended Wanted Level Status	Press R2, ●, ↑, L1, →, R1, →, ↑, ■, ▲. A box will appear under your felony stars showing how long you have had a felony and how close the cops are.
Faster Game Clock	Press ●, ●, L1, ■, L1, ■, ■, ■, L1, ▲, ●, ▲
Faster Gameplay	Press ▲, ↑, →, ↓, L2, L1, ■
Foggy Weather	Press R2, ×, L1, L1, L2, L2, L2, ×
Health	Press R1, R2, L1, ●, ←, ↓, →, ↑, ←, ↓, →, ↑
Hilary King Costume	Press R1, ●, R2, L1, →, R1, L1, ×, R2
Hotring Racer (Style 1)	Press R1, ●, R2, →, L1, L2, ×, ×, ■, R1
Hotring Racer (Style 2)	Press R2, L1, ●, →, L1, R1, →, ↑, ●, R2
Increase Your Vehicle's Top Speed	Press →, R1, ↑, L2, L2, ←, R1, L1, R1, R1
Ken Rosenberg Costume	Press →, L1, ↑, L2, L1, →, R1, L1, ×, R1

Grand Theft Auto: Vice City (continued)

Description	Code
Lance Vance Costume	Press ●, L2, ←, X, R1, L1, X, L1
Love Fist Limousine	Press R2, ↑, L2, ←, ←, R1, L1, ●, →
Love Fist Musician 1 Costume	Press ↓, L1, ↓, L2, ←, X, R1, L1, X, X
Love Fist Musician 2 Costume	Press R1, L2, R2, L1, →, R2, ←, X, ■, L1
Lower Wanted Level	Press R1, R1, ●, R2, ↑, ↓, ↑, ↓, ↑, ↓
Mercedes Costume	Press R2, L1, ↑, L1, →, R1, →, ↑, ●, ▲
Normal Weather	Press R2, X, L1, L1, L2, L2, L2, ↓
Overcast Skies	Press R2, X, L1, L1, L2, L2, L2, ■
Pedestrian Costume	Press →, →, ←, ↑, L1, L2, ←, ↑, ↓, → Repeat this code to cycle through the various pedestrian costumes.
Pedestrians Attack You	Press ↓, ↑, ↑, ↑, X, R2, R1, L2, L2 You cannot disable this code.
Pedestrians from "Thriller"	Press ■, L1, ▲, R2, ■, L1, L1 No confirmation message appears.
Pedestrians Have Weapons	Press R2, R1, X, ▲, X, ▲, ↑, ↓ You cannot disable this code.
Pedestrians Riot	Press ↓, ←, ↑, ←, X, R2, R1, L2, L1 You cannot disable this code.
Phil Cassady Costume	Press →, R1, ↑, R2, L1, →, R1, L1, →, ●.
Pink Traffic	Press ●, L1, ↓, L2, ←, X, R1, L1, →, ● or X .
Police Return from Dead	Press ●, L1, ↓, L2, ←, X, R1, L1, →, X.
Rainy Weather	Press R2, X, L1, L1, L2, L2, L2, ●.
Raise Wanted Level	Press R1, R1, ●, R2, ←, →, ←, →, ←, →.
Rhino Tank	Press ●, ●, L1, ●, ●, ●, L1, L2, R1, ▲, ●, ▲.
Ricardo Diaz Costume	Press L1, L2, R1, R2, ↓, L1, R2, L2.
Romero's Hearse	Press ↓, R2, ↓, R1, L2, ←, R1, L1, ←, → .
Sabre Turbo	Press →, L2, ↓, L2, L2, X, R1, L1, ●, ←.
Slower Gameplay	Press ▲, ↑, →, ↓, ■, R2, R1.
Sonny Forelli Costume	Press ●, L1, ●, L2, ←, X, R1, L1, X, X.
Suicide	Press →, L2, ↓, R1, ←, ←, R1, L1, L2, L1.
Sunny Weather	Press R2, X, L1, L1, L2, L2, L2, ▲.
Tommy Groupies	Press ●, X, L1, L1, R2, X, X, ●, ▲.
Trashmaster	Press ●, R1, ●, R1, ←, ←, R1, L1, ●, →.
Weapons (Tier 1)	Press R1, R2, L1, R2, ←, ↓, →, ↑, ←, ↓, →, ↑ The least powerful weapons in each category are unlocked.
Weapons (Tier 2)	Press R1, R2, L1, R2, ←, ↓, →, ↑, ←, ↓, ↓, ←.
Weapons (Tier 3)	Press R1, R2, L1, R2, ←, ↓, →, ↑, ←, ↓, ↓, ↓.

NOTE

After enabling this code while driving on the water, repeat the code to deactivate it. The car you drive goes directly to the bottom of the water and keeps going without losing any health. You soon hit a piece of land and either end up stuck in the ground or can drive again. You do not lose any health during the entire time.

Grand Theft Auto: Vice City Stories

Enter these codes while playing.

Unlockable	Code
Acquire Weapon Set 1	⇦, ⇨, X, ⇧, ⇩, ■, ⇦, ⇨
Acquire Weapon Set 2	⇦, ⇨, ■, ⇧, ⇩, ▲, ⇦, ⇨
Acquire Weapon Set 3	⇦, ⇨, ▲, ⇧, ⇩, ●, ⇦, ⇨

Grand Theft Auto: Vice City Stories (continued)

Unlockable	Code
All Green Lights	↑, ↓, ▲, X, L1, R1, ←, ●
Cars Avoid You	↑, ↑, →, ←, ▲, ●, ●, ■
Clear Weather	←, ↓, R1, L1, →, ↑, ←, X
Destroy Cars Near You	L1, R1, R1, ←, →, ■, ↓, R1
Foggy Weather	←, ↓, ▲, X, →, ↑, ←, L1
Full Armor	↑, ↓, ←, →, ■, ■, L1, R1
Full Health	↑, ↓, ←, →, ●, ●, L1, R1
$250,000	↑, ↓, ←, →, X, X, L1, R1
Guy Magnet	→, L1, ↓, L1, ●, ↑, L1, ■
Never Wanted (turns off after rampages)	↑, →, ▲, ▲, ↓, ←, X, X
No Traction	↓, ←, ↑, L1, R1, ▲, ●, X
Overcast Weather	←, ↓, L1, R1, →, ↑, ←, ■
Pedestrians Attack You	↓, ▲, ↑, X, L1, R1, L1, R1
Pedestrians Have Weapons	↑, L1, ↓, R1, ←, ●, →, ▲
Pedestrians Riot	R1, L1, L1, ↓, ←, ●, ↓, L1
Rainy Weather	←, ↓, L1, R1, →, ↑, ←, ▲
Raise Wanted Level	↑, →, ■, ■, ↓, ←, ●, ●
Slow Down Game	←, ←, ●, ●, ↓, ↑, ▲, X
Spawn Rhino Tank	↑, L1, ↓, R1, ←, L1, →, R1
Spawn Trashmaster Truck	↓, ↑, →, ▲, L1, ▲, L1, ▲
Speed Up Clock	R1, L1, L1, ↓, ↑, X, ↓, L1
Speed Up Game	←, ←, R1, R1, ↑, ▲, ↓, X
Sunny Weather	←, ↓, R1, L1, →, ↑, ←, ●
Color Changed to Black (Except for Cop Cars)	L1, R1, L1, R1, ←, ●, ↑, X
Vehicles Color Changed to Chrome	→, ↑, ←, ↓, ▲, ▲, L1, R1
Wasted! (Commit Suicide)	→, →, ●, ●, L1, R1, ↓, X

Great Escape

Press the following button combinations at the Main menu.

Unlockable	Code
All Movies	L2, L2, ■, ●, ●, R2, R1, ■, ■, ●, L2, R1
Level Select	■, L2, ■, R1, ●, R2, ●, L2, L2, R2, ●, ■
Unlimited Ammo	■, ●, L2, R1, R2, L2, ●, ■, L2, R1, L2, R1

Guitar Hero

Enter these codes on Game Mode selection screen.

Unlockable	Code
Crowd has Monkey Heads	Blue, Orange, Yellow, Yellow, Yellow, Blue, Orange
Crowd has Skull Heads	Orange, Yellow, Blue, Blue, Orange, Yellow, Blue, Blue
Character uses Air Guitar	Orange, Orange, Blue, Yellow, Orange
Rock meter will always stay green	Yellow, Blue, Orange, Orange, Blue, Blue, Yellow, Orange
Unlock Everything	Yellow, Orange, Blue, Blue, Orange, Yellow, Yellow
Unlocks Hero Guitar	Blue, Orange, Yellow, Blue, Blue
Venue Disappears	Blue, Yellow, Orange, Blue, Yellow, Orange

Guitar Hero 2

Enter codes at the main menu.

Unlockable	Code
Air Guitar	Yellow, Yellow, Blue, Orange, Yellow, Blue
Crowd Has Eyeball Heads	Blue, Orange, Yellow, Orange, Yellow, Orange, Blue
Crowd Has Monkey Heads	Orange, Blue, Yellow, Yellow, Orange, Blue, Yellow, Yellow
Flaming Head	Orange, Yellow, Orange, Orange, Yellow, Orange, Yellow, Yellow
Horse Head	Blue, Orange, Orange, Blue, Orange, Orange, Blue, Orange, Orange, Blue
Hyper Speed	Orange, Blue, Orange, Yellow, Orange, Blue, Orange, Yellow
Performance mode	Yellow, Yellow, Blue, Yellow, Yellow, Orange, Yellow, Yellow

Guitar Hero Encore: Rocks the 80s

At the main menu, enter a code to get the desired effect.

G: Press the Green fret button.
R: Press the Red fret button.
Y: Press the Yellow fret button.
B: Press the Blue fret button.
O: Press the Orange fret button.

Code	Code Effect
Y,B,Y,O,B,B	Air Guitar
Y,B,O,O,O,B,Y	Crowd Has Eyeball Heads
B,B,O,Y,B,B,O,Y	Crowd Has Monkey Heads
Y,O,Y,O,Y,O,B,O	Flame Head
B,O,O,B,Y,B,O,O,B,Y	Horse Head
Y,B,O,O,B,Y,Y,O	Hyperspeed Activate/De-Activate
B,B,O,Y,Y,B,O,B	Performance Mode
B,O,Y,R,O,Y,B,Y,R,Y,B,Y,R,Y,B,Y	Unlock Everything

Unlockable Guitars

Complete the following to be able to buy the guitar in the shop.

Axe Guitar	Beat Expert Career
Casket Guitar	Beat Medium Career
Eyeball Guitar	Five star every song on Hard Career
Fish Guitar	Beat Easy Career
Snaketapus Guitar	Beat Hard Career
The LOG Guitar	Five star every song on Expert Career
USA Guitar	Five star every song on Easy Career
Viking Guitar	Five star every song on Medium Career

Half-Life

Go to Options, then Cheat Codes, and enter the following:

Unlockable	Code
Alien Mode	↑,▲,↑,▲,↑,▲,↑,▲
Infinite Ammo	↓,×,←,●,↓,×,←,●
Invincibility	←,■,↑,▲,→,●,↓,×
Invisibility	←,■,→,●,←,■,→,●
Slow Motion	→,■,↑,▲,→,■,↑,▲
Xen Gravity	↑,▲,↓,×,↑,▲,↓,×

Haunted Mansion

While playing hold right on the d-pad and enter these codes.

Unlockable	Code
God Mode	■, ●, ●, ●, ■, ●, ▲, ×
Level Select	●, ●, ■, ▲, ▲, ■, ●, ×
Upgrade Weapon	■, ■, ▲, ▲, ●, ●, ●, ×

Headhunter

Description	Code
Activate Cheat Mode	Hold R1 + ■ and press START during gameplay.

Heroes of the Pacific

Enter these codes at the Main menu. Note that you will disable game-saving when these codes are entered.

Unlockable	Code
Cheat Menu	L1, R2, L2, R3, R1, L3
Unlock all planes and missions	Right Analog stick up, Right Analog stick down, Right Analog stick left, R2, L1, Right Analog stick right
Unlock Japanese Planes	●, R2, L1, L2, ⇦, ⇧
Upgrade planes	L1, Right Analog stick left, R2, Right Analog stick right, ⇨, ⇩

Hitman: Blood Money

On the Opera House mission, in the basement at the back part of the stage, there is a room that leads to staircases to bathrooms on the first floor. After heading down the stairs, enter a room, kill the three rats on the ground, and check the bench at the end of the room. There is a keycard for the rat club. Head to the second level where you collect the lightroom keycard. There is a door that cannot be opened. Use the rat club keycard and in there are rats boxing and gambling.

Hitman: Contracts

Unlockable	Code
Complete Level	During gameplay, press R2, L2, ↑, ↓, ×, L3, ●, ×, ●, ×
Level Select	In the Main menu, press ■, ▲, ●, ←, ↑, →, L2, R2

Hitman 2: Silent Assassin

Enter the following codes during gameplay.

Description	Code
All Weapons	R2, L2, ↑, ↓, ×, ↑, ■, ×
Bomb Mode	R2, L2, ↑, ↓, ×, ↑, L1
Full Heal	R2, L2, ↑, ↓, ×, ↑, ↓
God Mode	R2, L2, ↑, ↓, ×, R2, L2, R1, L1
Lethal Charge	R2, L2, ↑, ↓, ×, R1, R1
Level Skip	R2, L2, ↑, ↓, ×, L3, ●, ×, ●, × Enable this code immediately after starting a level to complete it with a Silent Assassin rank.
Megaforce Mode	R2, L2, ↑, ↓, ×, R2, R2 Restart the level to remove its effect.
Nailgun Mode (Weapons pin people to walls.)	R2, L2, ↑, ↓, ×, L1, L1
Punch Mode	R2, L2, ↑, ↓, ×, ↑, ↑
Slow Motion	R2, L2, ↑, ↓, ×, ↑, L2
SMG and 9mm Pistol SD	L2, R2, ↑, ↓, ×, ↑, R2, R2
Toggle Gravity	R2, L2, ↑, ↓, ×, L2, L2
Level Select	R2, L2, ↑, ↓, ■, ▲, ●

Hot Shots Golf 3

Description	Code
In-Game Reset	Press L1 + R1 + L2 + R2 + START + SELECT during gameplay.
Left-Handed Golfer	Press START when selecting a golfer.

Hot Shots Golf FORE!

In the Options menu, go into the Password screen to enter these passwords.

Unlockable	Password
Capsule 1	WXAFSJ
Capsule 2	OEINLK
Capsule 3	WFKVTG
Capsule 4	FCAVDO
Capsule 5	YYPOKK
Capsule 6	GDQDOF
Capsule 7	HHXKPV
Capsule 8	UOKXPS
Capsule 9	LMIRYD
Capsule 10	MJLJEQ
Capsule 11	MHNCQI
Price Reduction	MKJEFQ
Tourney Rank Down	XKWGFZ
Unlock 100t Hammer Club	NFSNHR
Unlock All Golfers	REZTWS
Unlock Aloha Beach Resort	XSREHD
Unlock Bagpipe Classic	CRCNHZ
Unlock Beginner's Ball	YFQJJI
Unlock Big Air Club	DLJMFZ
Unlock Bir Air Ball	CRCGKR
Unlock Blue Lagoon C.C.	WVRJQS
Unlock Caddie Clank	XCQGWJ
Unlock Caddie Daxter	WSIKIN
Unlock Caddie Kayla	MZIMEL
Unlock Caddie Kaz	LNNZJV
Unlock Caddie Simon	WRHZNB
Unlock Caddie Sophie	UTWIVQ
Unlock Dream G.C.	OQUTNA
Unlock Everybody's CD - Voice Version	UITUGF
Unlock Extra Pose Cam	UEROOK
Unlock Extra Swing Cam	RJIFQS
Unlock Extra Video	DPYHIU
Unlock Heckletts	DIXWFE
Unlock HSG Rules	FKDHDS
Unlock Infinity Ball	DJXBRG
Unlock Infinity Club	RZTQGV

Unlockable	Password
Unlock Landing Grid	MQTIMV
Unlock Menu Character Brad	ZKJSIO
Unlock Menu Character Phoebe	LWVLCB
Unlock Menu Character Renee	AVIQXS
Unlock Mike Costume	YKCFEZ
Unlock Mini-Golf 2 G.C.	RVMIRU
Unlock Nanako Costume	BBLSKQ
Unlock Phoebe Costume	GJBCHY
Unlock Pin Hole Ball	VZLSGP
Unlock Replay Cam A	PVJEMF
Unlock Replay Cam B	EKENCR
Unlock Replay Cam C	ZUHHAC
Unlock Sidespin Ball	JAYQRK
Unlock Silkroad Classic	ZKOGJM
Unlock Suzuki Costume	ARFLCR
Unlock Turbo Spin Ball	XNETOK
Unlock United Forest G.C.	UIWHLZ
Unlock Wallpaper Set 2	RODDHQ
Unlock Western Valley C.C.	LIBTFL
Unlock Wild Green C.C.	YZLOXE
Upgrade 100t Hammer Club to mid-level	BVLHSI
Upgrade Big Air Club from mid-level to top level	JIDTQI
Upgrade Big Air Club to mid-level	TOSXUJ
Upgrade Infinity Club from mid-level to top level	EIPCUL
Upgrade Infinity Club to mid-level	WTGFOR
Upgrade Pin Hole Club from mid-level to top level	RBXVEL
Upgrade Pin Hole Club to mid-level	TTIMHT
Upgrade Turbo Spin Club from mid-level to top level	DTIZAB
Upgrade Turbo Spin Club to mid-level	NIWKWP

DS PSP PS2 PS3 Wii Xbox Xbox 360 Index

Hot Wheels Velocity X

Unlockable	Code
All Cars and Tracks	In the Main menu, hold L1+R1 and press ●,■,■,▲,✕

The Hulk

From Options, select Code Input and enter the following. When done, go to Special Features and select Cheats to activate them.

Unlockable	Code
Double Hulk HP	HLTHDSE
Full Rage Meter	ANGMNGT
Half Enemies HP	MMMYHLP
Invulnerability	GMMSKIN
Puzzle Solved	BRCESTN
Regenerator	FLSHWND
Reset High Score	NMBTHIH
Unlimited continues	GRNCHTR
Unlock all levels	TRUBLVR
Wicked Punch	FSTOFRY

Enter the following codes at the Code Terminal.

Unlockable	Code
Play as Gray Hulk	"JANITOR"
Desert Battle Art	"FIFTEEN"
Hulk Movie FMV Art	"NANOMED"
Hulk Transformed Art	"SANFRAN"
Hulk vs. Hulk Dogs Art	"PITBULL"

Ice Age 2

Pause the game to enter these codes.

Unlockable	Code
Unlimited Energy	⇩, ⇦, ⇨, ⇩, ⇩, ⇨, ⇦, ⇩
Unlimited Health	⇧, ⇨, ⇩, ⇧, ⇦, ⇩, ⇨, ⇦
Unlimited Pebbles	⇩, ⇩, ⇦, ⇧, ⇧, ⇨, ⇧, ⇩

I-Ninja

To enter the following codes, pause the game and enter code.

Unlockable	Code
Big Head	Hold R1 and press ▲,▲,▲,▲. Release R1, hold L1, and press ▲,▲. Hold R1+L1, and press ▲,●,▲.
Level Skip	Hold R1 and press ■,■,■,●. Release R1, hold L1, and press ▲,▲. Release L1, hold R1, and press ■,■.
Sword Upgrade	Hold L1+R1 and press ●,■,●,▲,▲,■,●,■.

The Incredible Hulk: Ultimate Destruction

At the Code Input screen, enter the following codes.

Unlockable	Code
5,000 Smash Points	SMASH5
10,000 Smash Points	SMASH10
15,000 Smash Points	SMASH15
Abomination (must complete Story mode first)	VILLAIN
All Vehicles Become Taxis	CABBIES
American Flag Shorts	AMERICA
Black and White Graphics	RETRO
Canadian Flag Shorts	OCANADA

The Incredible Hulk: Ultimate Destruction (continued)

Unlockable	Code
Cow Missiles	CHZGUN
Double Hulk's Damage Abilities	DESTROY
Double Value of Health Pickups	BRINGIT
French Flag Shorts	DRAPEAU
German Flag Shorts	DEUTSCH
Gorilla Invasion Mode	KINGKNG
Gray Hulk (without suit)	CLASSIC
Grey Hulk Mr. Fix It	SUITFIT
Italian Flag Shorts	Mutanda
Japanese Flag Shorts	FURAGGU
Low Gravity	PILLOWS
Mass Transit On/Off	TRANSIT
Sepia Mode	HISTORY
Spanish Flag Shorts	BANDERA
Union Jack Flag Shorts	FSHNCHP
Wild Traffic	FROGGIE

The Incredibles

Some of these codes only work on certain levels and certain characters. Pause the game, choose Secrets, and enter the following:

Unlockable	Code
Blurry Game	LOSTGLASSES
Credits	YOURNAMEINLIGHTS
Ethereal View	EMODE
Eye Laser	GAZERBEAM
Fast Motion Game	SASSMODE
Game 20% Easier	BOAPLACE
Giant Head	EINSTEINIUM
Heads up Display	BHUD
Heavy Iron Logo	HI
Henchmen Bounce More	SPRINGBREAK
Infinite Incredi-Power for Elastigirl	FLEXIBLE
Inverts Aiming Controls for Turrets	INVERTURRET
Inverts Camera Control on the X-axis	INVERTCAMERAX
Inverts Camera Control on the Y-axis	INVERTCAMERAY
Invincible Dash (Damage and Collisions)	GILGENDASH
Mr. Incredible Glows When Swimming	TOWNIE
Mr. Incredible Lights Plants on Fire	PINKSLIP
One Hit Kills	KRONOS
Refill 30 Health	UUDDLRLRBAS
Slow Motion	BWTHEMOVIE
Tiny Head	DEEVOLVE
Unlimited Incredi-Power (Limited Time)	DANIELTHEFLASH
Violet has Infinite Invisibility Power (Limited Time)	TONYLOAF
Weakens Bomb Damage	LABOMBE

DS PSP PS2 PS3 Wii Xbox Xbox 360 Index

The Incredibles: Rise of the Underminer

To enter these codes, pause the game. Press ● to open the menu, then select Secrets to enter a password.

Unlockable	Password
All of Frozone's moves upgraded	FROZMASTER
All of Mr. Incredible's moves upgraded	MRIMASTER
Frozone's Super Move	FROZBOOM
Give Frozone 1,000 Experience Points	FROZPROF
Give Mr. Incredible 1,000 Experience Points	MRIPROF
Mr. Incredible's Super Move	MRIBOOM

James Bond 007: Everything or Nothing

Cheats are unlocked depending on how many platinum 007s you've earned. To activate a cheat once it is unlocked, pause the game and enter the code listed underneath the cheat.

Platinum	Cheat	Code
1	Golden Gun	●,▲,×,●,▲
3	Improved Traction	●,×,×,■,▲
5	Improved Battery	●,■,●,■,▲
7	Double Ammo	●,●,×,●,▲
9	Double Damage	●,▲,▲,■,●
11	Full Ammo	●,●,▲,■,■
13	Cloak	●,▲,×,▲,■
15	Full Battery	●,▲,▲,×,●
17	All Weapons	●,▲,×,×,●
19	Unlimited Battery	●,■,●,■,▲
23	Unlimited Ammo	●,×,■,×,●
25	Slow Motion Driving	●,■,▲,×,▲
27	Platinum Gun	●,■,■,●,×

Unlockable	Objective
All Weapons	17 Platinum
Baron Samedi	50 Points
Burn Chamber	370 Points
Cayenne Upgrade	12 Gold
Cistern	30 Points
Cloak	13 Platinum
Diavolo Moscow	400 Points
Double Ammo	7 Platinum
Double Damage	9 Platinum
Egypt Commander	90 Points
Egypt Guard	180 Points
Full Ammo	11 Platinum
Full Battery	15 Platinum
Gallery	27 Gold
Golden Gun	1 Platinum
Hazmat Guard	110 Points
Helicopter Upgrade	6 Gold
Improved Battery	5 Platinum
Improved Traction	3 Platinum
Katya	20 Gold
Katya Jumpsuit	320 Points
Le Rouge	260 Points
Moscow Guard	230 Points
MI6 Combat Simulator	Complete all Missions
MI6 Survival Test	Complete all Missions
Miss Nagai	450 Points
Miss Nagai	17 Gold
Mya	130 Points
Mya	14 Gold
Nanotank Upgrade	24 Gold
Odd Job	70 Points
003	290 Points
Platinum Gun	27 Platinum

James Bond 007: Everything or Nothing (continued)

Unlockable	Objective
Production Stills 1	1 Gold
Production Stills 2	2 Gold
Production Stills 3	3 Gold
Production Stills 4	4 Gold
Production Stills 5	5 Gold
Production Stills 6	7 Gold
Production Stills 7	9 Gold
Production Stills 8	13 Gold
Production Stills 9	16 Gold
Production Stills 10	18 Gold
Production Stills 11	19 Gold
Production Stills 12	22 Gold
Production Stills 13	23 Gold
Production Stills 14	25 Gold
Serena	350 Points
Serena	430 Points
Serena	8 Gold
Slow Motion Driving	25 Platinum
South Commander	210 Points
Tank Upgrade	10 Gold
Test Lab	160 Points
Triumph Upgrade	21 Gold
Underworld	11 Gold
Unlimited Ammo	23 Platinum
Unlimited Battery	19 Platinum
Vanquish Upgrade	15 Gold

Jaws Unleashed

Enter these passwords as Profile names.

Unlockable	Password
1 Million Points	Blooood
Unlock all Bonuses	Shaaark

Jeremy McGrath Supercross World

Enter the following codes at the Main menu.

Unlockable	Code
Unlimited Turbo Boost	R2, L1, ■, ●, ●, ●
Weird Gravity	↑, ↑, ↑, ↑, R2, ■, ●

Juiced

Enter this password in the Password menu.

Unlockable	Password
All Cars in Arcade Mode	PINT

Juiced 2: Hot Import Nights

Driver DNA Car Unlockables

Enter the passwords in the DNA lab to unlock the special challenges. If you win the challenges, you unlock a custom version of the following cars.

Unlockable	How to Unlock
Audi TT 1.8L Quattro	YTHZ
BMW Z4 Roadster	GVDL
Frito-Lay Infiniti G35	MNCH
Holden Monaro	RBSG
Hyundai Coupe 2.7L V6	BSLU
Infiniti G35	MRHC
Koenigsegg CCX	KDTR
Mitsubishi Prototype X	DOPX
Nissan 350Z	PRGN
Nissan Skyline R34 GT-R	JWRS
Saleen S7	WIKF
Seat Leon Cupra R	FAMQ

Justice League Heroes

To enter these codes, pause the game and hold [L1], [L2], [R1], [R2]

Unlockable	Code
Gives 20 points to shields	⇧, ⇧, ⇩, ⇩
Gives 25 Random Boosts	⇦, ⇨, ⇦, ⇨
Invincibility	⇦, ⇩, ⇨, ⇧, ⇦, ⇩, ⇨, ⇧
Maxes out abilities	⇨, ⇩, ⇨, ⇩
Unlimited Energy	⇩, ⇩, ⇨, ⇨, ⇧, ⇧, ⇦, ⇦
Unlock everything	⇩, ⇦, ⇧, ⇨

Karaoke Revolution Volume 2

Enter the following codes at the main title screen.

Unlockable	Code
GMR (Aneeka)	→,←, [R3],←,↑,↑, [L3],↓,●,■
Harmonix (Ishani)	[L3],●,↑,●,■, [L3],↓,↓, [R3]
Konami (Dwyane)	→, [R3],→, [R3],■,→,●,■,↓,←

Kelly Slater's Pro Surfer

To enter the following codes select the "Extras" option, and then choose "Cheats." Enter each code for the desired unlockable. An "Unlocked" message confirms correct code entry.

Unlockable	Code
All Boards	6195554141
All Objectives Completed	8565558792
All Suits	7025552918
All Surfers	9495556799
All Tricks	6265556043
First-Person View	8775553825 Pause gameplay and choose the "Camera Settings" option to change the view.
Higher Jumps	2175550217

Unlockable	Code
Select	3285554497
Master Code	7145558092
Maximum Stats	2125551776
Perfect Balance	2135555721
Play as Freak	3105556217
Play as Rainbow	8185555555
Play as Tiki God	8885554506
Play as Tony Hawk	3235559787
Play as Travis Pastrana	8005556292
Trippy Graphics	8185551447

Killzone

Enter these codes at the Main menu.

Unlockable	Code
Big Head Enemies	Hold [L1] and press ●, ■, ×, ●, ●
More Powerful Weapons	Hold [L1] and press ●, ▲, ●, ▲, ×
Unlock All Levels and Characters	Enter Shooterman as a profile name
Unlocks All Movies	Hold [L1] and press ●, ■, ▲, ●, ■

King of Route 66

Description	Objective
Tornado Truckers for VS Battle	Win Rival Chase 5 times in a row to unlock all of the Tornado Truckers for VS Battle mode.

NOTE

Each win will unlock the Tornado Truckers in this order: Bigfoot, Lizard Tail, Luna Queen, Danny Edge, and Mr. Crown.

Klonoa 2

Description	Objective
Hidden Levels	In each stage are six stars. If you collect all six, you gain a doll that appears on the R1 screen. Collect eight dolls to unlock the first hidden level, and all sixteen for the second.
Music Box	Complete both hidden levels to unlock the Music Box sound test. The first hidden level gives you the first 27 tracks, while the second one gives you the remaining songs.
Pictures in Image Gallery	Each stage has 150 little gems scattered about. If you collect all 150, you'll open up more images in the special image gallery.

Kung Fu Panda

Codes

From the main menu, select extras, and then select cheats.

Effect	Code
All Multiplayer Characters	←,↓,←,→,↓
Big Head Mode (Story Mode)	↓,↑,←,→,→
Dragon Warrior Outfit (Multiplayer Mode)	←,↓,→,←,↑
Infinite Chi	↓,→,←,↑,↓
Invulnerability	↓,↓,→,↑,←
4x Damage Multiplier	↑,↓,↑,→,←

L.A. Rush

Enter codes while playing. Do not pause.

Unlockable	Code
$5,000	⇧, ⇩, ⇦, ⇨, ●, ⇦, R2, ⇧
Disable Police	⇩, ⇦, ⇨, R2, ■, ⇨, R1, ⇦
Fast Traffic	⇧, ⇩, ⇦, ⇨, ■, ⇨, ●, ⇦
No Catching Up on Races	Enter C-VHARD as a profile name.
Unlimited N20	⇧, ⇩, ⇦, ⇨, ■, ⇧, ⇩, ●, ⇧

Le Mans 24 Hours

Enter the following codes as your name at the Championship mode name screen.

Unlockable	Code
All Cars	ACO
All Championships	NUMBAT
All Tracks	SPEEDY
Le Mans	WOMBAT
See the Credits	HEINEY

Legacy of Kain: Defiance

Pause gameplay to enter the following codes.

Unlockable	Code
All Bonuses	R2,↓,L2,R1,←,L2,↓,L1,▲
All Combo Moves	→,↓,↑,↓,↓,R1,▲,●,↓
All Dark Chronicles	R1,↓,R2,L1,→,R2,▲,↓,L1
All Power Ups	←,←,↑,↑,L1,R2,●,↓,▲
Cartoon Version	↑,↓,↑,↓,R1,R2,↓,●,▲
Full Health and Reaver Charge	←,→,←,→,R1,L1,●,▲,↓
No Textures	L1,↓,R2,→,R2,↑,▲,L1,↓

Legacy of Kain: Defiance (continued)

Unlockable	Code
Tube Reaver	↑,↓,←,→,R2,L2,▲,↓,●
Unlimited Reaver Charge and Balance Emblem	↓,↓,↑,←,R1,R2,↓,▲,●
Wireframe	L1,↓,L1,↑,R1,L2,L1,↓,▲

The Legend of Spyro: A New Beginning

Enter these codes while the game is paused.

Unlockable	Code
Infinite Breath	⇧, ⇧, ⇩, ⇩, ⇦, ⇨, ⇦, ⇨, L1, R1, L1, R1
Infinite Health	⇧, ⇧, ⇩, ⇩, ⇦, ⇨, ⇦, ⇨, L1, L1, R1, R1

LEGO Batman

Codes

Enter the codes on the second level of the Batcave at the computer above the outfit changer.

Effect	Code	Effect	Code
Alfred	ZAQ637	Penguin Goon	NKA238
Bat-Tank	KNTT4B	Penguin Goon Submarine	BTN248
Batgirl	JKR331	Penguin Henchman	BJH782
Bruce Wayne	BDJ327	Penguin Minion	KJP748
Bruce Wayne's Private Jet	LEA664	Poison Ivy Goon	GTB899
Catwoman (Classic)	M1AAWW	Police Bike	LJP234
Catwoman's Motorcycle	HPL826	Police Boat	PLC999
Clown Goon	HJK327	Police Car	KJL832
Commissioner Gordon	DDP967	Police Helicopter	CWR732
Fishmonger	HGY748	Police Marksman	HKG984
Freeze Girl	XVK541	Police Officer	JRY983
Garbage Truck	DUS483	Police Van	MAC788
Glideslam	BBD7BY	Police Watercraft	VJD328
Goon Helicopter	GCH328	Riddler Goon	CRY928
Harbor Helicopter	CHP735	Riddler Henchman	XEU824
Harley Quinn's Hammer Truck	RDT637	Riddler's Jet	HAHAHA
Joker Goon	UTF782	Robin's Submarine	TTF453
Joker Henchman	YUN924	S.W.A.T.	HTF114
Mad Hatter	JCA283	Sailor	NAV592
Mad Hatter's Glider	HS000W	Scientist	JFL786
Mad Hatter's Steamboat	M4DM4N	Security Guard	PLB946
Man-Bat	NYU942	The Joker (Tropical)	CCB199
Military Policeman	MKL382	The Joker's Van	JUK657
Mr. Freeze's Iceberg	ICYICE	Two-Face's Armored Truck	EFE933
Mr. Freeze's Kart	BCT229	Yeti	NJL412
Nightwing	MVY759	Zoo Sweeper	DWR243

LEGO Batman (continued)

Extra Codes

Effect	Code	Effect	Code
Always Score Multiply	9LRGNB	Ice Rink	KLKL4G
Area Effect	TL3EKT	Immune to Freeze	JXUDY6
Armor Plating	N8JZEK	Invincible	WYD5CP
Bats	XFP4E2	Minikit Detector	ZXGH9J
Beep Beep	RAFTU8	More Batarang Targets	XWP645
Character Studs	DY13BD	More Detonators	TNTN6B
Decoy	TQ09K3	Piece Detector	KHJ544
Disguise	GEC3MD	Power Brick Detector	MMN786
Extra Toggle	EWAW7W	Regenerate Hearts	HJH7HJ
Extra Hearts	ML3KHP	Score x2	N4NR3E
Fast Batarangs	JRBDCB	Score x4	CX9MAT
Fast Build	GHJ2DY	Score x6	MLVNF2
Fast Grapple	RM4PR8	Score x8	WCCDB9
Fast Walk	ZOLM6N	Score x10	18HW07
Faster Pieces	EVG26J	Silhouettes	YK4TPH
Flaming Batarangs (Used with heat batman)	D8NYWH	Slam	BBD7BY
		Sonic Pain	THTL4X
Freeze Batarang	XPN4NG	Stud Magnet	LK2DY4

LEGO Indiana Jones: The Original Adventures

Character Codes

Enter the codes on the blackboard in the math classroom of Barnett College (the 2nd door on the left in the main hallway).

Effect	Code	Effect	Code
Bandit	12N68W	Donovan	3NFTU8
Bandit Swordsman	1MK4RT	Elsa (Desert)	JSNRT9
Barranca	04EM94	Elsa (Officer)	VMJ5US
Bazooka Trooper (Crusade)	MK83R7	Enemy Boxer	8246RB
Bazooka Trooper (Raiders)	S93Y5R	Enemy Butler	VJ48W3
Belloq	CHN3YU	Enemy Guard	VJ7R51
Belloq (Jungle)	TDR197	Enemy Guard (Mountains)	YR47WM
Belloq (Robes)	VEO29L	Enemy Officer	572 E61
British Officer	VJ5TI9	Enemy Officer (Desert)	2MK45O
British Troop Commander	B73EUA	Enemy Pilot	B84ELP
British Troop Soldier	DJ5I2W	Enemy Radio Operator	1MF94R
Captain Katanga	VJ3TT3	Enemy Soldier (Desert)	4NSU7Q
Chatter Lal	ENW936	Fedora	V75YSP
Chatter Lal (Thuggee)	CNH4RY	First Mate	0GIN24
Chen	3NK48T	Effect	Code
Colonel Dietrich	2K9RKS	Grail Knight	NE6THI
Colonel Vogel	8EAL4H	Hovitos Tribesman	H0V1SS
Dancing Girl	C7EJ21	Indiana Jones (Desert Disguise)	4J8S4M

LEGO Indiana Jones: The Original Adventures (continued)

Effect	Code	Effect	Code
Indiana Jones (Officer)	VJ85OS	Pankot Guard	VN28RH
Jungle Guide	24PF34	Sherpa Brawler	VJ37WJ
Kao Kan	WMO46L	Sherpa Gunner	ND762W
Kazim	NRH23J	Slave Child	0E3ENW
Kazim (Desert)	3M29TJ	Thuggee	VM683E
Lao Che	2NK479	Thuggee Acolyte	T2R3F9
Maharaja	NFK5N2	Thuggee Slavedriver	VBS7GW
Major Toht	13NS01	Village Dignitary	KD48TN
Masked Bandit	N48SF0	Village Elder	4682 E1
Mola Ram	FJUR31	Willie (Dinner Suit)	VK93R7
Monkey Man	3RF6YJ	Willie (Pajamas)	MEN4IP
Pankot Assassin	2NKT72	Wu Han	3NSLT8

Item Codes

Enter the codes on the blackboard in the math classroom of Barnett College (the 2nd door on the left in the main hallway).

Effect	Code	Effect	Code
Artifact Detector	VIKED7	Regenerate Hearts	MDLP69
Beep Beep	VNF59Q	Secret Characters	3X44AA
Character Treasure	VIES2R	Silhouettes	3HE85H
Disarm Enemies	VKRNS9	Super Scream	VN3R7S
Disguises	4ID1N6	Super Slap	0P1TA5
Fast Build	V83SL0	Treasure Magnet	H86LA2
Fast Dig	378RS6	Treasure x2	VM4TS9
Fast Fix	FJ59WS	Treasure x4	VLWEN3
Fertilizer	B1GW1F	Treasure x6	V84RYS
Ice Rink	33GM7J	Treasure x8	A72E1M
Parcel Detector	VUT673	Treasure x10	VI3PS8
Poo Treasure	WWQ1SA		

LEGO Racer 2

Enter these codes at the Main menu.

Unlockable	Code
Mars Tracks	←, ←, →, →, ←, ←, →, ←, ↓, ←, →
Martian	→, ←, →, ↑, ↓, ←, →, ↑, ↑
Wide Angle	←, ←, ←, →, →, →, ↑, ↑, ↑, ↓, ↓, ↓, ←, ←, ←, →, →, →

LEGO Star Wars

In Dexter's Diner, go to Codes and enter the following. This will unlock characters for purchase in Free Play mode.

Character	Code	Character	Code
Battle Droid	987UYR	Boba Fett	LA811Y
Battle Droid (Commander)	EN11K5	Brushes	SHRUB1
Battle Droid (Geonosis)	LK42U6	Classic Blasters	L449HD
Battle Droid (Security)	KF999A	Clone	F8B4L6
Big Blasters	IG72X4	Clone (Episode III, Pilot)	BHU72T

DS PSP PS2 PS3 Wii Xbox Xbox 360 Index

LEGO Star Wars (continued)

Character	Code	Character	Code
Clone (Episode III, Swamp)	N3T6P8	Luminara	A725X4
Clone (Episode III, Walker)	RS6E25	Mace Windu (Episode III)	MS952L
Clone (Episode III)	ER33JN	Minikit Detector	LD116B
Count Dooku	14PGMN	Moustaches	RP924W
Darth Maul	H35TUX	Padme	92UJ7D
Darth Sidious	A32CAM	PK Droid	R840JU
Disguised Clone	VR832U	Princess Leia	BEQ82H
Droideka	DH382U	Purple	YD77GC
General Grievous	SF321Y	Rebel Trooper	L54YUK
Geonosian	19D7NB	Royal Guard	PP43JX
Gonk Droid	U63B2A	Shaak Ti	EUW862
Grievous' Bodyguard	ZTY392	Silhouettes	MS999Q
Invincibility	4PR28U	Silly Blasters	NR37W1
Jango Fett	PL47NH	Super Battle Droid	XZNR21
Ki-Adi Mundi	DP55MV	Tea Cups	PUCEAT
Kit Fisto	CBR954		

LEGO Star Wars II: The Original Trilogy

Enter these passwords in the Cantina.

Unlockable	Password	Unlockable	Password
Beach Trooper	UCK868	Imperial Spy	CVT125
Ben Kenobi (Ghost)	BEN917	Jawa	JAW499
Bespin Guard	VHY832	Lobot	UUB319
Bib Fortuna	WTY721	Palace Guard	SGE549
Boba Fett	HLP221	Rebel Pilot	CYG336
Death Star Trooper	BNC332	Rebel Trooper (Hoth)	EKU849
Ewok	TTT289	Sandtrooper	YDV451
Gamorrean Guard	YZF999	Skiff Guard	GBU888
Gonk Droid	NFX582	Snowtrooper	NYU989
Grand Moff Tarkin	SMG219	Stormtrooper	PTR345
Greedo	NAH118	The Emperor	HHY382
Han Solo (Hood)	YWM840	Tie Fighter	HDY739
IG-88	NXL973	Tie Fighter Pilot	NNZ316
Imperial Guard	MMM111	Tie Interceptor	QYA828
Imperial Officer	BBV889	Tusken Raider	PEJ821
Imperial Shuttle Pilot	VAP664	Ugnaught	UGN694

Madagascar

Enter these codes while playing.

Unlockable	Code
All power-ups	●, ×, ×, ●, ▲, L1, ■, R1, L1
Invincibility	⇧, ⇩, ×, ×, R1, L1, R2, L2, ▲, ■, ●
Level select	R1, R1, ●, L2, L1, ×, ▲, R1, ▲

Madden NFL 06

To enter this code, go into My Madden, select Madden Cards, then select Enter Code.

Unlockable	Code	Unlockable	Code
1st and 5 Bronze	2Y7L8B	**Extra Credit Bronze**	3D3Q3P
1st and 15 Bronze	2W4P9T	**Human Plow Bronze**	3H3U7F
3rd Down Bronze	3F9G4J	**Super Dive Bronze**	3H8M5U
5th Down Bronze	3E9R4V	**Tight Fit Bronze**	3D8X6T
Da Boot Bronze	3J3S9Y	**Unforced Errors Bronze**	2Z2F4H
Donovan McNabb Gold Card (alternate)	8Q2J2X		

Madden NFL 07

Under Madden Cards, select Madden Codes to enter these passwords. Passwords are case sensitive.

Unlockable	Password
When this card is played, you can't fumble or throw interceptions for one half	XL7SP1
When this card is played, your opponent will throw a lob pass for one half	5LAWO0
When this card is played, your QB accuracy will be 100% for one half	WROA0R

Major League Baseball 2K5: World Series Edition

Create a new profile and enter the following names.

Unlockable	Code
Unlock All Cheats	Ima Cheater
Unlock All Classic Teams	Old Timers
Unlock All Extras	Gimme Goods

Major League Baseball 2K7

To enter these codes, select My 2K7. Then select Enter Cheat Code.

Unlockable	Code
Boosts a team's power rating by 25% for 1 inning	mightymick
Boosts the hitting of the 3, 4, 5 hitters in the lineup by 50% for 1 game	triplecrown
Boosts your ability to hit home runs during the game just like The Mick	m4murder
Mickey will pinch hit	phmantle
Unlocks everything	Derek Jeter
Unlocks Mickey Mantle in free agency	themick

Manhunt

Unlockable	Code
God Mode	After finishing the game on Fetish mode, enter ↓,↓,●,↑,■,▲,■, R2,↑,↑,L1,▲ at the Title Screen.

Marc Ecko's Getting Up: Contents Under Pressure

Enter these passwords in the Cheats menu under Options.

Unlockable	Password
All Art	SIRULLY
All Black Book	SHARDSOFGLASS
All Characters in Versus Mode	STATEYOURNAME
All Combat	Upgrades DOGTAGS
All Legends	NINESIX
All Levels	IPULATOR
Max Skills	VANCEDALLISTER
All Movies	DEXTERCROWLEY
All iPod Songs	GRANDMACELIA
All Versus Arenas	WORKBITCHES
Infinite Health	MARCUSECKOS
Infinite Skills	FLIPTHESCRIPT
Max Health	BABYLONTRUST

The Mark of Kri

Enter the following codes at the Title Screen (where it says "Press Start"). If you enter them correctly, you will hear Rau give a vocal cue.

Unlockable	Code
All Enemies Tougher	×,●,■,■,×,■,●,●,×,●,●,×
Invincible Rau	■,●,×,■,●,■,×,●,×,■,●,×
Stronger Health Pickups	×,×,×,×,■,■,■,■,●,●,●,●
Turn off Arena A.I.	×,●,●,●,×,■,■,■,×,●,■,×
Unlimited Arrows	×,●,■,■,×,■,●,●,×,■,■,×
Wimpy Enemies	×,●,●,■,×,■,■,●

Marvel Nemesis: Rise of the Imperfects

To enter these passwords, go into the Options menu and select Cheats.

Unlockable	Password
Elektra swimsuit model card	THEHAND
Solara swimsuit model card	REIKO
Storm swimsuit model card	MONROE
Unlocks all Fantastic Four comics	SAVAGELAND
Unlocks all Tomorrow People comics	NZONE

Marvel Ultimate Alliance

Enter these codes while playing.

Unlockable	Code
God Mode	↑, ↓, ↑, ↓, ↑, ←, ↓, →, START
Super Speed	↑, ←, ↑, →, ↓, →, START
Touch of Death	←, →, ↓, ↓, →, ←, START

Enter these codes at the Team menu.

Unlockable	Code
100K	↑, ↑, ↑, ←, →, ←, START
All Characters	↑, ↑, ↓, ↓, ←, ←, ←, START
All Costumes	↑, ↓, ↑, ↓, ←, →, ←, →, ↑, ↓, START
All Powers	←, →, ←, →, ↑, ↓, ↑, ↓, ←, →, START
Level 99	↑, ←, ↑, ←, ↓, →, ↓, →, START
Unlocks Daredevil	←, ←, →, →, ↑, ↓, ↑, ↓, START
Unlocks Silver Surfer	↓, ←, ←, ↑, →, ↑, ↓, ←, START

Marvel Ultimate Alliance (continued)

Enter these codes at the Review menu.

Unlockable	Code
All Cinematics	↑, ←, ←, ↑, →, →, ↑, START
All Comics	←, →, →, ←, ↑, ↑, →, START
All Concept Art	↓, ↓, ↓, →, →, ←, ↓, START
All Wallpapers	↑, ↓, →, ←, ↑, ↑, ↓, START

Mat Hoffman's Pro BMX 2

Quickly press the following buttons when "Press Start" appears. A sound confirms correct code entry.

Unlockable	Code
All Music Tracks	L1, ←, ←, →, →, →, X, X
Big Foot's FMV Sequences	R1, ↑, ↓, ←, X, X, X, R1
BMX Costume	●, ▲, ←, →, ←, ●
Boston Level in Road Trip Mode	■, ↑, ↓, ↓, ↑, ■
Chicago Level in Road Trip Mode	■, ↑, ▲, ↑, ▲, ■
Cory Nastazio's FMV Sequences	R1, ■, ●, ●, ■, ■, ■, R1
Day Smith's FMV Sequences	R1, ●, ←, ←, ■, →, →, R1
Elvis Costume	●, L1, L1, ↑, ↑
Fiery Hands and Feet	↓, ▲, ▲, X, X, R1, R1
Invisible Bikes	↓, ↑, ←, ↓, →, ↓, ←, ↑
Joe Kowalski's FMV Sequences	R1, ↑, X, ▲, ↓, R1
Kevin Robinson's FMV Sequences	R1, X, ▲, ↓, ↑, R1
Kid's Bike	X, ←, ←, L1, R1, ← Alternately, after you release the Medi-vac chopper and save the downed biker in Chicago, go to the location of the ambulance to find the bike.
Las Vegas Level in Road Trip Mode	■, R1, ←, L1, →, ■
Los Angeles Level in Road Trip Mode	■, ←, ▲, ▲, ←, ■
Mat Hoffman's FMV Sequences	R1, ←, ●, ←, ●, ←, R1
Level Select	■, →, →, ▲, ↓, ■ See Note.
Mike Escamilla's FMV Sequences	R1, ●, X, X, ●, X, X, R1
Nate Wessel's FMV Sequences	R1, ↓, ▲, ●, ↓, ▲, ●, R1
New Orleans Level in Road Trip Mode	■, ↓, →, ↑, ←, ■
Perfect Balance	↓, ↑, ●, ↓, ↑, ●, ↓, ↑, ●
Play as Big Foot	▲, →, ↑, →, ↑, ■
Play as Day Smith	▲, ↑, ↓, ↑, ↓, ■
Play as the Mime	▲, ←, →, ←, →, ← Alternately, find all the gaps in the game.
Play as Vanessa	▲, ↓, ←, ←, ↓, ■
Play as Volcano	▲, ↑, ↑, X, ↑, ↑, X
Portland Level in Road Trip Mode	■, X, X, ▲, ▲, ■
Rick Thorne's FMV Sequences	R1, L1, →, R1, ←, R1
Ruben Alcantara's FMV Sequences	R1, ←, →, ←, →, ←, →, R1
Seth Kimbrough's FMV Sequences	R1, ↑, ↑, ●, ●, ●, R1
Simon Tabron's FMV Sequences	R1, L1, L1, R1, L1, L1, R1
Special Meter Always Full	↓, X, X, X, R1, R1, R1
Tiki Battle Mode	L1, L1, ↓, R1, X, L1

Mat Hoffman's Pro BMX 2 (continued)

TIP

To disable the codes, quickly enter almost any code when "Press Start" appears, and add an extra R1 at the end. A different sound confirms correct code entry.

NOTE

Level Select Note

This code does not unlock all levels in Road Trip mode; only in Freeride, Session, and Multiplayer modes.

Max Payne

Unlockable	Code
All Weapons and Full Ammo	Pause the game and press L1, L2, R1, R2, ▲, ●, ×, ■.
Infinite Health	Pause the game and press L1, L1, L2, L2, R1, R1, R2, R2.
Level Select	Finish the first chapter of the Subway. Return to the Main Menu and press ↑, ↓, ←, →, ↑, ←, ↓, ●.
Slow Motion Sounds	Pause the game and press L1, L2, R1, R2, ▲, ■, ×, ●.
Unlimited Bullet Time	Pause the game and press L1, L2, R1, R2, ▲, ×, ×, ▲.

Medal of Honor: European Assault

To unlock the ability to enter cheats, go to the Pause menu and enter the Activate Cheat Entry code.

Unlockable	Code
Active Cheat Entry	Hold L1+R1 then press ●, ●, ←, ▲, ●, ×
Player Suicide (SP only)	×, ▲, ●, →, ▲, ●
Hide HUD	●, ↓, ●, ↑, ▲, ●
Kill Nemesis	↓, L2, R2, ↑, ■
Pickup OSS Document	↑, ×, R2, R1, ↑, ■
Disable Shellshock	L2, R1, L2, ▲, ▲, ▲

Medal of Honor: Frontline

Enter the following codes at the Enigma Machine. Green lights will confirm correct code entry. Select the "Bonus" option under the Enigma Machine to enable or disable the cheat.

Description	Code
Achilles' Head mode (Nazis can be killed only with a headshot when this cheat is active.)	GLASSJAW
Bullet Shield Mode (Bullets will not damage you.)	BULLETZAP
Complete Current Mission with Gold Star	MONKEY
Complete Previous Mission with Gold Star	TIMEWARP
Invisible Enemies (You will see only your enemies' guns and helmets.)	WHERERU
Making of D-Day FMV Sequence	BACKSTAGEO
Making of Needle in a Haystack FMV Sequence	BACKSTAGER
Making of Rolling Thunder FMV Sequence	BACKSTAGEI
Making of Several Bridges Too Far FMV Sequence	BACKSTAGEF
Making of Storm in the Port FMV Sequence	BACKSTAGET
Making of The Horten's Nest FMV Sequence	BACKSTAGES
Master Code	DAWOIKS
Men with Hats (Characters will have various objects on their heads.)	HABRDASHR
Mission 2 (A Storm in the Port)	ORANGUTAN
Mission 3 (Needle in a Haystack)	BABOON

Medal of Honor: Frontline (continued)

Description	Code
Mission 4 (Several Bridges Too Far)	CHIMPNZEE
Mission 5 (Rolling Thunder)	LEMUR
Mission 6 (The Horten's Nest)	GORILLA
Mohton Torpedoes (Your bullets will change into "photon torpedoes.")	TPDOMOHTON
Perfectionist (Nazis kill you with one shot.)	URTHEMAN
Rubber Grenade Mode	BOING
Silver Bullet Mode (Silver Bullet mode allows enemies to be killed with one shot.)	WHATYOUGET
Snipe-O-Rama Mode (All guns can zoom like a sniper rifle.)	LONGSHOT

Enter the following codes while the game is paused. The game will automatically resume after correct code entry.

Unlockable	Code
Invincibility	■, L1, ●, R1, ▲, L2, SELECT, R2
Unlimited Ammunition	●, L2, ■, L1, SELECT, R2, ▲, SELECT

TIP

To get the EA LA Medal of Valor, complete the game with a Gold Star in every mission.

Medal of Honor: Rising Sun

Go to the Options screen and select Password. Enter the following codes. You will hear a chime to confirm code entry.

Unlockable	Code
All Missions	BUTTERFLY—Go to Mission Select and pick the desired level.
Invisible Soldiers	TRIGGER
Unlimited Ammo	GOBY

Medal of Honor: Vanguard

Codes

Pause the game and then enter ↑,↓,↑,↓ on the D-pad. If entered correctly a message will pop up saying "Enter Cheat Code," then enter the following codes.

Effect	Code
Extra Armor	→,←,→,↓,↑,→
Invincibility	↑,→,←,↓,↓,↑

Mega Man Anniversary Collection

Unlockable	Code
Atomic Planet Credits	Defeat the first 3 bosses of Mega Man 1.
G4TV Interview/Retrospective	Complete Mega Man 8.
Homage to Mega Man Song	Complete Mega Man 2.
Mega Man 2: All energy tanks	A5 B1 B3 C4 D2 D3 E1 E4 E5
Mega Man 2: All weapons, items, and 4 energy tanks	A5 B2 B4 C1 C3 C5 D4 D5 E2
Mega Man 2: The Power Fighters	Complete Mega Man 7.
Mega Man 3: All weapons, items, 9 energy tanks, and no Dr. Wily Robots	Blue: A3 B5 D3 F4 Red: A6
Mega Man 4: All weapons and items	A1 A4 B5 E2 F1 F3
Mega Man 5: All weapons and items	Blue: B4 D6 F1 Red: C1 D4 F6

Mega Man Anniversary Collection (continued)

Unlockable	Code
Mega Man 6: All weapons and items	B6 D4 F2 F4 F6
Mega Man 7: R.U.S.H., super rocket arm, 999 bolts, 4 Birds, 4 energy & weapon tanks, SP tank, energy bolt, exit, all weapons, shield, robot screw, all bosses dead	7853 5842 2245 7515
Mega Man Drum & Bass Song	Defeat the first three bosses of Mega Man 8.
Mega Man Power Fighters	Complete Mega Man 3.
Mega Man Radio Cut song	Complete Mega Man 7.
Mega Man: The Power Battles	Complete Mega Man 3.
Picture Set 1	Complete Mega Man 2.
Picture Set 2	Complete Mega Man 4.
Picture Set 3	Complete Mega Man 8.
Plant Man remix song	Defeat Plant Man in Mega Man 5.
Power Battle	Defeat Needle Man in Mega Man 3.
Power Fighters	Defeat Junk Man in Mega Man 7.
Protoman Song	Complete Mega Man 4.
Select Jungle Remix	Complete Mega Man 7
Unlock Interview	Make your way to Wily's Tower in Mega Man 8.
Wily Vs Bass Song	Complete Mega Man 4.
Wily's Revenge Song	Complete Mega Man 2.

Men in Black II: Alien Escape

Enter these codes at the Title Screen. The screen will flash when code entry is successful. If codes are entered, you will not be able to save your game or unlock features.

Unlockable	Code
Agent Data	↑,↓,●,R2,←,L2,→,X,R2,■,↑,R1
Alien Data	■,L1,●,L2,↓,▲,R1,→,X,←,R2,▲
All CST	■,↑,L2,←,▲,X,R2,●,→,R1,■,●
All Levels	R2,▲,←,●,■,L2,←,↑,X,↓,L2,■
All Weapons at Full Power	↑,↓,X,■,R1,▲,▲,←,●,L1,L1,→
Boss Mode	R1,▲,↓,↓,X,L2,←,■,→,▲,R2,L1
Don't Drop Pickups When Hit	↓,↑,X,■,↓,↑,X,■,L1,L2,■,●
Invincibility	→,X,R1,▲,↑,L2,X,←,L1,●,X,R2
Full Powerup on Bolt Weapons	←,→,↑,↓,L1,●,▲,R2,←,↓,■,■
Full Powerup on Spread Weapons	L2,R1,●,L2,↓,↑,L1,→,←,X
Full Powerup on Homing Weapon	←,↑,■,L1,←,←,L1,←,●,←
Full Powerup for Plasma Weapon	←,●,▲,→,L1,■,←,R1,R1,▲
Full Powerup on Area Effect Weapon	←,X,▲,↑,↓,■,L2,←,R2
Making Of	●,R2,L2,●,▲,↓,■,X,→,L1,X,↑
Big Otasi Easter Egg (N.Y. Streets, Stage 2, Section 6)	After killing Shark Guy and the two teleporters, the barrier in front of the Subway stairs will explode and you can proceed to the next stage. Instead of going down the Subway stairs, walk to the building doorway that is behind the stairs. Stand next to the doorway for twenty seconds or so, then walk left to the line of cars that stretch across the street. Look past the cars to see a giant Otasi running across the street. It is purely a visual thing—you don't get any bonuses—but what a sight!

Mercenaries 2: World in Flames

Faction Codes

Codes must be entered in the Faction menu. You'll get a confirmation sound if code was entered correctly.

Effect	Code
One Million Dollars	→,↓,←,↑,↑,←,↓,→
Full Fuel	→,↓,←,↑,→,↓,←,↑
Infinite Ammo	→,←,→,→,←,→,←,←
Infinite Health	↑,↓,↑,↓,←,→,←,→
Reset All Factions to Neutral	↑,↑,↑,↑,↓,↓,→,←

Midnight Club II

Enter the following codes from the Cheat menu.

Unlockable	Code
All Cars	theCollector
All Game Modes	dextran
All Locations	Globetrotter
All Locations and Cars (Arcade mode only)	pennyThug
Better Control in the Air	carcrobatics
Change Difficulty Levels	howhardcanitbe0 (easiest)
Change Difficulty Levels	howhardcanitbe1
Change Difficulty Levels	howhardcanitbe2
Change Difficulty Levels	howhardcanitbe3
Change Difficulty Levels	howhardcanitbe4
Change Difficulty Levels	howhardcanitbe5
Change Difficulty Levels	howhardcanitbe6
Change Difficulty Levels	howhardcanitbe7
Change Difficulty Levels	howhardcanitbe8
Change Difficulty Levels	howhardcanitbe9 (hardest)
Infinite Nitrous	greenLantern
Invincibility	gladiator
Machine Gun and Rocket Code	savethekids
LAPD car in Arcade Mode	Beat all five circuit races for LA in Arcade mode.
Paris Cop Car	Beat all 6 of the Paris arcade circuit tracks.
SLF450X	Complete 100% of the game.
The Veloci	Beat all of the World Champion's races.
Tokyo Cop Car	Beat all 7 Tokyo arcade circuit tracks.

Midnight Club 3 Dub Edition

Enter these case sensitive passwords in the Cheats section under Options.

Unlockable	Password
All cities in arcade mode	crosscountry
Bunny ears	getheadl
Chrome Body	haveyouseenthisboy
Faster pedestrians/All cities in arcade mode	urbansprawl
Flaming Head	trythisathome
Increase car mass in arcade mode	hyperagro
No damage	ontheroad

Midnight Club 3 Dub Edition (continued)

Unlockable	Password
Pumpkin Heads	getheadk
Skull head	getheadn
Snowman head	getheadm
Special move Agro	dfens
Special move Roar	Rjnr
Special move Zone	allin
Unlock all cities	roadtrip
Yellow Smile	getheadj

Mike Tyson Heavyweight Boxing

Enter the following codes at the Title Screen

Unlockable	Code
Big Head Mode	■,●,↑,↓
Codies Credits	×,▲,■,●
Custom boxer textures	L1,R1,×,×,▲,×
Platinum Unlock (All boxers, arenas, and game modes)	■,●,L2,R2
Small Head Mode	■,●,↓,↑
Square 2D/flat Mode	↓,↑,●,■
Super Mutant Mode	■,←,↑,▲

Minority Report

Enter the following as codes.

Description	Code
All Combos	NINJA
All FMV Sequences	DIRECTOR
All Weapons	STRAPPED
Armor	STEELUP
Baseball Bat	SLUGGER
Bouncy Men	BOUNZMEN
Cluttered Locations	CLUTZ
Concept Art	SKETCHPAD
Dramatic Finish	STYLIN
Ending Sequence	WIMP
Extra Health	BUTTERUP
Free Aim	FPSSTYLE
Invincibility	LRGARMS
Level Select	PASSKEY
Level Skip	QUITER
Maximum Ammunition	MRJUAREZ
Maximum Damage	SPINACH
Pain Arenas	MAXIMUMHURT
Play as Clown	SCARYCLOWN
Play as Convict	JAILBREAK
Play as GI	GNRLINFANTRY
Play as Lizard	HISSSS
Play as Moseley	BIGLIPS
Play as Nara	WEIGHTGAIN
Play as Nikki	HAIRLOSS
Play as Robot	MRROBOTO
Play as Superhero	SUPERJOHN
Play as Zombie	IAMSODEAD
Rag Doll	CLUMSY
Slow Motion Button	SLIZOMIZO

Mister Mosquito

Enter these codes on the Selection menu. Hold L2 will entering the codes.

Unlockable	Code
Doctor Mosquito	⇧, ⇨, ⇦, ⇩, ■, ■, R2, R2, R2
Mama Mosquito	⇧, ⇨, ⇦, ⇩, ■, ■, R1, R1, R1

MLB 2006

Pause the game to enter this code.

Unlockable	Code
Fart Mode	⇧,⇧,⇩,⇩,⇦,⇨,⇦,⇨

MLB Slugfest Loaded

Enter the following codes at the Versus screen.

Unlockable	Code
Big Head Mode	■,■,→
Max Batting	■,■,■,←
Max Power	▲,▲,▲,←
Max Speed	●,●,●,←
Rubber Ball Mode	■,■,▲,▲
Unlockable	**Code**
Softball Mode	■,■,▲,▲,▲,▲,●,●,↓
Tiny Head Mode	■,■,←
Unlimited Turbo	■,■,■,■,▲,▲,▲,▲,●,●,●,●,↓

Mortal Kombat: Deadly Alliance

Unlockable	Code
Random Character Select	Highlight "Shang Tsung" (for player one) or "Quan Chi" (for player two) at the Character Selection screen, and then hold ↑+START.
Versus Mode Stage Select	Press R1 before either player chooses a character to get a screen with a screenshot of a stage. Press ← or → to change to the desired stage.
Versus Mode Skill Select	Press L2 before either player chooses a character.

TIP

Fatalities!

You can do fatalities from anywhere on screen! Press L1 at the Finish Him/Her screen to change into your fatality stance, or you have to figure out the distance range.

Fatality	Button Combination
Bo Rai Cho (Belly Flop)	Press Away (x3), ↓, ●.
Cyrax (Smasher)	Press Toward (x2), ↑, ▲.
Drahmin (Iron Bash)	Press Away, Toward (x2), ↓, ✕.
Frost (Freeze Shatter)	Press Toward, Away, ↑, ↓, ■.
Hsu Hao (Laser Slice)	Press Toward, Away, ↓, ↓, ▲.
Jax (Head Stomp)	Press ↓, Toward (x2), ↓, ▲.
Johnny Cage (Brain Ripper)	Press Away, Toward (x2), ↓, ▲.
Kano (Heart Grab)	Press Toward, ↑ (x2), ↓, ■.
Kenshi (Telekinetic Crush)	Press Toward, Away, Toward, ↓, ✕.
Kitana (Kiss of Doom)	Press ↓, ↑, Toward (x2), ▲.
Kung Lao (Hat Throw)	Press ↓, ↑, Away, ✕.
Li Mei (Crush Kick)	Press Toward (x2), ↓, Toward, ●.
Mavado (Kick Thrust)	Press Away (x2), ↑ (x2), ■.
Nitara (Blood Thirst)	Press ↑ (x2), Toward, ■.
Quan Chi (Neck Stretch)	Press Away (x2), Toward, Away, ✕.
Raiden (Electrocution)	Press Away, Toward, Toward (x2), ✕.
Reptile (Acid Shower)	Press ↑ (x3), Toward, ✕.

Mortal Kombat: Deadly Alliance (continued)

Fatality	Button Combination
Scorpion (Spear)	Press Away (x2), ↓, Away+●.
Shang Tsung (Soul Steal)	Press ↑, ↓, ↑, ↓, ▲.
Sonya (Kiss)	Press Away, Toward (x2), ↓, ▲.
Sub Zero (Spine Rip)	Press Away, Toward (x2), ↓, ×.

Motor Mayhem

Description	Code
Buzzsaw as a playable character	Beat the Deathmatch, Endurance, and Eliminator modes with the same character on either Hard or Very Hard difficulty.

MTX Mototrax

Go to the Options menu and select Cheats. Enter the following:

Unlockable	Code	Unlockable	Code
All Tracks	BA7H	Officer Dick	BADG3
Butterfingers Gear	B77393	Sky Camera	HIC
Fast Acceleration	JIH345	Slipknot Maggot	86657457
Left Field Gear	12345	Slipknot Movie	23F7IC5
Max Air	BFB0020	SoBe Gear	50B3
Nokia Trickbot	HA79000	Speed Demon	773H999

MTX vs. ATV Unleashed

Enter in the Cheats menu.

Unlockable	Code
50cc Bikes	Minimoto
Unlock all freestyle tracks	Huckit
Unlock Everything	Toolazy

MX Unleashed

Go to Options and select Cheat Codes. Pick the cheat you want and press ● to enter the code.

Unlockable	Code
500cc Bikes	BIGDOGS
50cc Bikes	SQUIRRELDOG
A.I. Bowling	WRECKINGBALL
All Bonuses/ Completion	CLAPPEDOUT
All Machines	MINIGAMES
Unlockable	Code
Expert A.I.	OBTGOFAST
Freestyle Tracks	BUSTBIG
National Tracks	ECONATION
Pro Physics	SWAPPIN
Supercross Tracks	STUPERCROSS

MX Vs. ATV Untamed

Unlockables

Type in the following codes in the Cheats menu to unlock the gear.

Unlockable	How to Unlock
All Handlebars	NOHANDS
FOX Riding Gear	CRAZYLIKEA

My Street

Description	Code
Custom Body Parts	Beat Story Mode once.

Nano Breaker

Enter code during game.

Unlockable	Code
Mini Map Shooter	⇧, ⇧, ⇩, ⇩, ⇦, ⇨, ⇦, ⇦, ⇨, ×, ●.

Narc

Enter these codes while playing. Do not pause the game.

Unlockable	Code
All Drugs	Repeatedly press L1 + R1 + L3
All Weapons	Repeatedly press L1 + R1 + R3
Infinite Ammo	Repeatedly press L1 + R1 + ⇩ (Only for the weapon you have equipped.)
Invincibility	Repeatedly press R1 + L1 + ×
Show all Drug Stashes	Repeatedly press L1 + R1 + ⇦

NASCAR 06: Total Team Control

In Fight to the Top mode, go to the Edit Driver screen and enter the following passwords as your first and last names. (Note: case sensitive)

Unlockable	Password
$10,000,000	Walmart Money
Dale Jarett in the UPS "Big Brown Truck"	Race TheTruck
Max Fan Level	Super Star
Max Prestige	MeMyself AndI
Max Team Prestige	All ForOne
Unlock All Chase Plates	Gimme Gimme
Unlocks Dale Sr.	The Intimidator
Walmart Raceway, Walmart Cars, and Walmart Sponsorship for Custom Car	Walmart Exclusive

NBA 2K8

Unlockables

Go to the Features menu and select the Codes section to enter the following codes.

Unlockable	How to Unlock
2K Sports Team	2ksports
ABA Ball	payrespect
CHA "Race Day" Uniform	agtaccsinr
IND Alternate Uniform	cpares
NBA Development Team	nba2k
St. Patrick's Day Uniforms (CHI/BOS/NY/TOR)	uclerehanp
Valentine's Day Uniforms (CLE/SEA)	amcnreo
Visual Concepts Team	vcteam

NBA Hoopz

At the Versus screen, use the following buttons to change the numbers for code entry: ■ to change the first number, × to change the second number, and ● to change the third number. Then use the D-Pad to enter the direction. If you entered the code correctly you'll see the name of the code displayed on the screen.

Unlockable	Objective	Unlockable	Objective
ABA Ball	1-1-1 →	No Goaltending	4-4-4 ←
Away Uniform	0-2-4 →	No Hotspots	3-0-1 ↑
Beach Court	0-2-3 ←	Play As Dr. Atomic	5-4-4 ←
Big Heads	3-0-0 →	Show Hotspot	1-1-0 ↓
Granny Shots	1-2-1 ←	Show Shot Percent	0-1-1 ↓
Home Uniform	0-1-4 →	Street Court	3-2-0 ←
Infinite Turbo	3-1-2 ↑	Tiny Heads	3-3-0 ←
No Fouls	2-2-2 →	Tiny Players	5-4-3 ←

NBA Jam

Create a new profile using these names.

Unlockable	Code
Unlock Everything	-LPP-
Unlock the NBA Jam Development Team	CREDITS

NBA Live 06

Go to "My NBA Live," then "NBA Codes" to enter the following codes.

Unlockable	Code
Adidas A3 Garnett 3 Shoes	DRI239CZ49
S. Carter III LE Shoes	JZ3SCARTVY
TMac5 Black Shoes	258SHQW95B
TMac5 White Shoes	HGS83KP234P

NBA Live 07

To enter these passwords, select My NBA Live, then NBA Codes.

Unlockable	Code
Charlotte Bobcats secondary road uniform	JKL846ETK5
New Jersey Nets secondary road uniform	NB79D965D2
Utah Jazz secondary road uniform	228GG7585G
Washington Wizards secondary road uniform	PL5285F37F

NBA Live 08

Shoes

From the main menu, go to "My NBA Live" then select "NBA Codes" and enter the following codes.

Unlockable	How to Unlock
Adidas GIL II ZERO: "Agent Zero" Shoe	ADGILLIT6BE
Adidas GIL II ZERO: "Black President" Shoe	ADGILLIT7BF
Adidas GIL II ZERO: "Cuba" Shoe	ADGILLIT4BC
Adidas GIL II ZERO: "CustOmize" Shoe	ADGILLIT5BD
Adidas GIL II ZERO: "GilWood" Shoe	ADGILLIT1B9
Adidas GIL II ZERO: "TS Lightswitch Away" Shoe	ADGILLIT0B8
Adidas GIL II ZERO: "TS Lightswitch Home" Shoe	ADGILLIT2BA

NBA Street

After entering one of the following icon codes, press Enter on the D-Pad to complete code entry.

Unlockable	Code
ABA Ball	Basketball, Turntable, Turntable, Basketball
ABA Socks	Microphone, Microphone, Microphone, Microphone
Athletic Joe "The Show"	Turntable, Shoe, Basketball, Turntable
Authentic Uniforms	Basketball, Basketball, Turntable, Turntable
Beach Ball	Basketball, Turntable, Turntable, Shoe
Big Heads	Microphone, Turntable, Shoe, Turntable
Captain Quicks	Backboard, Basketball, Shoe, Turntable
Casual Uniforms	Turntable, Turntable, Basketball, Basketball
Disable All Cheats	Turntable, Turntable, Turntable, Turntable
EA Big Ball	Basketball, Turntable, Microphone, Basketball
Easy Distance Shots	Shoe, Turntable, Backboard, Basketball
Explosive Rims	Turntable, Shoe, Microphone, Basketball
Harder Distance Shots	Shoe, Shoe, Backboard, Basketball
Less Blocks	Backboard, Turntable, Shoe, Backboard
Less Gamebreakers	Turntable, Backboard, Microphone, Shoe
Less Steals	Backboard, Turntable, Microphone, Basketball
Mad Handles	Backboard, Shoe, Turntable, Basketball
Medicine Ball	Basketball, Turntable, Turntable, Backboard
Mega Dunking	Backboard, Basketball, Turntable, Basketball
More Gamebreakers	Turntable, Microphone, Backboard, Shoe
No Alley-oops	Backboard, Microphone, Turntable, Shoe
No Auto Replays	Turntable, Shoe, Turntable, Turntable
No Dunks	Backboard, Basketball, Turntable, Shoe
No Gamebreakers	Turntable, Microphone, Microphone, Shoe
No HUD Display	Turntable, Microphone, Turntable, Shoe
No Player Indicators	Microphone, Basketball, Basketball, Microphone
No Shot Clock	Microphone, Microphone, Basketball, Backboard
No Shot Indicator	Microphone, Backboard, Shoe, Microphone
No Turbo	Turntable, Microphone, Microphone, Backboard
No Two-pointers	Backboard, Backboard, Basketball, Backboard
NuFX Ball	Basketball, Turntable, Backboard, Basketball
Player Names	Basketball, Turntable, Shoe, Backboard
Soccer Ball	Basketball, Shoe, Turntable, Basketball
Springtime Joe "The Show"	Turntable, Turntable, Basketball, Turntable
Sticky Fingers	Backboard, Microphone, Turntable, Basketball
Summertime Joe "The Show"	Turntable, Basketball, Basketball, Turntable
Super Swats	Backboard, Backboard, Turntable, Basketball
Tiny Heads	Microphone, Shoe, Basketball, Shoe
Tiny Players	Microphone, Basketball, Microphone, Basketball
Ultimate Power	Backboard, Turntable, Turntable, Basketball
Unlimited Turbo	Shoe, Basketball, Backboard, Basketball
Volleyball	Basketball, Turntable, Turntable, Microphone
WNBA ball	Basketball, Turntable, Shoe, Basketball

NBA Street (continued)

Unlockable	Objective
All Courts	In Hold the Court mode, go to the screen where you choose your court. Hold R2 and press ↑,↓,←,→,→,←,↓,↑. While still holding ↑, press ✕.
Biggs and Beacon Hill Court	Play the City Circuit and reach the Region 1 City Challenge. Defeat Biggs' team to unlock him as a selectable player and unlock the Beacon Hill court.
Bonafide and Broad Street Court	Play the City Circuit and reach the Region 2 City Challenge. Defeat Bonafide's team to unlock him as a selectable player and unlock the Broad Street court.
Created Player Pieces	Complete the Hold the Court challenges to unlock more pieces and development points for created players.
DJ and Venice Beach Court	Play the City Circuit and reach the Region 4 City Challenge. Defeat DJ's team to unlock him as a selectable player and unlock the Venice Beach court.
Drake and the Yard Court	Play the City Circuit and reach the Region 3 City Challenge. Defeat Drake's team to unlock him as a selectable player and unlock The Yard court.
More Player Creation Points	Note: This code can only be used for new players. Hold L1+↙ and press ←,↓,→, then press ■,▲,● at the Create Player menu.
NBA Superstars	Play the City Challenge and defeat an NBA team to unlock a player from their roster.
Stretch and Rucker Park Court	Play the City Circuit and reach the Region 2 City Challenge. Defeat Stretch's team to unlock him as a selectable player and unlock the Rucker Park court.
Takashi and Yakatomni Plaza Court	Play the City Circuit and reach the Region 5 City Challenge. Defeat Takashi's team to unlock him as a selectable player and unlock the Yakatomni Plaza court.

For the following unlockables, enter the "Enter User ID" screen and go to the User Record box (displays either a user ID's record information, or "no user record").

Unlockable	Code
NYC Legends Team	Hold L2 and press ↓,↓,↓,←,✕. Alternately, get 30 wins in any mode.
Team 3LW	Hold R1 and press ←,←,→,↓,✕. Alternately, get 20 wins in any mode.
Team Big	Hold L2 and press ↑,↓,↓,←,✕. Alternately, get 10 wins in any mode.
Team Dream	Hold R1, then press ↑,↑,→,→,✕. Alternately, win (complete all the objectives) Hold the Court mode to unlock a team that includes Graylien Alien, Magma Man, and Yeti Snowman.
Team Street Legends	Hold R1, then press →,←,↑,↓,✕. Alternately, win the City Circuit to unlock the Street Legends team. This team includes Biggs, Bonafide, Drake, DJ, Takashi, Stretch, and Michael Jordan.

NBA Street Vol 2

For the following unlockables, hold ↙, then enter code.

Unlockable	Code	Unlockable	Code
All Jerseys	■,▲,●,●	Hard 2-Pointers	▲,■,●,▲
All Quicks	▲,●,▲,■	No Counters	▲,▲,●,●
Always Legend Trails	▲,▲,▲,■	Street Kids	▲,▲,●,■
Big Heads	●,■,■,●	Turbo	■,■,▲,▲
Easy 2-Pointers	▲,●,■,▲	Unlimited Turbo	■,■,▲,▲
Easy Shots	▲,●,■,▲	Unlock All Legends	■,▲,▲,●
Explosive Rims	●,●,●,▲	WNBA Ball	●,▲,▲,●

DS

PSP

PS2

PS3

Wii

Xbox

Xbox 360

Index

NBA Street Vol 2 (continued)

Unlockable	Objective
"Chocolate Thunder" and "The Glide" Boss Moves	Beat the Broad Street Challenge in Be a Legend mode.
'85 Jordan	Beat NBA challenge, Street School, and Be a Legend.
All Courts	Beat Be a Legend and NBA Challenge.
Biggie Little	Beat the Foster Beach Tournament in Be a Legend mode.
Bill Russell's Jersey	Beat the Northwest region with no losses.
Bill Walton's Jersey	Score over 1,000,000 trick points in a game.
Bobbito	Spend 250 Reward points to unlock him or win 10 games in Pick Up mode.
Bonafide	Beat the tournament in Rucker Park in Be a Legend.
Boss Move "Big Dipper"	Beat the Foster Beach Street Challenge in Be a Legend.
Boss Move "Biggie Little"	Beat the Foster Beach Tournament in Be a Legend.
Boss Move "Bonafide"	Beat the Rucker Park Tournament in Be a Legend.
Boss Move "Droppin' Dimes"	Beat the Lincoln College Tournament in Be a Legend.
Boss Move "Jordan"	Beat the Rucker Park '78 Street Challenge in Be a Legend mode.
Boss Move "Magic"	Beat the Lincoln College Street Challenge in Be a Legend mode.
Boss Move "Nique"	Beat the Mosswood Tournament in Be a Legend.
Boss Move "Stretch"	Beat the Soul in the Hole Tournament in Be a Legend.
Boss Move "The Doctor"	Beat the Mosswood Street Challenge in Be a Legend.
Boss Move "The Legend"	Beat the Greenlake Street Challenge in Be a Legend.
Boss Move "The Oz"	Beat the Mosswood Tournament in Be a Legend.
Boss Move "The Pistol"	Beat the Soul in the Hole Street Challenge in Be a Legend mode.
Boss Move "Whitewater"	Beat the Greenlake Tournament in Be a Legend.
Clyde Drexler's Jersey	Reach Reputation Level 1 in Be a Legend mode.
Connie Hawkins' Jersey	Win a game and get 20 blocks.
Darryl Dawkins' Jersey	Beat the Broad Street Challenge in Be a Legend mode.
David Thompson's Jersey	Reach Reputation Level 1 in Be a Legend mode.
Dime	Beat the tournament held at the Lincoln College in Los Angeles in the Be A Legend mode.
Dominique Wilkins, James Worthy, and Moses Malone	Beat the Southwest Region.
Dominique Wilkins' Jersey	Reach Reputation Level 4 in Be a Legend mode.
Earvin "Magic" Johnson's Jersey	Beat the Lincoln College Street Challenge in Be a Legend mode.
Elgin Baylor Jersey	Shutout the opponent.
George Gervin's Jersey	Reach Reputation Level 5 in Be a Legend mode.
James Worthy's Jersey	Beat the Northeast region with no losses to unlock the jersey.
Jerry West Jersey	Win a game without getting blocked.
Julius Erving's Jersey	Beat the Mosswood Street Challenge in Be a Legend.
Julius Erving, Connie Hawkins, and Earl Monroe	Beat the Rucker Park '78 Street Challenge in Be a Legend mode.
Just Blaze	Beat the Rucker Park '78 Street Challenge in Be a Legend mode.
Larry Bird's Jersey	Beat the Greenlake Street Challenge.

NBA Street Vol 2 (continued)

Unlockable	Objective
Larry Bird, Clyde Drexler, and Isiah Thomas	Beat the Central Region.
Michael Jordan's Jersey	Beat the Rucker Park '78 Street Challenge in Be a Legend mode.
MJ Throwback Jersey	Play Pick-up Game mode in each of the scoring rule categories.
Moses Malone's Jersey	Max out your created baller's stats and then win a game with him.
Nelly and the St. Lunatics	Get 750 reward points and buy their card.
Oscar Robertson's Jersey	Beat the Southwest Region with no losses.
Osmosis	Beat the tournament held in Mosswood in Oakland in the Be A Legend mode.
Pete Maravich, David Thompson, and George Gervin	Beat the Northwest Region.
Rucker Park '78	Beat Be a Legend mode to get Rucker park '78.
Street Champ Clothes	Beat Be a Legend mode to unlock the clothes.
Stretch	Win the Soul in the Hole Tournament to unlock Stretch.
Tiny Archibald Throwback Jersey	Beat street school without messing up.
Walt Frazier's Jersey	Beat the Central region with no losses.
Whitewater	Win the Greenlake Tournament to unlock whitewater.
Wilt Chamberlain's Jersey	Beat the Foster Beach Street Challenge in Be a Legend mode.

NCAA Football 08

Pennants

In your Pennant Collection, press Select and then enter the codes.

Unlockable	How to Unlock
#200, First and 15	Thanks
2004 All-American Team	Fumble
All-Time Alabama Team	Roll Tide
All-Time Arkansas Team	Woopigsooie
All-Time Auburn Team	War Eagle
All-Time Baylor Team	Sic Em
All-Time Clemson Team	Death Valley
All-Time Colorado Team	Glory
All-Time Florida State Team	Uprising
All-Time Florida Team	Great To Be
All-Time Georgia Team	Hunker Down
All-Time Illinois Team	Oskee Wow
All-Time Iowa Team	On Iowa
All-Time Kansas State Team	Victory
All-Time LSU Team	Geaux Tigers
All-Time Miami (Fl) Team	Raising Cane
All-Time Michigan Team	Go Blue
All-Time Mississippi State Team	Hail State
All-Time Missouri Team	Mizzou Rah
All-Time Nebraska Team	Go Big Red
All-Time North Carolina Team	Rah Rah
All-Time Notre Dame Team	Golden Domer
All-Time Ohio State Team	Killer Nuts
All-Time Oklahoma State Team	Go Pokes

NCAA Football 08 (continued)	
Unlockable	**How to Unlock**
All-Time Oklahoma Team	Boomer
All-Time Oregon Team	Quack Attack
All-Time Penn State Team	We Are
All-Time Pittsburgh Team	Lets Go Pitt
All-Time Purdue Team	Boiler Up
All-Time Syracuse Team	Orange Crush
All-Time Tennessee Team	Big Orange
All-Time Texas A&M Team	Gig Em
All-Time Texas Team	Hook Em
All-Time Texas Tech Team	Fight
All-Time UCLA Team	Mighty
All-Time USC Team	Fight On
All-Time Virginia Team	Wahoos
All-Time Virginia Tech Team	Tech Triumph
All-Time Washington Team	Bow Down
All-Time Wisconsin Team	U Rah Rah
Blink (referee spots the ball short for opponent)	For
Boing (opponent drops more passes)	Registering
Butter Fingers (opponent fumbles more often)	With EA
Crossed The Line #205 (QB can pass the line of scrimmage)	Tiburon
Cuffed #206 (you cannot throw interceptions or fumble)	EA Sports
Extra Credit (four point interceptions, three point sacks)	Touchdown
Helium #208 (more catches likely)	In The Zone
Hurricane (your team's pass rush improved for one game)	Turnover
Instant Freeplay (five downs instead of four)	Impact
Jumbalaya #211 (get points when your players are injured)	Heisman
Kicker Hex #229	Sideline
Michigan State Mascot Team	Mizzou Rah
Molasses (improve your opponent's fatigue for one game)	Game Time
Nike Free (increase ability to break tackles for one game)	Break Free
Nike Magnigrip (better chance your players will intercept)	Hand Picked
Nike Pro (increase your QB's accuracy for one game)	No Sweat
QB Dud #219	Elite 11
Steel Toe #221	Gridiron
Stiffed #222	NCAA
Super Dive	Upset
Tough as Nails #226	Offense
What a Hit #228	Blitz
Wyoming Mascot	All Hail
Zips Mascot	Hail WV

Glitches

To use an injured player on your roster, start the game normally, then after the first kickoff hit pause and click restart. Once the game has restarted, the injured players are available.

NCAA March Madness 06

Enter "My NCAA" and go into the Lounge. In the Lounge select Cheat Codes to enter these passwords.

Unlockable	Password
Air Jordan III Shoes	39N56BXC4S
First Air Jordans	2J9UWAS44L
All Historic Teams	PSDF9078VT

Need for Speed Carbon

Enter at the main menu.

Unlockable	Code
Extra Money	⇩, ⇧, ⇦, ⇩, ⇨, ⇧, ■, ▲
Infinite Crew Charge	⇩, ⇧, ⇧, ⇨, ⇦, ⇦, ⇨, ■
Infinite NOS	⇦, ⇧, ⇦, ⇩, ⇦, ⇩, ⇨, ■
Infinite SpeedBreaker	⇩, ⇨, ⇨, ⇦, ⇨, ⇧, ⇩, ■
Need For Speed Carbon Logo Vinyls Unlocked	⇨, ⇧, ⇩, ⇧, ⇩, ⇦, ⇨, ■
Need For Speed Carbon Special Logo Vinyls Unlocked	⇧, ⇧, ⇩, ⇩, ⇩, ⇩, ⇧, ■

Need for Speed Hot Pursuit 2

Enter these codes at the Main menu.

Aston Martin V12 Vanquish	R2,→,R2,→,▲,←,▲,←
BMW Z8	■,→,■,→,R2,▲,R2,▲
Cheat Mode	L2,R2,L2,R2,▲,■,▲,■
Ferrari F550	L1,■,L1,■,→,R1,→,R1
HSV Coupe GTS	L1,L2,L1,L2,R1,▲,R1,▲
Lamborghini Diablo 6.0 VT	→,R2,→,R2,R1,L1,R1,L1
Lotus Elise	▲,R2,▲,R2,←,■,←,■
McLaren F1 LM	■,L1,■,L1,▲,→,▲,→
Porsche Carrera GT	←,→,←,→,R1,R2,R1,R2

Need for Speed Most Wanted

All codes should be entered at the Start screen.

Unlockable	Code
Unlocks Burger King Challenge Event (#69)	⇧, ⇩, ⇩, ⇩, ⇦, ⇨, ⇦, ⇨
Unlocks Free Engine Upgrade Bonus Marker (Can be used in the backroom of the customization shops)	⇧, ⇧, ⇩, ⇩, ⇦, ⇨, ⇧, ⇩
Unlocks Special Edition Castrol Ford GT (Which is added to your bonus cars)	⇦, ⇨, ⇦, ⇨, ⇧, ⇩, ⇧, ⇩

Need for Speed ProStreet

Codes

Go to the "Enter Codes" section of the Career menu and enter the following codes.

Unlockable	How to Unlock
Extra $2,000	1MA9X99
Extra $4,000	W2iOLLO1
Extra $8,000	L1iS97A1
Extra $10,000	1Mi9K7E1
Extra $10,000	REGGAME
Extra $10,000	CASHMONEY
5 Repair Tokens	SAFETYNET

Need for Speed ProStreet (continued)

Unlockable	How to Unlock
Castrol Syntec Vinyl	CASTROLSYNTEC
Dodge Viper SRT10 (Speed Races)	horsepower
Dodge Viper SRT10 (In Garage)	WORLDSLONGESTLASTING
Receive Bonus Vinyl Sticker	ENERGIZERLITHIUM
Receive Coke Zero Golf GTI in Career Mode	ZEROZEROZERO
Receive Mitsubishi Lancer Evolution in Career Mode	MITSUBISHIGOFAR
Unlock Map, Cars (Dodge Viper SRT10, 2004 Pontiac GTO, Chevrolet Cobalt SS, and Nissan 240SX), and Stage 4 Parts	UNLOCKALLTHINGS
Unlock Progressive Vinyl	ITSABOUTYOU

King Cars

After you beat each of the five Kings, you get their car as the reward.

Unlockable	How to Unlock
06 Mustang GT (Karol Monroe)	Beat Drag King in Career mode.
08 Evo X (Ryo Watanabe)	Beat Showdown King in Career mode.
08 M3 E92 (Ray Krieger)	Beat Grip King in Career mode.
65 GTO (Nate Denver)	Beat Speed King in Career mode.
95 RX-7 (Aki Kimura)	Beat Drift King in Career mode.

Need for Speed Underground

At the Main menu:

Unlockable	Code
Drift Physics in All Modes	R1, ↑, ↑, ↑, ↓, ↓, ↓, L1
Level 1 Performance Parts	R2, R2, R1, R1, ←, →, ←, →
Level 2 Performance Parts	R1, R1, R1, R1, R2, R2, ←, →
Level 2 Visual Parts	↓, ←, ↑, ↓, R1, R2, R2, ■
Acura Integra	R2, R2, R1, R2, L2, L1, ↓, ↑
Acura RSX	R1, R2, ↓, ←, ↑, →, ←, →
Ford Focus	←, →, ↑, R1, R2, R1, R2, ↑
Honda S2000	↑, ↑, ↓, ↓, ↑, ←, ■, R2
Hyundai Tiburon	←, →, ←, →, ↑, ↓, ↑, ↓
Lost Prophets Car	↑, ↑, ↑, →, ↓, ↓, ↑, →
Mitsubishi Lancer	←, ←, ←, R1, R1, R2, R2, L2
Mystikal Car	↑, →, ↑, ↑, ↓, →, ↑, →
Nissan Nismo	↑, ↓, ↑, ←, ↓, ↓, ↑, →
Nissan 240SX	↑, ↓, ←, →, ■, R1, L2, R1
Nissan 350Z	→, →, ↓, ↑, ■, L1, R1, L2
Nissan Sentra	→, →, →, L2, L2, R2, R2, ↑
Nissan Skyline	↓, ↓, L1, L2, L1, L2, L1, ↓
Petey Pablo Car	↑, ↑, ↑, ↑, ↓, ↑, ↑, →
Rob Zombie Car	↑, ←, ↑, ↑, ↓, ←, ↑, →
Subaru Impreza	↑, ↓, ↓, ↑, L2, ↑, L2, ↓
Toyota Supra	R1, R1, R2, R1, R2, R1, L2, L1
All Circuit Tracks	↓, R1, R1, R1, R2, R2, R2, ■
All Drag Tracks	→, ■, ←, R1, ■, L1, L2, R2
All Drift Tracks	←, ←, ←, ←, →, R2, R1, L2
All Sprint Tracks	↑, R2, R2, R2, R1, ↓, ↓, ↓

Need for Speed Underground 2

Enter these codes at the Title screen.

Unlockable	Code
$1000	←,←,→,■,■,→,L1,R1
All Circuit Tracks	↓,R1,R1,R1,R2,R2,R2,■
Best Buy Vinyl	↑,↓,↑,↓,↓,↑,→,←
Burger King Vinyl	↑,↑,↑,↑,↓,↑,↑,←
D3 GTO	↑,↓,→,↑,←,↓,→,→
Hummer H2 Capone	↑,←,↑,↑,↓,←,↓,←

Neo Contra

Enter this code at the Title screen.

Unlockable	Code
19 Lives	↑,↑,↓,↓,L1,R1,L1,R1,L3,R3

NFL Street

Enter these codes at the User Name screen.

Unlockable	Code
All 8 Division All-Star Teams	AW9378
All Stadiums	Travel
All Star Teams	AW9378
KaySlay Team	KaySlay
NFL Legends Team	Classic
NFC West Team	NW9378
X-Ecutioners Team	Excellent

NFL Street 2

Create a profile then enter these case sensitive codes in the Cheats menu.

Unlockable	Code	Unlockable	Code
AFC East All-Stars	EAASFSCT	NFC North All-Stars	NNAS66784
AFC North All-Stars	NAOFRCTH	NFC South All Stars	SNOFUCTH
AFC South All-Stars	SAOFUCTH	NFC West All Stars	ENASFSCT
AFC West All-Stars	WAEFSCT	EA Field	EAField
All players will have a maxed out catching stat	MagnetHands	No Fumble Mode (Quick Game)	GlueHands
NFC East All Stars	NNOFRCTH	Reebok Team	Reebok

NHL 2K6

Enter this as a profile name. Case Sensitive.

Unlockable	Password
Unlock everything	Turco813

NHL 08 (PS2)

Gear

Enter the code at the EA Extras menu under RBK Edge.

Unlockable	How to Unlock
RBK Edge Jerseys	h3oyxpwksf8ibcgt

NHL Hitz Pro

At the Choose Team screen, enter the following words as a profile name. Then go to Settings, Game Tuning, Visuals, then "Cheats" to activate the cheat.

Unlockable	Code
Big Player Head	HERK
Big Team Heads	INGY
Different Puck Size	211S
Different Puck Shadow	SASG
Glowing Puck	CARB

Nightshade

Unlockable	Objective
Hisu	Complete the game on Easy mode.
Hotsuma	Complete the game on Normal but be sure to have a Shinobi save on the same Memory Card.
Hibana's 2nd Costume	Complete the game on Normal mode.
Hibana's 3rd Costume	Complete the game on Hard mode.
Joe Musashi	Complete 88 Stages.

Unlockable	Objective
EX Mission Stage 1	3 Clan Coins
EX Mission Stage 2	14 Clan Coins
EX Mission Stage 3	24 Clan Coins
EX Mission Stage 4	35 Clan Coins
EX Mission Stage 5	45 Clan Coins
EX Mission Stage 6	56 Clan Coins
EX Mission Stage 7	68 Clan Coins
EX Mission Stage 8	80 Clan Coins
Hisui's 2nd Costume	88 Clan Coins
Survival Stage 1	10 Clan Coins
Survival Stage 2	21 Clan Coins
Survival Stage 3	31 Clan Coins
Survival Stage 4	42 Clan Coins

Unlockable	Objective
Survival Stage 5	52 Clan Coins
Survival Stage 6	64 Clan Coins
Survival Stage 7	76 Clan Coins
Survival Stage 8	88 Clan Coins
Time Attack Stage 1	7 Clan Coins
Time Attack Stage 2	17 Clan Coins
Time Attack Stage 3	28 Clan Coins
Time Attack Stage 4	38 Clan Coins
Time Attack Stage 5	49 Clan Coins
Time Attack Stage 6	60 Clan Coins
Time Attack Stage 7	72 Clan Coins
Time Attack Stage 8	84 Clan Coins

Oni

For the following unlockables, press SELECT during gameplay, highlight the "Help" button, then enter code. A sound confirms correct code entry.

Unlockable	Code
Big Head Mode	L2, L1, L2, ■, ●, ■, START, ■, ●, START
Change the Character	L2, L1, L2, ■, ●, ■, L2, L2, L2, L2—do not move your cursor yet. Hit the L2 button until you select your character.
Extra Powerful Punches and Kicks	L2, L1, L2, ■, ●, ■, R3, L3, ●, ■
Godly Guns	L2, L1, L2, ■, ●, ■, L2, L2, L2, L1, L3—gives you unlimited ammo and you never have to reload.
Hard Mode	L2, L1, L2, ■, ●, ■, R3, L3, ●, ■

Oni (continued)	
Huge Characters	L2, L1, L2, ■, ●, ■, R3, ■, ●, L3
Instant Level Completion	L2, L1, L2, ■, ●, ■, L3, R3, L2, L1
Itty Bitty Characters	L2, L1, L2, ■, ●, ■, L3, R3, ■, ●
One Shot, One Kill	L2, L1, L2, ■, ●, ■, L3, R3, ●, ■
Unlimited Health	L2, L1, L2, ■, ●, ■, R3, L3, R3, ●
Unlimited Phase Cloak	L2, L1, L2, ■, ●, ■, L1, R3, L2, L3—enables you to stay invisible for as long as you want

TIP

Here's an extra tip. To avoid fall damage, press ↙ to do a flip as you near the ground.

Onimusha: Dawn of Dreams

Input these codes by going into the Special menu, highlighting exit, and entering a code.

Unlockable	Code
Gives Jubei a Racket	L1, R1, ⇨, L2, ▲, ⇨, L1, ⇨, L3, R1
Gives Jubei Cammy's Costume	L2, L2, ⇨, ⇨, L3, ▲, ⇦, L1, L2, ■
Gives Ohatsu Chun-Li's Costume	R3, ⇨, L2, ⇦, ⇦, R3, L1, R1, ⇨, R3

Input these codes by going into the Special menu, highlighting exit, and entering a code.

Unlockable	Code
Gives Ohatsu a Piggy Bank	⇨, ▲, ⇦, L3, L1, ▲, ■, R2, ■, R2
Gives Roberto Boxing Gloves	▲, R3, ▲, ⇨, R1, L3, ▲, L1, ⇨, L3
Gives Roberto Guile's Costume	R2, L2, ⇦, L1, ⇦, ⇨, R3, ■, ■, ▲
Gives Soki a Steel Pipe	L2, ■, ▲, R1, R1, R3, ⇦, ■, L1, ▲
Gives Soki Ryu's Costume	⇦, ▲, R2, R3, ■, R1, R1, ⇨, ⇦, L2
Gives Tenkai a Microphone Stand	R2, R3, ■, ⇦, ⇦, ⇨, L2, ⇦, R2, ⇦
Gives Tenkai Ken's Costume	L3, L3, R3, R3, R3, ⇦, R2, L1, ■, ⇨

The Operative: No One Lives Forever

In the Main menu, highlight Load Game, then enter the code.

Unlockable	Code
Level Select	Hold L3+R3, then press ×.

Orphen: Scion of Sorcery

Unlockable	Objective
Restart the Battle	Pause the game and pick "Equip" before resuming the game at the start of the battle. All your energy will be restored.

Outlaw Golf 2

Unlockable	Objective
Everything unlocked	Enter I Have No Time as a profile name.

Outlaw Volleyball Remixed

Enter these codes at the Exhibition Court Select screen.

Unlockable	Code
Hell Pit court	Hold R1 and press ■, ■, ■, ■, ■, ■, ▲, ▲, ▲, ▲, ▲, ▲, L2, L2, L2, L2, L2, L2
Warehouse court	Hold L1 and press ↑, ■, ■, ▲, ▲, ↓

Enter this at the Character Select screen.

Unlockable	Code
Better Stats	Hold R1 and press ←, L2, →, L2

Enter this code during gameplay.

Unlockable	Code
Big Heads	Hold L1 and press ●, ×, ●, ▲

Peter Jackson's King Kong

At the Main menu screen, hold L1+R1 and press ↓, ×, ↑, ■, ↓, ↓, ↑, ↑, then release L1+R1. This opens the Cheat Menu. Now enter any of these case sensitive passwords.

Unlockable	Password	Unlockable	Password
999 ammunition	KK 999 mun	One-hit kills	GrosBras
Bonuses completed	KKmuseum	Revolver	KKtigun
God mode	8wonder	Shotgun	KKsh0tgun
Level select	KKst0ry	Sniper rifle	KKsn1per
Machine gun	KKcapone	Unlimited spears	lance 1nf

Pirates: The Legend of Black Kat

To access the following unlockables, hold R1+R2, then enter code.

Unlockable	Code
Advance to Katarina's Next Sword	R3, SELECT, L2, L3, ■, ×, L1, ●, L3, ▲, L3, ■, ×, L1, ●
All Treasure Chest Keys	●, SELECT, ×, ■, R3, L1, L3, L2, ▲, L3
Alternate Glacial Gulf Music	Press L1, ×, ▲, L2, ■, ●, L2, SELECT, R3, L3—you can now hear music from SSX when sliding down in Glacial Gulf.
Extra Gold	▲, R3, L3, ×, ■, R3, SELECT, L1, ●—you can now sail to another map to get the Galleon.
High-Pitched Voices	R3, ●, SELECT, ×, R3, ▲, L1, ■, L2, L3
Invincibility for Katarina	×, ●, L3, ▲, R3, SELECT, R3, L1, L2, ■
Invincibility for the Wind Dancer	SELECT, ▲, L1, ×, R3, L2, ■, R3, ●, L3
Kane Poison Head	▲, L2, L1, ■, L3, ×, L3, ●, R3, SELECT—the poison status will be indicated by the head of Kane from Command and Conquer.

To access the following unlockables, hold R1+R2, then enter code.

Unlockable	Code
Reveal All Treasure Chests	R3, ×, ▲, L3, ●, L1, SELECT, L3, ■, L2
Reveal Buried Treasure Chests	●, ×, ■, ▲, L1, SELECT, L3, L2, L3, R3—green Xs will appear on the captain's log maps to indicate the location of buried treasure chests.
Unlimited Items	▲, L1, SELECT, L2, R3, L3, ■, ×, R3, ●—once found, an item will be available in unlimited amounts.
Unlimited Wind Boost	SELECT, L1, R3, ●, L2, ▲, ×, L3
Wind Dancer	L2, ▲, R3, L3, ×, ■, R3, SELECT, L1, ●

Pirates: The Legend of Black Kat (continued)

To access alternate Karina costumes, please see table below. The following code requires two players and controllers. Simultaneously hold L1+L2+↑+SELECT+L3 on controller one and R1+R2+▲+START+R3 on controller two. A short sequence of music will confirm correct code entry. Click down on R3 on controller one to change the value of the numbers that appear on screen, then start a new game or resume a saved game to view the corresponding costume. The costumes that can be accessed are as follows:

Costume	Code
Blackbeard in Purple	00000001
Blonde Hair, Orange and Yellow Bikini	00000101
Blonde Hair, Pink Bikini	00000110
Blue Hair with Orange and Red Bikini	00000011
Blue Hair, Shiny Copper Body Suit	00001010
Blue Hair, Shiny Silver Bikini	00000111
Original Costume and Hair Color	00000000
Pink Hair, Shiny Black Body Suit	00001001
Purple Hair, Shiny Silver Body Suit	00001011
Red Hair with Red and Orange Bikini	00000010
Red Hair, Black Bikini, Black Stockings	00001000
Tan, Brown Hair, Orange and Yellow Bikini	00000100

Pitfall: The Lost Expedition

Enter the following codes at the Title Screen. If you entered the code correctly, a message will appear.

Unlockable	Code
Hyper Punch Mode	Hold L1+R1, then press →,←,●,↑,●,→,←
Original Pitfall game	Hold L1+R1, then press ●,●,←,→,●,■,×,↑,●
Original Pitfall 2: Lost Caverns game	Hold L1+R1, then press ←,→,←,→,▲,▲,▲
Play as Nicole	Hold L1+R1, then press ←,↑,↓,↑,●,↑,↑
Unlimited Water in Canteen	Hold L1+R1, then press ←,■,●,↓,■,×,■,●

Prince of Persia: The Sands of Time

Unlockable	Code
Unlock the first **Prince of Persia**	Start a new game and stay on the balcony, press L3 and quickly enter ×, ■, ▲, ●, ▲, ×, ■, ●.

Pryzm Chapter 1: The Dark Unicorn

Unlockable	Code
Complete current level	←, →, ←, →, ↑, ↓, ↑, ↓
Invincibility, unlimited magic, and all levels	Start a new game and enter as your name SUPREMEMAGIC

Psi-Ops: The Mindgate Conspiracy

In Main menu, highlight Extra Content and press R1. Then enter these codes.

Unlockable	Code
All Powers	537893
Infinite Ammo	978945
Bulletproof	548975
Super Psi	456456
No Head	987978
Arcade mode	05051979
Co-op mode	07041979
Dark Mode	465486

Psi-Ops: The Mindgate Conspiracy (continued)

Extra Missions	Code
Aura Pool	659785
Bottomless Pit	54897
Bouncy Bouncy	568789
Gasoline	9442662
Gearshift	154684
Gnomotron	456878
Panic Room	76635766
Pitfall	05120926
Psi Pool	565485
Stop Lights	945678
Survival	7734206
Tip the Buddha	428584
TK Alley	90702
Up and Over	020615

Skins	Code
Burned Soldier	454566
Dock Worker	364654
Edgar Barrett	497878
Edgar Barret (Training 1)	196001
Edgar Barret (Training 2)	196002
Edgar Barret (Training 3)	196003
Edgar Barret (Training 4)	196004
Edgar Barret (Training 5)	196005
Edgar Barret (Training 6)	196006
The General	459797
The General (Clown)	431644
Jack	698798
Jov Leonov	468987
Marlena Kessler	489788
Marlena Kessler (Bikini)	135454
Marlena Kessler (Leather)	136876
MP1	321646
MP2	678999

Skins	Code
MP3	654659
Nick Scryer (Stealth)	456498
Nick Scryer (Training)	564689
Nick Scryer (Urban)	484646
Nick Scryer (Wasteland)	975466
Sara Blake	135488
Sara Blake (Psi)	468799
Sara Blake (Suicide)	231644
Scorpion	546546
Tonya	678999
UN Soldier	365498
Wei Lu	231324
Wei Lu (Dragon)	978789
Wei Lu (Tranquility)	654654

The Punisher

Effect	Code
Everything Unlocked (except upgrades)	V Pirate as a Profile Name.

Quake III Revolution

Enter the following code during gameplay.

Unlockable	Code
Level Skip	Hold L1+R1+R2+SELECT, then press ×,●,■,▲,×,●,■,▲

Ratchet and Clank: Up Your Arsenal

Unlockable	Code
Duel Blade Laser Sword	Pause the game and press ●,■,●,■,↑,↓,←,←.
Sly 2: Band of Thieves Demo	At the Title Screen, hold L1+L2+R1+R2.

Rayman Arena

Enter these codes as a name, then press L2+●+■ to activate it.

Unlockable	Code
3D Mode	3DVISION
Every Battle Mode Unlocked	ALLFISH
Every Character Unlocked	PUPPETS
Every Mode Unlocked	ALLRAYMANM
Every Skin Unlocked	CARNIVAL
Every Battle Level Unlocked	ARENAS
Every Level Unlocked	FIELDS
Every Race Level Unlocked	TRACKS
Monochrome Mode	OLDTV

Ready 2 Rumble Boxing: Round 2

Unlockable	Code
Big Gloves	At the Character Selection screen, press ←,→,↑,↓,R1,R2. A sound confirms correct entry.
Fat Boxer	At the Character Selection screen, press →,→,↑,↓,→,R1, R1,R2. A sound confirms correct entry.
Play As Freak E. Deke and Michael Jackson	At the character selection screen, press R1 x (13), R2, R1 x (10), R2.
Skinny Boxer	At the Character Selection screen, press →,→,↑,↓,→,R1,R2. A sound confirms correct entry.
Undead Boxer	At the Character Selection screen, press ←,↑,→,↓,R1,R1,R2. A sound confirms correct entry.
Bill Clinton	Beat Arcade mode eight times.
Champion Costumes	Complete Championship mode.
Freak E. Deke	Beat Arcade mode once.
Freedom Brock	Beat Arcade mode six times.
G.C. Thunder	Beat Arcade mode three times.
Hillary Clinton	Beat Arcade mode nine times.
Michael Jackson	Beat Arcade mode twice.
Rocket Samchay	Beat Arcade mode seven times.
Rumbleman	Beat Arcade mode ten times.
Shaquille O'Neal	Beat Arcade mode five times.
Wild "Stubby" Corley	Beat Arcade mode four times.

Ready 2 Rumble Boxing: Round 2 (continued)

Unlockable	Code
Christmas Costume	Set the system date to December 25. Selene Strike will be in an elf costume and Rumbleman will be in a snowman costume.
Easter Costume	Set the system date to April 23. Mama Tua will be in a Playboy Bunny costume.
Fourth of July Costume	Set the system date to July 4. G.C. Thunder will be in an Uncle Sam costume.
Halloween Costume	Set the system date to October 31. J.R. Flurry will be in a skeleton costume.
New Year's Costume	Set the system date to January 1. Joey T will be in a baby costume.
St. Patrick's Day Costume	Set the system date to March 17. The referee will be in a leprechaun costume.
Valentine's Day Costume	Set the system date to February 14. Lulu will be in a sexy costume.

Red Faction II

Enter the following codes at the Cheats screen under the Options menu.

Unlockable	Code
Bouncy Grenades	●,●,●,●,●,●,●,●
Directors Cut	■,×,●,▲,●,×,■,▲
Gibby Bullets	●,●,●,●,▲,×,●,●
Gibby Explosions	▲,●,×,■,▲,●,×,■
Instagib Ammunition	×,×,×,×,■,●,×,×
Joke Message	■,×,■,×,■,×,■,×
Level Select	●,■,×,▲,■,●,×,×
Master Code unlocks all normal game options.	▲,▲,×,×,■,●,■,●

Unlockable	Code
Master Cheat Code	■,●,▲,●,■,×,▲,×
Rain of Fire	■,■,■,■,■,■,■,■
Rapid Rails	●,■,●,■,×,×,▲,▲
Super Health	×,×,■,▲,■,▲,●
Unlimited Ammunition	■,▲,×,●,■,●,×,▲
Unlimited Grenades	●,×,●,■,×,●,×,●
Wacky Deaths	▲,▲,▲,▲,▲,▲,▲,▲
Walking Dead	×,×,×,×,×,×,×,×

Reign of Fire

Unlockable	Code
Level Select	At Main menu, enter ↑, ←, ●, ●, ←, ←, ■, ↓, ↑, ●

Reservoir Dogs

Enter these codes in the Cheats menu under extras.

Unlockable	Code
All levels	L2, R2, L2, R2, L1, R1, START
Art gallery	●, ×, L2, R2, ●, ×, START
Movie gallery	L1, L1, ●, ×, L1, R1, START
Unlimited ammo	R2, L2, ●, L2, ×, R2, START

Ridge Racer V

Unlockable	Objective
99 Lap Option	Get the top score in all the Time Attack GP races in Extra mode and finish in first place.
Changing Saved Game Icon	Beat the game with all secrets unlocked. The saved game icon will change from a car to Ai Fukami, a programmer.
Modifying the Intro Sequence	Press L1+R1 during the intro sequence with the girl. Press R1 once for black-and-white graphics. Press R1 a second time and the game will have a yellow tint. Press R1 a third time to add a blur effect. That blur effect eliminates the jaggies in the graphics. You can press L2 to cycle back through the various effects.

Ridge Racer V (continued)	
Unlockable	**Objective**
Onscreen Information	During a race, press and hold SELECT for a few seconds. A window shows up on the screen with various information. Press and hold SELECT again to make the information window go away.
Unlock 50's Super Drift Caddy	Place first in the Danver Spectra race in Duel mode to unlock this car in Free Run, Duel, and Time Attack modes.
Unlock a Beetle	Place first in the Solort Rumeur race in Duel mode to unlock this car in Free Run, Duel, and Time Attack modes.
Unlock a McLaren Type Car	Place first in the Kamata Angelus race in Duel mode to unlock this car in Free Run, Duel, and Time Attack modes.
Unlock Devil Drift	Place first in the Rivelta Crinale race in Duel mode to unlock this car in Free Run, Duel, and Time Attack modes.
Unlock Duel Mode	Enter Standard Time Attack GP and finish first in lap and overall time.
Unlock Pac-Man Mode	Race more than 3,000 kilometers in total distance. The Pac-Man race becomes available. Beat the Pac-Man race and the Pac-Man car and the ghosts on scooters become unlocked.
Unlocking Bonus Cars	Beat each of the Grand Prix circuits, or break the Time Attack high scores.

Rise of Kasai

Enter the following codes at the Press Start screen.

Unlockable	Code
Invincible Rau	■, ●, ×, ■, ●, ■, ×, ●, ×, ■, ●, ×
Infinite Ammunition	×, ●, ■, ■, ×, ■, ●, ●, ×, ■, ■, ×
Weaker Enemies	×, ●, ●, ■, ×, ■, ■, ●

Rise to Honor

Unlockable	Objective
Extra Costumes	Complete the game.
Hard Mode	Complete the game on Normal.
Kit Yun and Michelle's FMV	Complete the game.

Roadkill

Pause the game on the Map screen then enter the following codes.

Unlockable	Code
All Weapons	▲, ×, ×, ▲, ■, ●, ●, ■, ×, ■, ●, ▲
All Vehicles	↑, ↓, ↑, ↓, ▲, ×, ▲, ×, ■, ●, ●, ■
Health	■, ●, ■, ●, ■, ●, ■, ●
Infinite Ammo	▲, ■, ■, ●, ▲, ■, ■, ●
More Money	▲, ●, ▲, ●, ■, ×, ■, ×, ↓, ↑

Robotech: Battlecry

To access Cheat mode, enter the New Game or Load Game screen. Hold L1+L2+R1+R2, then press ←,↑,↓,×,→,▲,START to display the Code Entry screen. Enter one of the following codes to activate the corresponding cheat function.

Unlockable	Code
All Models and Awards	WHERESMAX
All Multiplayer Levels	MULTIMAYHEM
Alternate Paint Schemes	MISSMACROSS
Disable Active Codes	CLEAR
Gunpod Ammunition Refilled Faster	SPACEFOLD
Gunpod and Missiles Refilled Faster	MIRIYA
Invincibility	SUPERMECH

Robotech: Battlecry (continued)

Unlockable	Code
Level Select	WEWILLWIN
Missiles Refilled Faster	MARSBASE
One-Shot Kills	BACKSTABBER
One-Shot Kills in Sniper Mode	SNIPER
Upside-Down Mode	FLIPSIDE

Robotech: Invasion

From Options, select Extras. Enter the following:

Unlockable	Code
1 Hit Kill	DUSTYAYRES
All Levels	RECLAMATION
Invincibility	SUPERCYC
Lancer's Multiplayer Skin	YLLWFLLW
Rand's Multiplayer Skin	KIDGLOVES
Rook's Multiplayer Skin	BLUEANGLS
Scott Bernard's Multiplayer Skin	LTNTCMDR
Unlimited Ammo	TRGRHPY

Rocky

Enter the following codes in the Main menu while holding R1:

Unlockable	Code
All Default Boxers and Arenas	→,↓,↑,←,↑,L1
All Default Boxers, Arenas, and Rocky Statue	→,→,→,←,→,L1
All Default Boxers, Arenas, Rocky statue, and Mickey	↑,↓,↓,←,←,L1
Double Punch Damage	→,↓,←,↑,←,L1
Double Speed Boxing	↓,←,↓,↑,→,L1
Max Stats for Movie Mode	→,↓,↓,↑,←,L1
Max Stats for Tournament and Exhibition Modes	←,↑,↑,↓,→,L1
Win Movie Mode (During a fight, press R2+L2 to win!)	→,→,←,←,↑,L1

Rogue Ops

At any time in the game pause and enter the following codes.

Unlockable	Code
God Mode	←,→,→,←,←,→,→,←,←,→,→,←,■,■
Level Skip	L2,■,L2,●,L2,←,L2,→,L2,R2,R2,■,R2,●,R2,←,R2,→,■
Unlimited Ammo	■,●,■,●,■,●,■,●,←,●,■,●,■,●,■,●,■

Rogue Trooper

Enter these codes in the Extras menu.

Unlockable	Code
Extreme Ragdoll Physics	↑, ↑, ↑, R2, R2, ↑
Hippy Blood	L2, →, ●, ↓, R1, SELECT
Infinite Health	←, →, ↑, ↓, L3, ■
Infinite Supplies	SELECT, R1, L1, SELECT, R3, L1
Low Gravity Ragdoll Physics	■, ■, ●, ●, ↑, ↓

Romance of the Three Kingdoms VIII

Unlockable	Objective
Better Created Characters	100% item completion.
Extra Created Character Portraits	100% event completion.

Romance of the Three Kingdoms VIII (continued)

Unlockable	Objective
Pre-Made Characters	Create an officer with one of the names below for a hidden pre-made character: *Abraham Lincoln, *Albert Einstein, *Ben Franklin, *Benedict Arnold, *Davy Crockett, *Jebidiah Smith, *Jim Bridger, *John Adams, *John Henry, *Kit Carson, *Patrick Henry, *Paul Bunyan, *Paul Revere, *Pecos Bill, *Red Cloud, *Sam Houston, *Sitting Bull, *Thomas Edison, *William Cody, *William Seward.

Romance of the Three Kingdoms IX

Unlockable	Objective
Bai Qi	New Officer with name "Bai" "Qi"
Change Kingdoms in Mid-game	Leave all forces under computer control, then during the action phase, press start to "go to main-menu." Press × and the game will resume, then press SELECT. (You may also press the shoulder buttons and it will say "Select Force or Forces to play as" and at the end of the action phase you can choose up to eight new forces to play as.)
Chen Qingzhi	New Officer with name "Chen" "Qingzhi"
Chengji Sihan	New Officer with name "Chengji" "Sihan"
Da Qiao	Load Dynasty Warriors 4 Data
Emperor Xian	Unlock all sages and pick He Jin in 281 "Hero" scenario
Fan Zeng	New Officer with name "Fan" "Zeng"
Guan Yiwu	New Officer with name "Guan" "Yiwu"
Han Xin	New Officer with name "Han" "Xin"
Huang Yueying	Beat Tutorial Mode
Huo Qubing	New Officer with name "Huo" "Qubing"
Japan Tribe	Search near Bei Hai when warlord tells you to. You must have Bei Hai to do this.
Japan Tribe	Search Langxie while controlling two provinces and with 700 reputation or higher.
Kong Qiu	New Officer with name "Kong" "Qiu"
Li Ji	New Officer with name "Li" "Ji"
Li Si	New Officer with name "Li" "Si"
Lin Xiangru	New Officer with name "Lin" "Xiangru"
Liu Bang	New Officer with name "Liu" "Bang"
Lu Ling Qi	Load Dynasty Tactics 2 Data
Ma Yunlu	Beat Tutorial Mode
Mistress Zhen	Get Good Ending with Yuan Shang on Inheritance Wars challenge scenario.
Mistress Zhen	In Inheritance Wars, get event where Mistress Zhen gives Yuan Xi a carp charm, then beat the scenario.
Mistress Zou	In Defense of Nan Yang Scenario, get event where Jia Xu offers Mistress Zou up for Cao Cao, then beat the scenario.
Nanman Tribe	Beat Nanman Barbarians in scenario then beat game.
Qiang Tribe	Beat Qiang Barbarians in scenario then beat game.
Qin Liangyu	New Officer with name "Qin" "Liangyu"
Shan Yue Tribe	Beat Shen Yue Barbarians in scenario, then beat game.
Sun Bin	New Officer with name "Sun" "Bin"
Wang Jian	New Officer with name "Wang" "Jian"
Wu Wan Tribe	Beat Wu Wan Barbarians in scenario, then beat game.
Xiang Ji	New Officer with name "Xiang" "Ji"
Xiao He	New Officer with name "Xiao" "He"
Xiao Qiao	Load Dynasty Warriors 4 Extreme Legends Data
Yang Daiyan	New Officer with name "Yang" "Daiyan"

Romance of the Three Kingdoms IX (continued)

Unlockable	Objective
Ying Bu	New Officer with name "Ying" "Bu"
Ying Zheng	New Officer with name "Ying" "Zheng"
Yue Fei	New Officer with name "Yue" "Fei"
Yue Yi	New Officer with name "Yue" "Yi"
Zhang Liang	New Officer with name "Zhang" "Liang"
Zhang Yi	New Officer with name "Zhang" "Yi"
Zhen Ji	Beat Inheritance Wars Scenario.

RTX Red Rock

Unlockable	Code
Add Items	→,→,→,→,→,←,←,←,↑,↑
Difficult Mode	↓,↑,↑,↑,↑,↑,↑,↑,↑,↓
Easy Mode	↑,↓,↓,↓,↓,↓,↓,↓,↓,↑
Normal Mode	↑,↓,↑,↓,↑,↓,↑,↓,↑,↓
Old Soul Super Weapons	→,↑,↓,↓,↑,→,→,↑,↓,↓
Progressive Scan Mode	→,↑,→,→,↑,→,→,→,↑,→ (Note: You'll have to reboot your PS2 once the screen turns blue.)
Unlock All Levels	↓,←,←,↓,←,↓,→,↓,←,↓
Unlock All Special Features	←,↓,↑,←,→,↑,↓,←,→,↓

R-Type Final

Pause the game and enter the following (you will hear a sound if you entered the code correctly):

Unlockable	Code
99.9% Charge Dose	Hold L2 and press R2,R2,←,→,↑,↓,→,←,↑,↓,▲.
Curtain Call Ship (#100)	In the R's Museum, enter 1009 9201 as a password.
Full Blue Power, Missiles, and Bits	Hold L2 and press R2,R2,←,→,↑,↓,→,←,↑,↓,●.
Full Red Power, Missiles, and Bits	Hold L2 and press R2,R2,←,→,↑,↓,→,←,↑,↓,■.
Full Yellow Power, Missiles, and Bits	Pause the game, then hold L2 and press R2,R2,←,→,↑,↓,→,←,↑,↓,×.
Invincibility	Hold L2 and press →,→,←,→,←,←,→,←,L1,↑,↑,↓,↓,↑,↓,↑,↓,L1.
Lady Love Ship (#3)	In the R's Museum, enter 5270 0725 as a password.
Mr. Heli Ship (#59)	In the R's Museum, enter 1026 2001 as a password.
Strider Ship (#24)	In the R's Museum, enter 2078 0278 as a password.

Savage Skies

Enter these codes at the Main menu.

Unlockable	Code
All Creatures	⇦, ⇨, ⇦, ⇦, ⇨, ⇨, ⇨, ×
All Multiplayer Maps	⇦, ⇨, ⇦, ⇦, ⇨, ⇦, ⇨, ×

Enter these codes while the game is paused.

Unlockable	Code
Invulnerability	⇦, ⇦, ⇨, ⇨, ⇧, ⇧, ⇧, ⇧, ×, ⇧, ×
Unlock Crystal	⇦, ⇦, ⇨, ⇨, ⇦, ⇧, ⇨, ⇩, ⇦, ×, ×
Win Mission	⇦, ⇦, ⇨, ⇨, ⇩, ⇩, ⇩, ⇧, ⇩, ⇩, ×

Scarface

Enter these on the Cheats screen of the Pause menu.

Unlockable	Password
1,000 Balls	FPATCH
Antique Racer	OLDFAST
Bacinari	666999
Black Suit	BLACK
Blue Suit	BLUE
Blue Suit w/shades	BLUESH
BReal "The World Is Yours" Music Track	TUNEME
Bulldozer	DOZER
Change Time of Day	MARTHA
Decrease Cop Heat	FLYSTRT
Decrease Gang Heat	NOBALLS
Dump Truck	DUMPER
Fill Ammo	AMMO
Fill Health	MEDIK
Grey Suit	GREY
Grey Suit w/shades	GREYSH
Increase Cop Heat	DONUT
Increase Gang Heat	GOBALLS
Lightning	SHAZAAM
Rain	RAINY
Sandy Shirt	TANSHRT
Sandy Shirt w/shades	TANSH
Stampede	BUMMER
Tiger Shirt	TIGSHRT
Tiger Shirt w/shades	TIGERSH
Vehicle Repair	TBURGLR
White Suit	WHITE
White Suit w/shades	WHITESH

Scooby Doo: Night of 100 Frights

Pause the game and hold L1+L2+R1+R2, then enter the following codes.

Unlockable	Code
All Power-Ups	●,■,●,■,●,■,■,■,●,●,■,●,●,●
FMV Sequences	■,■,■,●,●,●,■,●,■
View Credits	■,●,●,■,●,■

Change the date on the PlayStation 2 for some special holiday decorations:

Unlockable	Code
Assorted Fireworks	July 4
Fireworks	January 1
Giant Bats	October 31
Snow	December 25

Scorpion King: Rise of the Akkadian

Enter these codes while the game is paused. A sound will confirm if the code was entered correctly. You must have one handed class weapons enabled.

Unlockable	Code
Big Heads	↑, ↓, ←, →, ←, →, ●, R2
Enable All Bonuses	↑, ↓, ←, →, ←, →, ■, R2
Max Health And Weapons	↑, ↓, ←, →, ←, →, ■, ●
Small Enemies	↑, ↓, ←, →, ←, →, ●, ■
Unlock Meat Club	↑, ↓, ←, →, ←, →, ←, ←

Secret Weapons Over Normandy

At the Title screen (New Game or Continue), enter the following:

Unlockable	Code
All Levels in Instant Action	↑,↓,←,→,L1,R1,L1,R1
All Planes and Missions	▲,▲,▲,■,■,■,L1,R1,R2,R2,L2,L2
Big Heads	→,↑,←,↓,→,↑,←,↓,→,L1,R1,L1,R1
Invulnerability	↑,↓,←,→,←,←,→,→,L1,L1,R1,R1,L2,R2
Unlimited Ammo	↑,→,↓,←,↑,→,↓,←,L1,R1

DS PSP PS2 PS3 Wii Xbox Xbox 360 Index

Shark Tale

During gameplay, press SELECT, hold L1, and enter code. After you enter the code, release L1 to activate the cheat.

Unlockable	Code
Attack Mode	●,●,●,●,×,●,●,●,●
Extra Clams and Fame	●,●,×,×,●,×,●,●
Replace All Pearls with Fish King Coins	●,×,●,●,●,×,●,●

Shellshock: Nam '67

Enter the following codes at the Title screen (Press Start Button screen):

Unlockable	Code
Add Weapon Option	↑,↓,←,→,●,■,↑,↓,←,→,●,■
All Missions and Pictures	L2,R2,L1,R1,L1,L2,L2,R2,L1,R1,R1,R2
God Mode	R3, L3,→,←,L1,R1, R3, L3,→,←,L1,R1
Infinite Ammunition	R2,R1,▲,L2,L1,↑,R2,R1,▲,L2,L1,↑
Psychedelic Mode	↑,R2,●,←,▲,■,L2,L1,●,R1

Shin Megami Tensei: Persona 3 FES

Unlockable

To unlock a new game with all of your items, equipment, status, etc., beat The Journey once through, and then create a new save game using your old save's information.

Shrek 2

During gameplay, pause the game. Then select the Scrapbook and enter the following:

Unlockable	Code
1,000 Coins	←,↑,×,●,←,↑,×,●,←,↑,×,●,↑,→,↓,←,↑
Bonus Games	←,↑,×,●,←,↑,×,●,←,↑,×,●,■,●,■,●,■,●
Full Health	←,↑,×,●,←,↑,×,●,←,↑,×,●,↑,→,↓,←,↑
Level Select	←,↑,×,●,←,↑,×,●,←,↑,×,●,↑,↑,↑,↑,↑

Shrek Super Slam

Enter these codes at the Title screen.

Unlockable	Code
Pizza One mini game	⇧, ⇧, ▲, ▲, ⇨, ⇨, ●, ●, ⇩, ⇩, L1, R1, ⇦, ⇦, ■, ■, L1, R1
Pizza Two mini game	●, ●, ■, ■, ⇨, ⇨, ⇦, ⇦, L1, L1
Pizza Three mini game	⇩, ⇩, ⇨, ●, ⇧, ▲, ⇦, ■, L1, L1
Slammageddon	⇧, ⇧, ⇩, ⇩, ⇦, ⇨, ⇦, ⇨, ▲, ■, ■, L1, R1
Super Speed Modifier	L1, L1, R1, R1, L1, R1, L1, R1, ■, ●, ▲, ▲
Unlock All Challenges	▲, ▲, ▲, ●, ●, ●, ▲, ■, ●, ■, ■, ■, ⇧, ⇩, ⇦, ⇨, L1, R1

Silent Scope 3

Unlockable	Objective
Real-Time Window Option	Complete the indoor shooting range with an "S" or better rank to unlock the "Real-Time Window" option at the EX Options menu.

The Simpsons: Hit and Run

From the Main menu, go to Options. Hold L1+R1 and enter the following:

Unlockable	Code
Blurry View	▲,●,▲,●
Explode on Impact Cars	▲,▲,■,■
Fast Cars	■,■,■,■

The Simpsons: Hit and Run (continued)

Unlockable	Code
Grid View	●,×,●,▲
Invincible Car	▲,×,▲,×
Jumping Car	■,■,■,▲
Speedometer	▲,▲,●,■
Very Fast Cars	▲,▲,▲,▲

TIP

Change the date of the PlayStation 2 to Halloween, Thanksgiving, and Christmas to see new living room decorations.

The Simpsons Game

Codes

Go into the "Extras" section of the main menu and insert the following codes. If the code is accepted, you should hear a sound effect.

Unlockable	How to Unlock
Unlimited Power for all characters	●,⇦,⇨,●,■,L1
All Cliché	⇦,■,⇨,●,⇨,L1
All Movies	■,⇦,■,⇨,●,R1

The Simpsons: Road Rage

Change the date of the PlayStation 2 to the following to unlock secret characters:

Unlockable	Code
New Year's Barney	Jan 1
Halloween Bart	Oct 31
Unlockable	Code
Thanksgiving Marge	Nov 22
Christmas Apu	Dec 25

The Simpsons Skateboarding

Enter these codes in the Character Selection screen while holding R1+R2+L1+L2.

Unlockable	Code
$99.00	▲, ×, ●, ■
Add Money	▲, ×, ●, ■
Ballerina Nelson	▲, ■, ×, ●
Big-Head Bart	×, ■, ●, ▲
Big-Head Frink	■, ×, ▲, ●
Big-Head Homer	●, ×, ▲, ■
Big-Head Lisa	■, ▲, ×, ●
Big-Head Nelson	▲, ■, ●, ×
Big-Head Wiggum	×, ●, ■, ▲
Business Suit Krusty	●, ▲, ■, ×
Demon Marge	×, ■, ▲, ●
Fuzzy Skaters	×, ▲, ■, ●
Gangsta' Bart	●, ×, ■, ▲
Gangsta' Lisa	■, ▲, ●, ×
Groovy Frink	×, ●, ▲, ■

The Simpsons Skateboarding (continued)

Unlockable	Code
Man-Eater Wiggum	▲, ●, ■, ×
Men in Black Otto	■, ×, ●, ▲
Tightie-whitie Homer	▲, ●, ×, ■
Transvestite Nelson	▲, ■, ×, ●
Tuxedo Krusty	●, ▲, ■, ×
Unlock All Boards	×, ▲, ●, ■
Unlock All Levels	▲, ×, ■, ●
Unlock All Skaters	●, ▲, ×, ■

The Sims 2: Castaway

Codes

Enter these codes during gameplay without pausing. The Cheat Gnome must be activated before any other cheats will work.

Effect	Code
Fill All Motives	R2,↑,×,■,L
Give All Plans	■,▲,L2,■,R1
Give All Resources	■,▲,↓,×,←
Max Current Inventory	←,→,■,R2,■
Max Relationships	L1,↑,R2,←,▲
Set Skills	▲,L1,L1,←,▲
Tank Top and Vest	Pause your game and enter the "Fashion and Grooming" menu; then, enter ■,R2,R2,▲,↓
Unlock Cheat Gnome	R1,L1,↓,■,R2

The Sims Bustin' Out

Pause the game at any time and enter these codes.

Unlockable	Code
All Skins	L1,R2,×,●,↑,↓
All Objects	L2,R2,↑,▲, L3
All Locations	R2,R2, L3,L2,R1,L1
Money	L1, R3,→,■, L3

Sled Storm

Enter the following codes at the Press Start screen while holding L1+R1.

Effect	Code	Effect	Code
All Characters	●,▲,●,▲,●,↓	Unlock Everything	●,■,↑,●,▲,↓
All Sleds	●,■,●,■,●,←	Unlock Hover Sled	●,▲,■,●,▲,→
All Tracks	●,←,●,→,●,↑		

Sly Cooper and the Thievius Raccoonus

Unlockable	Objective
Ending Bonuses	Get all the bottles hidden in a level to unlock an FMV sequence, special move, or background information.

Smuggler's Run

To access the following unlockables, pause the game, then enter code. A sound confirms correct entry.

Unlockable	Code
Invisibility	R1, L1, L1, R2, L1, L1, ↙
Less Time Warp	R2, L2, L1, R1, ←, ←, ←
Light Cars	L1, R1, R1, L2, R2, R2
More Time Warp	R1, L1, L2, R2, →, →, →
No Gravity	R1, R2, R1, R2, ↑, ↑, ↑

TIP

To unlock vehicles from Midnight Club: Street Racing, use a saved game from Midnight Club: Street Racing. Now you are able to use vehicles from that game.

Smuggler's Run 2 Hostile Territory

Enter these codes after pausing the game.

Unlockable	Code
Antigravity for ambient vehicles	R1, R2, R1, R2, ↑, ↑, ↑
Double the frame rate	R3, L3, L3, R3, ←, ●, ←, ●
Fast Motion	R1, L1, L2, R2, →, →, →
Glass Car	←, ↑, →, ↓, →, ↑, ←, L2
Increase Speed	R1, L1, L2, R2, →, →, →
Invisibility	R1, L1, L1, R2, L1, L1, L2
Level select and all cars	L2, R2, R2, L2, R1, L2, L1, ←, →, L2, ↓, R2
Low Gravity	L1, R1, R1, L2, R2, R2
Slow Motion	R2, L2, L1, R1, ←, ←, ←
Unlimited Countermeasures	R3, R3, R3, R1, R1, R2, R2

The Sopranos: Road to Respect

Enter these codes while playing.

Unlockable	Code
Infinite Ammo	Hold L2 and R2 and press ●, ■, ×, ■, ▲, ▲
Infinite Respect	Hold L2 and R2 and press ×, ■, ×, ■, ▲, ▲

Spawn: Armageddon

Pause the game and enter the following:

Unlockable	Code
All Comics	↑, ↓, ←, →, →, ←, ←, ↑
All Missions	↑, ↓, ←, →, ←, ←, →, →
All Weapons	↑, ↓, ←, →, ←, →, ←, ←
No Blood	↑, ↓, ←, →, ↑, ↑, ↑, ↑
Open Encyclopedia	↑, ↓, ←, →, ←, →, ↓, ↑
Unlimited Ammo	↑, ↓, ←, →, ↑, ←, ↓, →
Unlimited Health/ Necroplasm	↑, ↓, ←, →, →, ←, ↓, ↑
Unlimited Necroplasm	↑, ↓, ←, →, ↓, ←, ↑, →

Spider-Man

To access the following unlockables, enter the Specials menu to enter the sequence. A laugh will confirm a correct code entry. To return to normal, repeat the code entry.

Unlockable	Code
All Fighting Controls	KOALA
Big Head and Feet for Spider-Man	GOESTOYOURHEAD
Bonus Training Levels	HEADEXPLODY
Enemies Have Big Heads	JOELSPEANUTS
First-Person View	UNDERTHEMASK
Goblin-Style Costume	FREAKOUT
Level Select	IMIARMAS
Level Skip	Enter ROMITAS —after entering code, pause gameplay and select the "Next Level" option to advance to the next level.
Master Code	ARACHNID—unlocks all levels in the level warp option, all gallery options (movie viewer/production art), and combo moves.
Matrix-Style Attacks	DODGETHIS
Play as a Police Officer	REALHERO
Play as a Scientist	SERUM
Play as Captain Stacey (Helicopter Pilot)	CAPTAINSTACEY
Play as Shocker's Thug	THUGSRUS
Play as Skulls Gang Thug	KNUCKLES
Play as the Shocker	HERMANSCHULTZ
Small Spider-Man	SPIDERBYTE
Unlimited Green Goblin Glider Power	CHILLOUT
Unlimited Webbing	ORGANICWEBBING—you can also just accumulate 50,000 points during gameplay.

TIP

Unlocking the Green Goblin costume option allows you to play as Harry Osborn in the Green Goblin costume (complete with appropriate weapons) in an alternate storyline where he tries to correct the Osborn family's reputation. To unlock this easily, start a new game under the Hero or Superhero difficulty setting. At the first level, pause gameplay, then quit to the main menu. Enable the ARACHNID code, then go to the "Level Warp" option. Choose the "Conclusion" level (that features Norman revealing himself to Spider-Man followed by the glider sequence), then exit. This marks the game as completed under the selected difficulty setting. The Green Goblin costume option will be unlocked at the "Secret Store" screen.

Spider-Man 2

Start a New Game and enter HCRAYERT as a name. Go back and enter any name of your choice. This cheat will start in progress, with over 40% completion, 201,000 Hero points, upgrades, and other goodies!

The Spiderwick Chronicles

Codes

Input the following cheats while holding down L1 and R1 during the game.

Effects	Code
Enhance Combat	▲,▲,×,×,■,●,■,●
Field Guide	●,●,●,■,▲,▲,▲,×
Infinite Ammunition	■,■,■,●,×,×,×,▲
Invincibility	▲,▲,▲,▲,×,×,▲,▲
Restore Health	▲,■,×,●,▲,■,×,●

Splashdown Rides Gone Wild

Enter codes in the Options menu screen.

Unlockable	Code
50,000 Warehouse Points	⇧, ⇧, ⇩, ⇩, ⇦, ⇨, ⇦, ⇨, ■, ●
All Warehouse Items	⇧, ⇩, ⇧, ⇩, ⇦, ⇨, ⇦, ⇨, ⇦, ⇩, ⇨, ⇧, ⇨, ⇩, ⇦, ⇧

Spyhunter

At the screen where you enter a name, enter this password. The sound of a chicken clucking will confirm that you have entered the code correctly.

Unlockable	Code
Unlock Saliva Video	GUNN
View Concept Art	SCW823
View Making of FMV	MAKING
View Spy Hunter Theme FMV	SALIVA
View Test Animatic FMV	WWS413

Spy Hunter 2

Unlockable	Code
All Missions and Weapons	In the Main Menu, press L1,R2,L2,R1,R1,L2,R2,L1.
Infinite Ammo	Pause the game and press R1,L1,R2,R2,L2,R1,L1,R2,L2. Enter the code again to deactivate it.
Invincibility	Pause the game and press L1,L1,L1,R2,L1,R1,R1,L1,R2. Enter the code again to deactivate it.

SSX

Unlockable	Code
Third Board	Obtain the Rookie rank.
Fourth Board	Obtain the Sensei rank.
Fifth Board	Obtain the Contender rank.
Sixth Board	Obtain the Natural rank.
Seventh Board	Obtain the Star rank.
Eighth Board	Obtain the Veteran rank.
Ninth Board	Obtain the Champ rank.
10th Board	Obtain the Superstar rank.
11th Board	Obtain the Master rank.
Aloha Ice Jam Track	Get a medal on Tokyo Megaplex.
Hiro	Win four gold medals.
JP	Win two gold medals.
Jurgen	Win one gold medal.
Mercury City Meltdown Track	Get a medal on Elysium.

DS PSP PS2 PS3 Wii Xbox Xbox 360 Index

SSX (continued)

Unlockable	Code
Mesablanca Track	Get a medal on Mercury City Meltdown.
Pipedream Track	Get a medal on Tokyo Megaplex.
Fourth Costume	Complete all blue square tricks.
Third Costume	Complete all green circle tricks.
Untracked Course	Get a medal on the Aloha Ice Jam.
Tokyo Megaplex Track	Get a medal on Mesablanca.
Zoe	Win three gold medals.

To access the following unlockables, go into the Options menu, hold R1+R2+L1+L2, and enter code. A sound confirms correct code entry.

Unlockable	Code
All Courses, Costumes, Characters, and Boards	↓,←,↑,→,×,●,▲,■
All Course Hints	●,×,●,×,●,×,●,×
Maximum Stats	×,×,×,×,×,×,×,×,■
Running Man	■,▲,●,×,■,▲,●,×

SSX 3

From the Main menu, go to Options. Select "Enter Cheat" and enter the following codes (these codes are case-sensitive):

Unlockable	Code
All Artwork	naturalkoncept
All Boards	graphicdelight
All Peaks	biggerthank7
All Playlist Songs	djsuperstar
All Posters	postnobills
All Toys	nogluerequired
All Trading Cards	gotitgotitneedit
All Videos	myeyesaredim
Brodi	zenmaster
Bunny San	wheresyourtail
Canhuck	greatwhitenorth
Churchill	tankengine
Cudmore the Cow	milkemdaisy
Eddie	worm
Gutless	boneyardreject
Hiro	slicksuit
Lodge One Clothes	shoppingspree
Luther	bronco
Jurgen	brokenleg
Marty	back2future
North West Legend	callhimgeorge
Snowballs	betyouneverseen
Stretch	windmilldunk
Svelte Luther	notsosvelte
Unknown Rider	finallymadeitin

SSX On Tour

Enter these passwords at the Cheats menu.

Unlockable	Code
All Clothing	FLYTHREADS
All Levels	BACKSTAGEPASS
All Movies	THEBIGPICTURE
Extra Cash	LOOTSNOOT
Infinite Boost	ZOOMJUICE
Monster Tricks	JACKALOPESTYLE
Snowball Fight	LETSPARTY
Stat Boost	POWERPLAY
Unlock Characters	ROADIEROUNDUP
Unlock Conrad (The MiniViking)	BIGPARTYTIME
Unlock Mitch Koobski (The Unicorn)	MOREFUNTHANONE
Unlock Nigel (Rocker)	THREEISACROWD
Unlock Ski Patrol Character	FOURSOME

SSX Tricky

Unlockable	Objective
Alternate Costumes	To earn more costumes, complete all chapters in your trick book. To unlock the final chrome costume, complete World Circuit mode with a Master rank.
Fugi Board	Get a gold medal on every course with all boarders with their uberboard to unlock a Fugi board.
Pipedream Course	Win a medal on all Showoff courses.
Play as Brodi	Win a gold medal in World Circuit mode.
Play as JP	Win three gold medals in World Circuit mode.
Play as Kaori	Win four gold medals in World Circuit mode.
Play as Luther	Win eight gold medals in World Circuit mode.
Play as Marisol	Win five gold medals in World Circuit mode.
Play as Psymon	Win six gold medals in World Circuit mode.
Play as Seeiah	Win seven gold medals in World Circuit mode.
Play as Zoe	Win two gold medals in World Circuit mode.
Uberboards	Unlock all of the tricks for a character to get their uberboard, which is their best board.
Untracked Course	Win a medal on all Race courses.

To access the following unlockable, go to the Title screen and hold L1+R1, enter code, then release L1+R1. A sound will confirm correct code entry.

Unlockable	Code
Full Stat Points	▲,▲,→,▲,▲,↓,×,×,←,×,×,↑—all the boarders will have full stat points.
Mallora Board	×,×,→,●,●,↓,▲,▲,←,■,■,↑—choose Elise and start a track. Elise will have the Mallora Board and a blue outfit.
Master Code	×,▲,→,●,■,↓,▲,■,←,●,×,↑
Mix Master Mike	×,×,→,×,×,↓,×,×,←,×,×,↑—**(See below for more info)**
Running Man Mode	■,▲,●,×,■,▲,●,×—enter at the Options screen.
Sticky Boards	■,■,→,▲,▲,↓,●,●,←,×,×,↑

NOTE

For the Mix Master Mike unlockable, once you've input the code, choose any boarder at the character selection screen and he or she will be replaced by Mix Master Mike on the course. He has decks on his back and a vinyl board. Repeat the code to disable its effect.

Star Wars Battlefront

Unlockable	Code
All Planets	Choose Historical Campaign, then press ■,●,■,● at the Planet Selection screen.

Star Wars Bounty Hunter

Enter the following sequences as codes.

Unlockable	Code	Unlockable	Code
Chapter 1	SEEHOWTHEYRUN	Chapter 5	BANTHAPOODOO
Chapter 2	CITYPLANET	Chapter 6	MANDALORIANWAY
Chapter 3	LOCKDOWN	Concept Art	R ARTISTS ROCK
Chapter 4	DUGSOPLENTY	Mission 1	BEAST PIT

DS
PSP
PS2
PS3
Wii
Xbox
Xbox 360
Index

Star Wars Bounty Hunter (continued)

Unlockable	Code	Unlockable	Code
Mission 2	GIMMEMY JETPACK	Mission 11	ONEDEADDUG
Mission 3	CONVEYORAMA	Mission 12	WISHIHADMYSHIP
Mission 4	BIGCITYNIGHTS	Mission 13	MOS GAMOS
Mission 5	IEATNERFMEAT	Mission 14	TUSKENS R US
Mission 6	VOTE4TRELL	Mission 15	BIG BAD DRAGON
Mission 7	LOCKUP	Mission 16	MONTROSSISBAD
Mission 8	WHAT A RIOT	Mission 17	VOSAISBADDER
Mission 9	SHAFTED	Mission 18	JANGOISBADDEST
Mission 10	BIGMOSQUITOS	TGC Cards	GO FISH

Star Wars: Episode III Revenge of the Sith

Enter the following codes in the Codes section of the Options menu.

Unlockable	Code
All Attacks and Force Power Upgrades Activated	JAINA
All Bonus Missions Unlocked	NARSHADDAA
All Concept Art Unlocked	AAYLASECURA
All Duel Arenas Unlocked	TANTIVEIV
All Duelist Unlocked	ZABRAK
All Story Missions Unlocked	KORRIBAN
Fast Force Energy and Health Regeneration Activated	BELSAVIS
Infinite Force Energy Activated	KAIBURR
Infinite Health Activated	XUCPHRA

Star Wars Jedi Starfighter

Enter the following in the Codes section of the Options menu.

Unlockable	Code
Invincibility	QUENTIN
Fly-By Mode	DIRECTOR
No Hud	NOHUD

Star Wars Starfighter

To access the following unlockables, go to the Code screen (via the Options menu) to enter the sequence.

Unlockable	Code
Default Message	SHOTS (or SIZZLE)
Director Mode	DIRECTOR
Hidden Christmas Video	WOZ
Hidden Message	LTDJGD
Invincibility	MINIME
Jar Jar Mode	JARJAR
My Day at Work (short slideshow)	JAMEZ
No Heads Up Display	NOHUD
Everything	OVERSEER
Experimental N-1 Fighter	BLUENSF
Multiplayer Mode	ANDREW
Gallery	SHIPS
View Character Sketches	HEROES
View Hidden Picture	SIMON—you'll see a picture of the LEC team.

Star Wars Starfighter (continued)

Unlockable	Code
View Planet Sketch-Work	PLANETS
View the Credits	CREDITS
View the Dev Team	TEAM

Star Wars: The Clone Wars

Enter the following as codes.

Unlockable	Code
Unlock Clone Trooper in Academy Geonosis Level	FAKE FETT
All FMV Sequences	12 PARSECS
Campaign Level Select	DOORDONOT
Invincibility	DARKSIDE
Multiplayer Level Select	JORG SACUL
Programming Team Photographs (viewable after Sketchbook open)	JEDICOUNCIL
Three Bonus Objectives for Current Mission Marked Complete	GIMME
Unlimited Secondary and Special Weapon	SUPERLASER
Battle Droid in Academy Geonosis Level	TRADEFED
Next Level	THRISNOTRY
Padme Amidala in Academy Geonosis Level	NATALIE
Wookie in Academy Geonosis Level	NERFHERDER

Star Wars: The Force Unleashed

Codes

From the main menu go to "Options," then select "Enter Code." You can also do this from the "Extras" menu inside the Rogue Shadow.

Effect	Code
1,000,000 Force Points	SPEEDER
Admiral Ackbar	ITSATWAP
All Combos at Maximum Level	COUNTDOOKU
All Force Powers	TYRANUS
All Force Powers at Maximum Level	KATARN
Amplified Lightsaber Samage	LIGHTSABER
Asajj Ventress	ACOLYTE
Chop'aa Notimo	NOTIMO
Classic Stormtrooper	TK421
Count Dooku	SERENNO
Heavy Trooper	SHOCKTROOP
Immunity to All Damage	CORTOSIS
Lando Calrissian	SCOUNDREL
Play as Captain Juno Eclipse	ECLIPSE
Qui-Gon Jinn	MAVERICK
Twi'lek	SECURA
Unlimited Force power	VERGENCE
Unlock Aayla Secura Costume	AAYLA
Unlock All Costumes	GRANDMOFF
Unlock Anakin Skywalker costume	CHOSENONE
Unlock Ceremonial Jedi Robes Costume	DANTOOINE

Star Wars: The Force Unleashed (continued)

Effect	Code
Unlock Darth Desolous Costume	PAUAN
Unlock Darth Phobos Costume	HIDDENFEAR
Unlock Drexl Roosh Costume	DREXLROOSH
Unlock Emperor Palpatine Costume	PALPATINE
Unlock General Rahm Kota Costume	MANDALORE
Unlock Han Solo Costume	NERFHERDER
Unlock Kento's Robe Costume	WOOKIE
Unlock Luke Skywalker Costume	T16WOMPRAT
Unlock Mace Windu Costume	JEDIMASTER
Unlock Mara Jade Costume	MARAJADE
Unlock Maris Brood Costume	MARISBROOD
Unlock Navy Commando Costume	STORMTROOP
Unlock Obi-Wan Kenobi Costume	BENKENOBI
Unlock PROXY Costume	HOLOGRAM
Unlock Shaak Ti Costume	TOGRUTA
Unlock Shadowtrooper Costume	INTHEDARK
Unlock Sith Robe Costume	HOLOCRON
Unlock Sith Stalker Armor Costume	KORRIBAN
Unlock Yavin Luke Costume	YELLOWJCKT
Unlocks Darth Maul as a Skin	ZABRAK
Unlocks the Darth Vader Costume	SITHLORD

Starsky and Hutch

Type in VADKRAM as your Profile Name to unlock everything.

State of Emergency

To access the following unlockables, enter code during gameplay. A message will confirm correct code entry.

Unlockable	Code
AK47	←,→,↓,R2,▲
All Weapons	L1,L1,R2,R2,×
Big Player	R1,R2,L1,L2,▲
Bull	→,→,→,→,×—enter in Kaos mode. Alternately, successfully complete the East Side level in Revolution mode to unlock Bull in Kaos mode.
Flame Thrower	←,→,↓,R2,●
Freak	→,→,→,→,●—enter in Kaos mode. Alternately, successfully complete the Chinatown level in Revolution mode to unlock Freak in Kaos mode.
Grenade	←,→,↓,R2,■
Grenade Launcher	←,→,↓,R1,■
Invincibility	L1,L2,R1,R2,×
Little Player	R1,R2,L1,L2,×
Looting on the Rise	R1,L1,R2,L2,▲
M16	←,→,↓,R2,●
Minigun	←,→,↓,R1,▲
Mission Select	L1,L2,L2,L2,L1,×
Mission Skip	←,←,←,←,▲

State of Emergency (continued)

Unlockable	Code
Molotov Cocktail	←,→,↓,R2,×
Normal Player	R1,R2,L1,L2,● Alternately, press R1,R2,L1,L2,■.
Pepper Spray	←,→,↓,L1,■
Pistol	←,→,↓,L1,▲
Policeman	Hold L1, then press R2,R2,L2,R1
Punches Decapitate	L1,L2,R1,R2,■
Rocket Launcher	←,→,↓,R1,×
Shotgun	←,→,↓,L2,▲
Spanky	→,→,→,→,▲—enter in Kaos mode. Alternately, complete the Mall level in Revolution mode to unlock Spanky in Kaos mode.
Tazer	←,→,↓,L1,●
Tear Gas	←,→,↓,L1,×
Unlimited Ammunition	L1,L2,R1,R2,▲—enter without a weapon in your hands.
Unlimited Time in Kaos Mode	L1,L2,R1,R2,●

Unlockable	Objective
Chinatown Level	Score 25,000 points in the Capitol City Mall level in Kaos mode.
Corporation Central Level	Score 100,000 points in the East Side level in Kaos mode.
East Side Level	Score 50,000 points in the Chinatown level in Kaos mode.
Last Clone Standing Levels	Successfully complete the three-minute and five-minute versions of a level to unlock the Last Clone Standing version of that map in Kaos mode.
Unlimited Kaos Mode Time	Successfully complete all Kaos levels in Arcade mode.

Street Fighter EX3

Unlockable	Objective
Bonus Characters	Beat the game on Normal difficulty without using a Continue to unlock one of the hidden characters. *(See below for more info)*
Evil Ryu	Beat Original mode eight times with Ryu and without continuing. Go to the Character Selection screen and highlight Ryu. Press ×, ■, or ●.
M. Bison II	Beat Original mode eight times with M. Bison and without continuing. Go to the Character Selection screen and highlight M. Bison. Press ×, ■, or ●.
Narrator Sakura	Beat Original mode eight times with Sakura and without continuing. Go to the Character Selection screen and highlight Sakura. Press SELECT.

NOTE

In order to unlock all the bonus characters, repeat the method described above nine times. However, each time you beat the game, you must use a different regular character. The order of bonus characters are: Sagat, Vega, Garuda, Shadow Geist, Kairi, Pullum, Area, Darun, and Vulcano.

Street Hoops

Go to Game Settings and choose "Cheats" to enter these codes.

Unlockable	Code
ABA Ball	●, R2, ■, R2
All Courts	■, ■, L1, R2, L1, ●, L2, ●
All Teams	■, ■, L1, R2, L1, ●, L2, ●
Black Ball	R2, R2, ●, L2
Blocking Galore	R1, ●, L2, R2
Faster Clock	●, ●, ●, ■, ■
Kung-Fu	●, ●, ■, L1, ■, L1, L2
Normal Ball	R1, ■, ■, L1
Super Steals	■, R2, ■, R1, ●, L1, ●, L2
Tuxedo	L2, L2, ●, ■

Street Racing Syndicate

At the Main menu, press ↑, ↓, ←, →. A code entry screen will appear. Enter the following:

Unlockable	Code
Free Car Repair	FIXITUP
Mazda RX-8	RENESIS
Mitsubishi Eclipse GS-T	IGOTGST
Only a warning for the first three busts	LETMEGO
Pac Man Vinyl	GORETRO
Police Car	GOTPOPO
Subaru Impreza S202 STI	SICKGDB
Toyota Celica GT-S Action Package	MYTCGTS
Toyota Supra RZ	SICKJZA

Stuntman

At the New Game menu, use the following codes as drivers' names. All of the codes for this game are case-sensitive—enter them exactly as you see them!

Unlockable	Code
All Cars	spiDER
All Driving Games, Cars, and Toys	Bindl
All Toys	MeFf
Filmography Section (all trailers)	"fellA"

The Suffering

Unlockable	Objective
Alternate title sequence	Complete the game.
Director Commentary	In the Prelude level, wait for a crow to land next to the three inmates, then stand on top of the crow.
Prelude Level	Complete the game.

Enter the following codes during gameplay while holding L1+R1+×.

Unlockable	Code
All Items and Weapons except Gonzo Gun	↑, ↓, ↑, ←, →, ←, R2, ↑, ←, ↓, →, ↑, →, ↓, ←, R2, ↓, ↓, ↓, R2, R2
Bloody Torque	↑, ↓, ←, →
Clean Torque	↓, ↑, →, ←
Dirty family picture	←, ↓, ←, ↓, ←, ↓, R2
Full Health	↓, ↓, ↓, R2, ↑, ↑, ↓, ↑, R2
Full Xombium bottle	→, →, ↓, ↓, R2, ←, →, R2, →, ↑, →, R2

The Suffering (continued)

Unlockable	Code
Gonzo Gun	←, R2, R2, R2, →, ←, →, ←, ↑, R2, R2, R2, ↓, ↑, ↓, ↑, R2
Grenades	→, →, →, ←, ←, ←
Increase Negative Karma	←, ←, ↓, ↑, R2
Molotov Cocktails	↓, ↓, ↓, ↑, ↑, ↑
New Family Picture	↑, →, ↑, →, ↑, →, R2
Overcome Insanity	→, →, →, R2, ←, ←, →, ←, R2
Old Movie Mode	↑, R2, ←, R2, ↓, R2, →, R2
Psychedelic Mode	←, ←, R2, →, →, R2, ↑, ↑, R2, ↓, ↓, R2
Reload Ammunition for Current Gun	→, →, ↓, ↑, ←, →, ←, ←, R2
Refill Ranged Weapon Ammunition	←, ←, ↑, ↓, →, ←, →, →, R2
Shotgun with Full Ammunition	←, ←, ←, ↓, ↓, ↓
Wrinkled Family Picture	↑, ↑, →, ↑

The Suffering: Ties that Bind

While playing, enter the following codes while holding L1+R1+×. Do not pause the game.

Unlockable	Code
All Items and Weapons Except the Gonzo Gun	↓, ↑, ↓, ←, →, ←, R2, ↑, ←, ↓, →, ↑, →, ↓, ←, R2, ↓, ↓, ↓, R2, R2
Arsenal	↓, →, ↑, ←, ↓, R2, ←, ←, →, →, R2, ↓, ↑, ←, →, R2
Dream State	←, ←, R2, →, →, R2, ↑, ↑, R2, ↓, ↓, R2
Full Bottles	→, →, ↑, ↑, R2, ←, →, R2, →, ↑, →, R2
Full Flashlight Power	↑, ←, ↓, →, ↑, →, ↓, ←, R2
Full Health	↓, ↓, ↓, R2, ↑, ↑, ↓, ↑, R2
Full Insanity	→, →, →, R2, ←, ←, →, →, R2
Gonzo Gun	←, R2, R2, R2, →, ←, →, ←, ↑, R2, R2, R2, ↓, ↑, ↓, ↑, R2
Invincibility	↓, ↑, ↓, ↑
Max Evil Rep	←, ↓, ←, ↓, ←, ↓, R2
Max Good Rep	↑, →, ↑, →, ↑, →, R2
Minus 50 Rep	←, ←, ↓, ↑
Molotov Cocktails	↓, ↓, ↓, ↑, ↑, ↑
More Ammunition for Current Gun	→, →, ↓, ↑, ←, →, ←, ←, R2
More Ammo for Current Thrown Weapon	←, ←, ↑, ↓, →, ←, →, →, R2
Plus 50 Rep	↑, ↑, →, ↑
Projector State	↑, R2, ←, R2, ↓, R2, →, R2
Shotgun & Ammo	←, ←, ←, ↓, ↓, ↓
Shrapnel	→, →, →, ←, ←, ←
Suicide	↓, ↓, ↓, ↓
Zero Blood	↓, ↑, →, ←

DS
PSP
PS2
PS3
Wii
Xbox
Xbox 360
Index

Summer Heat Beach Volleyball

Enter the following codes at the Cheat menu to unlock the bonus.

Unlockable	Code
Disable Arrows	Whine
High Gravity	Zippy
High-pitched Voices	Mouse
Low Gravity	Space
Low-pitched Voices	Horse
Nails Mode	Nails
Spinning Heads	Exosz
All Accessories	Werit
All Beach House Bonuses	Mypad
All Characters	Peeps

Unlockable	Code
All Difficulty settings	Champ
All Locations	80Day
All Mini-games	Major
All Movies	Musak
All Swimsuits/Shorts	Greed
All Trailers	Gamon
Coconut Ball	Milky
Nerd Ball	Golem
Sun Ball	Hot 1

Unlockable	Objective
Artemis	Beat Arcade Mode on Expert.
Dummy	Beat all the tournaments on Medium.
Enigma	Beat all the tournaments on Hard.
Hephestus	Beat Arcade Mode on Hard.
Incognito	Beat all the tournaments on Expert.
Mannequin	Beat all tournaments on Easy.
Tina	Complete Training Mode.

Supercar Street Challenge

Unlockable	Code
Additional colors for your car	Select change color in styling studio and press ↑, →, ↓, ←, ▲, ●, ×, ■
Debug menu	At the main menu, enter ■, ■, ↑, →, ↓, ←, L2, R2, L1, R1

SWAT: Global Strike Team

These codes must be entered in the in game option screen.

Unlockable	Code
Infinite Ammo	←, →, ↑, ↓, ↑, ↓, R2, L2
God Mode	↑, ↓, ←, →, L2, R2

Tak and the Power of Juju

Enter these codes during gameplay then go into the Extra menu to activate them.

Unlockable	Code
100 Feathers	■,▲,●,■,▲,●,■,▲
All Moonstones	▲,▲,■,■,●,●,←,→
All Plants	■,▲,●,←,↑,→,↓,↓
All Juju Powers	↑,→,←,↓,▲,●,■,↓
All Yorbels	↑,▲,←,■,→,●,↓,↑
Everything	←,→,■,■,●,●,←,→

Teenage Mutant Ninja Turtles 2: Battle Nexus

From the Options menu, choose "Password" and enter the following:

Key: ***M***=Michaelangelo ***R***=Raphael ***L***=Leonardo ***D***=Donatello ***S***=Shredder

POWER UP CHEAT CODES:

Unlockable	Code
All Stamina Restore Items Are Upgraded to Pizza	MRLMRMR
Attack Power Doubled	SDLSRLL
Defense Power Doubled	LDRMRLM
Stamina Meter Gradually Restores Itself	DRMSRLR
Turtles No Longer Receive Damage	LSDRRDR
Turtles No Longer Suffer from Damage Effects	DSRDMRM
Unlimited Number of Shuriken	RSRLRSM

POWER DOWN CHALLENGE CODES:

Unlockable	Code
Any Damage is Fatal	LRSRDRD
Enemies' Attack Power Doubled	SLSDRDL
Enemies' Defense Power Doubled	RDSRMRL
No Falling Off	SDSDRLD
Shuriken No Longer Available	RLMRDSL
Stamina Restore Items No Longer Available	MRMDRMD
Turtles Suffer from Poisonous Effects	DRSLLSR

HUMOROUS CHEAT CODES:

Unlockable	Code
Attack Enemies to See What Happens	MLDSRDM
Walk About to Find Out the Effect	SSSMRDD

Tekken 4

Unlockable	Objective
Fight as Eddy Gordo	Successfully complete the game in Story mode as Christie Monteiro. Highlight Christie and press ▲ at the Character Selection screen. Eddy Gordo plays exactly like Christie.
Fight as Ling Xiaoyu in School Uniform	Complete the game in Story mode as Ling Xiaoyu. Highlight Ling Xiaoyu and press ▲ at the Character Selection screen.
Fight as Miharu	Complete the game in Story mode as Ling Xiaoyu. Highlight Ling Xiaoyu and press ● at the Character Selection screen. Miharu looks like Ling in her schoolgirl outfit from Tekken 3 and Tekken Tag Tournament and plays just like her.
Fight as Panda	Highlight Kuma at the Character Selection screen, then press ▲ or ●.
Fight as Violet	Highlight Lee at the Character Selection screen, then press ●.
Unlocking All Characters	Complete the game with the indicated character to unlock the corresponding fighter.

Tekken Tag Tournament

To unlock the different stages, first highlight Practice mode at the Main menu, then enter the code listed.

Unlockable	Objective
Eddy's Stage (Day)	Hold L2 and press R2 13 times.
Eddy's Stage (Sunset)	Hold L2 and press R2 ten times.
Heihachi's Stage	Hold L2 and press R2 12 times.
Hwoarang's Stage	Hold L2 and press R2,R2,R2,R2.
Jin's Stage (Day)	Hold L2 and press R2 17 times.
Jin's Stage (Night)	Hold L2 and press R2 eight times.
King's Stage	Hold L2 and press R2 11 times.
Law's Stage (New)	Hold L2 and press R2 once.
Law's Stage (Old)	Hold L2 and press R2 15 times.
Lei's Stage	Hold L2 and press R2,R2,R2,R2,R2.
Ling's Stage	Hold L2 and press R2,R2,R2.
Nina's Stage (Day)	Hold L2 and press R2 nine times.
Nina's Stage (Night)	Hold L2 and press R2 18 times.
Ogre's Stage	Hold L2 and press R2 six times.
Paul's Stage	Hold L2 and press R2 20 times.
School Stage (Day)	Hold L2 and press R2 16 times.
School Stage (Night)	Hold L2 and press R2 seven times.
Supercharging	During a match, press all buttons to charge up. Press ×+●+▲+■ if you kept the default buttons.
Unknown Stage	Hold L2 and press R2 14 times.
Yoshimitsu's Stage (Heavy Snow)	Hold L2 and press R2 19 times.
Yoshimitsu's Stage (Light Snow)	Hold L2 and press R2,R2.

NOTE

When unlocking the bonus characters, expect them to appear in this order: Kunimitsu, Bruce Irvin, Jack-2, Lee Chaolan, Wang Jinrey, Roger and Alex, Kuma and Panda, Kazuya Mishima, Ogre, True Ogre, Prototype Jack, Mokujin and Tetsujin, Devil and Angel, then Unknown.

Tenchu Fatal Shadows

While the game is paused, enter code on the second controller.

Unlockable	Code
View Score Status	■,■,⇩,⇩,⇧,⇧

Tenchu: Wrath of Heaven

Unlockable	Code
Increase Items	From the Items screen, hold R2+L2, then press ■,■,■,↑,←,↓,→.
Play Demo Stage	From the title screen, press ↑,↓,→,←,×,×,×.
Portable Ninja Brainwipe Machine	Pause the game with the left controller. Using the same controller, press L2, R3, R2, L3,→,■,↑,■,L2,←,■,↓,R2. The game will unpause and you may control the nearest enemy using the left controller in Story mode.
Regain Health	Pause the game and press ↑,↓,→,←,■,■,■.
Score Cheats	Pause the game and enter →,→,←,← on the left controller.

Tenchu: Wrath of Heaven (continued)

Unlockable	Code
Special Move Cheat	Pause the game and hold L2+L2, press ↑,↑,↓,↓ then release the L2+L2 and press ■,■,R1,R2.
Stock Infinite Items	From the item selection screen, hold L2+L1+R1+R2 then press ■,■,■,↑,←,↓,→,■,↑,→,↓,←.
All Characters	From the title screen, press L2,R2,L2,R1,→,←, L3, R3.
All Items	From the Items screen, hold R1+L2, then press ↑,■,■,←,■,■,↓,■,■,→,■,■.
All Layouts	From the Mission Select screen, press R3, L3,R2,L2,R1,L1.
All Missions	From the Mission Select screen, press L2,R1,L2,R2,→,■, L3, R3.
All Stages (Multiplayer)	From the Mission Select screen for multiplayer, press L2,R1,L2,R2,→,■, L3, R3.
Bonus Stage	From the title screen, press L2,↑,R1,↓,↙,→,R2,←.
Outtakes	From the title screen, hold L2+R2, then press ↓,■,↑,■,→,■,←,■. The choice will be listed as the "B-SIDE" under the Audio/Language menu.

Terminator 3: Rise of the Machines

From the Main menu, choose "Options," then select "Cheats." Enter the following:

Unlockable	Code
50% Less Health in Combat with TX	×,▲,■,●,▲,×,■,▲
50% More Health in Combat with TX	■,▲,■,▲,●,×,●,×
All Future Weapons	×,×,×,▲,●,●,■,×
All Present Weapons	●,●,▲,■,×,▲,▲,■
Centipide (Located in Special Features)	●,●,●,■,■,■,▲,■
Invincibility	■,■,×,▲,×,●,×,●
Missile Command (Located in Special Features)	●,●,●,■,■,■,×,×
Unlimited Ammo	×,▲,▲,▲,×,●,×,■

Terminator 3: The Redemption

In the Main menu, choose "Credits." While watching the credits, enter the following:

Unlockable	Code
All Levels	●+R2+▲
All Upgrades	●+▲+L1
Invincibility	●+R2+R1

Tiger Woods PGA Tour 2004

From the Options menu, choose "Passwords." (These are case-sensitive.)

Unlockable	Code
Ace Andrews	ACEINTHEHOLE
All Courses and Golfers	THEKITCHENSINK
All Courses	ALLTHETRACKS
All Golfers	CANYOUPICKONE
Cedric the Entertainer	CEDDYBEAR
Dominic "The Don" Donatello	DISCOKING
Edwin "Pops" Masterson	EDDIE
Erica "Ice" Von Severin	ICYONE
Felicia "Downtown Brown"	DTBROWN
Hamish "Mulligan" MeGregor	DWILBY

Tiger Woods PGA Tour 2004 (continued)

Unlockable	Code
Kellie Newman	TRAVELER
Melvin "Yosh" Tanigawa	THENEWLEFTY
Moa "Big Mo" Ta'a Vatu	ERUPTION
Solita Lopez	SHORTGAME
Sunday Tiger Woods	4REDSHIRTS
Takeharu "Tsunami" Moto	EMERALDCHAMP
Target World Challenge	SHERWOOD TARGET
Val "Sunshine" Summers	BEVERLYHILLS

Tiger Woods PGA Tour 2005

From the Options menu, choose "Passwords." (These are case-sensitive.)

Unlockable	Code
Adriana "Sugar" Dulce	SOSWEET
Alastair "Captain" McFadden	NICESOCKS
All Courses	THEWORLDISYOURS
All Golfers and Courses	THEGIANTOYSTER
Aphrodite Papadapolus	TEMPTING
Arnold Palmer	THEKING
Ben Hogan	PUREGOLF
Bev "Boomer" Bouchier	THEBEEHIVE
Billy "Bear" Hightower	TOOTALL
Bunjiro "Bud" Tanaka	INTHEFAMILY
Ceasar "The Emperor" Rosado	LANDOWNER
Gary Player	BLACKKNIGHT
Hunter "Steelhead" Elmore	GREENCOLLAR
Jack Nicklaus	GOLDENBEAR
Jeb "Shooter" McGraw	SIXSHOOTER
Justin Timberlake	THETENNESSEEKID
Kendra "Spike" Lovette	ENGLISHPUNK
Raquel "Rocky" Rogers	DOUBLER
Reginald	"Reg" Weathers REGGIE
Seve Ballesteros	THEMAGICIAN
Sunday Tiger Woods	4REDSHIRTS
The Roof	NIGHTGOLFER
Tiffany "Tiff" Williamson	RICHGIRL
All ADIDAS Items	91treSTR
All CALLOWAY Items	cgTR78qw
All CLEVELAND Items	CL45etUB
All MAXFLI Items	FDGH597i
All NIKE Items	YJHk342B
All ODYSSEY Items	kjnMR3qv
All PING Items	R453DrTe
All PRECEPT Items	BRi3498Z
All TAG Items	cDsa2fgY
All TourStage Items	TS345329

Tiger Woods PGA Tour 06

Go to the Options menu, then enter the Passwords menu to enter these passwords.

Unlockable	Code
All Clubs	CLUB11
All Courses	ITSINTHEHOLE
All Golfers	WOOGLIN
Tiger Woods with Alternate Old Golf Outfit	OLDSKOOL
Tiger Woods with Hat	GOLDENAGE
Tiger Woods with Old Striped Pants	TECHNICOLOR
Tiger Woods with Very Old Golf Outfit	THROWBACK

Tiger Woods PGA TOUR 09

Codes

Go to Extras at the main menu, then Passwords, and enter the following codes.

Effect	Code
1 Million Dollars	JACKPOT
All Clothing & Equipment Unlocked	SHOP2DROP
All Cover Stories Unlocked	HEADLINER
All PGA Tour Events Unlocked	BEATIT
Max Skill Points, All Clothing & Equipment Unlocked	IAMRUBBISH

Tim Burton's The Nightmare Before Christmas: Oogie's Revenge

Enter this code while playing.

Unlockable	Code
Pumpkin Jack and Santa Jack costumes	⇩, ⇧, ⇨, ⇦, L3, R3

Time Crisis 2

Unlockable	Objective
Auto Bullets	Clear the Story mode twice at any difficulty level to be able to fire 20 bullets in one trigger.
Auto Reload	Clear the Story mode at any difficulty level using Auto Bullets to earn unlimited firepower with your gun.
Increase Your Credits in Arcade Mode	Receive extra credits if you clear the Story mode at any difficulty level. *(See below for more info)*
Mirror Mode	To activate the Mirror mode, clear the Story mode without using the "Continue" function.
Music Player	To access the Music Player, clear the final mission of the "Crisis" Mission.
Shoot Away 2 Arrange Mode	To access Arrange mode, score very high points in the Arcade Original mode (Retro). Hit two clay pigeons with one bullet to double your points for that shot.
Shoot Away 2 Extra Mode	To access Extra mode, score good points in the Arcade Original mode (Retro).
Stage Trial 2	To reach Stage Trial 2, clear Stage 1 of the Story mode at any difficulty level.
Stage Trial 3	To reach Stage Trial 3, clear Stage 2 of the Story mode at any difficulty level.
Wide Shots	Clear the Story mode at any difficulty level with the Auto Reload function to enable your firearm to shoot wide shots (shotgun type with nine bullets per reload).

Time Crisis 2 (continued)

NOTE

For the "Increase Your Credits in Arcade Mode" code, once you've cleared the mode several times, you are eventually entitled to "Free Play" and a maximum of nine lives that you can set in the "Game" options.

Timesplitters 2

Beat each level listed in Story mode under Medium difficulty to unlock its secret character. You'll be able to play these unlockable characters in Arcade mode.

Level	Playable Character
1853 Wild West Level Reward	The Colonel
1895 Notre Dame Paris Level Reward	Notre Dame
1920 Aztec Ruins Level Reward	Stone Golem
1853 Wild West Level Reward	The Colonel
1895 Notre Dame Paris Level Reward	Notre Dame
1920 Aztec Ruins Level Reward	Stone Golem

NOTE

Beat the 2401 Space Station Level on "Easy" difficulty to unlock the ending sequence.

Tokyo Extreme Racer: Zero

Unlockable	Objective
Change Horn to Siren	Select rear spoiler type 5 for R30 and R30M.
Clean Pause Screen	When Pausing, press ▲+■ to remove the Pause menu. (See below for more info)
Driver View Replay	When viewing replay in "DRIVER VIEW," press L1+R1 to move the camera left/right.
Get a Special Nickname	Put a team sticker on the car you were driving for this team.
Manipulate Parts Camera	In the Parts Type select screen, selecting Aero parts or exhaust makes the camera move toward the car, but pressing ▲ will not cause the camera to move close to the parts (you'll see the entire car on your screen). Press ▲ again to see the close-up.
Reset Records	In Time Record screen, hold down L1+L2+R1+R2 with START. (This also resets the Quick race high score.) These will not be saved, though.
See Meters During Replay	When viewing replay, press SELECT.
See Other Car in One-on-One	When having one-on-one battle with a rival, hold down ■ on 1P's controller to show other cars on the course.
See Other Cars in Free Run	In "FREE RUN," press ■ on 1P's controller when you enter the course select.
Show Analyze Option	In Pause menu (except in the VS mode), hold ■ while you move the cursor to the bottom to show "ANALYZE."
Show Mirror Ornaments	Hold down L1+L2+R1+R2 when selecting the "Shift Assist" option.
Watch Replay with Regular Angle	When you're about to see the replay, hold ▲ on 1P's controller. (You can't switch camera angles when you do this.)

NOTE

You can't unpause the game while removing the Pause menu; you'll have to press ▲+■ to show the Pause menu before unpausing.

Tom and Jerry War of the Whiskers

To enter these codes, go into Options then open Cheats menu.

Unlockable	Code
Auto Refill Health Bars	×, ●, ×, ▲, ▲, ■, ●, ▲
Infinite Ammo	●, ■, ●, ▲, ×, ■, ×, ×
Unlock All Character Costumes	●, ●, ×, ■, ●, ▲, ×, ●

Tom Clancy's Ghost Recon

Enter the codes at the Title screen:

Unlockable	Code
All Missions	×, L2, ▲, R2, SELECT
All Special Features	L1, L2, R1, R2, ×, SELECT
Invincibility	Pause the game and press L1, R2, L2, R1, SELECT

Tom Clancy's Rainbow Six 3

Unlockable	Code
All Custom Mission maps	Press L1, R2, L2, R1, ←, →, ■, ● at the Main menu.

Tomb Raider: The Angel of Darkness

Unlockable	Code
Infinite Air	When Lara is swimming, save the game while underwater. When you load that save, the oxygen gauge will be restored to full.
Skip Level	Pause the game and press and hold L1+R2+↓+▲ then press ●, ↑, ■, ▲, →, ↓.

Tomb Raider Legends

Enter these codes in game. Codes can not be used until they are unlocked.

Unlockable	Code
Bulletproof	Hold L1 press ×, R1, ▲, R1, ■, L2
Draws Enemies Health	Hold L1 press ■, ●, ×, L2, R1, ▲
Excalibur	Hold L2 press ▲, ×, ● R1, ▲, L1
Infinite Assault Ammo	Hold L2 press ×, ●, ×, L1, ■, ▲
Infinite Grenade Launcher Ammo	Hold L2 press L1, ▲, R1, ●, L1, ■
Infinite Shotgun Ammo	Hold L2 press R1, ●, ■, L1, ■, ×
Infinite SMG Ammo	Hold L2 press ●, ▲, L1, R1, ×, ●
One Shot Kill	Hold L1 press ▲, ×, ▲, ×, L2, ●
Textureless Mode	Hold L1 press L2, ×, ●, ×, ▲, R1
Wield Soul Reaver	Hold L2 press ×, R1, ●, R1, L1, ■

Tony Hawk's American Wasteland

Enter this code in the Cheats menu. (Note: case sensitive)

Unlockable	Code
Mat Hoffman	the_condor

Tony Hawk's Pro Skater 3

From the Options menu, choose "Cheats" and enter the following codes. (Cheats can be activated in the Pause menu.)

Unlockable	Code
All Characters	YOHOMIES
All FMV Movies	Peepshow
All Levels	ROADTRIP
Cheat Menu	backdoor
Lots of Stat Points	PUMPMEUP

Tony Hawk's Pro Skater 4

Go to the Options menu and choose "Cheats." Enter the following:

Unlockable	Code
Cheat Mode	watch_me_xplode
Daisy	(o)(o)
Full Special Meter	doasuper
Hidden Skaters	homielist
Perfect Manual	mullenpower
Perfect Rail Balance	ssbsts
Matrix Mode	nospoon
Moon Gravity	superfly

At the Create a Skater screen, enter the following names to unlock hidden skaters:

- #$%@!
- Aaron Skillman
- Adam Lippman
- Andrew Skates
- Andy Marchal
- Angus
- Atiba Jefferson
- Ben Scott Pye
- Big Tex
- Brian Jennings
- Captain Liberty
- Chauwa Steel
- Chris Peacock
- ConMan
- Danaconda
- Dave Stohl
- DDT
- DeadEndRoad
- Fakes the Clown
- Fritz
- Gary Jesdanun
- Grjost
- Henry Ji
- Jason Uyeda
- Jim Jagger
- Joe Favazza
- John Rosser
- Jow
- Kenzo
- Kevin Mulhall
- Kraken
- Lindsey Hayes
- Lisa G Davies
- Little Man
- Marilena Rixfor
- Mat Hoffman
- Matt Mcpherson
- Maya's Daddy
- Meek West
- Mike Day
- Mike Lashever
- Mike Ward
- Mr. Brad
- Nolan Nelson
- Parking Guy
- Peasus
- Pete Day
- Pooper
- Rick Thorne
- Sik
- Stacey D
- Stacey Ytuarte
- Stealing Is Bad
- Team Chicken
- Ted Barber
- Todd Wahoske
- Top Bloke
- Wardcore
- Zac ZiG Drake

Tony Hawk's Project 8

In the Options menu, select Cheats to enter these passwords.

Unlockable	Password
Big Realtor	shescaresme
Christian Hosoi	hohohosoi
Colonel and Security Guard	militarymen
Dad and Skater Jam Kid	strangefellows
Full Air Stats	drinkup
Grim Reaper	enterandwin
Inkblot Deck	birdhouse
Jason Lee	notmono
Kevin Staab	mixitup
Mascot	manineedadate
Most Decks	needaride
Nerd	wearelosers
Photographer and Cameraman	themedia
Travis Barker	plus44
Unlock Specials in Skate Shop	yougotitall

Tony Hawk's Proving Ground

Cheats

Enter the codes in the Options menu of the main menu.

Unlockable	How to Unlock
100% Branch Completion (NTT)	FOREVERNAILED
Invisible Man	THEMISSING
Mini Skater	TINYTATER
No Bails	ANDAINTFALLIN
No Board	MAGICMAN
Perfect Manual	STILLAINTFALLIN
Perfect Rail	AINTFALLIN
Super Check	BOOYAH
Unlimited Focus	MYOPIC
Unlimited Slash Grind	SUPERSLASHIN
Unlock Judy Nails	LOVEROCKNROLL

Items

Unlockable	How to Unlock
50 Extra Skill Points	NEEDSHELP
All CAS Items	GIVEMESTUFF
All Decks	LETSGOSKATE
All Fun Items	OVERTHETOP
All Game Movies	WATCHTHIS
All Lounge Bling Items	SWEETSTUFF
All Lounge Themes	LAIDBACKLOUNGE
All Rigger Pieces	IMGONNABUILD
All Special Tricks Available	LOTSOFTRICKS
All Video Editor Effects	TRIPPY
All Video Editor Overlays	PUTEMONTOP
Full Stats	BEEFEDUP

Levels

Unlockable	How to Unlock
Unlock Air & Space Museum	THEINDOORPARK
Unlock FDR	THEPREZPARK
Unlock Lansdowne	THELOCALPARK

Skaters

Unlockable	How to Unlock
Boneman	CRAZYBONEMAN
Bosco	MOREMILK
Cam	NOTACAMERA
Cooper	THECOOP
Eddie X	SKETCHY
El Patinador	PILEDRIVER
Eric	FLYAWAY
Mad Dog	RABBIES
MCA	INTERGALACTIC
Mel	NOTADUDE

DS PSP PS2 PS3 Wii Xbox Xbox 360 Index

Tony Hawk's Proving Ground (continued)

Unlockable	How to Unlock
Rube	LOOKSSMELLY
Shayne	MOVERS
Spence	DAPPER
TV Producer	SHAKER

Tony Hawk's Underground

From the Options menu, choose "Cheat Codes" and enter the following:

Unlockable	Code
All Thug Movies	digivid
Moon Gravity	getitup
Perfect Manual	keepitsteady
Perfect Rail	letitslide
Perfect Skitch	rearrider

From the Options menu, choose "Cheat Codes" and enter the following:

1337	Dan Nelson	Jason Uyeda	Stacey D
Akira2s	Dave Stohl	Jeremy Andersen	Steal2Liv
Alan Flores	DDT	Joel Jewett	tao zheng
Alex Garcia	deadendroad	Johnny Ow	The Kraken
Andy Marchel	fatass	leedsleedsleeds	The Swink
arrr	FROGHAM	MARCOS XK8R	THEDOC
Bailey	GEIGER	Mike Ward	Todd Wahoske
Big Tex	Glycerin	moreuberthaned	TOPBLOKE
Chauwa Steel	GMIAB	M'YAK	TSUEnami! (
Chris Rausch	Greenie	Noly	woodchuck
ChrisP	grjost	NSJEFF	Y2KJ
CodePirate	Guilt Ladle	POOPER	Yawgurt
crom	Hammer	sik®	ZiG
Daddy Mac	Henry Ji	Skillzombie	

Tony Hawk's Underground 2

Go to Cheat Codes and enter the following:

Unlockable	Code
All Levels	d3struct
All Movies	boxoffice
Always Special	likepaulie
Bonus Characters	costars
Infinite Rail	straightedge
Natas Kaupas	oldskool
Nigel Beaverhausen	sellout
Paulie	4-wheeler
Phil Margera	aprilsman

TNA iMPACT!

Unlockables

Unlockable	How to Unlock
Abyss	Defeat Abyss in Story mode Part 6
AJ Styles X	Defeat AJ Styles in a singles match in Story mode
Brother Ray	Defeat Team 3D in a tag team match in Story mode
Chris Sabin X	Defeat Chris Sabin in a singles match in Story mode
Don West	Gain 250,000 Style points

TNA iMPACT! (continued)

Unlockable	How to Unlock
Eric Young	Win the TNA Tag Team Titles in Story mode
Jay Lethal	Win the 3 man gauntlet match in Story mode
Jeff Jarrett	Defeat Jeff Jarett in Story mode
Senshi	Gain 200,000 Style points
Sonjay Dutt	Defeat Sonjay Dutt in a singles match in Story mode
Tomko	Defeat AJ Styles and Tomko in a tag team match in Story mode

Transformers

Pause the game and enter any of the following codes:

Unlockable	Code
All Extras	Select Extras from the Main menu and press ■,■,●,■,■,●,L1,L2
Invincibility	R1,●,●,R1,R2,L1,L1,L2
One Shot Kills	■,●,■,●,L1,L1,L2,L1
Stealth Enemies	←,→,←,R1,R2,R1,→,→

Enter the following codes at the Autobot HQ screen:

Unlockable	Code
All Mini-Cons	L1,L2,●,●,■,●,L2,L1
Big Head Mode	●,●,●,■,L1,L1,L1,L2
Disable Mini Con Overload	R1,R1,L2,R1,R1,L2,●,●
Infinite Stealth	↑,↑,↓,↓,L1,L2,L1,L2
Turbo Mode	L1,R2,R2,■,■,■,■,L1
Unlimited Powerlink	↑,↓,↑,↓,●,■,■,●

At the Difficulty Select screen, enter the following:

Unlockable	Code
Alaska Level Complete	R1,●,R1,■,←,←,→,←
Amazon Boss Fight	←,←,→,L1,R2,←,←,→
Amazon Level Complete	L1,L1,L2,■,■,●,R1,R2
Antarctica Boss Fight	L1,←,L2,→,■,■,●,●
Antarctica Level Complete	R1,R1,R2,L2,L1,L1,R1,R1
Cybertron	R2,R1,L1,L2,■,●,■,●
Deep Amazon Level Complete	←,→,←,←,→,R1,R2,●
Mid-Atlantic Boss Fight	L2,←,→,→,←,L2,L2,L2
Mid-Atlantic Level Complete	●,■,●,■,→,←,←,→
Starship Boss Fight	→,→,■,R1,R2,●,←,←
Starship Level Complete	←,←,→,●,●,→,→,←

True Crime: New York City

While on the Compstat/Map, hold L1+R1 and enter these codes.

Unlockable	Code
A Million Dollars	■, ■, ▲, ■, ▲, ■
Double Damage	×, ×, ■, ×, ×, ×
Redman Gone Wild Mini-Game	▲, ×, ×, ●, ▲, ■

Unlockable	Code
Super Cop	▲, ×, ▲, ×, ▲, ▲
Ultra Easy Mode	●, ■, ×, ×, ▲, ●
Unlimited Ammo	●, ■, ×, ■, ■, ▲
Unlimited Endurance	●, ■, ×, ■, ×, ●

DS
PSP
PS2
PS3
Wii
Xbox
Xbox 360
Index

True Crime: Streets of LA

Enter the following codes at the City Map screen:

Unlockable	Code	Unlockable	Code
All Driving Upgrades	←,→,←,→,×	Bigger Vehicle	↓,↓,↓,×
All Fighting Moves	↑,↓,↑,↓,×	Nick Kang's Location	×,●,■,▲
All Gun Upgrades	→,←,→,←,×	Smaller Vehicle	↑,↑,↑,×

Go to Create a License Plate and try the following codes:

Unlockable	Code	Unlockable	Code
Asian Worker	HARA	Lola Gees	B00B
Bartender	HAWG	Pimp	PIMP
Bum	B00Z	Policeman	FUZZ
Chief, The	B1G1	Rose in Lingerie	HURT M3
Commando	M1K3	Rosie	ROSA
Dirty Morales	BRUZ	Sewer Ghoul	J1MM
Donkey	JASS	Street Punk	MNKY
Gangsta	TFAN	SWAT Officer	5WAT
George	FATT	Tattoo Concubines	TATS
Jimmy Fu	MRFU	Triad Butcher	PHAM

Turok: Evolution

Enter the following codes at the Cheat menu.

Unlockable	Code
All Available Weapons	TEXAS
Big Head Mode	HEID
Demo Mode and Target Mini-Game	HUNTER
Invincibility	EMERPUS
Invisibility	SLLEWGH
Level Select	SELLOUT—after entering, load a saved game to unlock all levels.
Master Code	FMNFB
Unlimited Ammunition	MADMAN
Zoo Mode	ZOO—you can now kill any animal in the game with the war club as a weapon.

NOTE

There are two parts to the "Demo mode and Target Mini-Game" code. Besides starting Demo mode, you can also play the Target minigame at the main title screen. Use the D-pad to move the pointer and Fire to shoot.

To access the following unlockables, pause gameplay, hold L1, then enter code. A message confirms correct code entry. Repeat the code to disable its effect.

Invincible NPCs	■,●,▲,×,■,●,▲,×
Unlimited Ammunition	←,●,→,■,↑,▲,↓,×
Unlimited Health	▲,■,▲,■,▲,●,▲,●
Unlimited Rage	←,↓,←,↓,→,↑,→,↑

Twisted Metal: Black

Unlockable	Code
Change Camera	To change the camera angle, press and hold SELECT, then press ↓. To switch between horizontal and vertical, hold SELECT, then press ←.
Convert Weapons into Health	During the game, hold down all four shoulder buttons, then press ▲,✕,■,●. Your weapons vanish and your health fills up a little.
Decipher Minion	To understand what Minion's numbered codes mean on the load screens (when playing as him), match the number with its corresponding letter. (A=1, B=2, and Z=26.)
Different Weapons Display	Press and hold SELECT, then press → during gameplay to change the weapons selection display.
Infinite Ammo	To have unlimited ammunition for your ride, press and hold the shoulder buttons, then press ↑,✕,←,●.
Invincibility	During gameplay (this includes story mode), press and hold the shoulder buttons, then press →,←,↓,↑.
Mega Machine Guns	To enable the Mega Machine Guns feature, press and hold the shoulder buttons, then press ✕,✕,▲.
One Hit Kills	During gameplay, hold the shoulder buttons and quickly press ✕,✕,↑. At the top of the screen, a message confirms correct code entry.
Unlock God Mode	During gameplay, hold the shoulder buttons and rapidly press ↑,✕,←,●. A message reading "God Mode On" appears at the top of the screen to confirm correct code entry.

Ty the Tasmanian Tiger

Unlockable	Code
Aquarang, Elemental Boomerangs, Dive, and Swim Abilities	Press L1,R1,L1,R1,▲,▲,■,■,▲,■ during gameplay.
Show Objects	Press L1,R1,L1,R1,▲,▲,●,■,■,●,R2,R2 during gameplay.
Technorangs	Press L1,R1,L1,R1,▲,▲,▲,■,▲,■ during gameplay.
Unlimited Health	Quickly press L1,R1,L1,R1,▲,▲,▲,▲,●,● when "Press Start" appears.
Unlock Gallery and Movies	Quickly press L1,R1,L1,R1,▲,▲,✕,✕,R2,■,R2,■ when "Press Start" appears.

NOTE

To unlock an Ending Bonus, complete the game with all cogs, eggs, and opals collected for a 100 percent completion. The Ending Bonus includes a bonus level, an extra FMV sequence after the ending credits, and the "Movies" option at the Extras menu.

NOTE

After you use the Show Objects code, the locations of hidden Opals, Bilbies, Golden Cogs, Rainbow Scales, and Thunder Eggs are shown with colored lines from the sky (Opals and Rainbow Scales with a green line, Golden Cogs with a gold line, Thunder Eggs with a purple line, and Bilbies with a whitish line).

Ultimate Spider-Man

Enter these codes in the Controller Setup screen.

Unlockable	Code
All Characters	⇨, ⇩, ⇨, ⇩, ⇦, ⇧, ⇦, ⇨
All Comic Covers	⇦, ⇦, ⇨, ⇦, ⇧, ⇦, ⇦, ⇩
All Concept Art	⇩, ⇩, ⇩, ⇧, ⇩, ⇧, ⇦, ⇦
All Landmarks	⇧, ⇨, ⇩, ⇦, ⇩, ⇧, ⇨, ⇦

Urban Reign

Enter these codes at the Title screen.

Unlockable	Code
All characters	R1, R2, ×, ⇦, ⇨, ■, ■, ■, ■, L1, ■, ▲, ●
All weapons	L1, R1, ×, ×, ▲, R1, R1, ▲, ■, ×, R1
Bonus weapon in multi-player mode	L2, L2, ×, ×, ▲, R1, R1, ■, R1
Two players in story and free modes	L1, R2, ●, ●, ▲, L2, R1, ●, ▲, ●

Van Helsing

During gameplay, enter the following:

Unlockable	Code
Bonus Movie 1	↑,↓,↑,↓,←,←,→,→,L1,L2, R3, R3
Bonus Movie 2	↑,→,↓,←,↑,←,↓,→,↑,R1,R2, R3
Bonus Movie 3	L1,L2,R2,R1,R2,L2,L1,↑,↑,↓,↓,SELECT
Bonus Movie 4	SELECT, L3, R3,SELECT,R1, L3,SELECT,←,←,↑,→,→
Bonus Movie 5	L2,R2,L1,R1,SELECT,SELECT,L1,L1,R2,R2,L3, R3
Bonus Movie 6	R2,R1,R2,R1,L1,L2,L1,L2,←,→,SELECT,SELECT
Bonus Movie 7	L3,←, R3,→,L2,↑,R2,↓,L1,←,R1,→

Viewtiful Joe

Unlockable	Objective
Unlock Dante	Beat game on any difficulty.
Unlock Sylvia	Beat game on Adult mode.

Virtua Fighter 4

Unlockable	Objective
Alternate Costumes	Hold START at the Character Selection screen. Press × to select that character while holding START to wear the alternate costume.
Alternate Main Menu Background	Enter the Game Option menu, and press R1 to cycle forward or L1 to cycle backward through the list of backgrounds for the Main menu.
Classic Victory Poses	Use a created fighter to reach the Second Kyu level. Hold Punch + Kick + Guard during the replay to do a classic victory pose from Virtua Fighter 1.
Dural's Stage in Versus Mode	Use a created fighter to reach the Emperor or High King rank and unlock the hangar stage in Versus mode.
Fight as Dural	Defeat Dural in Kumite mode to unlock her in Versus mode.
Training Stage 1 in Versus Mode	Use a created fighter to reach the First Dan rank and unlock the first training stage in Versus mode.
Training Stage 2 in Versus Mode	Use a created fighter to reach the Fifth Dan rank and unlock the second training stage in Versus mode.
Training Stage 3 in Versus Mode	Use a created fighter to reach the Champion rank and unlock the third training stage in Versus mode.

Virtua Fighter 4 (continued)

Unlockable	Objective
Training Trophy	Complete the trial events in Training mode with a created fighter. A small trophy icon is displayed over your character's health bar.
Virtua Fighter 1 Fighter Model	Use a character fighter to reach at least the First Dan rank. Select that fighter and hold Punch + Kick until the match begins.

V-Rally 3

Unlockable	Objective
Extra Challenges	Win the Michelin Challenge in Challenge mode.
Mitsubishi Lancer Evolution VI	Select Career mode and win the 1.6L FWD championship in V-Rally mode.
Reversed Tracks	Four tracks exist in each country. Beat a track's record to unlock the next one. Unlock all of them to access the four reversed tracks for that country.
SEAT Cordoba Repsol	Win the Pirelli Challenge in Challenge mode.
Subaru Impreza 2000	Select Career mode and win the 2.0L 4WD championship in V-Rally mode.
Toyota Corolla V-Rally	Set a record time in all circuits.
Car Preview	At the Car Selection screen, hold → or ← to open either door; hold ↑ to open the hood; and hold ↓ to open the trunk.
Flat Cars	Enter 21051975 PTITDAV as a name.
Floating Cars	Enter 210741974 MARTY as a name.
Jelly Cars	Enter 07121974 FERGUS as a name.
Small Cars	Enter 01041977 BIGJIM as a name.
Small Cars with High-Pitched Commentary	Enter no first name and PALACH as a last name.
Smashed Cars	Enter 25121975 PILOU as a name.
Stretched Cars	Enter Gonzales SPEEDY as a name.

Wakeboarding Unleashed

Enter the following codes at the Main menu.

Unlockable	Code
Have All Gaps	R1, L2, L2, R2, R1, L2, L2, R2, R1, L2, L2, R2, R1, L2, L2, R2.
Level Select	■, ■, ■, ■, ●, ●, ●, ●, ▲, ▲, ▲, ▲, ■, ●, ▲.
Unlock Everything	↑, ↓, ↑, ↓, ↑, ↓, ↑, ↓, ↑, ↓, ←, →, ←, →, ←, →, ←, →, ←, →.
Unlock Other Boards	↑, ↑, ←, ←, →, →, ↓, ↓, ↑, ←, →, ↓, ↑, ←, →, ↓.

Unlockable	Objective
All Boarders	Rotate the left analog stick clockwise fifteen times from the Main menu.
Boarder Movies	Complete the game with a particular boarder to unlock his or her movie.
Credits	Beat the game once with any boarder.
Jordan	Collect every star in the Star Search Challenges.
Summer	Beat the game once with any boarder.

WALL-E

Cheats

Enter the code for the following effects in the Options menu.

Effect	Code
All Bonus Features	WALL-E, Auto, EVE, ZPM
All Game Content	M-O, Auto, ZPM, EVE
Alternate Costumes	ZPM, WALL-E, M-O, Auto
Invincibility	WALL-E, M-O, Auto, M-O
Make Any Cube at Any Time	Auto, M-O, Auto, M-O
Wall-E with Super Laser Blaster	WALL-E, EVE, EVE, WALL-E

Enterable Cheats

Enter the codes in the following order.

Effect	Code
Code 1: Kills or Stuns Everything within Range	BOTOFWAR
Code 2: Can Move Undetected by any Enemy	STEALTHARMOR
Code 3: Laser Switches Color Continuously	RAINBOWLASER
Code 4: Every Cube Is an Explosive Cube	EXPLOSIVEWORLD
Code 5: Lights Dark Areas	GLOWINTHEDARK
Code 6: Wears Ski Goggles	BOTOFMYSTERY
Code 7: Wall-E has Golden Tracks	GOLDENTRACKS

The Warriors

Enter codes during gameplay.

Unlockable	Code
200 Dollars, 3 Pieces of Flash, and Some Cans	R1, R2, L1, ×, ↓, L1
Bat	■, R2, ↓, ↓, L1, L1
Complete Current Mission	↓, ■, ×, SELECT, R1, ←
Finish with 100%	L1, SELECT, ■, ↓, L2, →
Infinite Rage	■, ●, ▲, SELECT, ×, ←
Knife	↓, ↓, SELECT, ↑, ↑, L3
Lose Cops	↑, SELECT, ×, ▲, ▲, ■
Machete	L1, ×, R1, R1, SELECT, R2
Pipe	R2, ●, SELECT, ↑, L1, →

Way of the Samurai

Unlockable	Code
Change Characters	In the New Game menu, press L1, R1, R1, L2, L2, L2, R2, R2, R2+■. To choose a character, press ← or →.
Full Health	Pause the game, hold L1+L2, and press ↓, ↑, ↓, ↑, →, ←, ●.
Increase Sword Toughness +1	Pause the game, hold R1+R2, and press →, →, ←, ←, ↓, ↑, ●.
Versus Mode	At the Title screen, hold L1+R1, and press ●+■.

Way of the Samurai 2

Unlockable	Code
All Characters	Select Character Customization, highlight name and press L1, R2, R1, L2, L1, R2, R1, L2, ■
More Store Items	In the Main Map, press L1, R1, L1, R1, R2, R2, ▲.

WDL: Warjetz

Unlockable	Code
Add 10 Money	WNNNGS
All Codes	TWLVCHTS
All Movies	GRTD
Antarctica 1	CMPPLHJJNBQN
Antarctica 2	RKFPMYBZHBQN
Antarctica 3	GNVPMQFSNBQN
Australia 1	MHZKWTJMQBQM
Australia 2	ZBCKXPBHNBQM
Australia 3	LDRKXYFZTBQM
Double Money	TWFSTD
Everything	SPRLZY
Faster Jets	ZPPY
Ghost mode	SNKY
Huge Guns	QD
Instantly Win	SMSHNG
Invincibility	DNGDM
Level Select	JMPTT
New York City 1	KKSPKRJHKBQN
New York City 2	VBFKPLHBWZBQN
New York City 3	WJYPLWFQGBQN
Overlords Mode	VRLRDS
Panama 2	JBVKWNBBCBQM
Panama 3	MDKKWYFTKBQM
Plane Automatically Wins	SMSHNG
Rapid Fire	FRHS
Rhine River 1	YJVPJCJGVBQN
Rhine River 2	FCNPKXBVWBQN
Rhine River 3	PGDPKGFPDBQN
San Francisco 1	TRLPMBJLVBQN
San Francisco 2	SVMPNFBFVBQN
San Francisco 3	RXDPNHFYDBQN
Show All Boxes	BXDRW
Spin Shots	DZZY
Super Armor	MRRMR
Thailand	ZHHKXJJTBBQM
Thailand 2	TBPKYZBVHBQM
Thailand 3	KFFPJRFNPBQN
Valhalla 1	XBXPNGKRKBQN
Valhalla 2	LPXKVMCQZBQM
Valhalla 3	QSMKVSGKHBQM
View All FMV	GRTD

Whiteout

Unlockable	Code
10,000 Points	Hold L2+▲ and press ←,←,↑,↓ during a race.
All Characters	Hold L1+R1 and press ↓,↓,↓,↓ at the Main menu.
All Parts	Hold L1+R1 and press ←,←,←,← at the Main menu.
All Tracks	Hold L1+R1 and press ↑,↑,↑,↑ at the Main menu.
Alternate View	Hold L2+▲ and press ↓,↓,←,← during gameplay.
Master Code	Hold R1+L1 and press →,→,→,→ at the Main menu to unlock all tracks, characters, and snowmobiles.
Restore Stamina	Hold L2+▲ and press →,→,←,↓ during a race.
Win Race	Hold L2+▲ and press ↑,↓,←,→ during a race.

Wild ARMs 5

Costumes

If you beat the game after collecting all of the Ex File Keys, you unlock the Nine Lives costume, which looks like the Knight Blazer from *Wild ARMs 2*. Once you have beaten the game with the keys you can use the costume by starting a new game over your old save file.

Wild Wild Racing

Unlockable	Code
New Engines	Each country in Time Attack rewards you with an engine for one of the three initially-selectable buggies. Complete the three races per Time Attack (Uphill, Downhill, and Flat) to gain a new engine that ups the stats on your buggy.
Secret Menu and Top Secret Menu	At the Main menu, highlight and select Options. At the Options menu hold down ■ and press ↑,●,↓,●,←,→,←,→,●. This will open the Secret menu option on the Options screen. Enter Single Player and type your name as NORTHEND.

Winback Covert Operations

Enter these codes at the Start screen.

Unlockable	Code
All Versus Characters	⇧, ⇩, ⇩, ⇨, ⇨, ⇨, ⇦, ⇦, ⇦, ⇦, then press ●+START
Max Power Mode	L1, R2, L2, R2, L2, ▲, ●, ▲, ●, then hold L1 and press START
Sudden Death Mode	L2, R2, L2, R2, ●, ▲, ●, ▲, then hold L1 and press START

Wipeout Fusion

Enter these codes in the Codes menu under Extras.

Unlockable	Code
Animal Ships	▲, ●, ●, ▲, ×
Infinite Shield	▲, ▲, ■, ■, ■
Infinite Weapons	▲, ●, ×, ●, ■
Mini Ships	●, ■, ■, ×, ●
Retro Planes	×, ●, ▲, ■, ×
Super Fast ships	■, ×, ×, ×, ▲
Unlock all Features	×, ▲, ●, ▲, ●

World Soccer Winning Eleven 7

Unlockable	Objective
Premier All Star Team	Win the LG Championship Cup.
World All Star Team	Win the Multi International Cup.

World Tour Soccer

At the Main menu, enter the following:

Unlockable	Code
All Bonuses	L2, L2, L1, R1, ←, ↑, ←, ↓
Infinite TIF Tokens	↑, ↓, ↑, ↓, R1, R1, R2, R2, ↑, ↓, ↑, ↓
QA Liverpool, TIF OldBoys, TIF Newbies, and Touchline Teams	↓, →, L2, R1, ←, R1
TimeWarp Teams	R2, L2, R2, L2, ↑, L1

Wrath Unleashed

Unlockable	Objective
Elephant Pool Arena	Win 20 Team Battles.
Metal Age Arena	Win 100 Arena Battles.

Wreckless

Unlockable	Objective
Alternate View	Press ↓ to cycle through different screen effects during gameplay and replays. To unlock more effects, complete Missions A-9, A-10, B-9, and B-10.
AUV	Complete Mission A-9.
Dragon-SPL Car	Complete Mission A-1.
Gold Rank on All Missions	Highlight the "Unlimited Time" option at the Main menu, then press L2+R1+→+● as the game loads.
Missions A-2 to A-4	Complete Mission A-1.
Missions B-2 to B-4	Complete Mission B-1.

Wreckless (continued)

Unlockable	Objective
Music Test	Complete all twenty missions to unlock the "Music Test" selection at the Options screen.
Super Car	Complete Mission B-1.
Tank-90	Complete Mission B-8.
Tiger-SPL	Complete Mission A-8 to unlock the car that Tiger Tagachi drives.
Yakuza Car	Complete Mission B-9.

WWE Crush Hour

Unlockable	Code
Special Meter Fills Quickly	Pause the game, hold L3, and press ▲,●,●,●,●.
Unlimited Turbo	Pause the game, hold L3, and press ×,R1,R2.
All Levels and Vehicles	From the main menu, press ■,L2,R2,●,■,L2,L2,L2.
Kevin Nash	From the character select screen, press L2,■,R2,●.

Unlockable	Objective
All Levels	Beat Season mode with any character to unlock all levels.
Bradshaw	Beat Season mode with Brock Lesnar.
Christian	Beat Season mode with Chris Jericho.
D-Von Dudley	Beat Season mode with Bubba Ray Dudley.
Hulk Hogan	Beat Season mode with The Rock.
Lita	Beat Season mode with Matt Hardy.
Ric Flair	Beat Season mode with The Big Show, Rob Van Dam and Triple H.
Stephanie McMahon	Beat Season mode with Kurt Angle.
Vince McMahon	Beat Season mode, facing Vince in the final battle.

X2: Wolverine's Revenge

Unlockable	Code
All Cerebro Files and FMV Sequences	▲,●,▲,■,■,■,R1+R2
All Costumes	▲,●,▲,■,■,■,L1+L2
Cheat Menu	▲,▲,●,●,■,■,●,●,L1+R1+L2+R2
Level Select	▲,●,▲,■,▲,●,L1+R1

XG3 Extreme G Racing

Unlockable	Code
Unlimited Turbo	To get unlimited turbo, go to the title screen. Press R1+L1, R2+L2, R1+L1, and R2+L2. When the code is entered correctly, you get a message confirming entry.
All Tracks	Go to the Main menu and press L1,L1,L2,L2,R2,R2,R1,R1, then hold L1+R1+L2+R2. If the code is entered correctly, a message appears.

X-Men Legends

Costumes

Unlockable	How to Unlock
Bobby Drake, Original Iceman	Beat the game
Colossus Without Metal, Colossus 90's	Beat the game
Gambit's Animated Series Outfit	Beat the game
Original Beast	Beat the game

X-Men Legends (continued)

Unlockable	How to Unlock
Original Cyclops, Cyclops 80's	Beat the game
Original Jean Grey, Phoenix	Beat the game
Original Nightcrawler	Beat the game
Street Clothes Magma	Beat the game
Wolverine 90's, Weapon X	Beat the game

Characters

Unlockable	How to Unlock
Colossus	Beat Nuclear Facility level
Cyclops	Beat Mystique
Emma Frost	Beat Nuclear Facility level (meet in X-mansion)
Gambit	Finish Third Level
Ice Man, Jean Grey, Beast, Rogue, and Storm	Finish first level
Jubilee and Nightcrawler	Finish second level
Magma (on field missions)	Beat Blob in Magma/Cyclops mission
Psylocke	Beast NYC Riot, Morlock Rescue, and Muir Isle fight levels

X-Men Legends II: Rise of Apocalypse

Enter these codes on the Pause screen.

Unlockable	Code
God Mode	↓, ↑, ↓, ↑, →, ↓, →, ←, START
Super Speed	↑, ↑, ↑, ↓, ↑, ↓, START
Unlimited Xtreme Tokens	←, ↓, →, ↓, ↑, ↑, ↓, ↑, START

Enter this code at the Forge's or Beast's equipment screen.

Unlockable	Code
100,000 techbits	↑, ↑, ↑, ↓, →, →, START

Enter these codes on the Team Management screen.

Unlockable	Code
All skills	←, →, ←, →, ↓, ↑, START
Level 99	↑, ↓, ↑, ↓, ←, ↑, ←, →, START

Enter this code while playing. Do not pause.

Unlockable	Code
One hit kills	←, ←, →, ←, →, ↑, START

Enter these codes while in the Review menu.

Unlockable	Code
All Comics	→, ←, ←, →, ↑, ↑, →, START
Game Cinematics	←, →, →, ←, ↓, ↓, ←, START

X-Men The Official Game

Enter these codes in the Cerebro Files menu.

Unlockable	Code
Iceman's Danger Room	→, →, ←, ←, ↓, ↑, ↓, ↑, START
Nightcrawler's Danger Room	↑, ↑, ↓, ↓, ←, →, ←, →, START
Wolverine's Danger Room	↓, ↓, ↑, ↑, →, ←, →, ←, START

Ys The Ark of Napishtim

To enter these codes, first select new game and then select cheat. Hit the crystals in this order: Red, Blue, Yellow, Red, Blue, and Yellow. Then do a downward strike on the center piece. This must be done before entering any of these codes.

Ys The Ark of Napishtim (continued)

Unlockable	Code
20 Item Tool Max Increase	Yellow, Yellow, Red, Red, Blue, Blue, Yellow, Red
All Items 1/2 Price	Yellow, Yellow, Blue, Blue, Red, Red, Red, Yellow, Yellow, Yellow, Red, Red, Blue, Blue
All Three Swords Maxed Out	Red, Red, Yellow, Blue, Yellow, Red, Blue, Blue, Blue, Red, Yellow, Yellow, Blue, Yellow, Red
Beach CG – English Voice with English Sub	Blue, Blue, Red, Yellow
Beach CG—English Voice with Japanese Sub	Blue, Blue, Blue, Red, Yellow
Beach CG Movie—Japanese Voice with English Sub	Blue, Red, Red, Yellow
Beach CG—Japanese Voice with Japanese Sub	Blue, Red, Yellow
Clearflag	Red, Red, Red, Red, Blue, Blue, Blue, Blue, Yellow, Yellow, Yellow, Yellow, Blue, Blue, Yellow, Yellow, Red, Red
Maxed Out Blirante Sword	Blue, Blue, Yellow, Yellow, Yellow, Red, Blue, Red, Red, Red, Yellow, Yellow
Maxed Out Ericcil Sword	Blue, Yellow, Yellow, Red, Red, Red, Blue, Blue, Blue, Red, Red, Yellow
Maxed Out Livart Sword	Blue, Blue, Blue, Yellow, Yellow, Red, Blue, Red, Red, Yellow, Yellow, Yellow
Napishtim Destroyed CG—English Voice with English Sub	Blue, Red, Yellow, Red, Red, Blue, Yellow, Yellow
Napishtim Destroyed CG—English Voice with Japanese Sub	Blue, Red, Yellow, Red, Red, Blue, Yellow, Yellow, Yellow
Napishtim Destroyed CG—Japanese Voice with English Sub	Blue, Red, Yellow, Red, Red, Blue, Yellow, Yellow, Yellow, Yellow
Napishtim Destroyed CG—Japanese Voice with Japanese Sub	Blue, Red, Yellow, Red, Red, Blue, Yellow
Ohla In A Bikini	Blue, Blue, Blue, Blue, Blue, Yellow, Yellow, Yellow, Red, Blue, Yellow, Yellow, Red, Red, Red
Olha Demo After Clearing Time Attack On Hard (Japanese)	Red, Red, Red, Red, Red, Blue, Blue, Blue, Yellow, Red, Blue, Blue, Yellow, Yellow, Yellow
Opening CG In English Voice with English Sub	Blue, Blue, Yellow, Red
Opening CG—English Voice with Japanese Sub	Blue, Blue, Blue, Yellow, Red
Opening CG—Japanese Voice with Japanese Sub	Blue, Yellow, Red
Romun Fleet Destroyed Anime	Blue, Red, Yellow, Red, Red, Yellow, Red, Red, Red
Romun Fleet Destroyed CG	Blue, Red, Yellow, Red, Red, Yellow, Red
Romun Fleet Entrance Anime	Blue, Red, Yellow, Red, Red, Yellow, Blue, Blue, Blue
Unlockable	**Code**
Romun Fleet Entrance CG	Blue, Red, Yellow, Red, Red, Yellow, Blue
Start at Level 10	Red, Blue, Blue, Red, Red, Blue
Start at Level 20	Red, Blue, Blue, Red, Red, Blue, Blue
Start at Level 30	Red, Red, Blue, Blue, Red, Red, Blue, Blue
Start at Level 40	Red, Red, Blue, Red, Red, Blue, Blue, Yellow
Start at Level 50	Red, Red, Blue, Red, Red, Blue, Blue, Yellow, Yellow
Start at Level 60	Red, Red, Blue, Blue, Yellow, Yellow, Red, Red, Blue, Blue, Yellow, Yellow
Unlock Nightmare Mode, Time Trial, And Red Spirit Monuments	Red, Red, Red, Red, Blue, Blue, Blue, Blue, Yellow, Yellow, Yellow, Yellow, Blue, Blue, Yellow, Yellow, Red, Red

Yu-Gi-Oh! The Duelist of the Roses

Press R3 at the Build Deck screen to enter a password for a card.

Unlockable	Password
Ancient Tree of Enlightenment	EKJHQ109
Aqua Dragon	JXCB6FU7
Barrel Dragon	GTJXSBJ7
Beastking of the Swamp	QXNTQPAX
Birdface	N54T4TY5
Black Hole	UMJ10MQB
Blast Sphere	CZN5GD2X
Change of Heart	SBYDQM8B
Crush Card	SRA7L5YR
Dragon Seeker	81EZCH8B
Earthshaker	Y34PN1SV
Elf's Light	E5G3NRAD
Exodia the Forbidden One	37689434
Fairy King Truesdale	YF07QVEZ
Fairy's Gift	NVE7A3EZ
Goblin Fan	92886423
Gravity Bind	0HNFG9WX
Greenkappa	YBJMCD6Z
Harpie's Feather Duster	8HJHQPNP
Horn of the Unicorn	S14FGKQ1
Left Arm of the Forbidden One	A5CF6HSH
Magician of Faith	GME1S3UM
Meteor Dragon	86985631
Mimicat	69YDQM85
Mirror Wall	53297534
Mystical Capture Chain	N1NDJMQ3
Robotic Knight	S5S7NKNH
Royal Decree	8TETQHE1
Seiyaryu	2H4D85J7
Serpentine Princess	UMQ3WZUZ
Slate Warrior	73153736
Swordsman from a Foreign Land	CZ81UVGR
Swordstalker	AHOPSHEB
Tactical Warrior	054TC727

Yu Yu Hakusho: Dark Tournament

From the Options screen, choose "Cheats" and enter the following:

Unlockable	Code
All Cards	●,■,●,■,■,↓
All Chapters	↑,↓,X,●,■,→
All Environments	↑,→,←,→,X,X
All Fighters	■,↑,■,●,↓,●
All Modes	←,→,↓,→,X,●
No Damage to Player One	●,■,↓,←,●,■
No Damage to Player Two	↑,■,←,■,●,■
Player 1 Free Spirit Energy	■,X,●,■,X,●
Player 2 Free Spirit Energy	↓,↑,●,←,X,→
Turbo Mode	●,X,→,X,↑,■

Zapper

Enter these codes while the game is paused.

Unlockable	Code
Unlimited Lives	Hold L1 and press ↑, ↑, ←, ←, →, ←, →
Unlimited Shield	Hold L1 and press ↑, ↓, ↑, ←, →, ↓, ↑

Zone of the Enders

Press pause during gameplay, then enter this code.

Unlockable	Code
Full Health and Ammo	L1, L1, L2, L2, L1, R1, L1, R1, R2, R1

Unlockable	Objective
Alternate Ending	Complete all of the S.O.S calls, ranking A in each of them, and you see a different ending sequence.
Versus Mode	Complete the game to receive Versus mode. Your score (the amount of continues used, saves, and the amount of civilians you rescued) determines which frames you get to play.

Table of Contents – PS3

Armored Core 4

Hard Difficulty

Unlockable	How to Unlock
Hard Difficulty	Successfully complete any chapter on normal difficulty. Press ■ to toggle between difficulties.

Battlefield: Bad Company

Find All Five Weapons

Unlockable	**How to Unlock**
Assault Rifle	Register your old *Battlefield games at http://www.veteran.battlefield.com/.*
Light Machine Gun	Sign up for the newsletter at *http://www.findallfive.com/.*
Semi-Automatic Shotgun	After playing an Online game, login and check your stats at *http://www.findallfive.com/.*

Battlefield: Bad Company (continued)

Unlockable	How to Unlock
Sniper Rifle	Pre-order the game from a participating retailer before June 23rd, 2008.
Uzi	Play the "Battlefield: Bad Company Demo" and get to rank 4. (2,300 EXP required to reach rank 4.)

Trophies

Trophies are unlockable in Multiplayer modes.

Unlockable	How to Unlock
Assault Rifle Efficiency Trophy	In a round, 6 kills with assault rifle.
Avenger Trophy	In a round, 3 avenger points.
Best Squad Trophy	Awarded in end of round.
Big Guns Trophy	In a round, 5 kills with artillery.
Carbine Efficiency Trophy	In a round, 6 kills with M16A2.
Clear Skies Trophy	In a round, 5 kills with stationary weapon.
Combat Aviator Trophy	In a round, 5 kills with air vehicle.
Combat Efficiency Trophy	In a round, 6 kill streak.
Combat Engineer Trophy	In a round, 20 vehicle repair points (2 repairs).
Compact Assault Rifle Efficiency Trophy	In a round, 6 kills with compact assault rifle.
Demo Pack Efficiency Trophy	In a round, 3 kills with C4.
Emplacement Trophy	In a round, 5 kills with stationary weapon.
Explosive Efficiency Trophy	In a round, 10 kills with explosives.
Firearm Efficiency Trophy	In a round, 3 kills with handgun.
Frag Out Efficiency Trophy	In a round, 3 kills with grenade while playing Demolitionists.
Grenade Launcher Efficiency	In a round, 6 kills with grenade launcher.
Grenadier Efficiency Trophy	In a round, 3 kills with grenade while playing Assault.
High Card Trophy	In a round, get the best IAR score.
Kill Assists Trophy	In a round, 5 kill assists.
Laser Designating Efficiency Trophy	In a round, 3 kills from laser designating.
Light Machine Gun Efficiency Trophy	In a round, 6 kills with a light machine gun.
Marksman Trophy	In a round, 5 kills with sniper rifle.
Medic Trophy	In a round, 10 points from med kit (2 heals).
Melee Combat Trophy	In a round, 5 melee kills.
Mine Placement Efficiency Trophy	In a round, 3 kills with AT mines.
Mortar Strike Efficiency Trophy	In a round, 3 kills with mortar strike.
Naval Surface Warfare Trophy	In a round, 5 kills with sea vehicle.
Objective Attack Trophy	In a round, destroy the last objective.
Objective Defender Trophy	In a round, 30 defend points.
Objective Destroyer Trophy	In a round, destroy 3 objectives.
Rocket Launcher Efficiency Trophy	In a round, 3 kills with rocket launcher.
Savior Trophy	In a round, 3 savior points.
Shotgun Efficiency Trophy	In a round, 5 kills with a shotgun.
Squad Medication Trophy	In a round, 40 squad member heal points.
Squad Member Trophy	In a round, assist or save 5 squad members.

Battlefield: Bad Company (continued)

Unlockable	How to Unlock
SVU Efficiency Trophy	In a round, 5 kills with the SVU.
Tank Warfare Trophy	In a round, 5 kills with tanks.
Target Tagging Efficiency Trophy	In a round, 2 kill assists from dart gun tagging.
Transport Vehicle Trophy	In a round, 5 kills with transport vehicle.
UMP	In a round, 6 kills with UMP.
Wheels of Hazard Trophy	In a round, 2 road kills.
Winning Team Trophy	Awarded in end of round.

Wild Cards

Unlockable	How to Unlock
1 on 1 Air	In a round, destroy an air vehicle of the same kind without assistance.
1 on 1 Land	In a round, destroy one land vehicle of the same kind without assistance.
1 on 1 Sea	In a round, destroy 1 sea vehicle of the same kind without assistance.
2 Pair	In a round, get 2 of any 2 trophies.
Airtime	In a round, 2 seconds air time in a land vehicle.
Armor Buster	In a round, kill 5 armored vehicles.
Avenger Trophies	Global: 50x avenger trophies.
Beat the House	In a round, 15 grenade kills.
Cab Driver	In a round, 5 min as driver in a vehicle with passengers.
Chopper Chopper Kills	In a round, kill 5 air vehicles.
Dead Eye Headshots	Global: Get 100 headshots with any sniper rifle.
Destruction Site	In a round, destroy 50 objects.
Deuces Are Wild	In a round, kill 2 enemies of each kind.
Five of a Kind	In a round, destroy 5 vehicles of the same kind.
Full Deck	In a round, 52 total kills.
Full House	In a round, destroy 3+2 vehicles of the same kind.
Gunslinger	Global: 80 kills with handgun.
Headshots	In a round, 20 kills from headshots.
Parashooter	In a round, 4 road kills with any air vehicle.
Santa's Little Helper	In a round, 10 kill assist points.
Savior Trophies	Global: 50x savior trophies.
Snake Eyes	In a round, get 11 kills as two different classes.
Squad Avenger Card	Global: Get 100 avenger points avenging squad members.
Squad Wild Card	In a round, 1 squad member trophy per squad member.
Staying Dry	In a round, 2 seconds air time with a sea vehicle.
Straight Flush	In a round, destroy 1 vehicle of each kind.
Strike	In a round, kill 10 enemies at the same time.
Tank Buster	In a round, kill 5 tanks.
Three of a Kind	In a round, destroy 3 vehicles of the same kind.

Blazing Angels: Squadrons of WWII

Enter these codes while the game is paused.

Unlockable	Code
Increase Damage of Weapons	Hold L2 and quickly press L1, L1, R1; release L2, then hold R2 and quickly press R1, R1, L1

DS PSP PS2 PS3 Wii Xbox Xbox 360 Index

Blazing Angels: Squadrons of WWII (continued)

Invincibility	Hold L2 and press ■, ▲, ▲, ■; release L2, then hold R2 and quickly press ▲, ■, ■, ▲

Enter this code at the Title menu while holding L2+R2

Unlockable	Code
All Campaign Missions and Planes	■, L1, R1, ▲, ▲, R1, L1, ■

Blazing Angels 2: Secret Missions of WWII

Codes

Enter the code for unlocking the planes and missions in the main menu, and enter the other two codes while paused when on a mission.

Effect	Code
Damage Increased/Normal	Hold L2 and press L1,L1,R1. Release L2, hold R2 and press R1,R1,L1.
God Mode Active/Inactive	Hold L2 and press ■,▲,▲,■. Release L2, hold R2 and press ▲,■,■,▲.
Unlock All Planes and Missions	Hold both R2,L2 then press ■,L1,R1,▲,▲,R1,L1,■.

Brothers in Arms: Hell's Highway

Codes

Select the "Enter Codes" option at the main menu, then enter the codes.

Effect	Code
All Recon Points	0ZNDRBICRA
Kilroy Alert (Notifies you when you are close to a Kilroy)	SH2VYIVNZF
Kilroy Detector (Alerts you when a Kilroy is nearby)	4V35JZHQD6
Two Extra Skins	HI9WTPXSUK

Burnout Paradise

Unlockable Cars

Acquire an A level license, then insert these codes in the in-game Cheats menu.

Unlockable	How to Unlock
Best Buy Car	Type BESTBUY
Circuit City Car	Type CIRCUITCITY
Game Stop Car	Type GAMESTOP
Wal-Mart Car	Type WALMART

Other Unlockable Cars

Insert this code in the in-game Cheats menu under the "sponsor codes" section.

Unlockable	How to Unlock
Steel Wheels Car	Type: U84D 3Y8K FY8Y 58N6

Licenses

To unlock licenses, win the corresponding number of events in the game.

Unlockable	How to Unlock
A	26 events
B	16 events
C	7 events
D	2 events
Burnout Paradise	45 events

Burnout Paradise (continued)	
Unlockable	**How to Unlock**
Elite	110 events

Paint Colors

Unlockable	How to Unlock
Gold Paint	Earn the elite license
Platinum Paint	Earn the elite license and achieve 100 percent completion.

Call of Duty 4

Enter this code in the Chapter Select screen.

Unlockable	Code
Unlock All Levels	Hold SELECT and press ⇨, ⇨, ⇦, ⇦, ■, ■

Arcade and Cheat Options

These unlock automatically for completing *Call of Duty 4: Modern Warfare* on any difficulty level. During gameplay, find the Cheat menu in the Options menu.
Call of Duty 4: Modern Warfare

Unlockable	How to Unlock
Arcade Mode	Complete game on any difficulty
Cheat Menu	Complete game on any difficulty

Easter Egg (Hidden Mission)

Beat the game on any difficulty and let the credits run all the way through. When they finish, you'll start another mission. This mission takes place on a plane that resembles Air Force One, wherein you must fight your way through a horde of baddies, save the V.I.P., and escape the plane in less than two minutes.

Cheats

Unlock cheats by collecting enemy intel (intelligence), which look like laptop computers that are hidden throughout the campaign. Note: Using cheats disables Achievements.

Unlockable Cheats

Unlockable	How to Unlock
A Bad Year: When you kill enemies, they explode into tires!	Collect 15 pieces of enemy intel.
Cluster Bombs: After one of your frag grenades explodes, four more explode in a cross-shaped pattern.	Collect 10 pieces of enemy intel.
CoD Noir: Turns all gameplay into black and white.	Collect 2 pieces of enemy intel.
Infinite Ammo: Weapons have unlimited ammo. Doesn't work with Perk 1 abilities such as C4 and Claymores.	Collect 30 pieces of enemy intel.
Photo-Negative: Inverses all of the game's colors.	Collect 4 pieces of enemy intel.
Ragtime Warfare: Gameplay goes black and white, dust and scratches fill the screen, it plays at 2x speed, and the music becomes piano music.	Collect 8 pieces of enemy intel.
Slow-Mo Ability: Use the melee button to change the game to slow-mo and play at half-speed.	Collect 20 pieces of enemy intel.
Super Contrast: Dramatically increases the game's contrast, making the darks much darker and the lights much lighter.	Collect 6 pieces of enemy intel.

Call of Duty 4: Modern Warfare (continued)

Golden weapons are a special camo (or skin) that you unlock when you fully complete all the challenges under the weapon subtype in the barracks (SMG, LMG, etc.). Access them by choosing the camo of the respective weapon. The effect is purely cosmetic and does not enhance the ability of the weapon in any way.

Golden Weapons

Unlockable	How to Unlock
Golden AK-47	Complete all Assault Rifle challenges.
Golden Desert Eagle	Get to Level 55.
Golden Dragunov	Complete all Sniper challenges.
Golden M1014	Complete all Shotgun challenges.
Golden M60	Complete all LMG challenges.
Golden Mini-Uzi	Complete all SMG challenges.

Multiplayer Unlockables

Unlockable	Unlocked at Rank
Assault Rifle (G3)	Rank 25
Assault Rifle (G36C)	Rank 37
Assault Rifle (M14)	Rank 46
Assault Rifle (M4)	Rank 10
Assault Rifle (MP44)	Rank 52
LMG (M60E4)	Rank 19
Pistol (Desert Eagle)	Rank 43
Pistol (Golden Desert Eagle)	Rank 55
Pistol (M1911)	Rank 16
Shotgun (M1014)	Rank 31
SMG (AK-74U)	Rank 28
SMG (Mini Uzi)	Rank 13
SMG (P90)	Rank 40
Sniper Rifle (Barret)	Rank 49
Sniper Rifle (Dragunov)	Rank 22
Sniper Rifle (M40)	Rank 04
Sniper Rifle (R700)	Rank 34

Calling All Cars!

Unlockable Vehicles

Complete the appropriate tasks in the correct game mode and difficulty to unlock extra vehicles.

Unlockable	How to Unlock
BLUE BOMBER	Win at the Trainyards on Captain difficulty, using only the helicopter to score in a single-level, 5-minute game
CHERRY PICKER	In a single-level, 5 minute-game on Chief difficulty, win at the Burbs with at least 20 points
DUMPER	On Sergeant difficulty, beat Tournament mode
FLEABAG	On Chief difficulty, beat Tournament mode
HIGHROLLER	Beat the Burbs on Captain difficulty without letting the opponent score in a single-level, 5-minute game
LITTER BOX	On Captain difficulty, beat Tournament mode
SHAMROCK	In a single-level, 5-minute game on Sergeant difficulty, beat any level without letting the opponent score

Calling All Cars! (continued)

Unlockable Vehicles

Complete the appropriate tasks in the correct game mode and difficulty to unlock extra vehicles.

Unlockable	How to Unlock
BLUE BOMBER	Win at the Trainyards on Captain difficulty, using only the
SWEET CHEEKS	In a single-level, 2-minute game on Captain difficulty, win any level without letting the opponent score
YELLOW ROSE	On Rookie difficulty, beat Tournament mode
YELLOWJACKET	In a single-level, 5-minute game on Captain difficulty, win using only the 3-point ramp in the Alpine

Dark Sector

Unlockable

Unlockable	How to Unlock
Brutal Difficulty	Complete the game once.

Entitlements

Complete each entitlement to get the Unlockable.

Unlockable	How to Unlock
Baggage Claim	Complete Chapter 3.
Champion	Best overall in a ranked team game (Multiplayer).
Comrade	Scored 500 points in ranked team games (Multiplayer).
Dark Sector—Brutal Difficulty	Complete the game on Brutal difficulty.
Double Decap Latte	Two decapitations in one shot.
Electrician	Electrocuted 30 enemies.
Exposure	Complete Chapter 2.
Finesse	30 Aftertouch kills.
Ghost	Used cloaking to get a finisher.
Glaive Master	Completed a level using only the Glaive.
Glory	Finished best overall in a ranked match (Multiplayer).
Greed	Collected over 50,000 rubles.
Hardball	30 Power-throw kills.
Headhunter	Decapitated 30 enemies.
Hero	Scored 5,000 points (Multiplayer).
Hero of the People	Scored 5,000 points in ranked team games (Multiplayer).
Incinerator	Incinerated 30 enemies.
Industrial Evolution	Complete Chapter 7.
Jack Frost	Killed 30 frozen enemies.
Jack the Jackal	Took the Jackal for a ride.
Master Researcher	Collected all the weapon upgrades.
Moths to the Flame	Complete Chapter 4.
Prologue	Complete Chapter 1.
Rebound	Killed an enemy with a reflected projectile.
Researcher	Collected 10 weapon upgrades.
Sharpshooter	30 Headshots.
Skeet Shooter	Shot 10 projectiles in mid-flight.
The Bait	Complete Chapter 6.
The Dark Sector	Complete Chapter 10.
The Finisher	Performed 30 finishers.
The Shipment	Complete Chapter 5.

Dark Sector (continued)

Unlockable	How to Unlock
Threshold Guardian	Complete Chapter 9.
Unnatural History	Complete Chapter 8.
Veteran	Scored 500 points (Multiplayer).
Weaponsmith	Applied five upgrades in the market.

The Darkness

Phone Numbers

Go to any phone and enter the 18 phone numbers, in no specific order, to unlock Keeper of Secrets accomplishment. Find these phone numbers throughout the game on posters, graffiti, etc. Out of the 25, you only need 18 to unlock the accomplishment.

Phone Number	Count	Phone Number	Count	Phone Number	Count
555-6118	1/18	555-4569	7/18	555-1206	13/18
555-9723	2/18	555-7658	8/18	555-9562	14/18
555-1847	3/18	555-9985	9/18	555-9528	15/18
555-5289	4/18	555-1233	10/18	555-7934	16/18
555-6667	5/18	555-1037	11/18	555-3285	17/18
555-6205	6/18	555-3947	12/18	555-7892	18/18

Dead Space

Codes

Press Start, then insert the following codes. You will hear a chime if you've done it correctly.

Effect	Code
1,000 Credits (one time only)	■,■,■,▲,■
2,000 Credits (one time only)	■,■,■,▲,▲
5,000 Credits (one time only)	■,■,■,▲,■,▲
10,000 Credits (one time only)	■,▲,▲,▲,■,■,▲
Adds 2 Power Nodes (one time only)	▲,■,■,■,▲
Adds 5 Power Nodes (one time only)	▲,■,▲,■,■,▲,■,■,▲,■,■,▲
Refill Your Oxygen	■,■,▲,▲,▲
Refill Your Stasis and Kinesis Energy	▲,■,▲,▲,■,▲

Def Jam: Icon

At the Press Start screen, enter these codes.

Unlockable	Code
It's Going Down music track	●, ⇧, ⇨, ⇦, ▲
Make It Rain music track	⇩, ●, ⇩, ⇨

Disgaea 3: Absence of Justice

Unlockable Classes

Unlockable	How to Unlock
Archer (Female)	Level 15 Female Fighter and Level 15 Female Healer
Archer (Male)	Level 15 Male Fighter and Level 15 Male Healer
Berserker	Heavy Knight and Monster Tamer Level 40
Cheerleader (Idol)	Geo Master and Healer Level 25
Geo Master	Fist Fighter and Healer Level 20
Gunner Female	Female Thief and Mage Level 15

Disgaea 3: Absence of Justice (continued)

Unlockable	How to Unlock
Gunner Male	Thief and Male Mage Level 15
Heavy Knight	Male Fighter and Fist Fighter Level 15
Magic Knight	Fighter and Mage Level 25
Majin	Clear second play through tutorial
Masked Hero	Thief and Gunner Level 45
Monster Tamer	Female Fighter and Fist Fighter Level 15
Ninja (Female)	Level 30 Female Monk and Level 30 Female Magician
Ninja (Male)	Level 30 Male Monk and Level 30 Male Magician
Samurai (Female)	Level 35 Female Fighter and Level 35 Female Archer
Samurai (Male)	Level 35 Male Fighter and Level 35 Male Archer
Shaman	Geo Master and Mage Level 25

Unlockable Cameo Characters

Unlockable	How to Unlock
Asagi	Beat extra map 4
Axel	Beat extra map 6
Laharl, Etna, and Flonne	Beat extra map 7
Marona	Beat extra map 5
Master Big Star	Beat extra map 1
Prism Red	Beat extra map 3
Salvatore	Beat extra map 2

Unlockable Endings

Unlockable	How to Unlock
Almaz's Ending	Win stage 8-4 with Almaz alone and the battle after
Human World Ending	Kill more then 99 allies and clear two alt. stages by stage 7-6
Laharl's Ending	Go to homeroom and propose "Watch a New Ending" and clear the stage
Mao's Ambition Ending	Clear stage 1-9 on 2nd or higher cycle before stage 4-4
Normal Ending	Don't meet any other ending's requirement
Raspberyl's Ending 1	Lose against Raspberyl on stage 1-5
Raspberyl's Ending 2	Lose against Raspberyl on stage 2-1
Super Hero Ending	Use Mao at Level 500 or higher to defeat final boss

Dragon Ball Z: Burst Limit

Unlockable Characters

Unlockable	How to Unlock
100% Final Form Frieza	Beat Chapter 16 on Frieza Saga.
1st Form Frieza	Beat Chapter 8 on Frieza Saga.
2nd Form Frieza	Beat Chapter 9 on Frieza Saga.
3rd Form Frieza	Beat Chapter 12 on Frieza Saga.
Android #17	Beat Chapter 3 on Cell Saga.
Android #18	Beat Chapter 2 on Cell Saga.
Bardock	Beat Chapter 1 on Bardock Storyline.
Broly	Beat Chapter 1 on Broly Storyline.
Captain Ginyu	Beat Chapter 4 on Frieza Saga.

DS PSP PS2 PS3 Wii Xbox Xbox 360 Index

Dragon Ball Z: Burst Limit (continued)

Unlockable	How to Unlock
Final Form Frieza	Beat Chapter 14 on Frieza Saga.
Imperfect Cell	Beat Chapter 4 on Cell Saga.
Kaioken Goku	Beat Chapter 7 on Saiyan Saga.
Nappa	Beat Chapter 5 on Saiyan Saga.
Perfect Cell	Beat Chapter 12 on Cell Saga.
Piccolo Fuse with Kami	Beat Chapter 4 on Cell Saga.
Piccolo Sync with Nail	Beat Chapter 11 on Frieza Saga.
Raditz	Beat Chapter 1 on Saiyan Saga.
Recoome	Beat Chapter 1 on Frieza Saga.
Saibamen	Beat Chapter 3 on Saiyan Saga.
Semi-Perfect Cell	Beat Chapter 6 on Cell Saga.
Super Perfect Cell	Beat Chapter 18 on Cell Saga.
Super Perfect Cell	Beat Chapter 19 on Cell Saga.
Super Saiyan 2 Teen Gohan	Beat Chapter 19 on Cell Saga.
Super Saiyan Goku	Beat Chapter 16 on Frieza Saga.
Super Saiyan Trunks	Beat Chapter 7 on Cell Saga.
Super Saiyan Vegeta	Beat Chapter 2 on Cell Saga.
Super Trunks	Beat Chapter 13 on Cell Saga.
Super Vegeta	Beat Chapter 10 on Cell Saga.
Teen Gohan	Beat Chapter 1 on Cell Saga.
Trunks	Beat Chapter 7 on Cell Saga.
Vegeta	Beat Chapter 8 on Saiyan Saga.

Unlockable Difficulties

Unlockable	How to Unlock
Hard	Beat Z Chronicles on Normal.
Very Hard	Beat Z Chronicles on Normal.
Z	Beat Z Chronicles on Very Hard.

Unlockable Movies

Unlockable	How to Unlock
Credits	Beat Broly's Storyline.
Movie 1	Beat Frieza Saga.
Movie 2	Beat Cell Saga.

Dynasty Warriors 6

Characters

Unlockable	How to Unlock
Cao Cao	Clear Musou mode with three Wei characters.
Cao Pi	Deafeat Cao Pi within five minutes on Wu side of He Fei.
Cao Ren	Succeed in Battle Objective 2 on the Lu Bu side of Fan Castle.
Diao Chan	Clear Musou mode with one character from each Kingdom.
Dong Zhuo	Clear Musou mode with Lu Bu.
Gan Ning	Clear Musou mode with one Wu character.
Guan Ping	Succeed in two battle objectives on the Shu side of Fan Castle and finish battle with Guan Ping alive.
Huang Gai	Succeed in Battle Objective 3 on the Wu side of The Battle of Chi Bi.

Dynasty Warriors 6 (continued)

Unlockable	How to Unlock
Huang Zhong	Succeed in one battle objective on the Wei side of Ding Jun Mountain.
Ling Tong	Succeed in Battle Objective 1 on the Wei side of the Battle of Shi Ting.
Liu Bei	Clear Musou mode with three Shu characters.
Lu Bu	Clear Musou mode with Liu Bei, Cao Cao, and Sun Jian.
Lu Meng	Succeed in two battle objectives on the Wei side of He Fei.
Ma Chao	Succeed in two battle objectives on the Wei side of Han Zhong Attack Defense Battle.
Pang Tong	Succeed in three battle objectives at Cheng Du battle and finish battle with Pang Tong alive.
Sun Ce	Succeed in Battle Objective 1 on the Sun Jian side of the Battle of Xia Pi.
Sun Jian	Clear Musou mode with three Wu characters.
Sun Quan	Succeed in Battle Objective 1 on the Lu Bu side of The Battle of Chi Bi.
Taishi Ci	Defeat him in the Battle for Wu Territory.
Wei Yan	Succeed in two battle objectives on the Shu side of Wu Zhang Plains and finish battle with Wei Yan alive.
Xiahou Yuan	Succeed in one battle objective on the Shu side of Ding Jun Mountain.
Xiao Quio	Succeed in Battle Objective 3 on the Wu side of the Battle of Shi Ting.
Xu Chu	He Fei, Wu side, personally kill Cao Ren and Xu Chu.
Xu Huang	Succeed in two battle objectives on the Wei/Wu side of Fan Castle.
Yuan Shao	As Wei, complete all three targets and capture Wu Chao before completing the stage.
Yue Ying	Succeed in Battle Objective 1 on the Wei side of the Battle of Wu Zhang Plains.
Zhang Jiao	Beat stage and complete all three targets in the Yellow Turban Rebellion. Playable in only Free mode and Challenge mode.
Zhang Liao	Clear Musou mode with 1 Wei character.
Zhen Ji	Succeed in Battle Objective 1 on the Lu Bu side of the Xu Du Invasion.
Zheng He	Succeed in two battle objectives on the Shu side of Han Zhong Attack Defense Battle.
Zhou Tai	Succeed in three battle objectives on the Shu side of Yi Ling.
Zhuge Liang	Clear Musou mode with one Shu character.

Difficulties

Unlockable	How to Unlock
Chaos Difficulty	Clear Musou mode with one character from Wu, Shu, Wei, and other.
Hell Difficulty	Beat Wei, Wu, Shu, and Other Musou mode.
Master Difficulty	Beat any Musou mode on Easy or Normal.
Very Hard Difficulty	Clear Musou mode with any one character.

Dynasty Warriors: Gundam

Extra Characters and Mobile Suits

Unlockable	How to Unlock
Any Mobile Suit for a Pilot	Finish a pilot's Story mode at least once
Char's Gelgoog	Complete Amuro Ray's Official mode
Char's Zaku II	Complete Char Aznable's Official mode
Gundam Mk-II (Black)	Complete Kamille Bidan's Official mode and Heero Yuy's Original mode

DS
PSP
PS2
PS3
Wii
Xbox
Xbox 360
Index

Dynasty Warriors: Gundam (continued)

Unlockable	How to Unlock
Gundam ZZ	Complete Judau Ashita's Official mode
Hyaku Shiki (Gold Gundam)	Complete Char Aznable's Official mode Mission 4
Master Asia and Master Gundam	Finish Domon Kasshu's Original mode
Milliardo Peacecraft and Epyon	Finish Heero's story in Original mode
Musha Gundam	Beat Original mode with all 6 protagonists: Amuro, Kamille, Judau, Domon, Heero, and Loran
Official: Char Aznable	Complete Amuro Ray's Official mode
Official: Haman Karn	Complete Kamille Bidan's Official mode
Official: Paptimus Scirocco	Complete Judau Ashita's Official mode
Original: Amuro Ray	Complete Amuro Ray's Official mode
Original: Char Aznable	Complete Char Aznable's Official mode
Original: Elpe Puru	Complete Judau Ashita's Official mode and Domon Kasshu's Original mode
Original: Emma Sheen	Complete Char Aznable's Official mode and Rolan Cehack's Original mode
Original: Haman Karn	Complete Haman Karn's Official mode
Original: Jerid Messa	Complete Kamille Bidan's Official mode and Heero Yuy's Original mode
Original: Judau Ashita	Complete Judau Ashita's Official mode
Original: Kamille Bidan	Complete Kamille Bidan's Official mode
Original: Paptimus Scirocco	Complete Paptimus Scirocco's Official mode
Original: Puru Two	Complete Elpe Puru's Original mode
Original: Roux Louka	Complete Judau Ashita's Original mode and Haman Karn's Official mode
Qubeley	Complete Judau Ashita's Official mode
Qubeley Mk-II (Red)	Complete Elpe Puru's Original mode and Rolan Cehack's Original mode
Qubeley Mk-II (Black)	Complete Judau Ashita's Official mode and Domon Kasshu's Original mode
The O	Complete Kamille Bidan's Official mode

Fantastic 4: Rise of the Silver Surfer

Unlockables

Collect the indicated number of Tokens to unlock the corresponding bonus.

Unlockable	How to Unlock
1990's Fantastic Four	Collect 12 Tokens
2000's Fantastic Four	Collect 12 Tokens
Comic Covers #1	Collect 4 Tokens
Comic Covers #2	Collect 4 Tokens
Game Concept Art	Collect 4 Tokens
Ultimate Costumes	Collect 12 Tokens

FIFA Street 3

Bonus Teams

Complete the following tasks to unlock the corresponding team.

Unlockable	How to Unlock
Predator (Gerrard, Beckham, etc.)	Complete Adidas Challenge in FIFA Street Challenge.
The Blasters (Gerrard, Ballack, etc.)	Win 40 Games in FIFA Street Challenge.
The Champions (Baresi, Voller, etc.)	Complete Champion Challenge in FIFA Street Challenge.
The Classics (Cantona, Zico, etc.)	Complete Classic Challenge in FIFA Street Challenge.
World Stars (Ronaldinho, Eto'o, etc.)	Complete All Stars Challenge in FIFA Street Challenge.

Fight Night Round 3

Unlockable	Code
All Venues	newview

Unlockable	How to Unlock
Madison Square Garden	Win a match there in Career mode.
The Staples Center	Win a match there in Career mode.
"Hard Straights" Style	Win that style match in ESPN Classic Fights mode or Career mode.
"Hook Master" Style	Win that style match in ESPN Classic Fights mode or Career mode.
"Judge Jab" Style	Win that style match in ESPN Classic Fights mode or Career mode.
"Lethal Uppercuts" Style	Win that style match in ESPN Classic Fights mode or Career mode.
"Philly Shell" Style	Win that style match in ESPN Classic Fights mode or Career mode.
"Sinister Cross" Style	Win that style match in ESPN Classic Fights mode or Career mode.
"Slickster" Style	Win that style match in ESPN Classic Fights mode or Career mode.
"Smooth" Style	Win that style match in ESPN Classic Fights mode or Career mode.
"Textbook" Style	Win that style match in ESPN Classic Fights mode or Career mode.
"Uptight" Style	Win that style match in ESPN Classic Fights mode or Career mode.
Ko Rey Mo	Defeat him in the Lightweight Career mode.
The Burger King (Trainer)	Finish the Burger King event in Career mode and select him as a trainer.

Folklore

Special Folks

Unlockable	How to Unlock
Ellen—Collbrande	Score 150,000 Campaign Points in Dungeon Trial mode.
Ellen—Duergar	Score 30,000 Campaign Points in Dungeon Trial mode.
Ellen—Kaladbolg	Upload a 4,500-point dungeon.
Keats—Alphard	Upload a 4,500-point dungeon.

Folklore (continued)

Unlockable	How to Unlock
Keats—Collbrande	Score 150,000 Campaign Points in Dungeon Trial mode.
Keats—Duergar	Score 30,000 Campaign Points in Dungeon Trial mode.
Keats—Valiant	Score 100,000 Campaign Points in Dungeon Trial mode.

Frontlines: Fuel of War

More Levels

To unlock two extra single-player levels, insert the following passwords at the in-game Passwords menu.

Unlockable	How to Unlock
Urban Level	sp-street
Village Level	sp-village

Full Auto 2: Battlelines

In the Option menu, select the Cheats option to enter these codes.

Unlockable	Code
Unlock Sceptre and Mini-Rockets	10E6CUSTOMER
Unlock Vulcan and Flamethrower	5FINGERDISCOUNT

The Godfather: The Don's Edition

Enter these codes while the game is paused.

Unlockable	Code
$5,000	■, ▲, ■, ■, ▲, L2
Full Ammo	▲, ⇦, ▲, ⇨, ■, R1
Full Health	⇦, ■, ⇨, ▲, ⇨, L2

Gran Turismo 5 Prologue

Unlockables

Unlockable	How to Unlock
BMW Concept 1 Series tii '07	Beat all Class B Races.
Daihatsu OFC-1	Beat all Class C Races.
Nissan GT-R Proto '05	Beat all Class S Races.
Nissan Skyline Coupe Concept '07	Beat all Class A Races.
S Class Events	Complete all main A, B, and C Classes with at least Bronze Medal or better.

Grand Theft Auto IV

Codes

During gameplay, pull out Niko's phone and dial these numbers for the corresponding effect. Cheats will affect missions and achievements.

Effect	Code
Change weather	468-555-0100
Get the Ak-47, knife, Molotov Cocktails, pistol, RPG, sniper rifle and Uzi	486-555-0150
Get the baseball bat, grenades, M4, MP5, pistol, RPG, and sniper rifle	486-555-0100
Raise wanted level	267-555-0150
Remove wanted level	267-555-0100
Restore armor	362-555-0100
Restore health	482-555-0100
Spawn a Cognoscenti	227-555-0142

Grand Theft Auto IV (continued)

Effect	Code
Spawn a Comet	227-555-0175
Spawn a Jetmax	938-555-0100
Spawn a Sanchez	625-555-0150
Spawn a SuperGT	227-555-0168
Spawn a Turismo	227-555-0147
Spawn an Annihilator	359-555-0100
Spawn an FIB Buffalo	227-555-0100
Spawn an NRG-900	625-555-0100

Map Locations

Enter the password into any of the in-game computers.

Effect	Code
Weapon, health, armor, vehicle, pigeon, ramp/stunt, and entertainment locations	www.whattheydonotwantyoutoknow.com

Unlockables

Unlockable	How to Unlock
Annihilator Helicopter	Kill all 200 Flying Rats (Pigeons)

Easter Eggs

Unlockable	How to Unlock
The Heart of Liberty City	Gain access to Happiness Island. Once you're able to go there legally, find the Helicopter Tours (which is directly east of Happiness Island) and steal a helicopter. Fly over the Statue of Liberty and jump out at the statue's feet. Land on the topmost tier of the statue, which is basically a square platform with a door in the center of each side. Look for a door with a plaque on either side of it that reads, "No Hidden Content Here." Don't try to open the door; just walk through it. Inside, you'll find an empty room with a tall ladder. Climb it, and when you reach the top, look up; there is a gigantic beating heart, held in place by chains.

Friendship Bonuses

Gain the following bonuses by gaining the corresponding amount of friendship.

Unlockable	How to Unlock
Boom? (Call Packie for him to make you a car bomb)	Gain 75% friendship with Packie.
Chopper Ride (He will pick you up in his helicopter)	Gain 70% friendship with Brucie.
Discount Guns (Buy weapons at a cheaper price from Little Jacob)	Gain 60% friendship with Little Jacob.
Extra Help (A car of gang members will be sent to help you out)	Gain 60% friendship with Dwayne.
Free Ride (Call for a taxi)	Gain 60% friendship with Roman.
50% Off for All Clothing Stores	Gain 80% Relationship Status with Alex.
Health Boost (Call Carmen and select "Health Boost")	Gain 80% Relationship Status with Carmen.
Remove Up to 3 Wanted Stars (Call Kiki and select "Remove Wanted")	Gain 80% Relationship Status with Kiki.

Grand Theft Auto IV (continued)

Unlockables

Unlockable	How to Unlock
Rastah Color Huntley SUV	Complete 10 Package Delivery missions.
Remove Ammo Limit	Get 100% completion.

Grid

Livery Codes

Go to the "Enter Code" section from the main menu under Options, then input the codes.

Effect	Code
Aston Martin DBR9 *play.com* Livery	P47203845
BMW 320si Buchbinder Livery	F93857372
Pagani Zonda Micromania Livery	M38572343
WTCC Spec BMW 320si Gamestation Livery	G29782655

Guitar Hero: Aerosmith

Cheat Chords

Strum the following chords in the "Cheats" menu. A message should appear if you strummed them correctly. You can then turn them on or off in from the menu.

Effect	Code
Air Guitar (Guitarist plays without a guitar in the game)	(RY) (GR) (RY) (RY) (RB) (RB) (RB) (RB) (RB) (YB) (YB) (YO)
Hyperspeed (Faster Gameplay)	(YO) (YO) (YO) (YO) (YO) (RY) (RY) (RY) (RY) (RB) (RB) (RB) (RB) (RB) (YB) (YO) (YO)
No Fail (Makes it impossible to fail a song, doesn't work in Career mode, and disables online scores)	(GR) (B) (GR) (GY) (B) (GY) (RY) (O) (RY) (GY) (Y) (GY) (GR)
Performance Mode (No notes, just the song playing)	(GR) (GR) (RO) (RB) (GR) (GR) (RO) (RB)
Precision Mode (Makes it harder to miss notes)	(RY) (RB) (RB) (RY) (RY) (YB) (YB) (YB) (RB) (RY) (RB) (RB) (RY) (RY) (YB) (YB) (YB) (RB)
Unlock All Songs (except for "Pandora's Box" by Aerosmith)	(RY) (GR) (GR) (RY) (RY) (GR) (RY) (RY) (GR) GR) (RY) (RY) (GR) (RY) (RB)

Unlockables

Unlockable	How to Unlock
Character: DMC	Complete all of the songs in the fourth tier list to unlock him for purchase for $15,000.
Guitar: Doubleneck	Get a "5 Star" rank on all songs, except the bonus song, under the Expert difficulty.
Guitar: Get a Grip	Complete Career mode under the Hard difficulty.
Guitar: Nine Lives (Daredevil)	Complete Career mode under the Easy difficulty.
Guitar: Permanent Vacation	Complete the game under the Medium difficulty.
Guitar: Rock in a Hard Place (Zeitgeist)	Get a "5 Star" rank on all songs, except the bonus song, under the Medium difficulty.
Guitar: Toys in the Attic (Rocking Horse)	Get a "5 Star" rank on all songs, except the bonus song, under the Easy difficulty.
Guitar: Walk This Way	Complete Career mode under the Expert difficulty.
Song: "Joe Perry Guitar Battle" by Joe Perry	Complete "Guitar Battle vs. Joe Perry" after the sixth tier warm-up acts.

Guitar Hero: Aerosmith (continued)

Unlockables

Unlockable	How to Unlock
Song: "Kings and Queens" by Aerosmtih	Complete Career mode.

Half-Life 2: The Orange Box

Half-Life 2 Codes

Enter the code while playing. Codes can be entered at any time on any level.

Effect	Code
Restore Ammo (for current weapon)	R1,▲,●,×,■,R1,▲,■,×,●,R1
Restore Health by 25 Points	↑,↑,↓,↓,←,→,←,→,●,×
Unlock All Levels	←,←,←,←,L1,→,→,→,→,R1

Portal Codes

Enter these codes any time during gameplay.

Effect	Code
Create a Cube	↓,●,×,●,▲,↓,●,×,●,▲
Fire Energy Ball	↑,▲,▲,■,■,×,×,●,●,↑
Unlock All Levels	←,←,←,←,L1,→,→,→,→,R1

Harry Potter and the Order of the Phoenix

Room of Rewards Trophies

Successfully complete the indicated task to unlock the corresponding trophy.

Unlockable	How to Unlock
Characters Cup	Meet all 58 characters in Hogwarts
Defense Against the Dark Arts Cup	Cast all defensive spells in 6 duels
House Ghost Cup	Find all 4 House Ghosts
Nature Trail Cup	Find all animal footprints

Heavenly Sword

Difficulties

To unlock Hell mode, beat the game on Normal mode.

Making of Heavenly Sword

Unlock "Making of" videos by collecting the specified number of glyphs.

Unlockable	How to Unlock
Bringing Design to Life	Obtain 37 glyphs.
Capturing Performance	Obtain 42 glyphs.
Creating the Music	Obtain 86 glyphs.
Introduction	Obtain 3 glyphs.
The Sound of Combat	Obtain 77 glyphs.

Art Gallery

Unlock 107 pieces of concept and pre-production art by obtaining the following number of glyphs.

Unlockable	How to Unlock
Andy Serkis as Bohan	Obtain 26 glyphs.
Andy Serkis as Bohan (2nd)	Obtain 40 glyphs.
Andy Serkis as Bohan (3rd)	Obtain 96 glyphs.

Heavenly Sword (continued)

Unlockable	How to Unlock
Andy Serkis Facial Sketch	Obtain 119 glyphs.
Anime Character Concept Art	Obtain 88 glyphs.
Arena Balcony Concept Art	Obtain 69 glyphs.
Arena Concept Art	Obtain 67 glyphs.
Assassin Concept Art	Obtain 85 glyphs.
Assassin Weapon Concept Art	Obtain 84 glyphs.
Axeman Concept Art	Obtain 35 glyphs.
Back of Snowy Fort	Obtain 2 glyphs.
Back of Snowy Fort (2nd)	Obtain 102 glyphs.
Bazooka Concept Art	Obtain 52 glyphs.
Bohan and Raven Concept Art	Obtain 90 glyphs.
Bohan Armor Concept Art	Obtain 17 glyphs.
Bohan Armor Concept Art (2nd)	Obtain 105 glyphs.
Bohan Early Concept Art	Obtain 33 glyphs.
Bohan Early Concept Art (2nd)	Obtain 44 glyphs.
Bohan Early Concept Art (3rd)	Obtain 123 glyphs.
Bohan Promo Screenshot	Obtain 39 glyphs.
Bohan Promo Screenshot (2nd)	Obtain 49 glyphs.
Bohan Weapon Concept Art	Obtain 21 glyphs.
Central Hall Early Concept Art	Obtain 53 glyphs.
Ch. 5 Port Concept Art	Obtain 19 glyphs.
Chainman Concept Art	Obtain 66 glyphs.
Clansmen Concept Art	Obtain 63 glyphs.
Commander Concept Art	Obtain 94 glyphs.
Cover Art—Bazooka	Obtain 71 glyphs.
Cover Art—Bohan	Obtain 97 glyphs.
Cover Art—Nariko	Obtain 73 glyphs.
Cover Art—Power Stance	Obtain 110 glyphs.
Cover Art—Ranged Attack	Obtain 70 glyphs.
Crossbowman Concept Art	Obtain 104 glyphs.
Decrepit Temple Concept Art	Obtain 89 glyphs.
Desert Battleground Concept Art	Obtain 81 glyphs.
Desert Buildings Concept Art	Obtain 99 glyphs.
Desert Fort Concept Art	Obtain 93 glyphs.
Desert Level Concept Art	Obtain 116 glyphs.
Early Bohan Weapon Concept Art	Obtain 106 glyphs.
Early Packaging Concept Art	Obtain 72 glyphs.
Early Pond Concept Art	Obtain 111 glyphs.
Encampment Concept Art	Obtain 103 glyphs.
Encampment Concept Art (2nd)	Obtain 114 glyphs.
Environment Early Concept Art	Obtain 55 glyphs.
Environment Early Concept Art (2nd)	Obtain 59 glyphs.
Environment Early Concept Art (3rd)	Obtain 115 glyphs.
Flying Fox Costume Concept Art	Obtain 25 glyphs.

Heavenly Sword (continued)

Unlockable	How to Unlock
Flying Fox Facial Concept Art	Obtain 30 glyphs.
Forest Patch Concept Art	Obtain 57 glyphs.
Funeral Boat Concept Art	Obtain 124 glyphs.
Funeral Landscape Concept Art	Obtain 125 glyphs.
Funeral Landscape Painting	Obtain 126 glyphs.
Heaven and Hell Concept Art	Obtain 118 glyphs.
Heavenly Sword Concept Art	Obtain 60 glyphs.
Kai Concept Art	Obtain 6 glyphs.
Kai Early Concept Art	Obtain 8 glyphs.
Kai Early Concept Art (2nd)	Obtain 34 glyphs.
Kai Promo Screenshot	Obtain 46 glyphs.
Kai Promo Screenshot (2nd)	Obtain 127 glyphs.
Kai with Bow Concept Art	Obtain 29 glyphs.
Nariko Approaching Cage	Obtain 101 glyphs.
Nariko Color Sketch	Obtain 9 glyphs.
Nariko Costume Concept Art	Obtain 23 glyphs.
Nariko Early Concept Art	Obtain 80 glyphs.
Nariko Early Concept Art (2nd)	Obtain 87 glyphs.
Nariko Early Concept Art (3rd)	Obtain 109 glyphs.
Nariko Early Cover	Obtain 13 glyphs.
Nariko Imprisoned Concept Art	Obtain 64 glyphs.
Nariko Pencil Sketch	Obtain 12 glyphs.
Nariko Promo Screenshot	Obtain 20 glyphs.
Nariko Promo Screenshot (2nd)	Obtain 31 glyphs.
Nariko Promo Screenshot (2nd)	Obtain 129 glyphs.
Nariko with Heavenly Sword	Obtain 27 glyphs.
Natural Bridge Concept Art	Obtain 62 glyphs.
Oraguman Concept Art	Obtain 78 glyphs.
Oraguman Sketch	Obtain 79 glyphs.
Packaging Artwork	Obtain 98 glyphs.
Prison Approach Concept Art	Obtain 56 glyphs.
Prison Exterior Concept Art	Obtain 112 glyphs.
Prison Interior Concept Art	Obtain 113 glyphs.
Rain Battle Concept Art	Obtain 100 glyphs.
Raven Concept Art	Obtain 117 glyphs.
Raven God Concept Art	Obtain 121 glyphs.
Raven God Early Concept Art	Obtain 122 glyphs.
Raven God Facial Sketch	Obtain 120 glyphs.
Roach Concept Art	Obtain 41 glyphs.
Roach Weapon Concept Art	Obtain 83 glyphs.
Shen Concept Art	Obtain 4 glyphs.
Shen Promo Screenshot	Obtain 128 glyphs.
Shen with Staff	Obtain 5 glyphs.
Snowy Fort Concept Art	Obtain 1 glyph.

Heavenly Sword (continued)

Unlockable	How to Unlock
Swordsman Concept Art	Obtain 11 glyphs.
Swordsman Concept Art (2nd)	Obtain 51 glyphs.
The Sword Early Concept Art	Obtain 50 glyphs.
The Sword Landscape Concept Art	Obtain 107 glyphs.
The Sword Landscape Painting	Obtain 108 glyphs.
Throne Room Concept Art	Obtain 43 glyphs.
Tower Interior Concept Art	Obtain 92 glyphs.
Water Lift Concept Art	Obtain 91 glyphs.
Water Temple Interior	Obtain 95 glyphs.
Whiptail Costume Art	Obtain 75 glyphs.
Whiptail Early Concept Art	Obtain 38 glyphs.
Whiptail Early Concept Art (2nd)	Obtain 45 glyphs.
Whiptail Eel Concept Art	Obtain 36 glyphs.
Whiptail Promo Screenshot	Obtain 76 glyphs.
Young Kai Concept Art	Obtain 15 glyphs.
Young Nariko Sketch	Obtain 82 glyphs.

Hot Shots Golf: Out of Bounds

Capsules

Capsules contain items that are added to the course. They have no effect on the gameplay, they are just there for show.

Unlockable	How to Unlock
Armored Zombie	Play 20 rounds at Euro Classic G.C. (Regular Tee).
Bear	Play 20 rounds at Highland C.C. (Long Tee).
Blue Whale	Play 20 rounds at The Crown Links (Long Tee).
Child Witch	Play 20 rounds at Euro Classic G.C. (Long Tee).
Glider	Play 20 rounds at The Crown Links (Regular Tee).
Gnome	Play 20 rounds at Silver Peaks G.C. (Regular Tee).
Helicopter	Play 20 rounds at Highland C.C. (Regular Tee).
Jet Formation	Play 20 rounds at Okinawa Golf Resort (Regular Tee).
Lion	Play 20 rounds at Great Safari C.C. (Long Tee).
Manta	Play 20 rounds at Okinawa Golf Resort (Long Tee).
Rhino	Play 20 rounds at Great Safari C.C. (Regular Tee).
Unicorn	Play 20 rounds at Silver Peaks G.C. (Long Tee).

Juiced 2: Hot Import Nights

Driver DNA Car Unlockables

Enter the passwords in the DNA lab to unlock the special challenges. If you win the challenges, you unlock a custom version of the following cars.

Unlockable	How to Unlock
Audi TT 1.8L Quattro	YTHZ
BMW Z4 Roadster	GVDL
Frito-Lay Infiniti G35	MNCH
Holden Monaro	RBSG
Hyundai Coupe 2.7L V6	BSLU
Infiniti G35	MRHC

Juiced 2: Hot Import Nights (continued)

Unlockable	How to Unlock
Koenigsegg CCX	KDTR
Mitsubishi Prototype X	DOPX
Nissan 350Z	PRGN
Nissan Skyline R34 GT-R	JWRS
Saleen S7	WIKF
Seat Leon Cupra R	FAMQ

Kung Fu Panda (PS3)

Codes

From the main menu, select Extras and then select Cheats.

Effect	Code
All Multiplayer Characters	←,↓,←,→,↓
Big Head Mode (Story Mode)	↓,↑,←,→,→
Infinite Chi	↓,→,←,↑,↓
Invulnerability	↓,↓,→,↑,←
Dragon Warrior Outfit (Multiplayer Mode)	←,↓,→,←,↑
4x Damage Multiplier	↑,↓,↑,→,←

Lair

Passwords

Enter into the game's Cheat menu:

Password	Effect
chicken	Chicken Curry video
686F7420636F66666565	Hot Coffee video
koelsch	Unlocks Stable option for all levels on the Mission Select screen

LEGO Batman

Codes

Enter the codes on the second level of the Batcave at the computer above the outfit changer.

Effect	Code
Alfred	ZAQ637
Bat-Tank	KNTT4B
Batgirl	JKR331
Bruce Wayne	BDJ327
Bruce Wayne's Private Jet	LEA664
Catwoman (Classic)	M1AAWW
Catwoman's Motorcycle	HPL826
Clown Goon	HJK327
Commissioner Gordon	DDP967
Fishmonger	HGY748
Freeze Girl	XVK541
Garbage Truck	DUS483
Glideslam	BBD7BY
Goon Helicopter	GCH328
Harbor Helicopter	CHP735
Harley Quinn's Hammer Truck	RDT637
Joker Goon	UTF782
Joker Henchman	YUN924
Mad Hatter	JCA283
Mad Hatter's Glider	HS000W
Mad Hatter's Steamboat	M4DM4N
Man-Bat	NYU942
Military Policeman	MKL382
Mr. Freeze's Iceberg	ICYICE
Mr. Freeze's Kart	BCT229
Nightwing	MVY759
Penguin Goon	NKA238
Penguin Goon Submarine	BTN248

LEGO Batman (continued)

Effect	Code	Effect	Code
Penguin Henchman	BJH782	Riddler Henchman	XEU824
Penguin Minion	KJP748	Riddler's Jet	HAHAHA
Poison Ivy Goon	GTB899	Robin's Submarine	TTF453
Police Bike	LJP234	S.W.A.T.	HTF114
Police Boat	PLC999	Sailor	NAV592
Police Car	KJL832	Scientist	JFL786
Police Helicopter	CWR732	Security Guard	PLB946
Police Marksman	HKG984	The Joker (Tropical)	CCB199
Police Officer	JRY983	The Joker's Van	JUK657
Police Van	MAC788	Two-Face's Armored Truck	EFE933
Police Watercraft	VJD328	Yeti	NJL412
Riddler Goon	CRY928	Zoo Sweeper	DWR243

Extra Codes

Effect	Code	Effect	Code
Always Score Multiply	9LRGNB	Ice Rink	KLKL4G
Area Effect	TL3EKT	Immune to Freeze	JXUDY6
Armor Plating	N8JZEK	Invincible	WYD5CP
Bats	XFP4E2	Minikit Detector	ZXGH9J
Beep Beep	RAFTU8	More Batarang Targets	XWP645
Character Studs	DY13BD	More Detonators	TNTN6B
Decoy	TQ09K3	Piece Detector	KHJ544
Disguise	GEC3MD	Power Brick Detector	MMN786
Extra Toggle	EWAW7W	Regenerate Hearts	HJH7HJ
Extra Hearts	ML3KHP	Score x2	N4NR3E
Fast Batarangs	JRBDCB	Score x4	CX9MAT
Fast Build	GHJ2DY	Score x6	MLVNF2
Fast Grapple	RM4PR8	Score x8	WCCDB9
Fast Walk	ZOLM6N	Score x10	18HW07
Faster Pieces	EVG26J	Silhouettes	YK4TPH
Flaming Batarangs (Used with heat batman)	D8NYWH	Slam	BBD7BY
		Sonic Pain	THTL4X
Freeze Batarang	XPN4NG	Stud Magnet	LK2DY4

LEGO Indiana Jones: The Original Adventures

Character Codes

Enter the codes on the blackboard in the math classroom of Barnett College (the 2nd door on the left in the main hallway).

Effect	Code	Effect	Code
Bandit	12N68W	Belloq (Jungle)	TDR197
Bandit Swordsman	1MK4RT	Belloq (Robes)	VEO29L
Barranca	04EM94	British Officer	VJ5TI9
Bazooka Trooper (Crusade)	MK83R7	British Troop Commander	B73EUA
Bazooka Trooper (Raiders)	S93Y5R	British Troop Soldier	DJ5I2W
Belloq	CHN3YU	Captain Katanga	VJ3TT3

LEGO Indiana Jones: The Original Adventures (continued)

Effect	Code
Chatter Lal	ENW936
Chatter Lal (Thuggee)	CNH4RY
Chen	3NK48T
Colonel Dietrich	2K9RKS
Colonel Vogel	8EAL4H
Dancing Girl	C7EJ21
Donovan	3NFTU8
Elsa (Desert)	JSNRT9
Elsa (Officer)	VMJ5US
Enemy Boxer	8246RB
Enemy Butler	VJ48W3
Enemy Guard	VJ7R51
Enemy Guard (Mountains)	YR47WM
Enemy Officer	572 E61
Enemy Officer (Desert)	2MK450
Enemy Pilot	B84ELP
Enemy Radio Operator	1MF94R
Enemy Soldier (Desert)	4NSU7Q
Fedora	V75YSP
First Mate	0GIN24
Grail Knight	NE6THI
Hovitos Tribesman	H0V1SS
Indiana Jones (Desert Disguise)	4J8S4M
Indiana Jones (Officer)	VJ85OS
Jungle Guide	24PF34
Kao Kan	WM046L
Kazim	NRH23J
Kazim (Desert)	3M29TJ
Lao Che	2NK479
Maharaja	NFK5N2
Major Toht	13NS01
Masked Bandit	N48SF0
Mola Ram	FJUR31
Monkey Man	3RF6YJ
Pankot Assassin	2NKT72
Pankot Guard	VN28RH
Sherpa Brawler	VJ37WJ
Sherpa Gunner	ND762W
Slave Child	0E3ENW
Thuggee	VM683E
Thuggee Acolyte	T2R3F9
Thuggee Slavedriver	VBS7GW
Village Dignitary	KD48TN
Village Elder	4682 E1
Willie (Dinner Suit)	VK93R7
Willie (Pajamas)	MEN4IP
Wu Han	3NSLT8

Item Codes

Enter the codes on the blackboard in the math classroom of Barnett College (the 2nd door on the left in the main hallway).

Effect	Code
Artifact Detector	VIKED7
Beep Beep	VNF59Q
Character Treasure	VIES2R
Disarm Enemies	VKRNS9
Disguises	4ID1N6
Fast Build	V83SL0
Fast Dig	378RS6
Fast Fix	FJ59WS
Fertilizer	B1GW1F
Ice Rink	33GM7J
Parcel Detector	VUT673
Poo Treasure	WWQ1SA
Regenerate Hearts	MDLP69
Secret Characters	3X44AA
Silhouettes	3HE85H
Super Scream	VN3R7S
Super Slap	0P1TA5
Treasure Magnet	H86LA2
Treasure x2	VM4TS9
Treasure x4	VLWEN3
Treasure x6	V84RYS
Treasure x8	A72E1M
Treasure x10	VI3PS8

LEGO Star Wars: The Complete Saga

Characters

To use the codes, enter the Cantina, go to the bar, access the codes command, and type in the codes.

Unlockable Characters	Codes
Admiral Ackbar	ACK646
Battle Droid Commander	KPF958
Boba Fett (Boy)	GGF539
Boss Nass	HHY697
Captain Tarpals	QRN714
Count Dooku	DDD748
Darth Maul	EUK421
Ewok	EWK785
General Grievous	PMN576
Greedo	ZZR636
IG-88	GIJ989
Imperial Guard	GUA850
Indiana Jones	After you watch the trailer for the upcoming Indiana Jones game in the Bonus Room, Indy will become a playable character.

Unlockable Characters	Codes
Jango Fett	KLJ897
Ki-Adi-Mundi	MUN486
Luminara	LUM521
Padmé	VBJ322
R2-Q5	EVILR2
Sandtrooper	CBR954
Stormtrooper	NBN431
Super Battle Droid	XZNR21
Taun We	PRX482
Vulture Droid	BDC866
Watto	PLL967
Zam Wesell	584HJF

Ships

Unlockable Ships	Codes
Droid Trifighter	AAB123
Imperial Shuttle	HUT845
Slave I	Collect all 10 Minikits on each level.
TIE Fighter	DBH897
TIE Interceptor	INT729
Zam's Speeder	UUU875

Skills

Unlockable Skills	Codes
Disguise	BRJ437
Force Grapple Leap	CLZ738

LittleBigPlanet

Costumes

Complete the corresponding level without dying to unlock the following costumes.

Unlockable	How to Unlock
Bunny Tail	The Collectors Lair
Chicken Beak	The Dancers Court
Chicken Gloves	Great Magicians Palace
Chicken Tail	Elephant Temple
Cowboy Boots and Leather Gloves	Boom Town
Cowboy Hat	Serpent Shrine
Dinosaur Mask	The Construction Site
Dinosaur Tail	Lowrider

LittleBigPlanet (continued)	
Unlockable	**How to Unlock**
Googly Eye Glasses	Sensei's Lost Castle
Green Sock Puppet	Subway
Japanese Festival Headband	The Terrible Oni's Volcano
Japanese Festival Robe	Endurance Dojo
Jeans with a Belt and Cowboy Bandana	The Mines
Moustache	Burning Forest
Neon Helmet	The Bunker
Pirate Hat	Skate to Victory
Pirate Hook and Pirate Eye Patch	First Steps
Pirate Waistcoat and Pirate Shorts	Get a Grip
Ringmaster Jacket	Swinging Safari
Ringmaster Top Hat and Gold Monocle	The Meerkat Kingdom
Roman Armor	The Darkness
Roman Helmet	Skulldozer
White Neon Eyes	The Frozen Tundra
Wooden Sword	The Wedding Reception
Yellow Head	The Collector

Level Completion Prizes

Gain the following prizes by achieving 100% level completion (collect all the prize bubbles on that level).

Unlockable	How to Unlock
Anteater concept and Anteater concept with frame	The Mines 100%
Bad Witch concept, Bad Witch concept with frame	The Bunker 100%
Big Cat and Big Cat concept with frame	Burning Forest 100%
Big Sumo, The Islands concept, and The Islands concept with frame	Sensei's Lost Castle 100%
Boom Town concept and Boom Town concept with frame	Boom Town 100%
Boss concept, Boss concept with frame, and a monster truck	The Construction Site 100%
Bunny Tail and The Gardens	Skate to Victory 100%
Circus concept, Circus concept with frame	The Frozen Tundra 100%
Costumes concept and Costumes concept with frame	Elephant Temple 100%
Early Sackboy and Early Sackboy with frame	Lowrider 100%
Fairy Tale concept and Fairy Tale concept with frame	Get a Grip 100%
Grabbing Machine, Rock God, and Rock God with frame	Subway 100%
Graveyard concept, The Wedding concept with frame, and Skulldozer	Skulldozer 100%
Jumping Tank, Very First LBP concept, Very First LBP concept with frame	The Collectors Lair 100%
LBP concept with frame, Background Environment concept	The Dancers Court 100%
LBP Cosmos concept, Magicians Box, and Cosmos concept with frame	Great Magicians Palace 100%
Savannah concept and Savannah concept with frame	Swinging Safari 100%

LittleBigPlanet (continued)

Unlockable	How to Unlock
Sheriff Zapata's Explosives Machine, The Mines concept with frame, and The Mines concept	Serpent Shrine 100%
Temple concept, Temple concept with frame, and a Mystical Dragon	Endurance Dojo 100%
Terrible Oni, Islands City concept, and Islands City concept with frame	The Terrible Volcano 100%
The Collector Boss, The Collector's Pod, and the Collector	The Collector 100%
The Gardens concept and The Gardens concept with frame	First Steps 100%
The Savannah and The Pink Scarf	The Meerkat Kingdom 100%
Theme Characters concept with frame and Theme Characters Concept	The Darkness 100%
Wrestling Ring with frame and Wrestling concept	The Wedding Reception 100%

Trophies

Complete each condition to get the allotted Trophies. There are 36 Bronze Trophies, 8 Silver Trophies, 3 Gold Trophies, and 1 Platinum Trophy.

Unlockable	How to Unlock
100% Complete (Platinum)	Earn all LittleBigPlanet trophies to unlock this platinum trophy
20X Multiplier! (Silver)	Get a 20X Multiplier
2X Multiplier! (Bronze)	Get a 2X Multiplier
8X Multiplier! (Bronze)	Get an 8X Multiplier
Artist (Bronze)	Place a sticker
Booty Master (Silver)	Collect all the prize bubbles on the story levels
Celebrity (Silver)	You were hearted by 5 or more people as a player
Cranium Collector (Bronze)	Kill 100 creatures across all levels
Create (Gold)	A level you published was hearted by 50 or more people and you were hearted by 30 or more people
Creator (Bronze)	Build and save a level with the thermometer more than 30% full
Crowd Pleaser (Silver)	A level you published was played by 50 or more people
Dr. Frankenstein (Silver)	Create a living creature with at least 2 eyes, 2 legs or wheels, and a brain
Expert Creator (Bronze)	Complete all levels in the Tutorials
Fashion Sense (Bronze)	Choose a costume for your sackperson with at least one item on your head, at least one item on your body, and a material
Feel the love (Silver)	A level you published was hearted by 10 or more people
FIRST! (Bronze)	Be among the first 10 people to complete a community level
Forager (Bronze)	Collect 25% of the prize bubbles on the story levels
Friendly (Bronze)	Complete a level with more than one player
Hi Score (Silver)	Collect 1,000,000 points over all levels you have played
Homemaker (Bronze)	Place 10 stickers or decorations in your pod
Incredible Height! (Bronze)	Travel to an incredible height
Incredible Speed! (Bronze)	Travel at incredible speed
Just Beginning (Silver)	Complete all the main path story levels

LittleBigPlanet (continued)

Unlockable	How to Unlock
Look What I Made! (Bronze)	A level you published was played by 5 or more people
Neighbourhood (Bronze)	Watch heart 5 community levels
Networking (Bronze)	Heart 3 authors
Opinionated (Bronze)	Tag a community level
Party Person (Bronze)	Complete a level online with 3 other players who are on your friends list
Play (Gold)	Complete all story levels without dying, with the exception of those levels that only end when you die
Publisher (Bronze)	Publish a level
Sackbird (Bronze)	Spend 8 seconds or more in the air
Secret Stickerist (Bronze)	Unlock the race in First Steps
Share (Gold)	Play 150 community levels, tag 50 community levels and heart 10 community levels
Socialite (Bronze)	Complete a level online with 3 other players who are not on your friends list
Sticky Fingers (Bronze)	Collect 50% of the prize bubbles on the story levels
Talkative (Bronze)	Post a comment on a community level
Team Creator (Bronze)	Build and save a level with more than one player with the thermometer more than 30% full
The Canyons (Bronze)	Complete all levels in The Canyons
The Gardens (Bronze)	Complete all levels in The Gardens
The Islands (Bronze)	Complete all levels in The Islands
The Metropolis (Bronze)	Complete all levels in The Metropolis
The Savannah (Bronze)	Complete all levels in The Savannah
The Temples (Bronze)	Complete all levels in The Temples
The Wedding (Bronze)	Complete all levels in The Wedding
Top of the Class (Bronze)	Win a 4-player game
Traveller (Bronze)	Complete a community level
Treasure Hunter (Bronze)	Collect 75% of the prize bubbles on the story levels
Trendsetter (Bronze)	Place a sticker or a decoration on another player's sackperson

Madden NFL '07

Codes

Code	Effect
XL7SP1	Cannot throw an INT or Fumble the ball for 1 half
WROAOR	QB will have 100% accuracy for 1 half
5LAWO0	The opponent throws lob passes for 1 half
B57QLU	Unlock the 1958 Colts Gold card
1PL1FL	Unlock the 1966 Packers Gold card
MIE6WO	Unlock the 1968 Jets Gold card
CL2TOE	Unlock the 1970 Browns Gold card
NOEB7U	Unlock the 1972 Dolphins Gold card
YOOFLA	Unlock the 1974 Steelers Gold card
MOA11I	Unlock the 1976 Raiders Gold card

Madden NFL '07 (continued)

Code	Effect
C8UM7U	Unlock the 1977 Broncos Gold card
VIU007	Unlock the 1978 Dolphins Gold card
NLAPH3	Unlock the 1980 Raiders Gold card
COAGI4	Unlock the 1981 Chargers Gold card
WL8BRI	Unlock the 1982 Redskins Gold card
H0EW7I	Unlock the 1983 Raiders Gold card
M1AM1E	Unlock the 1984 Dolphins Gold card
QOETO8	Unlock the 1985 Bears Gold card
ZI8S2L	Unlock the 1986 Giants Gold card
SP2A8H	Unlock the 1988 49ers Gold card
2L4TRO	Unlock the 1990 Eagles Gold card
J1ETRI	Unlock the 1991 Lions Gold card
W9UVI9	Unlock the 1992 Cowboys Gold card
DLA3I7	Unlock the 1993 Bills Gold card
DR7EST	Unlock the 1994 49ers Gold card
F8LUST	Unlock the 1996 Packers Gold card
FIES95	Unlock the 1998 Broncos Gold card
S9OUSW	Unlock the 1999 Rams Gold card
YI8P8U	Unlock the Aloha Stadium Gold card
RLA9R7	Unlock the Super Bowl XLI Gold card
WRLUF8	Unlock the Super Bowl XLII Gold card
NIEV4A	Unlock the Super Bowl XLIII Gold card
M5AB7L	Unlock the Super Bowl XLIV Gold card

Major League Baseball 2K7

To enter these codes select My 2K7. Then select Enter Cheat Code.

Unlockable	Code
Boosts a team's power rating by 25% for 1 inning	mightymick
Boosts the hitting of the 3, 4, 5 hitters in the lineup by 50% for 1 game	triplecrown
Boosts your ability to hit home runs during the game just like The Mick	m4murder
Mickey will pinch hit	phmantle
Unlocks everything	Derek Jeter
Unlocks Mickey Mantle in free agency	themick

Marvel Ultimate Alliance

Enter these codes while playing.

Unlockable	Code
God Mode	↑, ↓, ↑, ↓, ↑, ←, ↓, →, START
Super Speed	↑, ←, ↑, →, ↓, →, START
Touch of Death	←, →, ↓, ↓, →, ←, START

Enter these codes at the Team menu.

Unlockable	Code
100K	↑, ↑, ↑, ←, →, ←, START
All Characters	↑, ↑, ↓, ↓, ←, ←, ←, START
All Costumes	↑, ↓, ↑, ↓, ←, →, ←, →, ↑, ↓, START

Marvel Ultimate Alliance (continued)

Unlockable	Code
All Powers	←, →, ←, →, ↑, ↓, ↑, ↓, ←, →, START
Level 99	↑, ←, ↑, ←, ↓, →, ↓, →, START
Unlocks Daredevil	←, ←, →, →, ↑, ↓, ↑, ↓, START
Unlocks Silver Surfer	↓, ←, ←, ↑, →, ↑, ↓, ←, START

Enter these codes at the Review menu.

Unlockable	Code
All Cinematics	↑, ←, ←, ↑, →, →, ↑, START
All Comics	←, →, →, ←, ↑, ↑, →, START
All Concept Art	↓, ↓, ↓, →, →, ←, ↓, START
All Wallpapers	↑, ↓, →, ←, ↑, ↑, ↓, START

Medal of Honor: Airborne

Codes

During gameplay, hold L1, R1 and push ■, ●, ▲, ×, × to call up the code screen, then enter the codes below.

Unlockable	How to Unlock
Health Restoration	Hold L1, R1 and push ▲, ■, ■, ▲, ×, ●
Infinite Ammo	Hold L1, R1 and push ●, ●, ▲, ■, ×, ▲

Metal Gear Solid 4: Guns of the Patriots

Bonus Weapons

Unlockable	How to Unlock
Bandanna	Complete a single-player session, on any difficulty, without killing anyone (including bosses).
Desert Eagle, Long Barrel	Earn the Fox emblem on a single-player session.
Digital Camera	In the Nomad vehicle during the mission intermission; you can unlock a special photo by picking up this item in stage 4 instead of earlier.
Patriot Future Assault Weapon	Earn the Big Boss emblem on a single-player session.
Race (Ricochet) Gun	Clear the single-player game once.
Scanning Plug S	Log more than 10 hours of *Metal Gear Online* play time on the same profile as your *Metal Gear 4* game. You purchase this from Drebin.
Solar Gun	Collect the five statues (those of the four Battle Beauties and the Frog Soldier/Haven Troopers in stage 1) using non-lethal means on their respective idols.
Stealth Item	Complete a single-player session without instigating a single alert (caution is okay, but not alert). You can do this on any difficulty.
Thor 45-70	Earn the Fox Hound emblem on a single-player session.
World War I Pistol	Earn the Hound emblem on a single-player session.

Completion Unlockables

Unlockable	How to Unlock
Big Boss Extreme Difficulty	Complete the single-player mode once (and saving the cleared data).
New Combat Vests	Clear the single-player game once.

Metal Gear Solid 4: Guns of the Patriots (continued)

Costumes

Unlockable	How to Unlock
Altair	Obtain the Assassin emblem.
Civilian Disguise	Start Eastern Europe level.
Corpse Camo	Get 41 continues or more in a single playthrough to unlock this Octocamo.
Middle East Militia Disguise	Middle East in the Militia Safe House.
South American Rebel Disguise	South America (Cove Valley Village).
Suit	Clear the game once.

Dolls/Statues

Unlockable	How to Unlock
Crying Wolf Doll/Statue	In a side of a building just where you start after killing her beast form
Frog Soldier Doll/Statue	At the garage at the end of the battle
Laughing Beast Doll/Statue	On a bed in a little room
Raging Raven Doll/Statue	On the upper floor on a corner
Screaming Mantis Doll/Statue	On the corridor where you started

Face Paint

Unlockable	How to Unlock
Big Boss's	Earn the Big Boss emblem on a single-player session.
Crying Wolf	Defeat the Battle Beauty (human form) Crying Wolf by non-lethal means.
Drebin	Purchase and keep more than 60 different weapons.
FaceCamo	Defeat the Battle Beauty Laughing Octopus (the overall battle, no specifics involved).
Laughing Octopus	Defeat the Battle Beauty (human form) Laughing Octopus by non-lethal means.
Otacon	Shock Dr. Emmerich using the Metal Gear II during the intermission scene.
Raging Raven	Defeat the Battle Beauty (human form) Raging Raven by non-lethal means.
Raiden Mask A	Shock Sunny using the Metal Gear II during the intermission scene.
Raiden Mask B	Shock Dr. Naomi Hunter using the Metal Gear II during the intermission scene.
Roy Campbell	Shock Colonel Campbell using the Metal Gear II during the intermission scene.
Screaming Mantis	Defeat the Battle Beauty (human form) Screaming Mantis by non-lethal means.
Young Snake	Beat Act 2.
Young Snake with Bandana	Beat Act 2.

iPod Tunes

Snake's iPod can download specific tunes throughout the course of the game. Some songs have an additional "secret" effect when it is played in the game.

Unlockable	How to Unlock
Beyond the Bounds (increases stun damage done by Snake from non-lethal weapons)	Stage 4 Shadow Moses, Tank Hangar. After power is restored, backtrack to the upper catwalk and explore all rooms.

Metal Gear Solid 4: Guns of the Patriots (continued)

Unlockable	How to Unlock
Big Boss (increases stun damage and increases Snake's accuracy when played)	Earn the Big Boss emblem.
Bio Hazard	Frisk the resistance fighter in Easter Europe.
Bio Hazard (cause soldiers held by Snake to scream in terror)	Stage 3 Europe, Midtown.
Boktai 2 Theme	Act 2, Mission Briefing, upstairs in the Nomad.
Bon Dance	Act 2, Marketplace.
Destiny's Call (causes soldiers held by Snake to go enraged)	A random gift from a militia or rebel soldier if Snake gives them a healing item.
Flowing Destiny (causes soldiers held by Snake to weep like a little girl)	Stage 4 Shadow Moses, Canyon. Before leaving the canyon area, examine the rocky walls for a hole hiding this item.
Fury, The (causes soldiers held by Snake to go enraged)	Stage 2 South America, Cove Valley Village. Inside the fire ravaged house.
Inorino Uta	Act 1, Mission Briefing.
Level 3 Warning	Act 1, Advent Palace.
Lunar Knights Main Theme	Act 4, Mission Briefing, upstairs in the Nomad.
Metal Gear 20 Years History: Part 2	Act 4, Warhead Storage Building B2.
Metal Gear 20 Years History: Part 3	Act 2, South America Confinement Facility. In room with beds inside the house.
Metal Gear Solid Main Theme (The Document Remix)	Act 5, under hatch to the left at the beginning of area.
MGS 4 Love Theme / Action (causes soldiers held by Snake to weep like a little girl)	A random gift from a militia or rebel soldier if Snake gives them a healing item.
On Alert	Act 3, Midtown N Sector.
One Night in Neo Kobe City (causes soldiers held by Snake to laugh)	Act 3, Midtown, hold-up PMC.
Opening—Old L.A. 2040 (increases Snake's accuracy)	Stage 4 Shadow Moses, Nuclear Warhead Storage B2. Input 78925 into Otacon's lab computer.
Policenaughts Ending (causes soldiers held by Snake to fall asleep on touch)	Stage 4 Shadow Moses, Nuclear Warhead Storage B2. Input 13462 into Otacon's lab computer.
Rock Me (increases Snake's amount of life recovered from items and other means)	Stage 2 South America, Confinement Facility. Island in the southeastern quadrant.
Sailor (increases Snake's amount of life recovered from items and other means)	Stage 2 South America, Vista Mansion. Between the east wall and a cargo container
Shin Bokura no Taiyou Theme	Act 3, Mission Briefing, upstairs in the Nomad.
Show Time (causes soldiers held by Snake to scream in terror)	A random gift from a militia or rebel soldier if Snake gives them a healing item.
Snake Eater (increase the life recovery rate of Snake through items and other actions)	Unlocked by earning all 40 game clear emblems.
Subsistence (increase Snake's accuracy)	Play at least one game of *Metal Gear Online*. You must start the match with at least two players.
Test Subject's Duality	Act 3, Midtown S Sector.

Metal Gear Solid 4: Guns of the Patriots (continued)

Unlockable	How to Unlock
The Best Is Yet To Come	Act 4, Snow Field. Just before the "Disc Change" Codec scene.
The Essence of Vince	Act 3, Echo's Beacon.
The Fury	Act 2, in the Cave Valley Village in badly burned building.
Theme of Solid Snake	Act 1, Millennium Park.
Theme of Tara	Act 1, Militia Safehouse. Just before seeing the unmanned flying-bomber on the table.
Warhead Storage	Act 4, Tank Hanger. Upper floor ventilation shaft.
Yell (Dead Cell)	Act 4, Casting Facility North.
Zanzibarland Breeze	Act 1, Urban Ruins before cutscene.

Unlockable Emblems

Unlockable	How to Unlock
Ant Emblem	Shake 50 enemies for items.
Assassin's Emblem	Beat the game with 50+ knife kills, 50+ CQC holds, and 25 or less alerts.
Bear Emblem	Choke 100 enemies to death.
Bee Emblem	Use the Scanning Plug S or Syringe on 50 enemies.
Big Boss Emblem	Beat the game on the highest difficulty with no deaths, no alerts, no kills, no recovery items, no stealth suit, no bandana items, in under 5 hours.
Blue Bird Emblem	Give friendly soldiers 50 items.
Centipede	Get less than 75 alert phases, less than 250 kills, and over 25 continues.
Chicken	Get over 150 alert phases, over 500 kills, over 50 continues, use over 50 recovery items and finish the game in over 35 hours.
Cow	Activate over 100 alerts.
Crocodile	Have over 400 kills.
Eagle Emblem	Get 150 headshots.
Fox Emblem	Beat the game on Normal or higher with no deaths, 5 or less alerts, no kills, no recovery items, no stealth suit, no bandana items, in under 6 hours.
Fox Hound Emblem	Beat the game on Hard or higher with no deaths, 3 or less alerts, no kills, no recovery items, no stealth suit, no bandana items, in under 5.5 hours.
Frog Emblem	Dive or roll 200 times.
Gecko Emblem	Press against walls for a total of 1 hour.
Giant Panda Emblem	Complete the game after 30 cumulative hours of play.
Gibbon Emblem	Hold up 50 enemies.
Hawk Emblem	Be admired by 25 friendly soldiers.
Hog Emblem	Get 10 combat highs.
Hound Emblem	Beat the game on hard or higher with no deaths, 3 or less alerts, no kills, no recovery items, no stealth suit, no bandana items, in under 6.5 hours.
Hyena Emblem	Pick up 400 dropped weapons.
Inch Worm Emblem	Crawl on the ground for a total of 1 hour.
Jaguar	Get over 75 alert phases, less than 250 kills, and less than 25 continues.

Metal Gear Solid 4: Guns of the Patriots (continued)

Unlockable	How to Unlock
Leopard	Get over 75 alert phases, less than 250 kills, and over 25 continues.
Little Gray Emblem	Collect all 69 weapons.
Lobster Emblem	Spend a total of 2.5 hours crouching.
Mantis	Finish the game with no alerts activated; no continues; no rations, noodles, or regains used; and in under 5 hours.
Octopus	Beat the game without activating any alert phases.
Panther	Get over 75 alert phases, over 250 kills, and less than 25 continues.
Pig	Use more than 50 recovery items.
Pigeon	Beat the game without killing a single person (Gekkos and Dwarf Gekkos don't count).
Puma	Get over 75 alert phases, over 250 kills, and over 25 continues.
Rabbit	Flick through 100 *Playboy* pages.
Rabbit Emblem	Look at 100 *Playboy* pages.
Raven	Beat the game in under 5 hours.
Scarab	Perform over 100 rolls.
Scorpion	Get less than 75 alert Phases, less than 250 kills, and less than 25 continues.
Spider	Get less than 75 alert phases, over 250 kills, and over 25 continues.
Tarantula	Get less than 75 alert phases, over 250 kills, and less than 25 continues.
Tortoise	Spend more than 60 minutes inside the drum can or cardboard box (this can be done throughout the game, not all at once),
Wolf	Beat the game with no continues and no rations, regains, or noodles used.

Mobile Suit Gundam: Crossfire

Unlockable	Code
Amuro Ray	Beat EFF campaign on Very Hard mode once, and load the clear data
Char Aznable	Beat Zeon campaign on Very Hard mode once, and load the clear data
Fraw Bow	Beat any campaign on Very Hard and load the clear data
Gelgoog	Become Brigadier General and play on Very Hard mode, and just after you get the Hildolfr you should unlock the Gelgoog
Gundam	Reach the rank of Warrant General
Hildolfr	Become Brigadier General and play on Very Hard mode in early December before the unidentified enemy mission
Kai Shiden	Beat any campaign on Very Hard and load the clear data

Motorstorm

Enter this code at the main menu.

Unlockable	Code
Unlock Everything	Hold L1, L2, R1, R2, R2 pushed up, L2 pushed down

Enter this code while the game is paused.

Unlockable	Code
Big Head on ATVs and Bikes	Hold L1, L2, R1, R2, R2 pushed right, L1 pushed left

MX Vs. ATV Untamed

Unlockables

Type the following codes in the Cheats menu to unlock the gear.

Unlockable	How to Unlock
All Handlebars	NOHANDS
FOX Riding Gear	CRAZYLIKEA

NASCAR 08

Passwords

Submit these cheats at the Cheat Code screen under Options at the main menu.

Password	Effect
checkered flag	Unlock all chase mode cars
EA SPORTS CAR	Unlock EA SPORTS CAR
race the pack	Unlock fantasy drivers
walmart everyday	Unlock Wal-Mart car and track

NBA 07

To enter these passwords, select Options, then Trophy Room and then select Team Jerseys. While in Team Jerseys, press ■ to enter these passwords.

Unlockable	Password
Charlotte Bobcats Secondary Road Uniform	JKL846ETK5
New Jersey Nets Secondary Road Uniform	NB79D965D2
Utah Jazz Secondary Road Uniform	228GG7585G
Washington Wizards Secondary Road Uniform	PL5285F37F

NBA 2K7

Enter these passwords in the Codes menu under Features.

Unlockable	Code
ABA Ball	payrespect
Defensive Awareness	getstops
Maximum Durability for One Game	ironman
Offensive Awareness	inthezone
Unlimited Stamina for One Game	norest
All-Star Uniforms	syt6cii
Bobcats Secondary	bcb8sta
Jazz Secondary	zjb3lau
Nets Secondary	nrd4esj
Wizards Secondary	zw9idla
St. Patrick Day Uniforms	tpk7sgn
International All-Stars	tns9roi
NBA 2K Team	bestsim
Superstar Team	rta1spe
Topps 2K Sports All-Stars	topps2ksports
2007 All-Star Ball	ply8mia
2007 All-Star Uniforms	syt6cii
New Orleans Hornets Uniforms (Valentine's Day)	vdr5lya

NBA 2K8

Unlockables

Go to the Features menu and select the Codes section to enter the following codes.

Unlockable	How to Unlock
2008 All-Star NBA Uniforms	haeitgyebs
2K Sports Team	2ksports
ABA Ball	payrespect
Bobcats Racing	agtaccsin
Bobcats Racing Uniform	agtaccsinr
NBA Development Team	nba2k
Pacers' Second Jersey	cpares
St. Patrick's Day Jerseys	uclerehanp
Valentine's Day Jerseys	amcnreo
Visual Concepts Team	vcteam

NBA Live 08

Shoes

From the main menu go to "My NBA Live" then "EA Sports Extras" then select "NBA Codes" and enter the following case-sensitive codes.

Unlockable	How to Unlock
Adidas Gil-Zero (All-Star Edition)	23DN1PPOG4
Adidas Tim Duncan Stealth (All-Star Edition)	FE454DFJCC

NBA Street Homecourt

Unlockable	Code
Brand Jordan Outfit 2	Get 10 blocks in a game
Brand Jordan Outfit 4	Get 10 steals in a game
Chicago All-Stars	Beat the Chicago Bulls in a Back to Basics game
Detroit All-Stars	Defeat the Detroit Pistons in a GB Battle
Jordan 9.5 Team	Win 5 Back to Basics games
Jordan 9.5 Team	Win 5 GB Battles
Jordan Hoops Lo	Win 15 GB Battles
Jordan Hoops Lo	Win 15 Back to Basics games
Jordan Laney 23	Win 30 Back to Basics games
Jordan Show Em Lo	Win 30 GB Battles
Jordan XXI PE	Win 100 Pick Up games
Los Angeles All-Stars	Defeat the Los Angeles Lakers in a Pick Up game
New Jersey All-Stars	Defeat the New Jersey Nets in a Trick Battle
New York All-Stars	Defeat the New York Knicks in a GB Battle
Oakland All-Stars	Defeat the Golden State Warriors in a Trick Battle
Jordan 9.5 Team	Win 5 Pick Up games
Jordan 9.5 Team	Win 5 Trick Battles
Jordan Hoops Lo	Win 15 Pick Up games
Jordan Hoops Lo	Win 15 Trick Battles
Jordan Laney 23	Win 30 Pick Up games
Jordan Show Em Lo	Win 30 Trick Battles

NCAA Football 08

Rivalry Trophies

Play the corresponding games to unlock the trophy.

Unlockable	How to Unlock
Administaff Bayou Bucket	Houston Vs. Rice
Anniversary Award	Bowling Green Vs. Kent State
Apple Cup	Washington Vs. Washington State
Backyard Bowl	West Virginia Vs. Pittsburgh
Battle for Illibuck	Ohio State Vs. Indiana
Battle for the Bell	Tulane Vs. Southern Miss
Battle of I-10	UTEP Vs. New Mexico State
Battle of I-25	New Mexico State Vs. New Mexico
Battle of I-75	Bowling Green Vs. Toledo
Bedlam Game	Oklahoma State Vs. Oklahoma
Beehive Bell	Utah Vs. Utah State
Beehive Boot	Utah State Vs. BYU or Utah
Big Game	Cal Vs. Stanford
Black and Blue Bowl	Southern Miss Vs. Memphis
Black Diamond Trophy	West Virginia Vs. Virginia Tech
Border War	Colorado State Vs. Wyoming
Civil War	Oregon State Vs. Oregon
Clean, Old-fashioned Hate	Georgia Vs. Georgia Tech
Commander in Chief Trophy	Air Force Vs. Navy or Army
Commonwealth Cup	Virginia Tech Vs. Virginia
Cy-Hawk Trophy	Iowa State Vs. Iowa
Deep South's Oldest Rivalry	Auburn Vs. Georgia
Egg Bowl	Ole Miss Vs. Mississippi
Florida-Georgia Game	Florida Vs. Georgia
Floyd of Rosedale	Minnesota Vs. Iowa
Fremont Cannon	UNKV Vs. Nevada
Golden Boot	Arkansas Vs. LSU
Governor's Victory Bell	Penn State Vs. Minnesota
Governor's Cup	Louisville Vs. Kentucky
Governor's Cup	Florida Vs. Florida State
Holy War	BYU Vs. Utah
Ireland Trophy	Boston College Vs. Notre Dame
Iron Bowl	Alabama Vs. Auburn
Iron Skillet	TCV Vs. SMU
Jefferson-Eppes Trophy	Florida State Vs. Virginia
Jewels Shillelagh	USC Vs. Notre Dame
Keg of Nails	Cincinnati Vs. Miami University
Legends Trophy	Stanford Vs. Notre Dame
Lone Star Showdown	Texas A&M Vs. Texas
Mayor's Cup	SMU Vs. Rice
Missouri-Nebraska Bell	Nebraska Vs. Missouri
Old Oaken Bucket	Purdue Vs. Indiana

NCAA Football 08 (continued)

Unlockable	How to Unlock
Palmetto State	Clemson Vs. South Carolina
Paul Bunyan Trophy	Penn State Vs. Michigan State
Paul Bunyan's Axe	Wisconsin Vs. Minnesota
Peace Pipe	Western Michigan Vs. Miami University
Purdue Cannon	Purdue Vs. Illinois
Ram-Falcon Trophy	Colorado State Vs. Air Force
Red River Rivalry	Texas Vs. Oklahoma
Rocky Mountain Showdown	Colorado Vs. Colorado State
Seminole War Canoe	Florida Vs. Miami
Shillelagh Trophy	Purdue Vs. Notre Dame
Schwartzwaler Trophy	West Virginia Vs. Syracuse
Sweet Sioux Tomahawk	Northwestern Vs. Illinois
Telephone Trophy	Missouri Vs. Iowa State
Textile Bowl	Clemson Vs. NC State
The Big Game	Arizona Vs. Arizona State
Third Saturday in October	Alabama Vs. Tennessee
Tigers Rag	Tulane Vs. LSU
Victory Bell	Cincinnati Vs. Miami University
Victory Bell	Duke Vs. North Carolina
Wagon Wheel	Akron Vs. Kent State
Williams Trophy	Tulsa Vs. Rice

Trophies

Unlockable	How to Unlock
AT&T Bowl	Win the AT&T Bowl.
Back-To-Back National Champs	Win two consecutive national championships.
BCS National Championship	Be the number-one ranked college football team.
Big East Championship	Have the most Big East conference wins.
C-USA Championship	Have the best conference wins in the C-USA conference.
Capital One Bowl	Win the Capitol One Bowl.
Chick-Fil-A Bowl	Win the Chick-Fil-A Bowl.
Davey O' Brien Award	Be the best quarterback.
Doak Walker Running Back Award	Be the number-one running back in the class, field, and community.
Gator Bowl Trophy	Win the Gator Bowl.
GMAC Bowl	Win the GMAC Bowl.
Hawaii Bowl	Win the Hawaii Bowl.
Heisman Memorial Trophy	Be the most outstanding college player in the United States.
Holiday Bowl	Win the Holiday Bowl.
Independence Bowl	Win the Independence Bowl.
Insight Bowl	Win the Insight Bowl.
Jim Thorpe Award	Be the number-one defensive back based on on-field performance, athletic ability, and character.

NCAA Football 08 (continued)

Unlockable	How to Unlock
Las Vegas Bowl	Win the Las Vegas Bowl.
MAC Championship	Have the best conference wins in the MAC conference.
Maxwell Award	Be the college player of the year.
Meineke Car Care Bowl	Win the Meineke Car Care Bowl.
Motor City Bowl	Win the Motor City Bowl.
MWC Championship	Have the best conference wins in the MWC conference.
New Orleans Bowl	Win the New Orleans Bowl.
Orange Bowl Trophy	Win the Orange Bowl.
Receiver of the Year	Be the number-one wide receiver.
SEC Championship	Have the best conference wins in the SEC conference.
Sugar Bowl Trophy	Win the Sugar Bowl.
Sun Belt Championship	Have the best conference wins in the Sun Belt conference.
Three-In-A-Row National Champs	Win three consecutive national championships.
Tight End of the Year	Be the number-one tight end.
WAC Championship	Have the best conference wins in the WAC conference.

NHL 08

Gear

At the in-game cheat menu, type in the following code.

Unlockable	How to Unlock
RBK Edge Jerseys	h3oyxpwksf8ibcgt

Need for Speed Carbon

Enter at the main menu screen.

Unlockable	Code
10K Booster	⇩, ⇧, ⇦, ⇩, ⇨, ⇧, ■, ▲
Infinite Crew Charge	⇩, ⇧, ⇧, ⇨, ⇦, ⇦, ⇨, ■
Infinite Nitrous	⇦, ⇧, ⇦, ⇩, ⇦, ⇩, ⇨, ■
Infinite SpeedBreaker	⇩, ⇨, ⇨, ⇦, ⇨, ⇧, ⇩, ■
Unlock Logo Vinyls	⇨, ⇧, ⇩, ⇧, ⇩, ⇦, ⇨, ■
Unlock Special Logo Vinyls	⇧, ⇧, ⇩, ⇩, ⇩, ⇩, ⇧, ■

Need for Speed ProStreet

Codes

Go to the "Enter Codes" section of the Career menu and enter the following codes.

Unlockable	How to Unlock
Extra $2,000	1MA9X99
Extra $4,000	W2iOLL01
Extra $8,000	L1iS97A1
Extra $10,000	1Mi9K7E1
Extra $10,000	REGGAME
Extra $10,000	CASHMONEY

Need for Speed ProStreet (continued)

Unlockable	How to Unlock
Extra $10,000 and Castrol Syntec Bonus Vinyl	CASTROLSYNTEC
5 Repair Tokens	SAFETYNET
Audi TT 3.2 Quattro (In Garage)	ITSABOUTYOU
Bonus Energizer Lithium Vinyl	ENERGIZERLITHIUM
Dodge Viper (In Garage)	WORLDSLONGESTLASTING
K&N Bonus Vinyl	HORSEPOWER
Lancer Evo (In Garage)	MITSUBISHIGOFAR
Pre-tuned Grip Coke Zero Golf GTI (In Garage) and Bonus Coke Zero Vinyl	ZEROZEROZERO
Re-Locks Everything Unlocked by "Unlockallthings"	LEIPZIG
Unlocks Everything (maps, cars, parts)	UNLOCKALLTHINGS

Ninja Gaiden Sigma

Mission Mode

To unlock Mission mode, beat the Normal difficulty setting in Story mode.

Unlockable Difficulties

Unlockable	How to Unlock
Hard	Beat the game on Normal.
Master Ninja	Beat the game on Very Hard.
Ninja Dog	Die three times.
Very Hard	Beat the game on Hard.

Extra Costumes

Unlockable	How to Unlock
Ashtar Ryu costume	Beat Story mode on the Hard difficulty setting.
Classic Ryuken costume	Beat Story mode on the Normal difficulty setting.

Golden Scarab Rewards

Collect the Golden Scarabs and Muramasa the shop owner will reward you with the following items and weapons. There are 50 Golden Scarabs in the game, but they are not available when playing as Rachel.

Unlockable	How to Unlock
Armlet of Benediction	Collect 30 Golden Scarabs.
Armlet of Celerity	Collect 25 Golden Scarabs.
Armlet of Fortune	Collect 40 Golden Scarabs.
Armlet of Potency	Collect 5 Golden Scarabs.
Dabilahro	Collect 20 Golden Scarabs.
Great Spirit Elixir	Collect 35 Golden Scarabs.
Jewel of the Demon Seal	Collect 45 Golden Scarabs.
Life of Gods	Collect 1 Golden Scarab.
Lives of the Thousand Gods	Collect 10 Golden Scarabs.
Plasma Saber MkII	Collect 50 Golden Scarabs.
Spirit of the Devils	Collect 15 Golden Scarabs.

DS
PSP
PS2
PS3
Wii
Xbox
Xbox 360
Index

Ninja Gaiden Sigma (continued)

Golden Scarab Rewards—Hard Mode

Unlockable	How to Unlock
Armlet of Benediction	Collect 40 Scarabs.
Armlet of Celerity	Collect 30 Scarabs.
Armlet of Fortune	Collect 45 Scarabs.
Dabilahro	Collect 25 Scarabs.
Dark Dragon Blade	Collect 50 Scarabs.
Plasma Saber MkII	Collect 49 Scarabs.
Spear Gun	Collect 35 Scarabs.
Technique Scroll—Counter Attacks	Collect 1 Scarab.
Technique Scroll—Guillotine Throw	Collect 10 Scarabs.
Technique Scroll—Izuna Drop	Collect 5 Scarabs.
Windmill Shuriken	Collect 15 Scarabs.
Wooden Sword	Collect 20 Scarabs.

Golden Scarab Rewards—Master Ninja Difficulty

Unlockable	How to Unlock
Ayane's Ration	Collect 30 Golden Scarabs.
Ayane's Ration Bundle	Collect 40 Golden Scarabs.
Dark Dragon Blade	Collect 50 Golden Scarabs.
Elixir of Spiritual Life	Collect 5 Golden Scarabs.
Elixir of the Devil Way	Collect 15 Golden Scarabs.
Fragrance Hydrangea	Collect 45 Golden Scarabs.
Fragrance of Dayflower	Collect 35 Golden Scarabs.
Great Devil Elixir	Collect 20 Golden Scarabs.
Great Spirit Elixir	Collect 10 Golden Scarabs.
Plasma Saber MkII	Collect 49 Golden Scarabs.
Smoke Bomb	Collect 25 Golden Scarabs.
Smoke Bomb	Collect 1 Golden Scarab.

Golden Scarab Rewards—Very Hard Difficulty

Unlockable	How to Unlock
Armlet of Fortune	Collect 30 Golden Scarabs.
Art of Inazuma	Collect 40 Golden Scarabs.
Art of the Ice Storm	Collect 10 Golden Scarabs.
Art of the Inferno	Collect 1 Golden Scarab.
Dark Dragon Blade	Collect 50 Golden Scarabs.
Jewel of the Demon Seal	Collect 25 Golden Scarabs.
Jewel of the Demon Seal	Collect 15 Golden Scarabs.
Jewel of the Demon Seal	Collect 35 Golden Scarabs.
Plasma Saber MkII	Collect 49 Golden Scarabs.
Spirit of the Devils	Collect 20 Golden Scarabs.
Spirit of the Devils	Collect 5 Golden Scarabs.
Spirit of the Devils	Collect 45 Golden Scarabs.

Pirates of the Caribbean: At World's End

Characters

Successfully complete the indicated task to unlock the corresponding character.

Unlockable	How to Unlock
Ammand the Corsair	Successfully complete the Pirate Poker sub-mission in the Shipwreck City level
Black Bart	Successfully complete the Combat Challenge in the Maelstrom level
Bootstrap Bill Turner	Successfully complete the Defeat Enemies sub-mission in the Prison Fortress level
Cannon Arm	Successfully complete the Combat Challenge in the Pearl vs. Kraken level
Captain Barbossa	Successfully complete the Shipwreck City level
Captain Chevalle	Successfully complete the Port Royal level
Captain Elizabeth Swann	Successfully complete the Combo Challenge in the Davy Jones' Locker level
Captain Jack Sparrow	Successfully complete the Prison Fortress level
Captain Sao Feng	Successfully complete the Singapore level
Captain Teague	Successfully complete the Combat Challenge in the Prison Fortress level
Cotton	Successfully complete the Rescue sub-mission in the Isla de Pelegostos level
Davy Jones	Successfully complete Pearl vs. Dutchman level
Elizabeth Swann	Successfully complete the Tortuga level
Gentlemen Jocard	Successfully complete the Davy Jones' Locker level
Gibbs	Successfully complete the Combat Challenge in the Port Royal level
Governor Swann	Successfully complete the Combat Challenge in the Pearl vs. Dutchman level
James Norrington	Successfully complete the Combat Challenge in the Tortuga level
Lian	Successfully complete the Combat Challenge in the Singapore level
Lord Cuttler Beckett	Successfully complete the Maelstrom level
Mercer	Successfully complete the Hit-Combo sub-mission in the Singapore level
Mistress Ching	Successfully complete the Jackanism sub-mission in the Tortuga level
Mordillah	Successfully complete the Combo Challenge in the Prison Fortress level
Pintel	Successfully complete the Isla Cruces level
Ragetti	Successfully complete the Combat Challenge in the Isla Cruces level
Sri Sumba Jee	Successfully complete the Combat Challenge in the Shipwreck City level
Tai Huang	Successfully complete the Sea Battle level
Tia Dalma	Successfully complete the Missing Person sub-mission in the Port Royal level
Villanueva	Successfully complete the Combo Challenge in the Tortuga level
Will Turner	Successfully complete the Isla de Pelegostos level

Pirates of the Caribbean: At World's End (continued)

Swords

Successfully complete the indicated task to unlock the corresponding sword.

Unlockable	How to Unlock
Bone Sword	Successfully complete the Davy Jones' Locker level
Davy Jones' Sword	Successfully complete the Maelstrom level
Dutchman Sword	Successfully complete the Pearl vs. Dutchman level
Ghost Sword	Successfully complete the Hit Combo sub-mission on the Isla Cruces level
Gun Sword	Successfully complete the Sea Battle level
Legend Sword	Successfully complete the Hit Combo sub-mission on the Maelstrom level
Norrington Sword	Successfully complete the Isla Cruces level
Pirate King's Sword	Successfully complete the Shipwreck City level

PixelJunk Eden

Custom Soundtrack

Find all 50 spectra to unlock in-game custom soundtrack.

Trophies

Unlockable	How to Unlock
500 Dead Pollen Prowlers (Bronze)	500 Pollen Prowlers killed.
All Gardens Clear (Bronze)	Get a Spectra in each garden.
All Seeds 01 (Bronze)	Open all seeds in garden 01.
All Seeds 02 (Bronze)	Open all seeds in garden 02.
All Seeds 03 (Bronze)	Open all seeds in garden 03.
All Seeds 04 (Bronze)	Open all seeds in garden 04.
All Seeds 05 (Bronze)	Open all seeds in garden 05.
All Seeds 06 (Bronze)	Open all seeds in garden 06.
All Seeds 07 (Bronze)	Open all seeds in garden 07.
All Seeds 08 (Bronze)	Open all seeds in garden 08.
All Seeds 09 (Bronze)	Open all seeds in garden 09.
All Seeds 10 (Bronze)	Open all seeds in garden 10.
All Spectra Found (Silver)	Get all the Spectra in all gardens.
Combo Fifteen (Bronze)	Pollen Prowler combo x 15.
Combo Ten (Bronze)	Pollen Prowler combo x 10.
Fifteen Crystals (Bronze)	Get 15 crystals in a single jump.
Ten Minute Grimp (Bronze)	Get all 5 Spectra from a garden within 10 minutes.
The Hundred Thousander (Bronze)	Get 100,000 pollen in one garden.
Three Play Ping Pong (Bronze)	In 3p mode, trapeze jump between two swinging Grimps.
Zero Wasted Pollen (Bronze)	Open all seeds in a garden without missing any pollen.

Ratatouille

Passwords

Load a saved profile or create a new profile. Then, select the "Extras" option at the main menu. Choose the "Gusteau's Shop" option, then select the "Secrets" option. Choose a "Code [number]" option and enter the corresponding cheat code to unlock that option. After a cheat option is unlocked, click on its name to enable it. Unlocked and enabled cheat options are saved with the current profile. However, some cheat options cannot be disabled.

* Codes marked with an asterisk cannot be unlocked until they are bought with Gusteau points earned during Story mode.

Password	Effect
Code 01 / Pieceocake	Very Easy difficulty *
Code 02 / Myhero	No impact or damage from enemies, but still take water and falling damage *
Code 03 / Shielded	No damage from enemies, but still take water and falling damage *
Code 04 / Spyagent	Move undetected by enemies *
Code 05 / Ilikeonions	Fart when jumping
Code 06 / Hardfeelings	Head butt when attacking instead of tailswipe
Code 07 / Slumberparty	Multiplayer mode
Code 08 / Gusteauart	All concept art
Code 09 / Gusteauship	All four championship modes
Code 10 / Mattelme	All single player and multiplayer minigames
Code 11 / Gusteauvid	All videos
Code 12 / Gusteaures	All bonus artworks
Code 13 / Gusteaudream	All Dream Worlds in Gusteau's Shop
Code 14 / Gusteauslide	All slides in Gusteau's Shop
Code 15 / Gusteaulevel	All single player minigames
Code 16 / Gusteaucombo	All items in Gusteau's Shop
Code 17 / Gusteaupot	+5,000 Gusteau points
Code 18 / Gusteaujack	+10,000 Gusteau points
Code 19 / Gusteauomni	+50,000 Gusteau points

Ratchet & Clank Future: Tools of Destruction

Extra Modes

Unlockable	How to Unlock
Challenge Mode	Beat the game.

Extras and Concept Art

Obtain the number of skill points listed below to unlock the art or the extra feature.

Unlockable	How to Unlock
2006 GDC Trailer	150 SP
2007 E3 Trailer	25 SP
Big Head Enemies	100 SP
Big Head Mode (Ratchet only)	50 SP
Character Concept Art	75 SP
Environment Concept Art	250 SP
James the Galactic Defender	400 SP
Levels Are Mirrored	500 SP
Ratchet Drawing Tutorial	350 SP
Script to Screen	600 SP
Tools of Production	200 SP
Weapon Concept Art	450 SP
Wrench Replacement	300 SP

Ratchet & Clank Future: Tools of Destruction (continued)

Skill Points

Unlockable	How to Unlock
Alphabet City	Teleport to each of the six asteroids in alphabetical order.
Been Around	Take off from every robo-wing pad in Stratus City.
Bolts in the Bank	Sell 20 Leviathan Souls to the Smuggler.
Can't Touch This	Don't take damage before fighting Greasepalms McGee.
Cheapskate	Purchase a single Combuster shot.
Chorus Line	Make 11 enemies dance together.
Collector's Addition	Collect all cargo containers.
Dancin' with the Stars	Make five enemies dance at once on an asteroid.
Dancing on the Ceiling	Successfully use the Groovitron on a Gravity Ramp.
Disco Inferno	Use the Groovitron followed by the Pyro Blaster.
Even Better the Second Time	Complete Challenge mode.
Everybody Dance Now	Make every type of enemy in the game dance.
Expert Marksman	Kill 75 percent of all the enemies.
Extinction	Kill all the Sargasso Grunthors.
Fast and Firey-ous	Use the charge boots to cross the bridge to the arena without being burned.
Fire With Fire	Kill two Kerchu Pyroguards with the Pyro Blaster.
For the Hoard!	Get every device.
Giant Hunter	Kill all Basilisk Leviathans in the Cobalia wilderness.
Global Thermonuclear War	Get every weapon.
Golden Children	Get all gold bolts.
Gotta Catch Them All	Hit all Cragmite soldiers with the Mag-Net Launcher.
Happy Feat	Get nine penguins dancing on screen.
Head Examiner	Land on all of the Troglosaur heads.
I Should Have Gone Down in a Barrel	Jump into each of the two gelatonium waterfalls in the Cobalia gelatonium plant.
I Think I'm Going To Be Sick	Ride the Ferris wheel five times without taking damage.
I've Got Places to Be	Destroy Iron Crotch Caruso in under 2:30.
It Sounded Like a Freight Train	Get 11 Anthropods in one tornado.
It's a Mutiny Cap'n!	Change five pirates into penguins in one shot.
It's Like the South Pole Here	Turn at least 15 enemies or citizens into penguins at one time.
It's Even Better the Second Time	Complete Challenge mode.
Knock You Down to Size	Wrench slam five Cerullean Centipedes.
Live Strong	Complete the Gyro-Cycle area in under 1:45.
Lombaxes Don't Like Cold	Break all the breakable icicles.
Low Flying Owls	Fly underneath an electrified barrier in the robo-wing segment.
Minesweeper	Clear out 10-15 mines.
Mow Down Hoedown	Use turrets to destroy 10 dancing pirates.
No, Up YOUR Arsenal	Upgrade every weapon to the max.
Now Boarding...	Complete the Gyro Cycle area in 0:55 seconds.
Nowhere to Hide	Destroy every piece of breakable cover.
One Heckuva Peephole	Use the Geo-Laser to blast through the wall.
Preemptive Strike	Destroy five of the Thwogs while they are still sleeping.
Pretty Lights	Don't destroy any Snatchers.

Ratchet & Clank Future: Tools of Destruction (continued)

Unlockable	How to Unlock
Promoted to Inspector	Get every gadget.
Pyew Pyew	Complete Verdigris Black Hole without secondary fire.
Roflcopter	Turn an enemy into a penguin, then use the Visi-copter to destroy the penguin.
Say Hello to My Little Friend	Kill 15 enemies with one RYNO shot.
Seared Ahi	Use the Pyro Blaster on three Drophyds after freeing them from their robotic suits.
Six Gun Salute	Get six pirates in a row to salute Ratchet while wearing the Holo-Pirate disguise.
Smashing Good Time	Destroy all crates and consumer robots on port and gel factory.
Stay Still So I Can Shoot You!	Use strafe flip 10 times while fighting.
Surface-to-air Plasma Beasts	Take out three flying targets using the Plasma Beasts.
Taste O' Yer Own Medicine	Destroy all Corsairs with the Combuster.
The Consumer Is Not (Always) Right	Destroy 18 consumer robots.
The Hardest Core	Get everything else in the game.
Untouchable	Don't take damage in the Gyro-Cycle.
We Don't Need No Stinkin' Bridges!	Cross the tripad sequence without activating the bridge.
Whats That, R2?	Barrel roll 10 times.
Wrench Ninja 3	Use only the wrench to make it to the robo-wings segment.
You Sunk My Battleship!	Shoot down at least 75 percent of the flying ships.

Ridge Racer 7

Unlockable	How To
Auto Rocket Start System	100 Points with Zolgear
Collision Decreaser	100 Points with all tyre and suspension manufacturers
Down Force Control System	100 Points with Bosconian
Nitrous Tank 100	100 Points with all nitrous manufacturers
Over Limit Start System	100 Points all engine tune up manufacturers
Prize Money x2	100 Points with all manufacturers
Race Data Analyzer	100 Points with Galaxian
SS Booster	100 Points with Arkbird
SS Canceler	100 Points all exterior parts manufacturers
10&20% discount and special Age machine	Obtain 100 Manufacturer Points from Age
10&20% discount and special Assoluto machine	Obtain 100 Manufacturer Points from Assoluto
10&20% discount and special Danver machine	Obtain 100 Manufacturer Points from Danver
10&20% discount and special Gnade machine	Obtain 100 Manufacturer Points from Gnade
10&20% discount and special Himmel machine	Obtain 100 Manufacturer Points from Himmel
10&20% discount and special Kamata machine	Obtain 100 Manufacturer Points from Kamata
10&20% discount and special Namco machine	Obtain 100 Manufacturer Points from Namco

DS
PSP
PS2
PS3
Wii
Xbox
Xbox 360
Index

Ridge Racer 7 (continued)

Unlockable	How To
10&20% discount and special SinseongMotors machine	Obtain 100 Manufacturer Points from SinseongMotors
10&20% discount and special Soldat machine	Obtain 100 Manufacturer Points from Soldat
10&20% discount and special Terrazi machine	Obtain 100 Manufacturer Points from Terrazi

Saints Row

Codes

Dial the following phone numbers to get the corresponding effects.

Effect	Code
1,000 dollars	#2274666399
12 Gauge	#920
.44 Cal	#921
Add Gang Notoriety	#35
Add Police Notoriety	#4
Annihilator RPG	#947
AR-200	#922
AR-50	#923
AR-50 with Grenade Launcher	#924
AS14 Hammer	#925
Baseball Bat	#926
Car Mass Increased	#2
Chainsaw	#927
Crowbar	#955
Drunk Pedestrians	#15
Everybody Is Shrunk	#202
Evil Cars	#16
Fire Extinguisher	#928
Flame Thrower	#929
Flashbang	#930
Full Health	#1
GAL 43	#931
GDHC	#932
Get Horizon	#711
Get Snipes 57	#712
Get Tornado	#713
Get Wolverine	#714
Giant	#200
Grenade	#933
Gyro Daddy Added to Garage	#4976
Heaven Bound	#12
Itty Bitty	#201
K6	#935
Knife	#936
Kobra	#934
Lighting Strikes	#666
Low Gravity	#18
Machete	#937
McManus 2010	#938
Milk Bones	#3
Mini-Gun	#939
Molotov	#940
Never Die	#36
Nightstick	#941
No Cop Notoriety	#50
No Gang Notoriety	#51
NR4	#942
Pedestrian Wars	#19
Pepper Spray	#943
Pimp Slap	#969
Pimpcane	#944
Pipe Bomb	#945
Player Pratfalls	#5
Raining Pedestrians	#20
RPG	#946
Samurai Sword	#948
Satchel Charge	#949
Shock Paddles	#950
SKR-9	#951
Sledge Hammer	#952
Stun Gun	#953
Super Explosions	#7
Super Saints	#8
TK3	#954
Tombstone	#956
Unlimited Ammo	#11
Unlimited Clip	#9
Unlimited Sprint	#6
Unlock D-STROY UFO	#728237
Unlock Peewee Mini Bike	#7266837
Vice 9	#957
XS-2 Ultimax	#958

Saints Row (continued)

Unlockables

Unlockable	How to Unlock
75% Mechanic Discount	Complete all 5 Chop Shop lists
Bodyguards and Ninjas	Game Progression
Brotherhood Gang Cars	Complete Last Mission for the Brotherhood
Brotherhood Melee	Complete Brotherhood Mission 6
Buggy	Complete Truck Yard Chop Shop list
Chainsaw in Weapon Cache	Complete Crowd Control (Marina) Level 6
Clothing Store Discount	Crowd Control Level 3 (Suburbs)
Crib Customization Discount	Mayhem Level 3 (Red Light)
Demo Derby Vehicles	Complete Demo Derby Level 6
Donnie's Vehicle	Complete Brotherhood Mission 2
Explosion Damage -5%	Level 3, Trail Blazing (Downtown)
Gang Customization Cars	15% hoods conquered
Gang Customization Cars	45% hoods conquered
Health Regeneration 2x	Snatch Level 3 (Chinatown)
Health Regeneration 3x	Snatch Level 6 (Chinatown)
Infinite Respect	Raise your respect past Level 99
Infinite SMG Ammo	Successfully complete "Snatch" Level 6 Downtown
Kobra (Pistol)	Fuzz Level 3 (Projects)
Legal Lee	Beat Stilwater Prison Fight Club Level 3
Mechanic Discount	Complete Demo Derby Level 3
One Follower	Complete Prologue Mission 4
Pepper Spray in Weapon Cache	Complete Crowd Control (Marina) Level 3
Police Notoriety Reduced	Complete FUZZ Level 3, Suburbs
Police Notoriety Reduced 2	Complete FUZZ Level 6, Suburbs
Pumped Up	Fight Club Level 6 (Arena)
Pumped Up	Fight Club Level 3 (Arena)
Red Light Apartment Crib	Complete Prologue Mission 2
Reduced Bullet Damage	Heli Assault Level 3 (Bario)
Ronin Gang Cars	Complete Last Mission for the Ronin
Ronin Melee	Complete Ronin Mission 6
Ronin Notoriety Reduced	Drug Trafficking Level 3 (Hotel and Marina)
Saints Hideout	Complete Prologue Mission 3
Sons of Samedi Gang Cars	Complete Last Mission for Sons of Samedi
Sons of Samedi Melee	Complete Mission Bad Trip
Sons of Samedi Notoriety Reduced	Complete Escort Level 3, University
Sprint Increased	Insurance Fraud Level 3 (Factories)
Sprint Increased (Unlimited)	Insurance Fraud Level 6 (Factories)
The News Helicopter	Complete Sons of Samedi Mission 3
Three Followers	50% hoods conquered
Tobias	Complete Sons of Samedi Mission 3
Troy	Beat Stilwater Prison Fight Club Level 6
Two Followers	25% hoods conquered

Saints Row (continued)

Unlockable	How to Unlock
Unlimited Pistol Ammo	Fuzz Level 6 (Projects)
Vehicle Delivery	Escort Level 3 (Red Light)
X2 Ultimax (Shotgun)	Drug Trafficking Level 3 (Airport)
Zombie Carlos	Call eye for an eye after you complete the brother hood story

Skate

Code

Enter code at main menu.

Code	Effect
Up, Down, Left, Right, ■, R1, ▲, L1	Unlock Best Buy clothes in store

Sonic the Hedgehog

Unlockable	How To
Last Episode	Beat Sonic's Episode, Shadow's Episode, and Silver's Episode
Audio Room	Complete Sonic, Shadow, or Silver's story 100%
Theater Room	Complete Sonic, Shadow, or Silver's story 100%
Shadow the Hedgehog	Complete "Crisis City" with Sonic
Silver the Hedgehog	Complete "Silver the Hedgehog" boss battle with Sonic

Star Wars: The Force Unleashed

Codes

From the pause menu go to the "Input Code" option then enter the following codes for the corresponding effect.

Effect	Code
All Databank Entries Unlocked	OSSUS
All Force Push Ranks Unlocked	EXARKUN
All Saber Throw Ranks Unlocked	ADEGAN
All Talents Unlocked	JOCASTA
Combo Unlock	RAGNOS
Incinerator Trooper	PHOENIX
Makes Levels Mirrored	MINDTRICK
New Combo	FREEDON
New Combo	MASSASSI
New Combo	MARAJADE
New Combo	SAZEN
New Combo	LUMIYA
New Combo	YADDLE
Proxy Skin Code	PROTOTYPE
Shadowtrooper Costume	BLACKHOLE
Snowtrooper	SNOWMAN
Stormtrooper Commander Costume	TK421BLUE
Unlocks All Lightsaber Crystals	HURRIKANE
Unlocks Emperor Costume	MASTERMIND
Unlocks All 32 Costumes	SOHNDANN
Unlocks All Force Combos	MOLDYCROW

DS PSP PS2 PS3 Wii Xbox Xbox 360 Index

Star Wars: The Force Unleashed (continued)

Effect	Code
Unlocks Bail Organa Costume	VICEROY
Unlocks Deadly Saber	LIGHTSABER
Unlocks Kashyyyk Trooper Costume	TK421GREEN
Unlocks Maximum Force Powers	KATARN
Unlocks Maximum Force Repulse Ranks	DATHOMIR
Unlocks Scout Trooper Costume	FERRAL
Unlocks Sith Master Difficulty	SITHSPAWN
Unlocks Stormtrooper Costume	TK421WHITE
Unlocks the Aerial Ambush Combo	VENTRESS
Unlocks the Aerial Assault Combo	EETHKOTH
Unlocks the Ceremonial Jedi Robes	DANTOOINE
Unlocks the Devastating Lightsaber Impale	BRUTALSTAB
Unlocks the Drunken Kota Costume	HARDBOILED
Unlocks the Jedi Adventure Robes	HOLOCRON
Unlocks the Master Kento Costume "The Apprentice's Father"	WOOKIEE
Unlocks the Rahm Kota Costume	MANDALORE
Unlocks the Saber Slam Combo	PLOKOON
Unlocks the Saber Sling Combo	KITFISTO
Unlocks the Sith Slash Combo	DARAGON
Unlocks the Sith Stalker Armor	KORRIBAN

Stranglehold

Difficulties

Unlockable	How to Unlock
Hard Boiled Difficulty	Complete the game on Casual mode once to unlock this difficulty.

Easter Eggs

Unlockable	How to Unlock
Movie Theater Trailers	In the first chapter in the Hong Kong Marketplace, go into the Ambushed section. When you finish killing everyone, go into the building. Break the door, and follow the corridor until you reach a movie theater. The screen is showing trailers for *Wheelman* and *Blacksite*.

Surf's Up

Passwords

Password	Effect
MYPRECIOUS	All Boards
FREEVISIT	All championship locations
GOINGDOWN	All leaf sliding locations
MULTIPASS	All multiplayer levels
NICEPLACE	Art gallery
ASTRAL	Astral board
TOPFASHION	Customizations for all characters
MONSOON	Monsoon board
IMTHEBEST	Plan as Tank Evans
TINYBUTSTRONG	Play as Arnold

DS PSP PS2 PS3 Wii Xbox Xbox 360 Index

Surf's Up (continued)

Password	Effect
SURPRISEGUEST	Play as Elliot
SLOWANDSTEADY	Play as Geek
KOBAYASHI	Play as Tatsuhi Kobayashi
THELEGEND	Play as Zeke Topanga
TINYSHOCKWAVE	Tine shockwave board
WATCHAMOVIE	Video Gallery

Tiger Woods PGA 07

Unlockable	How to Unlock
EA Black Series Clubs	Complete the game 100% to get the EA Black Series Clubs

Tiger Woods PGA Tour '08

Passwords

Go to the Password sub-menu from the EA Sports Extras menu and enter the following passwords to get the corresponding effects. Passwords are not case sensitive.

Password	Effect
Cream	Infinite money
PlayFIFA08	Unlock Wayne Rooney
Greensfees	Unlock all course
AllStars	Unlock all golfers

TNA iMPACT!

Unlockables

Unlockable	How to Unlock
Abyss	Defeat Abyss in Story mode Part 6.
Black Machismo	Defeat him in Story mode.
Brother Ray	Defeat TEAM 3D in Story mode.
Don West	Gain 250,000 style points.
Eric Young	During Story mode, you will eventually be paired up with Eric Young. After successfully winning your first tag team match, he will be unlocked.
Jay Lethal	Defeat Lethal in your TNA tryout gauntlet match in Story mode.
Jeff Jarrett	Defeat him in Story mode.
Kevin Nash	Defeat him during Story mode.
Moves for Your Created Superstar	Various moves are unlocked as your progress through Story mode.
Senshi	Gain 200,000 style points.
Suicide	Defeat Jeff Jarrett in Story mode.
Tomko	Win the tag team match.

Tom Clancy's Rainbow Six Vegas 2

Codes

At the Title screen, hold R1 and press the following.

Unlockable	How to Unlock
M468 Assault Rifle	↑,▲,↓,×,←,■,→,●,←,←,→,■
MTAR-21 Assault Rifle	↓,↓,↑,↑,■,●,■,●,▲,↑,↑,▲

Tom Clancy's Rainbow Six Vegas 2 (continued)

Single Player Codes

During gameplay, pause the game, hold R1, and insert the following codes.

Red and Blue Tracers (also works online, host must enter code)	L3, L3, ×, R3, R3, ●, L3, L3, ■, R3, R3, ▲
Third-Person View	■, ●, ■, ●, L3, L3, ▲, ×, ▲, ×, R3, R3
Super Ragdoll Mode	×, ×, ●, ●, ■, ■, ▲, ▲, ×, ●, ■, ▲

Comcast Multiplayer Map

At the game's main menu, go to the Extras menu, select Comcast Gift, then enter the following password.

Password	Effect
Comcast faster	Comcast multiplayer map

Tony Hawk's Project 8

In the Options menu, select Cheats to enter these passwords.

Unlockable	Password
Big Realtor	shescaresme
Christian Hosoi	hohohosoi
Colonel and Security Guard	militarymen
Dad and Skater Jam Kid	strangefellows
Full Air Stats	drinkup
Grim Reaper	enterandwin
Inkblot Deck	birdhouse
Jason Lee	notmono
Kevin Staab	mixitup
Mascot	manineedadate
Most Decks	needaride
Nerd	wearelosers
Photographer and Cameraman	themedia
Travis Barker	plus44
Unlock Specials in Skate Shop	yougotitall

Tony Hawk's Proving Ground

Cheats

Enter the codes in the options menu of the main menu

Unlockable	How to Unlock
100% Branch Completion (NTT)	FOREVERNAILED
Invisible Man	THEMISSING
Mini Skater	TINYTATER
No Bails	ANDAINTFALLIN
No Board	MAGICMAN
Perfect Manual	STILLAINTFALLIN
Perfect Rail	AINTFALLIN
Super Check	BOOYAH
Unlimited Focus	MYOPIC
Unlimited Slash Grind	SUPERSLASHIN
Unlock Judy Nails	LOVEROCKNROLL

Tony Hawk's Proving Ground (continued)

tems

Unlockable	How to Unlock
50 Extra Skill Points	NEEDSHELP
All CAS Items	GIVEMESTUFF
All Decks	LETSGOSKATE
All Fun Items	OVERTHETOP
All Game Movies	WATCHTHIS
All Lounge Bling Items	SWEETSTUFF
All Lounge Themes	LAIDBACKLOUNGE
All Rigger Pieces	IMGONNABUILD
All Special Tricks Available	LOTSOFTRICKS
All Video Editor Effects	TRIPPY
All Video Editor Overlays	PUTEMONTOP
Full Stats	BEEFEDUP

Levels

Unlockable	How to Unlock
Unlock Air & Space Museum	THEINDOORPARK
Unlock FDR	THEPREZPARK
Unlock Lansdowne	THELOCALPARK

Skaters

Unlockable	How to Unlock
Boneman	CRAZYBONEMAN
Bosco	MOREMILK
Cam	NOTACAMERA
Cooper	THECOOP
Eddie X	SKETCHY
El Patinador	PILEDRIVER
Eric	FLYAWAY
Mad Dog	RABBIES
MCA	INTERGALACTIC
Mel	NOTADUDE
Rube	LOOKSSMELLY
Shayne	MOVERS
Spence	DAPPER
TV Producer	SHAKER

Uncharted: Drake's Fortune

Drake's Jersey

To unlock a baseball jersey for Drake, go to the Costume section of the game, and input the following code.

Unlockable	How to Unlock
Baseball Jersey	←,→,↓,↑,▲,R1,L1,■

Secret Videos

To unlock secret videos in the Making a Cutscene section of the game, input the following codes.

Unlockable	How to Unlock
Video for Grave Robbing	←,R2,→,↑,L2,▲,■,↓
Video for Time's Up	L1,→,■,↓,←,▲,R1,↑

Uncharted: Drake's Fortune (continued)

Concept Art

Go to the Rewards section of the game, and insert the following codes.

Unlockable	How to Unlock
More Art	■, L1, →, ←, ↓, R2, ▲, ↑
Video	L2, →, ↑, ■, ←, ▲, R1, ↓

Virtua Fighter 5

Unlockable	Code
DOJO training stages	Complete the Time Attack mode
Costume C	Reach the rank of 1st Dan
Costume D	Complete the first orb disc

Warhawk

Trophies

Complete each condition to get the allotted trophies. There are 36 Bronze, 13 Silver, 7 Gold, and 1 Platinum trophy (including the secret trophies).

Unlockable	How to Unlock
Aerial Ballet (Silver)	While flying a jetpack, kill an enemy (who is also flying a jetpack) with any weapon other than the Rocket Launcher.
Anti-Air Ninja (Bronze)	Shoot down a Warhawk with any infantry weapon other than a Rocket Launcher.
Are You Aim-Botting? (Silver)	Snipe an enemy who is flying a jetpack.
Bandit Award (Bronze)	Earn all in-game badges at Bandit level.
Bandwidth Donor (Gold)	Host a ranked dedicated server for four consecutive hours.
Behind Enemy Lines (Silver)	Drive an APC into the enemy's home base, then have at least one teammate spawn into that APC.
Chief Sergeant (Bronze)	Achieve a rank of Chief Sergeant.
Collector (Bronze)	Capture four cores at once in Collection mode.
Combat Driver (Bronze)	Complete Vehicle Combat Training.
Commander (Silver)	Achieve a rank of Commander.
Cowboy (Bronze)	Play a perfect Team Deathmatch (top player, no deaths).
Dead-Eye (Bronze)	Achieve a sniper kill from more than 2,500 feet away.
Decorated Soldier (Silver)	Earn any 15 in-game medals.
Dumbfire (Bronze)	Destroy an enemy aircraft with a dumbfired Swarm or Homing Missile.
Emergency Evasion (Bronze)	Break at least 6 simultaneous missile locks using Chaff.
Enlistee (Bronze)	Join a clan.
Executive Honor (Gold)	Earn all in-game medals.
Flying Fortress (Silver)	Awarded to the driver and all six passengers of a fully loaded Dropship.
General (Gold)	Achieve a rank of General.
Giant Killer (Silver)	Shoot down an enemy Dropship while using a Warhawk.
Ground Pounder (Bronze)	Complete Ground Combat Training.
Hat Trick (Bronze)	Get three flag captures in a single round of CTF.
How Did You Do That? (Bronze)	Destroy an enemy aircraft with a Cluster Bomb.
Invincible (Bronze)	While on foot, take at least 250 damage within 10 seconds without dying.

Warhawk (continued)

Unlockable	How to Unlock
Irony (Bronze)	Kill an enemy with his own Proximity Mine.
Lone Wolf (Bronze)	Play a perfect Deathmatch (top player, no deaths).
Lt. Colonel (Silver)	Achieve a rank of Lt. Colonel.
Master Award (Silver)	Earn all in-game badges at Master level.
One in a Million (Bronze)	Shoot down an enemy aircraft using the tank's main cannon.
Overkill (Bronze)	Destroy an enemy aircraft with a volley of 8 Swarm Missiles.
Pilot's License (Bronze)	Complete Warhawk Combat Training.
Porcupine (Gold)	Destroy an enemy Warhawk with the APC's E-POD shield.
Recognition of Merit (Bronze)	Earn any five in-game medals.
Remote Pilot (Bronze)	Destroy an enemy aircraft with a TOW Missile.
Resourceful Driver (Bronze)	Achieve a road kill and a .50 cal kill using the same 4x4, without dismounting.
Rivalry (Bronze)	Win a clan match (red server) as either clan leader or a regular member.
Saboteur (Bronze)	Destroy an enemy vehicle with the Field Wrench.
Secret Anti-Camper (Bronze)	Kill an enemy in a Missile or Flak Turret after that enemy has achieved at least five kills in that type of turret.
Secret Canyon Run (Silver)	Using a Warhawk, shoot down an enemy Warhawk in the central gorge in Vaporfield Glacier.
Secret Daredevil (Bronze)	Get 100 feet off the ground in a ground vehicle. Does not count if the vehicle is being carried by a Dropship.
Secret Hit List (Bronze)	Kill every member of the opposing team at least once during a round.
Secret King of the Jungle Gym (Silver)	Retrieve the Proximity Mines from the top of the dome on the Omega Factory Rumble Dome layout.
Secret Minesweeper (Bronze)	Get killed by Proximity Mines five times in a single round.
Secret Reckless Pilot (Bronze)	Commit suicide in a Warhawk by running into your own Aerial Mine.
Secret Safety Violation (Silver)	Kill a distant enemy from on top of the salvage crane in Tau Crater.
Secret Vengeance (Bronze)	Kill an enemy within 60 seconds of that enemy killing you.
Secret What's That Green Line? (Bronze)	Get killed by a Binoculars strike while piloting an aircraft.
Shield Breaker (Silver)	Break an enemy E-POD shield using the Lightning Shell.
Surgical Strike (Gold)	Shoot down a Dropship with a Binoculars strike.
Survivalist (Bronze)	Survive for one minute as the hero in Hero mode.
Tail Shaker (Bronze)	Destroy an enemy aircraft with an Aerial Mine within 5 seconds of deploying it.
Taxi Driver (Bronze)	Help a teammate capture the flag (in CTF) or cogs (in Collection) by transporting him back to the base, using any vehicle.
That Was Some Bug (Gold)	Kill an enemy who is flying a jetpack by hitting him with any vehicle or aircraft.
Warhawk Award (Gold)	Earn all in-game badges at Warhawk level.
Warhawk Supreme Achievement (Platinum)	All your base trophies are belong to platinum.

Warhawk (continued)	
Unlockable	**How to Unlock**
Warlord (Bronze)	Create a clan and get nine other members to join. (Awarded at 10 members while you are the clan leader.)
World Victory (Bronze)	Control all capturable bases in a Zones match, and reduce the enemy's home base to level 1.

WWE SmackDown! Vs. Raw 2008

Arenas

To unlock arenas, get the following number of points in Hall of Fame mode.

Unlockable Arenas	Points Needed
No Way Out	5 points
Vengeance	6 points
ECW One Night Stand	7 points
December to Dismember	8 points
New Year's Revolution	9 points
Summerslam	10 points
Wrestlemania 23	12 points

Outfits and Costumes

Enter the codes in the in-game Cheats menu to unlock the outfits.

Unlockable Outfits	Codes
DX Costumes	DXCostume69K2
Kelly Kelly's Alternate Outfit	KellyKG12R

Table of Contents - Wii

DS
PSP
PS2
PS3
Wii
Xbox
Xbox 360
Index

ActRaiser

Hidden Extra Lives

Do the following to find four hidden extra lives in the game's towns.

Town	Action
Fillmore	When you get the Compass, use it here.
Bloodpool	Make it rain over the big lake.
Kasandora	Cause an earthquake after uncovering the pyramid.
Northwall	Strike the town's shrine with a lightning bolt.

Professional Mode

Unlockable	How to Unlock
Professional Mode	First, beat the game. Then on the title screen, highlight "New Game" and press ✚ or SELECT.

DS
PSP
PS2
PS3
Wii
Xbox
Xbox 360
Index

Adventure Island

Passwords

Password	Effect
3WSURYXZY763TE	Advanced items/abilities
RMAYTJEOPHALUP	Disable sounds
NODEGOSOOOOOOO	Start the game as Hu man
3YHURYW7Y7LL8C	Start the game as Hawk man
3YHURYW7Y7LRBW	Start the game as Lizard man
3YHURYW7Y7LN84	Start the game as Piranha man
3YHURYW7Y7LK88	Start the game as Tiger man

Adventures of Lolo

Level Passwords

Password	Effect
BCBT	Level 1-2
BDBR	Level 1-3
BGBQ	Level 1-4
BHBP	Level 1-5
BJBM	Level 2-1
BKBL	Level 2-2
BLBK	Level 2-3
BMBJ	Level 2-4
BPBH	Level 2-5
BQBG	Level 3-1
BRBD	Level 3-2
BTBC	Level 3-3
BVBB	Level 3-4
BYZZ	Level 3-5
BZZY	Level 4-1
CBZV	Level 4-2
CCZT	Level 4-3
CDZR	Level 4-4
CGZQ	Level 4-5
CHZP	Level 5-1
CJZM	Level 5-2
CKZL	Level 5-3
CLZK	Level 5-4
CMZJ	Level 5-5
CPZH	Level 6-1
CQZG	Level 6-2
CRZD	Level 6-3
CTZC	Level 6-4
CVZB	Level 6-5
CYYZ	Level 7-1
CZYY	Level 7-2
DBYV	Level 7-3
DCYT	Level 7-4
DDYR	Level 7-5
DGYQ	Level 8-1
DHYP	Level 8-2
DJYM	Level 8-3
DKYL	Level 8-4
DLYK	Level 8-5
DMYJ	Level 9-1
DPYH	Level 9-2
DQYG	Level 9-3
DRYD	Level 9-4
DTYC	Level 9-5
DVYB	Level 10-1
DYVZ	Level 10-2
DZVY	Level 10-3
GBVV	Level 10-4
GCVT	Level 10-5

Level Skip

Unlockable	How to Unlock
Level Skip	This only works if you have a password that starts with A, B, C, or D and if the second letter in the password appears earlier in the alphabet than the fourth letter. If so, switch the second and fourth letters in the password. Use the new password to start at a level one higher than the original.

Adventures of Lolo 2

New Difficulty Levels

Password	Effect
PPHP	Floor 01, Room 1
PHPK	Floor 01, Room 2
PQPD	Floor 01, Room 3
PVPT	Floor 01, Room 4
PRPJ	Floor 01, Room 5
PZPC	Floor 02, Room 1
PGPG	Floor 02, Room 2
PCPZ	Floor 02, Room 3
PLPY	Floor 02, Room 4
PBPM	Floor 02, Room 5

Adventures of Lolo 2 (continued)

Password	Effect	Password	Effect
PYPL	Floor 03, Room 1	HKKH	Floor 07, Room 2
PMPB	Floor 03, Room 2	QPKP	Floor 07, Room 3
PJPR	Floor 03, Room 3	QHDK	Floor 07, Room 4
PTPV	Floor 03, Room 4	QQDD	Floor 07, Room 5
PDPQ	Floor 03, Room 5	QVDT	Floor 08, Room 1
PKPH	Floor 04, Room 1	QRDJ	Floor 08, Room 2
HPPP	Floor 04, Room 2	QBDM	Floor 08, Room 3
HHKK	Floor 04, Room 3	QLDY	Floor 08, Room 4
HQKD	Floor 04, Room 4	QCDZ	Floor 08, Room 5
HVKT	Floor 04, Room 5	QGDG	Floor 09, Room 1
HRKJ	Floor 05, Room 1	QZDC	Floor 09, Room 2
HBKM	Floor 05, Room 2	QYDL	Floor 09, Room 3
HLKY	Floor 05, Room 3	QMDB	Floor 09, Room 4
HCKZ	Floor 05, Room 4	QJDR	Floor 09, Room 5
HGKG	Floor 05, Room 5	QTDV	Floor 10, Room 1
HZKC	Floor 06, Room 1	QDDQ	Floor 10, Room 2
HYKL	Floor 06, Room 2	QKDH	Floor 10, Room 3
HMKB	Floor 06, Room 3	VPDP	Floor 10, Room 4
HJKR	Floor 06, Room 4	VHTK	Floor 10, Room 5
HTKV	Floor 06, Room 5	VQTD	Last Level
HDKQ	Floor 07, Room 1		

Air Zonk

Codes

Unlockable	How to Unlock
Expert Mode	On the Configuration screen, hold ✚ and press SELECT
Sound Test	Hold ① and ② and SELECT as you turn on the game

Alex Kidd in the Enchanted Castle

Skip Boss Sequences

Unlockable	How to Unlock
Skip Boss Sequences	Wait until the conversation with the boss has ended. After that, Press START to get to the Options screen, then press START again and you should skip the sequence.

Alien Crush

Bonus

Unlockable	How to Unlock
1 Million Points + Bonus Ball	Get to the bonus round with skulls and green aliens. Kill everything except for one skull. Keep going until a pterodactyl appears. Hit the pterodactyl with the ball to get a million points and a bonus ball once the stage is cleared.

DS PSP PS2 PS3 Wii Xbox Xbox 360 Index

Alien Soldier

Level Passwords

Password	Effect	Password	Effect	Password	Effect
1985	Level 1	**8316**	Level 10	**9002**	Level 19
3698	Level 2	**6402**	Level 11	**2878**	Level 20
0257	Level 3	**9874**	Level 12	**3894**	Level 21
3745	Level 4	**1930**	Level 13	**4913**	Level 22
7551	Level 5	**2623**	Level 14	**2825**	Level 23
8790	Level 6	**6385**	Level 15	**7406**	Level 24
5196	Level 7	**7749**	Level 16	**5289**	Level 25
4569	Level 8	**3278**	Level 17		
8091	Level 9	**1039**	Level 18		

Alien Syndrome

Unlock Extra Difficulties

Unlockable	How to Unlock
Unlock Expert Difficulty	Beat the game on Hard difficulty
Unlock Hard Difficulty	Beat the game on Normal difficulty

Altered Beast

Codes

Enter these on the title screen.

Unlockable	How to Unlock
Beast Select	Hold Ⓐ+Ⓑ+Ⓒ+✚ and then press START
Character Kicks Credits	When the credits are being displayed on the screen after you have beaten the game, you can control your character to kick away the credited names
Continue from Last Stage Played	Hold Ⓐ and press SELECT after a Game Over
Level Select	Press Ⓑ and START
Sound Test	Hold Ⓐ+Ⓒ+✚ and then press START

Art of Fighting

Character Unlockables

Unlockable	How to Unlock
Mr. Big	Get to Mr. Big in 1-player mode and lose the match. Restart the game and Mr. Big will now be unlocked in 2-player mode.
Mr. Karate	Get to Mr. Karate in 1-player mode and lose the match. Restart the game and Mr. Karate will now be unlocked in 2-player mode.

Avatar: The Last Airbender

Passwords

Password	Effect	Password	Effect
37437	All treasure maps	**24463**	Unlimited chi
97831	Character concept gallery	**23637**	Unlimited copper
34743	Double damage	**94677**	Unlimited health
54641	One hit dishonor	**53467**	Unlimited stealth

Avatar: The Last Airbender (continued)

Unlockable Galleries

Unlockable	How to Unlock
Character Story Board Gallery	Collect all Set Items through level 6
Level Art Gallery	Collect all Set Items through level 3
Story Board Gallery	Collect all Set Items through level 5

Avatar: The Last Airbender– The Burning Earth

Codes

In the Password screen in the main menu, click the left arrow and then go to Cheat Entry.

Unlockable	How to Unlock
All Bonus Games	99801
All Gallery Items	85061
Double Damage	90210
Infinite Life	65049
Infinite Special Attacks	66206
Max Level	89121
One-Hit Dishonor	28260

Barnyard

Gameplay Cheat Codes

During gameplay hold C+Z and enter codes.

Unlockable	How to Unlock
9,999 Gopher Bucks	↓, ↓, ←, ←, ←, ←, ↑, ←
All Flower Pack and Knapsack Items	↓, ↓, ↑, →, ←, ←, →, ↑

Main Menu Cheat Codes

While on the main menu screen, hold C+Z and enter codes.

Unlockable	How to Unlock
Unlock All Antics	↑, ←, ↓, →, →, ↓, ←, ↑
Unlock All Bonus Items	↑, →, ↓,←, ←, ↓, →, ↑

Baroque

Baroques

Successfully complete the indicated task to unlock the corresponding Baroque.

Unlockable	How to Unlock
Appraiser	Identify over 50 items.
Arrow of Eros	Successfully complete the Neuron Tower while in Lust mode.
Bomber	Purify over 50 Meta-beings using the explosion brand.
Box bOx boX BOX	Successfully complete the Neuro Tower or die while holding over 15 types of boxes.
Broken Doll	Watch "Consciousness Simulation End VV."
Bug Nurturer	Raise over 10 larva until they grow into another parasite.
Careless Death	Die outside the Neuro Tower when your level is over 2.
Cat Fan	Use the Cat Torturer three times on one floor.
Cat Lover	Use the Cat Torturer six times on one floor.

DS
PSP
PS2
PS3
Wii
Xbox
Xbox 360
Index

Baroque (continued)

Unlockable	How to Unlock
Close to God	Die at the lowest level.
Collector	Get items from Urim, The Mind Reader, The Worker Angel, and Doctor Angelicus.
Confused World	Successfully complete the Neuro Tower while confused.
Cursebringer	Combine items over 30 times using a Curse Bringer angel on a single floor.
Deadly Meta-Beings	Purify Manas, Perisomats, Malecificia, and Tabula Smaragdina.
Defenseless Champ	Conquer the Defenseless dungeon.
Disk Collector	Successfully complete the Neuro Tower or die while holding over 15 types of disks.
Distant Wanderer	You have not qualified for any other Baroques.
Executioner	Successfully complete the Neuro Tower after purifying over 100 Meta-beings with torturers.
Explosive End	Die by consuming a boom bone.
Fashion Plate	Successfully complete the Neuro Tower or die while holding over 15 types of coats.
Fasting Penance	Successfully complete the Neuro Tower without eating hearts, flesh, or bones.
Fragile Splendor	Successfully complete the Neuro Tower while wearing Glass Sword, Glass Coat, and Glass Wings.
Fragments of Truth	Hear over 200 messages about the Baroques from the Baroque Monger.
Friendly Fire	Purify all the Koriel Members by using the Angelic Rifle.
Frugal Champ	Conquer the Frugal dungeon.
Hell Champ	Conquer the Hell dungeon.
Hunger Champ	Conquer the Hunger dungeon.
Hunger Strike	Die by losing HP from 0 Vitality (only if Vitality is over 499).
Hurting Dervish	Successfully complete the Neuro Tower after purifying over 100 Meta-beings by throwing items.
I am the World	Fuse with the absolute God when blind and deaf.
Icarus's Student	Successfully complete the Neuro Tower or die while holding over 15 types of wings.
Irony	Die while invincible.
Liberator	Once buried, purify Longneck, Horned Girl, and The Bagged One.
March On	Switch floors over 10 times while a Meta-being is in the room.
Masochist	Successfully complete the Neuro Tower or die while holding over 15 types of brands.
Medical Partner	Successfully complete the Neuro Tower or die while holding over 15 types of fluids.
Mugged	Let Gliro steal an item over 20 times.
Orb Seeker	Successfully complete the Neuro Tower after using every Consciousness Orb.
Parasite Museum	Successfully complete the Neuro Tower or die while holding over 15 types of parasites.
Power House	Successfully complete the Neuro Tower without a weapon and an attack above 50.
Promise of Peace	Successfully complete the Neuro Tower without purifying any Meta-beings.

Baroque (continued)

Unlockable	How to Unlock
Reverse Disk Champ	Conquer the Reverse Disk dungeon.
Rotten Champ	Conquer the Rotten dungeon.
Screaming Tower	Enter the Neuro Tower over 100 times.
Self Reliant	Reach the lowest level without using any consciousness orbs.
Serial Thrower	Throw over 100 items.
Shadow Boxer	Swing your sword over 100 times without hitting anything.
Skeleton Man	Successfully complete the Neuro Tower or die while holding over 15 types of bones.
Special Hunter	Successfully complete the Neuro Tower after purifying over 300 Meta-beings by sword.
Sword's Miracle	Land five consecutive critical hits with the sword.
The World's Tears	Find all the idea Sephirah that are in the item list.
Torture Master	Successfully complete the Neuro Tower or die while holding over 15 types of torturers.
Trap Champ	Conquer the Trap dungeon.
Unforgettable	Have a conversation with a specific phantom brother.
Unfortunate Death	Die from a Meta-being stepping on a disk.
Unrewarded Effort	Successfully complete the Neuro Tower without opening a Trials Box for over 2,000 cu.
Unstoppable	Successfully complete the Neuro Tower after taking over 5,000 damage.
Useless	Die without doing anything in the outer world.
Vacant Coffin	Conquer all training dungeons.
Warrior's Spirit	Successfully complete the Neuro Tower or die while holding over 15 types of swords.
Wasted Core	Successfully complete the Neuro Tower or die while holding over 15 types of crystals.
Wasted Effort	Lose either a coat or a sword with over 30.

Bases Loaded

Passwords

Password	Effect
LFBDJHE	Boston, one game away from the World Series
PFACNHK	DC, one game away from the World Series
CHXAACC	Game 162
LNADJPD	Hawaii, one game away from the World Series
CBIDNEP	Jersey, last game of the World Series
LFADNHH	Jersey, one game away from the World Series
PNCBNHD	Kansas, one game away from the World Series
PFBCNPD	LA, one game away from the World Series
PFCANHK	Miami, one game away from the World Series
PFDAJHH	New York, one game away from the World Series
LNDAJPD	Omaha, one game away from the World Series
JAELECO	Password for Pennant, must have selected "Pennant" option from menu
LFDBJHE	Philly, one game away from the World Series

Bases Loaded (continued)

Password	Effect
Select Pennant Mode and Enter JALECO as Password	Skip to the last team
LNCBJPD	Texas, one game away from the World Series
LNBCJPD	Utah, one game away from the World Series

Other Actions

Action	How to Enact
Don't Get Ejected During a Fight	Continually press Ⓑ during the fight
Hitter Charges the Mound and Gets Ejected	After the 3rd inning, bean the 3rd or 4th hitter in the lineup

Battle City

Stage Select

Unlockable	How to Unlock
Stage Select	When you start the game and see the screen with "Stage 1," press Ⓐ and Ⓑ to choose any stage you want

Ben 10: Protector of Earth

Codes

Press Start at the Map screen to bring up the Option menu, then select the "Enter Secret Code" menu and enter the following codes to get the corresponding effects.

Unlockable	How to Unlock
Dark Heroes	Cannonbolt, Cannonbolt, Fourarms, Heatblast
DNA Force	Wildvine, Fourarms, Heatblast, Cannonbolt
Invincibility	XLR8, Heatblast, Wildvine, Fourarms
Master Control	Cannonbolt, Heatblast, Wildvine, Fourarms
Unlock Alien Forms	Wildvine, Fourarms, Heatblast, Wildvine
Unlock ALL Combos	Cannonbolt, Heatblast, Fourarms, Heatblast
Unlock All Locations on Map	Heatblast, XLR8, XLR8, Cannonbolt

Bionicle Heroes

Secret Character

Unlockable	How to Unlock
Vezon	Complete the game once

BlastWorks: Build, Trade, Destroy

Unlockables

Unlockable	How to Unlock
Original TUMIKI Fighters	Beat all five campaigns on any difficulty.
Rootage	Complete the Arcade mode.
Black & White Cheat	Complete Campaign 2 in Arcade mode on Pilot difficulty.
Choose Ship Cheat	Complete Campaign 4 in Arcade mode on Pilot difficulty.
Extra Bullet Sounds	Complete Campaign 5 in Arcade mode on Pilot difficulty.
Extra Hit Sounds	Complete Campaign mode on Pilot difficulty.
Extra Skin Settings	Complete Campaign mode on Pilot difficulty.
Gunroar	Complete Campaign 4 in Campaign mode on Pilot difficulty.
Ninety Nine Cheat	Complete Campaign 2 in Campaign mode on Pilot difficulty.

BlastWorks: Build, Trade, Destroy (continued)

Unlockable	How to Unlock
Torus Trooper	Complete Campaign 3 in Campaign mode on Pilot difficulty.
TUMIKI Folder	Complete Campaign 5 in Campaign mode on Pilot difficulty.
Turtle Speed Cheat	Complete Campaign 1 in Campaign mode on Pilot difficulty.
Virtual Cheat	Complete Campaign 3 in Arcade mode on Pilot difficulty.
Wireframe Cheat	Complete Campaign 1 in Arcade mode on Pilot difficulty.
Flip Cheat	Complete Campaign 2 in Arcade mode on Ace difficulty.
Hyper Speed Cheat	Complete Campaign 1 in Arcade mode on Ace difficulty.

Blazing Angels: Squadrons of WWII

Unlockables

Unlockable	How to Unlock
All Aircraft/Missions/Paint Jobs	At the menu immediately following choose pilot, hold ⊖ and ⊕, then press [D-pad Left], [D-pad Right], ①, ②, ②, ①
B-17 Flying Fortress and Spitfire IX	Complete Campaign Mission 18—Counter Attack with at least a Veteran Pilot Ranking
B-25 Mitchell and Hs-129	Complete the Bombing Mini Campaign
Beaufighter and P-40C Warhawk	Complete Campaign Mission 6—Desert Rats with at least a Veteran Pilot Ranking
Boulton-Paul Defiant and Ki-43 Hayabusa (Oscar)	Complete Campaign Mission 10—Midway: Turning Point with at least a Veteran Pilot Ranking
De Havilland (DH) Mosquito and N1K Shiden (George)	Complete Campaign Mission 13—Rabaul Raid with at least a Veteran Pilot Ranking
Devastator and D3A1 Val	Complete Campaign Mission 7—Day of Infamy with at least a Veteran Pilot Ranking
Dornier Do-335 Pfeil (Arrow)	Complete Campaign mode
F2A Buffalo and B5N2 Kate	Complete Campaign Mission 8—Surprise Attack with at least a Veteran Pilot Ranking
Fw-190A and Me-109G	Complete Campaign Mission 14—Preemptive Strike with at least a Veteran Pilot Ranking
Hurricane I and Me-110C	Complete Campaign Mission 1—Training Day with at least a Veteran Pilot Ranking
Hurricane II and Me-110E	Complete Campaign Mission 5—Desert Recon with at least a Veteran Pilot Ranking
Me-262 Schwalbe (Sparrow) and Me-163 Komet	Complete the Dogfight Mini Campaign
Meteor and Kikka	Complete Campaign Mission 20—Berlin 1945 with at least a Veteran Pilot Ranking
P-51D Mustang and Me-109K	Complete Campaign Mission 16—D-Day Normandy with at least a Veteran Pilot Ranking
P-51H Mustang and Fw-190D-9	Complete Campaign Mission 19—Flying Fortresses with at least a Veteran Pilot Ranking
P-82 Twin Mustang and J2M Raiden (Jack)	Complete Campaign Mission 12—The Battle of New Georgia with at least a Veteran Pilot Ranking
SB2C Helldiver and SB2A Buccaneer	Complete Campaign Mission 11—Holding Guadalcanal with at least a Veteran Pilot Ranking
SBD-3 Dauntless and A6M Zero	Complete Campaign Mission 9—Midway: Opening with at least a Veteran Pilot Ranking
Seafire and Ju-87 Stuka	Complete Campaign Mission 4—London 1940 with at least a Veteran Pilot Ranking

DS
PSP
PS2
PS3
Wii
Xbox
Xbox 360
Index

DS PSP PS2 PS3 Wii Xbox Xbox 360 Index

Blazing Angels: Squadrons of WWII (continued)

Unlockables

Unlockable	How to Unlock
Spitfire I and Me-109E	Complete Campaign Mission 2—Skies of Dunkirk with at least a Veteran Pilot Ranking
Swordfish and Spitfire V	Complete Campaign Mission 3—Dunkirk Evacuation with at least a Veteran Pilot Ranking
Tempest and A-1 Skyraider	Complete Campaign Mission 17—Paris: La Liberation with at least a Veteran Pilot Ranking
Typhoon and Me-110G	Complete Campaign Mission 15—Top Secret with at least a Veteran Pilot Ranking
Upgraded Bombs, Rockets, and Torpedos for All Aircraft	Complete the Bombing Mini Campaign
Upgraded Cannons and Machine Guns for All Fighters	Complete the Dogfight Mini Campaign

Bleach: Shattered Blade

Characters

Unlockable	How to Unlock
Aizen Sousuke	Clear Arcade mode with Ulquiorra.
Arturo Plateado	Clear Episode mode with Arturo Plateado.
Grimmjow Jaggerjack	Clear Arcade mode with Aizen Sousuke.
Hinamori Momo	Clear Hitsugaya Toushiro's story.
Hisagi Shuuhei	Clear Episode mode with Yamada Hanatarou.
Ichimaru Gin	Clear Arcade mode with Matsumoto Rangiku and Kira Izuru.
Kuchiki Rukia	Beat Story mode with Abarai Renji.
Kurotsuchi Mayuri	Clear Arcade mode with Ishida Uryuu.
Kusajishi Yachiru	Clear Arcade mode with Yumichika Ayasegawa and Zaraki Kenpachi.
Kyouraku Shunsui	Clear Arcade mode with Sado Yasutora.
Madarame Ikkaku	Clear Episode mode with Zaraki Kenpachi.
Shihouin Yoruichi	Clear Training mode.
Soi Fon	Clear Episode mode with Shihouin Yoruichi.
Tousen Kaname	Clear Arcade mode with Hisagi Shuuhei and Komamura Sajin.
Ukitake Juushiro	Clear Arcade mode with Kyouraku Shunsui.
Ulquiorra	Clear Arcade mode with Tousen Kaname and Ichimaru Gin.
Urahara Kisuke	Clear Arcade mode with Kurotsuchi Mayuri.
Yamada Hanatarou	Beat Story mode with Youshiro Hitsugaya.
Yamamoto Genryuusai Shigekuni	Clear Arcade mode with Ukitake Juushiro.
Yumichika Ayasegawa	Clear Arcade mode with Madarame Ikkaku.

Costumes

Unlockable	How to Unlock
Hitsugaya School Costume	Win 15 matches with Toushiro Hitsugaya.
Ikkaku School Costume	Win 10 matches with Madarame Ikkaku.
Masked Komamura Costume	Win 15 matches with Komamura Sajin.
Matsumoto School Costume	AFTER unlocking Inoue Orihime's costume, win 15 matches with Matsumoto Rangiku.

Bleach: Shattered Blade (continued)

Unlockable	How to Unlock
Orihime School Costume	Win 15 matches with Inoue Orihime.
Renji School Costume	Win 15 matches with Abarai Renji.
Rukia School Costume	Win 15 matches with Kuchiki Rukia.
Shihouin Yoruichi Shunpo Costume	After completing practice mode, win 15 matches with Yoruichi.
Urahara Kisuke Shinigami Costume	Unlock everything, and it becomes available for free in Urahara's Shop.
Yumichika School Costume	Win 10 matches with Ayasegawa Yumichika.

Stages

Unlockable	How to Unlock
Arturo Battle Stage	Defeat Arturo Plateado on the final stage of Episode mode.
Ice Haven	Complete Hitsugaya's Episode mode.

Bloody Wolf

Codes

Unlockable	How to Unlock
10 Flash Bombs	When your strength is at "1," climb a barricade and press ✚+✚+RUN+②
10 Super Grenades	When your strength is at "1," climb a barricade and press ✚+✚+RUN+②
50 Bazooka Rounds	When your strength is at "2," climb a fence and press ✚+①+②
50 Flame Thrower Charges	Hold ✚+①+② and press RUN when parachuting at the start of level 2 or level 5
50 Shotgun Rounds	When your strength is at "2," climb a fence and press ✚+①+②
Fast Mode	At the title screen, press ✚, ✚, ✚, ✚, ①, ①, ② SELECT, RUN
Hover Mode (in game, press jump to hover)	At the title screen, press ✚, ✚, ✚, ✚, ②, ②, ①, SELECT, RUN
Sound Test	At the title screen, press ✚, then hold ①+②+SELECT

Level Select Codes

Press ②, ①, ①, ②, ①, ②, ②, ① at the title screen. Then press the following for the appropriate level.

Code	Effect	Code	Effect
Up	Level 1	Down	Level 5
Up/Right	Level 2	Down/Left	Level 6
Right	Level 3	Left	Level 7
Down/Right	Level 4	Up/Left	Level 8

Bonk's Revenge

Codes

Code	Effect
Bonus Levels	Press ①+② during the title screen
Clear Pause Screen	Pause the game and hold ①+②+SELECT
Ending Sequence Preview	First activate the "practice bonus rounds" code and then highlight the Exit option and press ②+RUN
Practice Bonus Rounds	Hold ② and then press RUN on the Difficulty Selection menu

Bonk's Revenge (continued)

Code	Effect
Remove Pause Text	Pause the game (by pressing RUN) and then press ①+②+SELECT
View Ending	Enable the Bonus Levels cheat, then Highlight "Exit" and press ②+RUN

Boogie

Unlockable Songs and Stages

Unlockable	How to Unlock
Song: Boogie Oogie Oogie	Beat Bubba's story
Song: Dancing in the Street	Beat Julius' story
Song: Love Shack	Beat Lea's story
Song: SOS (Rescue Me)	Beat Jet's story
Song: Tu y Yo	Beat Kato's story
Stage: Big Dub Hustle Club	Beat all 5 stories

Bratz: The Movie

Hidden Clothing Lines

To unlock these clothing lines, go to the small laptop near the computers in the Bratz Office and type in the following codes.

Code	Clothing Line
PRETTY	Feelin' Pretty Clothing Line
SCHOOL	High School Clothing Line
ANGELZ	Passion 4 Fashion Clothing Line
SWEETZ	Sweetz Clothing Line

Bravoman

Codes

Unlockable	How to Unlock
Bravo Kombat Minigame	Keep tapping ②, SELECT at the title screen
Continue Game	Press ②+RUN as Bravoman is dying
Unlimited Continues	Get 10,000 points, then lose and wait for the title screen to come up, then press ✜, ✜, ✜, ✜, ②, SELECT, ②, SELECT

Breath of Fire II

Unlockable	How to Unlock
Old Friends	At Giant Island, in the northern area above the town gate, you'll find Bo and Karn from the first *Breath of Fire* game. They don't do anything, but you can talk to them. You need the whale or the bird to get there.

Bully Scholarship Edition

Unlockables

Unlockable	How to Unlock
Black Ninja Suit	Take a picture of all the students of Bullworth.
BMX Helmet	Complete all bike races.
Crash Helmet	Win the first set of Go-Kart races.
Double Carnival Tickets	Collect all G & G cards.
Fireman's Hat	Pull the fire alarm 15 times to unlock the fireman's hat.

Bully Scholarship Edition (continued)

Unlockable	How to Unlock
Mo-Ped	Buy from carnival for 75 tickets.
Pumpkin Head	Smash all pumpkins either on Halloween or in basement.
Robber Mask	Break into 15 people's lockers without getting caught.
Rubber Band Ball	Collect all rubber bands.

Bust-A-Move Bash!

More Stages

Unlockable	How to Unlock
250 More Stages	After completing the first 250 stages in Puzzle mode, return to the Select screen and press Ⓐ with the cursor hovering over Stage Select. The area should be mostly orange now instead of blue, and only the first stage will be available. This is how you access stages 251-500.

Call of Duty 3

Enter this code in the Chapter Select screen.

Unlockable	Code
Unlock All Levels	Hold ⊕ and press ✚→, ✚→, ✚←, ✚←, ②, ②
Unlock All Extras	At the Chapter Select screen, hold ⊕, and press ✚→, ✚→, ✚←, ✚←, ②, ②

Cars

Input codes in the password section under the Options menu.

Unlockable	Code
All Cars	YAYCARS
All Concept Art	CONC3PT
All Movies	WATCHIT
All Paint Jobs	R4MONE
All Races	MATTL66
All Tracks and Mini-games	IF900HP
Mater's Speedy Circuit and Mater's Countdown Clean Up	TRGTEXC
Super Fast Start	IMSPEED
Unlimited Boost	VROOOOM

Chew-Man-Fu

Codes

Unlockable	How to Unlock
Golden Balls	At the title screen, hold ①+SELECT and press ✚←+✚↑

Passwords

Password	Effect
573300	Area 1, Round 1 (2nd Playthrough)
344710	Area 1, Round 1 (3rd Playthrough)
274510	Area 1, Round 1 (4th Playthrough)
321310	Area 1, Round 1 (5th Playthrough)
536300	Area 1, Round 1 (6th Playthrough)
301710	Area 1, Round 1 (7th Playthrough)
231510	Area 1, Round 1 (8th Playthrough)
256310	Area 1, Round 1 (9th Playthrough)
441300	Area 1, Round 1 (10th Playthrough)
677261	Area 5, Round 50
075653	Fight enemy opponents only

China Warrior

Codes

Unlockable	How to Unlock
Enable Invincibility and Level Select	Press RUN+SELECT to reset the game, keep the buttons held, then release RUN and press ✚ when the title screen is displayed. Release Select and press ✚, ✚, ✚, ✚, ✚, ✚, ✚, ✚, ✚, ✚, ✚, ✚, ✚.
Level Skip	Hold ✚ then SELECT+①+② to skip the first level. For the other levels, hold ✚ instead of ✚.
Continue (up to three times) from the Start of the Last Level Played	Hold ①+②+✚ and press RUN, RUN when the phrase "The End" appears after gameplay is over. Alternately, hold ①+2+✚ and press RUN at the title screen after game play is over.

Comix Zone

Unlockables

Unlockable	How to Unlock
Fart	In some areas, press ✚.
Sega Plug	At any time during the main game, press START to pause. After a few seconds, Sketch will yell, "Sega!"
Stage Select	Go to the Jukebox mode and place the red checker on the following numbers in order, pressing ✚ at each one: 14, 15, 18, 5, 13, 1, 3, 18, 15, 6. Now, highlight a number from 1 to 6 and press ✚ to warp to the corresponding stage.
Unlimited Health	Go to Jukebox in the Options menu and push ✚ on these numbers: 3, 12, 17, 2, 2, 10, 2, 7, 7, 11. You hear Sketch say "oh yeah."
View Credits	At the Options mode, press Ⓐ+Ⓑ+Ⓒ.
Paper Airplane	During gameplay press and hold the Punch button. After a second or so Sketch will tear a piece of paper from the background and make a paper airplane out of it. The plane will travel to the edge of the panel and circle back around. The plane does massive damage to all enemies, objects, and Sketch himself, so be careful. You lose a considerable amount of health when creating the plane.

Cratermaze

Passwords

Password	Effect
Unlock All Normal Levels	Press RUN on the title screen and select Password. Enter this password, then use ① and ② to select a level before pressing RUN. Blue/Left, Blue/Left, Blue/Right, Red/Front
Expert Level Select	Blue/Back, Blue/Back, Red/Right, Blue/Forward

Cybernator

Codes

Unlockable	How to Unlock
Extra Continues	At the title screen, hold ✚+✚+✚and then press START.
Napalm Gun	Complete the first level without shooting anything except the boss, then complete level 2 without dying.
Secret Bad Ending	Go through the first level, and do not destroy the boss. Finish the rest of the game to see the failed ending.

Dance Dance Revolution Hottest Party

Unlockables

Unlockable	How to Unlock
Super Samurai—jun	Play 3 songs on Expert and get a AA or higher on the third song
tokyoEVOLVED—Naoki UNDERGROUND	Unlock all songs, then play 3 songs on Expert and get an AA or higher on the third song
Harmony's Alternate Outfit	Beat Harmony at the song Little Steps at the Genesis Venue
Root's Alternate Outfit	Beat Root at Break Down with a B ranking at the Tectonic Venue

Dead Moon

Unlockable

Unlockable	How to Unlock
Option Screen	Hold the following: ✚+①+② and press SELECT

Devil's Crush

Unlockable

Unlockable	How to Unlock
Sound Mode	Press ✚, ✚, ✚ after pausing
Sound Test	Press RUN, SELECT during gameplay to display the High Score screen, then press ✚, ✚, ✚, ✚, ①

Passwords

Password	Effect
EFGHIJKLMB	924,000,000 points and 73 balls
AAAAAAAAAAAAAAAAAB	A 2-player game with unlimited balls
THECRUSHEL	Beat the game—launch the ball and once you hit something, the game ends
DAVIDWHITE	Beat the game—launch the ball and once you hit something, the game ends
FFFFFFFEEE	Beat the game—launch the ball and once you hit something, the game ends
NAXATSOFTI	Infinite balls, 206,633,300 points
AAAAAAHAAA	Infinite balls, 734,003,200 points
DEVILSATAN	Infinite balls, 955,719,100 points
THEDEVILSI	Over 145,000,000 points and 70 balls
ONECRUSHME	Over 594,000,000 points and 27 balls
AAAAAAAAAAAAAAABCE	2-player mode—gives player 1 unlimited balls and player 2 32 balls
PPPPPPPPPA	Unlimited balls
CKDEIPDBFM	25 balls and a score of 300,138,400
OJFJGDEJPD	34 balls and a score of 404,330,300
PNBIJOKJNF	38 balls and a score of 533,501,000
CGIAGPECGK	42 balls and a score of 610,523,600
OEHALCBGPF	45 balls and a score of 710,529,000
OLGGGEAPOF	52 balls and a score of 804,379,700
CBEOBLJGHA	62 balls and a score of 900,057,102
PFFMGHGOLK	65 balls and a score of 999,927,400
NLJBCFHGPO	65 balls and a score of 999,999,000
KGCMMCMLBN	65 balls and a score of 999,999,600
OMGANLOIJA	67 balls and a score of 976,769,800

Dewy's Adventure

Unlockables

Unlockable	How to Unlock
Character Gallery	Complete Groovy Grasslands
Hall of Records	Complete Groovy Grasslands
Music Gallery	Complete Groovy Grasslands
Photo Gallery	Complete Groovy Grasslands
Tips and Tricks	Complete Groovy Grasslands

Disney's Chicken Little: Ace in Action

Input the codes under Cheat option.

Unlockable	Code
All Levels Available	→, ↑, ←, →, ↑
All Weapons Available	→, ↓, →, ←
Unlimited Shield Available	→, ↓, →, ↓, →

Dokapon Kingdom

Unlockables

Here's how to unlock specific jobs.

Unlockable	How to Unlock
Acrobat	Get a Casino Ticket
Alchemist	Master Magician and Thief
Cleric	Master 1 of the Starter Jobs
Monk	Master Priest
Ninja	Master Warrior and Thief
Spellsword	Master Warrior and Magician

Double Dungeons

Passwords

At the Password screen, carefully enter the following passwords.

Password	Effect
cHR0EScxgoAq or iky7ihOfeBGe	In front of the last boss door
2R3KD4RG0J9D3YT0664LJ	Beginning of Level 22
YNzYSMChriGIgLV-ih0dfCGe	End of Level 22
Enter either Player01 or Player 02 as a password, with the remaining spaces filled in with either +'s or -'s	Get 65,535 HP
Enter any working password for player 1, then enter KKKKKKKKKKKKKKKKKKKKKKK as a password for player 2	Player 2 invincibility

Dr. Robotnik's Mean Bean Machine

Easy Mode Passwords

Password	Effect
RRRH	Stage 2: Frankly
CPCG	Stage 3: Humpty
RCHY	Stage 4: Coconuts
CBBP	Stage 5: Davy Sproket
CRCP	Stage 6: Sqweel
PYRB	Stage 7: Dynamight
YPHB	Stage 8: Grounder
YPHB	Stage 9: Spike
RYCH	Stage 10: Sir Fuzzy Logik
GPBC	Stage 11: Dragon Breath
RHHY	Stage 12: Scratch
YHBB	Stage 13: Dr. Robotnik

Dr. Robotnik's Mean Bean Machine (continued)

Hard Mode Passwords

Password	Effect	Password	Effect
RRRH GCYY	Stage 2: Frankly	CYHY	Stage 8: Grounder
CPCG YPCP	Stage 3: Humpty	PBBG	Stage 9: Spike
RCHY BGCB	Stage 4: Coconuts	CGRY	Stage 10: Sir Fuzzy Logik
RPGG	Stage 5: Davy Sproket	BYYH	Stage 11: Dragon Breath
YYCG	Stage 6: Sqweel	GCCB	Stage 12: Scratch
PCBB	Stage 7: Dynamight	HCPH	Stage 13: Dr. Robotnik

Hardest Mode Passwords

Password	Effect	Password	Effect
BBGY	Stage 2: Frankly	CPHY	Stage 8: Grounder
GYGC	Stage 3: Humpty	PGHC	Stage 9: Spike
PPRH	Stage 4: Coconuts	GBYH	Stage 10: Sir Fuzzy Logik
GRPB	Stage 5: Davy Sproket	GPHR	Stage 11: Dragon Breath
PCGY	Stage 6: Sqweel	RGHB	Stage 12: Scratch
BPGH	Stage 7: Dynamight	RRCY	Stage 13: Dr. Robotnik

Unlockables

Unlockable	How to Unlock
Jumping Bean Title Screen	At the title screen, press Ⓐ, Ⓑ, or ✜ on controller 1 to make the "e," "a," and "n" in "Mean" jump. Press Ⓐ, Ⓑ, or ✜ on controller 2 to make the "e", "a", and "n" in "Bean" jump.
Last Boss	On Easy mode, enter Yellow Bean, Has Bean, Blue Bean, Blue Bean as your password. On Normal mode, enter Purple Bean, Yellow Bean, Has Bean, Clear Bean.

Scenario Mode Passwords—Normal Difficulty

Enter these passwords after selecting "Continue" to skip ahead to the desired level.

R = Red Bean

Y = Yellow Bean

G = Green Bean

B = Blue Bean

P = Purple Bean

C = Clear (Garbage) Bean

H = Has Bean (the little orange fellow)

Password	Effect	Password	Effect
HCYY	Stage 2: Frankly	GHCY	Stage 8: Grounder
BCRY	Stage 3: Humpty	BPHH	Stage 9: Spike
YBCP	Stage 4: Coconuts	HRYC	Stage 10: Sir Fuzzy Logik
HGBY	Stage 5: Davy Sprocket	CRRB	Stage 11: Dragon Breath
GPPY	Stage 6: Sqweel	GGCY	Stage 12: Scratch
PBGH	Stage 7: Dynamight	PYHC	Stage 13: Dr. Robotnik

DS PSP PS2 PS3 Wii Xbox Xbox 360 Index

Dragon Ball Z: Budokai Tenkaichi 2

"What If" Sagas

These special sagas become available when you win an "impossible" battle. Without these, you cannot attain 100% completion in Story mode. They're best attempted after you've run through Story mode and leveled up your characters.

Unlockable	How to Unlock
Beautiful Treachery	Defeat Dodoria with Gohan and Krillin in Mission 01 of the Frieza Saga "A Pursuer Who Calls Death"
Destined Rivals Saga	Defeat Gohan with Goten in Mission 01 of the Majin Buu "Training with Goten"
Fateful Brothers	Defeat Raditz with Piccolo in Mission 00 of the Saiyan Saga "Mysterious Alien Warrior" (first mission of the game)

Fight Intruders in Ultimate Battle Z

Some towers in the Ultimate Battle Z mode have hidden battles that require specific conditions to trigger. They are available only in difficulty level 3.

Unlockable	How to Unlock
Fight Broly Legendary SSJ in Saiyan Blood	Defeat Bardock with an Ultimate Blast
Fight Goku SSJ2 and Vegeta (Second 2 Form) SSJ2 in Dragon Tag	Defeat any opponent with an Ultimate Blast
Fight Hercule in Unlimited	Defeat Gogeta SSJ4
Fight Omega Shenron in Ultimate Dragon	Defeat Syn Shenron with an Ultimate Blast
Fight SSJ3 Gotenks in Ultimate Children	Defeat Kid Goku with an Ultimate Blast
Fight Super Baby 2 in Normal-ism	Defeat Super 13 with an Ultimate Blast
Fight Tao Pai Pai in Assault Force!	Defeat any opponent with an Ultimate Blast
Fight Uub in Kakarot Road	Defeat Kid Buu with an Ultimate Blast

Unlockable Characters

Unlockable	How to Unlock
100% Full Power Frieza	Super Transformation + Final Form Frieza
Android 13	Computer + Hatred
Android 13 Fusion	Android 13 + Parts of 14 and 15
Baby Vegeta	Baby + Vegeta (second form)
Bardock	Defeat Lord Slug Saga
Bojack	Unsealed + Galactic Warrior
Broly	Son of Paragus + Hatred of Goku
Burter	Defeat Burter and Jeice with Goku
Cell	Defeat Cell with Piccolo and Android 17
Cell (2nd Form)	Defeat Cell (2nd Form) with Trunks and Vegeta
Cell (3rd Form or Perfect Form)	Defeat Cell (Perfect Form) with Gohan
Cell (Perfect or Perfect Cell)	Self Destruction + Cell Perfect Form
Cell Jr.	Defeat Cell Jrs. (5) with Gohan
Cooler	Frieza's Brother + Hatred of Goku
Cooler Final Form	Super Transformation + Cooler
Cui	Vegeta's Rival + Frieza's Soldier
Demon King Dabura	Defeat Dabura with Adult Gohan
Doboria	Defeat Doboria in Dragon Adventure

Dragon Ball Z: Budokai Tenkaichi 2 (continued)

Unlockable	How to Unlock
Dr. Gero	Defeat Dr. Gero with Krillin
Evil Buu	Evil Human Cannonball + Majin Buu
Full Power Bojak	Ultimate Transformation + Bojack
Garlic Jr.	Makyo Star + Dead Zone
General Tao	Bros. of Crane Hermit + Memorial Campaign
Giant Lord Slug	Slug + Giant Form
Ginyu	Defeat Ginyu (with Goku's body) and Jeice with Krillin, Vegeta, and Gohan
Gohan Super Buu	Gohan Absorbed + Evil Buu
Gotenks	Defeat Buu (Pure Evil) with Majin Buu and Hercule
Gotenks Super Buu	Gotenks Absorbed + Evil Buu
Grandpa Gohan	Master Roshi's Pupil + Fox Mask
Great Ape Baby	Super Baby 2 + Artificial Blutz Wave
Great Ape Bardock	Power Ball + Bardock
Great Ape Nappa	Power Ball + Nappa
Great Ape Raditz	Power Ball + Raditz
Great Ape Turles	Power Ball + Turles
Great Ape Vegeta	Power Ball + Vegeta (Scouter)
Great Saiyaman (Gohan)	Defeat Zangya and Bojack with Teen Gohan
Great Saiyaman 2 (Videl)	Defeat Broly with Goten and Adult Gohan
Guldo	Defeat Guldo with Vegeta, Krillin, and Gohan
Hercule	Defeat Perfect Cell with Super Trunks
Hirudegarn	Hirudegarn's Top Half + Hirudegarn's Lower Half
Janemba	Saike Demon + People's Bad Energy
Jeice	Defeat Jeice and Ginyu (with Goku's body) with Krillin, Vegeta, and Gohan
Kibitoshin	Kibito + Supreme Kai
Kid Buu	Defeat Kid Buu with Goku and Vegeta
Kid Goku	Defeat Grandpa Gohan
Legendary Super Saiyan Broly	Super Saiyan Broly + Breakthrough the Limit
Lord Slug	Namekian + Mutation
Majin Buu (Pure evil)	Human Gunman's Gun + Majin Buu
Majin Vegeta	Defeat Buu with Adult Gohan + Supreme Kai
Majin Vegeta	Defeat Majin Buu with Supreme Kai and Gohan
Majuub	Defeat Super Baby 2 with Pan and Uub
Master Roshi	Defeat Raditz with Goku
Master Roshi Full Power	Master Roshi + Seriousness
Mecha Frieza	Reconstructive Surgery + 100% Full Power Frieza
Metal Cooler	Big Gete Star + Cooler
Nappa	Defeat him in Dragon Adventure
Omega Shenron	Syn Shenron + Ultimate Dragon Ball
Pan	Defeat Hirudegarn with Tapion and Kid Trunks
Pikkon	Defeat Pikkon with Goku
Recoome	Defeat Recoome with Goku and Vegeta

Dragon Ball Z: Budokai Tenkaichi 2 (continued)

Unlockable	How to Unlock
Salza	Coolers Soldier + Armored Cavalry
Super Android 17	HFIL Fighter 17 + Android 17
Super Baby 1	Baby Vegeta + Lower Class Saiyan
Super Baby 2	Super Baby 1 + Power from Lower Class
Super Buu	Defeat Super Buu with Ultimate Gohan
Super Buu Gohan Absorbed	Absorb Gohan + Super Buu
Super Buu Gotenks Absorbed	Absorb Gotenks + Super Buu
Super Garlic Jr.	Garlic Jr. + Giant Form
Super Gogeta	Defeat Super Janemba with Pikkon + Buu
Super Gotenks	Defeat Pure Evil Buu with Buu + Hercule
Super Janemba	In item fusion combine Janemba + Ultimate Transformation
Super Perfect Cell	Suicide Bomb + Perfect Cell
Super Saiyan 1 Teen Gohan	Defeat Perfect Cell with Super Trunks
Super Saiyan 2 Goku	Defeat Majin Buu with Supreme Kai and Adult Gohan (Buu Saga)
Super Saiyan 2 Teen Gohan	Defeat Cell Jr. (5) with Super Saiyan 1 Gohan
Super Saiyan 2 Vegeta	Defeat Buu (Gotenks absorbed) with Goku
Super Saiyan 3 Goku	Defeat Majin Buu with Majin Vegeta
Super Saiyan 3 Gotenks	Defeat Super Buu with Gotenks
Super Saiyan 4 Gogeta	Defeat Omega Shenron with Super Saiyan 4 Goku and Vegeta
Super Saiyan 4 Goku	Defeat Super Baby with Majuub
Super Saiyan 4 Vegeta	Defeat Omega Shenron with Super Saiyan 4 Goku
Super Saiyan Broly	Broly + Super Saiyan
Super Saiyan Goku	Defeat Frieza Final Form with Piccolo, Krillin, and Kid Gohan (Frieza Saga)
Super Saiyan Goten	Defeat General Tao with Videl and Great Saiyaman
Super Saiyan Kid Trunks	Defeat General Tao with Videl and Great Saiyaman
Super Saiyan Trunks	Defeat Second Form Cell with Tien
Super Saiyan Trunks (Sword)	Defeat Androids 17 and 18 with Gohan
Super Saiyan Vegeta (Second Form)	Defeat Vegeta with Super Saiyan Teen Trunks (Buu Saga)
Super Trunks	Defeat Perfect Cell with Super Vegeta
Super Vegeta	Defeat Cell Form 2
Super Vegetto	Defeat Super Buu (Gohan Absorbed) with Goku and Vegeta
Supreme Kai	Defeat Android 18 with Hercule
Syn Shenron	Evil Dragon + Negative Energy
Tapion	Defeat Tapion with Trunks and Goten
Trunks	Unlock History of Trunks Saga
Turles	Lower-Class Saiyan Soldier + Fruit of the Gods
Ultimate Gohan (Mystic)	Defeat Buu with Piccolo or Super Saiyan 3 Gotenks
Uub	Defeat Hirudegarn with Super Saiyan 3 Goku

Dragon Ball Z: Budokai Tenkaichi 2 (continued)

Unlockable	How to Unlock
Vegeta (2nd Form)	Defeat Vegeta with Super Saiyan Teen Trunks (Buu Saga)
Vegeta (Post Namek)	Defeat Metal Cooler with Super Saiyan Goku (Return of Cooler Saga)
Vegetto	Defeat Super Buu + Gohan with Goku and Vegeta
Videl	Defeat Android 18 with Hercule (Buu Saga)
Videl	Defeat Bojack and Zangya with Piccolo + Gohan
Yajirobe	Defeat Great Ape Gohan with Piccolo
Zangya	The Fowers of Evil + Galactic Warrior
Zarbon Post-Transformation	Unsealed + Zarbon

Wii Exclusive Characters

In the European, Australian or Japanese versions of the game, you can unlock 6 extra secret characters by playing through Ultimate Battle Z mode.

Unlockable	How to Unlock
Appule	Complete Course 4
Cyborg Tao	Complete Course 6
Demon King Piccolo	Complete Course 8
Frieza Soldier	Complete Course 2
Pilaf Machine	Complete Course 10
Pilaf Machine Combined	Complete Course 10

Easter Egg

Unlockable	How to Unlock
Bra in the Training Mode	Complete Basic Training

Dragon Blade: Wrath of Fire

Codes

At the Stage Select screen, Hold Ⓩ and press ⊕ to start inputting the codes. To clear the codes, hold Ⓩ and press ⊖. You will hear a confirmation when you do the combination to enter the codes, when you enter the codes, and when you clear them.

Unlockable	How to Unlock
Tail Power	Swing your Wii Remote Down, Up, Left, and Right
Double Fist Power	Swing your Nunchuk Right-> Swing your Wii Remote left-> Swing your Nunchuk right while swinging your Wii Remote left->Swing both Wii Remote and Nunchuk down

Unlockables

Unlockable	How to Unlock
Long Sword	Beat the game once

Dragon Ball Z: Budokai Tenkaichi 3

Characters

Unlockable	How to Unlock
Android 8	Clear "Affectionate Android" in Dragon History's What If Saga.
Arale	Clear "Dream Match: Goku Vs. Arale" in Dragon History's What If Saga.
Babidi	Clear "Farewell to the Proud Warrior" in Dragon History's Majin Buu Saga.
Cyborg Tao	Obtain victory in Otherworld Tournament level 2.

Dragon Ball Z: Budokai Tenkaichi 3 (continued)

Unlockable	How to Unlock
Devilman	Clear "Unexpected Help" in Dragon History's What If Saga.
Dr. Wheelo	Clear "Strongest in the World" in Dragon History's Special Saga.
Fasha	Obtain victory in Yamcha Game level 3.
Future Gohan	Wish from Shenron.
General Blue	Clear "Penguin Village" in Dragon History's Dragon Ball Saga.
Goku GT	Clear "Immortal Monster" in Dragon History's Dragon Ball GT Saga.
Kid Chi-Chi	Wish from Red Shenron.
King Cold	Obtain victory in Cell Games level 3.
King Piccolo	Clear "Goku Strikes Back" in Dragon History's Dragon Ball Saga.
King Vegeta	Clear "Galaxy Battle" in Dragon History's What If Saga.
Nail	Clear "Super Saiyan?!" in Dragon History's Frieza Saga.
Nam	Clear "Ceiling Vs. Ground" in Dragon History's Dragon Ball Saga.
Nuova Shenron	Clear "Solar Warrior 6000 Degrees of Power!" in Dragon History's Dragon Ball GT Saga.
Pilaf Machine	Obtain victory in World Martial Arts Big Tournament level 2.
Spopovich	Obtain victory in World Tournament level 3.
Super Saiyan 4 Gogeta	Beat "Ultimate Super Gogeta" in Dragon Ball GT Saga.
Super Saiyan 4 Goku	Beat "Ultimate Android" in Dragon Ball GT Saga.
Super Saiyan 4 Vegeta	Beat "Ultimate Super Gogeta" in Dragon Ball GT Saga.
Tambourine	Clear "Goku Strikes Back" in Dragon History's Dragon Ball Saga.

Dragon Spirit

Codes

Unlockable	How to Unlock
100 Continues	Press ↓, →, SELECT, ↓, ②, ↓, ①, ←, SELECT, ↑, ①, ②, ① at the title screen
Arcade Mode Screen	Hold Select and press RUN 57 times to reset the game for a narrow screen
Sound Test	←, →, ↓, ↑, SELECT, ← at the title screen
Two Continues	Hold ① and press ② at the title screen

Dragon's Curse

Unlockable

Unlockable	How to Unlock
Full Life	After dying, use a potion while holding ②

Passwords

Password	Effect
3YHURYW7Y7LL8C	Start game at beginning with Max. Gold (983,040)/All Equipment/Full Health (8 Hearts)/Max. Stones (99)/All Items/Hawk-Man Status
3YHURYW7Y7LPBS	Start game at beginning with Max. Gold (983,040)/All Equipment/Full Health (8 Hearts)/Max. Stones (99)/All Items/Hu-Man Status
3YHURYW7Y7LRBW	Start game at beginning with Max. Gold (983,040)/All Equipment/Full Health (8 Hearts)/Max. Stones (99)/All Items/Lizard-Man Status

Dragon's Curse (continued)

Password	Effect
3YHURYW7Y7LM80	Start game at beginning with Max. Gold (983,040)/All Equipment/Full Health (8 Hearts)/Max. Stones (99)/All Items/Mouse-Man Status
3YHURYW7Y7LN84	Start game at beginning with Max. Gold (983,040)/All Equipment/Full Health (8 Hearts)/Max. Stones (99)/All Items/Piranha-Man Status
3YHURYW7Y7LK88	Start game at beginning with Max. Gold (983,040)/All Equipment/Full Health (8 Hearts)/Max. Stones (99)/All Items/Tiger-Man Status
W0CV5ATVKYR1SV	Start with all the necessary transformations and items to enter the final dungeon
MODE FOR 0000 000	Be Hu Man at Start (JP ONLY)
PLAY THE ONGA KUN	Disable door noise (JP ONLY)
NODEGOSOOOOOOO	Start as Be Hu Man
3WSURYXZY763TE	Start with advanced abilities and items
RMAYTJEOPHALUP	Take away the noises from doors
3ZHURYNZY726VH	Start as Hu-Man with 8 hearts, all equipment, all transformations unlocked, and only the final dungeon to beat

Driver: Parallel Lines

Password

Password	Effect
steelman	Invincibility

Collecting Stars

Collect the scattered golden stars throughout the map to unlock the following rewards. Note: Everything resets once you get to the 2006 era, and collecting another 50 Stars will unlock the same attributes. (There are 100 total in the game.)

Unlockable	How to Unlock
Double Ammunition Capacity	Collect 30 Stars
Double Car Durability	Collect 40 Stars
Free Vehicle Upgrades	Collect 50 Stars
Health Increase	Collect 10 Stars
Nitrous Increase	Collect 20 Stars

Unlockable Cars

Unlockable	How to Unlock
Andec Racer	Win the Jersey Racetrack race in 1978 on Hard
Bonsai Racer	Win the La Guardia race in 1978 on Medium
Brooklyn Racer	Win the Jersey Racetrack race in 1978 on Medium
Hot Rod	Win the Driver GP Long Island Race in 2006
Raven Racer	Win the Driver GP Long Island Race in 1978
San Marino Racer	Win the Hunts Points race in 1978 on Hard

Unlockables

Unlockable	How to Unlock
Far Out Mode	Reach 900 miles
Night Night Mode	Reach 700 miles
Play as a Pedestrian/Policeman	Reach 666 miles + melee attack the person you want to play as
Shortest Day Mode	Reach 800 miles

Drop Off

Unlockables

Unlockable	How to Unlock
Level Select	Press SELECT 16 times then press RUN
Sound Mode	Hold SELECT+①
Sound Test	Hold ② and press SELECT
Unlimited Continues	RUN+①, RUN+②

Dungeon Explorer

Passwords

Password	Effect
CHECK NAMEA	Change names
ADGDP-CJLPG	Final Dungeon is open
DEBDE DEBDA then press RUN+①	Invincibility
JBBNJ HDCOG	Play as Princess Aki
IMGAJ MDPAI	Play as the Hermit
HOMING AAAA	Precision guided weapons (smart weapons)

Level Select

Enable the "Invincibility" code. Enter one of the following 15 bushes in front of Axis castle to jump to the corresponding location. (Bush 1 is on the left end, bush 15 is on the right end.)

Bush	Location
1	Natas
2	Balamous Tower
3	Rotterroad (path to Judas)
4	Mistose Dungeon
5	Ratonix Dungeon
6	Reraport Maze
7	Rally Maze
8	Bullbeast
9	Melba Village
10	After Gutworm
11	Nostalgia Dungeon
12	Water Castle
13	Road to Cherry Tower
14	Stonefield
15	Karma Castle

Unlockables

Unlockable	How to Unlock
Secret Ending	Input the Invincibility code so you can pass through objects. When you take the ORA stone back to the King and he leaves, pass through the blockade to his throne, which initiates the secret ending.
Use the Harmit (Hermit) the hard way	To use the Harmit (*sic*), level a Bard until you have at least 50 HP. Go into the second house to the west of Axis Castle.

Dynamite Headdy

Unlockables

Unlockable	How to Unlock
Head Animations	At the title screen select "Options" and press: Ⓒ, Ⓐ, ←, →, Ⓑ. You hear "nice" when you've entered the code correctly. Then press START to view the head animations.
Stage Select	When the title screen appears, press START once. Leaving the cursor at Start Game, enter the code: Ⓒ, Ⓐ, ←, →, Ⓑ. You hear a sound. Press START and you'll access the Stage Select. Choose your level and stage, then press START to play! (Note: This trick was done on an early version of the game. It may or may not work on later versions.)
Hard Mode (1-hit Death Mode)	At the title screen, press START once, then leave the cursor on "Start Game." Just like the Stage Select code, press Ⓒ, Ⓐ, ←, →, Ⓑ. You hear Headdy say "Nice" when you've entered the code correctly. Then press and hold START. Continue holding START until you see the "Opening Demo" scene appear. Now release START and continue as normal. Be warned: 1 hit is all it takes to kill you now.
Secret Final Scene	After the end credits have finished rolling, you are prompted to enter a 4-digit secret code on a keypad. The code is different each time the game is played. Complete the basketball minigame four times while going through the game to determine your game's secret code.

Ecco the Dolphin

Unlockables

Unlockable	How to Unlock
Enable the Super Cheat Menu	Begin the game and move Ecco left and right. Press START to pause the game while Ecco is turning. You have to pause it when Ecco is directly facing you. When you do that, press →, Ⓑ, Ⓒ, Ⓑ, Ⓒ, ↓, Ⓒ, ↑. If you did it right, a Cheat menu appears that has options such as stage select, message test, sound test, and more.
Invincibility	Input a valid password, then press START, and wait for the screen that shows the name of the level you're currently in with your password. Next, hold Ⓐ and START. Keep hold of Ⓐ and START until Ecco appears on the screen. Now press START to unpause and you will be invincible.

Passwords

Level	Password
Final Level	KNLMLMLC
The Undercaves	UYNAINCC
The Undercaves 2	DQDIACCI
The Vents	FKWLACCA
The Lagoon	NDRBRIKR
Ridge Water	HYAUGFLV
Open Ocean	FNCQWBMT
The Ice Zone	DWFFZBMV
Hard Water Zone	QGDJRQLA
Cold Water Zone	MCLFRQLW
The Island Zone	UWXIOQLK
Deep Water Zone	EILQOQLC
The Marble Sea	XAKUQQLS

Level	Password
The Library	FDGXQQLC
Deep City	ZUVPQQLU
City of Forever	AABBRQLU
Jurassic Beach	PLABUNLT
Pteranodon Pond	FQREUNLI
Origin Beach	QXKIUNLX
Trilobite Circle	OBEMUNLX
Dark Water	JNXPUNLA
Deep Water 2	WSGAKNLC
City of Forever 2	ZBPIGPLD
The Tube	KUVEKMLK
The Machine	SDDBKMLG

Ecco: The Tides of Time

Unlockables

Unlockable	How to Unlock
Debug Menu	Pause while Ecco is facing you. Once Ecco is facing you, press Ⓐ, Ⓑ, Ⓒ, Ⓑ, Ⓒ, Ⓐ, Ⓒ, Ⓐ, Ⓑ If you entered the code correctly, a menu will pop up with all sorts of options such as a sound test, level select, tempo, etc. This code can be entered as many times as you'd like, as long as the game is paused while Ecco is facing you.
Hard Mode	In the starting area, break the two shells above you, and then swim through the tunnel to start the game in Hard mode.

Passwords

Level	Password	Level	Password
Crystal Springs	UEPMCVEB	Gateway	KDCGTAHB
Fault Zone	OZUNSKZA	Big Water	QQCQRDRA
Two Tides	KDKINTYA	Deep Ridge	UXQWJIZD
Skyway	SZXHCLDB	Hungry Ones	WBQHMIUE
Sky Tides	OZWIDLDB	Secret Cave	CHGTEYZE
Tube of Medusa	QSJRYHZA	Gravitorbox	UIXBGWXE
Skylands	MULXRXEB	Globe Holder	SBFPWWJE
Fin to Feather	YCPAWEXA	Dark Sea	MXURVMLA
Eagle's Bay	YCJPDNDB	Vortex Queen	OKIMTBPA
Asterite's Cave	AOJRDZWA	Home Bay	CSNCMRUA
Four Islands	UOYURFDB	Epilogue	CEWSXKPA
Sea of Darkness	UQZWIIAB	Fish City	SGTDYSPA
Vents of Medusa	MMVSOPBB	City of Forever	WSSXZKVA

Passwords for Hard Mode

* = New level found only in Hard mode

Level	Password	Moray Abyss	YCFSBRAB
Crystal Springs	WPHSAAFB	The Eye	AGNEXBTE
Fault Zone	CRNPTFZA	Big Water	YCBXONIA
Two Tides	QUKGZZYA	Deep Ridge	UPODMUQD
Skyway	MCMBPJDB	The Hungry Ones	YOHVUVLE
Sky Tides	OZMRKIDB	Secret Cave	SPKHKISE
Tube of Medusa	ODFADPYA	Lunar Bay	WTHXKISE
Aqua Tubeway*	KNHRKJYA	Black Clouds	USKIKDOE
Skylands	WXRDJYEB	GraviatorBox	WNQWZMME
Fin to Feather	UQTFBRXA	Globe Holder	MIPGDOME
Eagle's Bay	QSNVMMDB	New Machine*	GOSTCXJA
Asterite's Cave	EGAQRVXA	Vortex Queen	OOSFBXAA
Maze of Stone*	EUTQQQWA	Home Bay	QNSGAPGA
Four Islands	CZVQNHCB	Epilogue	AXBGKHBA
Sea of Darkness	WFMYIDAB	Fish City	WKGETHCA
Vents of Medusa	SHWZZNBB	City of Forever	WQHFTZHA
Gateway	QKLLFPHB	"Secret" Password	AVQJTCBA

Ecco: The Tides of Time (continued)

Unlockable

Unlockable	How to Unlock
Unlimited Air and Health	Turn Ecco left or right and pause the game while Ecco is facing the screen. Press Ⓐ, Ⓐ, →, Ⓐ, Ⓒ, Ⓐ, ↓, Ⓐ, Ⓐ, →, Ⓐ and then unpause. You will now never die from lack of air or injuries.

Elebits

Unlockable	Code
Alpha Wave Unit	Beat 15 Missions in Challenge mode
Aroma Unit	Earn the title "King of Surveillance" after beating the last boss
Berserk Elebits	Earn the title "King of Capture" after beating the last boss
Extreme Silence	Earn the title "King of Noise" after beating the last boss
High Power Mode	Beat the third boss, then watch the cutscene at the beginning of the next level
Limit Release (Strongest Level Capture Gun)	Beat 25 Challenge Missions
Main Unit Only	Beat 5 Challenge Missions
Permanent Homing Laser (Deactivates Vacuum Laser)	Beat 20 Challenge Missions
Permanent Vacuum Laser (Deactivates Homing Laser)	Get 25 S ranks in Normal Mission
Worn Capture Gun	Beat 10 Missions in Challenge mode

Escape from Bug Island

Unlockable

Unlockable	How to Unlock
Samurai Sword and Death Scythe in Inventory	If you clear the game with either an "A" or "S" ranking, the next time you start the game, both the Samurai Sword and Death Scythe will be in your inventory.

ESWAT: City Under Siege

Unlockables

Unlockable	How to Unlock
Level Select	Start a game, and the Hero and Mission screen appears. Now hold down Ⓐ+Ⓑ+Ⓒ and press ←, →, ↑, ↓. Select the level by pressing ←/→. Then during the ending sequence, press and hold Ⓐ+Ⓐ+Ⓒ+↓+←. Keep holding these and press START until the Sound Test screen appears.

Fantastic 4: Rise of the Silver Surfer

Unlockables

Unlockable	How to Unlock	Unlockable	How to Unlock
1990's Fantastic 4	12 Tokens	Comic Covers 2	4 Tokens
2000's Fantastic 4	12 Tokens	Concept Art	4 Tokens
Comic Covers 1	4 Tokens	Ultimate Costumes	12 Tokens

Far Cry Vengeance

Password

Password	Effect
GiveMeTheMaps	Unlock All Maps

Fatal Fury

Unlockable

Unlockable	How to Unlock
Good Ending	Beat the game on Normal or Hard without using a continue

Final Fantasy Fables: Chocobo's Dungeon

Additional Dungeons

Unlockable	How to Unlock
Chocobo's Memories (Standard Dungeon)	Accessed through the Chocobo statue in the park
Croma's Future (Special Dungeon)	Accessed through Croma in Stella's House

Jobs

Jobs are like classes. You begin with the "Natural" job and can unlock nine others during the game.

Unlockable	How to Unlock
Black Mage	Make it to 10F in Guardian of the Flame.
Dancer	Enter "Pirouette" (capital P at the beginning, the rest lowercase, AND a musical note at the end) as a Romantic Phrase.
Dark Knight	Defeat Croma Shade in 30F in Guardian of the Light.
Dragoon	Complete Meja's Memories.
Knight	Complete Freja's Memories.
Ninja	Complete Volg's Memories.
Scholar	Defeat the four elements in 20F Guardian of the Water.
Thief	Steal the item behind Merchant Hero X in any of his dungeon shops.
White Mage	Complete Pastor Roche's Memories.

Final Fight

Unlockable

Unlockable	How to Unlock
Secret Option Menu	Hold ←, press START (on title screen)

Final Soldier

Level Select

Unlockable	How to Unlock
Level Select	Before the demo starts, press ←, ←, ①, →, →, ②, ↑, ↓, ↑, ↓

Flappy

Passwords

Press Select on the title screen and then enter one of the following passwords. Note: each password allows you to chose your starting side (that's how levels are called in this game) from five corresponding levels. Just press ✚ or ✚ after you input a password.

Password	Effect	Password	Effect
4NADA	Side 001-005	7GB17	Side 101-105
MATUI	Side 006-010	NZ100	Side 106-110
0MORI	Side 011-015	HINAM	Side 111-115
OK8MA	Side 016-020	K0D00	Side 116-120
YO4DA	Side 021-025	ATTAK	Side 121-125
MA2N0	Side 026-030	N0130	Side 126-130
MORII	Side 031-035	PAPAT	Side 131-135
KA582	Side 036-040	MAMAA	Side 136-140
H8SHI	Side 041-045	110NN	Side 141-145
MEGU3	Side 046-050	LUCKY	Side 146-150
EAMRA	Side 051-055	B5BAY	Side 151-155
KITA9	Side 056-060	EBIRA	Side 156-160
SAPP6	Side 061-065	YA3ZW	Side 161-165
CHUO9	Side 066-070	YA379	Side 166-170
KITA1	Side 071-075	WOMAN	Side 171-175
ZAXES	Side 076-080	00ZAR	Side 176-180
VOLGD	Side 081-085	B0KUD	Side 181-185
08ATA	Side 086-090	X3Y48	Side 186-190
OIKA8	Side 091-095	LAST1	Side 191-195
MRSRM	Side 096-100	04MA5	Side 196-200

Gain Ground

Level Select

Unlockable	How to Unlock
Level Select	On the Options screen press Ⓐ, Ⓒ, Ⓑ, Ⓒ

Galaga '90

Unlockables

Unlockable	How to Unlock
Galactic Bonus	Just stand still (don't move) and don't shoot in the bonus stage.
Red Capsule	Hold ✚ and press RUN at the title screen. The capsule on the ship will turn red instead of blue to confirm code entry. Shoot the last target on the first level to capture the red capsule and power-up to a triple ship.

Gate of Thunder

Unlockables

Unlockable	How to Unlock
Hidden Bomberman Game	Press ✚, ✚, ✚, ✚, ②. You'll hear a sound and in a moment you'll be at the Bomberman title screen.
Stage Select	At the title screen press: ①, ②, ②, ①, SELECT, ①, ②, ①, ②, SELECT, SELECT, RUN.

Genpei Toumaden

Unlockable

Unlockable	How to Unlock
Options Menu	At the title screen, press ↑, →, ↓, ←, ①, ②

Ghouls 'n Ghosts

Unlockables

Unlockable	How to Unlock
Japanese Mode	Enter the Options menu. Choose "26" for the music and "56" for sound selections, then hold ↙+ Ⓐ+Ⓑ+Ⓒ+START.
Slow-Mo	At the title screen, press ↑, Ⓐ, ↓, Ⓐ, ←, Ⓐ, →, Ⓐ. Begin the game, press START to pause, and hold Ⓑ and unpause.

Level Select

Press ↑, ↓, ←, ↓ repeatedly at the title screen. You'll hear a harp if you did it right. Enter one of the following controller actions to select the corresponding level.

Effect	Code
The Execution Place	Press START
The Floating Island	Press Ⓐ, START
The Village of Decay	Press ↑, START
Town of Fire	Press ↑+Ⓐ, START
Baron Rankle's Tower	Press ↓, START
Horrible Faced Mountain	Press ↓+Ⓐ, START
The Crystal Forest	Press ←, START
The Ice Slopes	Press ←+Ⓐ, START
Beginning of Castle	Press →, START
Middle of Castle	Press →+Ⓐ, START
Loki	Press ↘, START

Debug Mode

While "Press Start Button" is flashing at the title screen, input Ⓐ, Ⓐ, Ⓐ, Ⓐ, ↑, ↓, ←, ↓ and you hear a chime. Start the game and you are in debug mode. Three functions can be accessed from the Pause menu now.

Code	Effect
Tap ↓ During Pause	Frame Advance
Pause, Ⓐ, Pause	Invincibility Toggle (falling is still fatal)
Hold Ⓑ During Pause	Slow Motion

The Godfather: Blackhand Edition

Enter these codes while the game is paused. For the film clips, enter that clip in the Film Archives screen.

Unlockable	Code
$5,000	⊖, ②, ⊖, ⊖, ②, ↑
Full Ammo	②, ←, ②, →, ⊖, ↓
Full Health	←, ⊖, →, ②, →, ↑
Unlock Film Clips	②, ⊖, ②, ⊖, ⊖, ↑

NOTE

These codes may only be entered roughly every five minutes. If you really need the health or ammo before five minutes, pause and wait a few minutes, then enter the game.

Godzilla: Unleashed

Codes

At the main menu, press Ⓐ and ✜ at the same time.

Code	Effect
31406	Add 90,000 store points.
0829XX	Set day (where the "xx" equals the actual day you wish to set to).
411411	Show monster moves.
787321	Toggle version number.
204935	Unlock everything.

Monsters

After you complete the following tasks, you unlock the corresponding monster.

Unlockable	How to Unlock
Baragon	Free Baragon from the crystals in "A Friend in Need" at Monster Island as an Alien. Defeat him in the "Baragon" stage and buy him for 15,000 points.
Biollante	Be an Earth Defender and play "Rumble in the Surf" at Tokyo. Destroy the building with vines, defeat Biollante later on, and buy her for 30,000 pts.
Krystalak	Play "Terran Mind-Control" at New York as an Alien. Destroy large crystal in crater and nine days later defeat Krystalak and buy him for 20,000 pts.
Mecha-King Ghidorah	Play "Invasion" as an Earth Defender at San Francisco and defeat Ghidorah. Play "M.K.G" and defeat Mecha Ghidorah and buy him for 50,000 points.
Megagurius	Be an ED and play "Enter General Gyozen" at London. Destroy three teal crystals. Return near the end and defeat Megaguirus. Buy her for 20,000 pts.
Obsidius	Play a mech from GDF and play "Big Trouble" at Seattle. Destroy three cone crystals. Defeat Obsidius later and buy him for 20,000 pts.
SpaceGodzilla	Play as a Mutant, obtain four Power Surges, and beat "Tyrant" at the end of the game. SpaceGodzilla gets added to the shop and costs 100,000.
Titanosaurus	Use a mech from GDF and play "Soloist" at Sydney. Destroy three circular ice structures. Return later and defeat the dinosaur. Buy him for 25,000 pts.
Varan	Play as an Alien and destroy the crystals on the Mothership in "On the Mothership." Return to the level and defeat Varan and buy him for 30,000 pts.
Godzilla 90s	Buy a monster from each faction or beat the game with a monster from each faction. Then buy him for 20,000 points.
Godzilla 1954	Unlock every monster for purchase or play a set number of hours. Then buy him for 100,000 points.

Golden Axe

Unlockables

Unlockable	How to Unlock
9 Continues	Hold ✜+3+Ⓒ. Release and press START.
Level Select	Select Arcade mode. Hold ✜+Ⓑ and press START at the Character Selection screen. A number that corresponds to the starting level appears in the screen's upper left. Use the D-pad to change it to the level you want.

Golden Axe II

Unlockables

Unlockable	How to Unlock
Level Select	While the opening screen scrolls, simultaneously hold down Ⓐ+Ⓑ+Ⓒ+START. Still holding Ⓐ, release Ⓑ+Ⓒ and press them again. This brings you to the Options screen. Still holding Ⓐ, let go of the other two, pick "exit," and press Ⓑ+Ⓒ once more. You'll be back at the main menu. Still holding Ⓐ, release Ⓑ+Ⓒ and hit them again to choose the number of players. Keep all the buttons down and press START. Release only START, select your character, then still holding down Ⓐ+Ⓑ+Ⓒ, press ↑ and hit START. You can now select the level you want to play.
Level Select and 8 Credits (ultimate procedure)	With the cursor go to "Options" sign. Now press and hold Ⓐ+Ⓑ+Ⓒ. In the Options screen, release only Ⓑ+Ⓒ. Now configure the game if you want. Use Ⓑ to confirm successive selections, until the warrior selection. For the 8 credits, the cheat is identical, but release only Ⓐ and use START to confirm successive selections.

Gottlieb Pinball Classics

Passwords

Password	Effect
NYC	Unlock Central Park Table
LIS	Unlock Free Play in Black Hole table
PHF	Unlock Free Play in Goin' Nuts table
HOT	Unlock Free Play in Love Meter
HEF	Unlock Free Play in Playboy table
PBA	Unlock Free Play in Strikes 'N Spares table
PGA	Unlock Free Play in Tee'd Off table
BIG	Unlock Free Play in Xoltan

Unlockables

Unlockable	How to Unlock
Goin Nuts: Free Play Mode	Complete the table goal for El Dorado
Teed Off: Free Play Mode	Complete the table goal for Big Shot

Gradius

Unlockables

Unlockable	How to Unlock
10,000 Bonus Points	Get 6 power-ups so that the ? box is selected, then, when the thousands digit of your score is a 5, get a 7th power-up
Continue	At the Game Over Screen, press ↓, ↑, Ⓑ, Ⓐ, Ⓑ, Ⓐ, Ⓑ, Ⓐ, START (once per game)
Full Option Command	Press START during the game, then press ↑, ↑, ↓, ↓, ←, →, ←, →, Ⓑ, Ⓐ, START.
Warp to Level 3 (after defeating Core Fighter)	In level 1, when the thousands digit of your score is even, destroy 4 hatches
Warp to Level 4	Destroy Xaerous Core at end of level 2 within 2 seconds of its core turning blue
Warp to Level 5 (after beating level)	Destroy 10 stone heads in level 3

Gradius II

Unlockables

Unlockable	How to Unlock
30 Lives	At the title screen, press ✚↑, ✚↑, ✚↓, ✚↓, ✚←, ✚→, ✚←, ✚→, Ⓑ, Ⓐ
Max Out Abilities	During game, press ✚↑, ✚↑, ✚↓, ✚↓, ✚←, ✚→, ✚←, ✚, Ⓑ, Ⓐ (once per level)
Sound Test Menu	Hold Ⓐ+Ⓑ and turn on. When the screen comes up, press START, hold Ⓐ+Ⓑ until title screen, then press START again.

Gradius III

Unlockables

Unlockable	How to Unlock
30 Extra Ships	At the title screen, hold ←Ⓒ and press Ⓧ, Ⓧ, Ⓧ, START
Arcade Mode	In the Options menu, highlight the Game Level, and rapidly tap Ⓐ until the level turns into ARCADE
Extra Credits	At the title screen, press ⇩ as many times as you can and then press START before the screen fades out
Easy Final Boss	The final boss, Bacterion, will die whether or not you attack him. Just dodge his blasts, and in 15 or so seconds, he will spontaneously die. Even cheaper, park your ship in the screen's bottom center, and you can't be hit!
Extended Demo Mode	Continue to hold Ⓐ through the initial demo, and you'll see the entire first stage including the boss.
Full Power-Up	Pause the game and press Ⓒ↑, Ⓒ↑, Ⓒ↓, Ⓒ↓, ←Ⓒ, Ⓒ→, ←Ⓒ, Ⓒ→, Ⓨ, Ⓧ
Full Power-Up (without using the code)	Choose "speed down" for the "!" option in the Weapon Select screen. If you can get enough power-ups to highlight the last weapon, which will not be visible, and use it without powering up on speed up, you get all four options, missiles, and the shield. But if you have the laser already, it will be taken away.
Random Weapon Select	At the Weapon Select screen, press Ⓒ→ to enter Edit mode, then press ⇩, Ⓒ↗, ⇩, ⇩, Ⓒ↗, Ⓒ↗, ⇩, Ⓒ↗
Spread the Options	Activate the R-Option and collect enough power-ups that the option selection is highlighted. Now press and hold Ⓐ.
Suicide	Pause the game and press Ⓒ↑, Ⓒ↑, Ⓒ↓, Ⓒ↓, ←Ⓒ, Ⓒ→, ←Ⓒ, Ⓒ→, Ⓨ, Ⓐ, START

Bonus Stages

When you clear a bonus stage, you end up in the next level. That's right, you don't have to fight the boss of the level you were in previously. However, if you get killed in the bonus stage, you go back to the regular level, and cannot reenter the bonus stage.

Stage	How to Unlock
Stage 2	When you see a hole in the wall at the bottom of the screen, fly down there. Prerequisite: None.
Stage 3	When you reach the lower level, a platform in the ceiling drops down. Fly just below the part where the platform was. Prerequisite: Destroy all of the ground targets in the stage up to that point.
Stage 4	In the last set of Moai heads (they look like Easter Island heads), one that's lying down lifts up. Fly behind it. Prerequisite: Nothing must be highlighted on your power-up bar.
Stage 5	Fly just below the ceiling before the narrow corridor. Prerequisite: The hundreds digit of your score reads 5, 7, or 3.

Gradius III (continued)

Stage	How to Unlock
Stage 7	Just after the long downward slope in the second half of the level, stay close to the ground and fly into the wall formation shaped like this: ..../ ....\ _____*/ (Key: dots are empty space, lines are walls, the asterisk is where your ship should be.) Prerequisite: Unknown.

The Grim Adventures of Billy and Mandy

View Concept Art Sketch

Enter this code at the main menu screen.

Unlockables

Unlockable	How to Unlock
Concept Art Sketch	Hold ①, press ↑, ↑, ↓, ↓, ←, →, ←, ↓, and release ①
Extra Costume	Choose the character that you wish to have the extra costume and use him/her to clear Story mode
Unlock Boogey	In Mission mode, finish Mission 9 in Tier 4
Unlock Chicken	Finish Story mode with all characters on any difficulty with 10 hours of gameplay
Unlock Clown	Beat Story mode once with every character and fight a total of 100 Vs. mode matches
Unlock Dracula	In Mission mode finish Mission 5 in Tier 3
Unlock Eris	Finish Story mode once with either Billy, Mandy, Grim, or Irwin
Unlock Fred Fredburger	Finish Story mode once with either Billy, Mandy, Grim, or Irwin
Unlock General Skarr	In Mission mode finish Mission 6 in Tier 4
Unlock Hoss Delgado	Finish Mission 9 in Tier 1 in Mission mode
Unlock Jack O'Lantern	In Mission mode finish Mission 9 in Tier 2
Unlock Lord Pain	Finish Mission 9 in Tier 5
Unlock Mogar	Finish Story mode once with either Billy, Mandy, Grim, or Irwin
Unlock Nergal	Finish Story mode once with either Billy, Mandy, Grim, or Irwin
Unlock Nergal Jr.	In Mission mode finish Mission 9 in Tier 3
Unlock Nerglings	Finish Story mode with all characters on any difficulty
Unlock Pumpkin	Beat Story mode once with every character and accumulate a total of 100,000 damage in Vs. mode
Unlock Vikings	Finish Story mode with all characters and destroy every letter in the credits sequence

GT Pro Series

Unlockables

Unlockable	How to Unlock
Brake Street	Win Championship Race (Beginner)
Filter Grade-A	Win Enjoy Cup (Beginner)
Headlight Blue	Win 3 Door Cup (Beginner)
Highspeed Class	Win all cups in Intermediate Class
Intermediate Class	Win all cups in Beginner's Class

GT Pro Series (continued)

Unlockable	How to Unlock
Mazda RX-7 Tune (FD3S)	Get at least a Great!, 20+ for max combo in Heights Mountain
Mazda RX-8	Win Championship Race (Beginner)
Nissan 180SX S13	Win Enjoy Cup (Beginner)
Nissan Silvia S14 Tune	Complete the first race in drift mode
Nissan Silvia Tune (S15)	Get at least a Good!, 15+ for max combo in Downtown Street
Professional Class	Win all cups in Highspeed Class
Toyota Celica LB TA27	Win 3 Door Cup (Beginner)

Gunstar Heroes

Unlockables

Unlockable	How to Unlock
Hidden Special Move	With either Gunstar Red or Gunstar Blue motion: ↓, ◎▸↓, ◎▸, ◎▸←, ←+shot button to execute a powerful standing slide.
Make the Logo Rotate	Hold ↓ on controller 1 before the Gunstar Heroes logo appears on the screen in order to rotate it.
Timeron's Secret	During the second Timeron encounter (which is in the Space Battle stage) a timer begins ticking from 00'00"00. As the timer keeps going, the Timeron's attacks change, and every 20 minutes or so, a circular drone appears, accompanied by Smash Daisaku's laughter. Avoid this drone for about 2 minutes until it self-destructs, because a single hit will reduce your health to zero. At about 50'00"00 or so, large blue balls appear. These rebound once against the screen, and do 11 points of damage instead of the normal 10 points from the smaller ones. Once the timer gets up to 99'50"00 or so, don't destroy the Timeron yet. Instead, wait out the remaining 10 seconds while avoiding the Timeron's attacks, but don't stay too close to the Timeron, or you'll get killed by the drone. Once the timer reaches 00'00"00 again, you'll hear that nasty laughter again, but this time, "GIVE UP!!" appears in the middle of the screen, and the Timeron self-destructs, accompanied by the message, "YOU OPENED THE - SATORI MIND -." A bit more of that nasty laughter accompanies the next message, "REPROGRAMMED BY NAMI - 1993." Now, instead of getting a Timer Bonus as you usually would, a Soul Bonus of exactly 930,410 points is added to your score.

Happy Feet

Unlockables

Unlockable	How to Unlock
"All Together Now"	33 Gold Medals
"Amigo Racing"	15 Gold Medals
"Boogie Wonderland"	21 Gold Medals
"Driving Gloria Away"	26 Gold Medals
"Mumble the Outsider"	06 Gold Medals
"Out of the Egg"	01 Gold Medal
"Somebody to Love"	12 Gold Medals
"The Zoo"	31 Gold Medals

Heatseeker

Unlockables

Unlockable	How to Unlock
The Big One (SR-71 Blackbird's fourth Weapon Pack)	Successfully complete the Ace bonus objective
Top Secret plane (SR-71 Blackbird)	Successfully complete the Pilot bonus objective

Ice Age 2: The Meltdown

Codes

Pause the game and press the following codes.

Unlockable	How to Unlock
Unlimited Health	↑, →, ↓, ↑, ←, ↓, →, ←

Image Fight

Unlockables

Unlockable	How to Unlock
Arcade Mode	Do a reset (START+SELECT), then immediately hold ①
Mr. Heli mode	Highlight song C in Sound Test mode and press ↓, SELECT, ②+①, then press ① on Mr. Heli and then press RUN
Sound Test	Press SELECT on the title screen

J.J. and Jeff

Unlockables

Unlockable	How to Unlock
Continue	When the Game Over screen appears, hold ①+②, then press RUN
Extra Lives	Stand at least five blocks away from a lamppost, then jump while kicking and hit the post perfectly.
Hidden Level Warps	Locate the brick bridge on level 1-4B. Kick the right corner of the bridge and underneath. This allows gameplay to continue in fields 2, 3, or 4. Locate the area halfway through level 3-3B where two rats begin to follow your character. Jump on top of them to reach the two bricks, then jump up. Gameplay resumes at 6-4.

Kid Chameleon

Unlockables

Unlockable	How to Unlock
5,000 Bonus Points	Complete any level without collecting any special items, or complete a stage without being hurt by an enemy
10,000 Bonus Points	Complete Blue Lake Woods in less than 20 seconds
Last Boss Warp	At the end of Blue Lake Woods there is a series of blocks just above the flag. Jump to the last one and then press down and right, jump and special together. You get warped to Plethora, the last level.

DS
PSP
PS2
PS3
Wii
Xbox
Xbox 360
Index

Kung Fu Panda

Codes

From the main menu, select Extras and then select Cheats.

Effect	Code
All Multiplayer Characters	←,↓,←,→,↓
Big Head Mode (Story Mode)	↓,↑,←,→,→
Infinite Chi	↓,→,←,↑,↓
Invulnerability	↓,↓,→,↑,←
Dragon Warrior Outfit (Multiplayer Mode)	←,↓,→,←,↑
4x Damage Multiplier	↑,↓,↑,→,←

Legend of Kage

Unlockables

Unlockable	How to Unlock
1-Up	If you stay in the water of the moat and kill seven ninjas with your sword, a blue creature flies across the screen. Catch him for a 1-Up. This works in all of the moat scenes.

LEGO Batman

Codes

Enter the codes on the second level of the Batcave at the computer above the outfit changer.

Effect	Code
Bruce Wayne	BDJ327
Commissioner Gordon	DDP967
More Batarang Targets	XWP645
Nightwing	MVY759
Penguin Minion	KJP748
Police Van	MAC788
The Joker (Tropical)	CCB199
Yeti	NJL412

Free Play Codes

Effect	Code
Unlocks Alfred in Free Play	ZAQ637
Unlocks Commissioner Gordon in Free Play	DPP967
Unlocks Free Girl in Free Play	XVK541
Unlocks Harley Quinn's Hammer Truck	RDT637
Unlocks More Batarang Targets	XWP645
Unlocks Penguin Henchman in Free Play	BJH782
Unlocks Yeti in Free Play	NJL412

LEGO Indiana Jones: The Original Adventures

Character Codes

Enter the codes in the math classroom (the 2nd door on the left in the main hallway). The characters still have to be purchased.

Effect	Code	Effect	Code
Bandit	12N68W	Fedora	V75YSP
Bandit Swordsman	1MK4RT	First Mate	0GIN24
Barranca	04EM94	Grail Knight	NE6THI
Bazooka Trooper (Crusade)	MK83R7	Hovitos Tribesman	H0V1SS
Bazooka Trooper (Raiders)	S93Y5R	Indiana Jones (Desert Disguise)	4J8S4M
Belloq	CHN3YU	Indiana Jones (Officer)	VJ850S
Belloq (Jungle)	TDR197	Jungle Guide	24PF34
Belloq (Robes)	VE029L	Kao Kan	WM046L
British Officer	VJ5TI9	Kazim	NRH23J
British Troop Commander	B73EUA	Kazim (Desert)	3M29TJ
British Troop Soldier	DJ5I2W	Lao Che	2NK479
Captain Katanga	VJ3TT3	Maharaja	NFK5N2
Chatter Lal	ENW936	Major Toht	13NS01
Chatter Lal (Thuggee)	CNH4RY	Masked Bandit	N48SF0
Chen	3NK48T	Mola Ram	FJUR31
Colonel Dietrich	2K9RKS	Monkey Man	3RF6YJ
Colonel Vogel	8EAL4H	Pankot Assassin	2NKT72
Dancing Girl	C7EJ21	Pankot Guard	VN28RH
Donovan	3NFTU8	Sherpa Brawler	VJ37WJ
Elsa (Desert)	JSNRT9	Sherpa Gunner	ND762W
Elsa (Officer)	VMJ5US	Slave Child	0E3ENW
Enemy Boxer	8246RB	Thuggee	VM683E
Enemy Butler	VJ48W3	Thuggee Acolyte	T2R3F9
Enemy Guard	VJ7R51	Thuggee Slavedriver	VBS7GW
Enemy Guard (Mountains)	YR47WM	Village Dignitary	KD48TN
Enemy Officer	572 E61	Village Elder	4682 E1
Enemy Officer (Desert)	2MK450	Willie (Dinner Suit)	VK93R7
Enemy Pilot	B84ELP	Willie (Pajamas)	MEN4IP
Enemy Radio Operator	1MF94R	Wu Han	3NSLT8
Enemy Soldier (Desert)	4NSU7Q		

Item Codes

Enter the codes on the blackboard in the math classroom of Barnett College (the 2nd door on the left in the main hallway).

Effect	Code	Effect	Code
Artifact Detector	VIKED7	Fast Dig	378RS6
Beep Beep	VNF59Q	Fast Fix	FJ59WS
Character Treasure	VIES2R	Fertilizer	B1GW1F
Disarm Enemies	VKRNS9	Ice Rink	33GM7J
Disguises	4ID1N6	Parcel Detector	VUT673
Fast Build	V83SL0	Poo Treasure	WWQ1SA

LEGO Indiana Jones: The Original Adventures (continued)

Effect	Code	Effect	Code
Regenerate Hearts	MDLP69	Treasure x2	VM4TS9
Secret Characters	3X44AA	Treasure x4	VLWEN3
Silhouettes	3HE85H	Treasure x6	V84RYS
Super Scream	VN3R7S	Treasure x8	A72E1M
Super Slap	0P1TA5	Treasure x10	VI3PS8
Treasure Magnet	H86LA2		

LEGO Star Wars: The Complete Saga

Characters

To use the codes, enter the Cantina, go to the bar, access the codes command, and type in the codes.

Unlockable Characters	Codes	Unlockable Characters	Codes
Admiral Ackbar	ACK646	Jango Fett	KLJ897
Battle Droid Commander	KPF958	Ki-Adi-Mundi	MUN486
Boba Fett (Boy)	GGF539	Luminara	LUM521
Boss Nass	HHY697	Padmé	VBJ322
Captain Tarpals	QRN714	R2-Q5	EVILR2
Count Dooku	DDD748	Sandtrooper	CBR954
Darth Maul	EUK421	Stormtrooper	NBN431
Ewok	EWK785	Super Battle Droid	XZNR21
General Grievous	PMN576	Taun We	PRX482
Greedo	ZZR636	Vulture Droid	BDC866
IG-88	GIJ989	Watto	PLL967
Imperial Guard	GUA850	Zam Wesell	584HJF
Indiana Jones	After you watch the trailer for the upcoming Indiana Jones game in the Bonus Room, Indy will become a playable character.		

Ships

Unlockable Ships	Codes
Droid Trifighter	AAB123
Imperial Shuttle	HUT845
Slave I	Collect all 10 Minikits on each level.
TIE Fighter	DBH897
TIE Interceptor	INT729
Zam's Speeder	UUU875

Skills

Unlockable Skills	Codes
Disguise	BRJ437
Force Grapple Leap	CLZ738

DS PSP PS2 PS3 Wii Xbox Xbox 360 Index

Lode Runner

Unlockables

Unlockable	How to Unlock
Game Speed	Press SELECT to view current level. Hold SELECT and press Ⓑ to decrease game speed, or Ⓐ to increase game speed.
Level Select	Press select to view current level. Press SELECT then press Ⓐ to increase a level and Ⓑ to drop one.

Madden NFL 07

To enter these codes, select My Madden, then select Madden Cards, and then select Madden Codes.

Unlockable	Code
#220 Super Bowl XLI (Gold)	RLA9R7
#221 Super Bowl XLII (Gold)	WRLUF8
#222 Super Bowl XLIII (Gold)	NIEV4A
#223 Super Bowl XLIV (Gold)	M5AB7L
#224 Aloha Stadium (Gold)	YI8P8U
#225 '58 Colts (Gold)	B57QLU
#226 '66 Packers (Gold)	1PL1FL
#227 '68 Jets (Gold)	MIE6WO
#228 '70 Browns (Gold)	CL2TOE
#229 '72 Dolphins (Gold)	NOEB7U
#230 '74 Steelers (Gold)	YOOFLA
#231 '76 Raiders (Gold)	MOA11I
#232 '77 Broncos (Gold)	C8UM7U
#233 '78 Dolphins (Gold)	VIU007
#234 '80 Raiders (Gold)	NLAPH3
#235 '81 Chargers (Gold)	COAGI4
#236 '82 Redskins (Gold)	WL8BRI
#238 '84 Dolphins (Gold)	M1AM1E
#240 '86 Giants (Gold)	ZI8S2L
#241 '88 49ers (Gold)	SP2A8H
1985 Bears Gold card	QOETO8
1990 Eagles Gold card	2L4TRO
1991 Lions Gold card	J1ETRI
1992 Cowboys Gold card	W9UVI9
1993 Bills Gold card	DLA3I7
1994 49ers Gold card	DR7EST
1996 Packers Gold card	F8LUST
1998 Broncos Gold card	FIES95
1999 Rams Gold card	S9OUSW
Lame Duck card	5LAWO0
Mistake Free card	XL7SP1
QB On Target card	WROA0R
Pump up the crowd for the 49ers	KL0CRL
Pump up the crowd for the Bears	B1OUPH
Pump up the crowd for the Bengals	DRL2SW

Madden NFL 07 (continued)

Unlockable	Code
Pump up the crowd for the Bills	1PLUYO
Pump up the crowd for the Broncos	3ROUJO
Pump up the crowd for the Browns	T1UTOA
Pump up the crowd for the Buccaneers	S9EWRI
Pump up the crowd for the Cardinals	57IEPI
Pump up the crowd for the Chargers	F7UHL8
Pump up the crowd for the Chiefs	PRI5SL
Pump up the crowd for the Colts	1R5AMI
Pump up the crowd for the Cowboys	Z2ACHL
Pump up the crowd for the Dolphins	C5AHLE
Pump up the crowd for the Eagles	PO7DRO
Pump up the crowd for the Falcons	37USPO
Pump up the crowd for the Giants	C4USPI
Pump up the crowd for the Jaguars	MIEH7E
Pump up the crowd for the Jets	COLUXI
Pump up the crowd for the Lions	3LABLU
Pump up the crowd for the Packers	4HO7VO
Pump up the crowd for the Panthers	F2IASP

Marvel Ultimate Alliance

Enter these codes while playing.

Unlockable	Code
God Mode	Up, Down, Up, Down, Up, Left, Down, Right, +
Fill Momentum	Left, Right, Right, Left, Up, Down, Down, Up, +
Super Speed	Up, Left, Up, Right, Down, Right, +
Touch of Death	Left, Right, Down, Down, Right, Left, +

Enter these codes in the Team menu.

Unlockable	Code
100k	Up, Up, Up, Left, Right, Left, +
Level 99	Up, Left, Up, Left, Down, Right, Down, Right, +

Enter these codes in the Team Selection screen.

Unlockable	Code
All Characters	Up, Up, Down, Down, Left, Left, Left, +
Unlock All Costumes	Up, Down, Up, Down, Left, Right, Left, Right, Up, Down, +
Unlock All Powers	Left, Right, Left, Right, Up, Down, Up, Down, Left, Right, +
Unlock Daredevil	Left, Left, Right, Right, Up, Down, Up, Down, +
Unlock Silver Surfer	Down, Left, Left, Up, Right, Up, Down, Left, +

Enter these codes in the Review menu.

Unlockable	Code
All Comics	Left, Right, Right, Left, Up, Up, Right, +
All Concept Art	Down, Down, Down, Right, Right, Left, Down, +
All Wallpapers	Up, Down, Right, Z, Up, Up, Down, +
All Cinematics	Up, Left, Left, Up, Right, Right, Up, +

DS PSP PS2 PS3 Wii Xbox Xbox 360 Index

Medal of Honor: Heroes 2

Map Awards

Unlockable	How to Unlock
Base Demolition	Put a permanent end to the Further's pet project.
Beach Attack	Land on the beach with the 5th Rangers, and push through the German defenses.
Destroy the Guns	To protect Allied bombers, five Anti-Air gun batteries need to be knocked out.

Map Awards

Unlockable	How to Unlock
Destroy Train	Fight your way through the fields to the Train Station. Whatever is on that train is too important to let go.
Monastery Assault	A key figure has set up a base of operation in a remote monastery. Crack the defenses and get whatever information you can.
Sink U-boats	Take out three U-boats in the port area.
Through the Sewers	The Germans have holed up underground. Go take them out while staying safe from Allied bombardment.

Special Awards

Unlockable	How to Unlock
Combat Basic	Awarded for killing 100 enemy soldiers on the battlefield.
Combat Master	Awarded for killing 500 enemy soldiers on the battlefield.
Combat Senior	Awarded for killing 250 enemy soldiers on the battlefield.
Endurance	Awarded for completing a mission without being critically injured once.
Green Survivor	Awarded for completing a mission on Green without dying once.
Grenade Combat	Awarded for killing 25 enemy soldiers with grenades.
Hero Survivor	Awarded for completing a mission on Hero without dying once.
Heroism	Awarded for completing Campaign mode on the Hero difficulty setting.
LMG Combat	Awarded for killing 150 enemy soldiers with the BAR or STG44 light machine guns.
Machine Gun Combat	Awarded for killing 50 enemy soldiers with the MG42 machine gun.
Marksmanship	Awarded for completing a mission with 75 percent accuracy.
Melee Combat	Awarded for killing 25 enemy soldiers in melee combat.
Participant	Awarded for completing Campaign mode on the Green difficulty setting.
Pistol Combat	Awarded for killing 50 enemy soldiers with the Colt .45 or Luger pistol.
Rifle Combat	Awarded for killing 50 enemy soldiers with the M1 Garand or Karabiner 98K rifles.
Rocket Combat	Awarded for killing 25 enemy soldiers with the Bazooka or Panzerschrek rocket launcher.
Sharpshooter	Awarded for achieving 100 headshots on the battlefield.
Shotgun Combat	Awarded for killing 50 enemy soldiers with the shotgun.
SMG Combat	Awarded for killing 250 enemy soldiers with the Thompson or MP40 submachine guns.
Sniper Combat	Awarded for killing 50 enemy soldiers with the scoped Gewehr rifle or the scoped Springfield rifle.

Medal of Honor: Heroes 2 (continued)

Unlockable	How to Unlock
Veteran	Awarded for completing Campaign mode on the Veteran difficulty setting.
Veteran Survivor	Awarded for completing a mission in Veteran without dying once.
Weapon Expert	Awarded for getting at least one kill with each weapon in the game.

Medal of Honor: Vanguard

Unlockable	Code
Cheat Menu (required for entering following codes)	In the pause menu, enter ↑, ↓, ↑, ↓
Extra Armor	→, ←, →, ↓, ↑, →
Invisibility	↑, →, ←, ↓, ↓, ↑

Mega Man

Unlockables

Unlockable	How to Unlock
Select Trick	When using a weapon that goes through an enemy, press the SELECT button (this pauses the game without bringing up the weapon menu) when the weapon is making contact with the enemy. While the game is paused this way the enemy continues to flash. When the flashing has stopped, press the SELECT button again to un-pause the game and the weapon hits the enemy again, causing more damage. You can do this trick repeatedly with many of the bosses, making them very easy to beat.

Mercury Meltdown Revolution

Unlockables

Unlockable	How to Unlock
30mph Speed Limit Sign Skin	Collect the bonus points in each stage
Basketball Skin	Collect the bonus points in each stage
Black and White Cat's Face	Collect the bonus points in each stage
Brown and White Dog's Face	Collect the bonus points in each stage
Football Skin	Collect the bonus points in each stage
Smiley Face Skin	Collect the bonus points in each stage
Snooker Ball Skin	Collect the bonus points in each stage
Wheel Skin	Collect the bonus points in each stage

Metal Marines

Codes

Code	Effect
Enter CSDV as a password	Start with more Money and Energy for each level
HBBT	Level 02
PCRC	Level 03
NWTN	Level 04
LSMD	Level 05
CLST	Level 06
JPTR	Level 07
NBLR	Level 08
PRSC	Level 09
PHTN	Level 10
TRNS	Level 11
RNSN	Level 12
ZDCP	Level 13
FKDV	Level 14
YSHM	Level 15
CLPD	Level 16
LNVV	Level 17
JFMR	Level 18
JCRY	Level 19
KNLB	Level 20

DS
PSP
PS2
PS3
Wii
Xbox
Xbox 360
Index

Metal Slug Anthology

Unlockables

Unlockable	How to Unlock
Special Music	Complete Metal Slug 1-5 and X on Hard with limited continues and also complete Metal Slug 6 with limited continues
Tonko Art Gallery	Complete Metal Slug 1-5 and X on Easy with limited continues and also complete Metal Slug 6 with limited continues

Mighty Bomb Jack

Unlockables

Unlockable	How to Unlock
Skip Levels	To perform this trick, get to the first treasure room in Round 1. Grab any of the bombs. Immediately you see another bomb light up with a sparkle. Grab the other bombs in the treasure room, making sure to grab the lit bomb last. You're transported to the Round 2 treasure room! Use this trick to skip as many of the normal stages as you wish. However, if you lose a life in one of the treasure rooms, you're transported back to the last level you were on before entering a treasure room.

Military Madness

Unlockables

Unlockable	How to Unlock
Alternate Colors	Power on the system, and hold SELECT to reset. While continuing to hold SELECT, choose the 1-player continue option and enter a map name.
Play as Axis	Select the new game or 1-player continue option on the title screen, then hold SELECT and press ①.
Switch Sides	Hold SELECT and press RUN before choosing the 1-player continue option.

Passwords

Password	Effect
REVOLT	Level 01
ICARUS	Level 02
CYRANO	Level 03
RAMSEY	Level 04
NEWTON	Level 05
SENECA	Level 06
SABINE	Level 07
ARATUS	Level 08
GALIOS	Level 09
DARWIN	Level 10
PASCAL	Level 11
HALLEY	Level 12
BORMAN	Level 13
APOLLO	Level 14
KAISER	Level 15
NECTOR	Level 16
MILTON	Level 17

Password	Effect
IRAGAN	Level 18
LIPTUS	Level 19
INAKKA	Level 20
TETROS	Level 21
ARBINE	Level 22
RECTOS	Level 23
YEANTA	Level 24
MONOGA	Level 25
ATTAYA	Level 26
DESHTA	Level 27
NEKOSE	Level 28
ERATIN	Level 29
SOLCIS	Level 30
SAGINE	Level 31
WINNER	Level 32
ONGAKU	Sound Test

Milon's Secret Castle

Unlockables

Unlockable	How to Unlock
Continue Game	Hold down left and press START when you die after getting the first crystal

Monster 4X4: World Circuit

Unlockables

Unlockable	How to Unlock
Reverse Tracks	Get first place on a track to get the same track in reverse

Mortal Kombat: Armageddon

Krypt Kodes (Using a GameCube Controller)

Enter the following by choosing the "?" in the Krypt. Enter the Krypt and press L on the GameCube Controller 4 times and you'll see it in the bottom right corner.

Code	Effect
L, →, A, R, ↑, ↑	Unlock Alternate Costume: Drahmin
↓, ↑, R, L, X, L	Unlock Alternate Costume: Frost
↓, L, ↑, L, L, →	Unlock Alternate Costume: Nitara
L, ←, ↑, X, ↑, L	Unlock Alternate Costume: Shang Tsung
↑, X, B, A, X, Y	Unlock Arena: Falling Cliffs
↑, X, R, ↑, A, A	Unlock Arena: General Reiko's Map Room
X, L, ↑, B, X, ↓	Unlock Arena: Krimson Forest
R, ←, ←, ↓, L, B	Unlock Arena: Nethership Interior
R, L, B, A, ↑, ↑	Unlock Arena: Pyramid of Argus
←, ←, X, ↑, Y, L	Unlock Arena: Shinnok's Spire
Y, B, ←, L, ←, X	Unlock Character: Blaze
L, L, Y, ↓, ↓, B	Unlock Character: Daegon
↑, B, B, X, X, ↑	Unlock Character: Meat
L, ←, ↑, ↑, X, ↓	Unlock Character: Taven
L, Y, L, L, R, B	Unlock Concept Art: Blaze
↑, A, ↑, ↓, L, A	Unlock Concept Art: Early Taven
↑, B, L, ↑, X, L	Unlock Concept Art: Firewall Arena
R, →, ↑, R, Y, ↑	Unlock Concept Art: Mileena's Car Design
Y, ←, ←, A, ↓, X	Unlock Concept Art: Pyramid Crack of Dawn
A, L, R, ↑, ↑, ↑	Unlock Concept Art: Pyramid of Argus
L, ←, ↑, X, ↑, L	Unlock Concept Art: Scorpion Throw Sketch
R, L, ←, A, ↑, R	Unlock Concept Art: Sektor's 2 Handed Pulse Blade
X, ↑, Y, ↓, X, ←	Unlock Concept Art: Unused Trap in Konquest Mode
↑, ↑, ↓, ↑, L, A	Unlock Movie: Armageddon Promo
←, L, ↑, ↓, ↑, L	Unlock Movie: Cyrax Fatality Blooper
Y, ↑, ↑, L, R, ↑	Unlock Movie: Motor Gameplay
A, B, ←, Y, B, A	Unlock Tune: Armory
L, ←, X, A, ↑, →	Unlock Tune: Lin Kuei Palace
↓, ←, ↑, L, ↑, L	Unlock Tune: Pyramid of Argus
↑, X, L, R, R, A	Unlock Tune: Tekunin Warship

Mortal Kombat: Armageddon (continued)

Krypt Kodes (Using a Wii Remote)

Enter the following by choosing the "?" in the Krypt. Enter the Krypt and press L on the GameCube Controller 4 times and you'll see it in the bottom right corner.

Code	Effect
D-Pad Down, Analog Right, D-Pad Down, Z, Analog Up, Analog Up	Unlock Alternate Costume: Drahmin
Analog Down, Z, Z, D-Pad Down, D-Pad Right, D-Pad Down	Unlock Alternate Costume: Frost
Analog Down, D-Pad Down, Analog Up, D-Pad Down, D-Pad Down, Analog Right	Unlock Alternate Costume: Nitara
D-Pad Down, Analog Left, Analog Up, D-Pad Right, Analog Up, D-Pad Down	Unlock Alternate Costume: Shang Tsung
Z, D-Pad Right, D-Pad Left, D-Pad Down, D-Pad Right, D-Pad Up	Unlock Arena: Falling Cliffs
Z, D-Pad Up, Z, Analog Up, D-Pad Down, D-Pad Down	Unlock Arena: General Reiko's Map Room
D-Pad Right, D-Pad Down, Analog Up, D-Pad Left, D-Pad Right, Analog Down	Unlock Arena: Krimson Forest
Z, Analog Left, Analog Left, Analog Down, D-Pad Down, D-Pad Left	Unlock Arena: Nethership Interior
Z, D-Pad Down, D-Pad Left, D-Pad Down, Z, Analog Up	Unlock Arena: Pryamid of Argus
Analog Left, Analog Left, D-Pad Right, Analog Up, D-Pad Up, D-Pad Down	Unlock Arena: Shinnok's Spire
D-Pad Up, D-Pad Left, Analog Left, D-Pad Down, Analog Left, D-Pad Right	Unlock Character: Blaze
D-Pad Down, D-Pad Down, D-Pad Up, Analog Down, Analog Down, D-Pad Left	Unlock Character: Daegon
Analog Up, D-Pad Left, D-Pad Left, D-Pad Right, D-Pad Right, Analog Up	Unlock Character: Meat
D-Pad Down, Analog Left, Z, Analog Up, D-Pad Right, Analog Down	Unlock Character: Taven
D-Pad Down, D-Pad Up, D-Pad Down, D-Pad Down, Z, D-Pad Left	Unlock Concept Art: Blaze
Analog Up, D-Pad Down, Z, Analog Down, D-Pad Down, D-Pad Down	Unlock Concept Art: Early Taven
Analog Up, D-Pad Left, D-Pad Down, Z, D-Pad Right, D-Pad Down	Unlock Concept Art: Firewall Arena
Z, Analog Right, Analog Up, Z, D-Pad Up, Analog Up	Unlock Concept Art: Mileena's Car Design
D-Pad Up, Analog Left, Analog Left, D-Pad Down, Analog Down, D-Pad Right	Unlock Concept Art: Pyramid Crack of Dawn
D-Pad Down, D-Pad Down, Z, Z, Analog Up, Analog Up	Unlock Concept Art: Pyramid of Argus
D-Pad Down, Analog Left, Analog Up, D-Pad Right, Z, D-Pad Down	Unlock Concept Art: Scorpion Throw Sketch
Z, D-Pad Down, Analog Left, D-Pad Down, Analog Up, Z	Unlock Concept Art: Sektor's 2 Handed Pulse Blade
D-Pad Right, Z, D-Pad Up, Analog Down, D-Pad Right, Analog Left	Unlock Concept Art: Unused Trap in Konquest Mode
Analog Up, Analog Up, Analog Down, Analog Up, D-Pad Down, D-Pad Down	Unlock Movie: Armageddon Promo
Analog Right, D-Pad Down, Z, Analog Down, Analog Up, D-Pad Down	Unlock Movie: Cyrax Fatality Blooper
D-Pad Up, Analog Up, Z, D-Pad Down, Z, Z	Unlock Movie: Motor Gameplay
D-Pad Down, D-Pad Left, Analog Left, D-Pad Up, D-Pad Left, D-Pad Down	Unlock Tune: Armory
D-Pad Down, Analog Left, D-Pad Right, D-Pad Down, Z, Analog Right	Unlock Tune: Lin Kuei Palace
Analog Down, Analog Left, Z, D-Pad Down, Analog Up, D-Pad Down	Unlock Tune: Pyramid of Argus
Analog Up, D-Pad Right, D-Pad Down, Z, Z, D-Pad Down	Unlock Tune: Tekunin Warship

Alternate Costumes

Unlockable	How to Unlock
Ashrah's Alternate Costume	Defeat the Ice Beast you encounter in Arctika and open the chest that appears
Baraka's Alternate Costume	Kill all of the enemies in the final room of the Tekunin Warship and open the chest that appears
Bo'Rai Cho's Alternate Costume	Open the chest that appears after you defeat the Wraiths of Shinnok's Spire
Cyrax's Alternate Costume	Kill all of the enemies in the third room of the Tekunin Warship and open the chest that appears
Dairou's Alternate Costume	Open the chest at the end of the second ice hallway at the beginning of the Lin Kuei Temple Entrance

Mortal Kombat: Armageddon (continued)	
Code	**Effect**
Darrius' Alternate Costume	In a chest behind a discolored wall at the beginning of the Lin Kuei Temple where you are attacked by Lin Kuei Archers
Drahmin's Alternate Costume	In the Netherrealm after you defeat Drahmin, shoot down the bat creature over the nearby cliff and open the chest that appears
Ermac's Alternate Costume	In a chest by the left wall in the room where you get attacked by the Red Commandos for the second time
Frost's Alternate Costume	Break all of the tombs lining the wall in the room where you meet Frost
Fujin's Alternate Costume	Defeat all of the Red Dragon Soldiers at the beginning of the Charred Mountain
Goro's Alternate Costume	In an invisible chest on the left side of the first area in Shao Khan's Fortress and directly to the right of a musical note
Havik's Alternate Costume	Defeat all of the demons in the second area of Shinnok's Spire
Hotaru's Alternate Costume	In a chest close to the wall in the second room of the Tekunin Warship
Hsu Hao's Alternate Costume	In a chest on the right walkway after you wake up on the Tekunin Warship
Jade's Alternate Costume	Defeat all of the Lin Kuei at the very beginning of the Lin Kuei Palace and open the chest that appears
Jarek's Alternate Costume	Open the right chest in the room where you fight with the Ice Scepter
Jax's Alternate Costume	Once you enter Arctika, turn around and go to the left to find an invisible chest
Johnny Cage's Alternate Costume	Defeat the Tengu Guards at the beginning of Arctika and open the chest that appears
Kai's Alternate Costume	In an invisible chest behind a breakable discolored wall to the right as you enter the third area of Lin Kuei Temple Entrance in Arctika
Kano's Alternate Costume	In an invisible chest to the left as you enter the last room of the Temple of Argus
Kenshi's Alternate Costume	Defeat all of the Tengu Ninjas with the given sword in Arctika
Kira's Alternate Costume	Step on the second Giant Spider in Botan Jungle and open the chest that appears
Kitana's Alternate Costume	Perform a Fatality on Wi Lae, leader of the Tengu Ninjas
Kobra's Alternate Costume	In an invisible chest behind the first monolith in the Botan Jungle
Kung Lao's Alternate Costume	Found in a chest to the right after you enter the Temple of Argus
Li Mei's Alternate Costume	In the second area of Shinnok's Spire, walk around the edge of the room until you find an invisible chest
Liu Kang's Alternate Costume	As you enter Shao Kahn's Fortress, turn around and run forward to find an invisible chest.
Mavado's Alternate Costume	Inside an invisible chest on the left part of the room where you do battle after you receive the Supermove: Time Stop

Mortal Kombat: Armageddon (continued)

Code	Effect
Mileena's Alternate Costume	After you defeat Mileena, hit the Ground Pound Switch in front of you and open the chest that appears
Motaro's Alternate Costume	After the third training obelisk, during the time you must gather crystals, go to the left side of this area and open the chest there
NightWolf's Alternate Costume	After you defeat the Giant Skulls in Edenia, travel up the path until all of the chests appear and open the first one on the right
Nitara's Alternate Costume	After you defeat the Undead Revenants for the first time in the Netherrealm, jump down the leftmost cliff instead of the right and open the nearby chest
Noob Saibot's Alternate Costume	Defeat all of the Shadow Ninjas the first time you encounter then in the Lin Kuei Palace and open the chest that appears
Quan Chi's Alternate Costume	Step on the rat in the tunnel after you travel through Door A1 in the Red Dragon Caverns and open the chest that appears
Raiden's Alternate Costume	When or after fighting the Shao Khan Colossus, go into the first room on the left
Rain's Alternate Costume	Open the chest at the end of the area in Arctika where you are attacked by Red Dragon Spies and before you meet Rain
Reiko's Alternate Costume	In a chest in Shao Khan's Fortress,; as you enter the first area with blades, travel down a hall to the left
Reptile's Alternate Costume	Defeat the Hybrid Dragons you encounter in the Red Dragon Caverns and open the chest
Sareena's Alternate Costume	Defeat Kai, Sareena, and Jatakka and open the chest that appears
Shang Tsung's Alternate Costume	At the beginning of Shao Khan's Fortress, hit the Ground Pound icon to the right and up the ramp
Shao Kahn's Alternate Costume	Open the chest that appears after you defeat Shao Khan's Statue
Shinnok's Alternate Costume	Once you get to the area in the Netherrealm with the falling rocks go to the leftmost side and open the chest
Shujinko's Alternate Costume	Hit the Ground Pound icon in one of the cells after you defeat The Executioner in Shao Khan's Dungeon
Sindel's Alternate Costume	Complete the third training obelisk
Smoke's Alternate Costume	Defeat Smoke and open the chest that appears
Sonya's Alternate Costume	In an invisible chest to the left of the gate in the area after you defeat Sonya
Stryker's Alternate Costume	Break the wall on the right of the hallway after the Shadow Stalkers, travel to the end of it, and open the chest in the left alcove
Sub-Zero's Alternate Costume	Open the chest to the right of the statue of your mother after your fight with Sub-Zero
Tanya's Alternate Costume	In Shao Khan's Dungeon, after you make it to the cell area, hit the Ground Pound icon and then go back to the third cell on the right
Taven's Alternate Costume	After you defeat the Giant Skulls in Edenia, travel up the path until all of the chests appear, and open the third one on the left

Mortal Kombat: Armageddon (continued)

Characters

Unlockable	How to Unlock
Blaze	Obtain 50 relics in Konquest
Daegon	Obtain 30 relics in Konquest
Meat	Obtain 10 relics in Konquest
Taven	Finish the storyline in Konquest

Konquest Mode Unlockable

Unlockable	How to Unlock
+20,000 Koins	Obtain 20 relics in Konquest mode

Kreate-A-Kharacter Unlockables

The following parts for kreate-a-kharacter are unlocked in Konquest mode.

Unlockable	How to Unlock
Elder God Female Armor: Torso	Open the golden chest in the right path of the fork in the Red Dragon Caverns
Elder Gods Female Armor: Belt	Inside a golden chest in a locked gate in Arctika after the second obelisk that opens after you defeat the Tengu Ninjas
Elder Gods Female Armor: Boots	After the Shadow Stalkers, break the cracked wall to the left and travel down to the right alcove where you find the golden chest
Elder Gods Female Armor: Cape	Inside a golden chest in the area after you meet and defeat Sonya
Elder Gods Female Armor: Glove	Once you get to the flaming sword area of Shinnok's Spire, turn and run to your left and open the golden chest
Elder Gods Female Armor: Helmet	When or after fighting the Shao Khan Colossus, go into the second room on the right
Elder Gods Female Armor: Legs	Open the golden chest in the cave that gets opened after you defeat the undead of the Netherrealm after you get your gauntlets
Elder Gods Female Armor: Shoulders	In Shao Kahn's Dungeon, after you make it to the cell area, hit the Ground Pound icon and then go back to the first cell on the left
Elder Gods Male Armor: Belt	Inside of a golden chest to the right after you open the first door in the Tekunin Warship
Elder Gods Male Armor: Boots	After the Shadow Stalkers, break the second cracked wall on the right and travel down to the end and open the golden chest in the left alcove
Elder Gods Male Armor: Cape	When or after fighting the Shao Khan Colossus, go into the second room on the left
Elder Gods Male Armor: Glove	Inside of a golden chest after the second fallen log and to the right in Botan Jungle
Elder Gods Male Armor: Helmet	After you defeat the Giant Skulls in Edenia, travel up the path until you find a golden chest
Elder Gods Male Armor: Legs	In a golden chest in the left corner of the second area of Shinnok's Spire
Elder Gods Male Armor: Shoulders	Stand in the middle of the room after you free Shujinko, shoot a fireball at the nearby torch, and get the chest that appears
Elder Gods Male Armor: Torso	After you defeat the Tengu Leader, break open the discolored wall on the right in the blade trap area.

Mortal Kombat: Armageddon (continued)

Soundtracks

All of the following soundtracks are unlocked in Konquest mode and found in the shape of a musical note.

Unlockable	How to Unlock
Arctika Tune	As you enter the second area of the Lin Kuei Temple Entrance, destroy the discolored wall on the right and open the chest
Bo'Rai Cho's Brewery Tune	Get the musical note after the bridge and in the cave to the right in Botan Jungle
Botan Jungle Track Tune	Get the musical note right before the second fallen log in Botan Jungle
Goro's Lair Fight Tune	In Shujinko's cell when you release him
Hell Fight Tune	In Shao Khan's Dungeon, after you make it to the cell area, hit the Ground Pound icon and then go back to the second cell on the right
Konquest Final Battle Tune	In Shao Khan's Fortress as you run up to the first area with the blades, travel to the right to find the musical note in the next room
Lin Kuei Palace Tune	Get the musical note in the Lin Kuei Palace directly to your left after you punch down the Ice Door
Lin Kuei Raceway Tune	Get the musical note near the entrance in the final area of Arctika after you defeat all of the Lin Kuei Warriors and Archers
Lumbermill Fight Tune	Get the musical note after the second crusher when you return to Arctika after the second obelisk
Meteor Storm Fight Tune	Get the musical note after you defeat the Undead Revenants for the first time in the Netherrealm, jump down the leftmost cliff instead of the right
Outworld Refinery Tune	Get the musical note behind you after you fight Drahmin in the Netherrealm
Outworld Spire Fight Tune	Get the musical note on the right side of the first room as you enter Shinnok's Spire
Pyramid of Argus Tune	After you defeat the Giant Skulls in Edenia, travel up the path and find the musical note to the right of a golden chest
Reptile's Lair Fight Tune	Get the musical note in the hallway right before the final room of the Red Dragon Caverns, behind a grouping of three blue barrels
Soul Chamber Fight Tune	Once you get to the flaming sword area of Shinnok's Spire, turn around and get the musical note
Subway Fight Tune	Get the musical note after you defeat Sonya Blade in A rctika
Tekunin Prison Fight Tune	In Shao Khan's Fortress, after you open the main door and enter the second area, go to the upper left side and get the musical note
Tekunin Warship Tune	Get the musical note in the area where you get attacked by Black Dragon Thug's in the Botan Jungle
The Lost Pyramid Tune	Behind an explosive barrel in the battle after you gain the Supermove: Time Stop
Wastelands Fight Tune	On the left of the elevator you get into at the end of Shao Khan's Dungeon

Mortal Kombat: Armageddon (continued)

Unlockable Arenas

Unlockable	How to Unlock
Artika Arena	Beat all 7 trials in Artika Obelisk
Edenian Ruins	After you defeat the Giant Skulls in Edenia, travel up the path until all of the chests appear and open the second one on the left
Netherrealm Cliffs	Defeat Drahmin in Konquest mode
Pyramid of Argus Arena	Collect 40 Relics in Konquest mode
Scorpion's Lair	After you defeat the Giant Skulls in Edenia, travel up the path until all of the chests appear and open the third one on the right

Moto Roader

Unlockables

Unlockable	How to Unlock
Get $50,000	Hold SELECT and press ② on the Course Selection screen
Music Select	Hold SELECT and press ① or ② while the game is paused
See Winning Time	Hold SELECT and press → on the Course Selection screen
Special Course	Hold SELECT and press ← on the Course Selection screen
Sound Test	Input MUSIC or ART88 as a player name

MySims

Codes

While running around town, pause the game, then push the following buttons on the Wiimote to get to the hidden password system: ②,①,↓,↑,↓,↑,←,←,→,→. A keyboard appears to allow you to type in the following case-sensitive codes.

Unlockable	How to Unlock
Bunk Bed (Furniture)	F3nevr0
Camouflage Pants	N10ng5g
Diamond Vest (Outfit)	Tglg0ca
Genie Outfit	Gvsb3k1
Hourglass Couch	Ghtymba
Kimono Dress (Outfit)	I3hkdvs
Modern Couch	T7srhca
Racecar Bed (Furniture)	Ahvmrva
Rickshaw Bed	Itha7da
White Jacket	R705aan

Tools

Once you reach a certain level, you get a message saying you've earned the following new tools.

Unlockable	How to Unlock
Blow Torch	Have your town reach four stars.
Crowbar	Have your town reach one star.
Pickaxe	Have your town reach three stars.
Saw	Have your town reach two stars.
Town Monument Blueprint	Have a five-star town.

MySims (continued)

Uber-Sims

After getting your interest level to 100% in any of the six categories, you get a message about a special guest waiting for you in the hotel. Check the next day and find the following Sims.

Unlockable	How to Unlock
Amazing Daryl	100% Fun Town
Chancellor Ikara	100% Tasty Town
Hopper	100% Cute Town
Mel	100% Spooky Town
Samurai Bob	100% Studious Town
Star	100% Geeky Town

MX Vs. ATV Untamed

Codes

Go to the Options screen and go to the Cheat Code input screen.

Effect	Code
1 Million Store Points	MANYZEROS
50cc Bike Class	LITTLEGUY
All Bikes	ONRAILS
All Challenges	MORESTUFF
All Gear	WELLDRESSED
All Machines	MCREWHEELS
All Riders	WHOSTHAT
Freestyle Tracks	FREETICKET
Paralyzer Monster Truck	PWNAGE
Unlock Everything	YOUGOTIT

Naruto: Clash of Ninja Revolution

Characters

To unlock the following characters, beat the Mission mode at least once, then do the following:

Unlockable	How to Unlock
Gaara	Beat Single Player mode with Naruto and Shikamaru.
Guy	Clear Mission 13.5.
Hinata Hyuuga	Beat Single Player mode with Neji.
Ino Yamanaka	Beat Single Player mode with Sakura.
Itachi Uchiha	Beat Mission "Rematch Itachi vs. Saskue," after unlocking all other starting characters plus Guy and Kankuro.
Kankuro	Clear Mission mode once.
Kisame	Beat Single Player mode with Naruto, Sasuke, Kakashi, Guy, and Jiraiya.
Orochimaru	Beat Single Player mode with Naruto, Sasuke, Kakashi, and Jiraiya.
Shino Aburame	Beat Arcade mode with Kankuro.
Temari	Beat Shikamaru's Single Player mode.
Tenten	Clear Mission 20.
Tsunade	Beat Single Player mode with Jiraiya.

Need for Speed Carbon

Unlockable	Code
Aston Martin DB9 (Exotic)	Defeat Wolf in Boss Battle mode
Dodge Charger RT Classic (Muscle)	Defeat the 21st Muscle Car Gang
Jaguar XK 2007 (Exotic)	Clear all three Turf War races
Mazda RX7 (Tuner)	Defeat Kenji in Boss Battle mode
Nissan 240SX (Tuner)	Clear all three Checkpoint challenges

Need for Speed ProStreet

Codes

Go to the "Enter Codes" section of the Career menu and enter the following codes.

Unlockable	How to Unlock
Audi TT 3.2 Quattro (In Garage)	ITSABOUTYOU
Bonus Energizer Lithium Vinyl	ENERGIZERLITHIUM
Dodge Viper (In Garage)	WORLDSLONGESTLASTING
Extra $2,000	1MA9X99
Extra $4,000	W2iOLLO1
Extra $8,000	L1iS97A1
Extra $10,000	1Mi9K7E1
Extra $10,000	REGGAME
Extra $10,000	CASHMONEY
Extra $10,000 and Castrol Syntec Bonus Vinyl	CASTROLSYNTEC
Five Repair Tokens	SAFETYNET
K&N Bonus Vinyl	HORSEPOWER
Lancer Evo (In Garage)	MITSUBISHIGOFAR
Pre-tuned Grip Coke Zero Golf GTI (In Garage) and Bonus Coke Zero Vinyl	ZEROZEROZERO
Re-Locks Everything Unlocked by "Unlockallthings"	LEIPZIG
Unlocks Everything (maps, cars, parts)	UNLOCKALLTHINGS

Neutopia

Passwords

Password	Effect
5ltgaKyUFxsWssUkjzmVAkcQ	Begin game with 16 life bars
yP5ESDjsMwPB NDCYSzhXr%PP	End Level
KgKc%h5oFfep Qy1XwcjZXDVn	Level 4
rZtW68PjCG%L 1d9gSJ2uzn7r	Level 5
TQinHIUCDOQJ I$ZEhVQJNAwl	Super Password (5 medallions, 78 bombs)

Neutopia II

Everything Collected

Password	Effect
At the Password screen, enter the following passwords: IbnoBJt$ AyUkJ7Wa XACpGDjm q1j1uR1Q M8ozNOQa cPUM&XcX	Puts you in the Town of Oasis ready to tackle the last dungeon, The Atra Labyrinth
Music_From_Neutopia	Sound Test
Thats_Entertainment_Neutopia	View Enemies

New Adventure Island

Unlockables

Unlockable	How to Unlock
Level Select	Press ←, ←, ①, →, → ②, ↑, ↓, ↑, ↓
Level Skip	Insert a NEC Avenue 6 pad in 6-button mode into port 1

Ninja Gaiden

Unlockables

Unlockable	How to Unlock
Sound Test	When the screen says Techmo Presents 1989: Hold Ⓐ+Ⓑ+←+↓+SELECT, and press START
Extra Lives	In Area 5-3, there's a 1UP on the third floor of the tower. Go back down the ladder to the second floor, and then back up to the third floor. The 1UP has returned. You can do this as many times as you want.

One Piece: Unlimited Adventure

Unlockable Characters

Unlockable	How to Unlock
Unlock Survival Mode	Unlock the following characters in Vs. mode. All characters must be defeated to unlock them. All locations given are the first location you encounter each enemy.
Bazooka Marine	Defeat one in the Seaside Zone
Blue Demon General	Defeat one in the Cave Zone
Cluster Demon Soldier	Defeat one in the Cave Zone
Crimson Demon General	Defeat one in the Cave Zone
Knuckle Pirate	Defeat one in the Ruins Zone
Marine Corps Chief	Defeat one in the Jungle Zone
Normal Marine	Defeat one in the Seaside Zone
Pistol Pirate	Defeat one in the Jungle Zone
Sabre Pirate	Defeat one in the Jungle Zone
Sword Demon Soldier	Defeat one in the Cave Zone
World Government Agent	Defeat one in the Ruins Zone

Unlockables

Unlockable	How to Unlock
Transform into Overlimit Chopper in Story Mode	Defeat Overlimit Chopper in Story mode and create the Rumble Ball. You are now eligible to transform into Overlimit Chopper. To do so, you first must be in a boss fight. While in the fight you have to use two Rumble Balls (wait for one to run out, heal SP gauge, take another one). While you are using the second Rumble Ball, the enemy has to kill Chopper. Instead of dying, as he normally would, a cinema scene occurs. The scene shows Chopper taking a third Rumble Ball and he transforms into his Overlimit form. He gains a new HP and SP bar. He can't use items.

Open Season

Unlockable Minigames

Unlockable	How to Unlock
Duck Chorus	Complete "Crazy Quackers"
Flowers for My Deer	Complete "Meet the Skunks"
Rise, Rise to the Top!	Complete "Beaver Damage"
Shake That Butt!	Complete "Hunted"
Wild Memory	Complete "Shaw's Shack"

Opoona (Wii)

Unlockables

Unlockable	How to Unlock
Fifth Citizen Ranking Star	Acquire the Five-Star Landroll Ranger License. Must be done before talking to woman for Sixth Star.
Five-Star Landroll Ranger License	Win 100 battles in the Intelligent Sea server room.
Sixth Citizen Ranking Star	Talk to a woman on the bottom floor of the Moon Forest Tokione Hotel after spending the night.

Ordyne

Unlockables

Unlockable	How to Unlock
Continue Game	While falling, hold ① and press RUN
Princess Mode	At the title screen, hold ① for about 10 seconds
Secret Test Mode	At the title screen, hold down RUN while pressing SELECT, SELECT, SELECT, SELECT, SELECT, SELECT, then release. Hold down ①+②+↑+←, then press RUN. Press SELECT and RUN simultaneously to reach each part of the Secret Test mode. You can access a Sound Test, select your starting stage and your starting number of ships, among other things.

Override

Levels

Enter the "Level Select mode" code before entering any of the level passwords.

Code	Effect
Level Select Mode	Hold RUN and press SELECT 10 times
Level 2	↑, SELECT, RUN
Level 3	→, SELECT, RUN
Level 4	↓, SELECT, RUN
Level 5	←, SELECT, RUN
Level 6	↑, →, SELECT, RUN

Unlockables

Unlockable	How to Unlock
Ending	Holding ↖+①+②+SELECT, press RUN
Invincibility	Press RUN, then quickly press and hold ①+②+SELECT+RUN
Sound Test	Hold SELECT and press RUN

Power Golf

Unlockables

Unlockable	How to Unlock
Left-handed Golfer	Hold ↓ and press ① when selecting a golfer

Prince of Persia Rival Swords

While in the Pause menu, use the d-pad to enter these codes.

Unlockable	Code
Unlock the Baby Toy Weapon	←, ←, →, →, Z, Nunchuck down, Nunchuck down, Z, ↑, ↓
Unlock Telephone Sword	→, ←, →, ←, ↓, ↓, ↑, ↑, Z, Nunchuck down, Z, Z, Nunchuck down, Nunchuck down

Prince of Persia Rival Swords (continued)

Unlockable	Code
Unlock Swordfish Weapon	↑, ↓, ↑, ↓, ←, →, ←, →, Z, Nunchuck down, Z, Nunchuck down
Unlock Chainsaw	↑, ↑, ↓, ↓, ←, →, ←, →, Z, Nunchuck down, Z, Nunchuck down

Pro Evolution Soccer 2008

Unlockables

Unlockable	How to Unlock
Classic Argentina	Win the World Cup with Argentina.
Classic Brazil	Win the World Cup with Brazil.
Classic England	Win the World Cup with England.
Classic France	Win the World Cup with France.
Classic Germany	Win the World Cup with Germany.
Classic Italy	Win the World Cup with Italy.
Classic Netherlands	Win the World Cup with the Netherlands.
Mii Match Mode	Finish top of the practice league in the Champions Road.

Pro Wrestling

Unlockables

Unlockable	How to Unlock
Battle the Great Puma	Once you are VWA Champion, defend your title for 10 matches. Then you will have a match with the Great Puma.

Pulseman

Unlockables

Unlockable	How to Unlock
Level SELECT	At the Sega logo, press (in joystick 2): Ⓐ, Ⓑ, Ⓒ, Ⓒ, Ⓑ, Ⓐ. After this, go to Options and use the Map option.

R-Type

Unlockables

Unlockable	How to Unlock
Extra Credits	Set the turbo switch for I to full. Then, hold SELECT+① and press RUN on the title screen.

Passwords

Password	Effect
CPL-3590-CM	Hard mode

R-Type II

Passwords

Password	Effect
JJL-6589-MB	All items and 99 lives

R-Type III

Unlockables

Unlockable	How to Unlock
Level Select	At the continue screen, press →, →, →, →, →, →, →, →, →, ↓ then press ← one or more times, then press START (the number of times L is pressed dictates the level you skip to

Rampage: Total Destruction

At the main menu, press the ⊖+⊕ to open the Password screen.

Unlockable	Password
All Monsters Unlocked	141421
Demo Mode with Two Random Monsters	082864
Disable All Active Codes	000000
Display Game Version	314159
Instant Demo Mode with Two Random Monsters	874098
Invincible to Military Attacks, Bombers, Infantry, Tanks, Etc.	986960
Obtain All Ability Upgrades	011235
One Hit Destroys a Building	071767
Unlock All Cities	271828
View Credits	667302
View Ending Theme	667301
View Opening Theme	667300

Rapala Tournament Fishing

Unlockable	How To
DT Flat Sure Set Series	Correctly answer 20 questions
Glass Shad Rap Lure	Correctly answer 10 questions
Lauri Rapala 100th Anniversary Lure	Correctly answer 40 questions
X-Rap Jointed Shad Lure	Correctly answer 30 questions
Video 1	Answer 5 questions correctly
Video 2	Answer 15 questions correctly
Video 3	Answer 25 questions correctly
Video 4	Answer 35 questions correctly
Video 5	Answer every question correctly

Rayman Raving Rabbids

Unlockables

Unlockable	How to Unlock
Alternate Ending	Score at least 1,000,000 points in Score mode
Artwork 1	5,000 Points
Artwork 2	93,000 Points
Bunnies Can't Cook Eggs	84,000 Points
Bunnies Can't Infiltrate Games Convention	48,000 Points
Bunnies Can't Play Soccer	138,000 Points
Bunnies Don't Do Vacuum Cleaning	21,000 Points
Bunnies Don't Like Taking a Bath	9,000 Points
Bunnies Never Close Doors	111,000 Points
Bunny Costume	Clear all games on day 12
Bunny Hunt Survival Mode	Clear all games on Bunny Hunt Time mode at least once
Bunny Hunt Time Mode	Clear all games on Bunny Hunt Score mode at least once

DS PSP PS2 PS3 Wii Xbox Xbox 360 Index

Rayman Raving Rabbids (continued)

Unlockable	How to Unlock
Caramba Costume	Clear all games on day 08
Challenge Mode	Complete Story mode
"Dark Iron Bunnies" for the Jukebox	Clear all games on day 11
Dee-Jay Costume	Clear all games on day 02
French Bastille Day	57,000 Points
Gold Cow Trophy on Top of the Wardrobe	Clear all games on day 15
"Girls Just Want To Have Fun" for the Jukebox	Clear all games on day 05
"Good Time" for the Jukebox	Clear all games on day 03
Gothic Costume	Clear all games on day 04
"Hip Hop Hooray" for the Jukebox	Clear all games on day 07
"La Bamba" for the Jukebox	Clear all games on day 09
"Misirlou" for the Jukebox	Clear all games on day 01
Raymaninho Costume	Clear all games on day 10
Rock 'n Roll Costume	Clear all games on day 06
"The Butcher Deejay" for the Jukebox	Clear all games on day 13
"Ubisoft Montpellier Choir" for the Jukebox	Clear all games on day 14
US Independence Day	165,000 Points

Red Steel

Unlockables

Unlockable	How to Unlock
Secret Staff Photos	When you first find the geishas on the mission Reiko sends you on, you'll see some lockers near them. Open the one with a darker door to see photos of the developers wearing blonde wigs.

Resident Evil: The Umbrella Chronicles

Unlockables

Unlockable	How to Unlock
Unlimited Ammo	Gain an S rank in all missions on Hard difficulty.

Extra Scenarios

To unlock the extra scenarios, complete the following scenarios with the corresponding ranks.

Unlockable	How to Unlock
Beginnings 1	Beat Train Derailment 3.
Beginnings 2	Beat Beginnings 1 with an A rank or higher.
Dark Legacy 1	Complete Fall of Umbrella 3.
Dark Legacy 2	Complete Death's Door and Nightmare 2.
Death's Door	Beat Raccoon's Destruction 3 with an A rank.
Fourth Survivor	Complete Dark Legacy 2.
Nightmare 1	Complete Mansion Incident 1.
Nightmare 2	Beat Nightmare 1 with an A rank or higher.
Rebirth 1	Beat Mansion Incident 3.
Rebirth 2	Beat Rebirth 1.

Resident Evil: The Umbrella Chronicles (continued)

Unlockable	How to Unlock

Past Items

To unlock items from past *Resident Evil* games, complete the following chapters and gain the corresponding rank.

Unlockable	How to Unlock
Battery	Complete Dark Legacy 2 with S rank.
Blue/Green Leech Charm	Complete Train Derailment 3 with A rank.
Blue/Red/Green Chemical	Complete Umbrella's End 2 with A rank.
Blue/Red/Yellow Gemstone	Complete Rebirth 2 with A rank.
Book of Wisdom/Future Compass	Complete Raccoon's Destruction 1 with S rank.
Briefcase	Complete Train Derailment 1 with S rank.
Chronos Key	Complete Raccoon's Destruction 3 with S rank.
Clark/Gail X-Ray	Complete Rebirth 1 with A rank.
Crystal/Obsidian/Amber Ball	Complete Raccoon's Destruction 3 with A rank.
Cylinder Shaft	Complete Nightmare 1 with A rank.
Death Mask	Complete Rebirth 2 with S rank.
Eagle/Serpent/Jaguar Stone	Complete Fourth Survivor with S rank.
Emblem/Gold Emblem	Complete Nightmare 2 with S rank.
Film A/B/C/D	Complete Umbrella's End 1 with S rank.
Fire/Water Key	Complete Beginning 2 with A rank.
Fuel Canteen	Complete Mansion Incident 3 with S rank.
G-Virus	Complete Fourth Survivor with A rank.
Hex Crank	Complete Nightmare 1 with S rank.
Ink Ribbon	Complete Umbrella's End 3 with S rank.
Joint N/S Plug	Complete Raccoon's Destruction 2 with A rank.
King/Knight/Bishop/Rook Plug	Complete Dark Legacy 1 with A rank.
Last Book, Vol. 1/2	Complete Nightmare 2 with A rank.
Lighter Fluid	Complete Raccoon's Destruction 2 with S rank.
Medium Base	Complete Dark Legacy 1 with S rank.
Microfilm A/B	Complete Beginning 2 with S rank.
Mixing Set	Complete Train Derailment 1 with A rank.
MO Disk	Complete Mansion Incident 3 with A rank.
Motherboard	Complete Beginning 1 with A rank.
Picture (Ada and John)	Complete Death's Door with A rank.
Plastic Bomb/Detonator	Complete Umbrella's End 1 with A rank.
Relief of Discipline/ Obedience/Unity	Complete Train Derailment 2 with S rank.
S.T.A.R.S. Card (Brad's)	Complete Death's Door with S rank.
S.T.A.R.S. Card (Jill's)	Complete Raccoon's Destruction 1 with A rank.
Slide Cartridge	Complete Rebirth 1 with S rank.
Spade/Diamond/Club/Heart Key	Complete Dark Legacy 2 with A rank.
Square Crank	Complete Umbrella's End 2 with S rank.
Statue of Good/Evil	Complete Train Derailment 2 with A rank.
Sterilizing Agent	Complete Train Derailment 3 with S rank.
Sun/Star/Moon Crest	Complete Mansion Incident 2 with A rank.
V-Jolt	Complete Mansion Incident 2 with S rank.
Vaccine	Complete Umbrella's End 3 with A rank.
Valve Handle	Complete Beginning 1 with S rank.

Ristar

Passwords

Password	Effect
STAR	A shooting star goes across the background (JP)
MUSEUM	Boss Rush mode
XXXXXX	Clears/Deactivates the current password
AGES	Copyright info is displayed
MIEMIE	Hidden items' grab points are shown with a blue star
FEEL	ILOVEU, MIEMIE, CANDY active all at once (JP)
CANDY	Invincibility (JP)
MACCHA	Mentions Miyake color (JP)
MASTER	Mentions next game (JP)
AAAAAA	No Continue limit (JP)
MAGURO	Onchi Music mode and credits music in sound test
HETAP	Reverses the high score in Demo mode (JP)
VALDI	Shows the solar system (JP)
ILOVEU	Stage select
SUPERB	Super Difficulty mode
SUPER	Super Hard mode
DOFEEL	Time Attack mode

River City Ransom

Passwords

Password	Effect
XfMdZTHwiR3 jaj6jfRUDEt tilm2tWRo8b	Final Boss, with Max Stats, Dragon Feet, Stone Hands, Grand Slam, and Texas Boots
XfMdZTHUPR3 rztzPeQUCTt 61lxhtWRo2b	Final Boss, with Max Stats, Stone Hands, Dragon Feet, Acro Circus, Grand Slam, 4 Karma Jolts, and $999.99 cash
t1izvpdOZnZ JxNkJp7Cpub XMPQgXErSMF	Ivan Beaten, High School Open
w412ysgtMqc MUSjKm2PqtE UJMNdUTGOQC	Power Up
jrYplfTgbdj nOorLTIYXwR SjTuqpilUHP	Start with all abilities and $500 in cash
fHUFBbvcnpa MS8iPplCZJP VKNOeVRQPDD	Strange item in inventory that gives stat increases

Unlockables

Unlockable	How to Unlock
Change Character Names	On the Character Select screen, press SELECT on the controller to go to a screen where you can change Alex and Ryan's names to whatever you want.
Merlin's Mystery Shop	To find Merlin's Mystery Shop go to the Armstrong Thru-Way. Once inside, press up at the top wall and the wall opens. Inside you can buy the best items in the game.

Rock Band

Codes

Using the colored fret buttons on the guitar, enter these codes QUICKLY on the title screen.

Effect	Code
Unlock All Songs (Disable Saving)	R, Y, B, R, R, B, B, R, Y, B

Romance of the Three Kingdoms IV: Wall of Fire

Unlockables

Unlockable	How to Unlock
Form Anti-Dong Zhuo Coalition	Select the first scenario (Dong Zhuo Triumphs in Luo Yang), then select Cao Cao as your leader. On your very first turn, move some generals and troops to Xu Chang. A few months later, Cao Cao will call a meeting, asking all the other leaders to form an alliance against Dong Zhuo. If Yuan Shao joins, he will become leader; otherwise, Cao Cao will become leader. This makes defeating Dong Zhuo a bit easier, depending on who joins you (such as Yuan Shao or Ma Teng).
Unlimited Soldiers	Use the War command and select a general to go into battle. Assign the maximum number of men to his unit. When they asked for confirmation for going to war select the "No" option. Remove the general from the list of commanders and reassign him to the post. Return to the troop assignment screen. The number of men available should be multiplied by the number that was assigned earlier. Repeat this process to increase the number of men, but don't go back to the main menu.

Samurai Warriors: Katana

Chaos Difficulty

Unlockable	How to Unlock
Chaos Difficulty	Complete all missions with an S rank.

Scarface: The World Is Yours

Passwords

Password	Effect
OLDFAST	Antique racer
666999	Bacinari
BLACK	Black suit
BLUESH	Blue suit with shades
DOZER	Bulldozer
MARTHA	Change time of day
NOBALLS	Decrease Gang Heat
FLYSTRT	Decreases Cop Heat
DUMPER	Dump truck
FPATCH	Fill Balls Meter
GRAYSH	Gray suit Tony with sunglasses
HAWAII	Hawaii print shirt
HAWAIIG	Hawaii print shirt with sunglasses
DONUT	Increase Cop Heat
GOBALLS	Increase Gang Heat
AMMO	Max Ammo
TUNEME	Real "The World Is Yours" music track
MEDIK	Refill health
TBURGLR	Repairs car
BUMMER	Stampede
RAINY	Toggle rain
WHITE	White suit
WHITESH	White suit with shades

DS
PSP
PS2
PS3
Wii
Xbox
Xbox 360
Index

SD Gundam: Scad Hammers

Unlockables

Unlockable	How to Unlock
Unlock Turn A Gundam	Fill up the Data Accumulation gauge (the one with the picture of a mobile suit beside it) under the Educational Data/Analysis Situation menu to 100%, then beat the Side 3 stage (Lv. 10 Ki mama ni Hammer 50) to unlock the Turn A Gundam

Shadow Dancer

Unlockables

Unlockable	How to Unlock
Earning 200,000 points	When you battle any boss (except Stavros) reduce your foe to within a flame or two of destruction, then stay out of reach until the last 10 seconds. At the very last second, use ninja magic to destroy the boss.
Practice on Any Stage	Enter the following code at the Title screen: Ⓐ+Ⓑ+Ⓒ+START. A new option appears, allowing you to practice on any level.
Extra Life	In the bonus round where you have to shoot the ninjas, kill either all ninjas or none of them.

Shadow Land

Secret Password Screen

Unlockable	How to Unlock
Password Screen	At the title screen hold ①+②+SELECT and press RUN

Passwords

Password	Effect
PC-ENGINE	(message)
NAMCO	(message)
NAMCOT	(message)
6502	(message)
6809	(message)
68000	(message)
756-2311	(message)
YAMASHITA	(message)
AKIRA	(message)
KOMAI	(message)
KAZUHIKO	(message)
KAWADA	(message)
SPEED-UP (4 way split screen)	Reset after entering the password
S.62.08.22 (Start from level 5)	Reset after entering the password

Shining in the Darkness

Unlockables

Unlockable	How to Unlock
Rename All Characters	At the Name Entry screen, input a name that takes up all the available spaces (5 letter spaces). Then, select the forward button and you can enter another name for the next character! This works for all the characters!

Shining Force

Unlockables

Unlockable	How to Unlock
Control All Opponents (JP Version Only)	When the battle begins, quickly tap Ⓐ, Ⓑ, Ⓒ, ✚(Up), Ⓐ, Ⓒ, Ⓐ, Ⓑ, Ⓐ
Fight Any Battle (JP Version Only)	Hold START on controller 2 then reset the system. Let go of START and hold Ⓐ+Ⓑ on controller 2. Select continue and wait until the girl says good luck. At that instant hold Ⓐ on controller 1 while continuing to hold Ⓐ+Ⓑ on controller 2.
Name Characters	Start a new game (must have completed game first) and go to the Name Your Character screen. Put the cursor on end and hold START+Ⓐ+Ⓑ+Ⓒ on controller 2 while holding: START+Ⓐ+Ⓒ on controller 1. You will see another character. Continue this to name all characters.

Other Unlockables

Unlockable	How to Unlock
2 Jogurts	If you put jogurt in your army and kill an enemy with him, you get a jogurt ring item. Use this in battle on any character to make that character look like a jogurt! Repeat as many times as you want, but you will have to get another ring when it breaks.
Anri's Alternate Costume	During the Laser Eye battle in Chapter 3, search to the left of the three dark elves. You'll receive a hidden item called Kitui Huku ("tight clothes" in Japanese). Give it to Anri and she'll have a new outfit.
Tao's Alternate Costume	In Chapter 3, after fighting the first battle to get the Moon Stone, go inside the cave and search the walls for a secret item called the Sugoi Mizugi. Give it to Tao and she will have an alternate costume.

Shinobi III: Return of the Ninja Master

Unlockables

Unlockable	How to Unlock
Bonus Points	Complete a level without throwing any shuriken to get 30,000 bonus points
Invincibility	Choose BMG selection on the options menu, then, press Ⓑ to select the following songs in order: He runs, Japonesque, shinboi walk, sakura, getufu
Unlimited Shuriken	Set the number of shuriken to 0 on the Options menu and set the sound effects option to Shuriken. Highlight the Shuriken option and keep it there, and the 0 will change into the symbol for infinity.

Shockman

Unlockables

Enter these cheats when the game is paused.

Unlockable	How to Unlock
Invincibility	✚(Up), ✚(Up), SELECT, ✚(Down), ②, SELECT
Level Skip	✚(Left), ✚(Down), SELECT, ✚(Right), ✚(Left), SELECT, SELECT
Refill Life Meter	✚(Left), SELECT, ②
Suicide	✚(Right), SELECT, ✚(Left), SELECT, SELECT

DS PSP PS2 PS3 Wii Xbox Xbox 360 Index

Shrek the Third

Unlockables

Unlockable	How to Unlock
10,000 Bonus Coins	Press ↑, ↑, ↓, ↑, →, ← at the Gift Shop
Bonus Damage	Buy at the Gift Shop for 10,500
Bonus Fairy Dust	Buy at the Gift Shop for 7,700
Academy Grounds Commentary	Buy at the Gift Shop for 1,500
Catacombs Commentary	Buy at the Gift Shop for 5,000
Docks Commentary	Buy at the Gift Shop for 1,000
Evil Queen's Castle Commentary	Buy at the Gift Shop for 5,000
Ice Lake Commentary	Buy at the Gift Shop for 3,000
Merlin's Hills Commentary	Buy at the Gift Shop for 4,000
Prison Cell Blocks Commentary	Buy at the Gift Shop for 2,000
Rundown Streets Commentary	Buy at the Gift Shop for 6,000
Stromboli's Workshop Commentary	Buy at the Gift Shop for 5,000
Donkey: Dragon Disguise	Buy at the Gift Shop for 3,650
Fiona: Funeral Dress	Buy at the Gift Shop for 2,150
Puss: Evil Knight Disguise	Buy at the Gift Shop for 2,850
Shrek: Knight Armor	Buy at the Gift Shop for 3,500
Shrek: Pirate Outfit	Buy at the Gift Shop for 4,250
Shrek: Regal	Buy at the Gift Shop for 3,200
Shrek: Swim Trunks	Buy at the Gift Shop for 3,350
Sleeping Beauty: Gown	Buy at the Gift Shop for 2,500
Charming	Buy at the Gift Shop for 15,500
Grimm	Buy at the Gift Shop for 1,500
Cyclops (Character)	Buy at the Gift Shop for 1,500
Dragon Keep (Castle)	Buy at the Gift Shop for 1,600
Dragon Keep (Map)	Buy at the Gift Shop for 1,350
Dwarves (Character)	Buy at the Gift Shop for 2,400

SimCity

Unlockables

Unlockable	How to Unlock
$999,999	At any time while playing a city, spend all of your money. When the tax screen appears at the end of December, hold down L. Select "Go with Figures" and then go back to the tax screen. Turn all of the dues to 100% and exit still holding L. When you release L your money will be at $999,999.
999 Extra City Maps	Start a new city, and choose any map number, then start the game. Now select the "Go to Menu" icon at the screen's top, and choose Start New City without saving. After a short time, the map will change, but the number won't.
Freeland	Beat the Las Vegas scenario
Las Vegas Scenario	Beat the six game scenarios and have at least one city with over 100,000 citizens living in it saved to the game.

The Sims 2: Pets

Unlockables

Unlockable	How to Unlock
10,000 Simoleons	Hold Ⓑ, press ↑, ←, ↓, ↓
Advance 6 Hours	→, →, →, →, →, ←
Change Skills	↓, ↓, ↓, ↑, ↑, ↑

The Simpsons Game

Codes

Go into the "Extras" section of the main menu and insert the following codes. If the code is accepted, you hear a sound effect.

Unlockable	How to Unlock
Unlimited Power for All Characters	⊕,←,→,⊕,⊖,Ⓩ
All Cliches	←,⊖,→,⊕,→,Ⓩ
All Movies	⊖,←,⊖,→,⊕,Ⓒ

Soldier Blade

Codes

Code	Effect
Level Select	Hold ↑, press SELECT, hold ↓, press SELECT, hold ←, press SELECT, hold →, press SELECT

Solomon's Key

Unlockables

Unlockable	How to Unlock
Continue Game	At the "Game Deviation Value" screen, hold ↑+Ⓐ+Ⓑ

Sonic 3D Blast

Unlockables

Unlockable	How to Unlock
Level Select	Go to the Press Start screen and enter Ⓑ, Ⓐ, →, Ⓐ, Ⓒ, ↑, ↓, Ⓐ (or baracuda). You're taken to the main screen. Press the Start option and the level select appears.
Quick Emerald Gain	Enter the Level Select code twice, and go to a level/act with Knuckles or Tails in it. Enter one of their bonus levels by collecting 50 rings. When the bonus level begins, press Ⓐ+START and you will receive the emerald for the bonus level.
Skip Levels	Do the Level Select code and start the game in any level. To skip levels, pause the game and press Ⓐ.
Stage Select (Alternative)	Beat the entire game with all the Chaos Emeralds. After the credits, the stage select is on.

Sonic and the Secret Rings

Unlockable	Code
Bookworm	Play a total time of 24 hours
Celebrity	Play attractions 35 times
Champion	Win 1st in 120 Party Games
Dark Master	Beat 20 missions using at least 5 Dark skills and no Wind/Fire skills
Dealer	Win World Bazaar 7 times
Explorer	Win at Treasure Hunt 7 times

Sonic and the Secret Rings (continued)

Unlockable	Code
Extreme Speeder	Use Speed Break 50 times
Flame Master	Beat 20 missions using at least 5 Fire skills and no Wind/Dark skills
Genie Buster	Defeat 1,000 Genies
Grind Performer	Grind a distance of 30 km (18.64 miles)
Hero	Defeat Erazor Djinn
Pirate	Win at Pirates Coast 7 times
Rebellion	Beat Erazor Djinn at level 25 or lower
Record Buster	Set records for all party games that have records
Ring Catcher	Collect 10,000 Rings
Skill Collector	Unlock every skill available
Skill Quinti	Beat 20 missions using 4 or fewer skills
Skill Saver	Beat 30 missions using fewer than 100 SP
Sonic Freak	Use Sonic 30 times in Party mode
Soul Collector	Collect every Fire Soul
Star	Play party games 200 times
Super	Reach level 99
The Ultimate	Collect all Gold Medals
Thief	Win at Genie's Lair 7 times
Time Controller	Use Time Break for 300 seconds
Trier	Win Tournament Palace 7 times
True Hero	Defeat Alf Layla wa Layla
Wind Master	Beat 20 missions using at least 5 Wind skills and no Fire/Dark skills
World Traveler	Travel 500 km (310.7 miles)

Sonic Spinball

Unlockables

Unlockable	How to Unlock
Level Select	Access the Options from the title screen, take controller 1, and press: Ⓐ, ✚, Ⓑ, ✚, Ⓒ, ✚, Ⓐ, Ⓑ, ✚, Ⓐ, Ⓒ, ✚, Ⓑ, Ⓒ, ✚. If you did it correctly, you hear a special sound. Go back to the title screen and hold Ⓐ and press START to begin on Level 2, Ⓑ and press START for Level 3, and ✚ and press START for level 4.
Multi-Ball Stage	Collect every ring in any stage.
Stop the Platform in The Machine	In Level 3, The Machine, a moving platform takes you to either side of the area. Stand on the platform and press up or down to make the platform stop, allowing you to get a good look around or plan your jump carefully.

Sonic the Hedgehog

Unlockables

Unlockable	How to Unlock
Config Mode	There is a code called Control mode, which is required before activating this code. To activate Control mode, press ✚, Ⓒ, ✚, Ⓒ, ✚, Ⓒ, ✚, Ⓒ at the title screen, but before pressing START to begin the game, hold Ⓐ as you hit START. Now, rather than just being in Control mode, you can enable Config mode by pressing Ⓑ. Sonic will morph into a ring, and the arrows can move him anywhere, even in the air, or through obstacles such as walls, floors, or even ceilings. You can change the item Sonic appears as by hitting Ⓐ while in Config mode. Ⓑ makes Sonic normal again, and ✚ will place the sprite that you have selected for Sonic to appear as. For example, you press Ⓑ, and Sonic becomes a ring, press ✚ to make a ring appear exactly where the ring icon is. WARNING!: This distorts several different things, such as the score, time, and other various icons throughout the game such as the finish signs at the end of the first two acts of each zone that spin when Sonic shoots past them, and the small score icons that appear whenever Sonic jumps high enough after finishing a level.
Drunk Sonic	During the demo, hold ✚. Sonic will crash into walls and get hit by enemies.
Level Select	At the title screen, press ✚, ✚, ✚, ✚. You should hear a noise like a ring being collected. Then, hold Ⓐ and press START for a level select!

Unlockables

Unlockable	How to Unlock
Secret Game Message	At the title screen, press Ⓒ, Ⓒ, Ⓒ, Ⓒ, Ⓒ, Ⓒ, ✚, ✚, ✚, ✚. When the demo starts, hold Ⓐ+Ⓑ+Ⓒ+✚ then press START. Instead of the Sonic Team logo, you will see a list of the game's developers in Japanese. When the title screen appears, a flashing "Press Start Button" will be there under Sonic's head.
Different Ending	Beat game with all Chaos Emeralds.

Sonic the Hedgehog 2

Unlockables

Unlockable	How to Unlock
Level Select	Some other cheats require you to enable this one first. Go to the Options menu from the main screen. From there, head to the Sound Select menu and play the following sounds: 19, 65, 09, 17. Once you have played each (1 time only), press ✚ and then press START to be brought back to the title screen. Now, when you see Sonic and Tails (Miles) appear on screen, hold Ⓐ and press START to finish off the code. You're brought to a menu where you have access to any level in the game, whether you've completed the level or not.
14 Continues	Go to the sound test (not the one on the level select) and put in 19, 65, 09, 17, 01, 01, 02, 04 (press Ⓐ after each one). There won't be a confirmation sound. Start the game by pressing START on the first option (character select) and you have 14 continues.
All 7 Chaos Emeralds	This code only works for Sonic. First, do the Level Select cheat. In the Level Select menu, go to Sound Test and play the sounds 04, 01, 02, 06. If done correctly, you'll hear a Chaos Emerald sound effect. Now, select any stage from this menu and you can turn into Super Sonic with 50 rings plus you'll get Sonic's second ending after beating Death Egg Zone.
Change Tails' Name to Miles	Press ✚, ✚, ✚, ✚, ✚, ✚, ✚ at the title screen.

Sonic the Hedgehog 2 (continued)

Unlockable	How to Unlock
Debug Mode	First enter the Level Select code. Now, go to Sound Test option, and play the following tunes: 01, 09, 09, 02, 01, 01, 02, 04. It should make a ring sound when track 4 is played to signify you've entered it correctly. Now select the stage you want to go to, and press START while holding Ⓐ until the stage starts, and you'll have debug activated. Press Ⓑ to turn Debug on/off, Ⓐ to switch object, and ✜ to put down object selected. Pressing Ⓐ while the game is paused will cause the game to reset.
Debug Mode (Alternate)	At Sound Test, enter: 19, 65, 09, 17, then press Ⓐ+START, then when Sonic and Tails pop up, press Ⓐ+START to go to the Level Select screen. On the Sound Test area, enter 01, 09, 09, 02, 01, 01, 02, 04, and then press Ⓐ+START.
Debug Mode and All Emeralds (when locked-on to Sonic and Knuckles)	First activate and go to the Stage Select. Play the following tracks in Sound Test with Ⓑ: 01, 09, 09, 04, 01, 00, 01, 08. This enables the Debug code, and you should hear a ring chime if the code is entered correctly. Start the selected level with Ⓐ+START. To get all 7 Chaos Emeralds, input this code the same way: 01, 06, 07, 07, 07, 02, 01, 06. You should hear the Emerald chime. Note: this code may not work without the Debug code.
Enable Super Sonic	First, head to the Options menu from the title screen, and then into the Sound Select menu from there. Play the following sounds in this order: 19, 65, 09, 17. After that, press ✜, START. You will be taken back to the title screen. Now, when you see Sonic and Tails (Miles) appear on the screen, press and hold Ⓐ and press START to be taken to the Level Select menu. From this menu, enter the Sound Test feature, and play the following sounds: 04, 01, 02, 06. If done correctly, a familiar tune plays. Exit this menu and start the game as normal. Once you collect a minimum of 50 coins in any level, Jump (Press Ⓐ) to activate the Super Sonic code.
Get Super Sonic on Emerald Hill	First, enter the Stage Select code, shown above. Then you go into the Special Stage in the Stage Select menu. Every time you finish the special stage, press reset and go back to the special stage. Keep doing this until you get the sixth emerald. Then don't press reset. It zaps you with your 6 emeralds into Emerald Hill. Get the last emerald on Emerald Hill, get 50 rings, and jump to be Super Sonic. Don't run out of rings or you will change into Sonic again. The rings start disappearing when you are Super Sonic.
Infinite Lives	First, enable the Level Select cheat and the Debug mode. Choose Sonic and Tails as the players. After entering the codes, choose any stage from the Level Select menu (preferably stage 1). As soon as you can move Sonic, hold ✜ and press Ⓐ (don't let go of down on the D-pad). This activates Sonic's spin; Tails will copy the Sonic spin also. Press Ⓑ and Sonic will become the Debug cursor. (Tails will be locked in the Sonic spin move). Press Ⓐ until the debug cursor displays an enemy sprite, like the monkey or that bee robot. Now that the debug cursor displays an enemy sprite, move the debug cursor to where Tails is, and repeatedly tap ✜. This produces enemies where Tails is, and because Tails is locked in the Sonic spin move, he destroys the enemies. As Tails destroys enemies in this position, press ✜ more until the score for destroying an enemy increases from 100 to 8,000 to a 1Up. Once you have enough 1Ups, press Ⓑ again to revert to Sonic.

Sonic the Hedgehog 2 (continued)

Unlockable	How to Unlock
Level Select (When Locked-On to Sonic and Knuckles)	At the title screen, press ↑, ↑, ↑, ↓, ↓, ↓, ←, →, ←, ↓. Then, hold Ⓐ and press START to be taken to the Level Select menu.
Night Mode	Activate level select and hold ↓ while selecting a stage to darken the level. The effect wears off when you die or when you beat the level.
Level Select Screen	At the title screen, select Options. Highlight Sound Test then play the following music and sounds: 19, 65, 09, and 17. You hear a ring-collecting sound for correct code entry. Then press START to return to the title screen. Highlight 1-Player, hold Ⓐ, and press START. You are directed to Level Select screen. Choose a level then press START to begin.

Code	Effect
17	Play Invincibility Music
65	Plays a Shifting Sound
09	Plays Casino Night Zone 1-Player Music
19	Plays Sonic 2 Theme

Slow Motion	First, enter the Level Select code. Then start your game in any level. When you start, press pause. Then hold Ⓑ and try to do anything with Sonic. The game plays in slow motion as long as you hold down Ⓑ.
Oil Ocean Music Forever	Go to the Sound Test in the Options menu and put in the sounds, 02, 01, 02, 04, and hold Ⓐ and press START. The Oil Ocean music will now be playing constantly, no matter what stage.
Pseudo Super Sonic	In Oil Ocean Zone, if you manage to take a hit and end up landing in one of those green-and-gold checkered cannons, you'll fall right out, but you'll be moving at twice your normal speed as well as jumping twice your normal height (with twice as much gravity). A good place for doing this would be in Oil Ocean Zone, Act 2, near the first set of pop-tops and cannons. Just jump into the semi-hidden bed of spikes on the right and land in the cannon. Note: Moving at twice normal velocity can often get you stuck in a wall. Also, this wears off if you Super Spin Dash or Spin Dash. It also only lasts for that act.
Super Tails	Normally, when you turn into Super Sonic you lose Tails behind you all the time. Well, after you put in the debug cheat and have started a level (preferably Emerald Hill), turn yourself into a box and place it somewhere on the floor while you are Super Sonic. It should be a switch places box. Hit it and Tails has a permanent invincible circle around him. He stays like this through the whole level.
Unlimited Speed Shoes in 2-Player vs. Mode	In 2-Player vs. mode, get speed shoes and die (while you still have them) and you get to keep your speed shoes until the end of the level.

Sonic the Hedgehog 3

Unlockables

Unlockable	How to Unlock
All 7 Chaos Emeralds and Super Sonic	To get all 7 Chaos Emeralds without having to complete their Special Stages, first enter the Level Select and Sound Test codes. Go to the Sound Test and play the following tunes in order: 02, 04, 05, 06. You will hear an emerald sound if the code is entered correctly. To get Super Sonic after entering the previous code, just select any level from the level select and start it. Once you acquire 50 Rings, do a double-jump to become Super Sonic.

Sonic the Hedgehog 3 (continued)

Unlockable	How to Unlock
Control Tails in a 1-Player Game	Start a 1-player game with Sonic and Tails as the characters. With controller 2, you can take control of Tails while also using Sonic.
Hidden Special Stage	On the Level Select menu, play sounds 01, 03, 05, 07. Highlight Special Stage 2 and press Ⓐ+START.
Infinite Lives	Get up to Launch Base Zone. Sound any of the alarms, so that the Kamikaze birds come after you. Charge up a Super Sonic Dash in between the alarm, but do not let go of the button. The birds continually crash into you. After about 30 seconds, you have gained enough points to get an extra life. Continue the process for as many lives as you want.
Level Select (When Locked-On to Sonic and Knuckles)	Start a game and go to Angel Island Zone, Act 1. Go to one of the swings that you hang from and grab on. While Sonic is swinging, press ✚, ✚, ✚, ✚, ✚, ✚, ✚, ✚, ✚. You will hear a ring if you entered the code correctly. Pause the game and press Ⓐ to take you back to the title screen. Press ✚, ✚ to find the newly unlocked Sound Test menu. Enter it, where you can play all of the sounds/music in the game and warp to any level.
Turn into Super Sonic	After entering the Level Select and Debug code, you can use the debug to turn yourself into Super Sonic without getting all of the Chaos Emeralds. With the debug on, go into any level and press Ⓑ to turn yourself into a ring. Then press Ⓐ to turn yourself into a monitor. Now, press ✚ to duplicate the monitor, and then Ⓑ again to change back into Sonic. Jump on the monitor and you will become Super Sonic.

Unlockables

Unlockable	How to Unlock
Level Select	When the "SEGA" screen fades, quickly press ✚, ✚, ✚, ✚, ✚, ✚,✚, ✚. If you have done this right, you should be able to scroll down to "Sound Test" below "Competition."
Sonic and Knuckles Mini-Boss Music	Get to the end of Act 1 of Hydrocity Zone (Zone 2). When facing the mini-boss, keep yourself underwater until the water warning music plays. Then jump out of the water. The game should now be playing the mini-boss music from Sonic and Knuckles, which wasn't out at the time (the music was evidently included in *Sonic 3* to make the backward compatibility feature easier).
Walk Thru Walls	In the Icecap Zone, Act 1, when you come to a wall that only Knuckles can bust through, hold ✚ until Sonic or Tails looks down, and the screen pans all the way down. Then press ✚ and jump at the same time. The screen starts to rotate. Walk in the direction of the wall and you will walk right through it.
100,000 Points	Beat a stage at with your time at exactly 9:59.
Frame by Frame	When playing a level after enabling the Level Select cheat, pause the game, then press ✚ to advance the game by one frame.
Slow Motion Mode	When playing any level that you have accessed using the Cheat menu, pause the game and hold Ⓑ. While Ⓑ is held down, the game plays in Slow Motion mode.

Codes

Code	Effect
Hold Ⓑ and press ✚	Your character shows all of his sprite animations
Hold Ⓑ and press ✚ again	Your character stops the sprite show if it is activated

Speed Racer

Codes

Enter the following codes in the "Enter Code" section of the "Options" menu. Enter the codes again to disable them.

Effect	Code
Aggressive Opponents	Up, Left, Down, Right, Up, Left, Down
Granite Car	Ⓑ, Up, ⊖, ⊕, ①, Up, ⊕
Helium	⊖, Up, ⊖, ②, ⊖, Up, ⊖
Invulnerability	Ⓐ, Ⓑ, Ⓐ, Up, Left, Down, Right
Monster Truck	Ⓑ, Up, ⊖, ②, Ⓑ, Up, ⊖
Moon Gravity	Up, ⊕, Up, Right, ⊖, Up, ⊖
Overkill	Ⓐ, ⊖, ⊕, Down, Up, ⊕, ①
Pacifist Opponents (other racers don't attack you)	Up, Right, Down, Left, Up, Right, Down
Psychedelic	Left, Ⓐ, Right, Down, Ⓑ, Up, ⊖
Tiny Opponents	Ⓑ, Ⓐ, Left, Down, ⊖, Up, ⊖
Unlimited Boost	Ⓑ, Ⓐ, Down, Up, Ⓑ, Ⓐ, Down
Unlock the Last 3 Cars	①, ②, ①, ②, Ⓑ, Ⓐ, ⊕

Unlockables

Complete the championships with a ranking of 3rd or higher to unlock the corresponding racer.

Unlockable	How to Unlock
Booster Mbube	Complete Class 2, Championship 6.
Colonel Colon	Complete Class 3, Championship 4.
Delila	Complete Class 3, Championship 3.
Denise Mobile	Complete Class 3, Championship 6.
Esther "Rev" Reddy	Complete Class 3, Championship 7.
Gothorm Danneskjblo	Complete Class 3, Championship 2.
Grey Ghost	Complete Class 1, Championship 3.
Kellie "Gearbox" Kalinkov	Complete Class 2, Championship 4.
Mariana Zanja	Complete Class 3, Championship 5.
Nitro Venderhoss	Complete Class 2, Championship 5.
Pitter Pat	Complete Class 3, Championship 1.
Prince Kabala	Complete Class 2, Championship 3.
Rosey Blaze	Complete Class 1, Championship 1.
Snake Oiler	Complete Class 1, Championship 2.
Sonic "Boom Boom" Renaldi	Complete Class 2, Championship 2.
Taejo Togokahn	Complete Class 2, Championship 1.

Spider-Man 3

Unlockables

Unlockable	How to Unlock
Collect all 50 Spider Emblems	Unlock black suit Spider-man after you destroy the suit

Spider-Man: Friend or Foe

Codes

Code	Effect
5,000 Tech Tokens, One Time Only	Up, Up, Down, Down, Left, Down
Unlock New Goblin	Left, Down, Right, Right, Down, Left
Unlock Sandman	Right, Right, Right, Up, Down, Left
Unlock Venom	Left, Left, Right, Up, Down, Down

Splatterhouse

Unlockables

Unlockable	How to Unlock
Hard Mode	At the title screen, hold SELECT until "HARD" appears on the screen
Sound Test	First enter the code to access the Stage Select option. When the screen comes up and asks you to select what stage you want to start on, press and hold the select button. After a second or two, the Stage Select option becomes a Sound Test menu, allowing you to listen to various "songs" and sound effects. Hold select again to change it back to the Stage Select menu.
Stage Select	When the prologue starts up and there's a house in the rain, press SELECT, SELECT, SELECT, hold ✚ and then press ① or ②. It brings up the option to select a level.

SpongeBob SquarePants: Creature from the Krusty Krab

Passwords

Password	Effect
ROCFISH	30,000 Z-Coins
HOVER	Alternate Plankton hovercraft
ROBOT	Astronaut suit for Plankton in Revenge of the Giant Plankton
LASER	Extra laser color in Revenge of the Giant Plankton level
ROCKET	Extra rocket for Patrick in Hypnotic Highway level
PILOT	Get Aviator SpongeBob costume
BRAIN	Get Exposed-Brain SpongeBob costume
INVENT	Get Inventor Plankton costume
SPIN	Get Patrick's different POW! effect
BUNRUN	Get Patrick's purple rocket
SAFARI	Get Safari Patrick costume
BONES	Get Skeleton Patrick costume
KRABBY	Get Skeleton SpongeBob costume
FLAMES	Get SpongeBob's flame effect color
HYPCAR	Get SpongeBob's Hypnotic car skin
DUCKGUN	Get SpongeBob's Squeaky Duck Gun
GASSY	Infinite Fuel (in Flying levels)
VIGOR	Infinite Health (in platforming levels)
SCOOTLES	Obtain all sleepy seeds
TISSUE	Obtain Sleepy Seed Detector
PIRATE	Play as Pirate Patrick in Rooftop Rumble level
SPONGE	Play as Punk SpongeBob in Diesel Dreaming level
PANTS	Play as SpongeBob Plankton in Super-Size Patty level
HOTROD	Unlock a bonus vehicle in the Diesel Dreaming level
PORKPIE	Unlock all bonus games
GUDGEON	Unlock all levels
SPACE	Unlock bonus ship in the Rocket Rodeo level
PATRICK	Unlock tuxedo for Patrick in Starfishman to the Rescue

SSX Blur

In the Options menu, select Cheat to enter this code.

Unlockable	Code
All Characters Unlocked	NoHolds

Star Soldier

Unlockables

Unlockable	How to Unlock
Powered Up Ship	At the title screen, press SELECT 10 times on controller 1. Then, hold ✚+✚ on controller 2. Then, hold ✚+✚+Ⓐ+Ⓑ on controller 1, finally press START, START on controller 1.

Star Wars: The Force Unleashed

Codes

From the "Extras" menu inside the Rogue Shadow, select "Cheat Codes" and enter the following codes.

Effect	Code
1,000,000 Force Points	SPEEDER
God Mode	CORTOSIS
Max All Force Powers	KATARN
Max Combos	COUNTDOOKU
Unlimited Force Power	VERGENCE
Unlock All Force Powers	TYRANUS
Your Lightsaber One Hit Kills All Normal Enemies	LIGHTSABER

Skin Codes

Effect	Code	Effect	Code
Aayla Secura	AAYLA	Episode VI Luke Skywalker	T16WOMPRAT
Admiral Ackbar	ITSATWAP	Imperial Shadow Guard	INTHEDARK
Anakin Skywalker	CHOSENONE	Juno Eclipse	ECLIPSE
Asajj Ventress	ACOLYTE	Kleef	KLEEF
Chop'aa Notimo	NOTIMO	Lando Calrissian	SCOUNDREL
Classic Stormtrooper	TK421	Mace Windu	JEDIMASTER
Clone Trooper	LEGION	Mara Jade	MARAJADE
Count Dooku	SERENNO	Maris Brood	MARISBROOD
Darth Desolus	PAUAN	Navy Commando	STORMTROOP
Darth Maul	ZABRAK	Obi-Wan Kenobi	BENKENOBI
Darth Phobos	HIDDENFEAR	PROXY	HOLOGRAM
Darth Vader	SITHLORD	Qui-Gon Jinn	MAVERICK
Drexl Roosh	DREXLROOSH	Rahm Kota	MANDALORE
Emperor Palpatine	PALPATINE	Shaak Ti	TOGRUTA
Episode IV Luke Skywalker	YELLOWJCKT		

Extra Costumes

Effect	Code
Ceremonial Jedi Robes	DANTOOINE
Kento Marek's Robes	WOOKIEE
Sith Stalker Armor	KORRIBAN
Unlocks All Costumes	GRANDMOFF

Streets of Rage

Unlockables

Unlockable	How to Unlock
Bad Ending	Choose to be Mr. X's righthand man the first time you meet him. Then complete the game.
Extra Continues	Press ←, ←, Ⓑ, Ⓑ, Ⓑ, Ⓒ, Ⓒ, Ⓒ, START at the title screen.
Final Boss Duel	When you get to the final boss in 2-player mode, have one player choose "yes" and the other choose "no." You duel against each other.
Level and Lives Select	Go to the main menu. Hold Ⓐ+Ⓑ+Ⓒ+↓ on controller 2 while selecting Options on controller 1 (best if done with two people). You can now select how many lives you start with and which stage to start on.

Streets of Rage 2

Unlockables

Unlockable	How to Unlock
Level and Lives Select	Go to the main menu. Hold Ⓐ+Ⓑ on controller 2 while selecting Options. Now select how many lives you start with (up to 9), choose your starting stage, and play at the Very Easy and Mania difficulty levels.
Same Character in 2 Player	At the title screen, hold →+Ⓑ on controller 1 and hold ←+Ⓐ on controller 2. Press ↓ on controller 2 with everything else still held down. Now both players can be the same person in 2 Player!

Streets of Rage 3

Unlockables

Unlockable	How to Unlock
Ending 1	Rescue the Chief in Stage 6 before his health runs out. Then, at the end of Stage 7, defeat Robot Y before the time limit runs out.
Ending 2	Rescue the Chief before his health runs out in Stage 6. Then, in Stage 7, defeat Robot Y but let the time limit run out.
Ending 3	Let the Chief's health run out in Stage 6. When you go to Stage 7, you will see that it is changed. Make it to the last boss and defeat him.
Ending 4	Set the difficulty to Easy and beat Robot X in Stage 5.
Extra Lives Select	Go to the Options screen and select the "Lives" option. Press and hold ↑+Ⓐ+Ⓑ+Ⓒ on controller 2, and press ← or → on controller 1 to select the number of lives you can start the game with. You can now select 9 lives, instead of the default max of 5.
Play as Ash	To select Ash, defeat him, then hold Ⓐ on controller 1. After losing all of your lives, continue, and you can choose Ash as your character.
Play as Roo	When you fight the clown and Roo, defeat the clown first and Roo should hop away off the screen. When you lose all your lives and continue, cycle through the characters and Roo is now available.
Play as Roo	At the title screen, hold ↑+Ⓑ, then press START. A kangaroo named Roo is now available at the Character Select screen.
Play as Shiva	After beating Shiva in the first stage when you get the last hit, hold Ⓑ+START. When the continue screen comes up, you can play as Shiva. (He is weaker than his *Streets of Rage 2* character).

Streets of Rage 3 (continued)

Unlockable	How to Unlock
Play as Super Axel	Press ↓ to select a player, then quickly hold Ⓐ and sweep the D-pad in a clockwise circle until Axel appears. Then press Ⓐ.

> **NOTE**
>
> *This cheat is very hard to get working.*

Unlockable	How to Unlock
Play as Super Skate	Pick Skate. As the first level starts, lose your first life having 0 points. You will now be Super Skate, with a much more powerful combo.
Play as the Same Character	Hold ↓+Ⓒ on controller 2 as you enter 2-player mode with controller 1.
Secret Items	In Stage 1, at the Warehouse area, go to the bottom-left region blocked by the crates in the background and press Ⓑ. You get 5,000 points and a 1-UP. Stage 7, (City Hall) also contains lots of hidden items. Search in areas blocked off by the background such as lampposts, flower pots, etc.
Secret Passageways	On Stage 5, in the first room with all the ninjas, there are three secret routes that you can access by killing all enemies here. These rooms have more items than the normal rooms. Route 1: Above the door where you follow your normal route, notice a white wall with cracks near the top. Punch it to access Secret Route 1. Route 2: Go to the bottom center of this room and punch a few times. You eventually bust a hole in the floor leading you to the basement of Stage 5 and also Secret Route 2. Route 3: Go to the top of the screen and go up to the red walls. A certain red wall has a few cracks in it. Punch it to access Secret Route 3. There are a lot of enemies here, so be careful.
Stage Select	Hold Ⓑ+↑, then press START. Stage Select appears on the Options screen.

Super C

Unlockables

Unlockable	How to Unlock
10 Lives (Player 1)	On the title screen, press →, ←, ↓, ↑, Ⓐ, Ⓑ, then START
10 Lives (Player 2)	On the title screen, press →, ←, ↓, ↑, Ⓐ, Ⓑ, SELECT, then START
Access Sound Test	On the title screen, hold down Ⓐ+Ⓑ then press START
Retain Old Score and # of Lives on New Game	On the title screen, after you've beaten the game, press Ⓐ, and then START
Retain Old Score on New Game	On the title screen, after you've beaten the game, press Ⓐ, Ⓑ, then START

Super Castlevania IV

Unlockables

Unlockable	How to Unlock
Higher Difficulty	Heart, Axe, Space, Water. Axe, Space, Space, Heart. Space, Axe, Space, Space. Space, Heart, Space, Space.

Difficult Level Passwords

Use these passwords to get to stages on the Difficult setting. You need to use a blank name.

Space, Axe, Space, Space. Water, Water, Space, Space. Space, Heart, Space, Axe. Water, Axe, Space, Space.	Difficult mode Stage 6 level 1

Super Castlevania IV (continued)

Difficult Level Passwords

Space, Axe, Space, Heart. Water, Heart, Space, Space. Space, Space, Space, Water. Space, Axe, Space, Space.	Difficult mode Stage 7 level 1
Space, Axe, Space, Space. Water, Water, Space, Space. Space, Heart, Space, Water. Water, Water, Space, Space.	Difficult mode Stage 8 level 1

Stage Passwords

> **NOTE**
> *When you come to "Enter your name," leave the space blank or these passwords won't work.*

Password	Effect
Space, Space, Space, Space. Firebombs, Space, Space, Space. Space, Space, Space, Space. Firebombs, Space, Space, Space	Level 2
Sspace, Space, Space, Heart. Firebombs, Space, Space, Space. Space, Space, Space, Space. Heart, Space, Space, Space	Level 3
Space, Space, Space, Firebombs. Firebombs, Firebombs, Space, Space. Space, Firebombs, Space, Axe. Space, Space, Space, Space	Level 4
Space, Space, Space, Space. Firebombs, Space, Space, Space. Space, Space, Space, Axe. Firebombs, Axe, Space, Space	Level 5
Space, Space, Space, Space. Firebombs, Firebombs, Space, Space. Space, Firebombs, Space, Axe. Firebombs, Axe, Space, Space	Level 6
Space, Space, Space, Firebombs. Firebombs, Hart, Space, Space. Space, Heart, Space, Firebombs. Space, Heart, Space, Space	Level 7
Space, Space, Space, Space. Firebombs, Firebombs, Space, Space. Space, Firebombs, Space, Firebombs. Firebombs, Firebombs, Space, Space	Level 8
Space, Space, Space, Heart. Firebombs, Firebombs, Space, Space. Space, Firebombs, Space, Firebombs. Heart, Firebombs, Space, Space	Level 9
Space, Space, Space, Axe. Firebombs, Space, Space, Space. Space, Space, Space, Heart. Heart, Heart, Space, Space	Level B
Space, Space, Space, Firebombs. Firebombs, Firebombs, Space, Space. Space, Firebombs, Space, Space. Space, Heart, Axe, Space	Level B (Dracula)

Unlockables

Unlockable	How to Unlock
Full Arsenal	In the last stage, before you climb the stairs to Dracula, jump down to the left. You land on an invisible platform. Move all the way left and you will get full health, 99 hearts, a cross, a fully upgraded whip, and a III stone.

Hidden Routes

There are three hidden branches from the main path.

Unlockable	How to Unlock
Hidden Route 1	In stage 3-1, when you must descend a short vertical shaft, halfway down here is a wall of pillars to the left. Demolish these, and you find a small side room containing hearts, cash bags, and some Roast.

Super Castlevania IV (continued)

Unlockable	How to Unlock
Hidden Route 2	The second secret, which is an actual hidden Block, is in stage 6-2. At the very beginning you pass a hallway with Axe Knights and falling chandeliers. The third archway has a chandelier but no guard. Hit the floor a couple of times and it'll crumble, revealing a stairwell into a secret area.
Hidden Route 3	The last one is in Block 9-2. You jump across a bed of spikes at the beginning. After this you see several whirlwind tunnels and some coffins. The last upper platform on the right has a coffin and a tunnel. Let the tunnel suck you in and you'll find a hidden area full of bonuses.

Super Ghouls 'N Ghosts

Unlockables

Unlockable	How to Unlock
Level Select	Highlight "Exit" on the Option screen with controller 1. Hold L + START on controller 2 and press START on controller 1.
Professional Mode	Beat the game on Normal mode.

Super Monkey Ball: Banana Blitz

Unlockables

Unlockable	How to Unlock
Baby Robo	To unlock the minigame version of Baby for the main game, play each minigame at least once (the game displays a play count on each minigame). After playing each minigame once, play one more minigame of your choice so that the game saves your stats. Baby Robo is now available in the main game. To select Baby Robo, you have to highlight Baby on the Character Select screen and press 1.
Staff Credits Game	Beat the first World
World 9	Complete Worlds 1-8 without continuing
World 10	Complete World 9 without continuing

Super Star Soldier

Cheat Menu

Following code unlocks a Cheat menu where you can mess with all the options for the game such as level selection and enemy difficulty. Input at the title screen.

Unlockable	How to Unlock
Unlock Cheat Menu	Press ←, ②, ↑, ②, →, ②, ↓,②, ←, ①, ↑, ①, →, ①, ↓, ①, ①+② x8, ①+SELECT x8

Super Swing Golf

Unlock Caddies

You unlock caddies by defeating the Pangya Festa with certain characters (except for Pipin). You must purchase them from the shop first just like the players. Outfits for the caddies will be unlocked and available for purchase when you unlock the caddies as well.

Unlockable	How to Unlock
Brie	Beat Arin's first Pangya Festa
Dolfini	Complete the first Pangya Storyline with Kooh
Lola	Complete the first Pangya Storyline with Uncle Bob
Pipin	Complete the Tutorial

Super Swing Golf (continued)

Unlockable	How to Unlock
Quma	Complete the first Pangya Storyline with Hana
Tiki	Complete the first Pangya Storyline with Max
TitanBoo	Beat Cecilia in Arin's first Pangya Festa

Unlockable Characters

To unlock a new character, beat Pangya Festa with another character. This means the first storyline of Pangya Festa, unless otherwise mentioned.

Unlockable	How to Unlock
Arin	Beat Pangya Festa with Kooh
Cecilia	Beat Pangya Festa with Hana or Uncle Bob
Kaz	Beat Arin's final storyline (to access this storyline, beat the first storyline with everyone but Kaz, and wear Arin's Magic School Uniform)
Kooh	Beat Pangya Festa with Max
Max	Beat Pangya Festa with Cecilia
Uncle Bob	Beat Pangya Festa with Scout

Super Thunder Blade

Level Select

Press these controller actions at the title screen to begin at the desired level.

Code	Effect
Press Ⓐ, ↑, ↓, ←, →, →, ←, ↓, ↑, START	Level 2
Press Ⓐ, Ⓐ, ↑, ↓, ←, →, →, ←, ↓, ↑, START	Level 3
Press Ⓐ, Ⓐ, Ⓐ, ↑, ↓, ←, →, →, ←, ↓, ↑, START	Level 4
Press Ⓐ, Ⓐ, Ⓐ, Ⓐ, ↑, ↓, ←, →, →, ←, ↓, ↑, START	Level 5

Unlockables

Unlockable	How to Unlock
Avoid Enemy Fire	Begin the game with Hard difficulty. Stay in the upper right or left corners and fire your weapon continuously in levels 1 through 3.
Extra Lives	Enable the Level Select code and get a continue. Highlight "Option" and hold Ⓐ+Ⓑ+Ⓒ and press START. A picture of a panda appears on the "Player" selection to confirm the code.

Surf's Up

Passwords

Password	Effect
NICEPLACE	Unlocks all art galleries
MYPRECIOUS	Unlocks all boards
GOINGDOWN	Unlocks all leaf-sliding locations
MULTIPASS	Unlocks all multiplayer levels
FREEVISIT	Unlocks all the locales
WATCHAMOVIE	Unlocks all video Galleries
TINYBUTSTRONG	Unlocks Arnold
ASTRAL	Unlocks Astral's board
DONTFALL	Unlocks bonus missions
TOPFASHION	Unlocks character customization
SURPRISEGUEST	Unlocks Elliot

Surf's Up

Password	Effect
SLOWANDSTEADY	Unlocks Geek
MONSOON	Unlocks Monsoon Board
IMTHEBEST	Unlocks Tank Evans
KOBAYASHI	Unlocks Tatsuhi Kobayashi
TINYSHOCKWAVE	Unlocks Tiny Shockwave board
THELEGEND	Unlocks Zeke Topanga

Unlockables

Unlockable	How to Unlock
Arnold	Obtain 30,000 points in Shiverpool 2
Big Z	Obtain 100,000 points in Legendary Wave
Elliot	Obtain 40,000 points in Pen Gu North 3
Geek	Obtain 60,000 points in Pen Gu South 4
Tank	Obtain 40,000 points in the Boneyards
Tatsuhi	Obtain 15,000 points in Pen Gu South 2

Sword of Vermilion

Unlockables

Unlockable	How to Unlock
Quick Cash	In Keltwick, when Bearwulf gives you the dungeon key to get to Malaga, sell it. It's worth 1,000 kims and Bearwulf has an unlimited number of them. Just go back, talk to him, and he'll say "Did you lose the key? I have another one." He'll give it to you, and you can repeat the process as much as you want.
Test Menu	Any time during the game, hold Ⓐ+Ⓑ+Ⓒ and press START on controller 2. A test menu appears with Input, Sound, and C.R.T. tests. And when you exit, it sends you back to the SEGA logo screen.

Teenage Mutant Ninja Turtles

Unlockables

Unlockable	How to Unlock
Restore Power	Find a doorway that has a pizza slice or full pizza right at the beginning. Enter, grab the pizza, and exit. The pizza regenerates when you reenter. Use this to restore power to all your turtles.
Remove Crushers in Level 3	Hop in the Party Wagon. Whenever you see a pesky Crusher, press SELECT. You exit the car, and the Crusher vanishes.
Share Boomerangs	When you get the boomerangs, throw up to 3 of them in the air, then switch turtles, and have the new turtle catch them. The new turtle can use those boomerangs without having picked up a boomerang icon.

Teenage Mutant Ninja Turtles II: The Arcade Game

Unlockables

Unlockable	How to Unlock
Extra Lives and Stage Select	At the title screen, press Ⓑ, Ⓐ, Ⓑ, Ⓐ, ↑, ↓, Ⓑ, Ⓐ, ←, →, Ⓑ, Ⓐ, START
Extra Lives Without Stage Select	On the title screen, press ↑, →, →, ↓, ↓, ↓, ←, ←, ←, ←, Ⓑ, Ⓐ, START
Stage Select	On the title screen, press ↓, ↓, ↓, ↓, ↓, →, →, →, →, →, →, →, Ⓑ, Ⓐ, START

Teenage Mutant Ninja Turtles II: The Arcade Game (continued)

Unlockable	How to Unlock
Easier Battle with Shredder	During the final battle against Shredder, Shredder splits up into two forms. They're identical in appearance, but only one is real and the other is fake. However, both forms use the lightning attack that instantly kills you by turning you into a normal turtle. However, when either form is weakened to near death, his helmet flies off. As you're beating up on the two forms of Shredder, one of them loses his helmet very quickly. When this happens, leave him alone. This Shredder is the fake, and he cannot use the lightning attack without his helmet on. Only the real Shredder can use the attack, but because it's only him using it, you can avoid it and slowly beat him down with ease. For the rest of the fight, ignore the fake. If you kill him, the real Shredder releases another fake.

TMNT

Unlockables

At the main menu, hold Ⓩ on the Nunchuk and enter the following codes. Release Ⓩ after each code to hear a confirmation sound.

Unlockable	Code
Unlock Don's Big Head Goodie	①, Ⓐ, Ⓒ, ②
Unlock Challenge Map 2	Ⓐ, Ⓐ, Ⓐ, ①, Ⓐ

Tiger Woods PGA Tour 07

Enter these codes under passwords in the Options menu.

Unlockable	Code
Acquire all Cobra gear	SnakeKing
Unlock all Adidas items	THREE STRIPES
Unlock all Bridgestone items	SHOJIRO
Unlock all Grafalloye items	JUST SHAFTS
Unlock all Level 3 EA Sports items	INTHEGAME
Unlock all Macgergor items	MACTEC
Unlock all Mizuno items	RIHACHINRZO
Unlock all Nike items	JUSTDOIT
Unlock all Oakley items	JANNARD
Unlock all PGA Tour items	LIGHTNING
Unlock all Ping items	SOLHEIM
Unlock all players in team play	GAMEFACE
Unlock all Taylormade items	MRADAMS

Tiger Woods PGA Tour 08

Passwords

Password	Effect
PROSHOP	All Clubs Unlocked
NOTJUSTTIRES	Unlock Bridgestone Items
THREESTRIPES	Unlock Buick Items
CLEVELAND	Unlock Cleveland Golf Items
SNAKEKING	Unlock Cobra Items
INTHEGAME	Unlock EA Items

Tiger Woods PGA Tour 08 (continued)

Password	Effect
JUSTSHAFTS	Unlock Grafalloy Items
JLINDEBERG	Unlock J.Lindeberg Items
RIHACHINRIZO	Unlock Mizuno Items
JUSTDOIT	Unlock Nike Items
GUYSAREGOOD	Unlock Precept Items

ToeJam and Earl

Unlockables

Unlockable	How to Unlock
Free Presents	Sneak up on Santa Claus before he takes off and he gives you a few presents.
Level 0	On Level 1, on the bottom left side, a small hole leads to level 0, which has hula dancers in a tub and a lemonade man who gives you another life.
Present Island	At the top right of the map on level 1, there is a hidden island with a load of presents for the taking. You need rocket skates, an inner-tube, or icarus wings to get there.
Ultimate Cheat	Pause the game, then press the following button combinations: ✚↑+Ⓐ+Ⓑ+Ⓒ, ✚→+Ⓐ, ✚↓+Ⓑ, ✚←+🔍. You hear a sound if you entered the code correctly. Unpause the game, and you have all but one of the ship pieces collected. The last piece will always be located on the next level.

ToeJam and Earl in Panic on Funkotron

Passwords

Password	Effect
R-F411W9Q986	Level 3
PJ04EK-5WT82	Level 5
MW0WEE6JRVF7	Level 7
VANDNEHF9807L	Level 9
MWAAK!8MDT76	Level 11
F!!NEHNW0Q73	Level 15
TOEJAMTEARL!	View Credits

High Funk Passwords

Enter these passwords at the password screen to go to your desired level with lots of Funk.

Password	Effect
RWJ21EW1R80X	Level 03 with 37 Funk
VJW6EK21-J07	Level 05 with 80 Funk
P0W09KAN-VQ	Level 07 with 95 Funk
VDJF7M2DyT6L	Level 09 with 99 Funk
VYJF73TH1PQQ	Level 11 with 99 Funk
DKYQHX4!EV!7	Level 13 with 89 Funk
J11L3R4C13H7	Level 15 with 49 Funk

Tom Clancy's Splinter Cell Double Agent

Unlockables

Unlockable	How to Unlock
Elite Mode	Clear the Solo mode once
Elite Mode (Co-op)	Beat the game in Co-op mode to unlock Co-op Elite mode

Tony Hawk's Downhill Jam

Enter these passwords in the Cheats menu.

Unlockable	Password
Always Special	PointHogger
Chipmunk Voices	HelloHelium
Demon Skater	EvilChimneySweep
Display Coordinates	DisplayCoordinates
Enables Manuals	IMISSMANUALS
Extreme Car Crashes	WatchForDoors
First Person Skater	FirstPersonJam
Free Boost	OotbaghForever
Giganto-Skater	IWannaBeTallTall
Invisible Skater	NowYouSeeMe
Large Birds	BirdBirdBirdBird
Mini Skater	DownTheRabbitHole
Perfect Manual	TightRopeWalker
Perfect Rail	LikeTiltingAPlate
Perfect Stats	IAmBob
Picasso Skater	FourLights
Power of the Fish!	TonyFishDownhillJam
Shadow Skater	ChimneySweep
Tiny People	ShrinkThePeople
Unlock All Boards and Outfits	RaidTheWoodshed
Unlock All Events	AdventuresOfKwang
Unlock All Movies	FreeBozzler
Unlock All Skaters	ImInterfacing

Tony Hawk's Proving Ground

Items

Unlockable	How to Unlock
50 Extra Skill Points	NEEDSHELP
All CAS Items	GIVEMESTUFF
All Decks	LETSGOSKATE
All Fun Items	OVERTHETOP

Tony Hawk's Proving Ground

Unlockable	How to Unlock
All Game Movies	WATCHTHIS
All Rigger Pieces	IMGONNABUILD
All Special Tricks Available	LOTSOFTRICKS
Full Stats	BEEFEDUP

Tony Hawk's Proving Ground (continued)

Levels

Unlockable	How to Unlock
Unlock Air and Space Museum	THEINDOORPARK
Unlock FDR	THEPREZPARK
Unlock Lansdowne	THELOCALPARK

Skaters

Unlockable	How to Unlock
Boneman	CRAZYBONEMAN
Bosco	MOREMILK
Cam	NOTACAMERA
Cooper	THECOOP
Eddie X	SKETCHY
El Patinador	PILEDRIVER
Eric	FLYAWAY
Mad Dog	RABBIES
MCA	INTERGALACTIC
Mel	NOTADUDE
Rube	LOOKSSMELLY
Shayne	MOVERS
Spence	DAPPER
TV Producer	SHAKER

Tower of Druaga

Codes

Enter this code at the title screen. If entered properly, the word "DRUAGA" will turn green. The game is now harder and the levels require different solutions.

Code	Effect
↑, ↑, ↑, ↑, ↑,↑, ←, ←, ←, ←, →, →, ↓	Another Druaga (Second Quest)

Transformers: The Game

Codes

Enter the following codes at the Campaign/Bonus Features/Credits menu.

Code	Effect
↓, ↑, ←, →, →, →, ↑, ↓	Unlock all missions
←, ←, ↑, ←, →, ↓, ↓	Infinite health—invincible
→, ←, →,←, →, ←, ↓	No vehicles running on the street and no tanks/cops attack
→, ↑, ↑, ↓, →, ←, ←	Unlock Cybertron missions
↓, →, ←, ↑, ↓, ↓, ←	Unlock G1 Optimus Prime
←, ↑, ↓, ↓, ←, ↑, ↓	Unlock Generation 1 Jazz Repaint
→, ↓, ←, ←, ↓, ↑, ↑	Unlock Generation 1 Starscream Repaint
↓, ↓, ↑, ↑, →, →, ↓	Unlock Robovision Optimus Prime
↓, ←, ←, ↓, →, →, ↑	Unlock G1 Megatron

Unlockables

Unlockable	How to Unlock
G1 Jazz Repaint	Clear all sub-missions in Autobot and Decepticon Story modes
G1 Megatron	Collect all of the Decepticon icons on all of the maps
G1 Optimus Prime	Collect all of the Autobot Icons on all of the maps
G1 Starscream Repaint	Beat the Decepticon's Story mode
Robovision Optimus Prime	Beat the Autobot's Story mode

Trauma Center: Second Opinion

Unlockable	How To
X Missions for both doctors	Once unlocked, the first X mission will be available to both doctors. If you complete an X mission with one doctor, the next mission will be available to both doctors.
Episode 6	Complete all operations in episodes 1-5 and Z to unlock episode 6.

Vectorman

Unlockables

Unlockable	How to Unlock
Blow Up SEGA Logo	At the SEGA screen, move Vectorman slightly to the right of the logo. Aim upward and shoot. There is a hidden TV monitor there. Once it is broken, grab and use an orb power-up. The SEGA logo goes dark and the background stops moving.
Debug Mode	On the Options screen press Ⓐ, Ⓑ, Ⓑ, Ⓐ, ↓, Ⓐ, Ⓑ, Ⓑ, Ⓐ. A menu then offers health, lives, level select, and weapon options.
Full Health	Pause the game and press Ⓐ, Ⓑ, →, Ⓐ, Ⓒ, Ⓐ, ↓, Ⓐ, Ⓑ, →, Ⓐ.
Invisibility and Invincibility	First grab a bomb morph, and detonate Vectorman. Pause the game while Vectorman is still exploding and enter CALLACAB (Ⓒ, Ⓐ, ←, ←, Ⓐ, Ⓒ, Ⓐ, Ⓑ). Unpause the game. Pause again and enter the CALLACAB code. Unpause it, and Vectorman is invisible and invincible. Reenter the CALLACAB code to turn it off. No bomb morph is needed to disable it.
Level Warp	When you turn on the game, you can move Vectorman around on the SEGA screen. Shoot the SEGA logo 24 times, jump and hit the SEGA logo with Vectorman's head 12 times, and the letters S, E, G, and A start falling. Catch 90 to 110 letters to start on Stage 5, catch more than 110 letters to start on Day 10.
Light Bulbs	During gameplay, pause and enter Ⓐ, Ⓑ, Ⓐ, Ⓒ, Ⓐ, Ⓑ and press pause. A group of lights should be around you. The four lights that surround Vectorman indicate the field of collision detection. The light at the bottom indicates the collision detection of Vectorman's jets.
Slow Motion	This code slows down the game whenever you're hit. While playing, pause and press ↓, →, Ⓐ, Ⓒ, ↑, ←, Ⓐ. Turn it off by entering the code again.
Stage Select	Ⓑ, Ⓐ, Ⓐ, Ⓑ, ↓, Ⓑ, Ⓐ, Ⓐ, Ⓑ
Taxi Mode	Pause and press Ⓒ, Ⓐ, ←, ←, Ⓐ, Ⓒ, Ⓐ, Ⓑ (Call a Cab). You turn into a small cursor/arrow and can travel anywhere in the level. Enemies can also be killed by coming in contact with them. Bosses cannot be killed this way. To return to normal, pause and enter the code again.

Virtua Fighter 2

Unlockables

Unlockable	How to Unlock
Different Costumes	To play in a character's different costumes, Hold ↑ and then select your character with Ⓐ or ↓. Or hold ↓ and select your character with Ⓐ, ↓, or START.
Extra Character Selection Time	Press ↓, ↑, ↓, Ⓐ+← at the Character Selection Screen for 99 seconds of extra time.
Hidden Options	Enter the Options screen, highlight the "Exit" selection, and tap ← until the hidden options are displayed.
No Damage	Hold Ⓑ while highlighting player 1's life selection at the Options screen, until the message "No Damage" appears. Then press START.

Virtua Fighter 2 (continued)

Unlockable	How to Unlock
Play as Dural	Highlight Akira using controller 1 or Jacky using controller 2. Then press ←, ↓. Repeat this a few times and Dural appears as a selectable character.

WALL-E

Cheats

In the password screen enter the codes for the following effects. ZPM = Zero Point Mover.

Effect	Code
All Bonus Features Unlocked	WALL-E, Auto, EVE, ZPM
All Game Content Unlocked	M-O, Auto, ZPM, EVE
All Holiday Costumes Unlocked	Auto, Auto, ZPM, ZPM
All Multiplayer Costumes Unlocked	ZPM, WALL-E, M-O, Auto
All Multiplayer Maps Unlocked	EVE, M-O, WALL-E, Auto
All Single Player Levels Unlocked	Auto, ZPM, M-O, WALL-E
EVE Permanent Super Laser Upgrade	EVE, WALL-E, WALL-E, Auto
Infinite Health	WALL-E, M-O, Auto, M-O
WALL-E & EVE Laser Gun Any Time	ZPM, EVE, M-O, WALL-E
WALL-E & EVE Make Any Cube Any Time	M-O, ZPM, EVE, EVE
WALL-E Always Has Super Laser	WALL-E, Auto, EVE, M-O
WALL-E Makes Any Cube Any Time	Auto, M-O, Auto, M-O
WALL-E with Laser Gun Any Time	WALL-E, EVE, EVE, WALL-E

Wonder Boy in Monster World

Unlockables

Unlockable	How to Unlock
Stay at the Inn for Free	Any Inn throughout the game will let you spend the night, even if you don't have enough gold. They just take whatever you have, even if you don't have any gold at all.

World Series of Poker: Tournament of Champions

Unlockables

Unlockable	How to Unlock
All Locations	Input ↑, ↑, ↓, ←, ↓ at the main menu

Wrecking Crew

Unlockables

Unlockable	How to Unlock
Gold Hammer	In Phase 6, there are five bombs, 2 on the bottom, 2 in the middle of the level, and 1 on the top. Hit the 2 bombs on the bottom and then hit the middle left bomb. In a few seconds, a hammer appears. Hit it to obtain it. You now have the gold hammer. The music changes and you can hit enemies. You have the hammer until you die.

DS
PSP
PS2
PS3
Wii
Xbox
Xbox 360
Index

Table of Contents - Xbox

Table of Contents - Xbox (con't.)

Table of Contents - Xbox (con't.)

007: Nightfire

Cheat Mode: For the following codes, select the "Codenames" option at the main menu. Select your character and enter one of the following codes at the Secret Unlocks screen. Save your Codename after entering the code. Then exit your Codename and begin gameplay.

Unlockable	Code
All Gadget Upgrades	Q LAB
All Multiplayer Options	GAMEROOM
Alpine Escape Level	POWDER
Bigger Clip for Sniper Rifle	MAGAZINE
Camera Upgrade	SHUTTER
Chain Reaction Level	MELTDOWN
Countdown Level	BLASTOFF
Decrypter Upgrade	SESAME
Deep Descent Level	AQUA
Double Cross Level	BONSAI
Enemies Vanquished Level	TRACTION
Equinox Level	VACUUM
Golden P2K	AU P2K
Golden PP7	AU PP7
Grapple Upgrade	LIFTOFF
Island Infiltration Level	PARADISE
Laser Upgrade	PHOTON
Level Select	PASSPORT
Multiplayer Bond Spacesuit	ZERO G
Multiplayer Mode All Characters	PARTY
Multiplayer Mode Assassination Option	TARGET
Multiplayer Mode Baron Samedi	VOODOO
Multiplayer Mode Bond Tuxedo	BLACKTIE
Multiplayer Mode Christmas Jones	NUCLEAR
Multiplayer Mode Demolition Option	TNT
Multiplayer Mode Drake	NUMBER 1
Multiplayer Mode Elektra King	Enter SLICK
Multiplayer Mode Explosive Scenery Option	BOOM
Multiplayer Mode GoldenEye Strike Option	ORBIT
Multiplayer Mode Goldfinger	MIDAS
Multiplayer Mode Jaws	DENTAL
Multiplayer Mode Max Zorin	BLIMP
Multiplayer Mode Mayday	BADGIRL
Multiplayer Mode Nick Nack	BITESIZE
Multiplayer Mode Oddjob	BOWLER
Multiplayer Mode Protection Option	GUARDIAN
Multiplayer Mode Pussy Galore	CIRCUS
Multiplayer Mode Renard	HEADCASE
Multiplayer Mode Scaramanga	ASSASSIN
Multiplayer Mode Team King of the Hill Option	TEAMWORK
Multiplayer Mode Uplink Option	TRANSMIT
Vanquish Car Missile Upgrade	LAUNCH

007: Nightfire (continued)

Unlockable	Code
Tranquilizer Dart Upgrade (Your tranquilizer darts are upgraded so enemies stay down longer.)	SLEEPY
Stunner Upgrade	ZAP
Rifle Scope Upgrade	SCOPE
Phoenix Fire Level	FLAME
P2K Upgrade	P2000
Night Shift Level	HIGHRISE
Multiplayer Mode Wai Lin	MARTIAL
Multiplayer Mode Xenia Onatopp	JANUS

Unlockable	Code
Berserk Racing	While racing on the Paris Prelude, Enemies Vanquished, Island Infiltration, or Deep Descent levels, press (START) to pause gameplay, hold (LT), press (X), (Y), (Y), (X), (Y), (B), then release (LT).
Faster Gameplay	Press (START) to pause gameplay, hold (LT), press (X), (Y), (B), (WHT), (X), (Y), (B), (WHT), then release (LT).
Frantic Racing	While racing on the Paris Prelude, Enemies Vanquished, Island Infiltration, or Deep Descent levels, press (START) to pause gameplay, hold (LT), press (X), (Y), (B), (Y), (X), then release (LT).
Drive a Shelby Cobra	While racing on the Enemies Vanquished level, press (START) to pause gameplay, hold (LT), press (Right), (Right), (Left), (Left), (Up), then release (LT). You can now use the Shelby Cobra from the Paris Prelude level in the race through the Alps.
Drive an SUV	While racing on the Enemies Vanquished level, press (START) to pause gameplay, hold (LT), press (X), (B), (Y), (X), (Y), and then release (LT).
Double Armor during Racing	While racing on the Paris Prelude, Enemies Vanquished, Island Infiltration, or Deep Descent levels, press (START) to pause gameplay, hold (LT), press (B), (Y), (X), (B), (B), then release (LT).
Bonus Race in Alps	While racing on the Enemies Vanquished level, press (START) to pause gameplay, hold (LT), press (B), (B), (X), (X), (Y), then release (LT).
Quadruple Armor during Racing	While racing on the Paris Prelude, Enemies Vanquished, Island Infiltration, or Deep Descent levels, press (START) to pause gameplay, hold (LT), press (B), (Y), (X), (B), (B), (B), (B), then release (LT).
Super Bullets during Racing	While racing on the Paris Prelude, Enemies Vanquished, Island Infiltration, or Deep Descent levels, press (START) to pause gameplay, hold (LT), press (B), (B), (B), (B), then release (LT). Note: You can also do this when you fly the plane with Alura.
Trails during Racing	While racing on the Paris Prelude, Enemies Vanquished, Island Infiltration, or Deep Descent levels, press (START) to pause gameplay, hold (LT), press (X), (B), (B), (X), then release (LT).
Triple Armor during Racing	While racing on the Paris Prelude, Enemies Vanquished, Island Infiltration, or Deep Descent levels, press (START) to pause gameplay, hold (LT), press (B), (Y), (X), (B), (B), (B), then release (LT).

4X4 Evolution 2

Enter these codes at the Main menu or Title screen.

Unlockable	Code
Extra Money in Career Mode	Y, X, WHT, Y, X, WHT, X, X, Y, BLK, X, Y
High Reputation (for team selection)	Y, Y, WHT, X, X, WHT, Y, Y, Y, X, X, X
Mission Select	X, X, WHT, WHT, Y, Y, WHT, X, Y, Y, X, WHT

50 Cent Bulletproof

To enter these passwords, pause the game. Go into Options, then enter the Cheat menu.

Unlockable	Password
Action 26	orangejuice
All Music Tracks	GrabAllThat50
All Music Videos	HookMeUp50
All Weapons	GotThemRachets
Bloodhound Counterkill	gunrunner
Bulletproof aka Invincible	ny'sfinestyo
Empty n' Clips Counterkill	workout
"G'd Up" Counterkill	GoodDieYoung
"Guillotine" Counterkill	GettingDropped
Infinite Ammo	GrizzSpecial
Mike Mode	the hub is broken
My Buddy video	sayhellotomylittlefriend
So Seductive video	yayoshome Tony Yayo
"Wanksta" Counter-Kill	AintGotNothin

Advent Rising

Enter this code while the game is paused.

Unlockable	Code
Cheat menu	↑, ↑, ↓, ↓, ←, →, ←, →, WHT, BLK, X

To enter this code, select a spot for a 'new game'. After you do that, enter this code.

Unlockable	Code
Unlock all levels and cutscenes	BLK, WHT, BLK, WHT, X

Aeon Flux

At the Main menu, press Y, then go into the Enter Cheats menu to enter these passwords.

Unlockable	Password
Action Movie	BRAVO ALPHA GOLF MIKE ALPHA NOVEMBER
Action Movie	UNIFORM KILO GOLF ALPHA MIKE ECHO ROMEO
Free Fatalities	CHARLIE UNIFORM TANGO INDIA OSCAR NOVEMBER ECHO
God Mode	TANGO ROMEO INDIA ROMEO OSCAR XRAY
One Strike Kills	BRAVO UNIFORM CHARLIE KILO FOXTROT SIERRA TANGO
Restore Health	HOTEL ECHO ALPHA LIMA MIKE ECHO
Unlimited Ammo	FOXTROT UNIFORM GOLF
Unlimited Health	CHARLIE LIMA OSCAR NOVEMBER ECHO

Aeon Flux (continued)

Unlockable	Password
Unlimited Power Strikes	LIMA CHARLIE VICTOR GOLF
Unlock All Replay Episodes	BRAVO ALPHA YANKEE OSCAR UNIFORM
Unlock All Slideshows	PAPA INDIA XRAY ECHO SIERRA
Unlock Bomber Jacket Outfit	JULIET ALPHA CHARLIE KILO ECHO TANGO
Unlock Fame Outfit	GOLF ROMEO ALPHA YANKEE
Unlock Monican Freya/Hostess Judy/Una/Fashion Una Outfits	CHARLIE LIMA OSCAR TANGO HOTEL ECHO SIERRA
Unlock Mrs. Goodchild Outfits	WHISKEY HOTEL INDIA TANGO ECHO
Unlock Revelation Outfits	ALPHA ROMEO MIKE SIERRA
Unlock Seed Outfits	MIKE OSCAR VICTOR INDIA ECHO
Unlock Seed Outfits	UNIFORM ROMEO BRAVO ALPHA NOVEMBER
Unlock War Outfits	BRAVO LIMA UNIFORM ROMEO

AirForce Delta Storm

Unlockables

Unlockable	How to Unlock
Get More Planes	Beat any 2 levels in a row without returning to air base to get more planes.

Alias

Level select

Successfully complete the game, then enter the code below

Code	Effect
Hold L1+RB+BLK+WHT	Level select

Alien Hominid

Passwords

Password	Effect
FBI	99 bombs and 10 lives

Unlockable Hats

Enter these as a player name. When you click submit, a foghorn sounds if the password was entered correctly.

Password	Effect	Password	Effect
Grrl	Hat 11, top hat	TomFulp	Hat 2, Tom Fulp
Abe	Hat 12, diamond tiara	Cletus	Hat 4, blonde hair
Betty	Hat 13, daisy headdress	April	Hat 5, red hair
Princess	Hat 13, daisy headdress	Superfly	Hat 7, Jheri curl
Dandy	Hat 14, Dick Tracy hat	Goodman	Hat 8, pirate bandana

Other Unlockables

Unlockable	How to Unlock
Chicken Hat, Level 1-4	When you come across the Behemoth building, destroy it and a foghorn will sound
Curly Hair, Level 1-4	When you find the Fish Are Like Plants building, destroy it, and a foghorn will sound
Super Soviet Missile Master Minigame	Complete level 1-5

Aliens vs. Predator: Extinction

Unlockable	Code
Cheats	Pause the game and press RT, RT, LT, RT, LT, LT, RT, LT, RT, RT, LT, RT, LT, LT, RT, LT. The cheats are now available via the Options menu.

Alter Echo

Enter these codes during gameplay.

Unlockable	Code
Remove Display	↑,↑,↓,↓,←,→,←,BACK+Y
Restore Health	↑,↑,↓,↓,←,→,←,BACK+→
Restore Time Dilation	↑,↑,↓,↓,←,→,←,BACK+↑

Amped: Freestyle Snowboarding

Passwords

Select "Options" at the main menu, then "Cheats." Enter these codes as case-sensitive codes. A sound confirms correct code entry. Press B to exit the Cheat menu.

Password	Effect
GimmeGimme	All Levels
BigLeg	Big Jumps
MegabOUnce	Bouncy Terrain
buzzsaW	Disable Tree Collisions
MegaLeg	Even Bigger Jumps
ZiPster	Go Faster (Even Uphill)
StickiT	Land All Jumps Perfectly
WhirlyGig	Major Spins
RidinwRaven	Play as Raven
ChillinwSteezy	Play as Steezy
KeepnReal	Realistic Mode
BigsteeZ	Super Snowboarder

Unlock Hidden Movie

Unlockable	How to Unlock
End Game Cinematic	Beat all the Pro Challenges, beat all the high scores, beat all the media challenges, and find all 8 snowmen on each level. (World Rank 1).

Amped 2

Go to Options and enter the following codes in the Cheats menu.

Unlockable	Code
All Courses Are Icy	AllIce
All Secret Boarders	AllMyPeeps
Cheats Are Deactivated	NoCheats
Low Gravity	LowGravity
Max Out Rider Stats	MaxSkills
No Collisions with Other Riders	NoCollisions
Open All Levels	AllLevels
Rider Moves Faster	FastMove
Rider Never Crashes	DontCrash
Spin Faster	SuperSpin
Unlock a Pink Bunny	Bunny

DS PSP PS2 PS3 Wii Xbox Xbox 360 Index

DS | PSP | PS2 | PS3 | Wii | Xbox | Xbox 360 | Index

Apex

Enter all codes as brand names in Dream mode.

Unlockable	Code
All Concept Cars in Arcade Mode	Dreamy
All Production Cars in Arcade Mode	Reality
All Tracks in Arcade Mode	World

Arctic Thunder

Enter these codes at the Mode Selection screen.

Unlockable	Code
All Atomic Snowballs	X, X, X, WHT, Y, START
All Boosts Mode	Y, BLK, BLK, Y, RT, START
All Grappling Hooks	Y, Y, LT, Y, Y, WHT, START
All Invisible	X, Y, X, RT, Y, Y, START
All Random Locations	BLK, RT, X, Y, BLK, RT, START
All Rooster Tails	BLK, RT, LT, WHT, X, START
All Snow Bombs	Y, Y, BLK, RT, START
Clone Mode	WHT, BLK, BLK, Y, WHT, Y, START
No Catch-Up Mode	Y, X, Y, Y, X, START
No Drones Mode	X, X, Y, Y, WHT, BLK, START
No Power-Up Mode	X, X, Y, X, RT, X, START
Super Boost	Y, WHT, X, RT, X, LT, START

Armed and Dangerous

Enter the following codes at the Cheats screen in the Options menu.

Unlockable	Code
Big Boots	RT, WHT, Y, A, LT, B, WHT, X
Big Hands	RT, WHT, X, LT, WHT, RT, RT, Y
Big Heads	LT, BLK, B, WHT, WHT, B, BLK, LT

Enter the following codes at the Cheats screen in the Options menu.

Unlockable	Code
Fill Ammo	BLK, B, A, RT, RT, A, LT, BLK
Fill Health Bar	X, RT, A, Y, BLK, B, A, RT
Invincible	X, X, X, RT, A, LT, LT, Y
Topsy Turvy	X, A, B, B, A, B, WHT, WHT

Azurik: Rise of Perathia

Unlockable	Code
Adjust Camera	Quickly press RT, ↓, ↑, ↓, ↑, click R, click L. The game stops, allowing you to alter the view. See Adjust Camera Tip for camera controls.
Adjust Lighting	Quickly press A, click R, B, click R, click L. Darker areas become easier to see, but at the expense of having less dramatic lighting. Repeat this code to return to normal.
Big Heads	Quickly click R, press RT, ↓, ↑, A. A sound confirms correct code entry.
God Mode	Quickly press X, BLK, WHT, RT + LT, click L + R. A sound confirms correct code entry. Repeat this code to disable its effect.

Azurik: Rise of Perathia (continued)

Unlockable	Code
Level Select (This cheat also allows you to change your stats and view all FMV sequences.)	Press L→ + ←R, ←L + R→, A, B, click R, click L. You must power off the Xbox to exit an FMV sequence.
Save at any point	Quickly press White, ↑, ↓, A, B, click R during the "swing" animation. A click confirms that the game has been saved.

TIP

Adjust Camera Tip: Camera Controls

Press LT or RT to move the view up or down. Press L or R to move the view forward and back. Press D-pad to zoom in and out. Press A to view and remove the elemental power display. Press Back to resume the game.

CAUTION

Gem Mode Caution!

Do not create more gems than are supported! This will crash the game.

CAUTION

Save Point Caution!

While this may be done at any time during the game, remember to choose your save point carefully. Avoid saving on moving platforms, in areas where enemies respawn, while falling, or while dying.

Backyard Wrestling

Enter this code at the Main menu.

Unlockable	Code
All Wrestlers and Stages	Hold LT, then press A,X,Y,B,A,X,Y,B.

Bad Boys: Miami Takedown

Enter the code at the Title screen.

Unlockable	Code
Cheat Menu	B,↑,X,Y,→,↓

The Bard's Tale

While playing, hold LT+RT, then enter the following codes.

Unlockable	Code
Damage x100	↑,↓,↑,↓,←,→,←,→
Full Mana and Health	←,←,→,→,↑,↓,↑,↓
Intangible	←,→,←,→,↑,↓,↑,↓
Invincible	→,←,→,←,↑,↓,↑,↓
Silver and Adderstones	↑,↑,↓,↓,←,→,←,→

Batman: Rise of Sin Tzu

At the Mode Select screen, hold LT+RT, then enter the codes.

Unlockable	Code
All Rewards	←, ↓, ←, →, ←, ←, ↓, →
All Upgrades	↓, ↑, ↓, ←, ↓, →, ↑, ↓
Dark Knight Mode	→, ↑, ↑, →, ←, ↓, →, ↑
Infinite Health	↑, →, ↑, ←, ↓, ←, ↓, →
Unlimited Combo Meter	←, →, ↓, ↑, ↑, ↓, →, ←

Batman Vengeance

Input the following codes at the Main menu. Many of them will make a sound to confirm correct code entry.

Unlockable	Code
Bonus Characters	Press ←, →, ↓, WHT, LT + RT, then press START
Master Code	Press LT, RT, LT, RT, X, X, Y, Y
Unlimited Batarangs	Press LT, RT, WHT, Y
Unlimited Electric Batarangs	Press LT, RT, B, WHT, LT

Battlefield 2: Modern Combat

Unlock All Weapons

Receive All Weapons Permanently
During gameplay, hold WHT+BLK and press →,→,↓,↑,←,←

Battlestar Galactica

Enter the following codes in the Extras menu. A sound will confirm successful code entry.

Unlockable	Code
Wingmen, Starbuck and Apollo	↓,↓,←,↓,↓,↑,→,→
Production Stills and Artwork	←,↑,←,←,↓,←,↑,↓ ↑,↑,↓,↓,→,↑,→,↓ ↓,↓,↓,↓,←,←,←,← ↑,↑,↑,↓,↓,↓,←,→ →,→,↓,↓,←,←,↑,↑ →,→,→,→,↓,↓,←,← →,→,↑,↑,←,←,↑,↑ ↑,←,↑,→,↑,←,↑,→

Big Mutha Truckers

Unlockable	Code
All Cheats	CHEATINGMUTHATRUCKER
Automatic Navigation	USETHEFORCE
Diplomatic Immunity	VICTORS
Evil Truck	VARLEY
Extra Money	LOTSAMONEY
Fast Truck	GINGERBEER
Infinite Time	PUBLICTRANSPORT
Level Select	LAZYPLAYER
Small Pedestrians	DAISHI
Toggle Damage	6WL

NOTE

You can also unlock Evil Truck by clearing the 60-Day Trial in Truckin' mode and win the race to Big Mutha Trucking HQ.

Big Mutha Truckers 2

To enter these passwords, highlight "Trial by Trucking" and press Y.

Unlockable	Code
$115,000	CASH
All Gallery Images	GALLERY
Invincible	NODAMAGE
Lots of Bikers	BIKERS
Lots of Cops	COPS
Opens All Bridges	BRIDGE
Removes All Police	NOCOPS
Unlocks All Missions	MISSIONS

Black

Enter this password as a profile name. Once it is entered you will be asked to enter a real profile name.

Unlockable	Password
Start with the BFG	5SQQ-STHA-ZFFV-7XEV

Black Stone: Magic and Steel

Unlockable	Code
New Character Class	From the Class selection screen, press RT as you highlight each of the following classes: Pirate, Thief, Warrior, Archer, Pirate, Warlock, Thief, Warlock, Thief.

Blade II

At the Main menu, hold down LT, then enter the following codes. Text will appear upon successful code entry.

Unlockable	Code
All Weapons	X, B, Down, Left, B, B, Y
Daywalker Difficulty	Left, B, Up, Down, X, B, A
Level Select	Down, Up, Left, Left, B, Right, Down, X

While paused, hold LT, then enter the following codes. Text will appear upon successful code entry.

Unlockable	Code
Infinite Ammunition	Left, B, Right, X, Up, Y, Down, A
Infinite Health	Y, X, Y, X, Y, B, Y, B
Infinite Rage	Left, Down, Left, Down, Right, Up, Right, Left
Invincibility for NPCs during escort missions	X, B, Y, A, X, B, Y, A

Blazing Angels: Squadrons of WWII

Enter this code at the Main menu.

Unlockable	Code
All Planes and Missions	Hold LT + RT and press X, WHT, BLK, Y, Y, BLK, WHT, X

Enter these codes while the game is paused.

Unlockable	Code
Extra Damage	Hold LT and press WHT, WHT, BLK, then release LT. Then hold RT and press BLK, BLK, WHT, then release RT
God Mode	Hold LT and press X, Y, Y, X, then release LT. Then hold RT and press Y, X, X, Y, then release RT

Blitz: The League

From the Main menu, go to "Extras," then "Codes" and enter the following passwords.

Unlockable	Password
Ball Trail Always On	ONFIRE
Beach Ball	BOUNCY
Double Unleash Icons	PIPPED
Stamina Off	NOTTIRED
Super Clash	CLASHY
Super Unleash Clash	BIGDOGS
Two Player Co-op	CHUWAY

Blood Wake

Input the following codes at the Start screen. Listen for the sound to confirm correct code entry.

Unlockable	Code
All Battle Modes	Press Y,A,X,B, click L, click R,BLK,WHT,RT,RT then press START.
All Boats	Press ↑, ↓, ←, →, LT, B, X, X, click R, then press START.
All Levels	Press X,Y,↑,→,←,↓,↑,↓, click L,LT, then press START.
Blood Ball Mode	Press X,Y,WHT,BLK,B,A,←,↑,→,↓, then press START.
Import Boat Mode	Press Y,B,X,A,LT,RT,←,→, click L, click R, then press START.
Invincibility	Click L, click R, press ↓,←,↓,←,B,Y, then press START.
Puffer Fish	Press A,B,BLK,WHT,Y,X, click R,R, click L,L, then press START.
Rubber Duck Mode	Click R, click L,RT,LT,BLK,WHT,↑,↓,←,→, then press START.
Unlimited Ammunition	Press BLK,WHT,LT,RT, click R,R,Y,X, then press START.
Unlimited Turbo	Press ↑,↑,↓,↓,←,→,←,→,B,A, then press START.

Unlockable	Objective
Basilisk	Complete the "Protection Racket" level under the captain difficulty setting.
Clanbake Battle Mode	Complete the "A Poke in the Eye" level under the ensign difficulty setting.
Fireshark	Complete the "Up the Nagau" level under the ensign difficulty setting.
Guncat Catamaran	Complete the "Protection Racket" level under the ensign difficulty setting.
Gunshark	Complete the "Ships in the Night" level under the ensign difficulty setting.
Hellcat Catamaran	Complete the "The Gauntlet" level under the ensign difficulty setting.
Hydroplane Switchblade	Complete the "Gladiator" level under the ensign difficulty setting.
Jackal	Complete the "Assault on Black Moon" level under the ensign difficulty setting.
Kingdom Come Battle Mode	Complete the "Baptism of Fire" level under the ensign difficulty setting.
Lightning	Complete the "A Friend in Need" level under the ensign difficulty setting.
Metal Massacre Battle Mode	Complete the "Hurricane of Fire" level under the ensign difficulty setting.
Pike	Complete the "Payment Is Due" level under the ensign difficulty setting.

Blood Wake (continued)

Unlockable	Objective
Salamander	Complete the "Fish in a Barrel" level under the ensign difficulty setting.
Switchblade Hydroplane	Complete the "Gladiator" level under the ensign difficulty setting.
Tigershark	Complete the "Sampan Surprise" level under the ensign difficulty setting.

BloodRayne

From the Options screen, go to Enter Cheats and input the following.

Unlockable	Code
Fill Bloodlust	ANGRYXXXINSANEHOOKER
Freeze Enemies	DONTFARTONOSCAR
God Mode	TRIASSASSINDONTDIE
Gratuitous Dismemberment	INSANEGIBSMODEGOOD
Juggy Mode	JUGGYDANCESQUAD
Level Select	ONTHELEVEL
Restore Health	LAMEYANKEEDONTFEED
Secret Louisiana Level	BRIMSTONEINTHEBAYOU
Show Weapons	SHOWMEMYWEAPONS
Time Factor	NAKEDNASTYDISWASHERDANCE

Blow Out

Unlockable	Code
All Weapons	charliehustleoverdressedromeo
All Levels	coollevelcheatcode
God Mode	nopainnocane
Unlimited Ammo	fishinabarrel

BMX XXX

Passwords

Enter the following as your name to obtain the desired cheat:

Password	Effect
65 SWEET RIDES	All bikes
THISISBMXX	Bonus Movie 1 FMV sequence
KEEPITDIRTY	Bonus Movie 2 FMV sequence
FREESAMPLE	Bronx, NYC 3 FMV
BOING	Dam 1 FMV sequence
THONG	Dam 2 FMV
DDUULRRLDRSQUARE	Final movie
GHOSTCONTROL	Ghost control mode
MAKEMEANGRY	Green skin mode
FLUFFYBUNNY	Happy bunny mode
HIGHBEAMS	Las Vegas 1 FMV sequence
TASSLE	Las Vegas 2 FMV sequence
SHOWMETHEMONEY	Las Vegas level
IFLINGPOO	Launch Pad 69 1 FMV sequence
PEACH	Launch Pad 69 2 FMV sequence
SHOWMETHEMONKEY	Launch Pad 69 level

BMX XXX (continued)

Password	Effect
Z AXIS	More speed
3RD SOG	Night vision mode
BULLETPOINT	Park editor
BURLESQUE	Rampage Skatepark 2 FMV sequence
IOWARULES	Rampage Skatepark level
XXXINTRO	Random intro
UNDERGROUND	Rotts level
ONEDOLLAR	Sheep FMV
69	Sheep Hills 2 FMV sequence
BAABAA	Sheep Hills level
MASS HYSTERIA	Stage select
HEAVYPETTING	Super crash mode
FUZZYKITTY	Syracuse 1 FMV sequence
MICHAELHUNT	Syracuse 2 FMV sequence
BOYBANDSSUCK	Syracuse level
LAPDANCE	The Bronx, NYC 1 FMV sequence
STRIPTEASE	The Bronx, NYC 2 FMV sequence
THATDAMLEVEL	The dam level
BOOTYCALL	UGP Roots Jam 2 FMV sequence
XXX RATED CHEAT	Unlock All Levels
CHAMPAGNE ROOM	Unlock All Movies
ELECTRICITYBAD	Unlock Amish Boy
AMISHBOY1699	Unlock Amish Boy's Bikes
HELLKITTY487	Unlock Hellkitty's Bikes
ITCHI594	Unlock Itchi's Bikes
JOYRIDE18	Unlock Joyride's Bikes
KARMA311	Unlock Karma's Bikes
LATEY411	Unlock La'tey's Bikes
MANUEL415	Unlock Manuel's Bikes
MIKA362436	Unlock Mika's Bikes
NUTTER290	Unlock Nutter's Bikes
RAVE10	Unlock Rave's Bikes
SKEETER666	Unlock Skeeter's Bikes
TRIPLEDUB922	Unlock Tripledub's Bikes
TWAN187	Unlock Twan's Bikes
PARABOLIC	Visible gap mode

Unlockables

Unlockable	How to Unlock
Topless Girl Mode	Win first place in both competition levels.

Brian Lara International Cricket 2005

Enter these passwords in the Cheat menu.

Unlockable	Password
Unlock All Classic Matches	BOWLEDHIM
Unlock All Teams	GOODLENGTH
Unlock All the Classic Players	GONEFORADUCK
Unlock All Trophys	DOLLY
Unlock the Classic XI Challenge	STUMPED
Unlock the Picture Gallery	SLEDGING

Brothers in Arms: Road to Hill 30

Unlockable	Code
Unlock All Levels and Difficulties	BAKERSDOZEN

Bruce Lee: Quest of the Dragon

Enter this code at the Title screen.

Unlockable	Code
Bruce's Challenges	X,Y,X,Y,X,X,Y,Y,L,R

Brute Force

Unlockable	Code
Better Aim	DEADAIM
Better Defense	ERINROBERTS
Cartoon Mode	HVYMTL
Harder Difficulty	BRUTAL
Quick Death	DBLDAY
Rapid Fire Weapons	RAPIDFIRE
Stupid AI	SPRAGNT
Tough Characters	MATTSOELL

Unlockable	Objective
Confed Marine	Find the DNA sequence in Mission 1 or Mission 6
Feral Colonist	Find the DNA sequence in Mission 2
Feral Outcast	Find the DNA sequence in Mission 3
Feral Shaman	Find the DNA sequence in Mission 9
Fire Hound	Find the DNA sequence in Mission 13
Gunthar Ghent	Find the DNA sequence in Mission 10
Hunter Lord	Find the DNA sequence in Mission 18
McTavish	Find the DNA sequence in Mission 14
Militia	Find the DNA sequence in Mission 5 or Mission 11
Outcast Shaman	Find the DNA sequence in Mission 7
Seer Follower	Find the DNA sequence in Mission 4
Seer Priest	Find the DNA sequence in Mission 8
Shadoon	Find the DNA sequence in Mission 12
Shrike Heavy	Find the DNA sequence in Mission 16
Shrike Hound	Find the DNA sequence in Mission 17
Shrike Soldier	Find the DNA sequence in Mission 15

DS PSP PS2 PS3 Wii Xbox Xbox 360 Index

Buffy the Vampire Slayer

Go to the Extras screen and input the following.

Unlockable	Code
All Four Multiplayer Arenas	Y, Y, WHT, BLK, BLK, Y, Y, Y, Y, Y, WHT, BLK
Slayer Power	Y, Y, Y, BLK, BLK, BLK, Y, WHT, BLK, BLK, WHT, Y
Unlimited Health	Y, WHT, BLK, BLK, WHT, Y, BLK, BLK, BLK, Y, Y, Y

Burnout: Revenge

Have a *Madden NFL 06* and *Burnout 3: Takedown* saved before starting a new game. You will unlock two special cars for Crash mode.

Unlockable	Code
Dominator Assassin	Burnout 3 Save
Madden Challenge Bus	Madden 06 Save

Capcom Classic Collection

Enter this code at the Press Start screen.

Unlockable	Code
Unlock Everything	LT, RT, ↑, ↓ on right analog stick, LT, RT, ↑, ↓ on left analog stick, LT, RT, ↑, ↓ on the D-Pad.

Call of Duty 3

Enter this code in the Chapter Select screen.

Unlockable	Code
Unlock All Levels	Hold BACK and press →, →, ←, ←, X, X

Call of Duty Big Red One

To enter this code, go into the Chapter Selection menu.

Unlockable	Code
Level Select	Hold LT+RT and press ↑, ↑, ↓, ↓, ←, ←, →, →, X, ←, X, ←, X

Cars

To enter these passwords, select Options, then select Cheat Codes.

Unlockable	Password
All cars	YAYCARS
All character skins	R4MONE
All tracks and mini games	MATTL66
Fast start	IMSPEED
Infinite boost	VROOOOM
Unlock art	CONC3PT
Unlock Master's speedy circuit and Master's countdown cleanup	TRGTEXC
Unlock movie clips	WATCHIT

Catwoman

Enter this code in the Vault menu.

Unlockable	Code
Extra Galleries	1941

Cel Damage

Enter these passwords as profile names.

Unlockable	Password
Unlock all Melee Weapons	MELEEDEATH
Unlock Everything	ENCHILADA!
Unlock Ranged Weapons	GUNSMOKE!

Chase Hollywood Stunt Driver

Enter these passwords as profile names.

Unlockable	Password
Unlock Everything	Dare Angel
All multiplayer levels	BAM4FUN

The Chronicles of Narnia: The Lion, The Witch, and The Wardrobe

To enter these codes, you must be at the title screen. Hold both LT+RT simultaneously and press Down, Down, Right, Up. The words "Please Press Start" should turn green. You will now be able to enter any of the following codes.

Unlockable	Code
Automatically Complete Level	While in-game hold LT and press Down, Left, Down, Left, Down, Right, Down, Right, Up
Fill Combo Meter	While in-game hold LT and press Up, Up, Right, Up
Receive 10,000 Coins	While in-game hold LT and press Down, Left, Right, Down, Down
Restore All Children's Health	While in-game hold LT and press Down, Left, Left, Right
Unlock All Abilities in Inventory	While in-game hold LT and press Down, Left, Right, Left, Up
Open All Levels	While on the Wardrobe screen hold LT and press Up, Up, Right, Right, Up, Right, Down
Unlock All Bonus Levels	While on the Bonus Drawer hold LT and press Down, Down, Right, Right, Down, Right, Up

Cold War

Enter these codes while the game is paused.

Unlockable	Code
All items, gadgets, and tech points	X, WHT, Y, BLK, Y
Complete current level	X, WHT, Y, BLK, X
Invulnerability	X, WHT, Y, BLK, Left

Commandos Strike Force

Enter this password as a profile name.

Unlockable	Password
All Missions	TRUCO

Conflict: Desert Storm

Enter this code at the Main menu.

Unlockable	Code
Cheat Mode	X, X, Y, Y, L, L, R, R, LT, LT, RT, RT

Conflict: Desert Storm II– Back to Baghdad

Unlockable	Code
Cheat Menu	At the Main menu, enter LT, LT, RT, RT, X, X, Y, Y, B, B. Go to Options and the Cheat menu will be at the bottom.

Conflict: Global Terror

Enter this code at the Main menu.

Unlockable	Code
Cheat Menu	LT, RT, LT, RT, X, WHT, BLK, X

Conflict: Vietnam

Enter this code at the Main menu.

Unlockable	Code
Cheat Menu	RT,RT,LT,LT,B,B,Y,Y,X,X,WHT

Constantine

To enter these codes, press BACK to open your journal.

Unlockable	Code
Big Headed Demons	BLK,←,→,←,←,→,←,BLK
Big Weapon Mode	←,X,X,X,Y,Y,Y
Explosive Holy Bomb	→,←,X,Y,X,Y,←,→
Rapid Fire Shotgun	WHT,←,BLK,←,Y,X,Y,X
Shoot Fireballs	Y,Y,Y,←,→,→,←,←,→

Corvette

In the Options menu, select "Change Name," then enter this code.

Unlockable	Code
All Cars and All Tracks	XOPENSEZ

Crash Bandicoot: The Wrath of Cortex

Unlockable	Code
Alternate Ending Sequence	Collect all 46 gems.

Crash Tag Team Racing

At the title screen, press and hold LT+RT, then enter the code.

Unlockable	Code
Chicken heads for characters	A, B, B, X
Disable HUD	A, X, Y, B
Japanese-version characters	X, B, X, B
One-hit knockouts	A, B, B, A
No top speed on cars	B, B, Y, Y
Toy block cars	B, B, Y, X

Crimson Skies: High Road to Revenge

Enter the following codes during gameplay.

Unlockable	Code
$5,000	A,Y,A,Y,BLK
10 Tokens	X,B,X,B,BLK
All Planes	Y,X,B,Y,BLK
God Mode	Y,A,X,B,BLK
Super Primary Weapon	B,X,A,B,BLK
Ultra Hard Mode	X,B,A,X,BLK

The Da Vinci Code

Codes

Code	Effect
Et In Arcadia Ego	All bonuses Unlocked
Apocrypha	All Visual Database entries Unlocked
Sacred Feminine	Double Health
Vitruvian Man	God Mode (infinite health)
Clos Luce 1519	Level Select
Phillips Exeter	One Hit Fist Kill
Royal Holloway	One Hit Weapon Kill

Dai Senryaku VII Modern Military Tactics

Enter these passwords in the Pass Code screen.

Unlockable	Password
Cobra (D7)	746C-3BBA-E396-9AFD AH-1S
Cobra (WT)	3D9A-D404-70E9-0162 AH-1S
Super Cobra	81FE-5327-CAD7-6500 AH-1W
Cyber Ninja	C554-D619-C0C7-33A9
SPRR (WT)	F4A3-6507-A7E5-E9CD Type 60
MBT (WT)	0993-4841-852E-14F9 Type 61
MBT (D7)	5285-2318-09F4-1DDC Type 74
MBT (WT)	6289-0549-0DF1-A797 Type 74
SPAAG (WT)	8399-71B4-500A-500A Type 87
MBT (D7)	B50A-6C45-CB7B-F94E Type 90
MBT (WT)	A124-2DC3-D9A6-D4F9 Type 90

Dakar 2

Enter these passwords in the Cheat menu under Extras.

Unlockable	Password
All Cars	SWEETAS
All Tracks	BONZER

Dance Dance Revolution Ultramix

Hook a controller to port 4. At the Main menu, go into options and select credits. Enter a code and you'll hear a sound if it was input correctly.

Unlockable	Code
All Music + Cleared Challenge Mode	Up, Up, Down, Down, Left, Right, Left, Right, B, A

Dark Summit

Input each of the following codes at the Main menu. After inputting a code, listen for a sound to confirm correct code entry.

Unlockable	Code
Alien Unlocked (Challenges 43 (Race the Chief), 48 (Bomb #5), 49 (Alien Half Pipe), and 50 (Storm HQ) will be completed. You'll also have Bomb Piece #5.)	Hold BACK + START and press Y, LT, X, B, RT, A, RT, X.
All Boarders	Hold BACK + START and press Y, LT, X, B, RT, A, RT, B

DS
PSP
PS2
PS3
Wii
Xbox
Xbox 360
Index

Dark Summit (continued)

Unlockable	Code
Challenges Completed (All challenges except for 43 (Race the Chief), 48 (Bomb #5), 49 (Alien Half Pipe), and 50 (Storm HQ) will be completed. You'll also have all Bomb Pieces, with the exception of Bomb #5.)	Hold [Back] + [Start] and press [Y], [LT], [X], [B], [RT], [A], [RT], [Y] at the main menu.
Extra Points (You'll get 9,100,000 lift points, which unlock all lifts except for the Moon Gate. You'll also get 9,100,000 equipment points, which unlock all boards, accessories, and special tricks.)	Hold [Back] + [Start] and press [Y], [LT], [X], [B], [RT], [A], [RT], [A] at the main menu.
Shoot Projectile	Hold [Back] + [Start] and press [Y], [X], [B], [RT]. Press [LT] + [RT] to shoot a barrel with a projectile.
Slow Motion	Hold [Back] + [Start] and press [Y], [X], [B], [LT]. Press [LT] + [RT] when in the air or during a railslide to activate Slow Motion mode. This mode automatically ends when you reach the ground.

Dave Mirra Freestyle BMX 2

Enter all codes at the Main menu. If done correctly, a sound confirms correct code entry.

CHARACTER BIKES	*CODE*
Colin Mackay	[Down], [Down], [Right], [Right], [Right], [Right], [Right], [Up], [X]
Dave Mirra	[Down], [Down], [Up], [Right], [Up], [Right], [Up], [Up], [X]
Joey Garcia	[Down], [Down], [Up], [Right], [Left], [Left], [Down], [Right], [X]
John Englebert	[Down], [Down], [Left], [Up], [Left], [Up], [Left], [Left], [X]
Kenan Harkin	[Down], [Down], [Left], [Up], [Down], [Right], [Down], [Down], [X]
Leigh Ramsdell	[Down], [Down], [Down], [Up], [Left], [Left], [Down], [Left], [X]
Mike Laird	[Down], [Down], [Right], [Left], [Down], [Up], [Up], [Right], [X]
Rick Moliterno	[Down], [Down], [Up], [Left], [Right], [Right], [Left], [Up], [X]
Ryan Nyquist	[Down], [Down], [Down], [Down], [Down], [Right], [Up], [Down], [X]
Scott Wirch	[Down], [Down], [Right], [Up], [Down], [Down], [Left], [Right], [X]
Tim Mirra	[Down], [Down], [Right], [Left], [Down], [Right], [Down], [Up], [X]
Todd Lyons	[Down], [Down], [Down], [Down], [Left], [Right], [Left], [Down], [X]
Troy McMurray	[Down], [Down], [Left], [Down], [Right], [Left], [Up], [Left], [X]
Zach Shaw	[Down], [Down], [Left], [Down], [Up], [Right], [Right], [Down], [X]
LEVELS	*CODE*
Colin Mackay	[Up], [Up], [Right], [Left], [Up], [Right], [Right], [Up], [X]
Dave Mirra	[Up], [Up], [Up], [Right], [Up], [Left], [Up], [Up], [X]
Joey Garcia	[Up], [Up], [Up], [Up], [Down], [Down], [Down], [Right], [X]
John Englebert	[Up], [Up], [Left], [Down], [Right], [Down], [Left], [Left], [X]
Kenan Harkin	[Up], [Up], [Left], [Left], [Down], [Up], [Down], [Down], [X]
Leigh Ramsdell	[Up], [Up], [Down], [Up], [Left], [Down], [Down], [Left], [X]
Mike Laird	[Up], [Up], [Right], [Down], [Down], [Right], [Up], [Right], [X]
Rick Molitero	[Up], [Up], [Up], [Down], [Right], [Right], [Left], [Up], [X]
Ryan Nyquist	[Up], [Up], [Down], [Down], [Left], [Right], [Up], [Down], [X]
Scott Wirch	[Up], [Up], [Right], [Up], [Left], [Left], [Left], [Right], [X]
Tim Mirra	[Up], [Up], [Right], [Down], [Right], [Left], [Down], [Up], [X]

Dave Mirra Freestyle BMX 2 (continued)

LEVELS	CODE
Todd Lyons	Up, Up, Down, Up, Right, Right, Left, Down, X
Troy McMurray	Up, Up, Left, Up, Up, Right, Up, Left, X
Zach Shaw	Up, Up, Left, Right, Down, Down, Right, Down, X
RIDER OUTFITS	*CODE*
Colin Mackay	Right, Right, Right, Left, Right, Up, Right, Up, X
Joey Garcia	Right, Right, Up, Down, Up, Right, Down, Right, X
John Englebert	Right, Right, Left, Right, Up, Up, Left, Left, X
Kenan Harkin	Right, Right, Left, Down, Up, Left, Down, Down, X
RIDER OUTFITS	*CODE*
Leigh Ramsdell	Right, Right, Down, Left, Up, Down, Down, Left, X
Mike Laird	Right, Right, Right, Up, Down, Down, Up, Right, X
Rick Moliterno	Right, Right, Up, Up, Up, Right, Left, Up, X
Ryan Nyquist	Right, Right, Down, Down, Left, Up, Up, Down, X
Scott Wirch	Right, Right, Right, Up, Left, Left, Left, Right, X
Tim Mirra	Right, Right, Right, Down, Down, Right, Down, Up, X
Todd Lyons	Right, Right, Down, Left, Left, Up, Left, Down, X
Troy McMurray	Right, Right, Left, Up, Left, Left, Up, Left, X
Zach Shaw	Right, Right, Left, Left, Down, Down, Right, Down, X
SIGNATURE TRICKS	*CODE*
Amish Air	Left, Right, Up, Up, Right, Down, Right, Right, X
Colin Mackay	Left, Right, Right, Up, Left, Right, Right, Up, X
Dave Mirra	Left, Right, Up, Up, Left, Right, Up, Up, X
Joey Garcia	Left, Right, Up, Right, Down, Up, Down, Right, X
John Englebert	Left, Right, Left, Left, Down, Up, Left, Left, X
Kenan Harkin	Left, Right, Left, Down, Up, Down, Down, Down, X
Leigh Ramsdell	Left, Right, Down, Left, Left, Right, Down, Left, X
Mike Laird	Left, Right, Right, Right, Left, Right, Up, Right, X
Rick Moliterno	Left, Right, Up, Up, Up, Down, Left, Up, X
Ryan Nyquist	Left, Right, Down, Down, Down, Up, Up, Down, X
Scott Wirch	Left, Right, Right, Right, Up, Down, Left, Up, X
Slim Jim Guy	Left, Right, Down, Left, Up, Left, Right, Left, X
Tim Mirra	Left, Right, Right, Up, Down, Up, Down, Up, X
Todd Lyons	Left, Right, Down, Down, Left, Right, Left, Down, X
Troy McMurray	Left, Right, Left, Left, Up, Down, Up, Left, X
Zach Shaw	Left, Right, Left, Down, Left, Up, Right, Down, X

Dead to Rights

Enter the code at the Main menu.

Unlockable	Code
Chapter Select	Up, Down, Up, Down, Left, Right, Right, Y, X, X

Def Jam: Fight for NY

Enter these codes in the Cheat menu.

Unlockable	Code
100 Reward Points	NEWJACK
Anything Goes by CNN	MILITAIN
Bust by Outkast	BIGBOI
Comp by Comp	CHOCOCITY

Def Jam: Fight for NY (continued)

Unlockable	Code
Dragon House by Chiang	AKIRA
Koto by Chiang	GHOSTSHELL
Man Up by Sticky Fingaz	KIRKJONES
Move by Public Enemy	RESPECT
Original Gangster by Ice T	POWER
Take a Look at my Life by Fat Joe	CARTAGENA
Walk with Me by Joe Budden	PUMP

NOTE

The following codes also yield the "100 Reward Points" unlockable: THESOURCE, CROOKLYN, DUCKET, GETSTUFF.

Destroy All Humans

To activate these codes, pause the game and hold LT, then enter the code and release LT.

Unlockable	Code
Ammo-A-Plenty	←, Y, WHT, →, BLK, X
Unlockable	**Code**
Aware Like a Fox	→, X, WHT, BLK, →, WHT
Bulletproof Crypto	X, Y, ←, ←, Y, X
Deep Thinker	BLK, WHT, Y, →, WHT, Y
Mmmm...Brains! (This code increases DNA.)	BLK, BLK, WHT, WHT, ←, →, ←, →, WHT, BLK (You must be on the Mothership.)
Nobody Loves You	WHT, →, WHT, BLK, X, →

Destroy All Humans 2

Pause the game, go to archives, press and hold L3, and enter following cheats.

Unlockable	Code
Salad Days with Pox and Crypto Video	A, X, Y, B, X, B, X, A, A

Disney's Extreme Skate Adventure

Enter these codes in the Cheats menu.

Unlockable	Code
All Create-a-Skater Items	gethotgear
All Levels	frequentflyers
All Skaters	xtremebuddies
Lion King Video	savannah
Unlockable	**Code**
Special Meter always full	happyfeet
Tarzan Video	nugget
Toy Story Video	marin

Doom 3

These codes must be entered very quickly while playing.

Unlockable	Code
God Mode	Hold LT and press X, Y, B, A
Level Skip	Hold LT and press B, A, X, Y

Dr. Muto

In the Options menu, select "Cheats" to enter these codes.

Unlockable	Code
All Gadgets	TINKERTOY
All Morphs	EUREKA
Death No Touch	NECROSCI
Go Anywhere	BEAMMEUP
Never Take Damage	CHEATERBOY
Secret Morphs	LOGGLOGG
See all Movies	HOTTICKET
Super Ending Unlocked	BUZZOFF

Driv3r

Enter the following codes at the Main menu.

Unlockable	Code
All Missions	X, X, Y, Y, RT, RT, LT
All Weapons	LT, LT, X, Y, Y, RT, RT
Immunity	X, Y, RT, RT, LT, LT, Y
Invincibility	X, Y, LT, RT, LT, RT, RT—(NOTE: Does not work in Story mode)
Unlimited Ammo	RT, RT, LT, LT, X, Y, Y
Unlock All Vehicles	X, X, Y, Y, LT, RT, LT

Driver Parallel Lines

Enter these passwords in the Cheat menu.

Unlockable	Password
All Vehicles	CARSHOW
All Weapons in Your Time Zone	GUNRANGE
Indestructible Cars	ROLLBAR
Infinite Ammunition	GUNBELT
Infinite Nitro	ZOOMZOOM
Invincibility	IRONMAN
Weaker Cops	KEYSTONE
Zero Cost	TOOLEDUP

Dungeons and Dragons Heroes

To enter these codes, hold LT and press A+Y during gameplay.

Unlockable	Code
10 Anti Venom	SPINRAD
10 Berserker Brew	THOMAS
10 Fire Bomb	WEBER
10 Fire Flask	BROPHY
10 Firey Oil	EHOFF
10 Flash Freeze	ESKO
10 Globe Potions	WRIGHT
10 Holy Water	CRAWLEY
10 Insect Plagues	DERISO
10 Keys	SNODGRASS
10 Large Healing Potions	THOMPSON
10 Large Will Potions	GEE

Unlockable	Code
10 Medium Potions of Will	LU
10 Potions of Haste	UHL
10 Pyrokins	SMITH
10 Rod of Destruction	AUSTIN
10 Rod of Fire	DELUCIA
10 Rod of Miracles	JARMAN
10 Rod of Missiles	MILLER
10 Rod of Reflection	WHITTAKE
10 Rod of Shadows	DINOLT
10 Thrown Axe of Ruin	RAMERO
10 Thrown Daggers	MOREL

Dungeons and Dragons Heroes (continued)

Unlockable	Code
10 Thrown Daggers of Stunning	BELL
10 Thrown Halcyon Hammer	PRASAD
10 Thrown Hammer	BRATHWAI
10 Thrown Viper Axe	HOWARD
10 Thunderstone	ELSON
10 Tome of Apprentice	BILGER
10 Tome of Lessons	PAQUIN
10 Tome of Teacher	MEFORD
10 Tome of the Master	SPANBURG
10 Warp Stones	HOPPENST
10,000 XP Points	DSP633
500,000 Gold Pieces	KNE637
Add 10 to Constitution	N STINE
Add 10 to Dexterity	YAN
Disable Cheats	UNBUFF
Invincibility	PELOR
Nightmare Setting	MPS LABS
Unlimited Mystical Will	OBADHI
View Concept Art	CONCEPTS
View Credits	Credits

EA Sports Bio Awards

Unlockable	Code
2002 All-American Team	Level 18
Butter Fingers Pennant	Level 4
Orange Bowl Pennant	Level 8
Rose Bowl Pennant	Level 2
Tostitos Bowl Pennant	Level 12

The Elder Scrolls III: Morrowind

During Gameplay, go to the Statistics page to enter the following codes. You can only enter one code at a time.

Unlockable	Code
Restore Fatigue	Highlight Fatigue and press BLK, BLK, WHT, WHT, BLK, then hold A to reach the desired level.
Restore Health	Highlight Health and press BLK, WHT, BLK, BLK, BLK, then hold A to reach the desired level.
Restore Magicka	Highlight Magicka and press BLK, WHT, WHT, BLK, WHT, then hold A to reach the desired level.

Enclave

Unlockable	Code
God Mode and Complete Mission	Pause the game and enter X, Y, X, X, Y, Y, X, Y, X, X, Y, Y.

Enter the Matrix

Enable Cheats: Enter the hacking system and enter cheat.exe from the A prompt. Then you can enter the codes below.

CAUTION

Warning! The game can crash with cheats enabled.

Unlockable	Code
All weapons	0034AFFF
Blind Enemies	FFFFFFF1
Bonus level	13D2C77F
Deaf Enemies	4516DF45
Faster Logos	7867F443
Faster Logos	7867F443
Infinite ammo	1DDF2556
Infinite focus	69E5D9E4
Infinite Health	7F4DF451
Invisibility	FFFFFFF1
Low gravity	BB013FFF
Multiplayer	D5C55D1E
Recover Focus Fast	FFF0020A
Taxi Driving	312MF451
Turbo mode	FF00001A

ESPN NBA 2Night 2002

Enter these passwords in the Cheats menu under Options.

Unlockable	Password
Ball Tails	BEFOREIMAGE
Basketball heads players	BALLHEAD
Better Performance	ABILITYBONUS
Big Feet	BIGFOOT
Big Hands	BIGHAND
Big Heads	BIGHEAD
Easy Dunks	DUNKERS
Flat Mode	PANCAKE
Increased shooting percentage	EXCELLENT
No Fans	NOSPECTATOR
Small Mode	MINIMINI

ESPN NBA Basketball

Unlockable	Code
All 24/7 Items	Create a Player with the first name HUNT and the lastname 4TREASURE.

ESPN NFL 2K5

Get these unlockables by changing your VIP profile name to the following:

Unlockable	Profile Name
1,000,000 Crib Credits	PhatBank
All Crib items	CribMax
All Milestones complete (full trophy room)	MadSkilz

Fantastic Four

Enter these codes quickly at the Main menu. You will hear a sound to confirm a correct entry.

Unlockable	Code
Barge Arena and Stan Lee Interview #1	X, B, X, Down, Down, B, Up
Bonus Level Hell	Right, Right, X, B, Left, Up, Down
Infinite Cosmic Powers	Up, X, X, X, Left, Right, B

Far Cry Instincts

To enter these passwords, pause the game and select the Cheat menu. Note that these passwords are case sensitive.

Unlockable	Password
100 Health Points	GiveMeHealth
All Maps	TheWorldIsMine
Disables Auto-Aim	NotForSissies
Feral Attack Ability	PunchMeHard
Infinite Adrenaline	VitruviAnRush
Infinite Ammo	BulletsofHell

Enter this code after you select Map Maker.

Unlockable	Code
Secret Message	LT, RT, Y, B, X, L3, R3, A

DS PSP PS2 PS3 Wii Xbox Xbox 360 Index

DS
PSP
PS2
PS3
Wii
Xbox
Xbox 360
Index

Fifa Street 2

Enter this code at the Main menu while holding LT + Y.

Unlockable	Code
All stages unlocked	←, ↑, ↑, →, ↓, ↓, →, ↓

Fight Night 2004

Unlockable	Code
All Venues	At the Main menu, highlight My Corner and press ←,←,←,→,→,→,←,→,→.
Big Tigger	In the Record Book menu, go to most wins and press ↑,↑.
Miniature Fighters	At the Main menu, hightlight Play Now and press ←,←,←,→,→,→,←,A.

Fight Night Round 2

Unlockable	Code
All Venus	At the game mode select screen hold ← until you hear a bell.
Mini Fighters	At the choose Venue screen hold ↑ until you hear a bell ring.
Unlock Fabulous	Create a character with the first name GETFAB then cancel out and Fabulous will be available for Play Now and Career mode.

Finding Nemo

Enter all the codes at the Main menu and the word Cheat will show up if done correctly.

Unlockable	Code
Credits	Y,X,B,Y,Y,X,B,Y,X,B,Y,X,X,B,Y,X,B,Y,X,B,B,X,Y
Invincibility	Y,X,X,B,B,B,Y,Y,X,X,X,B,B,B,B,X,Y,B, B,B,X,B,Y,B,B,X,B,B,Y,B,X,B,B,B,Y
Level Select	Y,Y,Y,X,X,B,X,Y,B,X,Y,X,Y,X,Y,B,Y,Y
Secret Level	Y,X,B,B,X,Y,Y,X,B,B,X,Y,Y,B,X,Y,X,B,B,X,Y

FlatOut

Create a profile using these passwords.

Unlockable	Passwords
Lots of Cash	GIVECASH
Unlock Everything	GIVEALL
Use the Shift Up Button to Launch the Driver	Ragdoll

FlatOut 2

Enter these passwords in the Cheats menu under extras.

Unlockable	Password
All Cars and 1 Million Credits	GIEVEPIX
All Tracks	GIVEALL
Big Rig	ELPUEBLO
Flatmobile Car	WOTKINS
Lots of Money	GIVECASH
Mob Car	BIGTRUCK
Pimpster Car	RUTTO
Rocket Car	KALJAKOPPA
School Bus	GIEVCARPLZ

Forza Motorsport

Start a new profile with this name. Note: the code is case sensitive.

Unlockable	Code
Start Career with 900,000,000 Credits	tEAm4za

Freaky Flyers

Unlockable	Objective
Pilot X	On the last level in Adventure mode, beat Pilot X by destroying his robot.

Freedom Fighters

Enter these codes during gameplay.

Unlockable	Code
Change Spawn Point	Y,A,X,B,A,Up
Fast Motion	Y,A,X,B,B,Down
Heavy Machine Gun	Y,A,X,B,Y,Down
Infinite Ammo	Y,A,X,B,A,Right
Invisibility	Y,A,X,B,B,Left
Max Charisma	Y,A,X,B,A,Down
Nail Gun	Y,A,X,B,A,Left
Ragdolls	Y,A,X,B,X,Up
Rocket Launcher	Y,A,X,B,Y,Left
Shotgun	Y,A,X,B,B,Up
Slow Motion	Y,A,X,B,B,Right
Sniper Rifle	Y,A,X,B,Y,Right
Sub Machine Gun	Y,A,X,B,Y,Up

Freestyle Metal X

Go to Options, then enter the following case-sensitive codes in the Cheat menu.

Unlockable	Code
$1,000,000	sugardaddy
All Bike Parts	garageking
All Costumes	johnnye
All FMV Sequences	watchall
All Levels and Events	universe
All Photos and Posters in the Gallery	seeall
All Riders and Bikes	dudemaster
All Songs	hearall
All Special Stunts	fleximan

Frogger Ancient Shadow

Art 1	Frogger, Frogger, Frogger, Frogger
Art 2	Finnus, Finnus, Finnus, Finnus
Art 3	Berry, Berry, Berry, Berry
Bird Nest Wig	Lily, Lily, Lily, Lily
Dev Picture 1	Wani, Frogger, Wani, Frogger
Dev Picture 2	Berry, Berry, Berry, Wani
Lobster Wig	Finnius, Wani, Lumpy, Frogger
Programmer Art 1	Wani, Wani, Wani, Wani
Programmer Art 2	Lumpy, Frogger, Berry, Lily
Programmer Art 3	Wani, Frogger, Lily, Finnius
Sail Boat Wig	Lumpy, Lumpy, Lumpy, Lumpy
Skull Wig	Frogger, Lumpy, Lily, Frogger

Full Spectrum Warrior

Enter the following codes at the Cheat menu.

Unlockable	Code
Big Head Mode	NICKWEST
Full Version of America's Army	ha2p1py9tur5tle
Play at a Harder Level with No HUD	SWEDISHARMY
Unlimited Ammo	MERCENARIES

DS
PSP
PS2
PS3
Wii
Xbox
Xbox 360
Index

Futurama

While playing, hold LT and enter the following codes.

Unlockable	Code
All Extras	A, RT+X, RT+Y, A, RT+X, RT+Y, RT+B, RT+A, BLK, RT+B, RT+BACK
Full Charge	A, RT+X, RT+Y, A, RT+X, RT+Y, RT+B, RT+A, BLK, X, RT+BACK
Full Health	A, RT+X, RT+Y, A, RT+X, RT+Y, RT+B, RT+A, BLK, Y, RT+BACK
Infinite Ammo	A, RT+X, RT+Y, A, RT+X, RT+Y, RT+B, RT+A, BLK, B, RT+BACK
Invincibility	A, RT+X, RT+Y, A, RT+X, RT+Y, RT+B, RT+A, BLK, RT+Y, RT+BACK
Unlimited Lives	A, RT+X, RT+Y, A, RT+X, RT+Y, RT+B, RT+A, BLK, A, RT+BACK
Bender's Breakout	A, RT+X, RT+Y, A, RT+X, RT+Y, RT+X, RT+Y, RT+Y, Y, BACK
Bogad Swamp Trail	A, RT+X, RT+Y, A, RT+X, RT+Y, RT+X, RT+Y, X, Y, BACK
Fry Fights Back	A, RT+X, RT+Y, A, RT+X, RT+Y, RT+X, RT+Y, RT+Y, A, BACK
Inner Temple	A, RT+X, RT+Y, A, RT+X, RT+Y, RT+X, RT+Y, A, RT+Y, BACK
Leela's Last Laugh	A, RT+X, RT+Y, A, RT+X, RT+Y, RT+X, RT+Y, RT+Y, B, BACK
Left Wing	A, RT+X, RT+Y, A, RT+X, RT+Y, RT+X, RT+Y, A, B, BACK
Market Square	A, RT+X, RT+Y, A, RT+X, RT+Y, RT+X, RT+Y, A, Y, BACK
Old New York	A, RT+X, RT+Y, A, RT+X, RT+Y, RT+X, RT+Y, Y, X, BACK
Planet Express	A, RT+X, RT+Y, A, RT+X, RT+Y, RT+X, RT+Y, Y, Y, BACK
Red Light District	A, RT+X, RT+Y, A, RT+X, RT+Y, RT+X, RT+Y, Y, Y, BACK
Red Rock Creek	A, RT+X, RT+Y, A, RT+X, RT+Y, RT+X, RT+Y, B, X, BACK
Right Wing	A, RT+X, RT+Y, A, RT+X, RT+Y, RT+X, RT+Y, A, A, BACK
Rumble in the Junkyard	A, RT+X, RT+Y, A, RT+X, RT+Y, RT+X, RT+Y, B, RT+B, BACK
Run, Bender, Run	A, RT+X, RT+Y, A, RT+X, RT+Y, RT+X, RT+Y, B, B, BACK
Sewers	A, RT+X, RT+Y, A, RT+X, RT+Y, RT+X, RT+Y, Y, A, BACK
Subway	A, RT+X, RT+Y, A, RT+X, RT+Y, RT+X, RT+Y, Y, B, BACK
Temple Courtyard	A, RT+X, RT+Y, A, RT+X, RT+Y, RT+X, RT+Y, A, X, BACK
The Junkyard	A, RT+X, RT+Y, A, RT+X, RT+Y, RT+X, RT+Y, B, RT+Y, BACK
The Mine Facility	A, RT+X, RT+Y, A, RT+X, RT+Y, RT+X, RT+Y, B, A, BACK
Uptown	A, RT+X, RT+Y, A, RT+X, RT+Y, RT+X, RT+Y, Y, RT+B, BACK
Weasel Canyon	A, RT+X, RT+Y, A, RT+X, RT+Y, RT+X, RT+Y, B, Y, BACK

Future Tactics The Uprising

Enter these codes during gameplay—do not pause.

Unlockable	Code
Big heads	↑, ←, ↓, ←, ↓, ↑, ↑, ←
Disco mode	LT, ←, LT, ←, RT, →, RT, →
Low gravity	↑, ↑, ↑, ↑, ↑, ↑, ↓, →, ↑

Fuzion Frenzy

Enter the following codes after pressing START to pause gameplay. Repeat each code to disable its effect.

Unlockable	Code
Enable "Real Controls"	Hold LT and press Y, Y, Y, B.
First-Person Mode	Hold LT and press Y, B, Y, B.
Mutant Mode	Hold LT and press Y, B, X, X. To get Mutant mode two, repeat the code. To return to Mutant mode, repeat the code again. To disable the code, repeat it one more time.
Squeaky Voices	Hold LT and press Y, X, Y, Y.
Turbo Mode (during a mini-game)	Hold LT and press Y, B, X, X.
Welsh Mode	Hold LT and press Y, Y, Y, Y.

Gauntlet: Dark Legacy

Enter the following codes as names to access these unlockables.

Unlockable	Name
10,000 Gold per Level	10000K
Always Have Nine Potions and Keys	ALLFUL
Dwarf in S&M Costume	NUD069
Dwarf Is a Large Jester	ICE600
Invincibility	INVULN
Jester Is a Stick Figure with Baseball Cap Head	KJH105
Jester Is a Stick Figure with Mohawk Head	PNK666
Jester Is a Stick Figure with Smiley Face	STX222
Knight Is a Bald Man in Street Clothes (Sean Gugler)	STG333
Knight Is a Ninja (Sword and Claws)	TAK118
Knight Is a Quarterback	RIZ721
Knight Is a Roman Centurion	BAT900
Knight Is an Orange-Skirted Waitress	KA0292
Knight Wears Black Karate Outfit with Twin Scythes	SJB964
Knight Wears Black Outfit and Cape	DARTHC
Knight Wears Street Clothes	ARV984
Knight Wears Street Clothes (Chris Sutton)	CSS222
Knight Wears Street Clothes and Baseball Cap	DIB626
Permanent Anti-Death	1ANGEL
Permanent Full Turbo	PURPLE
Permanent Invisibility	000000
Permanent Pojo the Chicken	EGG911
Permanent Reflect Shot	REFLEX
Permanent Shrink Enemy and Growth	DELTA1

Gladius

Enter these codes while paused in different locations.

Unlockable	Code
1,000 Dinars every time you input this code	Paused in the school →, ↓, ←, ↑, ←, ←, ←, ←, Ⓨ, ←
1,000 exp. points every time you input this code	Paused in the school →, ↓, ←, ↑, ←, ←, ←, ←, Ⓨ, →
Control camera	Pause during combat ↑, ←, ↓, →, →, →, →, →, ↑, ↑, ↑, ↑
Higher level enemies	Pause at a league office →, →, →, ↑, ↑, ←, ←, ←, ←, →, ↑, ↑, ↑, ↑, ↓
Lower Level Enemies & Recruits	Pause at a league office →, →, →, ↑, ↑, ←, ←, ←, ←, →, ↓, ↓, ↓, ↓, ↑

Goblin Commander: Unleash the Horde

To access the following unlockables, hold the left and right triggers and Ⓨ for three seconds during gameplay, then enter code.

Unlockable	Code
1,000 Gold and Souls	RT, RT, LT, RT, RT, Ⓨ, Ⓨ, Ⓨ, LT, LT
God Mode	RT, RT, RT, LT, LT, LT, RT, LT, Ⓨ, RT
Introduction Sequence	Press LT at the Midway Games screen to see how the story begins.
Permanent Super Shot with Large Crossbow	SSHOTS
Permanent Triple Shot	MENAGE
Permanent X-Ray Vision	PEEKIN
Run Quickly	XSPEED

DS PSP PS2 PS3 Wii Xbox Xbox 360 Index

DS
PSP
PS2
PS3
Wii
Xbox
Xbox 360
Index

Goblin Commander: Unleash the Horde (continued)

Unlockable	Code
Throw Quickly	QCKSHT
Valkyrie as a Cheerleader with Baton	CEL721
Valkyrie as a Japanese School Girl	AYA555
Valkyrie as the Grim Reaper with Bloody Scythe	TWN300
Warrior as an Orc Boss	MTN200
Warrior with a Rat Head	RAT333
Warrior with an Ogre Costume	CAS400
Wizard as a Pharaoh	DES700
Wizard as an Alien	SKY100
Wizard as an Undead Lich	GARM00
Wizard as Sumner	SUM224
Wizard with an Evil Appearance	GARM99

The Godfather

Unlockable	Code
$5,000	X, Y, X, X, Y, L3
Full Ammo	Y, ←, Y, →, ↓, R3
Full Health	←, X, →, Y, →, L3

Enter this code on the Join Family menu.

Unlockable	Code
Unlock All Movies	Y, X, Y, X, X, L3

Godzilla: Destroy All Monsters Melee

Cheat List: At the main menu, highlight Versus mode. Then in order, press and hold LT, B, and RT. Then release them in this order: B, RT, LT. Then enter the following codes.

Unlockable	Code
Black and white mode	860475
Boxing Level	440499
Extra Military Damage	970432
Godzilla 2000	637522
Unlock All monsters	209697

Unlockable	Objective
Destroyah	Beat Adventure mode with Godzilla 2000.
Gigan	Beat Adventure mode with Aguirus.
Godzilla 2000	Complete the Adventure mode with Godzilla 90's.
King Ghidorah	Beat Adventure mode with Megalon.
Mecha Godzilla	Beat the Adventure mode with Destoroyah, Rodan and Mecha-King Ghidorah.
Mecha Godzilla 2	Beat adventure mode with all monsters, then beat it again with Mecha King Ghidrah.
Mecha Godzilla 3	Beat adventure mode with Orga on Hard.
Mecha-King Ghidora	Beat Adventure mode with King Ghidorah.
Mothership Level	Beat the game on adventure mode with Mecha Godzilla.
Orga	Beat Adventure mode with all the characters, then beat the mode once more on medium difficulty with Godzilla 2000.
Rodan	Complete Adventure mode with Gigan.
Vortaak Level	Beat adventure mode with Mecha Godzilla 3 on Medium.

Godzilla: Save the Earth

To activate the Cheat menu, press and hold LT, then B, then RT in that order, then release the keys starting with B, then RT, then LT.

Unlockable	Code
All Cities	659996
All Monsters	525955
Buildings are Indestructible	812304
Energy doesn't regenerate	122574
Health Regenerates	536117
Player 1 deals 4x damage	259565
Player 1 has Infinite Energy	819324
Player 1 is Invisible	531470
Player 1 is Invulnerable	338592
Player 2 deals 4x damage	927281
Player 2 has Infinite Energy	324511
Player 2 is Invisible	118699
Player 2 is Invulnerable	259333
Player 3 deals 4x damage	500494
Player 3 has Infinite Energy	651417
Player 3 is Invisible	507215
Player 3 is Invulnerable	953598
Player 4 deals 4x damage	988551
Player 4 has Infinite Energy	456719
Player 4 is Invisible	198690
Player 4 is Invulnerable	485542

Golden Eye: Rogue Agent

In the Extras menu, enter the following:

Unlockable	Code
Paintball Mode	Right, Left, Right, Left, Down, Down, Up, Up
Unlock All Skins in Multiplayer	Down, Left, Up, Left, Right, Down, Left, Up

Grabbed by the Ghoulies

Unlockable	Code
20 Challenges	Collect 100 Rare Bonus Books
21st Challenge	Get Gold on all 20 Challenges

Grand Theft Auto 3

Unlockable	Code
All Weapons	BLK, BLK, LT, BLK, Left, Down, Right, Up, Left, Down, Right, Up
Full Health	BLK, BLK, LT, RT, Left, Down, Right, Up, Left, Down, Right, Up
Full Armor	BLK, BLK, LT, WHT, Left, Down, Right, Up, Left, Down, Right, Up

DS
PSP
PS2
PS3
Wii
Xbox
Xbox 360
Index

Grand Theft Auto: San Andreas

Enter these codes during gameplay; do not pause the game.

Unlockable	Code
$250,000 Plus Full Health and Armor	RT, BLK, LT, A, Left, Down, Right, Up, Left, Down, Right, Up
Adrenaline Mode	A, A, X, RT, LT, A, Down, Left, A
Aggressive Drivers	Left, BLK, Up, Up, BLK, B, X, BLK, LT, Left, Down, LT
Aggressive Traffic	BLK, B, RT, WHT, Left, RT, LT, BLK, WHT
Aiming while Driving	Up, Up, X, WHT, Right, A, RT, Down, BLK, B
All Cars Are Pink	B, LT, Down, WHT, Left, A, RT, LT, Right, B
All Cars Fly Away When Hit	X, BLK, Down, Down, Left, Down, Left, Left, WHT, A
All Cars Have Nitrous	Left, Y, RT, LT, Up, X, Y, Down, B, WHT, LT, LT
All Cars Have Tank Properties	LT, WHT, WHT, Up, Down, Down, Up, RT, BLK, BLK
All Cars You Drive Can Drive on Water	Right, BLK, B, RT, WHT, X, RT, BLK
All Cars You Drive Can Fly	X, Down, WHT, Up, LT, B, Up, A, Left
All Vehicles Are Black	B, WHT, Up, RT, Left, A, RT, LT, Left, B
All Vehicles Are Farm Vehicles and Everyone Is Dressed Like Farmers	LT, LT, RT, RT, WHT, LT, BLK, Down, Left, Up
All Vehicles Are Invisible (except motorcycles)	Y, LT, Y, BLK, X, LT, LT
All Vehicles Are Junk Cars	WHT, Right, LT, Up, A, LT, WHT, BLK, RT, LT, LT, LT
Always Midnight	X, LT, RT, Right, A, Up, LT, Left, Left
Beach Mode	Up, Up, Down, Down, X, B, LT, RT, Y, Down
Better Car Suspension	X, X, BLK, Left, Up, X, BLK, A, A, A
Chaos Mode	WHT, Right, LT, Y, Right, Right, RT, LT, Right, LT, LT, LT
Cloudy	WHT, Down, Down, Left, X, Left, BLK, X, A, RT, LT, LT
Clown Mode	Y, Y, LT, X, X, B, X, Down, B
Destroy All Cars	BLK, WHT, RT, LT, WHT, BLK, X, Y, B, Y, WHT, LT
Faster Cars	Right, RT, Up, WHT, WHT, Left, RT, LT, RT, RT
Faster Clock	B, B, LT, X, LT, X, X, X, LT, Y, B, Y
Faster Gameplay	Y, Up, Right, Down, WHT, LT, X
Flying Boats	BLK, B, Up, LT, Right, RT, Right, Up, X, Y
Foggy Weather	BLK, A, LT, LT, WHT, WHT, WHT, A
Full Wanted Level	B, Right, B, Right, Left, X, A Down
Hitman Rank (all weapons)	Down, X, A, Left, RT, BLK, Left, Down, Down, LT, LT, LT
Increase Car Speed	Up, LT, RT, Up, Right, Up, A, WHT, A, LT
Infinite Air	Down, Left, LT, Down, Down, BLK, Down, WHT, Down
Infinite Ammo	LT, RT, X, RT, Left, BLK, RT, Left, X, Down, LT, LT
Infinite Health	Down, A, Right, Left, Right, RT, Right, Down, Up, Y
Jetpack	Left, Right, LT, WHT, RT, BLK, Up, Down, Left, Right
Lower Wanted Level	RT, RT, B, BLK, Up, Down, Up, Down, Up, Down
Max Fat	Y, Up, Up, Left, Right, X, B, Down
Max Muscle	Y, Up, Up, Left, Right, X, B, Right
Max Respect	LT, RT, Y, Down, BLK, A, LT, Up, WHT, WHT, LT, LT
Max Sex Appeal	B, Y, Y, Up, B, RT, WHT, Up, Y, LT, LT, LT
Max Stamina	Up, A, Y, A, Y, A, X, BLK, Right
Max Vehicle Stats	X, WHT, A, RT, WHT, WHT, Right, RT, Right, LT, LT, LT
Morning	BLK, A, LT, LT, WHT, WHT, WHT, X
Never Hungry	X, WHT, RT, Y, Up, X, WHT, Up, A

Grand Theft Auto: San Andreas (continued)

Unlockable	Code
No Muscle and No Fat	Y, ↑, ↑, ←, →, X, B, →
No Pedestrians and Low Traffic	A, ↓, ↑, BLK, ↓, Y, LT, Y, ←
Noon	BLK, A, LT, LT, WHT, WHT, WHT, ↓
Orange Sky	←, ←, WHT, RT, →, X, X, LT, WHT, A
Overcast	BLK, A, LT, LT, WHT, WHT, WHT, X
Parachute	←, →, LT, WHT, RT, BLK, BLK, ↑, ↓, →, LT
Pedestrian Attack (This code cannot be turned off.)	↓, ↑, ↑, ↑, A, BLK, RT, WHT, WHT
Pedestrian Riot Mode (This code cannot be turned off.)	↓, ←, ↑, ←, A, BLK, RT, WHT, LT
Pedestrians Dress Like Elvis	LT, B, Y, LT, LT, X, WHT, ↑, ↓, ←
Pedestrians Have Guns	A, LT, ↑, X, ↓, A, WHT, Y, ↓, RT, LT, LT
Pedestrians Have Weapons	BLK, RT, A, Y, A, Y, ↑, ↓
Perfect Handling in Vehicles	Y, RT, RT, ←, RT, LT, BLK, LT
Pimp Mode	X, →, X, X, WHT, A, Y, A, Y
Prostitutes Pay You	→, WHT, WHT, ↓, WHT, ↑, ↑, WHT, BLK
Recruit Anyone (9mm)	↓, X, ↑, BLK, BLK, ↑, →, →, ↑
Recruit Anyone (rockets)	BLK, BLK, BLK, A, WHT, LT, BLK, LT, ↓, A
Sand Storm	↑, ↓, LT, LT, WHT, WHT, LT, WHT, RT, BLK
Skinny	Y, ↑, ↑, ←, →, X, B, →
Slow Down Gameplay	Y, ↑, →, ↓, X, BLK, RT
Spawn Bloodring Banger	↓, RT, B, WHT, WHT, A, RT, LT, ←, ←
Spawn Caddy	B, LT, ↑, RT, WHT, A, RT, LT, B, A
Spawn Dozer	BLK, LT, LT, →, →, ↑, ↑, A, LT, ←
Spawn Hotring Racer #1	RT, B, BLK, →, LT, WHT, A, A, X, RT
Spawn Hotring Racer #2	BLK, LT, B, →, LT, RT, →, ↑, B, BLK
Spawn Hunter	B, A, LT, B, B, LT, B, RT, BLK, WHT, LT, LT
Spawn Hydra	Y, Y, X, B, A, LT, LT, ↓, ↑
Spawn Monster	→, ↑, RT, RT, RT, ↓, Y, Y, A, B, LT, LT
Spawn Quadbike	←, ←, ↓, ↓, ↑, ↑, X, B, Y, RT, BLK
Spawn Rancher	↑, →, →, LT, →, ↑, X, WHT
Spawn Rhino	B, B, LT, B, B, B, LT, WHT, RT, Y, B, Y
Spawn Stretch	BLK, ↑, WHT, ←, ←, RT, LT, B, →
Spawn Stunt Plane	B, ↑, LT, WHT, ↓, RT, LT, LT, ←, ←, A, Y
Spawn Tanker	RT, ↑, ←, →, BLK, ↑, →, X, →, WHT, LT, LT
Spawn Vortex	Y, Y, X, B, A, LT, WHT, ↓, ↓
Stormy	BLK, A, LT, LT, WHT, WHT, WHT, B
Super Bike Jumps	Y, X, B, B, X, B, B, LT, WHT, WHT, RT, BLK
Super Jumps	↑, ↑, Y, Y, ↑, ↑, ←, →, X, BLK, BLK
Super Punches	↑, ←, A, Y, RT, B, B, B, WHT
Traffic Lights Stay Green	→, RT, ↑, WHT, WHT, ←, RT, LT, RT, RT
Unlock Romero	↓, BLK, ↓, RT, WHT, ←, RT, LT, ←, →
Unlock Trashmaster	B, RT, B, RT, ←, ←, RT, LT, B, →
Weapon Set 1	RT, BLK, LT, BLK, ←, ↓, →, ↑, ←, ↓, →, ↑
Weapon Set 2	RT, BLK, LT, BLK, ←, ↓, →, ↑, ←, ↓, ↓, ←
Weapon Set 3	RT, BLK, LT, BLK, ←, ↓, →, ↑, ←, ↓, ↓, ↓
Yakuza Mode	A, A, ↓, BLK, WHT, B, RT, B, X

Grand Theft Auto: Vice City

Enter these codes while playing; do not pause.

Unlockable	Code
Aggressive Drivers	BLK, B, RT, WHT, ←, RT, LT, BLK, WHT
Bikini Girls with Guns	→, LT, B, WHT, ←, A, RT, LT, LT, A
Black Cars	B, WHT, ↑, RT, ←, A, RT, LT, ←, B
Blow Up Cars	BLK, WHT, RT, LT, WHT, BLK, X, Y, B, Y, WHT, LT
Cars Can Drive on Water	→, BLK, B, RT, WHT, X, RT, BLK
Change Clothes	→, →, ←, ↑, LT, WHT, ←, ↑, ↓, →
Change Vehicle Wheel Size (Repeat to change again)	RT, A, Y, →, BLK, X, ↑, ↓, X
Cloudy Weather	BLK, B, LT, LT, WHT, WHT, WHT, Y
Dodo Cheat	→, BLK, B, RT, WHT, ↓, LT, RT (Press the analog stick back to fly)
Foggy Weather	BLK, A, LT, LT, WHT, WHT, WHT, A
Higher Top Speed for Your Vehicle	→, RT, ↑, WHT, WHT, ←, RT, LT, RT, RT
Ladies Man (Certain women follow you)	B, A, LT, LT, BLK, A, A, B, Y
Pedestrians Hate You (code cannot be undone)	↓, ↑, ↑, ↑, A, BLK, RT, WHT, WHT
Pedestrians Have Weapons (code cannot be undone)	BLK, RT, A, Y, A, Y, ↑, ↓
Pedestrians Riot (code cannot be undone)	↓, ←, ↑, ←, A, BLK, RT, WHT, LT
Perfect Handling	Y, RT, RT, ←, RT, LT, BLK, LT

Enter these codes while playing; do not pause.

Unlockable	Code
Pink Cars	B, LT, ↓, WHT, ←, A, RT, LT, →, A
Play As Candy Suxxx	B, BLK, ↓, RT, ←, →, RT, LT, A, WHT
Play As Hilary King	RT, B, BLK, LT, →, RT, LT, A, BLK
Play As Ken Rosenberg	→, LT, ↑, WHT, LT, →, RT, LT, A, RT
Play As Lance Vance	B, WHT, ←, A, RT, LT, A, LT
Play As Love Fist Guy #1	↓, LT, ↓, WHT, ←, A, RT, LT, A, A
Play As Love Fist Guy #2	RT, WHT, BLK, LT, →, BLK, ←, A, X, LT
Play As Mercedes	BLK, LT, ↑, LT, →, RT, →, ↑, B, Y
Play As Phil Cassady	→, RT, ↑, BLK, LT, →, RT, LT, →, B
Play As Ricardo Diaz	LT, WHT, RT, BLK, ↓, LT, BLK, WHT
Play As Sonny Forelli	B, LT, B, WHT, ←, A, RT, LT, A, A
Police Return from Dead	B, LT, ↓, WHT, ←, A, RT, LT, →, A
Raise Wanted Level	RT, RT, B, BLK, ←, →, ←, →, ←, →
Repair Vehicle Tires	BLK, WHT, LT, B, ←, ↓, →, ↑, ←, ↓, →, ↑
Slow Down Time	Y, ↑, →, ↓, X, BLK, RT
Spawn A Bloodring Banger	↑, →, →, LT, →, ↑, X, WHT
Spawn A Bloodring Racer	↓, RT, B, WHT, WHT, A, RT, LT, ←, ←
Spawn A Caddie	B, LT, ↑, RT, WHT, A, RT, LT, B, A
Spawn A Hotring Racer #1	RT, B, BLK, →, LT, WHT, A, A, X, RT
Spawn A Hotring Racer #2	BLK, LT, B, →, LT, RT, →, ↑, B, BLK

Grand Theft Auto: Vice City (continued)

Unlockable	Code
Spawn A Love Fist	BLK, Up, WHT, Left, Left, RT, LT, B, Right
Spawn A Rhino Tank	B, B, LT, B, B, B, LT, WHT, RT, Y, B, Y
Spawn A Romero's Hearse	Down, BLK, Down, RT, WHT, Left, RT, LT, Left, Right
Spawn A Sabre Turbo	Right, WHT, Down, WHT, WHT, A, RT, LT, B, Left
Spawn A Trashmaster	B, RT, B, RT, Left, Left, RT, LT, B, Right
Speed Up Time	B, B, LT, X, LT, X, X, X, LT, Y, B, Y
Stormy Weather	BLK, A, LT, LT, WHT, WHT, WHT, B
Suicide	Right, WHT, Down, RT, Left, Left, RT, LT, WHT, LT
Sunny Weather	BLK, A, LT, LT, WHT, WHT, WHT, Down
Very Cloudy Weather	BLK, A, LT, LT, WHT, WHT, WHT, X
Weapons #1	RT, BLK, LT, BLK, Left, Down, Right, Up, Left, Down, Right, Up
Weapons #2	RT, BLK, LT, BLK, Left, Down, Right, Up, Left, Down, Down, Left
Weapons #3	RT, BLK, LT, BLK, Left, Down, Right, Up, Left, Down, Down, Down

Great Escape

Unlockable	Code
Restore Health	While playing, pause when you are equipping a gun and a health kit. Then press Y,X,LT,RT,LT,RT,X,Y,LT,Y,Y,RT,A
Select Levels	From the Main menu, press Y,RT,Y,X,Y,RT,X,LT,X,X,X,Y
Unlock All Movies	From the Main menu, press LT,LT,Y,X,X,RT,RT,Y,Y,X,LT,RT

Half-Life 2

Enter these codes while playing; do not pause the game.

Unlockable	Code
Restores 25 points of health (per use)	Up, Up, Down, Down, Left, Right, Left, Right, B, A
Restores ammo for current weapon	Y, B, A, X, WHT, Y, X, A, B, WHT
Unlocks all chapters	Left, Left, Left, Left, BLK, Right, Right, Right, Right, WHT

Haunted Mansion

To access the following unlockables, hold RT on the D-Pad, then enter code.

Unlockable	Code
Level Select	B,B,X,Y,Y,X,B,A
God Mode	X,B,B,B,X,B,Y,A

Heroes of the Pacific

Enter these codes at the Main menu.

Unlockable	Code
Cheat Menu	Y, LT, Left, RT, Right, WHT
Unlock All Planes and Missions	R-Up, R-Down, WHT, BLK, R-Left, R-Right
Unlock Japanese Planes	WHT, BLK, LT, RT, R-Up, R-Left
Upgrade Planes	LT, R-Left, RT, R-Right, WHT, Y

Hitman 2: Silent Assassin

Unlockable	Code
All Weapons	Press RT, LT, Up, Down, A, Up, X, A during gameplay.
Bomb Mode	Press RT, LT, Up, Down, A, Up, WHT during gameplay.
Full Heal	Press RT, LT, Up, Down, A, Up, Down during gameplay.
God Mode	Press RT, LT, Up, Down, A, RT, LT, BLK, WHT during gameplay.
Hitman AI	During gameplay press RT, LT, Up, Down, A, Up, Up.
Lethal Charge	Press LT, RT, Up, Down, A, BLK, BLK during gameplay.
Level Select	Press RT, LT, Up, Down, Y, B at the main menu.

DS
PSP
PS2
PS3
Wii
Xbox
Xbox 360
Index

Hitman 2: Silent Assassin (continued)

Unlockable	Code
Level Skip	Press RT, LT, Up, Down, A, X, click L, and press B, A, B, A during gameplay. Enable this code immediately after starting a level to complete it with a Silent Assassin rank.
Megaforce Mode	Press RT, LT, Up, Down, A, RT, RT during gameplay. Restart the level to remove its effect.
Nailgun Mode (Weapons pin people to walls when you activate this code.)	Press RT, LT, Up, Down, A, WHT, WHT during gameplay.
Punch Mode	Press RT, LT, Up, Down, A, Up, Up during gameplay.
Slow Motion	Press RT, LT, Up, Down, A, Up, LT during gameplay.
SMG and 9mm Pistol SD	Press LT, RT, Up, Down, A, Up, RT, RT during gameplay.
Toggle Gravity	Press RT, LT, Up, Down, A, LT, LT during gameplay.

Hitman: Contracts

Enter the following codes at the Main menu.

Unlockable	Code
Level Select	X, Y, B, Left, Up, Right, LT, RT
Level Skip and Silent Assasin Rating	RT, LT, Up, Down, X, A, LT, B, A, B, A

The Hulk

Enter these cheats at the Code Input screen in the Options menu.

Unlockable	Code
Double Health for Enemies	BRNGITN
Double Health for Hulk	HLTHDSE
Full Rage Meter Cheat	ANGMNGT
Half Enemies' HP	MMMYHLP
High Score reset	NMBTHIH
Invincibility	GMMSKIN
Level Select	TRUBLVR
Play as Gray Hulk	JANITOR
Puzzle Solved Cheat	BRCESTN
Regenerator	FLSHWND
Unlimited Continues	GRNCHTR
Unlock Desert Battle art	FIFTEEN
Unlock Hulk Movie FMV art	NANOMED
Unlock Hulk Transformed art	SANFRAN
Unlock Hulk vs. Hulk Dogs art	PITBULL
Wicked Punch Cheat	FSTOFRY

I-Ninja

Codes

Unlockable	How to Unlock
Big Head Mode	Press START to pause gameplay, then hold RB and press Y, Y, Y, Y. Release RB, then hold L1 and press Y, Y. Hold RB+L1, then press Y, B, Y.
Level Skip	Press start to pause game, hold RT then press X, X, X, B. Release RT then hold LT and press Y, Y. Release LT then hold RT, X, X.

Unlockables

Unlockable	How to Unlock
Battle Arena	Collect all 64 Grades to unlock Battle Arena in Robot Beach

Ice Age 2: The Meltdown

Codes

Unlockable	How to Unlock
Unlimited Energy	Down, Left, Right, Down, Down, Right, Left, Down
Unlimited Health	Up, Right, Down, Up, Left, Down, Right, Left
Unlimited Pebbles	Down, Down, Left, Up, Up, Right, Up, Down

IHRA Drag Racing Sportsman Edition

Enter these case-sensitive passwords as profile names.

Unlockable	Password
$999,999	Loaded
All bonuses	IWantIt
All trophy room items	FilMeUp
Rocket cars	HotRodz

The Incredible Hulk: Ultimate Destruction

At the Code Input screen, enter the following codes.

Unlockable	Code
5,000 Smash Points	SMASH5
10,000 Smash Points	SMASH10
15,000 Smash Points	SMASH15
Abomination (must complete Story mode first)	VILLAIN
All Vehicles Become Taxis	CABBIES
American Flag Shorts	AMERICA
Black and White Graphics	RETRO
Canadian Flag Shorts	OCANADA
Cow Missiles	CHZGUN
Double Hulk's Damage Abilities	DESTROY
Double Value of Health Pickups	BRINGIT
French Flag Shorts	DRAPEAU
German Flag Shorts	DEUTSCH
Gorilla Invasion Mode	KINGKNG
Gray Hulk (without suit)	CLASSIC
Grey Hulk Mr. Fix It	SUITFIT
Italian Flag Shorts	Mutanda
Japanese Flag Shorts	FURAGGU
Low Gravity	PILLOWS
Mass Transit On/Off	TRANSIT
Sepia Mode	HISTORY
Spanish Flag Shorts	BANDERA
Union Jack Flag Shorts	FSHNCHP
Wild Traffic	FROGGIE

The Incredibles

Pause the game and go to the Secrets menu and enter the following codes.

Unlockable	Code
Big Heads	EINSTEINIUM
Credits	YOURNAMEINLIGHTS
Destroy All Enemies on Screen	SMARTBOMB
Eye Laser	GAZERBEAM
Feet of Fire	ATHLETESFOOT
One Hit Knockout	KRONOS
Restore Health	UUDDLRLRBAS
Slow down Gameplay	BWTHEMOVIE
Small Heads	DEEVOLVE
So many Colors	EMODE
Speed up Gameplay	SASSMODE
Turn off the HUD	BHUD
Unlimited Incredi-Power for Mr. Incredible	SHOWTIME
Unlimited Incredi-Power for Elastigirl	FLEXIBLE
Watch the Intro Again	HI

Indiana Jones and the Emperor's Tomb

Enter this code at the Main menu.

Unlockable	Code
God Mode	Hold LT+RT and press ↑, ↑, ↓, ↑, A, X, A, B, ↑, ↓, Y, START

Jaws Unleashed

Enter these passwords as Profile names.

Unlockable	Password
1 Million Points	Blooood
Unlock All Bonuses	Shaaark

Juiced

Enter this passwords in the Password menu.

Unlockable	Password
All Cars in Arcade Mode	PINT

Jurassic Park: Operation Genesis

Codes

Unlockable	How to Unlock
$10,000	Press LB+↑ and then LB+↓
All Dinosaurs have 55% DNA	→, ↑, ←, ↓
All Missions, Exercises, and Sites	RB, →, →, →, → RB
All Research	↓, ↓, ↓, ←, →, LB, ↓, ↑
Car Crash	Press L1+RB, and repeatedly tap ↑, ↓, w, ↓
Clear Storms	RB, RB, ←, →, ↑, →
Constant Rain	RB, LB, RB, ↓, ↑, ↓
Create a Heat Wave	Press RB+↓ (x2)
Create a Twister	←, ↑, →, ↓, and RB+L1
Create Stormy Weather	RB, RB, LB, RB, ↓, ↑, ↓
Damage All Paths	→, →, RB, RB, LB, ↓

Jurassic Park: Operation Genesis (continued)

Unlockable	How to Unlock
Diseased Dinosaurs	↓, ↑, ↓, ←, RB, RB, RB
Destroy All Fences	↑, +, ↓, LB, ←, ←
Downgrade All Fences to Low Security	↓, ↓, ←, →, LB, LB, ↑, ↑
Extinction Event	LB, RB, ↓, RB, LB
Guaranteed Immunity	↑, ↑, RB, LB, ↑, ↑
Increase Park Budget by $250,000	LB, →, →, LB, RB, ↓
Increase Park Rating by 1 Star	→, LB, ↑, LB, LB, ↓
Kill All Tourists	→, ←, →, ←, →, RB
Make Visitors Happy	RB, ↓, LB, ↑, ↑, ↑
Make Your Finances Zero	RB+L1, ↓
No More Rampages	LB, ←, ↑, ←, ↑, ←, LB
No Red Tape	LB, RB, ←, ↓, ↓, ↓, ↓
No Twisters	LB+R1, release LB+R1, and then press LB+R1 again.
Restock Your Market with Fossils	LB, RB, LB, RB, ↓, ↓
Set All Excavated Dinosaur DNA to 0%	LB, +, LB, →, ↓, RB
Set All Excavated Dinosaur DNA to 100%	RB, ↑, RB, →, LB, ↑
Shoot from Cars Using Camera	L1+RB, ←, ↓, →, →
Stress Out All Carnivores	LB, LB, LB and ←, ←, ←
Three Stars	LB, RB, ↓, ↓, LB, →
Tourist Casualties Don't Affect Your Budget	RB, ←, ↓, ↓, ↓, ↓
Undead Dinosaurs	RB, RB, RB, LB, →
Upgrade all Fences to Maximum Security	LB, ←, ←, RB, RB →

Justice League Heroes

Codes

Code	Effect
All Cinematics	↓, →, ↓, ←
Get 20 Shields	↑, ↑, ↓, ↓
Gives 35 Random Boosts	←, →, ←, →
Infinite Energy	↓, ↓, →, →, ↑, ↑, ←, ←
Invincibility	←, ↓, →, ↑, ←, ↓, →, ↑
Maxes Out Abilities	→, ↓, →, ↓
One Hit Kills	↑, ↑, ↓, ←, ↑, ↑, ↓, ↓
Purchase All Heroes	→, ↓, ←, ↑
Take Less Damage	←, ↑, →, ↓
Unlock all Costumes	↓, ←, ↑, →

Kelly Slater's Pro Surfer

Enter these passwords in the Options menu under cheats.

Unlockable	Password	Unlockable	Password
All Boards	619 555 4141	Max Stats	212 555 1776
All Levels	328 555 4497	Mega Cheat	714 555 8092
All Suits	702 555 2918	Pastrana	800 555 6292
All Surfers	949 555 6799	Perfect Balance	213 555 5721
All Tricks	626 555 6043	Play as Rainbow	213 555 5721
First-Person Mode	877 555 3825	Trippy	818 555 1447
Freak	310 555 6217	Unlock Tiki God	888 555 4506
High Jumps	217 555 0217	Unlock Tony Hawk	323 555 9787

Kill.switch

Unlockable	Code
Infinite Ammo	After completing the game, pause the game and press LT, RT, X, X

Kung-Fu Chaos

Enter these codes at the Main menu.

Unlockable	Code
All Available Costumes for Unlocked Characters	BADBABY
All Characters	BAWDYBALLAD
All Character Bios	BLARBDRAWL
All Island Scenes	BAYSAWAY
All Levels in the Style of a 1920's Movie	SALADDAYS
Play Ninja Challenge in Co-op	BUDDY
Unlock All Levels	LADYRADAR
Unlock Candi Roll	LADYSDAY
Unlock Captain Won	LARDYBUD
Unlock Championship Mode	SLAYDAY
Unlock Every Cheat	LUXURYLARD
Unlock Everything That Requires Rour Stars	ALLBRAWL
Unlock Miniseries Mode	SLYSUBURB
Unlock Shao Ting	WALRUSBALDY

Land of the Dead: Road to Fiddler's Green

Enter these codes during gameplay.

Unlockable	Code
All Weapons	Up, Down, Left, Right, A, B
God Mode	Up, Down, Left, Right, Up, Down, Left, Right
Kill All Spawned Enemies	A, B, Y, X, A, B, Y, X
Kungfu Fists	Right, Down, Left, A
Minigun	Up, Up, Down, Down, A, B, A, B
No Knockdown	Up, A, Up, B, Up, Y, Up, X

Legacy of Kain: Defiance

To access the following, pause the game any time and enter code.

Unlockable	Code
All Bonuses	Black, Down, White, RT, Left, White, Down, LT, Y
Infinite Reaver Charge	Down, Down, Up, Left, RT, Black, Down, Y, B
Card Board Tube Reaver	Up, Down, Left, Right, Black, White, Y, Down, B
God Mode	Up, Down, Right, Down, RT, Black, Down, Y, LT

Legends of Wrestling

Unlockable	Code
All Wrestlers	At the Main menu, press ↑, ↑, ↓, ↓, ←, →, ←, →, Y, Y, X. The save prompt appears to let you know the code worked.

LEGO Star Wars

To unlock characters for purchase in Free Play mode, go to Dexter's Diner, then the Codes menu, and enter the following.

Unlockable	Code
Battle Droid	987UYR
Battle Droid (Commander)	EN11K5
Battle Droid (Geonosis)	LK42U6
Battle Droid (Security)	KF999A
Big Blasters	IG72X4
Boba Fett	LA811Y
Brushes	SHRUB1
Classic Blasters	L449HD
Clone	F8B4L6
Clone (Episode III)	ER33JN
Clone (Episode III, Pilot)	BHU72T
Clone (Episode III, Swamp)	N3T6P8
Clone (Episode III, Walker)	RS6E25
Count Dooku	14PGMN
Darth Maul	H35TUX
Darth Sidious	A32CAM
Disguised Clone	VR832U
Droideka	DH382U
General Grievous	SF321Y
Geonosian	19D7NB
Gonk Droid	U63B2A
Grievous' Bodyguard	ZTY392
Invincibility	4PR28U
Jango Fett	PL47NH
Ki-Adi Mundi	DP55MV
Kit Fisto	CBR954
Luminara	A725X4
Mace Windu (Episode III)	MS952L
Minikit Detector	LD116B
Moustaches	RP924W
Padme	92UJ7D
PK Droid	R840JU
Princess Leia	BEQ82H
Purple	YD77GC
Rebel Trooper	L54YUK
Royal Guard	PP43JX
Shaak Ti	EUW862
Silhouettes	MS999Q
Silly Blasters	NR37W1
Super Battle Droid	XZNR21
Tea Cups	PUCEAT

LEGO Star Wars II: The Original Trilogy

Enter these passwords in the Cantina.

Unlockable	Password
Beach Trooper	UCK868
Ben Kenobi (Ghost)	BEN917
Bespin Guard	VHY832
Bib Fortuna	WTY721
Boba Fett	HLP221
Death Star Trooper	BNC332
Ewok	TTT289
Gamorrean Guard	YZF999
Gonk Droid	NFX582
Grand Moff Tarkin	SMG219
Greedo	NAH118
Han Solo (Hood)	YWM840
IG-88	NXL973
Imperial Guard	MMM111
Imperial Officer	BBV889
Imperial Shuttle Pilot	VAP664
Imperial Spy	CVT125
Jawa	JAW499
Lobot	UUB319
Palace Guard	SGE549
Rebel Pilot	CYG336
Rebel Trooper (Hoth)	EKU849
Sandtrooper	YDV451
Skiff Guard	GBU888
Snowtrooper	NYU989
Stormtrooper	PTR345
The Emperor	HHY382
Tie Fighter	HDY739
Tie Fighter Pilot	NNZ316
Tie Interceptor	QYA828
Tusken Raider	PEJ821
Ugnaught	UGN694

Links 2004

Unlockable	Code
80 Attribute Points	Create a new profile using the name SafariTK.
All courses	At the Main Menu, hold LT+RT and press X+Y

Madden NFL 06

To enter this code, go into My Madden, select Madden Cards, then select Enter Code.

Unlockable	Code
1st and 5 Bronze	2Y7L8B
1st and 15 Bronze	2W4P9T
3rd Down Bronze	3F9G4J
5th Down Bronze	3E9R4V
Da Boot Bronze	3J3S9Y
Donovan McNabb Gold Card (alternate)	8Q2J2X
Extra Credit Bronze	3D3Q3P
Human Plow Bronze	3H3U7F
Super Dive Bronze	3H8M5U
Tight Fit Bronze	3D8X6T
Unforced Errors Bronze	2Z2F4H

Madden NFL 07

Under Madden Cards, select Madden Codes to enter these passwords. Passwords are case sensitive.

Unlockable	Password
When this card is played, you can't fumble or throw interceptions for one half	XL7SP1
When this card is played, your opponent will throw a lob pass for one half	5LAW00
When this card is played, your QB accuracy will be 100% for one half	WROA0R

Magic the Gathering: Battlegrounds

Unlockable	Code
All Quest	During the Quest select, press LT+RT, ↓, ↑, L, White, ↑, →, ←, ↓, LT+RT.
Secret Level for Vs. Mode	At the Arena select, press LT+RT, ←, ↑, X, ↑, RT, Y, LT+RT.
All Duelists in Arcade Mode	At the Character select screen, press LT+RT, ↓, ↑, X, White, ↑, X, Black, ↑, X, LT+RT.

Major League Baseball 2K5: World Series Edition

Create a new profile and enter the following names.

Unlockable	Code
Unlock All Cheats	Ima Cheater
Unlock All Classic Teams	Old Timers
Unlock All Extras	Gimme Goods

Major League Baseball 2K7

Codes

Code	Effect
triplecrown	Increase ability of 3,4,5 hitters
Derek Jeter	Unlock everything (except the cheats you need special codes for)
themick	Unlock Mickey Mantle in free agency

Manhunt

In order to unlock these codes, you must complete each level with 3 stars or better. Then, once you unlock the codes, enter them at the main menu.

Unlockable	Objective	Code
Fully Equipped (All weapons in level and infinite ammo)	Beat Drunk Driving and Graveyard Shift	RT, WHT, LT, BLK, Down, Up, Left, Up
God Mode	Complete whole game	Down, Down, B, Up, X, Y, X, WHT, Up, Up, LT
Helium Hunters (Explode when hit and speak with squeaky voices)	Beat Strapped for Cash and View of Innocence	RT, RT, Y, B, X, BLK, LT, Down
Invisibility (Hunters are blind)	Beat Trained to Kill and Border Patrol	X, X, X, Down, X, Down, B, Up
Monkey Skin	Beat Press Coverage and Wrong Side of the Tracks	X, X, WHT, Down, Y, X, B, Down
Piggsy Skin	Beat Key Personnel and Deliverance	Up, Down, Left, Left, RT, WHT, LT, LT
Rabbit Skin	Beat Kill the Rabbit and Divided They Fall	Left, RT, RT, Y, RT, RT, X, LT
Regeneration (Cash's health regenerates)	Beat Fueled by Hate and Grounds for Assault	WHT, Right, B, WHT, BLK, Down, B, Left
Runner (Player has infinite stamina)	Beat Born Again and Doorway Into Hell	WHT, WHT, LT, WHT, Left, Right, Left, Right
Silence (Hunters are deaf)	Beat Road to Ruin and White Trash	RT, LT, WHT, LT, Right, Left, Left, Left
Super Punch	Beat Mouth of Madness and Doing Time	LT, Y, Y, Y, B, B, B, RT

Marc Ecko's Getting Up: Contents Under Pressure

Enter these passwords in the Cheats menu under Options.

Unlockable	Password
All Art	SIRULLY
All Black Book	SHARDSOFGLASS
All Characters in Versus Mode	STATEYOURNAME
All Combat	Upgrades DOGTAGS
All Legends	NINESIX
All Levels	IPULATOR
All Movies	DEXTERCROWLEY
All Ipod songs	GRANDMACELIA
All Versus Arenas	WORKBITCHES
Infinite Health	MARCUSECKOS
Infinite Skills	FLIPTHESCRIPT
Max Health	BABYLONTRUST
Max Skills	VANCEDALLISTER

Marvel Nemesis: Rise of the Imperfects

Enter these passwords in the Cheat menu under Options.

Unlockable	Password
All Fantastic Four comics	SAVAGELAND
All Tomorrow People comics	NZONE
Electra swimsuit card	THEHAND
Solara swimsuit card	REIKO
Storm's swimsuit card	MONROE

Marvel vs. Capcom 2

Unlockable	How to Unlock
Attack After Fight Is Finished	After you win a fight, press start to attack the other person until the end of the match
Choose Character to Start Match With	At the beginning of a battle, hold a character's assist button, and he/she will be first instead
Use the Same Character 3x Per Team	Unlock all hidden characters and all extra costumes

Mat Hoffman's Pro BMX 2

Enter these codes quickly at the "Press Start" screen. If done correctly you will hear a sound confirming the code worked.

Unlockable	Code
Adrenaline meter always full	↓, A, A, A, RT, RT, RT
Big Foot's videos	RT, ↑, ↓, ←, A, A, A, RT
BMX Costume	X, B, ←, →, ←, X
Boston (in Road Trip)	Y, ↑, ↓, ↓, ↑, Y
Chicago (in Road Trip)	Y, ↑, B, ↑, B, Y
Cory's videos	RT, Y, X, X, Y, Y, Y, RT
Day Smith's videos	RT, X, ←, ←, Y, →, →, RT
Fiery hands & feet	↓, B, B, A, A, RT, RT
Invisible Bikes	↓, ↑, ←, ↓, →, ↓, ←, ↑
Kevin's videos	RT, A, B, ↓, ↑, RT
LA (in Road Trip)	Y, ←, B, B, ←, Y
Mat's videos	RT, ←, X, ←, X, ←, RT
Mike's videos	RT, X, A, A, X, A, A, RT
Nate's videos	RT, ↓, B, X, ↓, B, X, RT

The Matrix: Path of Neo

Unlockables

Unlockable	How to Unlock
Bullet Reflection	Successful completion of The One difficulty
Consume/Drain Mode	Successful completion of Normal difficulty
God Mode	Successful completion of The One Difficulty
Infinite Ammo	Successful completion of Normal Difficulty
Start with Most Weapons	Successful completion of Easy difficulty
Unbreakable Melee Combat Weapons	Successful completion of Easy difficulty

The Matrix: Path of Neo (continued)

Special Combos and their Locations

Combo	Code
The Codebreaker:	LB+B, tap Y, B, tap Y
Quick Kicks:	Y, 4, 4, Y, LB+Y, B+Y
Machine Gun Kick:	Y, 4, 4, 4, Y, LB+Y, B+Y, tap Y
Ultimate Hyper Strike:	Y, 4, 4, Y, LB+Y, B+Y, LB+B, Y
The Beginning of the End:	Y, 4, 4, Y, LB+Y, B+Y, LB+B, tap Y
The One:	Y, 4, 4, 4, Y, LB+Y, B+Y, tap Y, LB+B, tap Y, B, tap Y press A as Neo does the uppercut, spin L 360 at peak of jump

Unlockable	How to Unlock
Machine Gun Kick	Stage—The Chase "I Need an Exit." Find the briefcase in the corner of the market area behind the fruit stands. clear the stage.
Quick Kicks	Stage—Storming the Drain. In the second to last room, touch the top two platforms in the room and clear the stage.
The Beginning of the End	Stage—Seraph's Apology. After returning to the teahouse from the theater, destroy one of the tables and all eight support columns in the room.
The Codebreaker	Stage—Weapon Training. Find the briefcase among the operator's secret stash in the upstairs corridor, when returning to teahouse. Clear the stage.
The One	Stage—The Burly Brawl: Defeat 30 Smiths. A briefcase appears in the center of the level. Pick it up and clear the stage.
Ultimate Hyper Strike	Stage—Redpill Rescue: The Security Guard. Defeat the SWAT team on the stairs in the given time limit and clear the stage.

"The Making of..." Unlockables

Unlockable	How to Unlock
Storyboard Sequence 1	In the Red Pill level, select mission The Key and then complete the bonus objective in the second room without using any guns
Storyboard Sequence 2	In The Frenchman Level, kill the first few enemies. In the dungeon area, go to the red cross, go right and pick up the briefcase, then finish.
Storyboard Sequence 3	Distorted Dimension: Find the Face 2 area with three doors. Press Focus and move the block and open the gate to the center door to find the briefcase.
Storyboard Sequence 4	Distorted Dimension: In the Face 3 area, move directly ahead from the entrance. Drop a few levels down to find the hidden briefcase in a niche.
Storyboard Sequence 5	After finding the previous briefcase in a niche, find the big stained-glass window. Wallrun up it, then follow a ledge to another hidden briefcase.
View Hand-to-Hand Combos	Distorted Dimensions: In the Face 1 area, wallrun up the wall with the windows, then Focus Jump to the focus pack. Look to the left, then Focus Jump.
View Staff Combos	Kung Fu Training: Execute three silent takedowns on all three enemies in the tool shop.
View Sword Combos	Sword Training: Break the pot behind the waterfall.

The Matrix: Path of Neo (continued)

Zion Archives

Unlockable	How to Unlock
Zion Archives	Choose the glyph in the 8 o'clock position in the Atman Principles

Maximum Chase

Go to Options, select Cheat Code, and enter the following.

Unlockable	Code
Black and white mode	9DE5
High Contrast mode	A8D7
Saturation mode	B6FC

Max Payne

Unlockable	Objective
Additional Difficulty Settings—"Dead on Arrival" and "New York Minute"	Complete the game under the "Fugitive" difficulty setting.
Bonus Level	Complete the game in New York Minute mode to unlock a new bonus level in which you have to kill a lot of enemies, all in bullet time.
Cheat Mode	Start a game. Press BACK during gameplay to display the main menu. Then, hold LT + RT + click L + click R, and quickly press WHT, BLK, BLK, WHT, WHT, BLK at the main menu. A cheat option will appear.
Last Challenge Bonus Level	Complete the game under the "Dead on Arrival" difficulty setting.
Secret Programmer Room	Complete the Last Challenge level. The doors in the back of the room will open up to the Remedy Room.

Max Payne 2

Unlockable	Code
All Modes	At any time during the game, pause and enter X,X,X,A,LT,RT,LT,RT

Mech Assault

Unlockable	Code
Completion Bonuses	Complete the game to unlock Ragnarok in local multiplayer mode.

Medal of Honor: European Assault

Codes

To enter Cheat mode, hold LT+RT then D-pad Down, A, X, BLK, B, D-pad Left. Release LT+RT when entering the actual cheat.

Effect	Code
Disable Shell Shock	X, Y, A, B, LT, X
Find OSS Document	A, B, RT, WHT, BLK, LT
Full Adrenaline	B, Y, D-pad Right, X, A, X
God Mode	WHT, BLK, Y, WHT, LT, LT
Kill Nemesis	D-pad Right, D-pad Left, RB, LB, X, Y ↗
Suicide	X, RT, WHT, Y, LT, WHT
Turn off HUD	BLK, LT, BLK, RT, D-pad Up, Y
Unlimited Ammo	LT, Y, B, D-pad Up, A, A

Medal of Honor: Frontline

Enter these passwords in the Options menu.

Unlockable	Password
Achilles Mode	TODADOME
Bullet Shield	NOHITSFORU
Full Bonus Menu	ENCHILADA
Gold on Previous Level	SALMON
Invisible Enemies	GHOSTSHOTS
M.O.H.ton Torpedo	TONSOFUN
Men with Hats	MERCER
Perfectionist Mode	ONEPMPCHMP
Rubber Grenades	ELASTIC
Silver Bullet Mode	KILLERSHOT
Sniper Mode	LONGVIEW

Pause the game to enter this code:

Unlockable	Code
Invincibility	X, LT, B, RT, BACK, Y, X

Medal of Honor: Rising Sun

Unlockable	Code
God Mode	banner
Infinite Ammo	jawfish
All Missions	tuskfish

Midnight Club II

Enter the following codes from the Cheat menu.

Unlockable	Code
All car abilities	greasemonkey
All cars	hotwired
All Locations	theworldismine
Change difficulty levels	howhardcanitbe0 (easiest)
Change difficulty levels	howhardcanitbe1
Change difficulty levels	howhardcanitbe2
Change difficulty levels	howhardcanitbe3
Change difficulty levels	howhardcanitbe4
Change difficulty levels	howhardcanitbe5
Change difficulty levels	howhardcanitbe6
Change difficulty levels	howhardcanitbe7
Change difficulty levels	howhardcanitbe8
Change difficulty levels	howhardcanitbe9 (hardest)
Change Game Speed	howfastcanitbe0 (slowest)
Change Game Speed	howfastcanitbe1
Change Game Speed	howfastcanitbe2
Change Game Speed	howfastcanitbe3
Change Game Speed	howfastcanitbe4
Change Game Speed	howfastcanitbe5
Change Game Speed	howfastcanitbe6
Change Game Speed	howfastcanitbe7
Change Game Speed	howfastcanitbe8
Change Game Speed	howfastcanitbe9 (fastest)

Midnight Club II (continued)

Unlockable	Code
Infinite Nitrous	zoomzoom4
Machine Gun and Rocket	lovenotwar
LAPD car in Arcade Mode	Beat all five circuit races for LA in Arcade mode.
Paris Cop Car	Beat all 6 of the Paris arcade circuit tracks.
SLF450X	Complete 100% of the game
Tokyo Cop Car	Beat all 7 Tokyo arcade circuit tracks.
Veloci	Beat all of the World Champion's races.

Midnight Club 3 Dub Edition

Enter these case sensitive passwords in the Cheats section under Options.

Unlockable	Password
All Cities Unlocked in Arcade Mode	crosscountry
Bunny Ears	getheadl
Chrome Body	haveyouseenthisboy
Faster Pedestrians/All Cities in Arcade Mode	urbansprawl
Flaming Head	trythisathome
Increase Car Mass in Arcade Mode	hyperagro
No Damage	ontheroad
Pumpkin Heads	getheadk
Skull Head	getheadn
Snowman Head	getheadm
Special Move Agro	dfens
Special Move Roar	Rjnr
Special Move Zone	allin
Unlock All Cities	roadtrip
Yellow Smile	getheadj

Midtown Madness 3

Unlockable	Objective
1959 El Dorado Seville	Complete the Washington Pizza Deliverer job.
1967 Ford Mustang	Complete the Washington Stunt Car Driver job.
All Cars	In the car select menu, click (L) while entering the following commands: LT, RT, LT, LT, LT, RT, RT, RT, LT, LT, RT, RT.
Ambulance	Complete the Paris Paramedic job.
Armored Car	Complete the Paris security guard job.
Audi S4 Avant	Complete the first six blitz races in Paris.
Audi TT	Complete the Paris Special Agent job.
Cadillac Escalade	Complete the Washington Limo Driver job.
Cement Truck	Win the first six checkpoint races in Washington.
Chevrolet Corvette Z06	Win the tenth checkpoint race in Washington.
Chevrolet SSR	Complete the first three blitz races in Washington.
Chrysler Crossfire	Win the tenth blitz race in Washington.
Chrysler PT Turbo	Complete the Washington Rental Car Driver job.
Dodge Viper SRT-10	Complete the Washington Private Eye job.
Fire Truck	Win the first six checkpoint races in Paris.
FLE	Complete the Paris Delivery Guy job.
Freightliner Century Class S/T	Complete the first six blitz races in Washington.
Hummer H2 SUV	Complete the Washington Salesman job.

Midtown Madness 3 (continued)

Unlockable	Objective
Koenigsegg CC	Complete all the game.
Limousine	Complete the Paris chauffeur job.
Lotus Esprit V8	Win the tenth Paris Blitz race.
Mini Cooper S	Complete the first three blitz races in Paris.
Paris Bus	Win the first three checkpoint races in Paris.
Paris Police	Complete the Paris Police Officer job.
Saab 9-3 Turbo	Win the tenth checkpoint race in Paris.
Taxi	Complete the Paris Taxi Driver job.
Washington Bus	Win the first three checkpoint races in Washington.
Washington Police	Complete the Washington Police Officer job.

Minority Report

To enter these codes, select the Special menu, then select the Cheats menu.

Unlockable	Code	Unlockable	Code
All Combos	NINJA	Infinite Ammo	MRJUAREZ
All Movies	DIRECTOR	Invincibility	LRGARMS
All Weapons	STRAPPED	Level Warp	PASSKEY
Armor	STEELUP	Level Skip	QUITTER
Baseball Bat	SLUGGER	Lizard Skin	HISSSS
Bouncy Men	BOUNZMEN	Moseley Skin	HAIRLOSS
Clown Skin	SCARYCLOWN	Nara Skin	WEIGHTGAIN
Concept Art	SKETCHPAD	Nikki Skin	BIGLIPS
Convict Skin	JAILBREAK	Pain Arena	MAXIMUMHURT
Do Not Select	DONOTSEL	Rag Doll	CLUMSY
Dramatic Finish	STYLIN	Robot Skin	MRROBOTO
Ending	WIMP	Super Damage	SPINICH
First Person Mode	FPSSTYLE	Super John Skin	SUPERJOHN
GI John Skin	GNRLINFINTRY	Wreck the Joint	CLUTZ
Health	BUTTERUP	Zombie Skin	IAMSODEAD

Mission Impossible: Operation Surma

Unlockable	Code
Level Select	In the Profiles menu, highlight Jasmine Curry and press LT+RT+Y+B. You will be able to choose your level from the Main menu.

MLB SlugFest 2006

Bonus Stadiums

Hit an out of the park home run in the indicated location to unlock the corresponding bonus stadium.

Unlockable	How to Unlock
Atlantis	Hit a home run in AT&T Park
Coliseum	Hit a home run in Fenway Park
Empire	Hit a home run in Yankee Stadium
Forbidden City	Hit a home run in PetCo Park
Rocket Park	Hit a home run in Minute Made Park

Bonus Teams

Unlockable	How to Unlock
Bobble Head	Hit 10 home runs in one game.
Casey	Hit a triple in Wrigley Field.
Dolphins	Hit a home run in Atlantis.

DS
PSP
PS2
PS3
Wii
Xbox
Xbox 360
Index

MLB SlugFest 2006 (continued)

Unlockable	How to Unlock
Eagles	Walk 3 times in one game.
Gladiator	Hit a home run in Coliseum Park.
Horse	Steal 10 times in one game.
Lion	Hit a home run with the Lions in Comerica Park.
Martian	Hit a triple in Rocket Park.
Minotaur	Hit a home run in Forbidden City.
Pinto	Hit a home run at Busch Field.
Rodeo Clowns	Perform a double play.
Tame Evil Clown	Hit a home run with a Yankee in Empire Park.

MLB Slugfest Loaded

Unlockable	Code
Unlock Everything	At the Main Menu, hold X+Y, then press the Right Trigger.

Mortal Kombat: Armageddon

Krypt Kodes

Enter at the ? in the krypt.

Unlockable	How to Unlock
Armageddon Promo Movie	↑, ↑, ↓, ↑, WHT, A
Armory Music	A, X, ←, Y, X, A
Blaze	Y, X, ←, RT, ←, B
Concept Art Blaze	RT, Y, WHT, WHT, RT, X
Concept Art Early Taven	↑, A, WHT, ↓, WHT, A
Concept Art Ed Boon Drawing	RT, ←, ↑, B, WHT, RT
Concept Art Firewall Arena	↑, X, RT, WHT, B, RT
Concept Art Mileena's Car Design	WHT, →, ↑, RT, Y, ↑
Concept Art Pyramid of Argus	A, RT, RT, WHT, ↑, ↑
Concept Art Pyramid of Argus	Y, ←, ←, A, ↓, B
Concept Art Sektor's Pulse Blade	WHT, RT, ←, A, ↑, RT
Concept Art Unused Konquest Trap	B, WHT, Y, ↓, B, ←
Daegon	RT, RT, Y, ↓, ↓, X
Drahmin's Alternate Costume	WHT, →, A, WHT, ↑, ↑
Ed Boon Drawing	RT, ←, ↑, B, WHT, RT
Falling Cliffs Arena	WHT, B, X, A, B, Y
Frost's Alternate Costume	↓, WHT, RT, RT, B, WHT
General Reiko's Map Room Arena	WHT, Y, RT, ↑, A, A
Lin Kuei Palace Tune	WHT, ←, B, A, WHT, →
Meat	↑, X, X, B, B, ↑
Motor Gameplay Movie	Y, ↑, WHT, RT, RT, WHT
Nethership Interior Arena	RT, ←, ←, ↓, RT, X
Nitara's Alternate Costume	↓, RT, ↑, RT, RT, →
Pyramid of Argus Arena	RT, RT, X, A, WHT, ↑
Pyramid of Argus Music	↓, ←, WHT, WHT, ↑, RT
Red Dawn Arena	B, RT, ↑, X, B, ↓
Shang Tsung's Alternate Costume	RT, ←, ↑, B, ↑, WHT
Shinnok's Spire Arena	←, ←, B, ↑, Y, RT
Taven	RT, ←, WHT, ↑, B, ↓
Tekunin Warship Music	↑, B, RT, RT, A

Mortal Kombat: Shaolin Monks

Enter to following codes for the fatalities for Kung Lao.

Unlockable	Code
Arm Cutter	Left, Right, Left, Down, X
Body Slice Fatality	Right, Right, Right, Right, X
Buzzsaw Fatality	Right, Right, Up, Up, X
Friendly Rabbit Fatality	Up, Up, Up, Down, X
Hat Control Mutality	Left, Right, Right, Left, Y
Head Toss Fatality	Left, Right, Left, Left, X
Headache Fatality	Up, Down, Up, Right, X
Many Chops Fatality	Up, Up, Left, Up, X
Mid-Air Slice Fatality	Up, Up, Up, Right, X
Razor Edge Brutality	Left, Left, Up, Up, B
Tornado Mutality	Up, Right, Down, Left, Y

Enter to following codes for the fatalities for Liu Kang.

Unlockable	Code
Arm Rip Fatality	Down, Left, Right, Up, X
Bonebreak Fatality	Left, Up, Up, Right, X
Dragon Fatality	Down, Right, Left, Left, X
Dragon's Fury Mutality	Left, Right, Up, Up, Y
Fire Trails Mutality	Up, Down, Up, Down, Y
Fire/Kick Combo Fatality	Left, Right, Down, Down, X
Flipping Uppercut Fatality	Up, Right, Down, Left, X
Headclap Fatality	Right, Up, Right, Up, X
Rage Mode Brutality	Right, Up, Down, Down, B
Shaolin Soccer Fatality	Down, Left, Up, Right, X
Stomp Fatality	Left, Left, Left, Up, X

Enter these codes at the Main menu.

Unlockable	Code
Mortal Kombat 2	X, Up, Down, Right, Left, RT, X
Scorpion	X, Up, LT, RT, Left, Right, X
Sub-Zero	X, Down, Up, LT, LT, Up, X

Motocross Mania 3

Enter these codes at the Main menu.

Unlockable	Code
All bike upgrades	Up, Left, Down, Right, Up, Down, Down, Left, Down, X
All bikes	Up, Left, Down, Right, Up, Left, Down, Up, X
All levels	Up, Left, Down, Right, Up, Left, Down, Left, Left, X
All weapons	Up, Left, Down, Right, Up, Left, Down, Left, Down, X

Moto GP 2

Unlockable	Objective
Alex Barros	Earn 250,000 points in stunt mode.
Carlos Chera	Earn 100,000 points in stunt mode.
Edgy	Earn 325 championship points.
Floating bike mode	Enter kingpin as your custom bike name.
Legend difficulty	Win the championship on the champion difficulty setting.
Max Biaggi	Get an overall total of 500,000 points in stunt mode to unlock Max Biaggi.
Mini-Games	To get a few minigames, go to the options menu and go to the text credits. When you find the text for the minigames, press A.

Moto GP 2 (continued)

Unlockable	Objective
Pop Video	Earn 375 championship points.
Saturate	Earn 300 championship points on rookie difficulty.
Season Highlights	Finish first in any track to see its highlight video.
Sheridan	Complete all the challenges in championship.
Tohru Ukawa	Earn 750,000 points in stunt mode.
Turbo	Earn 275 championship points.
Valentino Rossi	Earn 1000000 points in stunt mode.

MTX Mototrax

Unlockable	Objective
Officer Dick	Complete Free Ride in Career mode.
Police Bike	Complete all Freestyle Events.
Race as a Slipknot rider	Enter 86657457 at the Cheat Menu.
Sky view	HIC
Slipknot Bike	Complete Master Supercross.
Slipknot movie	Enter 23F7IC5 at the Cheat Menu.
Speed Demon	Complete Career mode.
Super Fast Acceleration	Enter JIH345 at the Cheat Menu.
Trick Bot	Complete Freestyle in Career mode.
Unlocks all Butter Finger gear	B77393
Unlocks all Sobe gear	50B3
Unlocks Officer Dick	BADG3

MTX vs. ATV Unleashed

Enter the codes in the Cheat menu.

Unlockable	Code
50cc Bikes	Minimoto
All Freestyle Tracks	Huckit
Everything	Toolazy

Murakumo

Unlockable	Objective
Expert mission	Complete scenario mode with all missions at A rank.
Free mission	Beat Scenario mode.
Sound Test mode	Beat Expert mode all with double S ranks.
"Special Art"	Beat expert mode with any rank.

MX Unleashed

Unlockable	Objective
All Bonuses	Enter clappedout under Career Completion in the cheats section.

Narc

Enter these codes while playing—do not pause the game.

Unlockable	Code
All Drugs and $10,000	Repeatedly press LT+RT+click L.
All Weapons	Repeatedly press LT+RT+click R.
Infinite Ammo	Repeatedly press LT+RT+♀. (Only works for the weapon equipped.)
Invincibility	Repeatedly press LT+RT+A.
The Refinery	Repeatedly press LT+RT+X.

NASCAR 2005 Chase for the Cup

Enter these codes in the Edit Driver screen. The passwords need to be entered as a first name and a last name.

Unlockable	Code
2,000,000 Prestige Points	You TheMan
$10,000,000	Walmart Nascar
All Thunder Plates	Open Sesame
Dale Earnhardt	The Intimidator
Exclusive Race Track	Walmart Exclusive

NASCAR 06: Total Team Control

In Fight to the Top mode, go to the Edit Driver screen and enter the following passwords as your first and last names. (Note: case sensitive)

Unlockable	Password
$10,000,000	Walmart Money
Dale Jarett in the UPS "Big Brown Truck"	Race TheTruck
Max Fan Level	Super Star
Max Prestige	MeMyself AndI
Max Team Prestige	All ForOne
Unlock All Chase Plates	Gimme Gimme
Unlocks Dale Sr.	The Intimidator
Walmart Raceway, Walmart Cars, and Walmart Sponsorship for Custom Car	Walmart Exclusive

NASCAR Heat 2002

Enter these codes at the Main Menu. The screen will flash to indicate correct code entry.

Unlockable	Code
Credits	↑,↓,←,→,White,↑,↓
Hardcore Realism Mode	↑,↓,←,→,White,↑,↓
High Suspension	↑,↓,←,→,White,←,→
Mini Cars	↑,↓,←,→,White,↓,↑
Paintball Mode for Single and Head to Head Race	↑,↓,←,→,White,↑,↑—while racing press ↑ to fire paintballs.
Wireframe Cars	↑,↓,←,→,White,→,←

NASCAR Thunder 2002

Enter these codes at the main menu. The screen flashes to indicate correct code entry.

Unlockable	Code
Credits	↑, ↓, ←, →, White, ↑, ↓
Hardcore Realism mode	↑, ↓, ←, →, White, ↑, ↓
High Suspension	↑, ↓, ←, →, White, ←, →
Mini Cars	↑, ↓, ←, →, White, ↓, ↑
Paintball mode for Single and Head to Head Race	↑, ↓, ←, →, White, ↑, ↑—while racing press ↑ to fire paintballs
Wireframe Cars	↑, ↓, ←, →, White, →, ←

NBA 2K2

Cheat Menu: Enter the Options menu and select "Gameplay." Hold [Left] + [Right] and press [Start]. The "Codes" selection is now unlocked at the Options menu.

Unlockable	Code
Airball	Select "Street" at the main menu. Press [White], then hold [LT] and press [Y], [Y]. Press [Start] and "Airball" appears to confirm correct code entry.
Bonus Teams	Enter MEGASTARS as a case-sensitive code to unlock the Sega Sports, Visual Concepts, and Team 2K2 in Exhibition and Street modes.
Muhammad Ali and Michael Jackson	Press [Start] and hold [LT] during an Exhibition game. The screen shakes to confirm correct code entry. Go onto the Sixers and they should be on the starting lineup.

Enter Options mode and choose the Game Play menu. Once in the menu, hold [Left], Left Analog Stick Right, Start. After you exit the Game Play menu, the Codes Entry screen selection is now available.

Unlockable	Password
NBA 2K2 Team, Sega Sports Team, Visual Concepts Team	MEGASTARS

NBA 2K6

From the Main menu, go to "Features," then "Codes" to enter the following codes.

Unlockable	Code
2005-2006 Pacers Uniform	31andonly
2K Sports Team	2ksports
Nike Up Tempo Pro Shoes	anklebreakers
Nike Zoom Kobe 1 Shoes	kobe

From the Main menu, go to "Features," then "THE CRIB." Go to the PowerBar vending machine and enter the following codes.

Unlockable	Code
+10 Bonus for Defensive Awareness	lockdown
+10 Bonus for Offensive Awareness	getaclue
Max Durability	noinjury
Powerbar Tattoo	pbink
Unlimited Stamina	nrgmax
Unlock All Items	criball

NBA Ballers

The following cheats are entered at the Versus Screen, right before the match starts. [Y] is the first number, [B] is the second number, and [X] is the third number. Press the corresponding button as many times as stated.

Unlockable	Code
2X Juice Replenish	4 3 1
Alley-Oop Ability	7 2 5
Alternate Gear	1 2 3
Baby Ballers	4 2 3
Back-In Ability	1 2 2
Back-In Ability	3 1 7
Big Head Mode	1 3 4

Unlockable	Code
Expanded Move Set	5 1 2
Fire Ability	7 2 2
Good Handling	3 3 2
Half House Meter	3 6 7
Hot Spot	6 2 7
Kid Ballers	4 3 3
Legal Goal Tending	7 5 6

NBA Ballers (continued)

Unlockable	Code	Unlockable	Code
No Weather	112	Rain	222
Paper Ballers	354	Random Moves	300
Perfect Free Throws	327	Shows Shot Percentage	012
Play As Afro Man	517	Snow	333
Play As Agent	557	Speedy Players	213
Play As BiznezMan-A	537	Stunt Dunk Ability	374
Play As BiznezMan-B	527	Super Back-Ins	235
Play As Coach	567	Super Blocks	124
Play As Secretary	547	Super Push	315
Put Back Ability	313	Super Steals	215
Pygmy	425	Tournament Mode	011
R2R Mode	008	Young Ballers	443

Go to "Inside Stuff" and select "Phrase-ology." Enter the following codes to unlock goodies:

Unlockable	Code
Allen Iverson's Alternate Gear	killer crossover
Allen Iverson's Studio	the answer
Alonzo Mourning	zo
Amare Stoudamire	rising sun
Baron Davis	Stylin & Profilin
Ben Wallace's alternate outfit	radio controlled cars
Bill Russell	celtics dynasty
Bill Walton	towers of power
Chris Webber	24 seconds
Clyde Drexler	clyde the glide
Darryl Dawkins	rim wrecker
Dikembe Mutumbo	in the paint
Dominique Wilkins	dunk fest
Elton Brand	rebound
George Gervin	the ice man cometh
Jalen Rose	bring it
Jason Kidd	pass the rock
Jason Williams	give and go
Jerry Stackhouse's Alt. Gear	Stop Drop and Roll
John Stockton	court vision
Julius Erving	one on one
Karl Malone	special delivery
Karl Malone's Devonshire Estate	ice house
Kevin Garnett's alternate outfit	boss hoss
Kevin McHale	holla back
Kobe Bryant's Alt. Gear	Japanese steak
Larry Bird	hoosier
Latrell Sprewell	spree
Lebron James	king james
Magic Johnson	laker legends
Manu Ginobili gear	manu
Michael Finley	student of the game
Nene Hilario	rags to riches

NBA Ballers (continued)

Unlockable	Code
Oscar Robertson's Alt. Gear	Ain't No Thing
Pete Maravich	pistol pete
Rashard Lewis	fast forward
Rasheed Wallace	bring down the house
Ray Allen	all star
Reggie Miller's Alt. Gear	From Downtown
Richard Hamilton	rip
Robert Parish's Alt. Gear	The Chief
Scottie Pippen	playmaker
Scottie Pippen's Yacht	nice yacht
Shaq's alternate outfit	diesel rules the paint
Special Movie #1	juice house
Special Movie #2	nba showtime
Special Shoe #1	dub deuce
Stephon Marbury	platinum playa
Steve Francis	ankle breaker
Steve Francis's Alt. Gear	Rising Star
Steve Nash	hair canada
Tim Duncan	make it take it
Tony Parker's Alt. outfit	run and shoot
Tracy McGrady	living like a baller
Wally Szczerbiak	world
Walt Frazier	Penetrate and Perpetrate
Wes Unseld	old school
Willis Reed	hall of fame
Wilt Chamberlain	wilt the stilt
Yao Ming	center of attention
Yao Ming's Grade School	prep school

NBA Jam

Create a new profile using these names.

Unlockable	Code
Unlock Everything	-LPP-
Unlock the NBA Jam Development Team	CREDITS

NBA Live 06

Go to "My NBA Live," then "NBA Codes" and enter the following codes.

Unlockable	Code
Adidas A3 Garnett 3 Shoes	DRI239CZ49
S. Carter III LE Shoes	JZ3SCARTVY
TMac5 Black Shoes	258SHQW95B
TMac5 White Shoes	HGS83KP234P

NBA Live 07

Passwords

Password	Effect
99B6356HAN	Adidas Artillery II (black)
NTGNFUE87H	Adidas Artillery II (white)
7FB3KS9JQ0	Adidas BTB Low (St. Patty's edition)

NBA Live 07 (continued)

Password	Effect
BV6877HB9N	Adidas C-Billups (All-Star edition)
85NVLDMWS5	Adidas C-Billups (Vegas edition)
CLT2983NC8	Adidas Campus Lt (St. Patty's edition)
CC98KKL814	Adidas Crazy 8 (St. Patty's edition)
22OIUJKMDR	Adidas Equipment Bball (St. Patty's edition)
HYIOUHCAAN	Adidas Garnett Bounce (All-Star edition)
KDZ2MQL17W	Adidas Garnett Bounce (Vegas edition)
23DN1PPOG4	Adidas Gil-Zero (All-Star edition)
QQQ3JCUYQ7	Adidas Gil-Zero (Vegas edition)
369V6RVU3G	Adidas Gil-Zero Mid (Away)
1GSJC8JWRL	Adidas Gil-Zero Mid (Home)
FE454DFJCC	Adidas Stealth (All-Star edition)
MCJK843NNC	Adidas T-Mac 6 (All-Star edition)
84GF7EJG8V	Adidas T-Mac 6 (Vegas edition)
PNBBX1EVT5	Air Jordan V Black/White
VIR13PC451	Air Jordan V White/Blue/Grey
IB7G8NN91Z	Air Jordan V White/Red/Black
WOCNW4KL7L	East away uniform
5654ND43N6	East home uniform
JUL38TC485	Jordan Melo M3 Black
WEDX671H7S	New Bobcats road uniform
VCBI89FK83	New Jazz road uniform
D4SAA98U5H	New Nets road uniform
QV93NLKXQC	New Wizards road uniform
XX93BVL20U	West away uniform
993NSKL199	West home uniform

NBA Street Vol 2

Unlockable	Code/Objective
All Quicks	Hold LT and press Y, B, Y, X.
Alternate Ball (NBA or ABA)	Hold LT and press B, X, B, X.
Always Legend Trails	Hold LT and press Y, Y, Y, X.
Big Heads	Hold LT and press B, X, X, B.
Easy 2 pointers	Hold LT and press Y, B, X, Y.
Explosive Rims	Hold LT and press B, B, B, Y.
Hard 2 Pointers	Hold LT and press Y, X, B, Y.
Nelly and the St. Lunatics	Get 750 reward points or win 20 games in Pick Up.
No Counters	Hold LT and press Y, Y, B, B.
No HUD	Hold LT and press X, B, B, B.
Street Kids	Hold LT and press Y, Y, B, X.
Unlimited Turbo	Hold LT and press X, X, Y, Y.
1985 Jordan	Collect the Street School trophy, NBA Challenge trophy and the Be A Legend trophy.
Biggie Little	Beat the tournament on Broad Street in Philly.

DS PSP PS2 PS3 Wii Xbox Xbox 360 Index

NBA Street Vol 2 (continued)

Unlockable	Code/Objective
Bill Walton Jersey	Earn 1,000,000 trick points or more in a game.
Clyde Drexler Jersey	Collect 1 reputation star in Legend Mode.
Dime	Complete the tournament in Lincoln College.
Elgin Baylor Jersey	Get 20 or more blocks in a game.
Jerry West Jersey	Win a game without getting blocked.
Just Blaze	Get 500 Reward Points or win 15 games in Pick Up.
Osmosis	Win the Mosswood tournament in Legend mode.
Street Champ Costume	Complete *Be A Legend* by earning all 500/500 progress points.
Stretch	Beat the Soul in the Hole Tournament.
Whitewater	Complete the tournament in Green Lake to Whitewater.
WNBA Ball	Hold LT and press B, Y, Y, B.

NCAA Football 06

Under MY NCAA, go into Pennant Collection. Click the Right Analog Stick to enter any of these passwords.

Unlockable	Password
1ST and 15 mode-Opponent must gain 15 yards for 1ST down	THANKS
2003 All Americans	FUMBLE
All Time Clemson Team	Death Valley
All Time Notre Dame	Golden Domer
All Time Ohio State	Killer Nuts
All Time Oklahoma State Team	Go Pokes
All Time Texas Team	Hook Em
All-Colorado Team	Glory
All-Florida Team	Great To Be
All-Kansas State Team	Victory
All-Michigan Team	Go Blue
All-Oklahoma Team	Boomer
All-Oregon Team	Quack Attack
All-Penn State Team	We Are
All-Syracuse Team	Orange Crush
All-Time Alabama	ROLL TIDE
All-Time Auburn	WAR EAGLE
All-Time Florida State Team	UPRISING
All-Time Miami	RAISING CANE
All-Time Mississippi State Team	HAIL STATE
All-Time Nebraska	GO BIG RED
All-Time Tennessee	BIG ORANGE
All-Time Texas A&M Team	Gig Em

Unlockable	Password
All-Time USC	FIGHT ON
All-UNC Team	Rah Rah
All-Virginia Tech Team	Tech Triumph
All-Washington Team	Bow Down
Arkansas All-Time Team	WOOPIGSOOIE
Arkansas Mascot	Bear Down
Baylor power-up	SIC EM
Blink mode-ref spots the ball short for opponent	FOR
Boing Pennant; opponent drops passes more	REGISTERING
Butter Fingers (#204)	With EA
Crossed The Line card	TIBURON
Cuffed mode	EA SPORTS
Extra Credit; Gives 4 points per interception, 3 for each sack	TOUCHDOWN
Free play pennant	IMPACT
Gives you points when your player is injured (#211)	Heisman
Hard to Tackle	Break Free
Helium (#208)	In the Zone
Illinois ratings boost	OSKEE WOW
Increased Pass Rush	Turnover
Iowa All-Time Team	On Iowa
Iowa State mascot team	RED AND GOLD

NCAA Football 06 (continued)

Unlockable	Password
KU Mascot	Rock Chalk
Makes wind go in your direction	Sideline
Minnesota All-Time Team	Rah Rah Rah
Mizzouri All-Time Team	Mizzou Rah
Molasses mode	HOME FIELD
MSU Mascot	Go Green
NC State Mascot	Go Pack
NU Mascot	Go Cats
Pittsburgh All-Time Team	LETS GO PITT
Purdue All-Time Team	BOILER UP
QB dud mode	ELITE 11
Stiffed mode	NCAA
Take Your Time (#223)	Football
Texas Tech Boost	Fight
Thread the needle mode	2006
Tough as Nails (#226)	Offense
Trip (#227)	Defense
UK Mascot	On On UK
Wake Mascot	Go Deacs Go
What A Hit mode	BLITZ
WSU Mascot	All Hail

NCAA Football '07

Passwords

At the Pennant Collection screen, press Back, then enter one of the following codes to activate the corresponding cheat function.

Unlockable	Code
2004 All-Americans #273	Fumble
Alabama All-Time Team	Roll Tide
Arizona Mascot Team	Bear Down
Arkansas All-Time Team	Woopigsooie
Auburn All-Time Team	War Eagle
Badgers All-Time Team	U Rah Rah
Clemson All-Time Team	Death Valley
Colorado All-Time Team	Glory
Cuffed #206	EA Sports
Florida All-Time Team	Great To Be
Florida State All-Time Team	Uprising
Georgia All-Time Team	Hunker Down
Georgia Tech Mascot Team	Ramblinwreck
Iowa All-Time Team	On Iowa
Iowa State Mascot Team	Red and Gold
Jumbalaya #211	Heisman
Kansas Mascot Team	Rock Chalk
Kansas State All-Time Team	Victory
Kentucky Mascot Team	On On UK
LSU All-Time Team	Geaux Tigers
Miami All-Time Team	Raising Cane
Michigan All-Time Team	Go Blue
Michigan State Mascot Team	Go Green
Minnesota Mascot Team	Rah Rah Rah
Mississippi State All-Time Team	Hail State
Mizzouri All-Time Team	Mizzou Rah
Nebraska All-Time Team	Go Big Red
North Carolina All-Time Team	Rah Rah

NCAA Football '07 (continued)

Unlockable	Code
North Carolina State Mascot Team	Go Pack
Notre Dame All-Time Team	Golden Domer
NU Mascot Team	Go Cats
Ohio State All-Time Team	Killer Nuts
Oklahoma All-Time Team	Boomer
Oklahoma State All-Time Team	Go Pokes
Ole Miss Mascot Team	Hotty Totty
Oregon All-Time Team	Quack Attack
Penn State All-Time Team	We Are
Pittsburgh All-Time Team	Lets Go Pitt
Purdue All-Time Team	Boiler Up
South Carolina Mascot Team	Go Carolina
Stiffed #222	NCAA
Syracuse All-Time Team	Orange Crush
Take Your Time #224	Football
Tennessee All-Time Team	Big Orange
Texas A&M All-Time Team	Gig Em
Texas Longhorns All-Time Team	Hook Em
Texas Tech #160	Fight
UCLA All-Time Team	Mighty
USC All-Time Team	Fight On
Virginia All-Time Team	Wahoos
Virginia Tech All-Time Team	Tech Triumph
Wake Forest Mascot Team	Go Deacs Go
Washington All-Time Team	Bow Down
Washington State Mascot Team	All Hail
West Virginia Mascot Team	Hail WV

Unlock Vince Young

Unlockable	How to Unlock
Vince Young	Beat Dynasty Mode with the Texas Longhorns

Need for Speed Carbon

Enter at the main menu.

Unlockable	Code
Extra Cash	↓, ↑, ←, ↓, →, ↑, Ⓧ, Ⓑ
Infinite Crew Charge	↓, ↑, ↑, →, ←, ←, →, Ⓧ
Infinite NOS	←, ↑, ←, ↓, ←, ↓, →, Ⓧ
Infinite SpeedBreaker	↓, →, →, ←, →, ↑, ↓, Ⓧ
Need For Speed Carbon Logo Vinyls Unlocked	→, ↑, ↓, ↑, ↓, ←, →, Ⓧ
Need For Speed Carbon Special Logo Vinyls Unlocked	↑, ↑, ↓, ↓, ↓, ↓, ↑, Ⓧ

Need for Speed: Hot Pursuit 2

Unlock All Tracks

Unlockable	How to Unlock
Unlock all tracks	X, B, B, LB, LB, Up, Down, Right, Up

Unlockable Cars

Unlockable	How to Unlock
Dodge Viper GTS	2,000,000 points
Ferrari F50	Lead a single race with full grid and advanced for 8 laps
Ford Crown Victoria	Complete Hot Pursuit Event 5
Lamborghini Murcielago	3,000,000 points
Lamborghini Diablo 6.0 VT	2,500,000 points
McLaren F1	4,000,000 points
McLaren F1 LM	5 million points OR win world championship
Mercedes CLK GTR	4,500,000 points
Porsche 911 Turbo	800,000 points
Porsche Carrera GT	3,500,000 points
Vauxhall VX220	Win a single race with first place in all laps

Unlockable Tracks

Complete the following events to unlock the corresponding race tracks.

Unlockable	How to Unlock
Alpine Trail	Championship event 22
Ancient Ruins II	Ultimate racer event 12
Autumn Crossing	Ultimate racer event 17
Autumn Crossing II	Ultimate racer event 14
Calypso Coast	Ultimate racer event 10
Calypso Coast II	Ultimate racer event 26
Coastal Parklands	Championship event 4
Desert Heat II	Championship event 25
Fall Winds II	Championship event 24
Island Outskirts II	Championship event 8
Mediterranean Paradise II	Championship event 14
National Forest	Ultimate racer event 1
National Forest II	Ultimate racer event 6
Outback	Championship event 11
Outback II	Ultimate racer event 25
Palm City Island	Ultimate racer event 28
Palm City Island II	Ultimate racer event 29
Rocky Canyons	Championship event 27
Rocky Canyons II	Championship event 9
Scenic Drive II	Championship event 6
Tropical Circuit	Championship event 29
Tropical Circuit II	Championship event 28

Need for Speed Most Wanted

All codes should be entered at the Start screen.

Unlockable	Code
Unlocks Burger King Challenge Event (#69)	Up, Down, Down, Down, Left, Right, Left, Right
Unlocks Free Engine Upgrade Bonus Marker (Can be used in the backroom of the customization shops)	Up, Up, Down, Down, Left, Right, Up, Down
Unlocks Special Edition Castrol Ford GT (Which is added to your bonus cars)	Left, Right, Left, Right, Up, Down, Up, Down

Need for Speed Underground

Enter the following codes at the Main menu.

Unlockable	Code
Circuit Tracks	Down, RT, RT, RT, BLK, BLK, X
Drift Tracks	Left, Left, Left, Left, Right, BLK, RT, WHT
Drag Tracks	Right, X, Left, RT, X, LT, WHT, BLK
Sprint Tracks	Up, BLK, BLK, BLK, RT, Down, Down, Down

Need for Speed Underground 2

Codes are entered at the Main menu.

Unlockable	Code
$1,000 for Career Mode	Left, Left, Right, X, X, Right, LT, RT
Best Buy Vinyl	Up, Down, Up, Down, Down, Up, Right, Left

NFL Street

Enter the following passwords as your User name.

Unlockable	Code
NFL Legends	classic
Xecutioner Team	excellent
Kay Slay Team	kayslay
All Stadiums	travel

NFL Street 2

Enter these codes in the Cheats menu.

Unlockable	Code
AFC East All-Stars	EAASFSCT
AFC North All-Stars	NAOFRCTH
AFC South All-Stars	SAOFUCTH
AFC West All-Stars	WAEFSCT
All players will have a maxed out catching stat	MagnetHands

NHL 2K6

Enter this as a profile name. Case Sensitive.

Unlockable	Password
Unlock everything	Turco813

NHL Hitz 2002

Activate Cheat Menu: Press X, Y, and B to change the icons in the first, second, and third boxes respectively at the Match-Up screen. The numbers in the following list indicate the number of times each button is pressed. After the icons have been changed, press the D-Pad in the indicated direction to enable the code. For example, to enter 1-2-3 Left, press X, Y(2), B(3), Left.

NHL Hitz 2002 (continued)

Unlockable	Code
Big Head Player	2-0-0 →
Big Head Team	2-2-0 ←
Big Hits	2-3-4 ↓
Big Puck	1-2-1 ↑
Bulldozer Puck	2-1-2 ←
Disable Previous Code	0-1-0 ↓
Domino Effect	0-1-2 →
First to Seven Wins	3-2-3 ←
Hitz Time	1-0-4 →
Hockey Ball	1-3-3 ←
Huge Head Player	3-0-0 →
Huge Head Team	3-3-0 ←
Huge Puck	3-2-1 ↑
Late Hits	3-2-1 ↓
More Time to Enter Codes	3-3-3 →
No Crowd	2-1-0 →
No Fake Shots	4-2-4 ↓
No One-Timers	2-1-3 ←
No Puck Out	1-1-1 ↓
Pinball Boards	4-2-3 →
Rain Mode	1-4-1 ←
Show Shot Speed	1-0-1 ↑
Show the Team's Hot Spot	2-0-1 ↑
Skills Versus	2-2-2 ↓
Snow Mode	1-2-1 ←
Tennis Ball	1-3-2 ↓
Turbo Boost	0-0-2 ↑
Unlimited Turbo	4-1-3 →
Win Fights for Goals	2-0-2 ←

NHL Hitz Pro

Enter these codes as User Names. To turn on these codes, pause the game and select Settings, then select Visuals, followed by Cheats.

Unlockable	Code
Big Player Head	HERK
Big Team Heads	INGY
Unlockable	**Code**
Different Puck Size	211S
Different Puck Shadow	SASG
Glowing Puck	CARB

Oddworld Stranger's Wrath

Codes

This is all done in game, with no need to pause. Insert a second controller into port #2 on your Xbox. Remove the second controller. On controller 1, press X, X, Y, Y, B, B, A, A to activate Cheat mode. You hear a sound confirming that Cheat mode has been activated.

Unlockable	How to Unlock
1,000 Extra Moolah	L, L, R, R, L, L, R, R
Invincibility	X, Y, A, B, X, Y
Level Select	Start a new game and enter the following Player Name: ©@®&
New Yolk City's Black Market	After bagging X'Plosives but before taking on a new bounty, Stranger can ask townfolk about where X got all his weapons. On the side of the road is a female clakker who knows about a black market in town, and she then tells you the password. The Black Market is located up a rope across from the Bounty Store. Go down the hallway, recite the password, and gain access. The store's items include: Bola Blasts, Wasps, Regen Upgrade, Stamina Upgrade, and Steel Knuckles.

Oddworld Stranger's Wrath (continued)

Unlockable	How to Unlock
Secret Grubb Statue	When you complete the Eugene Ius bounty you end up in a Grubb village. Proceed into the village by jumping across the rooftops. Turn right and keep going forward and you see a break to the right, leading to a little maze-like area. Turn right and there's a small forked path. Go left and you're right next to a rope. Climb it and jump on to the roof. You can see another rope that you have to jump onto. When you jump on it you can see a boarded-up window. Break it by shooting it or meleeing it. When you enter the room there is a shiny Grubb statue. It's worth a bit of moolah.
Sepia Graphics Filter	This code makes the graphics a brownish-yellow color that's synonymous with the western theme seen in Stranger's Wrath. While in-game and only one controller is plugged in (the first port), press LT, L, R, A, B, RT, B, A, R, L, LT After entering this, take a second controller, plug it into the fourth controller slot, then pull it back out. If done correctly, you will see the graphics filter change. To deactivate the code, repeat this process.

Oddworld: Munch's Oddysee

Unlock Alternate Endings

The game endings below can be obtained depending on your Quarma level near the end of the game. You can check your detailed Quarma level on the Quarma Bar in the Pause menu.

Unlockable	How to Unlock
Angelic Quarma Ending	Beat the game with the Quarma Bar filled higher that 75%
Bad Quarma Ending	Beat Level 23 with the Quarma Bar filled less than 50%
Neutral Quarma Ending	Beat the game with the Quarma Bar filled between 50% and 75%

Open Season

Unlockable Minigames

Unlockable	How to Unlock
Duck Chorus	Complete "Crazy Quackers"
Flowers for My Deer	Complete "Meet the Skunks"
Rise, Rise to the Top!	Complete "Beaver Damage"
Shake That Butt!	Complete "Hunted"
Wild Memory	Complete "Shaw's Shack"

Outlaw Golf

Unlockable	Objective
Atlas Driver	Complete the Stroke Me event.
Atlas Fairway Woods	Complete the Not-So-Goodfellas event.
Atlas Irons	Complete the High Rollers event.
Atlas Putter (Black)	Complete the All the Marbles event.
Atlas Putter Gold	Complete the Suave's Revenge event.
Atlas Wedge	Complete the Pretty in Pink event.
Boiler Maker Fairway Woods	Complete the Hole Lotta Luv event.
Boiler Maker Irons	Complete the Jersey Ball Bash event.
Boiler Maker Putter	Complete the Sun Stroke event.
Boiler Maker Wedge	Complete the Back 9 Shuffle event.
Bonus Costumes	Hold LT and press Y, Y, WHT, Y, BLK, Y at the character selection screen.

Outlaw Golf (continued)

Unlockable	Objective
C.C.	Complete the Hot, Hot, Hot event.
Cincinnati Balls	Complete the Rough Riders event.
Cincinnati Driver	Complete the Ol' Blood and Guts event.
Cincinnati Fairway Woods	Complete the Full Frontal event.
Cincinnati Irons	Complete the Stroke Me Again event.
Cincinnati Wedge	Complete the Blister in the Sun event.
Coiler Maker Driver	Complete the Money Talks event.
Distract Opponent	Start a game with two or more players. While the other person is hitting the ball, press (A) to say things to distract them.
Doc Diggler	Complete the Ladies Night event.
Ecstasy Balls	Complete the Scorched Earth Classic event.
Ecstasy Putter	Complete the Motley Crew event.
Killer Miller	Complete the Test Drive event.
Master Code	Start a new game and enter Golf_Gone_Wild as a case-sensitive name, including underscores, to unlock all characters, clubs, and stages.
Nelson Balls	Complete the Different Strokes event.
Python Driver	Complete the Heat Rash Invitational event.
Python Fairway Woods	Complete the Tough Crowd event.
Python Irons	Complete the A Hole in the Sun event.
Python Wedge	Complete the Garden State Stroke Fest event.
Scrummy	Complete the Odd Ball Classic event.
Suave's Balls	Complete the Garden State Menage a Trois event.
Suki	Complete the Baked on the Bone event.
Trixie	Complete the Chicks with Sticks event.

Outlaw Golf 2

Unlockable	Code
Big Head Mode	At any time during the game, hold (LT) and press (B),(A),(B),(Y),↓,←.
Everything	Enter I Have No Time as your name.

Outlaw Volleyball

Unlockable	Code
All Characters	At the character select screen, hold (LT) and press ←,(WHT),→,(WHT).
All Courts	On Court Selection Screen, hold (LT) and press ↑,↓,↑,↓,←,←,→,→.
Big Head Mode	During gameplay, hold (LT) and press (B),(A),(B),(Y).
Maximum Stats	In Exhibition mode, hold (RT) and press ←,(WHT),→,(WHT).
Time Bombs	In Exhibition mode, hold (LT) and press (A),(B),(B),(Y), and (A)+(X) together.

Outrun 2

To enter these codes, select Outrun Challenge, then select Gallery, and last, select Enter Code.

Unlockable	Code
All Cars	DREAMING
All Mission Stages	THEJOURNEY
All Music	RADIOSEGA
Bonus Tracks	TIMELESS
Original Outrun	NINETEEN86
Reverse Tracks	DESREVER

Outrun 2006 Coast to Coast

To enter these passwords create a license. Then go into Edit License and change the name to the password. Do not press the Done button—instead, press the B to back out of the screen.

Unlockable	Password
100% Complete	ENTIRETY
1,000,000 Outrun Miles	MILESANDMILES

Over the Hedge

Unlock Minigames and Attacks

Unlockable	How to Unlock
Unlock Attack: Finishing Moves	Complete 20 Objectives
Unlock Attack: Ground Pound	Complete 50 Objectives
Unlock Minigame: Bumper Carts 1	Complete 15 Objectives
Unlock Minigame: Bumper Carts 2	Complete 45 Objectives
Unlock Minigame: Race Track 1	Complete 25 Objectives
Unlock Minigame: Race Track 2	Complete 60 Objectives
Unlock Minigame: Range Driver 1	Complete 10 Objectives
Unlock Minigame: Range Driver 2	Complete 40 Objectives

Panzer Dragoon Orta

Unlockable	Objective/Code
Box Game Mode	Complete the game under the Hard difficulty setting or accumulate fifteen hours of gameplay.
Flight Records Option	Complete the game under any difficulty setting or accumulate five hours of gameplay.
Pandora's Box Options	Accumulate twenty hours of gameplay to unlock most of the Pandora's Box Appendix options, including the Panzer Dragoon game.
Panzer Dragoon Dragon-Only Mode (Only the lock-on weapons are available with this code.)	Enable the "Power-ups" code, followed by ←, ←, →, →, ↑, ↓, ↑, ↓, LT, RT. The sound of the dragon being hit confirms correct code entry.
Panzer Dragoon Episode 0	Press ↑, ↑, ↑, ↓, ↓, ↓, ←, →, ←, →, ←, →, LT, RT at the Panzer Dragoon main menu. Shoot enemies to restore your health, which gradually decreases during gameplay.
Panzer Dragoon Episode Select	Press ↑, ↑, ↓, ↓, ←, →, ←, →, X, Y, White at the Panzer Dragoon main menu.
Panzer Dragoon Game	Complete the game or accumulate five hours of gameplay to unlock the original Panzer Dragoon game in the Pandora's Box Appendix.
Panzer Dragoon Invincible Mode	Press LT, LT, RT, RT, ↑, ↓, ←, → at the Panzer Dragoon main menu. The sound of the dragon being hit and the phrase "Invincible Mode" appears to confirm correct code entry.
Panzer Dragoon Power Ups	Press ↑, X, →, Y, ↓, White, ←, Y, ↑, X at the Panzer Dragoon Easy Game Options screen. The Sega logo turns into a polygon woman. This normally occurs after you complete the game without dying. Go to the Episodes screen, and hold B for red lasers, Black for missiles, Y for rapid fire, or White for a wide-shot weapon.

Panzer Dragoon Orta (continued)

Unlockable	Objective/Code
Panzer Dragoon Red Sega Polygon Man	Press Up, X, Right, Y, Down, White, Left, Y, Up, X at the Panzer Dragoon main menu. The sound of the dragon being hit confirms correct code entry. After finishing the last continue, the polygon Sega figure is red instead of blue.
Panzer Dragoon Rolling Mode	Press Start at the Panzer Dragoon Title screen. Sweep the D-pad in three clockwise full circles when the screen with normal game and options appears. A sound and the phrase "Rolling Mode" appears to confirm correct code entry. Tap the D-pad twice to perform a roll during gameplay. To activate a smart bomb, begin a roll, and hold any button to highlight all enemy targets on the radar. Release the button to destroy the targets.
Panzer Dragoon Unlimited Continues	Press Up, X, Right, Y, Down, White, Left, Y, Up, X at the Panzer Dragoon main menu.
Panzer Dragoon View Hard Difficulty Ending Sequence	Press Up, Up, Down, Up, Left, Left, Right, Left, Down, Down, Up, Down, Right, Right, Left, Right at the Panzer Dragoon main menu.
Panzer Dragoon View Normal Ending Sequence	Press Up, Up, Down, Up, Right, Right, Left, Right, Down, Down, Up, Down, Left, Left, Right, Left at the Panzer Dragoon main menu.
Panzer Dragoon Wizard Mode	Press Start at the Title screen. Press LT, RT, LT, RT, Up, Down, Up, Down, Left, Right at the Panzer Dragoon main menu. The phrase "Wizard Mode" appears to confirm correct code entry. Gameplay is very fast when you enable this mode.
White Dragonmare	Unlock the Dragonmare in Box mode. Highlight the "Dragon Select" option, hold White, and press Start. Release White when the game starts.

Pariah

To enter these codes go to the Codes option.

Unlockable	Code
EB Games Multiplayer Level	White, Y, X, Black
Gamestop Multiplayer Level	Left, LT, X, Left

Enter these codes in the Cheat Codes menu under "settings."

Unlockable	Code
All Ammo	Down, Up, Down, Y
God Mode	Up, LT, X, LT

Peter Jackson's King Kong

At the Main menu screen, hold LT+RT and press Down, X, Up, Y, Down, Down, Up, Up, then release LT+RT. This opens the Cheat menu. Now enter any of these case sensitive passwords.

Unlockable	Password
999 ammunition	KK 999 mun
Bonuses completed	KKmuseum
God mode	8wonder
Level select	KKst0ry
Machine gun	KKcapone
One-hit kills	GrosBras
Revolver	KKtigun
Shotgun	KKsh0tgun
Sniper rifle	KKsn1per
Unlimited spears	lance 1nf

Phantasy Star Online Episode I and II

Unlockable	Objective
Open the Dressing Room	Have 10,000 Meseta on your character (not in the bank) when you start the game.
Hard Mode (offline)	Beat Normal Mode.
Hard Mode (online)	Get to level 20.
Ultimate Mode (offline)	Beat Very Hard Mode.
Ultimate Mode (online)	Get to level 80.
Very Hard Mode (offline)	Beat Hard Mode.
Very Hard Mode (online)	Get to level 40.

Pinball Hall of Fame

To enter these codes, go to Options, Code Entry.

Unlockable	Code	Unlockable	Code
Love Meter machine	LUV	Tournament mode	TMA
Playboy machine	PKR	Custom Balls option	BLZ
Xolton Fortune Teller machine	XTN	Infinite Final Ball option	INF
Payout mode	LAS	Unlock Gottlieb Tour	DGC

Pirates: The Legend of Black Kat

Unlockable	Code
Advance to Katarina's Next Sword	Hold LT + RT and click R, press BACK, BLK, click L, press X, A, WHT, Y, click L, press B
All Treasure Chest Keys	Hold LT + RT and press Y, BACK, A, X, click R, press WHT, click L, press BLK, B, click L.
Alternate Glacial Gulf Music	Hold LT + RT and press WHT, A, B, BLK, X, Y, click L, press BACK, click R, click L to hear music from SSX when sliding down in Glacial Gulf.
Alternate Katarina Costumes	Press LT + RT, click L, press BACK, START. A short sequence of music confirms correct code entry. Click R to change the value of the numbers that appear on screen, then start a new game or resume a saved game to view the corresponding costume. The available costumes and their values are in the table below.
Extra Gold	Hold LT + RT and press B, click R, press WHT, X, A, click R, press BACK, click L, press Y, BLK. Sail to another map to get the Galleon.
High-Pitched Voices	Hold LT + RT and click R, press Y, BACK, A, click R, press B, WHT, X, BLK, click L.
Invincibility for Katarina	Hold LT + RT and press A, Y, click L, press B, click R, press BACK, click R, press WHT, BLK, X.
Invincibility for the Wind Dancer	Hold LT + RT and press BACK, B, WHT, A, click R, press BLK, X, click R, press Y, click L.
Kane Poison Head	Hold LT + RT and press B, BLK, WHT, X, click L, press A, click L, press Y, click R, press BACK. The poison status will be indicated by the head of Kane from Command and Conquer.
Reveal All Treasure Chests	Hold LT + RT and click R, press A, B, click L, press Y, WHT, BACK, click L, press X, BLK.
Reveal Buried Treasure Chests	Hold LT + RT and press Y, A, X, B, WHT, BACK, click L, BLK, click L, click R. Green Xs appear on the captain's log maps to indicate the location of buried treasure chests.
Unlimited Items	Hold LT + RT and press B, WHT, BACK, BLK, click R, click L, press X, A, click R, press Y. Once found, an item becomes available in unlimited amounts.
Unlimited Wind Boost	Hold LT + RT and press BACK, WHT, click R, press X, click L, press Y, BLK, B, A, click L.
Wind Dancer	Hold LT + RT and press BLK, B, click R, click L, press A, X, click R, press BACK, WHT, Y.

Pirates: The Legend of Black Kat (continued)

Alternate Costume	Numerical Value
Blackbeard in Purple	00000001
Blonde Hair, Orange and Yellow Bikini	00000101
Blonde Hair, Pink Bikini	00000110
Blue Hair with Orange and Red Bikini	00000011
Blue Hair, Shiny Copper Body Suit	00001010
Blue Hair, Shiny Silver Bikini	00000111
Original Costume and Hair Color	00000000
Pink Hair, Shiny Black Body Suit	00001001
Purple Hair, Shiny Silver Body Suit	00001011
Red Hair with Red and Orange Bikini	00000010
Red Hair, Black Bikini, Black Stockings	00001000
Tan, Brown Hair, Orange and Yellow Bikini	00000100

Pirates of the Caribbean

Codes

Code	Effect
AXYBYBXBBA	+100,000 gold
AYXXYYBYXA	God Mode
ABYXYBBYBA	50 skill points
AXYXYBBYBA	Change your reputation back to neutral. This can only be done on land and no menus should be open at the start.

Easter Egg

Unlockable	How to Unlock
Portraits and AKELLA Logo	When you first enter the Labyrinth in the Incan Temple, Dannielle and Clement should make you go through the middle entryway. Keep going straight until you enter a different room. Go right. Keep an eye on the floor. You see a skull and a sun. Follow the sun. If you went the right way, you see a room with break in the wall. Look on the floor and you should see a sun and a skull. As you enter the room, run into the right wall. You go through the wall. Look at all of the portraits. Those are the crew who helped make the game. Look on the floor, you will see the AKELLA logo.

Pitfall: The Lost Expedition

Enter the following codes at the Main menu while holding LT+RT.

Unlockable	Code
Bottomless Canteen	←,X,B,↓,X,A,X,B
Original Pitfall	B,B,←,→,B,X,A,↑,B
Play as Nicole	←,↑,↓,↑,B,↑,↑
Punch Mode	←,→,B,↑,B,→,←

Prince of Persia

Unlockable	Objective
Original Prince of Persia	Complete the game and you will open up the very first Prince of Persia.

DS PSP PS2 PS3 Wii Xbox Xbox 360 Index

Prince of Persia: The Two Thrones

Extra Secondary Weapons

Pause the game while you have a secondary weapon equipped and ready.

Unlockable	How to Unlock
Chainsaw	Up, Up, Down, Down, Left, Right, Left, Right, Y, X, Y, X
Phone	Right, Left, Right, Left, Down, Down, Up, Up, Y, X, Y, Y, X, X
Rattle	Left, Left, Right, Right, Y, X, X, Y, Up, Down
Swordfish	Up, Down, Up, Down, Left, Right, Y, X, Y, X

Sand Gate Rewards

Unlockable	How to Unlock
100 Sand Credits	Deactivate Two Sand Gates
150 Sand Credits	Deactivate Five Sand Gates
200 Sand Credits	Deactivate Eight Sand Gates
Eye of the Storm Power	Deactivate Three Sand Gates
Fifth Sand Tank	Deactivate Four Sand Gates
Fourth Sand Tank	Deactivate One Sand Gate
Sand Storm Attack	Deactivate Nine Sand Gates
Sixth Sand Tank	Deactivate Seven Sand Gates
Winds of Sand Attack	Deactivate Six Sand Gates
Video Gallery	Successfully complete the game

Prince of Persia: Warrior Within

Refill Sand Tanks

Code	Effect
Refills Sand Tanks	(Hold Left Analog Stick Down) B, B, A, X, X, A, Y, Y

Hidden Bonus: Indestructible Weapons

At certain points throughout the game you find Weapon Racks containing "unique" weapons. These weapons are indicated in the Secondary Weapon Display with a question mark icon and are indestructible, unlike other secondary weapons. There are five of these weapons in all. For all but the Giant Hand, you need the Scorpion Sword. The Garden Flamingo and Teddy Bear must be completed before you find the Mask, and require you to backtrack along the path you would take when trying to complete the towers in which they are located. The Teddy Bear also requires you to break a wall during the Dahaka chase zone in that area. You get one chance only to find the Giant Hand and Glowing Sword.

Unlockable	How to Unlock
Garden Flamingo	Hanging Garden (present)—Behind a wall in the first alcove you reach if you were trying to reach the giant ladder in the past.
Giant Hand (little damage, instant knock down)	During the escape from the Tomb, find it in a small alcove to your left during the second (or third) Dahaka chase (depending on how you play).
Glowing Sword (Very high stats, also damages Prince)	Behind a wall in a pit immediately after the room covered in fog.
Hockey Stick	Central Hall (past), rotate the switch toward the Hourglass Room. Use the new path to reach a breakable wall at the bottom of the room.

Prince of Persia: Warrior Within (continued)

Unlockable	How to Unlock
Teddy Bear (little damage, heals the Prince with each hit)	Mechanical Pit (present), in the area where you fought the second Brute, take the stairs up and look for a breakable wall in the water-filled pit.

Secret Ending

Unlockable	How to Unlock
Secret Ending	Collect all 9 life upgrades. Then go to the hourglass room as you would normally would, get the Water Sword from Kaileena, and beat a secret final boss.

Prisoner of War

At the Main menu, select Passwords to enter these codes.

Unlockable	Code
All Chapters	GER1ENG5
All Secrets	FARLEYMYDOG
Default Chapters	DEFAULTM
Defiance	FATTY
First Person Mode	BOSTON
Game Creation Date and Time	DT
Guard Perception	QUINCY
Guard Size	MUFFIN
Informed of all Events	ALLTIMES
Informed of Core Current Events	CORETIMES
Top Down Mode	FOXY
Unlimited Goodies	DINO

Project Gotham Racing

Unlockable	Code
All Cars and Courses	Enter the name Nosliw.

Project Gotham Racing 2

Bonus Cars

Unlockable	How to Unlock
Delfino Feroce	Beat Kudos Challenge on Steel
Ferrari 250 GTO	Beat Kudos Challenge on Bronze
Mercedes CLK-GTR	Beat Kudos Challenge on Gold
Porsche 911 GT1	Beat Kudos Challenge on Silver
TVR Cerbera Speed 12	Beat Kudos Challenge on Platinum

Unlockables

Unlockable	How to Unlock
Geometry Wars	Access this minigame by going into the Garage. While you're in Walk mode, go over to the arcade machine and press Ⓐ.
Reverse	On any track in online Xbox Live play, you can drive backward, but it takes 2 laps for every actual lap. So 3 laps is really 6 laps. Drive over the start line, do a U-turn, and go. Whoever crosses the finish line first, (sixth place) is first on the leaderboard and gets the bonus kudos as well.

Psi Ops: The Mindgate Conspiracy

At the Main menu, highlight Extra Content, press RT, and enter any of these codes.

Unlockable	Code
All Powers from the start	537893
Arcade Mode	05051979
Bulletproof	548975
Co Op Play Mode	07041979
Dark Mode	465486
Super Psi	456456
Unlimited Ammo	978945
Crispy Soldier	454566
Dockworker	364654
Edgar Barret	497878

Skin Unlockable	Code
Edgar Barret	(Training 1) 196001
Edgar Barret	(Training 2) 196002
Edgar Barret	(Training 2) 196002
Edgar Barret	(Training 3) 196003
Edgar Barret	(Training 4) 196004
Edgar Barret	(Training 5) 196005
Edgar Barret	(Training 6) 196006
Jack	698798
Jov Leonov	468987
Kimiko Jones	978798
Labcoat	998789
Marlena Kessler	489788
Marlena Kessler (Bikini)	135454
Marlena Kessler (Leather)	136876
Marlena Kessler (Saranae)	65496873
MP1	321646
MP2	698799
MP3	654659
Nick Scryer (Stealth)	456498
Nick Scryer (Training)	564689
Nick Scryer (Urban)	484646
Nick Scryer (Wasteland)	975466
No Head	987978
Sara Blake	135488
Sara Blake (Psi)	468799
Sara Blake (Suicide)	231644
Scorpion	546546
The General (Clown)	431644
The General (Default)	459797
Tonya	678999
UN Soldier	365498
Wei Lu	231324
Wei Lu (Dragon)	978789
Wei Lu (Tranquility)	654654
Aura Pool	659785
Bottomless Pit	154897
Bouncy, Bouncy	568789
Floor of Death	05120926
Gasoline	9442662
Gearshift	154684
Gnomotron	456878
Panic Room	76635766
Psi Pool	565485
Survival Mode	7734206
Stoplights	945678
Tip the Idol	428584
TK Alley	090702
Up and Over	020615

Psychonauts

During gameplay, hold LT+RT and enter the codes. A "you cheated" sound will confirm correct entry.

Unlockable	Code
9999 Ammo	→,Ⓐ,←,←,Ⓨ,Ⓑ
9999 Arrow Heads	Ⓐ,→,→,WHT,Ⓨ,Ⓧ
9999 Lives	←,WHT,WHT,Ⓑ,Ⓐ,→
All Items Except Dream Fluffs, Colorizer, and Psi-Ball	→,Ⓑ,WHT,WHT,←,Ⓨ
All Powers and Max Rank	←,→,←
All PSI Powers	Ⓑ,Ⓑ,Ⓨ,WHT,←,Ⓨ
Invincibility	Ⓑ,WHT,Ⓑ,Ⓑ,Ⓨ,BLK,WHT,Ⓑ,WHT
Text Changes	WHT,Ⓐ,←,WHT,WHT,Ⓑ

The Punisher

Enter V Pirate as a Profile Name to unlock everything except Upgrades.

Quantum Redshift

Enter Cheat as your name, then in the Options menu, select the Cheats menu to enter these codes. Codes are case sensitive.

Unlockable	Code	Unlockable	Code
All Characters	Nematode	Infinite Shields	ThinkBat
All Speeds	zoomZOOM	Upgrade All Characters	RICEitup
Infinite Turbo	FishFace		

Red Card 2003

Unlockable	Objective
Apes Team and Victoria Falls Stadium	Defeat the Apes team in World Conquest mode.
Dolphins Team and Nautilus Stadium	Defeat the Dolphins team in World Conquest mode.
Finals Mode	Win all matches in World Conquest mode.
Martians Team and USAFB001 Stadium	Defeat the Martians team in World Conquest mode.
Matadors Team and Coliseum Stadium	Defeat the Matadors team in World Conquest mode.
Samurai Team and Youhi Gardens Stadium	Defeat the Samurai team in World Conquest mode.
SWAT Team and Nova City Stadium	Defeat the SWAT team in World Conquest mode.
Cheat Mode	Enter BIGTANK as a name to unlock all teams, stadiums, and finals mode.

Red Faction II

Input the following codes at the Cheat menu.

Unlockable	Code
Bouncy Grenades	BLK, BLK, BLK, BLK, BLK, BLK, BLK, BLK
Bullet Gibs	BLK, BLK, BLK, BLK, WHT, X, BLK, BLK
Bullets Instantly Gib	X, X, X, X, Y, BLK, X, X
Directors Cut	Y, X, BLK, WHT, BLK, X, Y, WHT
Explosives Instantly Gib	WHT, BLK, X, Y, WHT, BLK, X, Y
Fat Mode	BLK, BLK, BLK, BLK, WHT, X, BLK, BLK
Fire Bullets	Y, Y, Y, Y, Y, Y, Y, Y
Hidden Message	Y, X, Y, X, Y, X, Y, X
Rapid Rails	BLK, Y, BLK, Y, X, X, WHT, WHT
Super Health	X, X, Y, WHT, Y, WHT, BLK
Unlimited Ammo	Y, WHT, X, BLK, Y, BLK, X, WHT
Unlimited Grenades	BLK, X, BLK, Y, X, WHT, X, BLK
Everything	WHT, WHT, X, X, Y, BLK, Y, BLK
Wacky Deaths	WHT, WHT, WHT, WHT, WHT, WHT, WHT, WHT
Zombie Walk	X, X, X, X, X, X, X, WHT

Reservoir Dogs

Codes

Unlockable	How to Unlock
Adrenaline Rush—Infinite Adrenaline	A, LT, Y, A, LT, A, START
Battering Ram—Instant Crash	BLK, BLK, A, A, Y, WHT, START
Bulletproof—Infinite Health	LT, RT, Y, Y, RT, WHT, START
Fully Loaded—Infinite Ammo	WHT, BLK, Y, BLK, A, WHT, START
Magic Bullet—One Shot Kills	RT, BLK, Y, A, RT, A, START
Time Out—Infinite Timer	RT, RT, WHT, Y, A, BLK, START
Unlock All Levels	BLK, WHT, BLK, WHT, LT, RT, START
Unlock Art Gallery	Y, A, BLK, WHT, Y, A, START
Unlock Movie Gallery	LT, LT, Y, A, LT, RT, START

Unlockables

Unlockable	How to Unlock
Battering Ram	Successfully complete the game with the Professional ranking to unlock the Battering Ram cheat under the Extra menu.
Bulletproof	Successfully complete the game with the Professional ranking to unlock the Bulletproof cheat under the Extra menu.
Fully Loaded	Successfully complete the game with the Psychopath ranking to unlock the Fully Loaded cheat under the Extra menu.
Time Out	Successfully complete the game with the Career Criminal ranking to unlock the Time Out cheat under the Extra menu.

Return to Castle Wolfenstein: Tides of War

Unlockable	Code
Wolfenstein 3D	Beat the single player Campaign mode.

Roadkill

Enter the following codes at the map screen when paused.

Unlockable	Code
Restore Health	X,B,X,B,X,B,X,B
More Money	Y,B,Y,B,X,A,X,A,Down,Up
Infinite Ammo	Y,X,X,B,Y,X,X,B

Robotech: Battlecry

Cheat Mode: Start a new game or load a previous one. Highlight "Options," hold LT + RT, and press Left, Up, Down, A, Right, B, Start to display the Code Entry screen. Enter one of the following codes to activate the corresponding cheat function.

Unlockable	Code
All Models and Awards	WHERESMAX
All Multiplayer Levels	MULTIMAYHEM
Alternate Paint Schemes	MISSMACROSS
Disable Active Codes	CLEAR
Gunpod Ammunition Refilled Faster	SPACEFOLD
Gunpod and Missiles Refilled Faster	MIRIYA
Invincibility	SUPERMECH
Level Select	WEWILLWIN
Missiles Refilled Faster	MARSBASE
One-Shot Kills	BACKSTABBER
One-Shot Kills in Sniper Mode	SNIPER
Upside-Down Mode	FLIPSIDE

Robotech: Invasion

In the Options menu, select Extras, then enter the following:

Effect	Password
1 Hit Kill	dustyayres
Access to all levels	reclamation
Invincibility	supercyc
Lancer's Multiplayer Skin	yllwfllw
Rand's Multiplayer Skin	kidgloves
Rook's Multiplayer Skin	blueangls
Scott Bernard's Multiplayer Skin	ltntcmdr
Unlimited Ammo	trgrhpy

Robots

Pause the game to enter these codes.

Unlockable	Code
Give Rodney a Big Head	Up, Down, Down, Up, Right, Right, Left, Right
Unlimited Health	Up, Right, Down, Up, Left, Down, Right, Left
Unlimited Scrap	Down, Down, Left, Up, Up, Right, Up, Down

Rocky

Unlockable	Code
All Default Boxers and Arenas	Hold RT and press Right, Down, Up, Left, Up, LT at the Main menu.
All Default Boxers, Arenas, and Rocky Statue	Hold RT and press Right, Right, Right, Left, Right, LT at the Main menu.
All Default Boxers, Arenas, Rocky Statue, and Mickey	Hold RT and press Up, Down, Down, Left, Left, LT at the Main menu.
Double Punch Damage	Hold RT and press Right, Down, Left, Up, Left, LT at the Main menu.
Double Speed Boxing	Hold RT and press Down, Left, Down, Up, Right, LT at the Main menu.
Full Stats in Movie Mode	Hold RT and press Right, Down, Down, Up, Left, LT at the Main menu.
Full Stats in Tournament and Exhibition Modes	Hold RT and press Left, Up, Up, Down, Right, LT at the Main menu.
Win Fight in Movie Mode	Hold RT and press Right, Right, Left, Left, Up, LT at the Main menu. Press Black + White during a fight in Movie mode to win automatically.
Fight as Mickey Goldmill	Complete Movie mode under the Champ difficulty setting.
Gold Class Knockout Tournament	Win the silver class knockout tournament.
Rocky Statue	Complete Movie mode under the Contender difficulty setting.
Silver Class Knockout Tournament	Win the bronze class knockout tournament.

Rogue Ops

To enter these codes, just pause the game. If done correctly, the screen will flash.

Unlockable	Code
Big Feet	Right, Right, Right, Left, Right, Left, Right, Left, Left, Left
Explosive Crossbow	Left, Right, Right, Left, X, Y, Black, White, X, Y, Left, Right
Half Damage	X, X, Y, Y, Left, Left, Right, Right, Y, Y, X, X
Missile Sniper	X, Left, Right, Black, White, Right, X, White, White, Black, Left, Left
No Bullet Damage	Left, Right, Right, Left, X, Y, Y, X

Rogue Ops (continued)

Unlockable	Code
One Hit Kills	Y, ←, →, →, ←, Y, RT, LT, Y, X, X
Skeleton Mode	←, ←, ←, →, ←, →, ←, →, →, →
Unlimited Bullets	X, Y, X, Y, X, Y, X, Y, ←, Y, X, Y, X, Y, X, Y, X
Unlimited Health	←, →, →, ←, ←, →, →, ←, ←, →, →, ←, X, X
Unlimited Spy Cam	←, ←, →, →, WHT, WHT, BLK, BLK, X, X, Y, Y
Unlimited TOC	Y, Y, X, X, ←, →, →, ←, BLK, WHT, BLK

Rogue Trooper

Codes

To activate these codes, enter them while in the "Extras" Menu. You can then select them from the "Cheats" menu.

Unlockable	How to Unlock
Extreme Ragdoll	↑, ↑, ↑, BLK, BLK, BLK, ↑
Hippy Blood	WHT, ←, B, ↓, RB, BACK
Infinite Health	←, →, ↑, ↓, L, X
Infinite Supplies	BACK, RB, LB, BACK, R, LB
Low Gravity Ragdoll	X, X, X, B, B, B, ↑, ↓

Unlockables

Unlockable	How to Unlock
All Weapons and Upgrades	Complete the game. Instead of starting a new game, use the Level Select cheat and start on the first level to keep everything you unlocked.
Extreme Ragdoll	Complete the game on any difficulty, start a new game, enter the Options menu, select Cheats.
Hippy Blood (Changes blood into colorful flowers)	Complete the game on any difficulty, start a new game, enter the Options menu, select Cheats.
Level Select	Successfully complete a level to unlock it at the Cheats menu.
Low Gravity Ragdoll (Enemies fly away when killed)	Complete the game on any difficulty, start a new game, enter the Options menu, select Cheats.
Massacre Mode	Complete the game on any difficulty setting to unlock the Massacre difficulty setting.

Run Like Hell

Unlockable	Code
Breaking Benjamin Video	←, B, A, LT, RT, ↑
Baby Nick	B, A, B, Y, ↓, ↓
Max Assault Rifle Damage	←, B, →, X, ↓, Y, ↑, A
Max Bolt Thrower Damage	X, Y, B, WHT, B, Y, X, BLK
Max Pulse Rifle Damage	B, ↓, ←, A, WHT, BLK, X, Y
Max Repeater Rifle Damage	←, Y, →, A, ↑, X, ↓, B
Max Rifle Damage	L, L, X, Y, B, A, R, R
Max Shotgun Damage	A, A, L, R, ↑, ↓, ←, →
Refill Armor	A, Y, B, X, Y, A, LT, RT
Refill Health	↑, ↓, ←, →, ←, →, A, B
Show Credits	X, B, A, ↑, ↓, Y

Scaler

Enter these codes while the game is paused. Select Options, then Audio, and then enter these codes.

Unlockable	Code
200,000 Klokkies	LT, LT, RT, RT, Y, X, Y
Full Health	RT, LT, RT, LT, Y, Y, X, X, RT, X
Infinite Electric Bombs	RT, RT, LT, LT, Y, Y, X

Scarface

Enter these on the Cheats screen of the Pause menu.

Unlockable	Password
1,000 Balls	FPATCH
Antique Racer	OLDFAST
Bacinari	666999
Black Suit	BLACK
Blue Suit	BLUE
Blue Suit w/shades	BLUESH
BReal "The World Is Yours" Music Track	TUNEME
Bulldozer	DOZER
Change Time of Day	MARTHA
Decrease Cop Heat	FLYSTRT
Decrease Gang Heat	NOBALLS
Dump Truck	DUMPER
Fill Ammo	AMMO
Fill Health	MEDIK
Grey Suit	GREY
Grey Suit w/shades	GREYSH
Increase Cop Heat	DONUT
Increase Gang Heat	GOBALLS
Lightning	SHAZAAM
Rain	RAINY
Sandy Shirt	TANSHRT
Sandy Shirt w/shades	TANSH
Stampede	BUMMER
Tiger Shirt	TIGSHRT
Tiger Shirt w/shades	TIGERSH
Vehicle Repair	TBURGLR
White Suit	WHITE
White Suit w/shades	WHITESH

Scarface: The World Is Yours

Passwords

Password	Effect
BUMMER	4x4 Stampede vehicle
S13	Babylon Club Redux
DW_fron	Cabana Cigar/Oakly drive in
FLYSTRT	CHEAT: Decrease Cop Heat
NOBALLS	CHEAT: Decrease Gang Heat
FPATCH	CHEAT: Fill Balls Meter
DONUT	CHEAT: Increase Cop Heat
GOBALLS	CHEAT: Increase Gang Heat
KILLTONY	CHEAT: Kill Tony
AMMO	CHEAT: Max Ammo
MEDIK	CHEAT: Refill Health
BLACK	Clothing: Black Suit Tony
BLUESH	Clothing: Blue Suit Tony with Sunglasses
GRAY	Clothing: Gray Suit Tony
GRAYSH	Clothing: Gray Suit Tony with Sunglasses
S12	Deliver
S07A	Freedom town redux

Scarface: The World Is Yours (continued)

Password	Effect
F_M_SHA	Havana Storehouse
HAWAII	Hawaiian shirt Tony
HAWAIIG	Hawaiian shirt Tony w/shades
F_M_SHC	Leopard Storage
F_M_SHB	Marina Storage
TUNEME	Music Track: "The World Is Yours"
S09	Nacho Contreras
S10	Nacho's Tanker
DW_fron	Ogrady's
TBURGLR	Repair Tony's Vehicle
SANDY	Sandy shirt Tony
SANDYSH	Sandy shirt Tony w/shades
F_M_SHD	Shoreline Storage
A51	The Dock Boss
S18	The End
A22	The Plantation
A23	Tranquilandia
S11	Un-Load
OLDFAST	Vehicle: Spawn Ariel MK III
666999	Vehicle: Spawn Bacinari
DOZER	Vehicle: Spawn Bulldozer
MARTHA	Weather Modifier: Change Time of Day
SHAZAAM	Weather Modifier: Toggle Lightning
RAINY	Weather Modifier: Toggle Rain
WHITE	White suit Tony
WHITESH	White suit Tony w/shades

Scooby-Doo: Night of 100 Frights

To access the following unlockables, pause the game, hold LT+RT, then enter code.

Unlockable	Code
All Power Ups	B,X,B,X,B,X,X,X,B,B,X,B,B,B
All Warp Gates	X,X,B,X,X,B,X,B,B,B
View Credits	X,B,B,X,B,X

Set the clock on your Xbox to the following dates and see what happens!

Holiday	Date
Christmas	December 25
Halloween	October 31
Independence Day	July 4
New Year's	January 1
New Year's Eve	December 31
St. Patrick's Day	March 17
Valentine's Day	February 14

Secret Weapons Over Normandy

Enter the following codes at the New Game/Continue screen.

Unlockable	Code
God Mode	Up, Down, Left, Right, Left, Left, Right, Right, LT, LT, RT, RT, WHT, BLK
Infinite Ammo	Up, Right, Down, Left, Up, Right, Down, Left, LT, RT
All Planes and Levels	Y, Y, Y, X, X, X, LT, RT, BLK, BLK, WHT, WHT

Sega Soccer Slam

Enter these codes at the Title screen.

Unlockable	Code
8-Ball	RT, Right, Up, Up, Y, Y
All Player Items	Left, X, Left, X, Left
All Stadiums	RT, RT, Right, Right, Up, Up, Up, Up, Up, X, X
Alpen Castle	Up, Up, Up, Down, X, X
Beachball	RT, Right, Right, Down, Y, X
Big Head Mode	RT, LT, Up, Up, Y, Y
Big Hits	LT, RT, Up, Up, X, Y
Black Box	RT, Left, Left, Down, X, X
Crate	RT, Left, Down, Right, Y, X
Eyeball	RT, Right, Down, Up, X, X
Get Unlimited Turbo	LT, RT, Right, Up, X, X
Globe	RT, Right, Right, Left, X, X
Jungle Canopy	LT, RT, Up, Down, Left, Right, X, Y
Kid's Block	RT, Left, Right, Right, Y, Y
Kid's Play (star)	RT, Right, Up, Down, X, Y
Maximum Power	LT, RT, Left, Right, Y, Y
Old-School	RT, Right, Left, Left, Y, X
Pacific Atoll	Up, Up, Left, Left, Y, Y
Reactor Core	Up, Left, Left, Right, X, Y
Riviera Ruins	Up, Down, Down, Right, Y, X
Rob's Head	RT, Left, Up, Left, Y, X
Rusty Can	RT, Left, Up, Up, Y, Y
Tribal Oasis	LT, RT, Up, Up, Down, Down, X, X
Unlimited Spotlight	LT, RT, Down, Right, Y, X

Serious Sam

Cheat Mode: Click and hold L, and press BLK, WHT, Y at the main menu. A "Cheats" option now appears at the main menu. After enabling Cheat mode, press START during gameplay to access the Cheat menu. You can restore lives and ammunition to avoid dying.

Unlockable	Objective
Hidden Level	Destroy all the statues in the "Valley of the Kings" level.
Mental Mode (Mental fades in and out under Serious. In Mental mode, all the enemies appear and disappear.)	Complete the game in Serious mode, and start a new game.

Serious Sam 2

Enter this code while the game is paused.

Unlockable	Code
Unlock Cheat Menu	Hold RT, then keep pressing BLK, WHT, BLK, WHT until the Cheat menu appears at the bottom of the screen.

DS PSP PS2 PS3 Wii Xbox Xbox 360 Index

Shadow Ops: Red Mercury

Enter the following codes at the Password screen.

Unlockable	Objective
All Co-op Levels	wanderlust
All Single Player Missions	happycamper

Shattered Union

To enter these codes, press the start button to bring up the menu during Campaign mode. Once the menu is up, select cheat and enter your code.

Unlockable	Code
$100,000 into your Treasury	X, X, A, A, Y
Arcadia Plains	B, X, X, X, A
Arizona Territory	B, X, X, A, X
Carolinas	B, X, Y, X, A
Central Cascades	B, X, X, X, Y
Central Heartland	B, X, X, B, Y
Cumberlands	B, X, Y, X, Y
Dakotas	B, X, X, B, X
Eastern Shenandoah	B, X, Y, Y, B
Florida	B, X, Y, X, B
Great Basin	B, X, X, Y, A
Great Lakes	B, X, X, B, A
Great Plains	B, X, X, B, B
Mississippi Delta	B, X, Y, X, X
New Mexico	B, X, X, Y, B
New York	B, X, Y, Y, Y
Northern California	B, X, X, Y, X
Northern Cascades	B, X, X, X, B
Northern New England	B, X, Y, Y, A
Northern Texas	B, X, X, A, A
Ohio Valley	B, X, Y, Y, X
Oklahoma Grasslands	B, X, X, A, Y
Southeastern Cascades	B, X, X, X, X
Southern California	B, X, X, Y, Y
Southern Texas	B, X, X, A, B

Shrek 2

Codes

Press Start during game play to access the Scrapbook, enter a code here.

Code	Effect
Left, Up, A, B, Left, Up, A, B, Left, Up, A, B, B, B, B, B, B	1,000 Coins
Left, Up, A, B, Left, Up, A, B, Left, Up, A, B, X, B, X, B, X, B	Bonus game (Found under "bonus")

Unlockable Bonuses

The following bonuses will be unlocked depending on the number of missions you have completed in *Shrek 2*.

Unlockable	How to Unlock
Cage Drop	59 missions completed
Cloud Maze	45 missions completed
Floating Floor	31 missions completed
Movie Stills and Crash Coliseum	70 missions completed
Ring Coliseum	21 missions completed

Shrek Super Slam

Enter these codes at the Title screen.

Unlockable	Code
Pizza One mini game	Up, Up, Y, Y, Right, Right, B, B, Down, Down, LT, RT, Left, Left, X, X, LT, RT
Pizza Two mini game	Down, Down, Right, B, Up, Y, Left, X, LT, LT
Pizza Three mini game	B, B, X, X, RT, RT, Left, Left, LT, LT
Slammageddon	Up, Up, Down, Down, Left, Right, Left, Right, Y, X, X, LT, RT
Super Speed Modifier	LT, LT, RT, RT, LT, RT, LT, RT, X, B, Y, Y
Unlock All Challenges	Y, Y, Y, B, B, B, Y, X, B, X, X, X, Up, Down, Left, Right, LT, RT

Sid Meier's Pirates

Enter these as names for the desired effects.

Unlockable	Password
Begin game with the best ship in the game and a full crew	D.Gackey
Bonus Frag	Snappy Dresser
Dueling Invincibility	Dragon Ma
Food Never Dwindles	Sweet Tooth
Invincibility in Ship Battles	Bloody Bones Baz
The Governor's daughters always love you no matter how badly you dance	Scooter
Your crew is always at highest possible morale	B.Caudizzle
Your fleet sails twice as fast	Sprinkler

Silent Hill 2

Completion Bonuses: Complete the game. Start another game and enter the Extra Options menu to access new features. You can set a "Bullet Adjust" option, allowing the normal amount of ammunition found at a location to double or triple. You can toggle a "Noise Effect" option. Another new option you can toggle allows you to view scenes without distortion.

Unlockable	Objective
Additional Riddle Difficulty	Complete the game under the Easy, Normal, and Hard riddle difficulty settings. Select the Hard riddle difficulty again, and begin a new game with a new combination of riddles.
Book of Lost Memories	Complete the game. Start a new game and look for the newspaper stand near the Texxon Gas Station. Find the Book of Lost Memories inside.
Book of the Crimson Ceremony	Find this book in the reading room on the second floor of the Nightmare hotel.
Chainsaw	Complete the game under the Normal difficulty and Normal riddle difficulty settings. Start a new game to find the Chainsaw among logs before the cemetery.
Dog Key	Complete the game with the "Rebirth" ending. Start a new game and a doghouse appears near Jack's Inn and the gas station. Look inside the doghouse to find the Dog Key. Use it to open the observation room in the Nightmare hotel.
Hyper Spray	Complete the game two times. Start a new game to find the Hyper Spray on the south side of the motor home.
Introduction FMV Sequence Audio	If you wait at the title screen for a while, the introduction FMV sequence begins. In some scenes, there will be no audio. Complete the game one time to restore the audio to those.
Joke Ending	To view the sixth secret joke ending, use the Blue Gem at Alternate Brook Haven Hospital's garden, the dock before getting on the boat, and room 312 in the Lakeview Hotel. Once you use it in room 312, the game ends and the joke ending appears.

Silent Hill 2 (continued)

Unlockable	Objective
Obsidian Goblet	Complete the game. Start a new game, and enter the Historical Society building. Find the Obsidian Goblet on a shelf.
Reveal Signs	Unlock all five endings, and start a new game. All signs are now revealed.
White Chrism	Complete the game. Start a new game to find the White Chrism vial in the kitchen of apartment 105 in Blue Creek Apartments.

The Simpsons Hit and Run

Pause the game and enter the Option menu, then hold LT+RT and enter the code.

Unlockable	Code
All cars for new game (must be typed in with complete save loaded)	A,B,A,B
One hit kills (all cars will explode if you ram them or if they ram you, including cops and bosses)	Y,Y,X,X
Press your horn for high flying jumps	X,X,X,Y
Secret cars replaced by red box racer	B,B,Y,X
Show grid view	B,A,B,Y
Show speedometer	Y,Y,B,X
Super fast Cars	X,X,X,X
Your car is invincible	Y,A,Y,A
Your cars are 5 times faster than normal	Y,Y,Y,Y

The Simpsons Road Rage

Codes

In the Options menu, hold both triggers and press the following buttons:

Code	Effect
X, X, X, X	2D Cardboard People
Y, Y, Y, Y	Cars in Slow Motion
B, B, X, B	Christmas Apu
B, B, A, A	Debug Mode
A, A, A, A	Drive at Night
B, B, Y, A	Drive Nuclear Bus
B, B, Y, X	Drive Red Soapbox Car
B, B, X, A	Halloween Bart
B, B, X, Y	Happy New Year Krusty!
B, B, X, X	Marge's Thanksgiving Car
Y, Y, Y, Y	More Camera Views
X, X, X, Y	Overhead View
B, B, Y, Y	Play as Smithers
X, B, Y, A	Stop Watch Mode

Unlockable	How to Unlock
New Car for Homer	Play through and complete all missions and you get "The Car Built for Homer" from the episode where Danny DeVito was Homer's brother and Homer designed a car for his company.
Play as Frankenstein Bart	Set the system date/clock to Halloween (October 31st).
Play as Pilgrim Marge	Set the system date/clock to Thanksgiving (3rd Thursday of November).
Play as a Santa Apu	Set the system date/clock to Christmas (December 25th).

The Simpsons Road Rage (continued)

Unlockable	How to Unlock
Play as Tuxedo Krusty	Set the system date/clock to New Year's Day (January 1st).
Skip Missions	Skip every mission (play the mission by trying it 5 times) and then beat the 10th mission. Then you will have beaten every mission and get the car built for Homer.

The Sims

Press both LT + RT to call up a cheat menu, then enter the codes below.

Unlockable	Code
2 Player mode	MIDAS
First person View (press Black)	FISH EYE
Free Items	FREEALL
Party Motel in 2 Player Mode	PARTY M
Play the Sims Mode	SIMS

The Sims 2

Codes

Enter these codes in game. Most codes require the player to enter the master code (LB, RB, Up, A, BLK) first.

Code	Effect
LB, RB, Up, A, BLK	Master code
Up, B, Up, Right, WHT	Max all motives
Right, Up, Right, Down, Right, Up, Down, Left	Remove messages
Y, B, X, BLK, Left	Change any Sim's skill
RB, LB, BLK, Right, Left	Give the household §10,000
B, X, LB, Up, Down	Go six hours forward in time
B, WHT, Left, Up, B	Unlock all Story mode locations
X, BLK, Down, Right, X	Unlock all clothes
WHT, B, Down, Left, Up	Unlock all objects
BLK, X, Up, Down, Right, A	Unlock all recipes
B, WHT, Left, B, Up, B	Unlocks all lots/locations

Unlock Locations

To Unlock New Locations, complete all of your Gold and Platinum goals. Do not worry too much with the Green ones. You also need to complete your roommates' Gold and Platinum goal.

Unlockable	How to Unlock
Alien Crash Site	Help XY-XY. Fulfill all Aspirations and become friends with Jonas.
Bio Dome	Have Noelle complete one full career.
Cliffside Retreat	Fulfill all of Isabella's Wants, but it might take a while for her to make a sandwich.
HMS Armore	Fulfill all of Betty's Wants until she is in a Platinum mood. Then marry Captain Nelson.
Jugen House	Fulfill Toothless Joe's Aspirations until your Sim gets "Visit New Location" as an Aspiration. Go back to Tranquility Falls, and help Chantel
Mesa Gallery	Help Hector complete his goals at HMS Amore.

The Sims 2 (continued)

Orbit Room	Become friends with Red S. and serve him food. Move back to Sunset Canyon and make Red S. and Helga get married and get Red S. in Platinum mood.
Rockwall Acres	Follow instructions on what it says
Shoreline Trails	Buy a foosball table and defeat Torin
Sunset Canyon	Bring Helga, Billy, and Sheila back to life, make a kitchen, clean up mess, buy them beds, and build bathroom
Tranquility Falls	Fulfill Larry's Want and put him in Platinum mood, same with Chantel.

The Sims Bustin' Out

Enter the following codes any time during the game (when paused).

Unlockable	Code
The Gnome	RT, LT, ↓, BLK, ← (This must be entered first before any of the other codes.)
All Locations	BLK, ↓, RT, LT, Y
All Objects	BLK, ↑, Y, ↓, RT
All Socials	LT, RT, A, ↓, BLK
Money	LT, BLK, →, X, ←

Smashing Drive

Unlockable Shift	Objective
Dusk and Wired Shift	Complete the Night Owl shift.
Night Owl Shift	Complete the Rush Hour shift.
Rush Hour Shift	Complete the Early Bird shift.

Soldier of Fortune II: Double Helix

While playing, click in the left analog stick, then enter these codes.

Unlockable	Code
All Weapons	X, Y, A, B
God Mode	B, A, Y, X
Level select	BLK, B, A, WHT
Unlimited Ammo	BLK, A, Y, WHT

Sonic Heroes

Unlockable	Objective
2 Player Team Battle Mode	Collect 20 Emblems.
2 Player Special Stage Mode	Collect 40 Emblems.
2 Player Ring Race Mode	Collect 60 Emblems.
2 Player Bobsled Race Mode	Collect 80 Emblems.
2 Player Quick Race Mode	Collect 100 Emblems.
2 Player Expert Race Mode	Collect 120 Emblems.
Last Song and Movie	Complete the Last Story.
Last Story Mode	Complete Story Mode with all four teams and all Choas Emeralds.
Metal Characters	Press A+Y after you chose a level for 2 players.
Super Hard Mode	Collect 141 Emblems and have all A ranks.
Team Chaotix Song and Movie	Complete Story Mode with Team Chaotix.
Team Dark Song and Movie	Complete Story Mode with Team Dark.
Team Rose Song and Movie	Complete Story Mode with Team Rose.
Team Sonic Movie and Song	Complete Story Mode with Team Sonic.

Spawn: Armageddon

Enter the following codes any time during the game (when paused).

Unlockable	Code
All Comics	↑,↓,←,→,→,←,←,↑
All Weapons	↑,↓,←,→,←,→,←,←
Infinite Health and Necroplasm	↑,↓,←,→,→,←,↓,↑
Infinite Ammo	↑,↓,←,→,↑,←,↓,→

Spider-Man

Enter the following codes at the Specials menu. Listen for the laugh to know you entered it correctly. Repeat code entry to return to normal.

Unlockable	Code
All Fighting Controls	KOALA
Big Head and Feet for Spider-Man	GOESTOYOURHEAD
Bonus Training Levels	HEADEXPLODY
Enemies Have Big Heads	JOELSPEANUTS
First-Person View	UNDERTHEMASK
Goblin-Style Costume	FREAKOUT
Level Select	IMIARMAS
Level Skip	ROMITAS (Pause gameplay and select the "Next Level" option to advance to the next level.)
Master Code	ARACHNID (All levels in the Level Warp option, all Gallery options (movie viewer/production art), and combo moves are unlocked.)
Matrix-Style Attacks	DODGETHIS
Play as a Police Officer	REALHERO
Play as a Scientist	SERUM
Play as Captain Stacey (Helicopter Pilot)	CAPTAINSTACEY
Play as Mary Jane	GIRLNEXTDOOR
Play as Shocker's Thug	THUGSRUS
Play as Skulls Gang Thug	KNUCKLES
Play as the Shocker	HERMANSCHULTZ
Play as Uncle Ben's Killer	STICKYRICE
Small Spider-Man	SPIDERBYTE
Unlimited Green Goblin Glider Power	CHILLOUT
Unlimited Webbing	ORGANICWEBBING

Unlockable	Code
Alternate Green Goblin Costume	If you're using the Alex Ross Spider-Man, play any level with the Green Goblin in it and he'll have an alternate costume that more closely resembles his classic costume
Green Goblin FMV Sequence	Complete the game under the hero or greater difficulty setting.
Pinhead Bowling Mini-Game	Accumulate 10,000 points during gameplay to unlock the Pinhead bowling mini-game in the Training menu.
Play as Alex Ross	Complete the game under the normal or higher difficulty setting to unlock the Alex Ross costume in the Specials menu.
Play as Peter Parker	Complete the game under the easy or higher difficulty setting to unlock the Peter Parker costume in the Specials menu.

Spider-Man (continued)

Play as Wrestler	Complete the game under the easy or higher difficulty setting to unlock the wrestler costume in the Specials menu. To unlock this easily, first unlock the Unlimited Webbing cheat. When you get to the ring, zip to the top and keep on shooting Spidey Bombs.
Shocker FMV Sequence	Accumulate 30,000 points during gameplay to unlock a Shocker FMV sequence in the CG menu.
Unlimited Webbing	Accumulate 50,000 points during gameplay.
Vulture FMV Sequence	Accumulate 20,000 points during gameplay to unlock a Vulture FMV sequence in the CG menu.

TIP

Play as Green Goblin!

Complete the game under the hero or superhero difficulty setting to unlock the Green Goblin Costume option at the Specials menu. Select that option to play as Harry Osborn in the Green Goblin costume, including his weapons, in an alternate storyline in which he tries to correct the Osborn family's reputation. To unlock this easily, start a new game under the hero or superhero difficulty setting. At the first level, pause gameplay, then quit to the main menu. Enable the ARACHNID code, then go to the Level Warp option. Choose the Conclusion level (that features Norman revealing himself to Spider-Man followed by the glider sequence), then exit. This marks the game as completed under the selected difficulty setting. The Green Goblin costume option will be unlocked at the Secret Store screen.

Spider-Man 2

Type in HCRAYERT as a name to gain upgrades, a lot of Hero Points, and 44% game completion.

Splashdown

On the option screen, hold down (RT). Then press ↑, ↑, ↓, ↓, ←, →, ←, →, Ⓧ, Ⓑ, Ⓧ, Ⓑ. Once this is done, you can enter these passwords.

Unlockable	Password
All Stages	Passport
Cannot be knocked off your SeaDoo	TopBird
Expert AI	AllOutAI
Max Out Performance Meter	PMeterGo
Race against an F-18 Jet in Time Trials	F18
Race against the Ghost of the currently selected Character	SEADOO
Race against a UFO in Time Trials	IBelieve
Unlock all characters	AllChar
Unlock all endings	Festival
Unlock hard tracks with normal AI difficulty	Hobble
Unlock all wetsuits	LaPinata

SpongeBob SquarePants Battle for Bikini Bottom

Pause the game and hold LT+RT, then input the code. You must do this quickly. You'll hear a sound if you entered the code correctly.

Unlockable	Code
10 Spatulas	X, Y, Y, X, X, Y, Y, X
1000 Shiny Objects	Y, X, X, Y, Y, X, X, Y
All monsters in Monster Gallery (Police Station)	X, Y, X, Y, Y, X, Y, X
Big Plankton	Y, Y, Y, Y, X, Y, X, Y, X, X, X, X
Bubble Bowl Power Up	X, Y, X, Y, X, X, Y, Y
Cruise Bubble Bowl Power Up	Y, X, Y, X, Y, Y, X, X
Cruise Bubble has Cruise Control	X, X, X, X, Y, Y, X, X, Y, X, Y, Y
Invert Camera Controls (Left/Right)	Y, Y, X, X, X, X, Y, Y
Invert Camera Controls (Up/Down)	Y, X, X, X, X, X, X, Y
Restore health	X, X, X, X, Y, X, Y, X, Y, Y, Y, Y
Small Patrick, Mr. Crab, Squidword, Squirrel Girl in Astronaut Costume	Y, Y, Y, Y, X, Y, X, Y, Y, Y, Y, Y
Small Towns People	Y, Y, Y, Y, Y, X, Y, Y, X, Y, X
Sponge Bob No Pants	X, X, X, Y, X, X, Y, X, Y, Y, X
Townspeople are Thieves (Shiny Objects)	Y, Y, Y, Y, Y, X, Y, X, Y, Y, X, X
Unlock Art Gallery (Theatre)	Y, X, Y, X, X, Y, X, Y

SpongeBob SquarePants: The Movie

Pause the game, hold LT+RT to enter the following codes.

Unlockable	Code
All Health	Y,Y,Y,Y,X,Y,X,Y
All Moves	X,X,Y,X,Y,Y,X,X
All Moves to Macho	X,X,Y,X,Y,Y,X,Y
All Tasks	Y,X,Y,Y,X,Y,X,X

Spy Hunter 2

To access the following codes, pause gameplay at any time during the game and enter code.

Unlockable	Code
God Mode	LT,LT,LT,BLK,LT,RT,RT,LT,BLK
Infinite Ammo	RT,LT,BLK,BLK,WHT,RT,LT,BLK,WHT

Spy vs. Spy

Go to the Extras menu, then enter the following codes in the Cheats menu.

Unlockable	Code
All Modern Maps	PROHIAS
All Multiplayer Maps	MADMAG
All Spy Attachments	DISGUISE
All Story Maps	ANTONIO
Invulnerability	ARMOR
Permanent Fairy	FAIRY

SSX 3

Unlockable	Code	Unlockable	Code
Snow Boards	graphicdelight	Hiro	slicksuit
Videos	myeyesaredim	Stretch	windmilldunk

Unlockable	Objective
Alternate Costumes	To earn more costumes, complete all chapters in your trick book. To unlock the final chrome costume, complete World Circuit mode with a "Master" rank.
Fugi Board	Get a gold medal on every course with all boarders with their überboards to unlock a Fugi board.

SSX On Tour

Enter these passwords at the Cheats menu.

Unlockable	Password
All Clothing	FLYTHREADS
All Levels	BACKSTAGEPASS
All Movies	THEBIGPICTURE
Extra Cash	LOOTSNOOT
Infinite Boost	ZOOMJUICE
Monster Tricks	JACKALOPESTYLE
Snowball Fight	LETSPARTY
Stat Boost	POWERPLAY
Unlock Characters	ROADIEROUNDUP
Unlock Conrad (the MiniViking)	BIGPARTYTIME
Unlock Mitch Koobski (the Unicorn)	MOREFUNTHANONE
Unlock Nigel (Rocker)	THREEISACROWD
Unlock Ski Patrol Character	FOURSOME

SSX Tricky

Unlockable	Objective
Pipedream Course	Win a medal on all Showoff courses.
Play as Brodi	Win a gold medal in World Circuit mode.
Play as JP	Win three gold medals in World Circuit mode.
Play as Kaori	Win four gold medals in World Circuit mode.
Play as Luther	Win eight gold medals in World Circuit mode.
Play as Marisol	Win five gold medals in World Circuit mode.
Play as Psymon	Win six gold medals in World Circuit mode.
Play as Seeiah	Win seven gold medals in World Circuit mode.
Play as Zoe	Win two gold medals in World Circuit mode.
Überboards	Unlock all of the tricks for a character to get his or her überboard, which is that character's best board.
Untracked Course	Win a medal on all Race courses.

Input these codes at the main options screen, with the "Start Game" and "DVD Extras" option. Listen for the sound to confirm correct code entry.

Unlockable	Code
Annette Board	Hold LT + RT and press X, A, Right, X, A, Down, X, A, Left, X, A, Up, then release LT + RT. Choose Kaori and start a track. Kaori will have a full Tricky meter, and a faster board.

SSX Tricky (continued)

Unlockable	Code
Full Stat Points	Hold LT + RT and press Y, Y, Right, Y, Y, Down, A, A, Left, A, A, Up. (All the boarders will have full stat points.)
Mallora Board	Hold LT + RT and press A, A, Right, B, B, Down, Y, Y, Left, X, X, Up, then release LT + RT. Choose Elise and start a track. Elise will have the Mallora Board and a blue outfit. This code only works for Elise.
Master Code	Hold LT + RT and press A, Y, Right, B, X, Down, Y, X, Left, B, A, Up, then release LT + RT.
Mix Master Mike	Hold LT + RT and press A, A, Right, A, A, Down, A, A, Left, A, A, Up, then release LT + RT. Choose any boarder at the character selection screen, and he or she will be replaced by Mix Master Mike on the course, with the number of the character that was originally selected. He has decks on his back and a vinyl board. Repeat the code to disable its effect.
Sticky Boards	Hold LT + RT and press X, X, Right, Y, Y, Down, B, B, Left, A, A, Up, then release LT + RT.

Star Trek: Shattered Universe

Enter these codes at the Main Menu.

Unlockable	Code
All Medals and Ranks Awarded	BLK, LT, RT, B, RT, Y, LT, WHT
All Missions Open	BLK, RT, LT, B, X, LT, RT, Y, WHT
All Ships Open	BLK, LT, X, LT, X, RT, RT, B, WHT
Invincibility	BLK, LT, B, LT, RT, Y, Y, B, WHT
Kobayashi Maru Open	BLK, LT, Y, LT, LT, X, Y, Y, RT, WHT

Star Wars Battlefront

Unlockable	Code
All Missions	In Historical Campaign, press X, Y, X, Y at the Level Select screen.

Star Wars Battlefront II

During gameplay, pause the game. Enter the following codes. There will be a sound if done correctly.

Unlockable	Code
Disable HUD	Up, Up, Up, Up, Left, Up, Up, Down, Left, Down, Up, Up, Left, Right
Lower Resolution Soldiers	Down, Down, Down, Up, Up, Left, Down, Down, Down, Down, Down, Left, Up, Up, Up, Left, Right
Invulnerable	Up, Up, Up, Left, Down, Down, Down, Left, Up, Up, Up, Left, Right
Slow Motion Sound Effects	Up, Up, Up, Left, Up, Down, Up, Up, Left, Down, Down, Down, Left, Up, Down, Down, Left, Right
Weird Captions	Up, Down, Left, Down, Left, Right

Star Wars: Episode I Obi-Wan

Unlockable	Code
Additional Versus Mode Characters	Defeat a character in the Jedi Arena during gameplay to unlock him or her in Versus mode.
All levels until Darth Maul	Enter M1A2U3L4!? as a saved game name
Battle Royal Mission (You have to fight eight other Jedi Masters in the Saber Arena.)	Defeat Darth Maul in Level 25.
Level Select (All levels, including the bonus levels, will be unlocked.)	Select the "New Game" option at the main menu, then enter GREYTHERAT as saved game name.

Star Wars: Episode III Revenge of the Sith

These codes can be entered in the Codes section of the Options menu.

Unlockable	Code
All Attacks and Force Power Upgrades Activated	JAINA
All Bonus Missions Unlocked	NARSHADDAA
All Concept Art Unlocked	AAYLASECURA
All Duel Arenas Unlocked	TANTIVEIV
All Duelist Unlocked	ZABRAK
All Story Missions Unlocked	KORRIBAN
Fast Force Energy and Health Regeneration Activated	BELSAVIS
Infinite Force Energy Activated	KAIBURR
Infinite Health Activated	XUCPHRA

Star Wars Jedi Knight II: Jedi Outcast

Passwords

Password	Effect
DINGO	All Levels
BUBBLE	God Mode
BISCUIT	Infinite Ammo
PEEPS	Multiplayer Characters
DEMO	Play Bonus Level
Fudge	Start With Lightsaber
SCOOTER	Unlimited Force
CHERRY	Unlock First Seven Levels

Unlockable	How to Unlock
Fight Desann Twice	When you are in Yavin Courtyard, run as fast as you can to the room with the Seeker Drones. Push the red button on the right wall 5 times and Desann appears. He is easier to fight right now than when you fight him at Yavin Final Conflict.

Star Wars Knights of the Old Republic

Unlock the Hidden Ending: Before the final battle with Darth Malak press LT + RT + Y on all controllers (you need to have more than one) that you have plugged into the Xbox. This must be done before you enter the door to face Darth Malak. If you did it right, your Jedi takes out her/his lightsaber. Then open the door and walk up to Malak and talk to him.

Star Wars Republic Commando

Enter this code while the game is paused.

Unlockable	Code
Refill Ammo (refills the weapon equipped)	Y,Y,X,(down),RT,LT,RT,(up)

Star Wars Starfighter: Special Edition

Enter the following as codes to access the specified unlockable.

Unlockable	Code
Alternate Camera Angles	DIRECTOR—the message "Director Mode" confirms correct code entry.
Bruiser Gun	BRUISER
Default Screen	SIZZLE
Disable Cockpit Displays	NOHUD
Enemy Ship Gallery	SHIPS

Star Wars Starfighter: Special Edition (continued)

Invincibility	EARCHIPS—the message "Invincibility" confirms correct code entry.
Master Code (Everything except the multiplayer levels will be unlocked.)	EUROPA
Pre-Production Art	PLANETS
Programmer FMV Sequence	LATEAM
Reversed Controls	JARJAR—the message "Jar Jar Mode" confirms correct code entry.
Secret Level Programmers	SLTEAM
Secret Spaceship for Bonus Missions (Unlock the Experimental N-1 Fighter.)	FSNEULB
Spaceship and Cast Pictures	HEROES
Trade Federation Freighter	UTILITY
View Credits	CREDITS

Unlockable	Code
Canyon Sprint Mission	Earn a silver medal in the Naboo Proving Grounds, the Royal Escort, Taking the Offensive, Midnight Munitions Run, Rescue on the Solleu, and the Final Assault missions.
Charm's Way Mission	Earn a bronze medal in the Royal Escort, Contract Infraction, Piracy above Lok, Taking the Offensive, the New Resistance, and the Final Assault missions.
Darth Maul's Infiltrator Ship	Earn a gold medal in all default missions.
Guardian Mantis Ship	Earn a gold medal in the Contract Infraction, Secrets on Eos, and the New Resistance missions.
Havoc Ship	Earn a gold medal in the Piracy above Lok, Valuable Goods, Eye of the Storm, the Crippling Blow, and Last Stand on Naboo missions.
Outpost Attack Mission	Earn a bronze medal in all default missions.
Secret Spaceship for Bonus Missions (Unlock the Experimental N-1 Fighter.)	Earn a gold medal in the Naboo Proving Grounds, the Royal Escort, Taking the Offensive, Midnight Munitions Run, Rescue on the Solleu, and the Final Assault missions.
Space Sweep Mission	Earn a silver medal in all default missions.

Star Wars: The Clone Wars

Unlockable	Code
All Bonus Menu Items	IGIVEUP
All Multiplayer Levels	LETSDANCE
Earn the three bonus objectives	ALITTLEHELP
Get All FMV Movies	GOTPOPCORN
Invincibility	LORDOFSITH
Team Photos	YOURMASTERS
Unlimited Ammo	NOHONOR

Starsky and Hutch

Unlockable	Code
Everything	Enter VADKRAM as a profile name.

State of Emergency

Unlockable	Code
AK47	←, →, ↓, RT, Y
All Weapons Cheat	While playing, press WHT, WHT, RT, RT.
Flamethrower	←, →, ↓, BLK, B
God Mode	While playing, press WHT, LT, BLK, RT, A.

State of Emergency (continued)

Unlockable	Code
Grenade	←, →, ↓, RT, X
Grenade Launcher	←, →, ↓, BLK, X
Looting Cheat	While playing, press BLK, WHT, RT, LT, Y, B
M16	←, →, ↓, RT, B
Minigun	←, →, ↓, BLK, Y
Molotov Cocktail	←, →, ↓, RT, A
Pepper Spray	←, →, ↓, WHT, X
Pistol	←, →, ↓, WHT, Y
Rocket Launcher	←, →, ↓, BLK, A
Select a Level	WHT, LT, LT, LT, WHT, A
Shotgun	←, →, ↓, LT, Y
Skip Level	←, ←, ←, ←, Y
Tazer	←, →, ↓, WHT, B
Tear Gas	←, →, ↓, WHT, A
Unlimited Ammunition	While playing, press WHT, LT, BLK, RT, Y.
Unlimited Time	While playing, press WHT, LT, BLK, RT, B.
Unlock Bull	While playing KAOS Mode, press →, →, →, →, A.
Unlock Freak	While playing KAOS Mode, press →, →, →, →, B.
Unlock Spanky	While playing KAOS Mode, press →, →, →, →, Y.

Stolen

Enter this code in the Equipment screen.

Unlockable	Code
99 of all equipment items	RT, LT, →

Street Hoops

In the Setting menu, select Cheats to enter these codes.

Unlockable	Code
ABA Ball	Y, WHT, X, WHT
Black Ball	WHT, WHT, Y, BLK
Block Party (easier to block)	RT, Y, BLK, WHT
Brick City Clothing	RT, BLK, RT, LT, Y, X, RT, LT
Clown Uniform	X, LT, X, Y
Cowboy Uniform	Y, WHT, WHT, RT
Elvis Uniform	Y, BLK, WHT, BLK, BLK, WHT, LT, BLK
Kung Fu Uniforms	X, Y, X, LT
Normal Ball	RT, X, X, LT
Pimp Uniforms	RT, X, Y, BLK
Power Game	WHT, Y, BLK, Y
Santa Uniform	WHT, BLK, WHT, BLK
Tuxedo Uniform	BLK, BLK, Y, X
Theft Mode (easier to steal)	RT, X, X, X, RT, BLK, Y, WHT

Street Racing Syndicate

Press ↑, ↓, ←, → at the Main menu to enter these codes.

Unlockable	Code
1996 Supra RZ	SICKJZA
1999 Mitsubishi Eclipse GS-T	IGOTGST
2004 Toyota Celica GT-S Action Package	MYTCGTS
Free car repair	FIXITUP
Mazda RX-8	RENESIS
Pac Man Vinyl	GORETRO

Street Racing Syndicate (continued)

Unlockable	Code
Police Car	GOTPOPO
Subaru Impreza Sti	SICKGDB
The first three times you are pulled over in street mode, you will be released with a warning.	LETMEGO

The Suffering

Unlockable	Objective
Alternate title sequence	Complete the game.
Director Commentary	In the Prelude level, wait for a crow to land next to the three inmates, then stand on top of the crow.
Prelude Level	Complete the game.

Enter the following codes during gameplay while holding LT+RT+X.

Unlockable	Code
All Items and Weapons except Gonzo Gun	↓,↑,↓,←,→,←,A,↑,←,↓, →,↑,→,↓,←,A,↓,↓,↓,A,A
Bloody Torque	↑,↓,←,→
Clean Torque	↓,↑,→,←
Dirty Family Picture	←,↓,←,↓,←,↓,A
Full Health	↓,↓,↓,A,↑,↑,↓,↑,A
Full Xombium bottle	→,→,↑,↑,A,←,→,A,→,↑,→,A
Gonzo Gun	←,A,A,A,→,←,→,←,↑,A,A,A,↓,↑,↓,↑,A
Grenades	→,→,→,←,←,←
Increase Negative Karma	←,←,↓,↑,A
Molotov Cocktails	↓,↓,↓,↑,↑,↑
New Family Picture	↑,→,↑,→,↑,→,A
Overcome Insanity	→,→,→,A,←,←,→,←,A
Old Movie Mode	↑,A,←,A,↓,A,→ Press Start to disable this effect.
Psychedelic Mode	←,←,A,→,→,A,↑,↑,A,↓,↓,A
Refill Ranged Weapon Ammunition	←,←,↑,↓,→,←,→,→,A
Reload Ammunition for Current Gun	→,→,↓,↑,←,→,←,←,A
Shotgun with Full Ammunition	←,←,←,↓,↓,↓
Wrinkled Family Picture	↑,↑,→,↑

The Suffering: Ties that Bind

Enter these codes while playing; do not pause.

Unlockable	Code
All Weapons and Items	Hold ↖ + RT + X, then press ↓, ↑, ↓, ←, →, ←, A, ↑, ←, ↓, →, ↑, →, ↓, ←, A, ↓, ↓, ↓, A, A
Full Ammunition for Equipped Gun	Hold LT + RT + X, then press →, →, ↓, ↑, ←, →, ←, ←, A
Refill Health	Hold LT + RT + X, then press ↓, ↓, ↓, A, ↑, ↑, ↓, ↑, A
Shotgun with Full Ammo	Hold LT + RT + X, then press ←, ←, ←, ↓, ↓, ↓

Superman: The Man of Steel

Pause the game to enter these codes.

Unlockable	Code
All Levels and Bonuses	RT, BLK, Y, BLK, LT, WHT
Unlimited Health	BLK, WHT, LT, Y, LT, WHT

SWAT: Global Strike Team

Enter these codes at the Mission Selection screen in either Single Player or Cooperative mode.

Unlockable	Code
All Missions	Up, LT, Down, RT, Left, LT, Right, RT

Tao Feng: Fist of the Lotus

Unlockable	Objective
Unlock Extra Stage	Clear advance training.
Unlock Zhao Yen	Beat Quest Mode with every member of the Black Mantis and Pale Lotus and beat Zhao Yen with both factions.

Teenage Mutant Ninja Turtles 2: Battle Nexus

In the Options menu, select Passwords to enter any of these codes. When selecting a turtle, hold the LT button to pick his New Nexus Outfit.

Unlockable	Code
Challenge Code Abyss	SDSDRLD
Challenge Code Endurance	MRMDRMD
Challenge Code Fatal Blow	LRSRDRD
Challenge Code Lose Shuriken	RLMRDSL
Challenge Code Nightmare	SLSDRDL
Challenge Code Poison	DRSLLSR
Challenge Code Super Tough	RDSRMRL
Cheat Code All You Can Throw Shuriken	RSRLRSM
Cheat Code Health	DSRDMRM
Cheat Code Mighty Turtle	LSDRRDR
Cheat Code Pizza Paradise	MRLMRMR
Cheat Code Self Recovery	DRMSRLR
Cheat Code Squeaking	MLDSRDM
Cheat Code Super Defense Power	LDRMRLM
Cheat Code Super Offense Power	SDLSRLL
Cheat Code Toddling	SSSMRDD
New Nexus Outfit for Donatello	DSLRDRM
New Nexus Outfit for Leonardo	LMRMDRD
New Nexus Outfit for Michelangelo	MLMRDRM
New Nexus Outfit for Raphael	RMSRMDR
Playmates Added to Bonus Materials	SRMLDDR

Teenage Mutant Ninja Turtles 3: Mutant Nightmare

Passwords

Password	Effect
MSRLSMML	2x Enemy Attack
SLRMLSSM	2x Enemy Defense
DMLDMRLD	Endurance—No health pickups available on map
LDMSLRDD	Instant Death—Die in 1 hit
MDLDSSLR	Invincibility—Never die or even lose health!
RRDMLSDL	Max Ougi—Unlimited Ougi!
LLMSRDMS	Shuriken loser—Shurikens no longer available on maps
SLLMRSLD	Sushi Party—All Health pickups become Sushi!
LMDRRMSR	Unlimited shuriken—Unlimited shuriken

Tenchu: Return from Darkness

Unlockable	Objective
All Characters	At the Start screen, hold WHT+BLK and press ↑,→,←,↓. Release WHT+BLK and press LT,RT.
All Enemy Locations	At the Mission Select screen, press →,←,LT,RT,WHT,BLK.
All Items	At the Item Selection screen, hold LT+RT and press ↑,↓,↑,↓,X,X,X,←,→,←,→,X,X,X.
All Missions	At the Mission Select screen, press WHT,WHT,LT,RT,→,X,←,→.
Bonus Mission	At the Title screen, press WHT,↑,BLK,↓,LT,→,RT,←.
B-Side Voices	At the Title screen, hold LT+RT and press ↓,X,X,↑,X,X,←,X,X,→,X,X.
Fill the Kuji Meter	During a mission, pause and hold LT+RT, then press ←,←,←,→,X.
Increase Items	At the Item Selection screen, hold LT+RT and press ↑,←,↓,→,X,X,X.
Increase Offensive Power	During a mission, pause and hold RT+WHT and press ↑,↓,↑,↓, then release RT+WHT and press X,X,X.
Increase Score	During a mission, pause and hold WHT+BLK and press →,→,→,←.
New Ability	During a mission, pause and hold RT+BLK and press ↑,↑,↓,↓, then release RT+BLK and press X,X,LT,RT.
One Kanji	During a mission, pause and press ←,←,←,→,X.
Restore Health	During a mission, pause and press ↑,↓,↑,↓,X,X,X.
Score	During a mission, pause and press →,→,→,←.
Unlimited Item Capacity	At the Item Selection screen, hold LT+RT+WHT and press ↑,↑,↓,↓,←,→,←,→, then release WHT and press X,X,X.

Terminator 3: Rise of the Machines

Enter these codes in the Cheats menu under "Options."

Unlockable	Code
All Future Weapons	A, A, A, X, B, X, B, B
All Present Day Weapons	Y, B, A, B, A, X, Y, X
Invincibility	Y, X, B, B, A, A, B, X
T-850's Hit Points Increased by 50 Percent	A, Y, A, Y
T-850's Hit Points Reduced by 50 Percent	B, Y, A, A
T-X Hit Points Increased by 50 Percent	B, X, X, X, B, A, Y, A
T-X Hit Points Reduced by 50 Percent	B, B, X, X, X, B, A, Y
Unlimited Ammo	X, A, Y, Y, Y, A, X, B
Unlimited Continues	B, B, B, X, B, A, Y, A
Unlock All Exclusive Movie Scenes	B, B, B, A, X, Y, X, Y
Unlock All Game Scenes	B, B, B, X, B, Y, B, B
Unlock All Levels	X, Y, Y, X, B, A, A, B
Unlock Centipede	A, B, B, B, X, Y, B, A
Unlock Missile Command	A, B, B, B, X, Y, A, B

Terminator 3: The Redemption

Unlockable	Code
All Upgrades	Highlight Credits and press B+Y+LT

Test Drive

Passwords

Password	Effect
Unlock 2 Jaguars and an Aston Martin Vanquish	Set a new record on the drag racing level in Story mode and enter SOUNDMAX
Unlock the G4TV Viper	Set a new record on any track and Enter KQXYKGVY as the name

Tiger Woods PGA Tour 06

Go to the Options menu, then enter the Passwords menu to enter these passwords.

Unlockable	Code
All Clubs	CLUB11
All Courses	ITSINTHEHOLE
All Golfers	WOOGLIN
Tiger Woods with Alternate Old Golf Outfit	OLDSKOOL
Tiger Woods with Hat	GOLDENAGE
Tiger Woods with Old Striped Pants	TECHNICOLOR
Tiger Woods with Very Old Golf Outfit	THROWBACK

Tiger Woods PGA Tour 07

Passwords

Password	Effect
ELDRICK	Unlocks 20+ golfers and 30+ course memberships
THREE STRIPES	Unlocks the Adidas sponsorship
JUSTDOIT	Unlocks the Nike sponsorship (Does not unlock the Nike TW items, only the regular Nike items)

Timesplitters 2

Complete these levels in Story mode under the Medium difficulty setting to access the playable characters.

Level Reward	Playable Character
1853 Wild West	The Colonel
1895 Notre Dame Paris	Notre Dame
1920 Aztec Ruins	Stone Golem
1932 Chicago	Big Tony
1972 Atom Smasher	Khallos
1990 Oblask Dam Siberia	The Mutant TimeSplitter
2019 NeoTokyo	Sadako
2280 Return to Planet X	Ozor Mox
2315 Robot Factory	Machinist
2401 Space Station	Reaper Splitter See Tip

TIP

Complete the 2401 Space Station level under the Easy difficulty setting to unlock the ending sequence.

Tom Clancy's Ghost Recon 2: Summit Strike

Pause the game during gameplay, choose "In Game Options," then choose "Enter Cheats."

Unlockable	Code
Complete Current Mission	B, B, X, Y
Refill Ammo	B, B, X, X
Superman (Player Invincibility)	B, B, X, A
Team Superman (Team Invincibility)	B, B, X, B

Tom Clancy's Rainbow Six 3: Black Arrow

Unlockable	Code
Guns fire lasers instead of bullets	Enter Up, Down, Up, Down, RT, RT
God Mode	Enter Up, Up, Down, Down, Left, Right, Left, Right, B, A during gameplay.

Tom Clancy's Rainbow Six 4

This code only works in single player mode.

Unlockable	Code
God mode	Press Up, Up, Down, Down, Left, Right, Left, Right, B, A

Tomb Raider Legends

Enter these codes in game. Codes can not be used until they are unlocked.

Unlockable	Code
Bulletproof	Hold LT press A, RT, Y, RT, X, BLK
Draw enemies' health	Hold LT press X, B, A, BLK, RT, Y
Excalibur	Hold BLK press Y, A, B, RT, Y, LT
Infinite Assault Ammo	Hold BLK press A, B, A, LT, X, Y
Infinite Grenade Launcher Ammo	Hold BLK press LT, Y, RT, B, LT, X
Infinite Shotgun Ammo	Hold BLK press RT, B, X, LT, X, A
Infinite SMG Ammo	Hold BLK press B, Y, LT, RT, A, B
One Shot Kills	Hold LT press Y, A, Y, X, BLK, B
Soul Reaver	Hold BLK press A, RT, B, RT, LT, X
Textureless Mode	Hold LT press BLK, A, B, A, Y, RT

Tony Hawk's American Wasteland

Enter this code at the Cheats menu. (Note: case sensitive)

Unlockable	Code
Mat Hoffman	the_condor

Tony Hawk's Project 8

In the Options menu, select Cheats to enter these passwords.

Unlockable	Password
Big Realtor	shescaresme
Christian Hosoi	hohohosoi
Colonel and Security Guard	militarymen
Dad and Skater Jam Kid	strangefellows
Full Air Stats	drinkup
Grim Reaper	enterandwin
Inkblot Deck	birdhouse

Tony Hawk's Project 8 (continued)

Unlockable	Password
Jason Lee	notmono
Kevin Staab	mixitup
Mascot	manineedadate
Most Decks	needaride
Nerd	wearelosers
Photographer and Cameraman	themedia
Travis Barker	plus44
Unlock Specials in Skate Shop	yougotitall

Tony Hawk's Pro Skater 2X

Unlockable	Code
All Cheats	While playing, pause the game and hold the (LT), then press (START), (A), (WHT), (Up), (Right), (Down), (A), (Y), (B), (A), (B), (Y).

Tony Hawk's Pro Skater 3

To enter these codes, select Cheats in the Options menu.

Unlockable	Code	Unlockable	Code
All Characters	teamfreak	Complete game with selected Character	stiffcomp
All Decks	neverboard	Max Stats	juice4me
All Movies	rollit		

Tony Hawk's Pro Skater 4

To enter these codes, select Cheats in the Options menu.

Unlockable	Code	Unlockable	Code
Always Special	i'myellow	Perfect Manuals	freewheelie
Daisy	(o)(o)	Perfect Rails	belikeeric
Everything	watch_me_xplode	Perfect Skitch	bumperrub
Matrix Mode	fbiagent	Stats 13	4p0sers
Moon Gravity	moon$hot		

Tony Hawk's Underground

Unlockable	Code
Moon Gravity	getitup
Perfect Manuals	keepitsteady
Perfect Rails	letitslide

Tony Hawk's Underground 2

To enter these codes, select Cheats in the Options menu.

Unlockable	Code
Paulie Ryan	4wheeler
Perfect Rails	straightedge

Toxic Grind

Enter these codes at the main menu. To enter them, you will need to hold (LT)+(RT).

Unlockable	Code
All Bikes	(Down), (Up), (Right), (Right), (Right), (Right), (Right), (Right), (Right), (L3)
All Levels	(Down), (Up), (Left), (Left), (Up), (Right), (Right), (Right), (L3)
All Music Tracks	(Right), (Right), (Right), (Right), (Right), (Right), (Up), (Down), (L3)
All Riders	(Left), (Up), (Down), (Right), (Up), (Down), (Up), (Right), (L3)
Unlock All Movies	(Right), (Up), (Down), (Down), (Up), (Right), (Down), (Down), (L3)

True Crime: New York City

While on the Compstat/Map, hold LT+RT and enter these codes.

Unlockable	Code
A Million Dollars	X, X, Y, X, Y, X
Double Damage	A, A, X, A, A, A
Redman Gone Wild Mini Game	Y, A, A, X, A, X
Super Cop	Y, A, Y, A, Y, Y
Ultra Easy Mode	B, X, A, A, Y, B
Unlimited Ammo	B, X, A, X, X, Y
Unlimited Endurance	B, X, A, X, A, B

True Crime: Streets of LA

Enter the following codes on the Map screen.

Unlockable	Code
All Driving skills	←,→,←,→,A
All Gunplay Skills	→,←,→,←,A
All Fighting Skills	↑,↓,↑,↓,A

Turok: Evolution

Go to the Cheats menu and enter the following codes.

Unlockable	Code	Unlockable	Code
All Cheats	FMNFB	Invisible	SLLEWGH
All Weapons	TEXAS	Level Select	SELLOUT
Big Head Mode	HEID	Opens All Codes	FMNFB
Demo Mode/Mini-Game	HUNTER	Unlimited Ammo	MADMAN
Invincible	EMERPUS	Zoo Level	ZOO

Ty the Tasmanian Tiger 2: Bush Rescue

Enter these codes during gameplay.

Unlockable	Code
100,000 Opals	START, START, Y, START, START, Y, B, A, B, A
All Bunnyip Licenses	START, START, Y, START, START, Y, X, B, X, A
All Level One Rangs	START, START, Y, START, START, Y, B, X, B, X
All Level Two Rangs	START, START, Y, START, START, Y, X, B, X, Y

Ultimate Spider-Man

Enter these codes in the Controller Setup menu. A sound confirms a correct entry.

Unlockable	Code
Unlock All Characters	→, ↓, →, ↓, ←, ↑, ←, →
Unlock All Comic Covers	←, ←, →, ←, ↑, ←, ←, ↓
Unlock All Concept Art	↓, ↓, ↓, ↑, ↓, ↑, ←, ←
Unlock All Landmarks	↑, →, ↓, ←, ↓, ↑, →, ←

Unreal Championship

Unlockable	Code
Agility Power-up	When your adrenaline reaches 100 and starts to flash, quickly tap ↓, ↓, ↓, ↑.
Berserk Power-up	When your adrenaline reaches 100 and starts to flash, quickly tap ↑, ↑, ↑, ↑.
Invincibility Power-up	When your adrenaline reaches 100 and starts to flash, quickly tap →, →, ←, ←.
Regeneration Power-up	When your adrenaline reaches 100 and starts to flash, quickly tap ↓, ↓, ↓, ↓.
Wall Jump	If a wall exists to your right, jump up and to the right, and then jump off the wall to your left.

DS
PSP
PS2
PS3
Wii
Xbox
Xbox 360
Index

Unreal Championship 2: The Liandri Conflict

Unlockable	Code
Cheat Menu	Pause, then hold down LT+RT and press WHT. Turn on any of the cheats you want.

Urban Chaos Riot Response

At the Main menu, enter Up, Up, Down, Down, Y, Down, Up, Y to open the Cheat menu. Then input these passwords.

Unlockable	Password
All Levels and Emergencies	KEYTOTHECITY
Assault Rifle Mk3 with Infinite Shells	ULTIMATEPOWER
Disco Mode	DANCINGFEET
Enhanced (Longest Ranged) Stun Gun Unlocked	FRYINGTIME
Headless Enemies	KEEPYOURHEAD
Mini-Gun Unlocked	MINIFUN
Pistol Mk4. Unlocked	ZEROTOLERANCE
Shot Sets Enemy on Fire	BURNINGBULLET
Squeaky Voices	WHATWASTHAT
Terror Difficulty Unlocked	BURNERSREVENGE

Van Helsing

During gameplay, enter the following. Access the movies in the Gallery.

Unlockable	Code
Bonus Movie 1	Up, Down, Up, Down, Left, Left, Right, Right, LT, L3, R3, RT
Bonus Movie 2	Up, Right, Down, Left, Up, Left, Down, Right, Up, RT, BLK, R3
Bonus Movie 3	LT, WHT, BLK, RT, BLK, WHT, LT, Up, Up, Down, Down, BACK
Bonus Movie 4	BACK, L3, R3, BACK, R3, L3, BACK, Left, Left, Up, Right, Right
Bonus Movie 5	WHT, BLK, LT, RT, BACK, BACK, LT, LT, BLK, BLK, L3, R3
Bonus Movie 6	BLK, RT, BLK, RT, LT, WHT, LT, WHT, Left, Right, BACK, BACK
Bonus Movie 7	L3, Left, R3, RT, WHT, Up, BLK, Down, LT, Left, RT, Right

Wakeboarding Unleashed

Unlockable	Code
All Boarders	Rotate Ⓛ clockwise fifteen times at the Main menu.
Boarder Movies	Complete the game with that character.
Credits	Beat the game once with any boarder.
Jordan	Collect every star in the Star Search Challenges.
Level Select	Go to the Main menu and enter: X, X, X, X, B, B, B, B, Y, Y, Y, Y, X, B, Y.
More Boards	Enter this code at the Main menu: Up, Up, Left, Left, Right, Right, Down, Down, Up, Left, Right, Down, Up, Left, Right, Down.
Summer	Beat the game once with any boarder.
Unlock Everything	Enter this code at the Main menu: Up, Down, Up, Down, Up, Down, Up, Down, Up, Down, Left, Right, Left, Right, Left, Right, Left, Right, Left, Right.

World Series Baseball

Unlockable	Objective
Batting Champ Medal	Complete Franchise mode in the top three teams in batting averages.
Big Spender Medal	Complete Franchise mode in the top three teams in BP spent.
Cellar Dweller Medal	Complete Franchise mode in the bottom three teams in wins.
Dominant Team Medal	Complete Franchise mode in the top three teams in wins.

World Series Baseball (continued)

Unlockable	Objective
Golden Slugger Medal	Complete Franchise mode in the top three teams in homeruns.
Great Glove Medal	Complete Franchise mode in the top three teams in fielding percentages.
Pitching Ace Medal	Complete Franchise mode in the top three teams in earned run averages.
Speed Demon Medal	Complete Franchise mode in the top three teams in stolen bases.
Strikeout King Medal	Complete Franchise mode in the top three teams in strikeouts.
Tightwad Medal	Complete Franchise mode in the bottom three teams in BP spent.

Wrath Unleashed

Unlockable	Code
Big World Map Critters	Left, X, Up, Y, Right, B, Down, B
Extended Fighting	Down, Down, Up, Down, Left, Right, Down, Up, Up, Up, Right, Left, X
Team Fighter Character Variation	LT, LT, Down, Down, BLK, WHT, BLK, WHT, RT, LT, BLK, RT, RT, RT, WHT
Versus Character Variations	LT, LT, Down, Down, BLK, WHT, BLK, WHT, RT, LT, BLK, RT, RT, WHT

WWE Wrestlemania 21

Enter the code at the Title screen.

Unlockable	Code
All items in the Shop Zone unlocked	Hold LT+RT, and then press A+B+X+Y

X2: Wolverine's Revenge

Cheats Option: On the main menu, press X, X, LT, LT, LT, LT, X, X, LT. The cheats option should now be available when you pause the game.

Unlockable	Code
All Cerebro Files and Movies	On the main menu, press X, LT, X, LT, X, X, RT, LT.
Level Select and All Challenges	On the main menu, press X, LT, X, LT, X, LT, LT, RT.
Unlock Everything	Press X, LT, X, LT, X, X, LT, RT at the title screen. Repeat the code a few times to unlock absolutely everything.

XGRA: Extreme-G Racing Association

Go to Options, select the Cheat menu, and enter the following.

Unlockable	Code
All Tracks	WIBBLE
All Racing Levels	FREEPLAY
02 Liveried	UCANDO

X-Men Legends 2: Rise of Apocalypse

Enter these codes in the Review menu.

Unlockable	Code
Unlocks All Comics	Right, Left, Left, Right, Up, Up, Right, START
Unlocks Game Cinematics	Left, Right, Right, Left, Down, Down, Left, START

X-Men The Official Game

Enter these codes in the Cerebro Files menu.

Unlockable	Code
Iceman's Danger Room	Right, Right, Left, Left, Down, Up, Down, Up, START
Nightcrawler's Danger Room	Up, Up, Down, Down, Left, Right, Left, Right, START
Wolverine's Danger Room	Down, Down, Up, Up, Right, Left, Right, Left, START

DS | PSP | PS2 | PS3 | Wii | Xbox | Xbox 360 | Index

DS PSP PS2 PS3 Wii Xbox Xbox 360 Index

Table of Contents - XBOX 360

1942: Joint Strike

Secret Plane

Beat the game on Wing King Difficulty setting, then select Shinden in the Plane Selection screen by pressing "Y." This enables you to use a black and red version of the Shinden with maxed out power.

2006 FIFA World Cup

Unlockable	Code
Beat the Host Nation	Beat the host nation Germany in a full match
Complete a Scenario	Complete any Challenge in Global Challenge
Complete all Scenarios	Complete all the Challenges in Global Challenge
Qualify for the World Cup	Qualify for the World Cup in 2006 FIFA World Cup mode
Win the World Cup	Win the World Cup in 2006 FIFA World Cup mode

Alien Hominid HD

Unlockable Hats

To unlock each hat do the following. Note: you must finish the level for it to unlock. Just doing the task isn't enough.

Unlockable	How to Unlock
Area 51 Agent Hat	Beat 3-2
Black Afro	Beat 1-5
Blond Wig/Pearls	Beat 1-2
Brown Hair	On Hard, jump off the spaceship before the screen fades after beating the final boss
Brown Hat	In 2-5, kill 7 birds

DS
PSP
PS2
PS3
Wii
Xbox
Xbox 360
Index

Alien Hominid HD (continued)

Unlockable	How to Unlock
Brown Wig/Pearls	Beat 1-3
Chef Hat	Beat 1-3
Conical Purple Hat	In 1-3, destroy "Castle of Crap" building
Crown of Flowers	1-1 with gore off
Daisy-petal	Beat 2-3
Jester's Cap	Beat 3-4 on Hard
Jheri Curl	In 1-4 destroy "fish are like plants" building
KGB Agent Hat	Beat 2-1
Nurse Cap	In 3-5, get to final boss (don't have to win)
Pirate Hat	1-1 destroy "Hairy Mommy Daycare"
Private Eye hat	Beat 3-2 on Hard
Red Bandana	Beat 1-4
Rooster Hat	In 1-4 destroy the Behemoth-logo building (must be out of tank)
Stove Pipe Hat	1-1 with gore off
Tiara	2-2 on Hard
Yellow Shark Fin	In 2-4 dig/suffocate before riding snowmobile

Alone in the Dark

Achievements

Unlockable	How to Unlock
A Day in Central Park	Complete the game.
Basic Combination	A bottle with tape.
Blackout	Finish Episode 1 without skipping any sequence.
Blazing Roots	Burn all roots of evil.
Bloody Mary	Heal 5 bleeding wounds.
Burning Root	Burn a root of evil.
Car Thievery	Break into a locker car by shattering the window.
Cockpit Addict	Complete the 59th Street run with Episode 2 in cockpit view.
Cocoon	Burn a monster cocoon.
Countdown to Death	Stop your bleeding wound.
Demolition Expert	Build the most destructive weapon.
Eradication	Kill 100 Humanz.
Fight Back and Loss	Finish Episode 4 without skipping any sequence.
Fire Bullets	Make Fire Bullet by combining fuel with your pistol.
Fisherman's Foe	Shoot a goldfish in one of the Central Park ponds.
Fissure	Burn one of the snaking fissures.
Flaming Roots	Burn half of the roots of evil.
Free Gasoline	Pierce a car gas tank with a knife or screwdriver and fill a bottle with fuel.
Goal!	Give 10 kicks to Bugz.
Handyman Carnby	Make all possible combinations in the inventory.
Hidden Cave	Discover what's under the blockhouse in Episode 8.
Massage	Save Sarah from a cocoon.
Meet Again	Meet Theo in Room 943 in the museum.
Never Leave a Key Here	Find car keys in the sun visor.

Alone in the Dark (continued)

Unlockable	How to Unlock
Not Alone Anymore	Finish Episode 5 without skipping any sequence.
Nuke	Kill 3 Humanz with a single attack.
Painful Answers	Finish Episode 3 without skipping any sequence.
Purification by Fire	Destroy a Vampirz Nest.
Questions	Finish Episode 2 without skipping any sequence.
Stuntman	Jump across the gap in front of the museum using the tow truck.
The 10 Miles Race	Drive at least 10 miles in a vehicle.
The Air Bomb	Shoot a bottle filled with flammable content out of the air.
The Biggest of All	Defeat the monster at the end of the Episode 5.
The Blind Man	Finish the "Wake up" sequence in the beginning of the game without closing your eyes.
The Cocktail Molotov	Combine a bottle with flammable content with handkerchief.
The Glowstick Bomb	Tape a glowstick to a fuel-filled bottle.
The Light Bringer	Finish Episode 8 without skipping any sequence.
The Path of Darkness	Kill Sarah.
The Path of Light	Don't kill Sarah.
The Path of Light	Finish Episode 7 without skipping any sequence.
The Sharp Shooter	Finish a monster by shooting its fissures with fire bullets.
The Smart Fighter	Kill a monster with spray + lighter combination.
The Sticky Bomb	Combine a bottle filled with flammable content with tape and use it against an enemy.
The Truth	Finish Episode 6 without skipping any sequence.
Toasted Eggs	Burn a Bugz nest.
Unlimited Offer	Call all contacts in your phone's address book.
Useless!	Combine an empty taped bottle, a wick, and an emergency flare.
Vampirz	Burn a Vampirz.
Wired	Hotwire a car.

Amped 3

At the Main menu, go into Options, then into the Cheats menu to enter this code.

Unlockable	Code
All Sleds	(RT), (X), (LT), (D-pad down), (D-pad right), (LB), (LT), (RT), (Y), (X)

Army of Two

Achievements

Unlockable	How to Unlock
Alright, Who Wants Some? (20)	Kill 250 enemies using SMGs.
Beast with Two Fronts (20)	Kill 50 enemies in Back-to-Back.
Big Boom! Big Bada Boom! (20)	Kill 25 enemies using RPGs.
Boots on the Ground (10)	Finish playing a versus ranked match.
Dead Man's Hand (20)	Kill 150 enemies using handguns.
Elite PMC (50)	Complete all missions as a Professional.
Fear Is the Mind Killer (45)	Spend one minute straight at full Aggro.

Army of Two (continued)

Unlockable	How to Unlock
Field Medic (30)	Drag and heal your partner 25 times.
Fission Mailed (20)	Kill 25 Martyrs by shooting the Bomb Packs on their chests.
Flip You. Flip You For Real. (20)	Kill 50 enemies using the Melee Attack.
If I Were a Rich Man (40)	Earn one million dollars over the course of Campaign mode.
If It Bleeds, We Can Kill It (30)	Kill 25 Heavy Armor enemies.
L'Abattoir (30)	Kill 100 enemies while in the power mode of Overkill.
Man of Many Masks (50)	Purchase every mask variant.
Mission 1 Complete (30)	Completed Mission 1 as Contractor or higher.
Mission 2 Complete (30)	Completed Mission 2 as Contractor or higher.
Mission 3 Complete (15)	Completed Mission 3 as Contractor or higher.
Mission 4 Complete (15)	Completed Mission 4 as Contractor or higher.
Mission 5 Complete (15)	Completed Mission 5 as Contractor or higher.
Mission 6 Complete (15)	Completed Mission 6 as Contractor or higher.
My Kind of Case! (40)	Collect all of the information cases in the entire game.
My Virtual Friend (35)	Complete all missions with the Partner AI.
One Gun Is Enough (35)	Win a ranked match without purchasing any additional weapons.
One Shot. One Kill. (20).	Kill 100 enemies using Sniper Rifles.
Out of Debt (15)	Heal your partner for the first time. Training does not count.
Retirement Savings Plan (40)	Earn one billion dollars in ranked matches.
Running Man (30)	Kill 75 enemies while in the stealth mode of Overkill.
Say Hello to My Little Friends (45)	Purchase the MP7, M134, DAO-X Protecta, MGL MK-X, and the M107 Light Fifty.
Seven-six-two Millimeter (20)	Kill 250 enemies using Assault Rifles.
Spray and Pray (20)	Kill 250 enemies using Machine Guns.
Starting a Riot (30)	Kill 50 enemies in Co-op Riot Shield.
Stonewall (30)	Kill 30 enemies using the Riot Shield melee attack.
Surviving the Game (25)	Complete a ranked match without ever needing to be revived.
The Devil's in the Details (20)	Complete 20 minor objectives in a ranked match.
This Is My Boom Stick! (20)	Kill 250 enemies total using Shotguns.
Two Eyes Are Better Than One (35)	Kill five enemies total using Co-op Snipe.
Weapon Specialist (15)	Purchase three weapons.

Assassin's Creed

Achievements

Complete each achievement to get the allotted gamerscore.

Unlockable	How to Unlock
Absolute Symbiosis (45)	Have a complete Synchronization bar.
Blade in the Crowd (30)	Kill one of your main targets like a true assassin.
Conversationalist (20)	Go through every dialog with Lucy.
Defender of the People: Acre (20)	Complete every free mission in Acre.
Defender of the People: Damascus (20)	Complete every free mission in Damascus.
Defender of the People: Jerusalem (20)	Complete every free mission in Jerusalem.
Disciple of the Creed (30)	Assassinate all your targets with a full DNA bar.

Assassin's Creed (continued)

Unlockable	How to Unlock
Eagle's Challenge (20)	Defeat 25 guards in a single fight.
Eagle's Dance (10)	Perform 50 leaps of faith.
Eagle's Dive (20)	Perform 50 combo kills in fights.
Eagle's Eye (15)	Kill 75 guards by throwing knives.
Eagle's Flight (20)	Last 10 minutes in open conflict.
Eagle's Prey (20)	Assassinate 100 guards.
Eagle's Swiftness (20)	Perform 100 counter kills in fights.
Eagle's Talon (15)	Perform 50 stealth assassinations.
Eagle's Will (20)	Defeat 100 opponents without dying.
Enemy of the Poor (5)	Grab and throw 25 harassers.
Fearless (25)	Complete all reach high points.
Gifted Escapist (5)	Jump through 20 merchant stands.
Hero of Masyaf (20)	You've protected Masyaf from the Templar invasion.
Hungerer of Knowledge (20)	See 85% of all the memory glitches.
Keeper of the 8 Virtues (10)	Find all Hospitalier flags in Acre.
Keeper of the Black Cross (10)	Find all Teutonic flags in Acre.
Keeper of the Creed (10)	Find all flags in Masyaf.
Keeper of the Crescent (20)	Find all flags in Damascus.
Keeper of the Four Gospels (20)	Find all flags in Jerusalem.
Keeper of the Lions Passant (25)	Find all of Richard's flags in the kingdom.
Keeper of the Order (10)	Find all Templar flags in Acre.
March of the Pious (5)	Use scholar blending 20 times.
Personal Vendetta (40)	Kill every Templar.
The Blood of a Corrupt Merchant (25)	You've slain Tamir, Black Market Merchant in Damascus.
The Blood of a Doctor (25)	You've slain Garnier de Naplouse, Hospitalier Leader in Acre.
The Blood of a Liege-Lord(25)	You've slain William of Montferrat, Liege-Lord of Acre.
The Blood of a Nemesis(25)	You've slain Robert de Sable, but there is one more.
The Blood of a Regent (25)	You've slain Majd Addin, Regent of Jerusalem.
The Blood of a Scribe(25)	You've slain Jubair, the Scribe of Damascus.
The Blood of a Slave Trader (25)	You've slain Tatal, Slave Trader of Jerusalem.
The Blood of a Teutonic Leader(25)	You've slain Sibrand, the Teutonic Leader of Acre.
The Blood of the Merchant King (25)	You've slain Abul Nuqoud, Merchant King of Damascus.
The Eagle and the Apple—1191 (100)	Complete *Assassin's Creed.*
The Hands of a Thief (15)	Pickpocket 200 throwing knives.
The Punishment for Treason (20)	You have found the traitor and have brought him before Al Mualim.
Visions of the Future (50)	After the credits roll, walk back into Desmond's bedroom and activate Eagle Vision by pressing Ⓨ and look at the wall above the bed.
Welcome to the Animus (20)	You've successfully completed the Animus tutorial.

Avatar: The Last Airbender–The Burning Earth

Codes

In the Password screen in the main menu, click the left arrow, and then go to "cheat entry."

Unlockable	How to Unlock
All Bonus Games	99801
All Gallery Items	85061
Double Damage	90210
Infinite Life	65049
Infinite Special Attacks	66206
Max Level	89121
One-Hit Dishonor	28260

Achievements

Unlockable	How to Unlock
One with Combat (300)	Achieve a Hit Counter of 50.
The Art of Combat (200)	Achieve a Hit Counter of 40.
The Flow of Combat I (150)	Achieve a Hit Counter of 10.
The Flow of Combat II (150)	Achieve a Hit Counter of 20.
The Flow of Combat III (200)	Achieve a Hit Counter of 30.

Battlefield: Bad Company

Find All Five Weapons

Unlockable	How to Unlock
Assault Rifle	Register your old *Battlefield* games at *http://www.veteran.battlefield.com/*.
Light Machine Gun	Sign up for the newsletter at *http://www.findallfive.com/*.
Semi-Automatic Shotgun	After playing an Online game, login and check your stats at *http://www.findallfive.com/*.
Sniper Rifle	Pre-order the game from a participating retailer before June 23rd, 2008.
Uzi	Play the "Battlefield: Bad Company Demo" and get to rank 4. (2,300 EXP required to reach rank 4.)

Trophies

Trophies are unlockable in Multiplayer modes.

Unlockable	How to Unlock
Assault Rifle Efficiency Trophy	In a round, 6 kills with Assault rifle.
Avenger Trophy	In a round, 3 avenger points.
Best Squad Trophy	Awarded at end of round.
Big Guns Trophy	In a round, 5 kills with artillery.
Carbine Efficiency Trophy	In a round, 6 kills with M16A2.
Clear Skies Trophy	In a round, 5 kills with stationary weapon.
Combat Aviator Trophy	In a round, 5 kills with air vehicle.
Combat Efficiency Trophy	In a round, 6 kill streak.
Combat Engineer Trophy	In a round, 20 vehicle repair points (2 repairs).
Compact Assault Rifle Efficiency Trophy	In a round, 6 kills with compact assault rifle.
Demo Pack Efficiency Trophy	In a round, 3 kills with C4.
Emplacement Trophy	In a round, 5 kills with stationary weapon.

Battlefield: Bad Company (continued)

Unlockable	How to Unlock
Explosive Efficiency Trophy	In a round, 10 kills with explosives.
Firearm Efficiency Trophy	In a round, 3 kills with handgun.
Frag Out Efficiency Trophy	In a round, 3 kills with grenade while playing Demolitionists.
Grenade Launcher Efficiency	In a round, 6 kills with grenade launcher.
Grenadier Efficiency Trophy	In a round, 3 kills with grenade playing Assault.
High Card Trophy	In a round, get the best IAR Score.
Kill Assists Trophy	In a round, 5 kill assists.
Laser Designating Efficiency Trophy	In a round, 3 kills from laser designating.
Light Machine Gun Efficiency Trophy	In a round, 6 kills with a light machine gun.
Marksman Trophy	In a round, 5 kills with sniper rifle.
Medic Trophy	In a round, 10 points from med kit (2 heals)
Melee Combat Trophy	In a round, 5 melee kills.
Mine Placement Efficiency Trophy	In a round, 3 kills with AT mines.
Mortar Strike Efficiency Trophy	In a round, 3 kills with mortar strike.
Naval Surface Warfare Trophy	In a round, 5 kills with sea vehicle.
Objective Attack Trophy	In a round, destroy the last objective.
Objective Defender Trophy	In a round, 30 defend points.
Objective Destroyer Trophy	In a round, destroy 3 objectives.
Rocket Launcher Efficiency Trophy	In a round, 3 kills with rocket launcher.
Savior Trophy	In a round, 3 savior points.
Shotgun Efficiency Trophy	In a round, 5 kills with a shotgun.
Squad Medication Trophy	In a round, 40 squad member heal points.
Squad Member Trophy	In a round, assist or save 5 squad members.
SVU Efficiency Trophy	In a round, 5 kills with the SVU.
Tank Warfare Trophy	In a round, 5 kills with tanks.
Target Tagging Efficiency Trophy	In a round, 2 kill assists from dartgun tagging.
Transport Vehicle Trophy	In a round, 5 kills with transport vehicle.
UMP	In a round, 6 kills with UMP.
Wheels of Hazard Trophy	In a round, 2 road kills.
Winning Team Trophy	Awarded at end of round.

Wild Cards

Unlockable	How to Unlock
1 on 1 Air	In a round, destroy an air vehicle of the same kind without assistance.
1 on 1 Land	In a round, destroy one land vehicle of the same kind without assistance.
1 on 1 Sea	In a round, destroy 1 sea vehicle of the same kind without assistance.
2 Pair	In a round, get 2 of any 2 trophies.
Airtime	In a round, 2 seconds air time in a land vehicle.
Armor Buster	In a round, kill 5 armored vehicles.
Avenger Trophies	Global: 50x avenger trophies.
Beat the House	In a round, 15 grenade kills.
Cab Driver	In a round, 5 min as driver in a vehicle with passengers.

DS PSP PS2 PS3 Wii Xbox Xbox 360 Index

Battlefield: Bad Company (continued)

Unlockable	How to Unlock
Chopper Chopper Kills	In a round, kill 5 air vehicles.
Dead Eye Headshots	Global: Get 100 headshots with any sniper rifle.
Destruction Site	In a round, destroy 50 objects.
Deuces Are Wild	In a round, kill 2 enemies of each kind.
Five of a Kind	In a round, destroy 5 vehicles of the same kind.
Full Deck	In a round, 52 total kills.
Full House	In a round, destroy 3+2 vehicles of the same kind.
Gunslinger	Global: 80 kills with handgun.
Headshots	In a round, 20 kills from headshots.
Parashooter	In a round, 4 road kills with any air vehicle.
Santa's Little Helper	In a round, 10 kill assist points.
Savior Trophies	Global: 50x savior trophies.
Snake Eyes	In a round, get 11 kills as two different classes.
Squad Avenger Card	Global: Get 100 avenger points avenging squad members.
Squad Wild Card	In a round, 1 squad member trophy per squad member.
Staying Dry	In a round, 2 seconds air time with a sea vehicle.
Straight Flush	In a round, destroy 1 vehicle of each kind.
Strike	In a round, kill 10 enemies at the same time.
Tank Buster	In a round, kill 5 tanks.
Three of a Kind	In a round, destroy 3 vehicles of the same kind.

Achievements

Unlockable	How to Unlock
Action, Not Words! (25)	Complete "Welcome To Bad Company" on Hard.
Always Get Paid in Gold Bars (15)	Complete "Welcome To Bad Company" on Normal.
Be the Best (20)	(Online) Place #1 in a ranked match.
Beans Bullets Bandages (30)	(Online) Get 10,002 kills.
Been There, Drove That! (20)	Drive all vehicle types (jeep, tank, heli, boat).
Capitalist Pigs, Very Nice (25)	Complete "Crash and Grab" on Hard.
Cart Wheels (25)	Complete "Par for the Course" on Hard.
Catch the "Bad" Moment (15)	(Online) Take 3 pictures using the image system.
Check My Grill (20)	Find half of the gold bars.
Clean Sweep (25)	Find all collectables.
Colonel (25)	(Online) Reach Rank 20.
Darwin's Parachute (10)	(Online) Glide in the parachute for 3 seconds.
Death from Above (20)	Kill 25 enemies in a helicopter.
Dog Owner! (20)	(Online) Collect 5 unique dog tags.
Drive By (25)	(Online) 100 kills using vehicle.
Forest Ranger (15)	(Online) Knock down 1,000 trees.
General of the Army (35)	(Online) Reach Rank 25.
Get Me Started (15)	(Online) Participate in one online match (Ranked).
Get the Dog! (20)	(Online) Collect 50 unique dog tags.
Gold Digger (30)	Find all gold bars.
Half Way Thru (20)	Find half of all collectables.
He Might Come in Handy (15)	Complete "Par for the Course" on Normal.

Battlefield: Bad Company (continued)

Unlockable	How to Unlock
Here Is Your DD-214 (30)	Complete "Ghost Town" on Hard.
Hold On! (15)	Complete "Air Force One" on Normal.
Home Wrecker (15)	Destroy 200 walls.
I Am Bad Company! (25)	(Online) Achieve all the awards.
I Love Gold! (10)	Find one gold bar.
Killer on the Loose (25)	Kill 25 enemies.
Leatherneck (25)	(Online) Play 100 online matches.
Let's Take That Boat (15)	Complete "Crash and Grab" on Normal.
Manic Lumberjack (15)	Knock down a small forest.
Master Sergeant (15)	(Online) Reach Rank 8.
Never Used a Door (15)	(Online) Destroy 1,000 walls.
Not Even a Nugget! (15)	Complete "Acta Non Verba" on Normal.
On Top of the World (20)	Climb to the highest spot in the game.
One In a Million (20)	Hit hostile helicopter with laser designator.
Ooh Rah (20)	(Online) Achieve half of all awards.
Russia? (25)	Complete "Air Force One" on Hard.
Say Goodbye to the Gold! (25)	Complete "Crossing Over" on Hard.
Sir, Yes Sir! (30)	Complete "Ghost Town" on Normal.
Specialist (10)	(Online) Reach Rank 3.
Staying Alive (15)	Complete one mission without dying (any difficulty).
The Anti-Mechanic (20)	Destroy 50 vehicles (containing enemy AI).
The Hypochondriac (20)	Use auto injector 50 times.
There Is No I in Squad (15)	(Online) Have 20 squad members spawn on you without dying in a single round.
Vehikill (20)	(Online) Get at least one kill in every vehicle.
Where Are They Going So Fast? (25)	Complete "Acta Non Verba" on Hard.
With My Devil Dogs (15)	(Online) Use squad in the menu, find a friend, and play one round.
You and What Army? (15)	Complete "Crossing Over" on Normal.
You Found It You Keep It (15)	Find 5 unique collectables.

Battlefield 2: Modern Combat

Unlock All Weapons (Campaign)

Code	Effect
Hold the LB and RB and press → → ↓ ↑ ← ← on the d-pad	Unlock all Weapons

Multiplayer ranks

To advance in rank in multiplayer you must get the right number of Medals, Points, and PPH (points per hour).

Unlockable	How to Unlock
Brigadier General	12 Medals, 19,390 Points, 85 PPH
Captain	8 Medals, 8,430 Points, 65 PPH
Chief Warrant Officer	5 Medals, 3,700 Points, 50 PPH
Colonel	11 Medals, 16,070 Points, 80 PPH
Commanding Sergeant Major	3 Medals, 1,820 Points, 40 PPH

Battlefield 2: Modern Combat (continued)

Unlockable	How to Unlock
Corporal	0 Medals, 70 Points, 15 PPH
First Lieutenant	7 Medals, 6,560 Points, 60 PPH
Five Star General	15 Medals, 32,000 Points, 100 PH
Lieutenant Colonel	10 Medals, 13,150 Points, 75 PPH
Lieutenant General	14 Medals, 27,330 Points, 95 PH
Major	9 Medals, 10,620 Points, 70 PPH
Major General	13 Medals, 23,150 Points, 90 PPH
Master Sergeant	1 Medal(s), 720 Points, 30 PPH
Private	0 Medals, 0 Points, 0 PPH
Private First Class	0 Medals, 20 Points, 10 PPH
Second Lieutenant	6 Medals, 4,900 Points, 55 PPH
Sergeant	0 Medals, 190 Points, 20 PPH
Sergeant First Class	0 Medals, 390 Points, 25 PPH
Sergeant Major	2 Medals, 1,180 Points, 35 PPH
Warrant Officer	4 Medals, 2,650 Points, 45 PPH

Battlestations: Midway

Enter this code at the mission select screen.

Unlockable	Code
Unlock All Levels	Hold (RB), ■, ↑, ↖ and push ↘

Bejeweled 2 Deluxe

Mode Unlockables

Unlockable	How to Unlock
Remove Background Grid	Hold (LB) (LT) (RB) (RT) then press (B)
Change Jewel Types	Hold (LB) (LT) (RB) (RT) then press (A)
Unlock Cognito Mode	Finish all the puzzles in Puzzle mode. It is okay to look at hints constantly to solve all the puzzles. Cognito mode is basically Puzzle mode with no hints.
Finity Mode	Complete 280 levels of Endless mode
Hyper Mode	Complete 8 levels of Action mode
Twilight Mode	Complete 17 levels of Classic mode
Original Mode	Go into Play Game when you first load up the game. Select the Classic, Action, Endless, and Puzzle mode buttons (in that order) at the menu screen repeatedly (so you're basically maneuvering the cursor across the screen clockwise). After several rounds, a window will come up saying "Please Wait," and Original mode will load up.

Beautiful Katamari

Formal Outfit

Unlockable	How to Unlock
Royal Outfit	Obtain 100 percent on item collection.

Eternal Mode

Get 100 points on any level to unlock Eternal mode for that specific level. After that you can roll about without a time limit or a goal.

Beautiful Katamari (continued)

Achievements

Unlockable	How to Unlock
1,000 Cookies (40)	Obtain 1,000 cookies.
10 Cousins (5)	Find 10 cousins.
10 Presents (5)	Collect 10 presents.
100 Cookies (5)	Obtain 100 cookies.
100 Hours Playtime (80G)	Played for 100 hours.
20 Cousins (10)	Find 20 cousins.
20 Presents (10)	Collect 20 presents.
30 Cousins (20)	Find 30 cousins.
30 Presents (20)	Collect 30 presents.
40 Cousins (40)	Find 40 cousins.
50 Hours Playtime (40G)	Played for 50 hours.
All Cousins (80)	Download stages and find all cousins.
All Presents (80)	Download stages and collect all presents.
All Requests (60)	Complete all requests.
Astronomic Katamari (90)	Download stages and make a katamari over 1,500,000 km.
Big Katamari (10)	Make a katamari that's 30m or more!
Collection 100% (80G)	Roll up 100% of the collection.
Collection 20% (5)	Roll up 20% of the collection.
Collection 40% (10)	Roll up 40% of the collection.
Collection 60% (20)	Roll up 60% of the collection.
Collection 80% (40)	Roll up 80% of the collection.
Colossal Katamari (60)	Make a katamari that's 10,000 km or more!
Frequent Online Roller (10)	Play online 10 times.
Jumbo Katamari (20)	Make a katamari that's 500 m or more!
Katamari Fan (40G)	Complete requests 100 times in Normal mode.
Katamari Lover (80)	Complete 200 requests.
Katamari Perfectionist (100)	Clear all stages, and then do each (of the possible ones) on time attack.
Manic Roller (20)	Hint: Running into walls will destroy your katamari.
Mini Katamari (5)	Make a katamari that's 30cm or more!
Non-stop Roller (30)	Hint: Roll through the course without stopping once.
Online Roller (5)	Play online.
Quick Turner (10)	Hint: Use Quick Turn to your advantage.
Request x 3 (5)	Complete three requests.
Request x 6 (5)	Complete six requests.
Request x 9 (20)	Complete nine requests.
Resident Online Roller (40)	Play online 50 times.
Responsible Roller (30)	Hint: Roll through the course without bumping into any objects.
Small Katamari (5)	Make a katamari that's 1m or more!
Sorta Big Katamari (5)	Make a katamari that's 5m or more!
Speedy Roller (10)	Hint: Zip through the course with Dash.

DS PSP PS2 PS3 Wii Xbox Xbox 360 Index

BioShock

Achievements

Achievement	How to Unlock
Ammo Inventor (25)	Successfully invented all possible ammo types.
Avid Inventor (10)	Successfully invent at least 100 items.
Basic Inventor (5)	Successfully invent at least one item.
Became a Big Daddy (30)	The player has become a Big Daddy.
Bought One Slot (5)	Purchase one slot in any Plasmid or Tonic track.
Brass Balls (100)	Beat the game on Hard difficulty without using a Vita Chamber.
Broke Fontaine's Mind Control (30)	The player has broken Fontaine's mind control.
Completed Cohen's Masterpiece (30)	The player has completed Sander Cohen's great masterpiece.
Completed Welcome (10)	Successfully complete the Welcome To Rapture level.
Dealt with Every Little Sister (40)	Either harvest or rescue every Little Sister in the game.
Defeated Andrew Ryan (30)	The player has defeated Andrew Ryan.
Defeated Atlas (100)	The player has defeated Atlas.
Defeated Dr. Steinman (15)	The player has defeated the crazed Dr. Steinman.
Defeated Peach Wilkins (15)	The player has defeated Peach Wilkins.
Five Fully Upgraded Weapons (10)	Fully upgrade five weapons.
Found Cohen's Room (10)	The player has entered Sander Cohen's personal quarters.
Four Fully Upgraded Weapons (10)	Fully upgrade four weapons.
Fully Researched Bouncer (10)	Fully research the Bouncer.
Fully Researched Gun Splicer (10)	Fully research the Leadhead Splicer.
Fully Researched Houdini Splicer (10)	Fully research the Houdini Splicer.
Fully Researched Little Sister (10)	Fully research the Little Sister.
Fully Researched Nitro Splicer (10)	Fully research the Nitro Splicer.
Fully Researched Rosie (10)	Fully research the Rosie.
Fully Researched Spider Splicer (10)	Fully research the Spider Splicer.
Fully Researched Thug Splicer (10)	Fully research the Thuggish Splicer.
Hacked a Safe (10)	Successfully hack a safe.
Hacked a Security Bot (10)	Successfully hack a security bot.
Hacked a Security Camera (10)	Successfully hack a security camera.
Hacked a Turret (10)	Successfully hack a turret.
Hacked a Vending Machine (10)	Successfully hack a vending machine.
Historian (50)	Find every audio diary.
Irony (10)	The player has taken a picture of Sander Cohen's corpse.
Little Sister Savior (100)	Complete the game without harvesting any Little Sisters.
Lucky Winner (10)	Hit the jackpot at a slot machine.
Maxed All Tracks (50)	Purchased every slot in all four Plasmid and Tonic tracks.
Maxed One Track (20)	Purchased every slot in one of the Plasmid or Tonic tracks.

BioShock (continued)

Achievement	How to Unlock
One Fully Upgraded Weapon (5)	Fully upgrade one weapon.
One Successful Hack (5)	Perform at least one successful hack.
Prolific Photographer (5)	Take at least one photo in every research group.
Quality Research Photo (20)	Take a Research Photo of the highest grade.
Research PhD (20)	Max out all possible research.
Researched a Splicer (5)	Take at least one Research Photo of a Splicer.
Restored the Forest (15)	The player has restored the forests of Arcadia.
Seriously Good At This (40)	Complete the game on the hardest difficulty setting.
Skilled Hacker (40)	Successfully complete 50 hacks.
Three Fully Upgraded Weapons (10)	Fully upgrade three weapons.
Toaster in the Tub (10)	Shock an enemy in the water.
Tonic Collector (50)	Collect or Invent 53 Tonics in the Physical, Engineering, and Combat tracks.
Two Fully Upgraded Weapons (5)	Fully upgrade two weapons.
Upgraded a Weapon (5)	Acquire at least one weapon upgrade.
Weapon Specialist (20)	Acquire all upgrades for all weapons.

Alternate Endings

Unlockable	How to Unlock
Bad Ending	Harvest more than one Little Sister.
Good Ending	Harvest one Little Sister, but rescue the rest.

Blazing Angels: Squadrons of WWII

Enter these codes while the game is paused.

Unlockable	Code
Firepower Increased	Hold LT, press L1, L1, RB, release LT, hold RT, and then press RB, RB, L1
God Mode	Hold LT, press X, Y, Y, X, release LT, hold RT, and then press Y, X, X, Y

Enter this code at the Main menu.

Unlockable	Code
Unlock all campaign levels and planes	Hold LT+RT, then press X, L1, RB, Y, Y, RB, L1, X

Blitz: The League

Enter these passwords in the Code menu under Extras.

Unlockable	Password
Ball Trail Always On	ONFIRE
Beach Ball	BOUNCY
Double Unleash Icons	PIPPED
Stamina Off	NOTTIRED
Two Player Co-op	CHUWAY
Unlimited Clash Icons	CLASHY
Unlimited Unleash	BIGDOGS

Brothers in Arms: Hell's Highway

Codes

Select the "Enter Codes" option at the main menu, then enter the codes.

Effect	Code
All Recon Points	0ZNDRBICRA
Kilroy Alert (Notifies you when you are close to a Kilroy)	SH2VYIVNZF
Kilroy Detector (Alerts you when a Kilroy is nearby)	4V35JZHQD6
Two Extra Skins	HI9WTPXSUK

Bullet Witch

Unlockable	Code
Hell Mode	Beat Chaos and Hard modes

Bully: Scholarship Edition

Codes

The following cheats can be input only on the 360's second controller, not the primary controller. Input all the codes during gameplay.

Unlockable	How to Unlock
All Weapons	LB,↑,↑,↑,↑
Full Health (not the extra from kissing)	LB,→,→,→
Infinite Ammo (enter again to turn off)	LB,↑,↓,↑,↓
Massive Money Gain	LB,Y,X,B,A

Achievements

Unlockable	How to Unlock
After Hours (20)	Spend five hours out after curfew.
Black & White & Read All Over (20)	Complete All Paper Route Missions.
Boy Genius (30)	Complete nine Classes.
Casanova (20)	Receive 25 kisses from the ladies.
Down for the Count (20)	Beat up 200 opponents.
Dual Nebula (20)	Achieve a high score on Consumo, Nut Shots, and Monkey Fling Arcade Games.
Eggsellent! (20)	Egg 25 cars.
Freshman (20)	Complete Chapter 1.
Glass Dismissed (25)	Break 300 bottles at the shooting gallery.
Graduate (40)	Complete Chapter 5.
Green Thumb (20)	Complete all Lawn Mowing Jobs.
Green Thumbs Up (20)	Pick 50 flowers.
Helping Hand (20)	Complete 10 Errand Missions.
It's All in the Wrists (20)	Complete all four of the Carnival Games once.
Junior (20)	Complete Chapter 3.
Keener (20)	Complete three Classes.
Kickin' the Balls (20)	Kick 100 soccer balls.
Little Angel (20)	Complete 20 Errand Missions.
Marathon (25)	Travel 100,000 meters on foot.
Mission Accomplished (75)	Complete all Missions.
Momma's Boy (25)	Complete 30 Errand Missions.
Over the Rainbow (20)	Receive 20 kisses from the gents.

Bully: Scholarship Edition (continued)

Unlockable	How to Unlock
Perfectionist (125)	100% completion.
Pole Position (20)	Complete all Go Kart Races.
Senior (20)	Complete Chapter 4.
Sharp Dressed Man (25)	Collect 250 clothing items.
Skate Pro (25)	Travel 50,000 meters on the skateboard.
Skidmark (25)	Give 50 wedgies.
Smart Mouth (25)	Say 100 taunts.
Smell Ya Later (25)	Hit people with stink bombs 50 times.
Soda-licious (20)	Buy 100 sodas.
Sophomore (20)	Complete Chapter 2.
Speed Freak (20)	Complete half of all Go Kart Races.
Teacher's Pet (20)	Complete six Classes.
The Champion (20)	Complete all Bike Races.
The Wheel Deal (25)	Perform 200 wheelies on the bike.
Tour De Bullworth (25)	Travel 100 km on the bike.
Watch Your Step (20)	Trip 25 people with marbles.

Burnout Paradise

Unlockable Cars

Acquire an A level license, then insert these codes in the in-game cheats menu.

Unlockable	How to Unlock
Best Buy Car	Type BESTBUY
Circuit City Car	Type CIRCUITCITY
Game Stop Car	Type GAMESTOP
Wal-Mart Car	Type WALMART

Other Unlockable Cars

Insert this code in the in-game cheats menu under the "sponsor codes" section.

Unlockable	How to Unlock
Steel Wheels Car	Type: U84D 3Y8K FY8Y 58N6

Licenses

To unlock licenses, win the corresponding number of events.

Unlockable	How to Unlock
A	26 events
B	16 events
C	7 events
D	2 events
Burnout Paradise	45 events
Elite	110 events

DS PSP PS2 PS3 Wii Xbox Xbox 360 Index

Burnout Revenge

Unlock Special Cars Offline

Unlockable	How to Unlock
Black Elite Racer	Gain the "Elite" Ranking
Criterion GT Racer	Complete Central Route's Challenge Sheet
Custom Classic	Complete Sunshine Keys' Challenge Sheet
EA GT Racer	Complete White Mountain's Challenge Sheet
Etnies Racer	Complete Motor City's Challenge Sheet
Euro Classic LM	Complete Eternal City's Challenge Sheet
Hot Rod	Complete Lone Peak's Challenge Sheet
Logitech World Racer	Complete Rank 10 Ultimate Revenge Grand Prix
Low Rider	Complete Angel Valley's Challenge Sheet
Nixon Special	Complete Eastern Bay's Challenge Sheet
Revenge Racer	Gain "100% Complete" Status
Unlock the Madden Van	Open Options, then Special Features, and bring up the Madden 06 preview

Call of Duty 2

Enter this code on the Mission Select screen.

Unlockable	Code
Unlock all levels	Hold both the left and right bumpers, then quickly input ◀(D-pad), ◀(D-pad), ▶(D-pad), ▶(D-pad), Ⓨ, Ⓨ

Call of Duty 3

Enter this code at the Chapter Select screen.

Unlockable	Code
Unlock All Levels and Pictures	Hold BACK then press ▶(D-pad), ▶(D-pad), ◀(D-pad), ◀(D-pad), Ⓧ, Ⓧ

Call of Duty 4: Modern Warfare

Arcade and Cheat Options

These unlock automatically for completing *Call of Duty 4: Modern Warfare* on any difficulty level. During gameplay, find the Cheat menu in the Options menu.

Unlockable	How to Unlock
Arcade Mode	Complete game on any difficulty
Cheat Menu	Complete game on any difficulty

Cheats

Unlock cheats by collecting enemy intel (intelligence), which look like laptop computers that are hidden throughout the campaign. Note: Using cheats disables Achievements.

Unlockable Cheats

Unlockable	How to Unlock
A Bad Year: When you kill enemies, they explode into tires!	Collect 15 pieces of enemy intel.
Cluster Bombs: After one of your frag grenades explodes, four more explode in a cross-shaped pattern.	Collect 10 pieces of enemy intel.
CoD Noir: Turns all gameplay into black and white.	Collect 2 pieces of enemy intel.
Infinite Ammo: Weapons have unlimited ammo. Doesn't work with Perk 1 abilities such as C4 and Claymores.	Collect 30 pieces of enemy intel.

Call of Duty 4: Modern Warfare (continued)

Unlockable	How to Unlock
Photo-Negative: Inverses all of the game's colors.	Collect 4 pieces of enemy intel.
Ragtime Warfare: Gameplay goes black and white, dust and scratches fill the screen, it plays at 2x speed, and the music becomes piano music.	Collect 8 pieces of enemy intel.
Slow-Mo Ability: Use the melee button to change the game to slow-mo and play at half-speed.	Collect 20 pieces of enemy intel.
Super Contrast: Dramatically increases the game's contrast, making the darks much darker and the lights much lighter.	Collect 6 pieces of enemy intel.

Golden weapons are a special camo (or skin) that you unlock when you fully complete all the challenges under the weapon subtype in the barracks (SMG, LMG, etc.). Access them by choosing the camo of the respective weapon. The effect is purely cosmetic and does not enhance the ability of the weapon in any way.

Golden Weapons

Unlockable	How to Unlock
Golden AK-47	Complete all Assault Rifle challenges.
Golden Desert Eagle	Get to Level 55.
Golden Dragunov	Complete all Sniper challenges.
Golden M1014	Complete all Shotgun challenges.
Golden M60	Complete all LMG challenges.
Golden Mini-Uzi	Complete all SMG challenges.

Multiplayer Unlockables

Unlockable	Unlocked at Rank:
AK-74U Submachine Gun	28
Bandolier Perk Class 1	32
Barret Sniper Rifle	49
Bomb Squad Perk Class 1	13
Boot Camp Challenges 1	08
Boot Camp Challenges 2	14
Boot Camp Challenges 3	17
Clan Tag	11
Claymore Perk Class 1	23
Commander Prestige Mode	55
Create a Class	03
Dead Silence Perk Class 3	44
Demolitions Class Weapon Class	01
Desert Eagle Pistol	43
Double Tab Perk Class 2	29
Dragunov Sniper Rifle	22
Eavesdrop Perk Class 3	35
Elite Challenges	51
Elite Challenges 2	53
Elite Challenges 3	54
Frag x 3 Perk Class 1	41
G3 Assault Rifle	25
G36C Assault Rifle	37
Golden Desert Eagle	55

Unlockable	Unlocked at Rank:
Gun Challenges	04
Humiliation Challenges	42
Humiliation Challenges 2	45
Humiliation Challenges 3	47
Humiliation Challenges 4	48
Humiliation Challenges 5	50
Iron Lungs Perk Class 3	26
Killer Challenges	30
Killer Challenges 2	33
Killer Challenges 3	36
Killer Challenges 4	39
Last Stand Perk Class 3	07
M1014 Shotgun	31
M14 Assault Rifle	46
M1911 Pistol	15
M4 Carbine Assault Rifle	09
M40 Sniper Rifle	06
M60E4 Light Machine Gun	18
Martyrdom Perk Class 2	16
Mini Uzi Submachine Gun	12
MP44 Assault Rifle	52
New Playlists	05

DS
PSP
PS2
PS3
Wii
Xbox
Xbox 360
Index

Call of Duty 4: Modern Warfare (continued)

Unlockable	Unlocked at Rank:
Operations Challenges	20
Operations Challenges	21
Operations Challenges 2	24
Operations Challenges 3	27
Overkill Perk Class 2	38
P90 Submachine Gun	40
R700 Sniper Rifle	34
Sleight of Hand Perk Class 2	19
Sniper Class Weapon Class	02
UAV Jammer Perk Class 2	10

Cars

Passwords

Password	Effect
CONC3PT	All art concept
WATCHIT	All movies
R4MONE	All paint jobs
IMSPEED	Super fast start
VROOOOM	Unlimited boost
YAYCARS	Unlock all cars
MATTL66	Unlock all races
IF900HP	Unlock everything in the game

Castlevania: Symphony of the Night

Play as Other Characters and Extras

You must complete the game as Alucard with 180% or more and have a "CLEAR" Save.

Password	Effect
Enter AXEARMOR as your name	Alucard with Axelord armor
Enter RICHTER as your name	Play as Richter Belmont
Enter X-X!V"Q as your name	Alucard with lower stats and MAX Luck

Cloning Clyde

Unlock Mutant Clyde

Unlockable	How to Unlock
Mutant Clyde	Beat all levels under par time

College Hoops 2K6

Unlockable Alternate Team Jerseys

These jerseys are unlockable via the Campus Store under the Extras menu. All items are unlockable using points you earn during game play.

Unlockable	How to Unlock
Arizona Wildcats Alternate Jersey (red)	45 points
Duke Blue Devils Alternate Jersey (black)	45 points
Florida Gators Alternate Jersey (black)	45 points
Illinois Fighting Illini Alternate Jersey (orange)	45 points
Michigan Wolverines Alternate Jersey (yellow)	45 points
Missouri Tigers Alternate Jersey (yellow gold)	45 points
Notre Dame Fighting Irish Alternate Jersey (gold)	45 points
Oregon Ducks Alternate Jersey (bright yellow)	45 points
Pittsburgh Panthers Alternate Jersey (navy blue)	45 points

Condemned: Criminal Origins

All Levels and Content

Code	Effect
Enter ShovelFighter as a case-sensitive profile name	Unlocks all levels and all additional content usually unlocked through earning achievements

Achievement	How to Achieve	Reward
Bird Bath Xbox 360	Find hidden Xbox 360 with the Bird Bath TV in Chapter 7	Initial crawler grabbing animation video
Bronze Detective Badge	Find hidden Bronze Detective Badge TV in Chapter 1	Video of some early forensic tool testing
Bronze Melee Master Award	Complete a single chapter with only melee weapons (no firearms)	Stick-fighting animation video with special performance by Detective Dickenson
Chapter 1 Bronze Bird Award	Find a dead bird in Chapter 1	Concept artwork of addicts
Chapter 1 Completion Award	Finish Chapter 1	Concept artwork for Weisman Office Building
Chapter 1 Silver Bird Award	Find all six birds in Chapter 1	Concept artwork of police officers
Chapter 2 Bronze Bird Award	Find a dead bird in Chapter 2	Concept artwork of the Glassman character (who was cut from the final game)
Chapter 2 Completion Award	Finish Chapter 2	Concept artwork for Central Metro Station
Chapter 2 Silver Bird Award	Find all six birds in Chapter 2	Concept artwork and character model of Detective Dickenson
Chapter 3 Bronze Bird Award	Find a dead bird in Chapter 3	Concept artwork of the Sandhog (burly enemy in fireman-style uniform)
Chapter 3 Completion Award	Finish Chapter 3	Concept artwork of the subway tunnels
Chapter 3 Silver Bird Award	Find all six birds in Chapter 3	Concept artwork and character model of Officer Becker
Chapter 4 Bronze Bird Award	Find a dead bird in Chapter 4	Concept artwork of vagrant characters (and others)
Chapter 4 Completion Award	Finish Chapter 4	Additional concept artwork for the subway tunnels
Chapter 4 Silver Bird Award	Find all six birds in Chapter 4	Concept artwork of Agent Ethan Thomas (you)
Chapter 5 Bronze Bird Award	Find a dead bird in Chapter 5	Concept artwork of mannequins
Chapter 5 Completion Award	Finish Chapter 5	Concept artwork for Bart's Department Store
Chapter 5 Silver Bird Award	Find all six birds in Chapter 5	Concept artwork of Vanhorn
Chapter 6 Bronze Bird Award	Find a dead bird in Chapter 6	Concept artwork and character models of the Rejects (the weakest crawlers)
Chapter 6 Completion Award	Finish Chapter 6	Concept artwork of the first crime scene
Chapter 6 Silver Bird Award	Find all six birds in Chapter 6	Concept artwork of Rosa
Chapter 7 Bronze Bird Award	Find a dead bird in Chapter 7	Concept artwork of the Trespassers
Chapter 7 Completion Award	Finish Chapter 7	Concept artwork for Metro City Library
Chapter 7 Silver Bird Award	Find all six birds in Chapter 7	Additional character concept artwork

Condemned: Criminal Origins (continued)

Achievement	How to Achieve	Reward
Chapter 8 Bronze Bird Award	Find a dead bird in Chapter 8	Concept artwork and character models of the crawlers
Chapter 8 Completion Award	Finish Chapter 8	Concept artwork for St. Joseph's Secondary School
Chapter 8 Silver Bird Award	Find all six birds in Chapter 8	Character model images for Samuel Tibbits
Chapter 9 Bronze Bird Award	Find a dead bird in Chapter 9	Additional character concept artwork
Chapter 9 Completion Award	Finish Chapter 9	Concept artwork for the Apple Seed Orchard
Chapter 9 Silver Bird Award	Find all six birds in Chapter 9	Concept artwork and character model of the Match Maker
Chapter 10 Bronze Bird Award	Find a dead bird in Chapter 10	Lunch lady concept artwork and character model
Chapter 10 Silver Bird Award	Find all six birds in Chapter 10	Concept artwork, character model, and screenshots of Serial Killer X
Chief Investigator Award	Find every crime scene clue in the game	Concept artwork of Dark enemies
Compassion Award	Let Serial Killer X live	Final pull video
DUO Report	Discover 29 metal pieces	Deep Undercover Operative Report & related evidence photos
Firearm Freedom Award	Wield every type of firearm in the game	Concept artwork of Dark enemies
Gold Detective Badge	Find hidden Gold Detective Badge TV in Chapter 9	Filipino stick-fighting video
Gold Game Completion Award	Finish entire game	Concept artwork for the different weapons in the game
Gold Melee Master Award	Complete game without using any firearms	Second prototype trailer video
Golden Bird Award	Find all birds in the game	Condemned E3 Trailer Video
Internal Affairs Report	Discover 20 metal pieces	Report that sheds light on current events/background
Melee Mayhem Award	Wield every type of debris and entry tool weapon in the game	Video of metal reduction animations (and some finishing moves)
Propaganda Report #1	Discover 9 metal pieces	Initial propaganda report and translated findings
Propaganda Report #2	Discover 20 metal pieces	Secondary propaganda report and additional translations
Propaganda Report #3	Discover 29 metal pieces	Third propaganda report and additional translations
Propaganda Report #4	Discover 30 metal pieces	Fourth propaganda report and a clue to shed additional light on the mystery
Revenge Award	Kill Serial Killer X	Serial Killer X wire-frame speech video
Ripple Xbox 360	Find hidden Xbox 360 with the Ripple TV in Chapter 2	Video of further concept artwork
Silver Detective Badge	Find hidden Silver Detective Badge TV in Chapter 6	Video of further concept artwork
Silver Melee Master Award	Complete three chapters without using any firearms	Crawler animation video
Static Xbox 360	Find hidden Xbox 360 with the Static TV in Chapter 4	A headless Ethan Thomas video

Condemned: Criminal Origins (continued)		
Achievement	**How to Achieve**	**Reward**
Test Pattern Xbox 360	Find hidden Xbox 360 with the Test Pattern TV in Chapter 8	Condemned credits video
Propaganda Report #2	Discover 20 metal pieces	Secondary propaganda report and additional translations
Propaganda Report #3	Discover 29 metal pieces	Third propaganda report and additional translations
Propaganda Report #4	Discover 30 metal pieces	Fourth propaganda report and a clue to shed additional light on the mystery
Revenge Award	Kill Serial Killer X	Serial Killer X wire-frame speech video
Ripple Xbox 360	Find hidden Xbox 360 with the Ripple TV in Chapter 2	Video of further concept artwork
Silver Detective Badge	Find hidden Silver Detective Badge TV in Chapter 6	Video of further concept artwork
Silver Melee Master Award	Complete three chapters without using any firearms	Crawler animation video
Static Xbox 360	Find hidden Xbox 360 with the Static TV in Chapter 4	A headless Ethan Thomas video
Test Pattern Xbox 360	Find hidden Xbox 360 with the Test Pattern TV in Chapter 8	Condemned credits video

Condemned 2: Bloodshot

Achievements

Unlockable	How to Unlock
A La Mode (25)	Five scoops of everything.
Anger Management (10)	Get emotional!
Beat Cop (10)	Beat your way through a mission.
Big Game Hunter (10)	Get up close and personal with the antler.
Bloodshot (25)	Unlock all Bloodshot Fight Clubs.
Brick Wall (10)	MP—Block it away!
Bum King (30)	No guns, no problem.
Can You Hear Me Now? (30)	Emitter Removal Service.
Chain Gang (30)	Use all chain attacks a few times.
Chief Investigator (50)	Complete all missions in Hard mode.
Collector (10)	Scan the MP goodies once, twice, thrice—and more!
Cut Throat (30)	Finish it!
Decisive Restraint (25)	Restraint is a virtue.
Defender (25)	MP Defense 10 times over on the evidence.
Detective (30)	Get through a mission in FPS.
Detective—First Grade (50)	Shoot your way through it all in FPS.
EPA (Environmental Pwnage Area) (25)	Grab your foes by the neck and do what's necessary.
Flambe (25)	Splash, Shock, and Fry.
Gold-Plated (50)	Go gold in all missions.
GOOOAAALLLL! (10)	Use the foosball table piece to your advantage.
Investigator (25)	You took on the hardest and beat them at their game.
Just the Facts (25)	MP Crime Scene Goodness.
Magellan (25)	Explore all maps more than once!
Master Investigator (30)	PERFECTION as a sleuth all the way through.

Condemned 2: Bloodshot (continued)

Unlockable	How to Unlock
MP Overachiever (50)	Win a Deathmatch game with 15 kills without dying.
Punch Drunk (10)	MP—Duke of Queensbury rules only
Restraint...Not (30)	Win Crime Scene games as SCU without firing a shot.
Rush Champ (25)	Take SCU out with the trash five times.
Self Medicated (25)	Heal thyself, physician.
Serial Killer (50)	Go kill, kill, kill in MP.
Sidekick (10)	Assist in scanning evidence in Crime Scene mode.
SKX (50)	Kill the killers.
Sleuth (10)	Be the PERFECT sleuth.
Survivor King (30)	Bum Rush Survivor multiple times.
The Final Word (10)	You never forget your first time.
The Plumber (25)	Find a pipe and use it frequently.
Trooper (30)	Complete the single-player game.
Tune In Tokyo (30)	Tune in all those TVs.

Contra

Codes

Code	Effect
Up, Up, Down, Down, Left, Right, Left, Right, B, A	Start game with 30 lives. Your score is not eligible for the High Score Leader Board.

Dark Sector

Unlockable

Unlockable	How to Unlock
Brutal Difficulty	Complete the game once.

Achievements

Unlockable	How to Unlock
Baggage Claim (10)	Complete Chapter 3.
Champion (30)	Finish Best Overall in a Ranked Epidemic match (Multiplayer).
Colossus (50)	Defeated the Colossus.
Comrade (30)	Score 500 points in Ranked Epidemic games (Multiplayer).
Dark Sector—Brutal Difficulty (110)	Complete the game on Brutal difficulty.
Double Decap Latte (15)	Get two decapitations in one shot.
Electrician (10)	Electrocute 30 enemies.
Exposure (10)	Complete Chapter 2.
Finesse (40)	Kill 30 enemies with Aftertouch.
Ghost (35)	Used Shifting to get a Finisher.
Glaive Master (10)	Complete a level using only the Glaive.
Glory (30)	Finish Best Overall in a Ranked Infection match (Multiplayer).
Greed (10)	Collect over 50,000 rubles.
Hardball (35)	Kill 30 enemies with Power-throw.
Headhunter (10)	Decapitate 30 enemies.

Dark Sector (continued)

Unlockable	How to Unlock
Hero (40)	Score 2,000 points in Ranked Infection games (Multiplayer).
Hero of the People (40)	Score 2,000 points in Ranked Epidemic games (Multiplayer).
Incinerator (10)	Incinerate 30 enemies.
Industrial Evolution (10)	Complete Chapter 7.
Jack Frost (10)	Kill 30 frozen enemies.
Jack the Jackal (35)	Took the Jackal for a ride.
Master Researcher (15)	Collect all the Weapon Upgrades.
Moths to the Flame (10)	Complete Chapter 4.
Nemesis (85)	Defeated the Nemesis.
Prologue (10)	Complete Chapter 1.
Rebound (15)	Kill an enemy with a reflected projectile.
Researcher (10)	Collect 10 Weapon Upgrades.
Sharpshooter (10)	Get 30 headshots.
Skeet Shooter (10)	Shoot 10 projectiles in mid-flight.
Stalker (65)	Defeated the Stalker.
The Bait (10)	Complete Chapter 6.
The Dark Sector (100)	Complete the game.
The Finisher (10)	Perform 30 Finishers.
The Shipment (10)	Complete Chapter 5.
Threshold Guardian (10)	Complete Chapter 9.
Veteran (30)	Score 500 points in Ranked Infection games (Multiplayer).
Weaponsmith (10)	Apply five upgrades in the Black Market.

The Darkness

Special Darklings

At any in-game phone, enter the number and you will unlock a special Darkling

Password	Effect
555-GAME	Unlocks Special 2K Darkling
555-5664	Unlocks the European Retailer (Golfer) Special Darkling

Dead Rising

Ending Requirements

These are the requirements needed in 72 hour mode to unlock different endings, with A the best and F the worst.

Unlockable	How to Unlock
Ending A	Solve all cases, talk to Isabella at 10 am, and return to the heliport at 12 pm on the 22nd
Ending B	Don't solve all cases and be at the heliport on time
Ending C	Solve all cases but do not talk to Isabella at 10 am on the last day
Ending D	Be a prisoner of the special forces at 12 pm on the 22nd
Ending E	Don't be at the heliport and don't solve all cases
Ending F	Fail to collect all of Carlito's bombs on act 7-2

Dead Rising (continued)

Unlock Weapon: Molotov Cocktail

Unlockable	How to Unlock
Molotov Cocktail (infinite supply)	Use fire extinguisher to save Paul, then bring him to the security room.

Unlockables

A handful of the Achievements have Unlockable content that becomes available once they've been activated. These, rewards, which include special costumes and items, can be found inside Shopping Bags behind the air duct in the Security Room after you've finished the game.

Unlockable	How to Unlock
Ammo Belt	Perfect Gunner
Arthur's Boxers	7 Day Survivor
Cop Hat	Saint
Hockey Mask	PP Collector
Laser Sword	5 Day Survivor
Mall Employee Uniform	Transmissionary
Mega Man Boots	Unbreakable
Mega Man Tights	Punisher
Prisoner Garb	Carjacker
Pro Wrestling Boots	Item Smasher
Pro Wrestling Briefs	Karate Champ
Real Mega Buster	Zombie Genocide
Special Forces Boots	Legendary Soldier
Special Forces Uniform	Hella Copter
White Hat	Census Taker

Unlockable Modes

Unlockable	How to Unlock
Infinity Mode	Complete Overtime mode
Overtime Mode	Complete all missions in 72 mode, talk to Isabella at 10am, and return to the helipad by noon on the 22nd

Dead Space

Codes

Press Start, then insert the following codes. You will hear a chime if you've done it correctly.

Effect	Code
1,000 credits (one time only per playthrough)	X,X,X,Y,X
10,000 credits (one time only per playthrough)	X,Y,Y,Y,X,X,Y
2 Nodes (one time only per playthrough)	Y,X,X,X,Y
2,000 credits (one time only per playthrough)	X,X,X,Y,Y
5 Nodes (one time only per playthrough)	Y,X,Y,X,X,Y,X,X,Y,X,X,Y
5,000 credits (one time only per playthrough)	X,X,X,Y,X,Y
Refill Your Oxygen	X,X,Y,Y,Y
Refill Your Stasis and Kinesis Energy	X,Y,Y,X,Y

Def Jam: Icon

Enter these codes at the Press Start screen.

Unlockable	Code
"It's Going Down" Music Track	B, Up, Right, Left, Y
"Make It Rain" Music Track	Down, B, A, Right

Devil May Cry 4

Unlockables

Unlockable	How to Unlock
Bloody Palace Survival Mode	Complete the game on Devil Hunter difficulty or Human difficulty.
Bonus Art and Character Art	Complete the game on Devil Hunter difficulty or Human difficulty.
Gallery	Complete the game on Devil Hunter difficulty or Human difficulty.
History of Devil May Cry	Complete the game on Devil Hunter difficulty or Human difficulty.
Son of Sparda Difficulty	Complete the game on Devil Hunter difficulty.

Dirt

Achievements

Unlockable	How to Unlock
4WD Rally Veteran (20)	Win all 4WD Rally events in Career mode.
5 Wins (10)	Win five races in any game mode.
10 Wins (15)	Win 10 races in any game mode.
20 Wins (20)	Win 20 races in any game mode.
All Tracks (20)	Race on every track (including shakedown stages) in any game mode.
Champion of Champions Winner (20)	Win the Champion of Champions event in Career mode.
Classic Rally Veteran (20)	Win all Classic Rally events in Career mode.
CORR Pro 4 Truck Veteran (20)	Win all CORR Pro 4 Truck events in Career mode.
CORR Super Buggy Veteran (20)	Win all CORR Super Buggy events in Career mode.
Crossover Veteran (20)	Win all Crossover events in Career mode.
Driven in Excess of 100 Miles (5)	Drive 100 miles in Career mode.
Driven in Excess of 250 Miles (10)	Drive 250 miles in Career mode.
Driven in Excess of 500 Miles (20)	Drive 500 miles in Career mode.
Driven in Excess of 1,000 Miles (25)	Drive 1,000 miles in Career mode.
European Rally Champion (25)	Win the European Rally Championship.
First 20m Jump (15)	Jump 20m.
First Clean Race (15)	Complete a race without crashing.
First Podium Finish (15)	Achieve a podium finish in any game mode.
First Victory (15)	Win a race in any game mode.
First Xbox Live Clean Race (20)	Complete a ranked race on Xbox Live without colliding with anything.
First Xbox Live Hill Climb Win (20)	Win a ranked Hill Climb race on Xbox Live.
First Xbox Live Rally Win (20)	Win a ranked rally race on Xbox Live.
FWD Rally Veteran (20)	Win all FWD Rally events in Career mode.
Global Rally Champion (60)	Win the Global Rally Championship.

Dirt (continued)

Unlockable	How to Unlock
Hat Trick (15)	Win three races in a row in any game mode.
Hill Climb Big Rig Veteran (20)	Win all Hill Climb Big Rig events in Career mode.
Hill Climb Veteran (20)	Win all Hill Climb events in Career mode.
International Rally Champion (40)	Win the International Rally Championship.
Manual Transmission (10)	Win a race using manual transmission in any game mode.
Maximum Career Points Milestone (45)	Achieve maximum points up to the end of Tier 11 in Career mode.
National Rally Veteran (20)	Win all National Rally events in Career mode.
Own 15 Vehicles (15)	Own 15 vehicles in Career mode.
Own 30 Vehicles (30)	Own 30 vehicles in Career mode.
Own All Vehicles (45)	Own all of the vehicles in Career mode.
Rally Raid T1 Veteran (20)	Win all Rally Raid T1 events in Career mode.
Rally Raid T4 Truck Veteran (20)	Win all Rally Raid T4 Truck events in Career mode.
Rallycross Veteran (20)	Win all Rallycross events in Career mode.
RWD Rally Veteran (20)	Win all RWD Rally events in Career mode.
Tier 2 Career Points Milestone (10)	Achieve maximum points up to the end of Tier 2 in Career mode.
Tier 4 Career Points Milestone (10)	Achieve maximum points up to the end of Tier 4 in Career mode.
Tier 6 Career Points Milestone (20)	Achieve maximum points up to the end of Tier 6 in Career mode.
Tier 8 Career Points Milestone (20)	Achieve maximum points up to the end of Tier 8 in Career mode.
Top Speed (10)	Reach a speed of at least 135 mph in a race in any game mode.
Win Arai Japanese Alpine Rally (20)	Win the Arai Japanese Alpine Rally in Championship mode.
Win BP Ultimate Rally UK (20)	Win the BP Ultimate Rally UK in Championship mode.
Win Brembo Rallye Italia (20)	Win the Brembo Rallye Italia in Championship mode.
Win Rally Deutschland (20)	Win the Rally Deutschland in Championship mode.
Win Shell Rally Australia (20)	Win Shell Rally Australia in Championship mode.
Win Sparco Rally Espana (20)	Win Sparco Rally Espana in Championship mode.

Doom

Gamer Pics

Unlockable	How to Unlock
Secret Gamer Pic of a Demon	Beat any level on Nightmare difficulty
Secret Gamer Pic of a Doom Marine	Get a 100% kill rating on any level with a "Hurt Me Plenty" or higher difficulty level

Dragon Ball Z: Burst Limit

Unlockable Characters

Unlockable	How to Unlock
100% Final Form Frieza	Beat Chapter 16 on Frieza Saga.
1st Form Frieza	Beat Chapter 8 on Frieza Saga.
2nd Form Frieza	Beat Chapter 9 on Frieza Saga.

Dragon Ball Z: Burst Limit (continued)

Unlockable	How to Unlock
3rd Form Frieza	Beat Chapter 12 on Frieza Saga.
Android #17	Beat Chapter 3 on Cell Saga.
Android #18	Beat Chapter 2 on Cell Saga.
Bardock	Beat Chapter 1 on Bardock Storyline.
Broly	Beat Chapter 1 on Broly Storyline.
Captain Ginyu	Beat Chapter 4 on Frieza Saga.
Final Form Frieza	Beat Chapter 14 on Frieza Saga.
Imperfect Cell	Beat Chapter 4 on Cell Saga.
Kaioken Goku	Beat Chapter 7 on Saiyan Saga.
Nappa	Beat Chapter 5 on Saiyan Saga.
Perfect Cell	Beat Chapter 12 on Cell Saga.
Piccolo Fuse with Kami	Beat Chapter 4 on Cell Saga.
Piccolo Sync with Nail	Beat Chapter 11 on Frieza Saga.
Raditz	Beat Chapter 1 on Saiyan Saga.
Recoome	Beat Chapter 1 on Frieza Saga.
Saibamen	Beat Chapter 3 on Saiyan Saga.
Semi-Perfect Cell	Beat Chapter 6 on Cell Saga.
Super Perfect Cell	Beat Chapter 18 on Cell Saga.
Super Perfect Cell	Beat Chapter 19 on Cell Saga.
Super Saiyan 2 Teen Gohan	Beat Chapter 19 on Cell Saga.
Super Saiyan Goku	Beat Chapter 16 on Frieza Saga.
Super Saiyan Trunks	Beat Chapter 7 on Cell Saga.
Super Saiyan Vegeta	Beat Chapter 2 on Cell Saga.
Super Trunks	Beat Chapter 13 on Cell Saga.
Super Vegeta	Beat Chapter 10 on Cell Saga.
Teen Gohan	Beat Chapter 1 on Cell Saga.
Trunks	Beat Chapter 7 on Cell Saga.
Vegeta	Beat Chapter 8 on Saiyan Saga.

Unlockable Difficulties

Unlockable	How to Unlock
Hard	Beat Z Chronicles on Normal.
Very Hard	Beat Z Chronicles on Normal.
Z	Beat Z Chronicles on Very Hard.

Unlockable Movies

Unlockable	How to Unlock
Credits	Beat Broly's Storyline.
Movie 1	Beat Frieza Saga.
Movie 2	Beat Cell Saga.

Achievements

Unlockable	How to Unlock
A Beginner Awakens!	Clear Basic tutorials: 5 points.
Advanced Victory!	Clear Advanced tutorials: 15 points.
All Cell Fighters	Unlock all of the Cell Saga fighters: 5 points.
All Frieza Fighters	Unlock all of the Frieza Saga fighters: 5 points.

Dragon Ball Z: Burst Limit (continued)

Unlockable	How to Unlock
All Saiyan Fighters	Unlock all of the Saiyan Saga fighters: 5 points.
Battler (Custom)	Play the Survival Trial (Custom Drama): 5 points.
Battler (Default)	Play the Survival Trial (Default Drama): 5 points.
Bloodless Victory!	Win a battle without taking any damage. (Z Chronicles/ Versus only): 20 points.
Cell Saga Allies	Unlock all of the Cell Saga ally characters: 5 points.
Destructive Win!	Win a battle while changing or destroying the background. (Z Chronicles/Versus only): 5 points.
Family Bonds	Clear all chapters of the Cell Saga: 15 points.
Fierce Warrior	Clear all of the Saga chapters with the difficulty set to Very Hard: 40 points.
Frieza Saga Allies	Unlock all of the Frieza Saga ally characters: 5 points.
Frieza Z Award: 35g	Clear all Frieza Saga chapters with a Z rank on Normal difficulty.
Full Drama Unlock	Unlock all of the Drama Pieces for one character: 5 points.
Goku's Father	Unlock Bardock: 20 points.
Intermediate Fire!	Clear Intermediate tutorials: 5 points.
Legendary Saiyan	Unlock Broly: 20 points.
Legendary Warrior	Clear all chapters of the Frieza Saga: 15 points.
Master of History	Clear all chapters: 15 points.
Meeting a Rival	Clear all chapters of the Saiyan Saga: 5 points.
Powerful Allies	Unlock all ally characters: 15 points.
Saiyan Saga Allies	Unlock all of the Saiyan Saga ally characters: 5 points.
Saiyan Saga Drama	Unlock all of the Drama Pieces from the Saiyan Saga: 20 points.
Saiyan Z Award	Clear all Saiyan Saga chapters with a Z rank on Normal difficulty: 35 points.
Score Beyond Terror	Clear the Battle Point Trial (Course A) and get a result: 5 points.
Speed Beyond Power	Clear the Time Attack Trial (Course B) and get a result: 5 points.
Speed Beyond Terror	Clear the Time Attack Trial (Course A) and get a result: 5 points.
Sturdy Warrior	Unlock all fighters: 20 points.
Survivor (Custom)	Play the Survival Trial (Custom Drama) and defeat 50 opponents: 35 points.
The First Z Award	Clear a chapter with a Z rank on Normal difficulty: 20 points.
The Story Begins	Clear the first chapter of the Saiyan Saga: 5 points.
Ultimate Unlock	Unlock all of one character's Ultimate Attacks: 5 points.
Ultimate Warrior	Unlock all characters' Ultimate Attacks: 15 points.
Unleashed Ki Win!	Transform, use Aura Spark, and win with an Ultimate Attack. (Z Chronicles/Versus only): 5 points.
Worldwide Contender	Join 10 sessions over Xbox LIVE: 5 points.
Worldwide Warrior	Create 10 sessions over Xbox LIVE: 5 points.

Dynasty Warriors 5 Empires

Unlockables

Unlockable	How to Unlock
1,000 K.O Ribbon	Defeat 1,000 enemies in one battle. You also must win the battle.
All Created Officer Attire	Create an officer, then complete the Yellow Turban campaign.
Extra Models (Unique Characters only)	Reach the maximum number of Experience Points (60,000) with any unique character to unlock all of their models.
A Divided Land Scenario	Successfully complete the Dong Zhou in Luo Yang scenario to unlock the A Divided Land scenario.
Battle of Guan Du Scenario	Successfully complete the A Divided Land scenario to unlock the Battle of Guan Du scenario.
Dong Zhou in Luo Yang Scenario	Successfully complete The Yellow Turban Rebellion scenario to unlock the Dong Zhou in Luo Yang scenario.
Flames over Chi Bi scenario	Successfully complete the Battle of Guan Du scenario to unlock the Flames over Chi Bi scenario.
Level 4 weapons	Raise a weapon type to maximum, then get 500 kills with the person who you want to get the 4th weapon.
Executions/Old Age Death	Beat Empire mode once.
Isolate	Beat Empire mode once.
Unlimited Time	Beat Empire mode once.

Unlockable Ending Events

All endings must be unlocked on Empire mode using any difficulty and on any era.

Unlockable	How to Unlock
Death	Fail to conquer all 25 territories when the campaign time limit runs out. Campaign time limit option must be on.
Unification (Evil Ruler)	Continuously use evil deeds such as Despotism and become Emperor. Then conquer all 25 territories without committing a good deed.
Unification (Good Ruler)	Continuously use good deeds such as Philanthropy and become Emperor. Then conquer all 25 territories without committing a evil deed.
Unification (Neutral)	Conquer all 25 territories without being extremely good or evil.

Dynasty Warriors 6

Characters

Unlockable	How to Unlock
Cao Cao	Clear Musou mode with three Wei characters.
Cao Pi	Defeat Cao Pi within five minutes on Wu side of He Fei.
Cao Ren	Succeed in Battle Objective 2 on the Lu Bu side of Fan Castle.
Diao Chan	Clear Musou mode with one character from each Kingdom.
Dong Zhuo	Clear Musou mode with Lu Bu.
Gan Ning	Clear Musou mode with one Wu character.
Guan Ping	Succeed in two battle objectives on the Shu side of Fan Castle and finish battle with Guan Ping alive.
Huang Gai	Succeed in Battle Objective 3 on the Wu side of The Battle of Chi Bi.

DS
PSP
PS2
PS3
Wii
Xbox
Xbox 360
Index

Dynasty Warriors 6 (continued)

Unlockable	How to Unlock
Huang Zhong	Succeed in one battle objective on the Wei side of Ding Jun Mountain.
Ling Tong	Succeed in Battle Objective 1 on the Wei side of the Battle of Shi Ting.
Liu Bei	Clear Musou mode with three Shu characters.
Lu Bu	Clear Musou mode with Liu Bei, Cao Cao, and Sun Jian.
Lu Meng	Succeed in two battle objectives on the Wei side of He Fei.
Ma Chao	Succeed in two battle objectives on the Wei side of Han Zhong Attack Defense Battle.
Pang Tong	Succeed in three battle objectives at Cheng Du battle and finish battle with Pang Tong alive.
Sun Ce	Succeed in Battle Objective 1 on the Sun Jian side of the Battle of Xia Pi.
Sun Jian	Clear Musou mode with three Wu characters.
Sun Quan	Succeed in Battle Objective 1 on the Lu Bu side of the Battle of Chi Bi.
Taishi Ci	Defeat him in the Battle for Wu Territory.
Wei Yan	Succeed in two battle objectives on the Shu side of WuZhang Plains and finish battle with Wei Yan alive.
Xiahou Yuan	Succeed in one battle objective on the Shu side of Ding Jun Mountain.
Xiao Quio	Succeed in Battle Objective 3 on the Wu side of the Battle of Shi Ting.
Xu Chu	He Fei, Wu side, personally kill Cao Ren and Xu Chu.
Xu Huang	Succeed in two battle objectives on the Wei/Wu side of Fan Castle.
Yuan Shao	As Wei, complete all three targets and capture Wu Chao before completing the stage.
Yue Ying	Succeed in Battle Objective 1 on the Wei side of the Battle of Wu Zhang Plains.
Zhang Jiao	Beat stage while completing all three targets in the Yellow Turban Rebellion. Playable in only Free mode and Challenge mode.
Zhang Liao	Clear Musou mode with one Wei character.
Zhen Ji	Succeed in Battle Objective 1 on the Lu Bu side of the Xu Du Invasion.
Zheng He	Succeed in two battle objectives on the Shu side of Han Zhong Attack Defense Battle.
Zhou Tai	Succeed in three battle objectives on the Shu side of Yi Ling.
Zhuge Liang	Clear Musou mode with one Shu character.

Difficulties

Unlockable	How to Unlock
Chaos Difficulty	Clear Musou mode with one character from Wu, Shu, Wei, and Other.
Hell Difficulty	Beat Wei, Wu, Shu, and Other Musou mode.
Master Difficulty	Beat any Musou mode on Easy or Normal.
Very Hard Difficulty	Clear Musou mode with any one character.

Achievements

Unlockable	How to Unlock
1st in RAMPAGE (10)	Rank first (personal best) in Rampage.
1st in GAUNTLET (10)	Rank first (personal best) in Gauntlet.
1st in HAVOC (10)	Rank first (personal best) in Havoc.
1st in SPEED RUN (10)	Rank first (personal best) in Speed Run.
1st in SUDDEN DEATH (10)	Rank first (personal best) in Sudden Death.
Musou Mode Master (50)	All Musou modes cleared.

Dynasty Warriors 6 (continued)

Unlockable	How to Unlock
Scenario Captain (40)	30 or more scenarios cleared.
Scenario Corporal (30)	20 or more scenarios cleared
Scenario General (50)	All scenarios cleared.
Scenario Private (20)	10 or more scenarios cleared.
Target Captain (50)	100 or more targets achieved.
Target Corporal (40)	70 or more targets achieved.
Target General (60)	All targets achieved.
Target Private (30)	50 or more targets achieved.
The Arm of Cao Cao (10)	Xiahou Yuan has been unlocked.
The Barbarian Lord (10)	Wei Yan has been unlocked.
The Beautiful Dancer (30)	Diao Chan has been unlocked.
The Courageous Lord (10)	Xu Huang has been unlocked.
The Ferocious Warrior (10)	Taishi Ci has been unlocked.
The Fledgling Phoenix (10)	Pang Tong has been unlocked.
The Forthright Lord (30)	Zhang Liao has been unlocked.
The General of Heaven (10)	Zhang Jiao has been unlocked.
The Little Conqueror (10)	Unlock Sun Ce.
The Lord of Beauty (10)	Zhang He has been unlocked.
The Loyal Warrior (10)	Zhou Tai has been unlocked.
The Master General (10)	Lu Meng has been unlocked.
The Patriarch of Yuan (10)	Yuan Shao has been unlocked.
The Reckless Pirate (30)	Gan Ning has been unlocked.
The Sleeping Dragon (30)	Zhuge Liang has been unlocked.
The Son of Guan Yu (10)	Guan Ping has been unlocked.
The Splendid One (10)	Ma Chao has been unlocked.
The Tiger General (10)	Huang Zhong has been unlocked.
The Tiger of Jiang Dong (10)	Unlock Sun Jian.
The Veteran General (10)	Huang Gai has been unlocked.
The Wise Lady (10)	Yue Ying has been unlocked.

Dynasty Warriors: Gundam

Unlockable Characters and Pilots

Unlockable	How to Unlock
Char Aznable and Char's Gelgoog	Complete Amuro Ray's Story mode on any difficulty in Official mode
Char's Zaku II	Complete Char Aznable's Story mode on any difficulty in Official mode
Elpe Ple and Qubeley Mk-II (Black)	Complete Both Judau Ashita and Domon Kasshu's Story modes on any difficulty
Emma Sheen	Complete Both Char Aznable and Rolan Cehack's Story modes on any difficulty
Haman Karn, Judau Ashita, Qubeley Gundam, and Gundam ZZ	Complete Judau Ashita's Story mode on any difficulty in Official mode
Hyaku Shiki	Complete Mission 4 of Char Aznable's Official mode on any difficulty

Dynasty Warriors: Gundam (continued)

Unlockable	How to Unlock
Jerid Messa and Gundam Mk-II (Black)	Complete Both Kamille Bidan and Heero Yuy's Story modes on any difficulty
Master Gundam/Master Asia	Beat Domon/Burning Gundam's Story mode on any difficulty
Milliardo Peacecraft and Gundam Epyon	Complete Heero Yuy's Story mode on any difficulty in Original mode
Musha Gundam	Complete Story mode for Amuro Ray, Kamille Bidan, Judau Ashita, Domon Kasshu, Heero Yuy, and Rolan Cehack on any difficulty
Paptimus Scirocco and The O	Complete Kamille Bidan's Story mode on any difficulty in Official mode
Ple Two	Complete Elpe Ple's Story mode on any difficulty in Original mode
Qubeley Mk-II (Red)	Complete Both Elpe Ple and Rolan Cehack's Story modes on any difficulty
Roux Louka	Complete Both Judau Ashita and Haman Karn's Story modes on any difficulty

Earth Defense Force 2017

Unlockable Bonus Weapons

Beat every mission on a certain difficulty to unlock the corresponding weapon.

Unlockable	How to Unlock
Genocide Gun	Beat all missions on Inferno
PX50 Bound Shot	Beat all missions on Hardest
Y20 Impulse	Beat all missions on Hard
ZE Launcher	Beat all missions on Normal
Zero Laser Rifle	Beat all missions on Easy

Ecco the Dolphin

Level Passwords

Password	Effect		
UYNAINCC	The Undercaves	FDGXQQLC	The Library
DQDIACCI	The Undercaves 2	ZUVPQQLU	Deep City
FKWLACCA	The Vents	AABBRQLU	City of Forever
NDRBRIKR	The Lagoon	PLABUNLT	Jurassic Beach
HYAUGFLV	Ridge Water	FQREUNLI	Pteranodon Pond
FNCQWBMT	Open Ocean	QXKIUNLX	Origin Beach
DWFFZBMV	The Ice Zone	OBEMUNLX	Trilobite Circle
QGDJRQLA	Hard Water Zone	JNXPUNLA	Dark Water
MCLFRQLW	Cold Water Zone	WSGAKNLC	Deep Water 2
UWXIOQLK	The Island Zone	ZBPIGPLD	City of Forever 2
EILQOQLC	Deep Water Zone	KUVEKMLK	The Tube
XAKUQQLS	The Marble Sea	SDDBKMLG	The Machine
		AJPPOWAX	Last Fight

Eragon

Unlimited Fury Mode

Pause the game while in a level.

Unlockable	How to Unlock
Unlimited Fury Mode	Hold (L) + (LT) + (R) + (RT) and press (X) (B) (B) (B) (Note: This makes magic cooldown go much faster.)

Eternal Sonata

Achievements

Unlockable	How to Unlock
Claves's Resurrection (50G)	Collect all seven pieces of Claves's Soul.
EZI Worshipper (321G)	Collect all EZI items in the game.
Fantaisie Impromptu (10G)	Complete chapter 3.
Grand Finale (70G)	Defeat Frederic with Claves unlocked.
Grande Valse Brilliante (10G)	Complete chapter 4.
Heaven's Mirror (10G)	Complete Final chapter: Heaven's Mirror.
Hero's Gate (30G)	Use the Hero's Crest to open the way to Mysterious Unison.
Heroic (10G)	Complete chapter 7.
Nocturne (10G)	Complete chapter 5.
Party Level 2 (10G)	Obtain party level 2.
Party Level 3 (10G)	Obtain party level 3.
Party Level 4 (10G)	Obtain party level 4.
Party Level 5 (10G)	Obtain party level 5.
Party Level 6 (20G)	Obtain party level 6.
Pirate's Treasure (80G)	Finally obtain Dolce's treasure.
Raindrops (10G)	Complete chapter 1.
Revolution (10G)	Complete chapter 2.
Rondo's Return (50G)	Defeat Rondo in Mysterious Unison.
Score Piece Collector (100G)	Collect all 32 score pieces.
Soul Released (79G)	Free Chord's Soul from Fort Fermata.
Tristesse (10G)	Complete chapter 6.
Xylophone Treasure (80G)	Use your orb to open the secret door in Xylophone Tower.

Fable II

Infinite Experience

Once you have access to Bowerstone Market, walk to Town Square. There is a potion shopkeeper on the left side. Walk around the right side of the buildings there and down an alley to find a house known as Monster Manor. Sleep there to gain its benefit (+1 star of Physique) Once you gain this benefit, go to your abilities list, select physique, and hit Y to unlearn it. The bonus star from the house does not disappear, but the experience is given to you anyway. Repeat this process as many times as you like, the more stars you have in physique the more exp you get each time. This experience is general experience and can be applied to any skills.

Infinite Experience II

Wait until your character is at least somewhat leveled up. Plug in a second controller and begin a co-op game without using a second profile. Using the second controller, go to your henchman's abilities and discard all of them, returning the experience to the pool. Then quit out of the co-op game. You should find that all the "leftover" experience has been transferred to your hero. Repeat as often as you like. Note: Your co-op henchman will have the same abilities that you do, so the stronger the hero, the more abilities there are to sell off and thus more experience.

DS PSP PS2 PS3 Wii Xbox Xbox 360 Index

Fallout 3 (XBOX360)

Infinite XP

You can gain infinite XP if your Speech skill is high enough (approximately level 30). Go Big Town, north of Vault 101. Speak with a girl named Bittercup. She'll tell you about her dating exploits. After speaking with her, go into the house marked "Common House" and speak to a man named Pappy. There should be a speech skill dialogue option that says "You came here with Bittercup, right?" You get XP every time you click it. Continue to do this as long as you like to gain free XP.

]Early Detection

When heading into seemingly hostile territory, try hitting the VATS button over and over again as you make your character turn around, searching all angles. Doing so will alert you to any enemies you may not yet see by zooming in on them in VATS mode. You won't be able to do damage to your foes from such a distance, but it's a good way to spot foes before they spot you so you know what you're getting yourself into.

Far Cry Instincts Predator

To enter these passwords, pause the game and select the Cheat menu. Note that these passwords are case sensitive.

Unlockable	Password
Enable Evolutions	FeralAttack
Evolution Game	GiveMeltAll
Heal Yourself	ImJackCarver
Infinite Adrenaline	Bloodlust
Infinite Ammo	UnleashHell
Unlock All Maps	GiveMeTheMaps

F.E.A.R.

To unlock all levels but disable achievements, enter F3ARDAY1 as a profile/gamertag.

FIFA 06

Bonus Team, Kits, and Balls

Unlockable	How to Unlock
Adidas Etrusco Ball	Win an 8 (or more) Team Custom Knockout Tournament
Adidas Tango Espana Ball	Win a 16 (or more) Team Custom Knockout Tournament
Adidas Tricoloure Ball	Win a 5 (or more) Team Custom League
Classic 11 Team	Qualify for the World Cup in Road to the World Cup Mode
England 1966 World Cup Kit	Win the International Masters Tournament with England in Road to the World Cup mode
England 1990 World Cup Kit	Win the International Open Tournament with England in Road to the World Cup mode

FIFA Street 3

Bonus Teams

Complete the following tasks to unlock the corresponding team.

Unlockable	How to Unlock
Predator (Gerrard, Beckham, etc.)	Complete Adidas Challenge in FIFA Street Challenge.
The Blasters (Gerrard, Ballack, etc.)	Win 40 Games in FIFA Street Challenge.
The Champions (Baresi, Voller, etc.)	Complete Champion Challenge in FIFA Street Challenge.

FIFA Street 3 (continued)

Unlockable	How to Unlock
The Classics (Cantona, Zico, etc.)	Complete Classic Challenge in FIFA Street Challenge.
World Stars (Ronaldinho, Eto'o, etc.)	Complete All Stars Challenge in FIFA Street Challenge.

Achievements

Unlockable	How to Unlock
Challenge Heavyweight (100)	With the lead *FIFA Street 3* profile, complete a match with World Stars.
Challenge Lightweight (35)	With the lead *FIFA Street 3* profile, complete a match with the Champions.
Challenge Middleweight (75)	With the lead *FIFA Street 3* profile, complete a match with F50.
Five-A-Side Match (15)	Complete a Five-A-Side match with the lead *FIFA Street 3* profile.
Gamebreaker (25)	Score a Gamebreaker goal with the lead *FIFA Street 3* profile in any game mode except Practice.
Gamebreaker Match (15)	Complete a Gamebreaker Goal match with the lead *FIFA Street 3* profile.
Gamebreaker Possession (25)	With the lead *FS3* profile, fill your Gamebreaker bar in one possession in any mode except Practice.
Gamebreaker Spoiler (50)	Score with the lead *FIFA Street 3* profile while your opponent is on Gamebreaker.
Get Online (25)	Complete a ranked or unranked match with the lead *FIFA Street 3* profile on Xbox LIVE.
Golden Gamebreaker (75)	Score a golden goal with the lead *FIFA Street 3* profile in a timed match while on Gamebreaker.
Guest Picks (25)	Win a completed Xbox LIVE Playground Picks match hosted by another player with the lead *FS3* profile.
Hat Trick Hero (50)	With the lead *FIFA Street 3* profile, score a hat trick with CROUCH in any game mode except Practice.
Head to Head Breaker (25)	With the lead *FS3* profile, complete the last Gamebreaker Goals match to three goals in a best of seven.
Head to Head Headache (50)	With the lead *FS3* profile, complete the last Headers and Volleys match to seven goals in a best of five.
Head to Head Series (25)	With the lead *FS3* profile, complete the last Head to Head match in a best of three of any type.
Headers and Volleys Match (15)	Complete a Headers and Volleys match with the lead *FIFA Street 3* profile.
Host Picks (25)	Win a completed match as the host of an Xbox LIVE Playground Picks match with the lead *FS3* profile.
Ranked Champ (100)	Complete and win 25 ranked matches on Xbox LIVE with the lead *FIFA Street 3* profile.
Ranked Goals (50)	Score 50 goals in completed ranked matches on Xbox LIVE with the lead *FIFA Street 3* profile.
Score Difference Match (15)	Complete a Score Difference match with the lead *FIFA Street 3* profile.
Score Match (15)	Complete a Score match with the lead *FIFA Street 3* profile.
Shooting Gallery (10)	Take 50 shots on goal in any game mode except Practice with the lead *FIFA Street 3* profile.

FIFA Street 3 (continued)

Unlockable	How to Unlock
Street Fever (45)	Complete an Xbox LIVE match against another player who has Street Fever with the lead *FS3* profile.
Timed Match (15)	Complete a Timed match with the lead *FIFA Street 3* profile.
Tourist (10)	Score a goal in every environment in any game mode except Practice with the lead *FS3* profile.
Triple Gamebreaker (50)	Score three Gamebreakers with the lead *FS3* profile on the same Gamebreaker in any mode except Practice.
Wally (35)	Run on the walls 50 times in any game mode except Practice with the lead *FIFA Street 3* profile.

Fight Night Round 3

Create a new boxer with this first name.

Unlockable	Code
All Venues	newview

Unlockables

Unlockable	How to Unlock
ESPN Classic Fight	Clear the Under Armor Bout in Career mode to unlock the fight of Big E vs. Goliath.
Judge Jab	Defeat Joe Frazier with Ali.
Ko Rey Mo	In the light heavy division, defeat him in Career mode.
Lethal Uppercuts	Win a classic fight with Roberto Duran.
Madison Square Garden Venue	Win a match at Madison Square Garden.
Sinister Cross	Win a classic fight with Roy Jones Jr.
Smooth Style	Defeat Muhammad Ali in a challenge event.
Textbook	Win a classic fight with Oscar De La Hoya.
Staples Center Venue	Win at the Staple's Center in Career mode.
Rey Mo and Burger King Trainer—Light Heavyweight	Create a boxer with the last name YAXKUKMO and complete, or have previously completed the Burger King sponsored bout in Career mode to unlock.

Achievements

Unlockable	How to Unlock
Burger King Achievement: 100 points	Win The BK Invitational Fight.
Dodge Achievement: 100 points	Win the Dodge sponsored fight.
EA SPORTS Achievement: 150 points	Win any EA SPORTS sponsored fight.
ESPN FNF Achievement: 150 points	Win any ESPN Friday Night Fight event.
ESPN PPV Achievement: 150 points	Win any ESPN Pay Per View fight event.
ESPN WNF Achievement: 150 points	Win any ESPN Wednesday Night Fight event.
Everlast Achievement: 100 points	Win the Everlast sponsored fight.
Under Armor Achievement: 100 points	Win the Under Armor sponsored fight.

FlatOut: Ultimate Carnage

Unlock Vehicles

Perform well enough to get a Bronze medal or better in each stage of three/four races to unlock the following cars. Please note that to unlock the cars, you don't need to complete the other objectives such as Time Trial, only races count. Also note that one or two of each class are unlocked in the Carnage mode. You'll have to earn gold to unlock them.

FlatOut: Ultimate Carnage (continued)

Unlockable	How to Unlock
Bonecracker (Derby)	Get Gold in the Bonecracker Demolition Derby
Bullet, Lentus, and Ventura (Race)	Complete the Race Class Stage 2
Canyon (Street)	Get Gold in the Canyon, beat the Bomb Race
Crusader (Street)	Get Gold in the Crusader Deathmatch Derby
Flatmobile (Special)	Get Gold in the Flatmobile, beat the Bomb Race
Grinder (Derby)	Get Gold in the Grinder Demolition Derby
Insetta (Race)	Get Gold in the Insetta Carnage Race
Lancea, Daytana, and Fortune (Race)	Complete the Race Class Stage 1
Mob Car (Special)	Get Gold in the Mob Car Carnage Race

FlatOut: Ultimate Carnage

Unlockable	How to Unlock
Road King (Street)	Get Gold in the Road King, beat the Bomb Race
Shaker, Blaster XL, and Banger (Derby)	Complete the Derby Class Stage 1
Sparrowhawk, CTR Sport, and Vexter XS (Street)	Complete the Street Class Stage 1
Speedshifter, Terrator, Speeddevil, Bullet GT, and Sunray (Street)	Complete the Street Class Stage 2
Splitter, Switchblade, and Venom (Derby)	Complete the Derby Class Stage 2
Truck (Special)	Get Gold in the Truck Deathmatch Derby

Forza Motorsport 2

Amateur Race Series

Get first place in all the races in the series.

Unlockable	How to Unlock
#22 3R-Racing Viper Competition Coupe	Complete 5X5 V10 Super Sprint
1973 Porsche 911 Carrera RS	Complete Sports Car Classic
1992 Toyota Do-Luck Supra	Complete Boosted Shootout
2000 Acura VIS Racing Integra Type-R	Complete Inline 4 Showcase
2002 Chevrolet Lingenfelter 427 Corvette	Complete Big Block Shootout
2002 Nissan Tommy Kaira Skyline GT-R R34	Complete 6-Cylinder Showoff
Corvette Goldstrand Edition	Complete American Iron Runoff
ME Four-Twelve Concept	Complete Extreme Performance Shoot-Out
Mugen S2000	Complete Free-Breathing Challenge
VeilSide Supra Fortune 99	Complete 20th Century Supercar Invitational

Asia Level Reward Cars

Reach these levels in Asia to unlock the cars.

Unlockable	How to Unlock
1969 Nissan Fairlady Z 432R	Reach Level 5
2004 Mitsubishi Lancer Evolution VIII MR	Reach Level 10
1998 Subaru Impreza 22B STi	Reach Level 15
2002 Nissan Skyline GT-R V-Spec II Nur	Reach Level 20
2002 Mazda RX-7 Spirit R Type-A	Reach Level 25
2005 Honda NSX-R GT	Reach Level 30

DS
PSP
PS2
PS3
Wii
Xbox
Xbox 360
Index

Forza Motorsport 2 (continued)

Unlockable	How to Unlock
2003 Subaru #77 CUSCO SUBARU ADVAN IMPREZA	Reach Level 35
2006 Toyota #25 ECLIPSE ADVAN SUPRA	Reach Level 40
1998 Nissan #32 NISSAN R390 GTI	Reach Level 45
1999 Toyota #3 Toyota Motorsports GT-ONE TS020	Reach Level 50

Europe Level Reward Cars

Reach these levels in Europe to unlock the cars.

Unlockable	How to Unlock
1961 Jaguar E-type S1	Reach Level 5
1974 Lancia Stratos HF Stradale	Reach Level 10
1982 Porsche 911 Turbo 3.3	Reach Level 15
1989 Lotus Carlton	Reach Level 20
1987 Porsche 959	Reach Level 25
1998 Ferrari F355 Challenge	Reach Level 30
2005 Porsche #3 Lechner Racing School Team 1 911 GT3 Cup	Reach Level 35
2005 BMW Motorsport #2 BMW Motorsport M3-GTR	Reach Level 40
McLaren #41 Team McLaren F1 GTR	Reach Level 45
Audi #1 Infineon Audi R8	Reach Level 50

Manufacturer Club Races

Get first place in all the races in the series.

Unlockable	How to Unlock
1967 Ferrari 330 P4	Complete Club Ferrari
1995 Toyota VIS Racing MR2 Turbo T-bar	Complete MR2 Cup
1999 Lamborghini Diablo GTR	Complete Running of the Bulls
2000 Audi AWE S4 Tuning Silver Bullet S4	Complete Audi Cup
2000 Dodge Hennessey Viper 800TT	Complete Viper Performance Cup
2000 Nissan Top Secret D1-Spec S15	Complete Nissan Racing Club
2002 Honda Mugen Integra Type-R	Complete Integra Cup
2003 Volkswagen Golf R32	Complete Volkswagen Driver's Club
2005 Chevrolet #99 Tiger Racing Corvette Z06	Complete Corvette Touring Cup
2006 Porsche #82 Red Bull 911 GT3 Cup	Complete Porsche Sports Car Club

North America Level Reward Cars

Reach these levels in North America to unlock the cars.

Unlockable	How to Unlock
1968 Shelby Mustang GT-500KR	Reach Level 5
1969 Dodge Charger R/T-SE	Reach Level 10
1970 Chevrolet Chevelle SS-454	Reach Level 15
2000 Ford Mustang Cobra R	Reach Level 20
1996 Chevrolet Corvette Grand Sport	Reach Level 25
1999 Dodge Viper GTS ACR	Reach Level 30
2005 Chevrolet #31 Whelen Engineering Corvette Z06	Reach Level 35
2005 Panoz #51 JML Team Panoz Esperante GTLM	Reach Level 40
2002 Saleen #11 Graham Nash Motorsport S7R	Reach Level 45
2002 Cadillac #6 Team Cadillac NorthStar LMP-02	Reach Level 50

Forza Motorsport 2 (continued)

Proving Grounds Unlockable Cars

Get first place in all the races in the series.

Unlockable	How to Unlock
1969 Chevrolet Camaro Z28	Complete North American Open
1970 Porsche 914/6	Complete European Open
1985 Toyota AE86 Sprinter Trueno	Complete Asian Open
1992 Lancia Delta Integrale EVO	Complete RWD Shootout
1994 Honda Do-Luck NSX	Complete Flyweight Invitational
1995 Toyota Border MR2 Turbo T-bar	Complete Mid-Engine Challenge
2001 Mazda Mazdaspeed Roadster	Complete FWD Shootout
2003 Renault Sport Clio V6 RS	Complete Hot Hatch Runoff
2004 Honda Wings West Civic Si	Complete AWD Shootout
2007 Shelby GT500	Complete Heavyweight Open

Semi-Pro Races

Get first place in all the races in the series.

Unlockable	How to Unlock
1995 Mazda AB Flug RX-7	Complete Kumho 250HP
1998 Nissan R390	Complete Nissan 350HP
1998 Subaru Tommy Kaira Impreza M20b	Complete Goodyear 150HP
2003 Dodge #23 Viper Comp Coupe	Complete Stoptech 400HP
2003 Mitsubishi Sparco Lancer Evo VIII	Complete Sparco 200HP
2004 Volvo #24 At-Speed S60-R	Complete Toyo 450HP
2005 Maserati #35 Risi Comp MC12	Complete Risi Comp 600HP
2006 Audi #2 FSI Champion Racing R8	Complete K&N 700HP
2006 Panoz #81 Team LNT Esperante GTLM	Complete Panoz 500HP
2007 Peugeot 207 Super 2000	Complete Castrol 300HP

Fracture

Codes

In Campaign mode, press Start. While in the Start menu, press the following code.

Effect	Code
Unlocks New Skin	↑,→,←,↓,↑,←,→,↓

Frogger

Make Frogger Bigger

Unlockable	How to Unlock
Make Frogger Bigger	At the screen where you are selecting to choose One or Two players, enter ↑ ↑ ↓ ↓ ← → ← → Ⓑ Ⓐ

Frontlines: Fuel of War

More Levels

To unlock two extra single-player levels in the game, insert the following passwords into the in-game passwords menu.

Unlockable	How to Unlock
Urban Level	sp-street
Village Level	sp-village

Frontlines: Fuel of War (continued)

Unlockable	How to Unlock

Achievements

Unlockable	How to Unlock
Anvil (15)	Complete the third mission on Normal difficulty or higher.
Anvil—Ironman (20)	Complete the third mission in a single session without dying.
Anvil—Stopwatch (25)	Complete the third mission in under 25 minutes.
Bull's-eye (90)	Complete the first or second half of a mission with an accuracy higher than 50%.
Bulletproof (90)	Kill 100 hostiles without dying in the first or second half of a single-player mission.
Captains of Industry (15)	Complete the second mission on Normal difficulty or higher.
Captains of Industry—Ironman (20)	Complete the second mission in a single session without dying.
Captains of Industry—Stopwatch (25)	Complete the second mission in under 25 minutes.
Darkness Falls (15)	Complete the first mission on Normal difficulty or higher.
Darkness Falls—Ironman (20)	Complete the first mission in a single session without dying.
Darkness Falls—Stopwatch (25)	Complete the first mission in under 15 minutes.
Flawless (50)	Win a ranked match without dying.
Graveyard (15)	Complete the fourth mission on Normal difficulty or higher.
Graveyard—Ironman (20)	Complete the fourth mission in a single session without dying.
Graveyard—Stopwatch (25)	Complete the fourth mission in under 50 minutes.
History Repeats (15)	Complete the final mission on Normal difficulty or higher.
History Repeats—Ironman (20)	Complete the final mission in a single session without dying.
History Repeats—Stopwatch (25)	Complete the final mission in under 40 minutes.
Killing Spree (50)	Score five kills in a row without dying in multiplayer.
Living Quarter (15)	Complete the sixth mission on Normal difficulty or higher.
Living Quarter—Ironman (20)	Complete the sixth mission in a single session without dying.
Living Quarter—Stopwatch (25)	Complete the sixth mission in under 25 minutes.
Marksman (75)	Finish a ranked match with an accuracy level higher than 40%.
Noob (0)	Suicide 10 times in a Multiplayer match.
Rampage (75)	Score 10 kills in a row without dying in multiplayer.
The Mountain King (15)	Complete the fifth mission on Normal difficulty or higher.
The Mountain King—Ironman (20)	Complete the fifth mission in a single session without dying.
The Mountain King—Stopwatch (25)	Complete the fifth mission in under 30 minutes.
Top Scorer (50)	Be the player with the highest score on the winning team of a ranked match.

Full Auto

To unlock everything, you must make a new profile from the Xbox 360 dashboard.

Unlockable	Password
Unlock everything	magicman

Gauntlet

Walls Become Exits

Unlockable	How to Unlock
Walls Become Exits	On any level, all players must stand still for 200 seconds. After 200 seconds, all the walls in the level will become exit doors. If players wish to, they can shoot enemies, and change the direction of their shooting, just as long as they do not move. This works on single and multiplayer.

Gear's of War

Unlockable	How To
Insane Difficulty	Complete the game on either Casual or Hardcore difficulty.
Secret Gamer Pic	Complete the game on Insane difficulty to unlock a secret gamer picture.
Secret Gamer Pic #2	Unlock the "Seriously..." achievement by getting 10,000 kills in ranked multiplayer matches to get that respective GamerPic.

The Godfather

Cheat Codes

Code	Effect
Y, Left, Y, Right, X, Right	Full Ammo
Left, X, Right, Y, Right, LB	Full Health
Y, X, Y, X, Y, LB **(click)**	Film Clips

Infinite Ammo

Unlockable	How to Unlock
Infinite Ammo	Become Don of NYC

Grand Theft Auto IV

Codes

During gameplay, pull out Niko's phone and dial these numbers for the corresponding effect. Cheats will affect missions and Achievements.

Effect	Code
Change weather	468-555-0100
Get the Ak-47, knife, Molotov Cocktails, pistol, RPG, sniper rifle and Uzi, and "Cleaned the Mean Streets" Achievement blocked	486-555-0150
Get the baseball bat, grenades, M4, MP5, pistol, RPG, and sniper rifle, and "Cleaned the Mean Streets" Achievement blocked	486-555-0100
Raise wanted level	267-555-0150
Remove wanted level; "One Man Army" and "Walk Free" Achievements blocked	267-555-0100
Restore armor; "Cleaned the Mean Streets," "Finish Him," "One Man Army," and "Walk Free" Achievements blocked	362-555-0100
Restore health; "Cleaned the Mean Streets" Achievement blocked	482-555-0100
Spawn a Cognoscenti	227-555-0142
Spawn a Comet	227-555-0175

DS PSP PS2 PS3 Wii Xbox Xbox 360 Index

Grand Theft Auto IV (continued)

Effect	Code
Spawn a Jetmax	938-555-0100
Spawn a Sanchez	625-555-0150
Spawn a SuperGT	227-555-0168
Spawn a Turismo	227-555-0147
Spawn an Annihilator; "One Man Army" and "Walk Free" Achievements blocked	359-555-0100
Spawn an FIB Buffalo	227-555-0100
Spawn an NRG-900	625-555-0100

Map Locations

Enter the password into any of the in-game computers.

Effect	Code
Weapon, health, armor, vehicle, pigeon, ramp/stunt, and entertainment locations	www.whattheydonotwantyoutoknow.com

Achievements

Unlockable	How to Unlock
Assassin's Greed	Complete all 9 assassin missions: 20 points
Auf Wiedersehen, Petrovic	Win all ranked multiplayer variations, all races, and Cops 'n' Crooks, as both sides: 30 points
Chain Reaction	Blow up 10 vehicles in 10 seconds: 20 points
Cleaned the Mean Streets	Capture 20 criminals through the police computer: 20 points
Courier Service	Complete all 10 package delivery jobs: 10 points
Cut Your Teeth	Earn a personal rank promotion in multiplayer: 5 points
Dare Devil	Complete 100% of the unique stunt jumps: 30 points
Dial B for Bomb	Unlock the special ability of phoning for a bomb to be placed: 10 points
Driving Mr. Bellic	Unlock the special ability of taxi: 10 points
Endangered Species	Collect every hidden package: 50 points
Fed the Fish	Complete the mission "Uncle Vlad": 5 points
Finish Him	Complete 10 melee counters in 4 minutes: 15 points
Fly the Coop	Beat Rockstars time in ranked versions of Deal Breaker, Hangman's NOOSE, and Bomb da Base II: 15 points
Full Exploration	Unlock all the islands
Genetically Superior	Come first in 20 single-player street races: 25 points
Gobble Gobble	Score 3 strikes in a row, a turkey, in 10-pin bowling: 10 points
Gracefully Taken	Complete mission "I'll Take Her": 10 points
Half Million	Reach a balance of $500,000: 55 points
Impossible Trinity	Complete mission "Museum Piece": 10 points
It'll Cost Ya	Complete a taxi ride without skipping from one island to another: 5 points
Join the Midnight Club	Win a ranked multiplayer race without damaging your vehicle too much and have damage enabled: 10 points
Key to the City	Achieve 100% in "Game progress" statistic: 100 points
King of QUB3D	Beat the High Score in QUB3D: 15 points

Grand Theft Auto IV (continued)

Unlockable	How to Unlock
Let Sleeping Rockstars Lie	Kill a Rockstar developer in a ranked multiplayer match: 10 points
Liberty City (5)	After you meet all friends, the ones left alive like you above 90%: 20 points
Liberty City Minute	Complete the story missions in less than 30 hours: 30 points
Lowest Point	Complete mission "Roman's Sorrow": 5 points
Manhunt	Complete the most wanted side missions from police computer: 15 points
No More Strangers	Meet all random characters: 5 points
Off the Boat	Complete the first mission: 5 points
One Hundred and Eighty	In a game of darts, score 180 with only 3 darts: 10 points
One Man Army	Survive 5 minutes on 6-star wanted level: 40 points
Order Fulfilled	Complete all 10 Exotic Export orders: 10 points
Pool Shark	Beat a friend at pool: 10 points
Retail Therapy	Unlock the ability to buy guns from a friend: 10 points
Rolled Over	Do 5 car rolls in a row from one crash: 30 points
Sightseer	Fly on all helicopter tours of Liberty City: 5 points
Taking It for the Team	Be on the winning team in all ranked multiplayer games: 10 points
Teamplayer	Kill five players who are not in your team, in any ranked multiplayer team game: 10 points
That Special Someone	Complete the mission "That Special Someone": 10 points
That's How We Roll!	Unlock the special ability of helicopter: 10 points
Top of the Food Chain	Kill 20 players with a pistol in a ranked multiplayer deathmatch : 10 points
Top the Midnight Club	Come first in 20 different ranked standard multiplayer races: 20 points Wanted
Under the Radar	Fly underneath the main bridges in the game that cross water with a helicopter : 40 points
Walk Free	Lose a 4-star wanted level by outrunning the cops: 50 points
Wanted	Achieve the highest personal rank in multiplayer: 20 points
Warm Coffee	Successfully date a girl to be invited into her house: 5 points
Wheelie Rider	Do a wheelie lasting at least 500 feet on a motorbike: 30 points
You Got the Message	Deliver all 30 cars ordered through text messages: 20 points
You Won!	Complete the final mission: 60 points

Unlockables

Unlockable	How to Unlock
Annihilator Helicopter	Kill all 200 Flying Rats (Pigeons)

Grand Theft Auto IV (continued)

Easter Eggs

Unlockable	How to Unlock
The Heart of Liberty City	Gain access to Happiness Island. Once you're able to go there legally, find the Helicopter Tours (which is directly east of Happiness Island) and steal a helicopter. Fly over the Statue of Liberty and jump out at the statue's feet. Land on the topmost tier of the statue, which is basically a square platform with a door in the center of each side. Look for a door with a plaque on either side of it that reads, "No Hidden Content Here." Don't try to open the door; just walk through it. Inside, you'll find an empty room with a tall ladder. Climb it, and when you reach the top, look up; there is a gigantic beating heart, held in place by chains.

Codes

During gameplay, pull out Niko's phone and dial these numbers for the corresponding effect. Cheats will affect missions and achievements.

Effect	Code
Banshee	265-555-2423
Feltzer	662-555-0147
Presidente	265-555-2423
Song Information	948-555-0100

Friendship Bonuses

Gain the following bonuses by gaining the corresponding amount of friendship.

Unlockable	How to Unlock
Boom? (Call Packie for him to make you a car bomb)	Gain 75% friendship with Packie.
Chopper Ride (He will pick you up in his helicopter)	Gain 70% friendship with Brucie.
Discount Guns (Buy weapons at a cheaper price from Little Jacob)	Gain 60% friendship with Little Jacob.
Extra Help (A car of gang members will be sent to help you out)	Gain 60% friendship with Dwayne.
Free Ride (Call for a taxi)	Gain 60% friendship with Roman.

Unlockables

Unlockable	How to Unlock
Rastah Color Huntley SUV	Complete 10 Package Delivery missions.
Remove Ammo Limit	Get 100% completion.

Grid

Livery Codes

Go to the "Enter Code" section from the main menu under Options, then input the codes.

Effect	Code
All Drift Cars	TUN58396
All Muscle Cars	MUS59279
Buchbinder 320si Livery	F93857372
Free Pagani Zonda R	M38572343

Grid (continued)

Effect	Code
Play.com Livery	P47203845
Unlock a BMW 320si for Use in Grid World and Raceday. Locked to Gamestation Livery	G29782655

Achievements

Unlockable	How to Unlock
1st and 2nd at Global (25)	Get a 2-1 at Global level.
Airborne (15)	Get the car airborne for 1 second.
Back to Front (10)	Cross the finish line in first place in reverse.
Beat Codies (30)	Beat the developer or anyone who has beaten the developer online.
Car Wreck (5)	Cause insane damage to your car.
City Slicker (20)	Race in every city.
Combo King (20)	Get a x50 Drift Multiplayer.
Corporate Power (10)	Fill all your sponsor slots.
Driver for Hire (10)	Race for a team from every region.
Filthy Rich (25)	Earn enough to buy a brand new Lamborghini Murcielago GTR.
First Wheels (5)	Buy your first car.
First Win! (10)	Win your first race.
First Xbox LIVE Win (10)	Win your first ranked Xbox LIVE race.
Five Xbox LIVE Wins (30)	Win 5 ranked Xbox LIVE races.
Flashback & Win (5)	Use the Flashback feature and win the race.
Full Rep (10)	Earn the full reputation available on EXTREME difficulty.
Gentleman Driver (30)	Win an entire GRID World Event without making contact with other cars.
Global License (20)	Unlock your Global License.
Globe Hopper (30)	Race at every location.
Gotta Drive 'Em All (30)	Drive every car.
Hard Charger (20)	Win a 12 car race starting from the back of the Grid.
Head 2 Head (30)	Win your first Head 2 Head race.
High Mileage (30)	Drive 750 miles in a single car.
Hire & Fire (10)	Hire a new teammate with a higher rank than your current one.
Hot Lap (20)	Beat the original lap record on any track.
Keep Drifting (10)	Drift your car for 5 seconds.
Keep Rolling (10)	Roll your car 20 times.
Last Man Standing (20)	Be the last survivor of a single-player Demolition Derby.
Le Mans Legend (30)	Win a Le Mans 24 hour race on Pro mode.
Le Mans Rookie (15)	Complete your first Le Mans 24 hour race.
Long Haul (40)	Drive a total of 1,000 miles.
New Kid on the Block (5)	Complete your first race.
Online Elite (30)	Obtain the Elite rank in the Xbox LIVE game mode.
Online Legend (50)	Obtain the Legend rank in the Xbox LIVE game mode.
Power Seller (25)	Sell a car for more than you paid for it.

Grid (continued)

Unlockable	How to Unlock
Record Breaker (10)	Complete a lap of Okatama Grand Circuit in under 90 seconds.
Road Block (10)	Be involved in a 3-car pile-up.
Seasoned Pro (30)	Win all Event Trophies.
Short Haul (30)	Drive a total of 500 miles.
Speed Demon (10)	Reach 200mph in any car in a GRID World race.
Spin & Win (10)	Complete a 360° spin and still win the race.
Stick Shift (10)	Win a race using manual transmission.
Sunday Drivers (30)	Finish a race at least one lap ahead of the rest of the field in GRID World or Race Day.
Team Win (20)	Take your team to win its first Event.
Top of Team Leaderboard (35)	Top the Team Leaderboard.
Top of the Tree (35)	Top the Driver Leaderboard.
Touge King (20)	Win a Touge Event on EXTREME difficulty.
When Will I Be Famous? (20)	Get onto a Hall of Fame Leaderboard.
Winning Streak (15)	Win all races in an Event.
You Again? (20)	Lap an opponent in a 12 car GRID World race.

Guitar Hero II

Codes

Enter code at the main menu screen where it shows "Career" and "Quick Play."

Unlockable	How to Unlock
Air Guitar	Y, B, Y, O, Y, B
Enables Hyperspeed	B, O, Y, O, B, O, Y, Y
Eyeball Head Crowd	Y, O, B, B, B, O, Y
Flaming Heads	O, Y, Y, O, Y, Y, O, Y, Y, B, Y, Y, B, Y, Y
Monkey Head Crowd	O, Y, B, B, Y, O, B, B
Performance Mode	B, B, Y, B, B, O, B, B
Unlock All Songs	B, Y, O, R, Y, O, B, Y, B, Y, B, Y, B, Y, B, Y

Unlockable Guitars

Unlockable	How to Unlock
"The Log" Guitar	5 Star every song on Expert mode
Axe Guitar	Beat Expert mode
Casket Guitar	Beat Medium mode
Eyeball Guitar	5 Star every song on Hard mode
Fish Guitar	Beat Easy mode
Snaketapus Guitar	Beat Hard mode
USA Guitar	5 Star every song on Easy mode
Viking Guitar	5 Star every song on Medium mode

Extra Bass Guitars Unlockable in Co-Op

NOTE

"Extra" songs do not count toward these unlockables.

Guitar Hero II (continued)

Unlockable	How to Unlock
Cream SG	Get 5 stars on 20 Co-Op songs
Gibson Grabber	Beat 20 Co-Op songs
Gibson SG Bass	Beat 10 Co-Op songs
Gibson Thunderbird	Beat 30 Co-Op songs
Hofner Bass	Beat all Co-Op songs
Lava Pearl Musicman Stingray	Get 5 stars on 10 Co-Op songs
Natural Maple Gibson Grabber Bass	Get 4 stars on all Co-Op songs
Natural Sunburst Gibson Thunderbird Bass	Get 5 stars on all Co-Op Songs

Guitar Hero III: Legends of Rock

Enter the following in the Cheats menu under Options. You must strum every note/chord. The letters correspond to colored frets G=Green, R=Red, Y=Yellow, B=Blue, O=Orange

Code	Effect
(BY) (GY) (GY) (RB) (RB) (RY) (RY) (BY) (GY) (GY) (RB) (RB) (RY) (RY) (GY) (GY) (RY) (RY)	Air guitar
(GR) (GR) (GR) (GB) (GB) (GB) (RB) R R R (RB) R R R (RB) R R R	Bret Michaels singer
(GR) (GY) (YB) (RB) (BO) (YO) (RY) (RB)	Easy Expert
O, B, O, Y, O, B, O, Y	Hyperspeed
(GR) (B) (GR) (GY) (B) (GY) (RY) (O) (RY) (GY) (Y) (GY) (GR)	No fail (does not work in Career mode)
RY, RB, RO, RB, RY, GB, RY RB	Performance mode
GR, GR, GR, RY, RY, RB, RB, YB, YO, YO, GR, GR, GR, RY, RY, RB, RB, YB, YO, YO	Precision mode
YO, RB, RO, GB, RY, YO, RY, RB, GY, GY, YB, YB, YO, YO, YB, Y, R, RY, R, Y, O	Unlock all songs
(GR_BO) (GRYB_) (GRY_O) (G_BYO) (GRYB_) (_RYBO) (GRYB_) (G_YBO) (GRYB_) (GRY_O) (GRY_O) (GRYB_) (GRY_O)	Unlock everything (no sound plays when you enter these chords)

Unlockable	How to Unlock
Lou	Defeat this boss and you can buy him for $15,000
Slash	Defeat this boss and you can buy him for $10,000
Tom Morello	Defeat this boss and you can buy him for $10,000

After unlocking these guitars, you can buy them in the shop.

Unlockable Guitars

Unlockable	How to Unlock
Assassin Bass	5-star Co-op Expert mode.
Bat Guitar	5-star all songs in Easy mode.
Beach Life Bass	Complete Co-Op Career Hard mode.
El Jefe Guitar	5-star all songs in Expert mode.
Jolly Roger Guitar	5-star all songs in Medium mode.
Moon Guitar	Complete Easy mode.
Pendulaxe Blade Bass	Complete Co-op Expert mode.
Risk Assessment Guitar	Complete Expert mode.
Rojimbo! Guitar	Complete Hard mode.
Saint George Guitar	Complete Medium mode.
Tiki Face Guitar	5-star all songs in Hard mode.
Tiki Fortune 4 Bass	Complete Co-op Easy mode.

Guitar Hero: Aerosmith

Cheat Chords

Strum the following chords in the "Cheats" menu. A message should appear if you strummed them correctly. You can then turn them on or off in from the menu.

Effect	Code
Air Guitar(Guitarist plays without a guitar in the game)	(RY) (GR) (RY) (RY) (RB) (RB) (RB) (RB) (RB) (YB) (YB) (YO)
Hyperspeed (Faster Gameplay)	(YO) (YO) (YO) (YO) (YO) (RY) (RY) (RY) (RY) (RB) (RB) (RB) (RB) (RB) (YB) (YO) (YO)
No Fail (Makes it impossible to fail a song, doesn't work in Career mode, and disables online scores)	(GR) (B) (GR) (GY) (B) (GY) (RY) (O) (RY) (GY) (Y) (GY) (GR)
Performance Mode (No notes, just the song playing)	(GR) (GR) (RO) (RB) (GR) (GR) (RO) (RB)
Precision Mode (Makes it harder to miss notes)	(RY) (RB) (RB) (RY) (RY) (YB) (YB) (YB) (RB) (RY) (RB) (RB) (RY) (RY) (YB) (YB) (YB) (RB)
Unlock All Songs (except for "Pandora's Box" by Aerosmith)	(RY) (GR) (GR) (RY) (RY) (GR) (RY) (RY) (GR) GR) (RY) (RY) (GR) (RY) (RB)

Characters

Once unlocked, the following characters will be available for purchase in Career mode.

Unlockable	How to Unlock
DMC	Beat "King of Rock" by Run DMC.
Joe Perry	Defeat Joe Perry in a Guitar Battle in Career mode.

Songs

Once unlocked, the following songs can be accessed by pushing the blue fret button on the main setlist.

Unlockable	How to Unlock
Aerosmith: "Kings and Queens"	Complete the Career Tour.
Joe Perry: "Joe Perry Guitar Battle"	Defeat Joe Perry in a Guitar Battle in Career mode.

Gun

Unlockables

Unlockable	How to Unlock
Magruder's Seven Barrel Nock Gun	Successfully complete the Story mode
Reed's Horse and Magruder's Cannon Nock Gun	Get 100% completion in the Story mode
.69 Ferguson Rifle	Defeat Hollister
Apache Shirt	Successfully complete the Hunting Missions
Cavalry Sword	Defeat Reed
Dual Peacemakers	Defeat Hoodoo
Magruder's Seven Barrel Nock Gun	Successfully complete Story mode
Reed's Armored Horse	Complete the game and get 100%
Silver Spurs	Successfully complete the Pony Express Missions

Half-Life 2: The Orange Box

Half-Life 2 *Codes*

Enter the code while playing *Half Life 2.* No specific requirements other than the game. Can be entered at any time on any level. Using cheats does not disable Achievements.

Code	Effect
LB, Up, RB, Up, LB, LB, Up, RB, RB, Up	Invincibility
Up, Up, Down, Down, Left, Right, Left, Right, B, A	Restores health by 25 points
Y, B, A, X, RB, Y, X, A, B, RB	Restores ammo for current weapon
Left, Left, Left, Left, P, Right, Right, Right, Right, RB	Unlocks all levels, which can then be accessed from the new game window

Portal Codes

Enter these codes anytime during gameplay.

Code	Effect
Down, B, A, B, Y, Down, B, A, B, Y	Create box
LB, Down, RB, Down, LB, LB, Up, RB, RB, Up	Enables invincibility
Up, Y, Y, X, X, A, A, B, B, Up	Fire energy ball
Y, A, B, A, B, Y, Y, A, Left, Right	Portal placement anywhere
X, B, LB, RB, Left, Right, LB, RB, LT, RT	Upgrade Portalgun

Halo 3

Armor Permutations Unlockables

Body Pieces: Spartan marked with (S) and Elite marked with (E).

Unlockable	How to Unlock
(E) Ascetic Body	Unlock "Up Close and Personal" Achievement
(E) Ascetic Head	Unlock "Steppin' Razor" Achievement
(E) Ascetic Shoulders	Unlock "Overkill" Achievement
(E) Commando Body	Unlock "Triple Kill" Achievement
(E) Commando Head	Unlock "Overkill" Achievement
(E) Commando Shoulders	Unlock "Killing Frenzy" Achievement
(E) Flight Body	Complete Tsavo Highway on Heroic or Legendary
(E) Flight Head	Complete Campaign mode on Heroic
(E) Flight Shoulders	Complete The Ark on Heroic difficulty or higher
(S) EOD Body	Complete Tsavo Highway on Legendary
(S) EOD Head	Complete Campaign mode on Legendary
(S) EOD Shoulders	Complete The Ark on Legendary
(S) EVA Body	Complete Tsavo Highway on Normal or higher
(S) EVA Head	Complete Campaign mode on Normal
(S) EVA Shoulders	Complete The Ark on Normal difficulty or higher
(S) Hayabusa Chest	Collect 5 hidden skulls
(S) Hayabusa Helmet	Collect 13 hidden skulls
(S) Hayabusa Shoulders	Collect 9 hidden skulls
(S) Mark V Head	Unlock "UNSC Spartan" Achievement
(S) ODST Head	Unlock "Spartan Graduate" Achievement
(S) Rogue Head	Unlock "Spartan Officer" Achievement
(S) Scout Body	Unlock "Too Close to the Sun" Achievement
(S) Scout Head	Unlock "Used Car Salesman" Achievement

Halo 3 (continued)

Unlockable	How to Unlock
(S) Scout Shoulders	Unlock "Mongoose Mowdown" Achievement
(S) Security Head	Earn 1,000 Gamerscore points
(S) Security Shoulders	Earn 850 Gamerscore points
Katana	Complete all Achievements (1,000/1,000)

BLACK-EYE SKULL

Effect: Melee hits instantly recharge your shield.

Level: Crow's Nest

Location: As soon as you start the level, head straight up to the higher level. Head toward the door with the red light, then turn around. Jump onto the racks, onto the red metal light holders, then onto the ventilation tube. The skull spawns at the end.

BLIND SKULL

Effect: "Shoot from the hip."

Level: First Stage

Location: When you get to the area where you see the Phantom overhead (one of the marines points it out) jump over the rocks and keep following the path on the right. When you get to the cliff, there's a rock over on the side. The skull is on the end of the rock. Note: This skull has to be activated before you start a Campaign map.

CATCH SKULL

Effect: all enemies have 2 grenades, throw more grenades.

Level: The Storm

Location: From the start, go through until you go outside again. Outside, look straight across to a small round building. The skull is on top. To get up there, either use a warthog as a platform or grenade-jump. DO NOT destroy the wraith near the door or the skull will disappear.

COWBELL SKULL

Effect: Explosive force increased (sputnik from H2).

Level: The Ark

Location: First pick up a grav lift from the small building near where you fight the scarab. Now proceed through the level until you reach the second sloping hallway (stairway). You should see some partitioned risers (platforms) halfway down. The skull is on the top level. Toss the grav-lift on the right side of the hall so it lands on the fourth little green dot from the door. Then run, jump, and use the grav-lift to propel you to the top. You reach a checkpoint just as you enter the room, so if you miss, just try again.

FAMINE SKULL

Effect: "Trust us. Bring a magazine." Dropped weapons have very little ammo compared to normal.

Level: The Ark

Location: When you first go into the valley to the right after the wrecked phantom, look left to see a huge boulder. Use a ghost and get to the side of the boulder closest to the bridge overhead. It is easy to pilot the ghost up the side of the wall using the thrust. To get the skull, pilot 2 ghosts up the wall to the top of the bridge and stack them one on top of another next to the beam where the skull is placed. Simply jump from the top of the ghosts toward the skull and land on the beam.

FOG SKULL

Effect: "You'll miss those eyes in the back of your head." Your motion sensor disappears.

Level: Floodgate

Halo 3 (continued)

Location: As you are walking down from the anti-air gun you destroyed in the previous mission, you encounter a ramp (next to a missile launcher). Around this ramp, you hit a checkpoint. At this point, you should also hear a marine yelling, "There! Over There!" Look up and to the right, directly at the roof of the building next to the missile launcher. A single flood form (not to be mistaken for the two other flood forms jumping in front of you) holds the skull. Kill him before he jumps, and he drops the skull down to the ground where you can retrieve it. If you shoot too early, and the skull gets stuck on the roof.

GRUNT BIRTHDAY PARTY SKULL

Effect: Headshots on grunts cause heads to explode with confetti.

Level: Crow's Nest

Location: Right after the first objective, while en route to the barracks, you fall onto a pipe. At the end of this pipe, look over the edge to see a small space a few feet below you. Drop over and as quickly as you can, pull back to land under the floor you were just on. The skull is at the end.

IRON SKULL

Effect: When either player dies in Co-Op on any difficulty both players restart at last checkpoint. In single player, you restart the level if you die.

Level: Sierra 117

Location: In the area where you rescue Sarge, behind the prison cell is a large ledge. Go to the far right side and jump on the boxes, then onto the pipes to get up on the ledge. Go to the far end of the ledge, turn two corners, and the skull is at the far end.

IWHBYD SKULL

Effect: "But the dog beat me over the fence." Unlocks bonus dialogue throughout the game. For most, this is the last skull, so this gives you the Hayabusa Helmet as well.

Level: The Covenant

Location: To get this, get to the room where you "fight" the Prophet of Truth. Let the Arbiter kill him, turn around, and kill all the flood here as well. This makes it a lot easier. Then jump through the Halo holograms in this order: 4 6 5 4 5 3 4. When you jump through the final hologram, they all light up in a sequential pattern. The skull is at the end, right before the energy bridge leading to Truth's corpse.

MYTHIC SKULL

Effect: Every enemy on the field now has double the normal amount of health.

Level: Halo

Location: As soon as the mission starts, walk up the hill in front of you and into the cave. Hug the right side of the cave, and after a large boulder you see a path on your right. Take the short path and find it at the end.

THUNDERSTORM SKULL

Effect: "Field promotions for everyone!" Upgrades enemies to their stronger versions.

Level: The Covenant

Location: After you shut down tower 1 and get access to the hornet, fly to tower 2 (the one the Arbiter shut down). While walking up the stairs, go to the middle part that connects both. A stair leads up to a platform where the skull is.

TILT SKULL

Effect: "What was once resistance is now immunity." Enemies have different body parts that may be resistant to certain bullet types.

Level: Cortana

Location: When in the circular type room with all the flood, look for a small structure piece next to two archways. Jump on top of it and up on the rocks to the top left, turn left and jump up again, then do a 180 and jump to the rocks across from you. Follow the rock sticking out and leading up on top of the original circular room. The skull is in a pile of blood.

Halo 3 (continued)

TOUGH LUCK SKULL

Effect: Enemies do saving throws.

Level: Tsavo Highway

Location: On Tsavo Highway, about halfway through the mission (right after you are forced to walk through a large blue barrier), you will come out of a tunnel on the highway, and see a large pipeline on your left. Drop down in between the two, and run to the wall in front of you. Follow the wall all the way to where it connects with the cliff on your right, and turn to the left. There should be a few ledges—simply crouch-jump from ledge to ledge, and the last one should have the "Tough Luck" skull on it.

THE SEVEN TERMINALS

The Ark:

1. Start the mission and once you enter the first building, take a left into another door and emerge in a curved corridor. On the inside is a Terminal.

2. After activating the bridge to let your comrades across the gap, do a 180 and you should see it. (It does not open until you activate the bridge.)

3. In the third building after defeating the scarab, kill the group of sleeping covenant, then follow the corridor downward. Once you reach a door in front that is locked, immediately on the left there's an open door. Go through and walk straight, then do a 180 to find a secret room. It is in there.

The Covenant:

1. When in the first tower standing on the lift, face the access panel and turn left. Jump over and it's right there.

2. Land your hornet on the second tower, walk toward the entrance, but when you see the locked door, do a 180.

3. When in the third tower standing on the lift, face the access panel and turn right. Jump over.

Halo:

1. After reaching the end of the first cave, hug the right wall and you see a building. Jump up onto the walkway and hang a left once inside.

Harry Potter and the Order of the Phoenix

Room of Rewards Trophies

Unlockable	How to Unlock
Characters Cup	Meet all 58 characters in Hogwarts
Defense Against the Dark Arts Cup	Cast all defensive spells in six duels
House Ghost Cup	Find all four House Ghosts
Nature Trail Cup	Find all animal footprints

Infinite Undiscovery

Unlockables

Unlockable	How to Unlock
Hard Mode	Finish the game in Normal mode

Iron Man

Unlockables

Unlockable	How to Unlock
Classic	Beat the "One Man Army vs. Mercs" challenge.
Classic Mark I	Beat the "One Man Army vs. AIM" challenge.
Extremis	Beat the "One Man Army vs. Maggia" challenge.
Hulkbuster	Beat the "One Man Army vs. AIM-X" challenge.
Mark II	Beat the "One Man Army vs. Ten Rings" challenge.

Iron Man (continued)

Unlockable	How to Unlock
Mark III	Unlocked by default.
Silver Centurion (Xbox 360 Exclusive)	Beat the Mission "Showdown" (or beat the game, since "Showdown" is the last mission).

Achievements

Unlockable	How to Unlock
AIM Obsoleted (25)	Complete the One Man Army vs. AIM challenge without an armor breach.
AIM-X Obsoleted (25)	Complete the One Man Army vs. AIM-X challenge without an armor breach.
Air Superiority (15)	Destroy all dropships before the Stark Gunship is stolen in the First Flight mission.
An Object in Motion (15)	Destroy any target using a ramming attack.
City Protector (25)	Destroy drones without civilian damage in the First Flight mission.
Classic Confrontation (15)	Defeat Titanium Man using the Classic armor.
Collateral Damage (15)	Destroy a Prometheus missile by destroying a fuel truck in the Maggia Compound mission.
Decommissioner (25)	Destroy all Prometheus missiles in the Maggia Compound mission.
Disarmed (25)	Destroy stockpiled Stark weapons in the Escape mission.
Eject! (25)	Spare the US fighter pilots in the Stark Weapons mission.
Escape Velocity (25)	Sever the tether before the satellite overloads in the Space Tether mission.
Excelsior! (70)	Complete Hero Objectives for all missions.
Ground Pound (15)	Defeat an opponent using the ground pound in the Extremis armor.
Grounded (15)	Successfully grapple and throw a plane.
Guardian (25)	Protect warehouse workers in the Maggia Factories mission.
Hero (75)	Complete all missions on Normal difficulty (or harder).
Hulk Smash! (15)	Successfully grapple an opponent in the Hulkbuster armor.
Impenetrable (15)	Complete a mission (other than Escape or First Flight) without an armor breach.
In the Drink (25)	Avoid civilian casualties in the Flying Fortress mission.
Launch Aborted (15)	Destroy all Prometheus missiles within 10 minutes in the Maggia Compound mission.
Long Shot (15)	Damage or destroy another enemy while grappling a howitzer.
Maggia Obsoleted (25)	Complete the One Man Army vs. Maggia challenge without an armor breach.
Mercs Obsoleted (25)	Complete the One Man Army vs. Mercs challenge without an armor breach.
Not a Scratch (25)	Avoid harming the destroyer and its crew in the Lost Destroyer mission.
Old School (15)	Defeat Iron Monger using the Silver Centurion armor.
Overkill (15)	Defeat a soldier using the Unibeam.
Personnel Vendetta (15)	Defeat 20 soldiers in the Arctic Battle mission.
Power Saver (25)	Avoid disrupting the city's power supply in the On Defense mission.

Iron Man (continued)

Unlockable	How to Unlock
Proton Shut Out (25)	Prevent cannon attacks on civilian targets in the Island Meltdown mission.
Pugilist (15)	Complete any mission (other than Escape) without using weapons systems.
Road King (15)	Destroy all convoy vehicles in less than 2 minutes in the Stark Weapons mission.
Shocking! (25)	Protect outlying occupied buildings in the Save Pepper mission.
Sidekick (75)	Complete all missions on Easy difficulty (or harder).
Smack Down (15)	Defeat Titanium Man before his second recharge in the On Defense mission.
Super Hero (75)	Complete all missions on Formidable difficulty.
Tatyana, Interrupted (25)	Protect the nuclear facility in the Arctic Battle mission.
Ten Rings Obsoleted (25)	Complete the One Man Army vs. Ten Rings challenge without an armor breach.
You're Fired! (25)	Destroy power regulators in the Iron Monger mission.
Your Own Medicine (15)	Damage or destroy another enemy while grappling a SAM launcher.

Jetpac Refuelled

Pictures and Dashboard

Unlockable	How to Unlock
Two Gamer Pictures and Dashboard Theme	Beat level 64. You can download these items in the Help and Options menu.

Juiced 2: Hot Import Nights

Driver DNA Car Unlockables

Enter the passwords in the DNA lab to unlock the special challenges. If you win the challenges, you unlock a custom version of the following cars.

Unlockable	How to Unlock
Audi TT 1.8L Quattro	YTHZ
BMW Z4 Roadster	GVDL
Frito-Lay Infiniti G35	MNCH
Holden Monaro	RBSG
Hyundai Coupe 2.7L V6	BSLU
Infiniti G35	MRHC
Koenigsegg CCX	KDTR
Mitsubishi Prototype X	DOPX
Nissan 350Z	PRGN
Nissan Skyline R34 GT-R	JWRS
Saleen S7	WIKF
Seat Leon Cupra R	FAMQ

Achievements

Unlockable	How to Unlock
Billionaire! (25)	One billion dollars!
Daredevil! (15)	Entered 25 pink slip races!
Dealer! (10)	Traded five cars online.
DNA Collector! (10)	Downloaded somebody's DNA.
Drift Marathon! (100)	20,000,000 point drift.
Elite (5)	Promoted to Elite.
Elite Legend (10)	Completed all Elite goals.
Feelin' Lucky! (5)	Entered a pink slip race.
Flawless Drift! (50)	5,000,000 point drift.

Juiced 2: Hot Import Nights (continued)

Unlockable	How to Unlock
HIN Champion (45)	Completed all HIN crew challenges.
Juiced! (25)	Maxed out 10 cars!
League 1 (5)	Promoted to League 1.
League 1 Legend (10)	Completed all League 1 goals.
League 2 (5)	Promoted to League 2.
League 2 Legend (10)	Completed all League 2 goals.
League 3 (5)	Promoted to League 3.
League 3 Legend (10)	Completed all League 3 goals.
League 4 (5)	Promoted to League 4.
League 4 Legend (10)	Completed all League 4 goals.
League 5 (5)	Promoted to League 5.
League 5 Legend (10)	Completed all League 5 goals.
League 6 (5)	Promoted to League 6.
League 6 Legend (10)	Completed all League 6 goals.
League 7 (5)	Promoted to League 7.
League 7 Legend (10)	Completed all League 7 goals.
Loaded! (20)	One hundred million dollars!
Lookin' Smooth! (10)	Traded five decal presets online.
Millionaire! (15)	One million dollars!
Nailed! (100)	100% completion.
Nice Bodywork! (5)	Traded a decal preset online.
Online Elite (5)	Promoted to Elite online.
Online Elite Legend (10)	Completed all online Elite goals.
Online League 1 (5)	Promoted to League 1 online.
Online League 1 Legend (10)	Completed all online League 1 goals.
Online League 2 (5)	Promoted to League 2 online.
Online League 2 Legend (10)	Completed all online League 2 goals.
Online League 3 (5)	Promoted to League 3 online.
Online League 3 Legend (10)	Completed all online League 3 goals.
Online League 4 (5)	Promoted to League 4 online.
Online League 4 Legend (10)	Completed all online League 4 goals.
Online League 5 (5)	Promoted to League 5 online.
Online League 5 Legend (10)	Completed all online League 5 goals.
Online League 6 (5)	Promoted to League 6 online.
Online League 6 Legend (10)	Completed all online League 6 goals.
Online League 7 (5)	Promoted to League 7 online.
Online League 7 Legend (10)	Completed all online League 7 goals.
Online Rookie Legend (10)	Completed all online Rookie goals.
Online World Class (5)	Promoted to World Class online.
Online World Class Legend (10)	Completed all online World Class goals.
Prestige (45)	Completed all celebrity challenges.
Revved! (20)	Maxed out five cars!
Risk Taker! (10)	Entered 10 pink slip races.

DS PSP PS2 PS3 Wii Xbox Xbox 360 Index

Juiced 2: Hot Import Nights (continued)

Unlockable	How to Unlock
Rookie Legend (10)	Completed all Rookie goals.
Style King! (15)	Traded 10 decal presets online!
Trader! (5)	Bought or sold a car online.
Tuned! (15)	Maxed out a car!
Tycoon! (10)	Traded 10 cars online!
Unstoppable Drift! (150)	50,000,000 point drift!
World Class (5)	Promoted to World Class.
World Class Legend (10)	Completed all World Class goals.

Kameo: Elements of Power

Thorn's Castle

Unlockable Required	Description	Pts.
Audio—The Troll Song	You have to hear it to believe it.	1,000,000
Cheats #1	Big Troll heads, Big Kameo head	2,500,000
Classic Kameo Skin	Have Kameo don her original purple outfit!	100,000
Video—Cutscene Style Test	A test clip of an early cutscene.	2,000,000
Video—Making Backgrounds	Shows how the background were made.	500,000
Video—Trailer Concept	An insight into the development process of the trailer.	1,500,000

Forgotten Forest

Unlockable Required	Description	Pts.
Cheats #2	Warrior Vision, Screen FX	2,000,000
FMV Player	The Story Begins, Kameo Meets Thorn, Pummel Weed Evolves, Rubble Evolves, Major Ruin Evolves, Deep Blue Evolves, Flex Evolves, 40 Below Evolves, Thermite Evolves, Shadow Troll Vision, Halis Vision, Lenya Vision, Yeros Vision, Airship, Warp, Death, The End…, Credits.	1,600,000
Pummel Weed Skin	Enable a new skin for Pummel Weed!	400,000
Rubble Skin	Enable a new skin for Rubble!	1,200,000
Video—Animation Creation	The magic of animation.	200,000
Video—The Wotnot Book	Learn more about the ancient tome.	800,000

Water Temple

Unlockable Required	Description	Pts.
Ash Skin	Enable a new skin for Ash!	1,000,000
Boss Battles	Old Mawood, Corallis, Queen Thyra, Lord Cheats #3	3,000,000
Drok, Thorn	Retro FX, Hard Trolls (disables Battle Points)	2,500,000
Cutscene Extras	Bonus bits for cutscene aficionados.	1,500,000
Gothic Kameo Skin	Kameo goes goth.	500,000
Major Ruin Skin	Enable a new skin for Major Ruin!	2,000,000

Kameo: Elements of Power (continued)

Snow Temple

Unlockable Required	Description	Pts.
Bonus Music Player	Bonus Tune #1—Umchacka, Bonus Tune #2—Alternative Theme	1,500,000
Cheats #4	Fire Proof (disables Battle Points), Troll Traitors—flip-kick a Troll to turn it against the others! (disables Battle Points), Scaredy-Trolls (disables Battle Points)	3,000,000
Chilla Skin	Enable a new skin for Chilla!	2,000,000
Deep Blue Skin	Enable a new skin for Deep Blue!	1,000,000
Group Shot Movie Player	An evolution of the group; Group Shot—2003, Group Shot—2004 #1, Group Shot—2004 #2	500,000
Video—Model Gallery	Check out the different character models.	2,500,000

Thorn's Pass

Unlockable Required	Description	Pts.
Animatic Player #1	Kameo Meets Thorn, Pummel Weed Evolves, Flex Evolves, 40 Below Evolves, Thermite Evolves, Transform Animatic	4,500,000
Cheats #5	Max Health (disables Battle Points), Elemental Override: fire (disables Battle Points), Elemental Override: ice (disables Battle Points)	5,000,000
Coyote Kameo Skin	Kameo blends in with the animals.	2,500,000
Flex Skin	Enable a new skin for Flex!	4,000,000
Old Evolve Sequences Player	Video—Evolving Rubble, Video—Evolving 40 Below, Video—Evolving Pummel Weed, Video—Evolving Deep Blue	3,500,000
Video—Old Chars. & Moves	View some old character and moves.	3,000,000

Thorn's Airship

Unlockable Required	Description	Pts.
40 Below Skin	Enable a new skin for 40 Below!	1,500,000
Video—Airship Concept	Working on Thorn's Airship.	2,000,000
Cheats #6	Easy Trolls (disables Battle Points), One-Hit Kills (disables Battle Points), Invulnerable (disables Battle Points), Upgrade All Warriors (disables Battle Points)	3,000,000
Other Deleted Scenes Player	Video—Kalus Attacks!, Video—Evolving Cloud Monster, Video—Kameo Rare Logo, Video—Vortex Capture	1,000,000
Video—Early Years	Check out footage of a very early version of Kameo.	500,000
Video—Ending Concept	An early idea for the ending sequence.	2,500,000

Kameo: Elements of Power (continued)

Unlockable	Overall Score Required Description	Pts.
Animatic Player #2	The Release of Thorn, Cailem Goes to the Citadel, Cailem Leads the Trolls, Tree Monster Evolves, Cloud Monster Evolves, Whirly Bird Evolves, Death Animatic	18,000,000
Concept Art Gallery #1	Concept art straight from the designers.	9,000,000
Concept Art Gallery #2	More awesome concept art.	12,000,000
Snare Skin	Enable a new skin for Snare!	15,000,000
Video—Deleted Cutscenes	See what didn't make the cut.	21,000,000
Thermite Skin	Enable a new skin for Thermite!	24,000,000

Kane & Lynch: Dead Men

Achievements

Unlockable	How to Unlock
50 to Won (25)	Win 50 rounds of Fragile Alliance.
A Lot (15)	Escape with $1,500,000 from a Fragile Alliance heist.
Behemoth (10)	Stop the roaring beast.
Berserkopath (30)	Make the most of Lynch's condition.
Boomstick (20)	Shotgun messiah.
Bulletproof (10)	Avoid using adrenaline on a level.
Bullseye (20)	Lynch reacts fast at the Exchange.
By the Grace of... (10)	Lynch puts them out of their misery.
Cash Addict (25)	Help to get all the money out in a Fragile Alliance round.
Celebrity (0)	Play as Lynch in Fragile Alliance.
Crime Buster (10)	Kill 10 traitors in Fragile Alliance.
Crowd Control (30)	Surgical precision in the nightclub.
Damned If You Do (20)	Let them burn.
Damned If You Don't (30)	No rest for the wicked.
Double Trouble (25)	Kill two traitors in a Fragile Alliance round.
End of the Road (50)	Complete the game in co-op.
Family Member (5)	Complete a Fragile Alliance session.
Frag Out (20)	Five with one fragmentation grenade.
Fragile Alliance (10)	Complete the first level in co-op.
Have Gun, Will Travel Part I (20)	Travel into the Rising Sun.
Have Gun, Will Travel Part II (20)	Counter-revolution.
Have Gun, Will Travel Part III (20)	The Beginning of the End.
Headmaster (10)	47 headshots.
Hindsight (10)	Get that bird out of the sky.
Impact (20)	Escape from death row.
Iron Flower (50)	Complete the game on hard.
Mercenary (15)	Complete one session in each Fragile Alliance scenario.
Most Wanted (50)	Escape with $150,000,000 from Fragile Alliance heists.
Mr. Play-It-Straight (50)	Win 50 rounds of Fragile Alliance as a merc.
Mr. Popularity (35)	Kill 100 traitors in Fragile Alliance.

Kane & Lynch: Dead Men (continued)

Unlockable	How to Unlock
Never Give Up (30)	Get three personal revenge kills in a Fragile Alliance session.
No Going Back Now (30)	Go to the point of no return in co-op.
Perfect Split (25)	All players split the money equally from a Fragile Alliance heist.
Pushblade Symphony (20)	Points for getting up close and personal.
Return to Sender (10)	Throw back enemy grenades.
Revenge Part I (20)	Silencing the silent one.
Revenge Part II & III (20)	Who's the old timer now?
Revenge Part IV (20)	Shouldn't have gotten personal.
Revenge Part V (30)	Glad it got personal.
Rush Hour (15)	Escape in all rounds of a Fragile Alliance session.

Achievements

Unlockable	How to Unlock
Some (5)	Escape with $50,000 from a Fragile Alliance heist.
Sun Tzu (20)	Let your crew do the dirty work.
Sweet Revenge (5)	Get personal revenge in Fragile Alliance.
Teflon (20)	Avoid damage on a level.
The Cleaner (30)	Get 30 personal revenge kills in Fragile Alliance.
True Elite (0)	Play as Kane in Fragile Alliance.
Veteran (35)	Complete 200 Fragile Alliance sessions.

Kingdom Under Fire: Circle of Doom

Unlockables

Unlockable	How to Unlock
Curian	Clear Celine's campaign on Normal difficulty or higher.
Extreme Mode	Beat the game on Normal and Hard difficulty.
Stone Golem	Use Petrifying Breath on the Wood Golem enemy to produce a Stone Golem enemy.

Kung Fu Panda

Achievements

Unlockable	How to Unlock
Awesomely Awesome (30)	Defeat 250 enemies.
Fastest Warrior (20)	Obtain a Hit Chain of 10 or higher using only Fast Attacks.
Fearless (20)	Make it through an entire level without blocking an attack.
Game Completed: Master (20)	Complete the entire game on the Master Difficulty setting.
Invincible (50)	Make it through the entire game without dying.
Kung Fu Warrior (20)	Obtain a Hit Chain of 15 or higher using any combination of attacks.
Level 1 100% Completion! (20)	Complete level "Po's Dream" 100%.
Level 2 100% Completion! (20)	Complete level "Tournament of the Dragon Warrior" 100%.
Level 3 100% Completion! (20)	Complete level "Level Zero" 100%.

Kung Fu Panda (continued)

Unlockable	How to Unlock
Level 4 100% Completion! (20)	Complete level "Protect the Palace" 100%.
Level 5 100% Completion! (20)	Complete level "Lake of Tears" 100%.
Level 6 100% Completion! (20)	Complete level "Wudang Temple" 100%.
Level 7 100% Completion! (20)	Complete level "Treacherous Waters" 100%.
Level 8 100% Completion! (20)	Complete level "Wudang Rescue" 100%.
Level 9 100% Completion! (20)	Complete level "Howling Moon" 100%.
Level 10 100% Completion! (20)	Complete level "Secret of the Sands" 100%.
Level 11 100% Completion! (20)	Complete level "The Palace" 100%.
Level 12 100% Completion! (20)	Complete level "The Warrior's Destiny" 100%.
Level 13 100% Completion! (20)	Complete level "The Final Battle" 100%.
Master of All (30)	Unlock Everything.
Panda Stumble Extreme (20)	Panda Stumble for 60 seconds. Forced Stumble doesn't count.
Panda Stumble Warrior (20)	Obtain a Hit Chain of 5 or higher using only Panda Stumble.
Strongest Warrior (20)	Obtain a Hit Chain of 5 or higher using only Strong Attacks.
Ultimate Dragon Warrior (30)	Purchase all upgrades.
Untouchable (20)	Make it through an entire level without getting hit.

Codes

From the main menu, select Extras and then select Cheats.

Effect	Code
All Multiplayer Characters	←,↓,←,→,↓
Big Head Mode (Story Mode)	↓,↑,←,→,→
Infinite Chi	↓,→,←,↑,↓
Invulnerability	↓,↓,→,↑,←
Dragon Warrior Outfit (Multiplayer Mode)	←,↓,→,←,↑
4x Damage Multiplier	↑,↓,↑,→,←

LEGO Batman

Codes

Enter the codes on the second level of the Batcave at the computer above the outfit changer.

Effect	Code
Alfred	ZAQ637
Bat-Tank	KNTT4B
Batgirl	JKR331
Bruce Wayne	BDJ327
Bruce Wayne's Private Jet	LEA664
Catwoman (Classic)	M1AAWW
Catwoman's Motorcycle	HPL826
Clown Goon	HJK327
Commissioner Gordon	DDP967
Fishmonger	HGY748
Freeze Girl	XVK541
Garbage Truck	DUS483
Glideslam	BBD7BY
Goon Helicopter	GCH328
Harbor Helicopter	CHP735
Harley Quinn's Hammer Truck	RDT637
Joker Goon	UTF782
Joker Henchman	YUN924
Mad Hatter	JCA283
Mad Hatter's Glider	HS000W
Mad Hatter's Steamboat	M4DM4N
Man-Bat	NYU942

LEGO Batman (continued)

Effect	Code	Effect	Code
Military Policeman	MKL382	Police Van	MAC788
Mr. Freeze's Iceberg	ICYICE	Police Watercraft	VJD328
Mr. Freeze's Kart	BCT229	Riddler Goon	CRY928
Nightwing	MVY759	Riddler Henchman	XEU824
Penguin Goon	NKA238	Riddler's Jet	HAHAHA
Penguin Goon Submarine	BTN248	Robin's Submarine	TTF453
Penguin Henchman	BJH782	S.W.A.T.	HTF114
Penguin Minion	KJP748	Sailor	NAV592
Poison Ivy Goon	GTB899	Scientist	JFL786
Police Bike	LJP234	Security Guard	PLB946
Police Boat	PLC999	The Joker (Tropical)	CCB199
Police Car	KJL832	The Joker's Van	JUK657
Police Helicopter	CWR732	Two-Face's Armored Truck	EFE933
Police Marksman	HKG984	Yeti	NJL412
Police Officer	JRY983	Zoo Sweeper	DWR243

Extra Codes

Effect	Code	Effect	Code
Always Score Multiply	9LRGNB	Ice Rink	KLKL4G
Area Effect	TL3EKT	Immune to Freeze	JXUDY6
Armor Plating	N8JZEK	Invincible	WYD5CP
Bats	XFP4E2	Minikit Detector	ZXGH9J
Beep Beep	RAFTU8	More Batarang Targets	XWP645
Character Studs	DY13BD	More Detonators	TNTN6B
Decoy	TQ09K3	Piece Detector	KHJ544
Disguise	GEC3MD	Power Brick Detector	MMN786
Extra Toggle	EWAW7W	Regenerate Hearts	HJH7HJ
Extra Hearts	ML3KHP	Score x2	N4NR3E
Fast Batarangs	JRBDCB	Score x4	CX9MAT
Fast Build	GHJ2DY	Score x6	MLVNF2
Fast Grapple	RM4PR8	Score x8	WCCDB9
Fast Walk	ZOLM6N	Score x10	18HW07
Faster Pieces	EVG26J	Silhouettes	YK4TPH
Flaming Batarangs (Used with heat batman)	D8NYWH	Slam	BBD7BY
		Sonic Pain	THTL4X
Freeze Batarang	XPN4NG	Stud Magnet	LK2DY4

DS PSP PS2 PS3 Wii Xbox Xbox 360 Index

LEGO Indiana Jones: The Original Adventures

Character Codes

Enter the codes on the blackboard in the math classroom of Barnett College (the 2nd door on the left in the main hallway).

Effect	Code	Effect	Code
Bandit	12N68W	Fedora	V75YSP
Bandit Swordsman	1MK4RT	First Mate	0GIN24
Barranca	04EM94	Grail Knight	NE6THI
Bazooka Trooper (Crusade)	MK83R7	Hovitos Tribesman	H0V1SS
Bazooka Trooper (Raiders)	S93Y5R	Indiana Jones (Desert Disguise)	4J8S4M
Belloq	CHN3YU	Indiana Jones (Officer)	VJ850S
Belloq (Jungle)	TDR197	Jungle Guide	24PF34
Belloq (Robes)	VEO29L	Kao Kan	WM046L
British Officer	VJ5TI9	Kazim	NRH23J
British Troop Commander	B73EUA	Kazim (Desert)	3M29TJ
British Troop Soldier	DJ5I2W	Lao Che	2NK479
Captain Katanga	VJ3TT3	Maharaja	NFK5N2
Chatter Lal	ENW936	Major Toht	13NS01
Chatter Lal (Thuggee)	CNH4RY	Masked Bandit	N48SF0
Chen	3NK48T	Mola Ram	FJUR31
Colonel Dietrich	2K9RKS	Monkey Man	3RF6YJ
Colonel Vogel	8EAL4H	Pankot Assassin	2NKT72
Dancing Girl	C7EJ21	Pankot Guard	VN28RH
Donovan	3NFTU8	Sherpa Brawler	VJ37WJ
Elsa (Desert)	JSNRT9	Sherpa Gunner	ND762W
Elsa (Officer)	VMJ5US	Slave Child	0E3ENW
Enemy Boxer	8246RB	Thuggee	VM683E
Enemy Butler	VJ48W3	Thuggee Acolyte	T2R3F9
Enemy Guard	VJ7R51	Thuggee Slavedriver	VBS7GW
Enemy Guard (Mountains)	YR47WM	Village Dignitary	KD48TN
Enemy Officer (Desert)	2MK450	Village Elder	4682 E1
Enemy Officer	572 E61	Willie (Dinner Suit)	VK93R7
Enemy Pilot	B84ELP	Willie (Pajamas)	MEN4IP
Enemy Radio Operator	1MF94R	Wu Han	3NSLT8
Enemy Soldier (Desert)	4NSU7Q		

Item Codes

Enter the codes on the blackboard in the math classroom of Barnett College (the 2nd door on the left in the main hallway).

Effect	Code	Effect	Code
Artifact Detector	VIKED7	Fast Dig	378RS6
Beep Beep	VNF59Q	Fast Fix	FJ59WS
Character Treasure	VIES2R	Fertilizer	B1GW1F
Disarm Enemies	VKRNS9	Ice Rink	33GM7J
Disguises	4ID1N6	Parcel Detector	VUT673
Fast Build	V83SL0	Poo Treasure	WWQ1SA

LEGO Indiana Jones: The Original Adventures (continued)

Effect	Code	Effect	Code
Regenerate Hearts	MDLP69	Treasure x2	VM4TS9
Secret Characters	3X44AA	Treasure x4	VLWEN3
Silhouettes	3HE85H	Treasure x6	V84RYS
Super Scream	VN3R7S	Treasure x8	A72E1M
Super Slap	0P1TA5	Treasure x10	VI3PS8
Treasure Magnet	H86LA2		

Achievements

Unlockable	How to Unlock
A source of unspeakable power! (20)	Build 250 LEGO objects.
Bad dates! (20)	Give 20 bananas to monkeys.
Belloq's staff is too long. (10)	Complete the "City of Danger" level in Story mode.
Blow it up! (40)	Blow up 5 enemies with 1 explosion.
DON'T call me Junior! (10)	Complete the "Castle Rescue" level in Story mode.
Fortune & glory kid. (100)	Complete the game to 100%.
Goodbye Dr. Jones. (20)	Destroy Indy with Lao Che.
He chose... poorly. (10)	Complete the "Temple of the Grail" level in Story mode.
He no nuts. He's crazy!! (20)	Smash 250 LEGO objects.
Hey! You call him Dr. Jones! (20)	Create and name a custom build character.
How dare you kiss me! (15)	Use your whip to kiss Marion, Willie, and Elsa.
How we say goodbye in Germany. (20)	Access restricted enemy locations 50 times.
I had bugs for lunch! (10)	Complete the "Pankot Secrets" level in Story mode.
I hate these guys. (20)	Destroy 200 bad guys.
I step on fortune cookie! (20)	Destroy 50 creepy-crawlies.
It's not the years honey... (40)	Complete any level with out dying, without invincibility.
It's important Marion, trust me. (10)	Complete the "Into the Mountains" level in Story mode.
I'm making this up as I go along (10)	Complete the "Pursing the Ark" level in Story mode.
Kali Ma will rule the world! (10)	Complete the "Kali's Temple" level in Story mode.
Keep your eyes shut! (10)	Complete the "Opening the Ark" level in Story mode.
Nice try, Lao Che! (20)	Destroy Lao Che with Indy.
No ticket. (10)	Complete the "Trouble in the Sky" level in Story mode.
Oh it breaks the heart. (15)	Oh it breaks the heart.
Prepare to meet Kali! (10)	Complete the "Battle on the Bridge" level in Story mode.
Unlockable	**How to Unlock**
Quit fooling around. (10)	Complete the "Free the Slaves" level in Story mode.
Short Round, step on it! (10)	Complete the "Shanghai Showdown" level in Story mode.
Show a little backbone will ya? (20)	Destroy 100 snakes.
Start the engines, Jock! (20)	Use a mechanic character's repair ability 50 times.
Take the left tunnel! (10)	Complete the "Escape the Mines" level in Story mode.
That belongs in a museum! (10)	Complete the "Young Indy" level in Story mode.
That's for blasphemy! (20)	Destroy Indy with Jones Senior.

LEGO Indiana Jones: The Original Adventures (continued)

Unlockable	How to Unlock
The best digger in Cairo. (20)	Uncover 50 pieces of buried treasures using the excavation ability.
There is nothing to fear here. (10)	Complete the "The Lost Temple" level in Story mode.
They're well out of range dad. (10)	Complete the "Desert Ambush" level in Story mode.
This... this is history... (40)	Collect all artifacts.
Trouble with her is the noise. (20)	Destroy 50 objects or characters using the scream and super scream ability.
We're not going in the boat? (10)	Complete the "Motorcycle Escape" level in Story mode.
What a cautious fellow I am. (20)	Destroy 50 objects with a bazooka or other explosive device.
Where Forrestal cashed in. (30)	Collect 1,000,000 studs in the Ancient City level.
Why did it have to be snakes? (10)	Complete the "The Well of Souls" level in Story mode.
X marks the spot! (10)	Complete the "The Hunt for Sir Richard" level in Story mode.
You call this archaeology? (20)	Use a scholar character's academic ability 50 times.
You chose... wisely. (30)	Unlock all of the available characters.
You will become a true believer. (20)	Use a Thuggee Statue 20 times.
Your mail is on your desk. (40)	Post all parcels.

LEGO Star Wars II: The Original Trilogy

Different Characters

Password	Effect	Password	Effect
Beach Trooper	UCK868	Palace Guard	SGE549
Ben Kenobi's Ghost	BEN917	Rebel Pilot	CYG336
Bespin Guard	VHY832	Rebel Trooper from Hoth	EKU849
Bib Fortuna	WTY721	Red Noses on All Characters	NBP398
Boba Fett	HLP221	Santa Hat and Red Clothes	CL4U5H
Death Star Trooper	BNC332	Skiff Guard	GBU888
Emperor	HHY382	Snowtrooper	NYU989
Ewok	TTT289	Stormtrooper	PTR345
Gamorean Guard	YZF999	TIE Fighter	HDY739
Gonk Droid	NFX582	TIE Fighter Pilot	NNZ316
Grand Moff Tarkin	SMG219	TIE Interceptor	QYA828
Han Solo with Hood	YWM840	Ugnaught	UGN694
IG-88	NXL973	Unlock Greedo	NAH118
Imperial Guard	MMM111	Unlock Jawa	JAW499
Imperial Officer	BBV889	Unlock Sandtrooper	YDV451
Imperial Shuttle Pilot	VAP664	Unlock Tusken Raider	PEJ821
Imperial Spy	CVT125	White Beard Extra	TYH319
Lobot	UUB319		

LEGO Star Wars: The Complete Saga

Characters

To use the codes, enter the Cantina, go to the bar, access the codes command, and type in the codes.

Unlockable Characters	Codes
Admiral Ackbar	ACK646
Battle Droid Commander	KPF958
Boba Fett (Boy)	GGF539
Boss Nass	HHY697
Captain Tarpals	QRN714
Count Dooku	DDD748
Darth Maul	EUK421
Ewok	EWK785
General Grievous	PMN576
Greedo	ZZR636
IG-88	GIJ989
Imperial Guard	GUA850
Indiana Jones	After you watch the trailer for the upcoming Indiana Jones game in the Bonus Room, Indy will become a playable character.

Unlockable Characters	Codes
Jango Fett	KLJ897
Ki-Adi-Mundi	MUN486
Luminara	LUM521
Padmé	VBJ322
R2-Q5	EVILR2
Sandtrooper	CBR954
Stormtrooper	NBN431
Super Battle Droid	XZNR21
Taun We	PRX482
Vulture Droid	BDC866
Watto	PLL967
Zam Wesell	584HJF

Ships

Unlockable Ships	Codes
Droid Trifighter	AAB123
Imperial Shuttle	HUT845
Slave I	Collect all 10 Minikits on each level.

Unlockable Ships	Codes
TIE Fighter	DBH897
TIE Interceptor	INT729
Zam's Speeder	UUU875

Skills

Unlockable Skills	Codes
Disguise	BRJ437
Force Grapple Leap	CLZ738

The Lord of the Rings, The Battle for Middle-Earth II

Unlockable Heroes

Unlockable	How to Unlock
Avatan	Win 10 capture and hold games
Brerthor	Complete the whole good campaign
Celebrim	Win 10 resource race games
Felek	Win 10 hero vs. hero games
Fhaleen	Win 10 king of the hill games
Hadhood	Complete level 1 of good campaign with all bonus objectives
Idrial	Complete level 8 of good campaign with all bonus objectives
Krashnack	Complete level 1 of dark campaign with all bonus objectives
Maur	Complete level 4 of the dark campaign with all bonus objectives
Mektar	Complete good campaign with no heroes dying
Ohta	Win 10 versus games
Olog	Complete level 8 of the dark campaign with all bonus objectives
Thrugg	Complete level 4 of the dark campaign with all bonus objectives
Tumna	Complete the whole bad campaign
Urulooke	Complete dark campaign with no heroes dying

Lost Planet: Extreme Condition

Enter these codes when the game is paused. They can be used only on Easy mode.

Unlockable	Code
500 Thermal Energy	↑, ↑, ↓, ↓, ←, →, ←, →, X, Y, RB, LB
Infinite Ammunition	LB, LT, RT, RB, Y, X, →, ↓, ←, LB, LT, RT, LT, LB, RB, X, ←, ↓, X, RB, LB
Infinite Health	↓, ↓, ↓, ↑, Y, ↑, Y, ↑, Y, ↑, ↑, ↑, ↓, X, ↓, X, ↓, X, ←, Y, →, X, ←, Y, →, X, RB, LB
Infinite Ammunition	RT, RB, Y, X, →, ↓, ←, LB, LT, RT, RB, Y, X, →, ↓, ←, LB, LT, RT, LT, LB, RB, X, ←, ↓, X, RB, LB

Madden NFL 08

Achievements

Unlockable	How to Unlock
1 Catch by Seven Players (20)	Catch one pass with seven players.
2 TD Catches with One Player (10)	Get two touchdown catches with one player.
3 2pt Conversions Passing (35)	Pass for three two-point conversions in one game.
3 2pt Conversions Rushing (35)	Rush for three two-point conversions in one game.
3 Rushing TDs (15)	Get three rushing touchdowns with one player.
4 Sacks (10)	Get four sacks with one player in one game. Max 5min Qtr.
4 TD Passes (10)	Throw four touchdown passes in one game.
7 Sacks with One Player (35)	Sack the quarterback seven times with one player in one game.
8 Tackles with One Player (10)	Get eight tackles with one player in one game.
10 Catches in a Row (15)	Catch 10 passes in a row with one player. Max 5min Qtr.

Madden NFL 08 (continued)	
Unlockable	How to Unlock
10 Catches with One Player (15)	Get 10 receptions with one player.
20 Completions in a Row (25)	Get 20 completions in a row with one player.
40 Rush Attempts with One Player (15)	Attempt 40 rushes with one player in one game. Max 5min Qtr.
40 Yard Field Goal (15)	Kick a 40-yard or more field goal.
50 Yard Field Goal (20)	Kick a 50-yard or more field goal.
60 Yard Pass (15)	Complete a 60-yard pass.
60 Yard Run (15)	Complete a 60-yard run.
80 Percent Pass Completion (15)	Complete 80 percent of the attempted passes in one game.
80 Yard Run (35)	Complete an 80-yard run.
90 Yard Pass (30)	Complete a 90-yard pass.
100 Percent Pass Completion (25)	Get 100 percent pass completion.
100 Rec Yards with 2 Players (15)	Get 100 reception yards by two players.
100 Rush Yards with One Player (15)	Get 100 rushing yards with one player.
100 Rush Yards with Two Players (30)	Get 100 rushing yards with two players.
150 Receiving Yards (15)	Achieve 150 receiving yards with one player.
150 Rush Yards in One Qtr (25)	Get 150 yards or more rushing in one quarter with one player.
200 Kick Return Yards (20)	Achieve 200 kick return yards with one player. Max 5min Qtr.
200 Pass Yards (10)	Get 200 passing yards in a game.
200 Punt Return Yards (20)	Get 200 punt return yards in one game with one player.
200 Receiving Yards (25)	Get 200 receiving yards with one player.
200 Rush Yards (15)	Rush for 200 yards or more with one player in one game.
250 Rush Yards (25)	Rush for 250 yards with one player in one game.
300 Pass Yards (10)	Achieve 300 passing yards in one game.
400 Yards on Offense (10)	Achieve 400 yards of offense in one game. Max 5min Qtr.
500 Pass Yards (30)	Pass for 500 yards in one game.
650 Yards on Offense (30)	Get 650 yards on offense. Max 5min Qtr.
Average 20 Yards Receiving (25)	Average 20 yards receiving with one player in one game.
Average 20 Yards Rushing (25)	Average 20 yards rushing per attempt with one player in one game.
Complete 25 Passes (30)	Complete 25 passes in one game.
Deflect 4 Passes (20)	Deflect four or more passes with one player.
Force 3 Fumbles (10)	Force three fumbles with one player.
Intercept 2 Passes (20)	Get two interceptions with one player.
Intercept 3 Passes (20)	Get three interceptions in one game.
Intercept 5 Passes (35)	Intercept five passes in one game.
No Dropped Passes (20)	Don't drop a pass for an entire game. Min 5min Qtr.
No Sacks Allowed (20)	Don't allow a sack for an entire game. Min 5min Qtr.
Recover 2 Fumbles (25)	Recover two fumbles in one game with one player.
Score 84 Points (35)	Score 84 or more points in one game. Max 5min Qtr.

Major League Baseball 2K6

To enter these passwords, go into My 2K6, then select Enter Codes. Note that passwords are case sensitive.

Unlockable	Password
Bouncy Ball	Crazy Hops
Crazy Pitches	Unhittable
Rocket Arms	Gotcha
Super Wall Climbs	Last Chance
Topps 2k6 All-Stars	Dream Team
Unlock All Cheats	Black Sox
Unlock All Extras	Game On
Unlock Everything	Derek Jeter

Major League Baseball 2K7

To enter these codes select My 2K7. Then select Enter Cheat Code.

Unlockable	Code
Boosts a team's power rating by 25% for 1 inning	mightymick
Boosts the hitting of the 3, 4, 5 hitters in the lineup by 50% for 1 game	triplecrown
Boosts your ability to hit home runs during the game just like The Mick	m4murder
Mickey will pinch hit	phmantle
Unlocks everything	Derek Jeter
Unlocks Mickey Mantle in free agency	themick

Marvel: Ultimate Alliance

These codes need to be entered in different areas of the game. Enter these in the Team menu.

Unlockable	Code
100k	Up, Up, Up, Left, Right, Left, Start
Level 99	Up, Left, Up, Left, Down, Right, Down, Right

Enter these in the Character Selection screen.

Unlockable	Code
All Character Code	Up, Up, Down, Down, Left, Left, Left, Start
All Costumes	Up, Down, Up, Down, Left, Right, Left, Right, Up, Down, Start
All Powers	Left, Right, Left, Right, Up, Down, Up, Down, Left, Right, Start
Unlock Daredevil	Left, Left, Right, Right, Up, Down, Up, Down
Unlock Silver Surfer	Down, Left, Left, Up, Right, Up, Down, Left

Enter these codes in the Review menu.

Unlockable	Code
All Cinematics	Up, Left, Left, Up, Right, Right, Up
All Comics	Left, Right, Right, Left, Up, Up, Right
All Concept Art	Down, Down, Down, Right, Right, Left, Down
All Wallpapers	Up, Down, Right, Left, Up, Up, Down

Enter these codes while playing.

Unlockable	Code
Filler	Left, Right, Right, Left, Up, Down, Down, Up
God mode	Up, Down, Up, Down, Up, Left, Down, Right
Super Speed	Up, Left, Up, Right, Down, Right
Touch of Death	Left, Right, Down, Down, Right, Left

Enter this code on the Comic Book missions.

Unlockable	Code
The Courses	Up, Right, Left, Down, Up, Right, Left, Down

Mass Effect

Achievements

Complete each of the following achievements to get the allotted gamerscore.

Unlockable	How to Unlock
AI Hacking Specialist (15)	Use AI hacking 75 times.
Asari Ally (20)	Complete the majority of the game with the Asari squad member.
Assault Rifle Expert (15)	Register 150 assault rifle kills.
Barrier Mastery (15)	Use Biotic Barrier 75 times.
Charismatic (10)	Use Charm or Intimidate to resolve an impossible situation.
Completionist (25)	Complete the majority of the game.
Council Legion of Merit (25)	Complete Virmire.
Damping Specialist (15)	Use Damping Field 75 times.
Distinguished Combat Medal (25)	Complete one Mass Effect playthrough on the Hardcore difficulty setting.
Distinguished Service Medal (25)	Complete Eden Prime.
Dog of War (25)	Register 150 organic enemy kills.
Extreme Power Gamer (50)	Reach 60th level with one character.
First Aid Specialist (15)	Use medi-gel 150 times.
Geth Hunter (25)	Register 250 synthetic enemy kills.
Honorarium of Corporate Service (25)	Complete Noveria.
Krogan Ally (20)	Complete the majority of the game with the Krogan squad member.
Lift Mastery (15)	Use Biotic Lift 75 times.
Long Service Medal (25)	Complete two playthroughs on any setting.
Medal of Exploration (50)	Land on an uncharted world.
Medal of Heroism (25)	Complete Feros.
Medal of Honor (100)	Complete one playthrough on any difficulty setting.
Medal of Valor (50)	Complete one playthrough on the Insanity difficulty setting.
Neural Shock Specialist (15)	Use Neural Shock 75 times.
Overlord Specialist (15)	Use Shield Overload 75 times.
Paragon (15)	Accumulate 75% of total Paragon points.
Paramour (10)	Complete any romance subplot.
Pistol Expert (10)	Register 150 pistol kills.
Power Gamer (20)	Reach 50th level with one character.
Quarian Ally (20)	Complete the majority of the game with the Quarian squad member.
Renegade (15)	Accumulate 75% of total Renegade points.
Rich (25)	Exceed 1,000,000 Credits.
Sabotage Specialist (15)	Use Sabotage 75 times.
Scholar (25)	Find all primary aliens: Council Races, Extinct Races, and Non-Council Races codex entries.
Search and Rescue (10)	Locate Dr. T'Soni in the Artemis Tau cluster.
Sentinel Ally (20)	Complete the majority of the game with the Alliance sentinel squad member.

DS PSP PS2 PS3 Wii Xbox Xbox 360 Index

Mass Effect (continued)

Unlockable	How to Unlock
Shotgun Expert (15)	Register 150 shotgun kills.
Singularity Mastery (15)	Use Biotic Singularity 75 times.
Sniper Expert (15)	Register 150 sniper rifle kills.
Soldier Ally (20)	Complete the majority of the game with the Alliance soldier squad member.
Spectre Inductee (15)	Become a Spectre.
Stasis Mastery (15)	Use Biotic Stasis 75 times.
Tactician (25)	Complete playthrough with shield damage greater than health damage.
Throw Mastery (15)	Use Biotic Throw 75 times.
Turian Ally (20)	Complete the majority of the game with the Turian squad member.
Warp Mastery (15)	Use Biotic Warp 75 times.

Character Benefit Unlockables

Attain certain achievements to gain benefits on future playthroughs.

Unlockable	How to Unlock
+10% Experience Bonus	Complete 75% of game.
+10% Hardening Bonus	Complete 75% of game with Ashley in squad.
+10% Health Bonus	Kill 150 organic beings.
+10% Shield Bonus	Kill 250 synthetics.
+25% Marksman Cooldown Bonus	Attain 150 kills with pistol.
10% Reduced Cooldown for Barrier and Stasis	Complete 75% of game with Liara in squad.
10% Reduced Cooldown for Lift and Throw	Complete 75% of game with Kaiden in squad.
10% Reduced Cooldown for Overload and Damping	Complete 75% of game with Garrus in squad.
10% Reduced Cooldown for Sabotage and AI Hacking	Complete 75% of game with Tali in squad.
10% Shield Increase	Sustain more shield damage than health damage during one playthrough.
5% Increase in Weapon Damage	Complete the game twice on any difficulty.
Assault Rifle Skill for New Characters	Attain 150 kills with assault rifle.
Barrier Skill for New Characters	Use Barrier 75 times.
Decryption Skill for New Characters	Use Sabotage 75 times.
Electronics Skill for New Characters	Use Overload 75 times.
First Aid Skill for New Characters	Use medi-gel 150 times.
Hacking Skill for New Characters	Use AI Hacking 75 times.
Lift Skill (for non-biotics)	Use Lift 75 times.
Medicine Skill for New Characters	Use Neural Hacking 75 times.
Regenerate 1 Health per Second	Complete 75% of game with Wrex in squad.
Shielding Skill for New Characters	Use Dampening 75 times.
Shotgun Skill for New Characters	Attain 150 kills with shotgun.
Sniper Rifle Skill for New Characters	Attain 150 kills with sniper rifle.
Spectre Grade Weapons for Purchase	Attain 1,000,000 credits in your wallet.
Singularity Skill for New Characters	Use Singularity 75 times.
Statis Skill for New Characters	Use Statis 75 times.

Mass Effect (continued)

Unlockable	How to Unlock
Throw Skill for New Characters	Use Throw 75 times.
Warp Skill for New Characters	Use Warp 75 times.

Unlockable Gamer Pics

Complete the game on the Hardcore and Insanity difficulties to unlock two special gamer pics for your profile.

Unlockable	How to Unlock
"N7" Gamer Pic	Gain the Medal of Valor achievement.
Saren Gamer Pic	Gain the Distinguished Combat Medal achievement.

Unlockables

Complete the game on Normal to unlock the secrets.

Unlockable	How to Unlock
Hardcore Mode	Complete the game once.
Increased Level Cap (51–0)	Complete the game once.
Insane Difficulty	Beat the game on the Hardcore difficulty without changing the difficulty.
New Game +	Start a New Game, then select existing Career. You'll be playing with your older character (with all items and skills intact).

Medal of Honor: Airborne

Codes

Unlockable	How to Unlock
Enter Cheat menu	Press (RB)+(LB), then press (X),(B),(Y),(A),(A)
Full Ammo	Press and hold (LB)+(RB) then press (B),(B),(Y),(X),(A),(Y)
Full Health	(Y),(X),(X),(Y),(A),(B)

Mercenaries 2: World in Flames

Unlockable Costumes

To unlock costumes, you must complete Level 3 of a weapon challenge, which can be done by talking to Fiona at your PMC. Each time you complete a Level 3 weapon challenge, you receive one of three costumes.

Monster Madness: Battle for Suburbia

At the pause screen press: (Up),(Up),(Down),(Down),(Left),(Right),(Left),(Right),(B),(A). The typing console appears. Then type in the cheat.

Code	Effect
patrickdugan	Animal sounds
ihatefunkycameras	Disable special tracking cameras
upthejoltcola	Faster music
MorgyTheMole	First person/headless
ArieannDeFazioWithFlair	Increase the size of Jennifer's chest
stevebrooks	Infinite secondary items
SouthPeak	Push objects away from player
reverb	Remove film grain
chipmunks	Squeaky voices

MX Vs. ATV Untamed

Unlockables

Type in the following codes in the cheats menu to unlock the gear.

Unlockable	How to Unlock
All Handlebars	NOHANDS
FOX Riding Gear	CRAZYLIKEA

NASCAR 08

Passwords

Password	Effect
checkered flag	All Chase mode cars unlocked
ea sports car	Unlocks the EA Sports car
race the pack	Unlocks the fantasy drivers
Walmart Everyday	Unlocks the Walmart car and track

NASCAR 09

Codes

Effect	Code
Unlocks All Fantasy Drivers	CHECKERED FLAG
Unlocks Walmart Track (Chicago Pier) and the Walmart Car	Walmart Everyday

NBA 2K6

Enter these passwords in the Codes menu from the Features menu.

Unlockable	Password
2K Sports Team	2KSPORTS
Air Zoom Kobe 1 Shoes	KOBE
Alt. All-Star Team Jerseys	fanfavorites
Boston, New York and Chicago St. Patricks Day Jerseys	gogreen
Celebrity Players Unlocked in 24/7 Mode	ballers
Champagne Uniform	sac 2nd
Dark Blue Uniform	den 2nd
Green Uniform	bos 2nd
Lebron James Summer Shoes	lebronsummerkicks
Lebron's Allstar shoes	lb allstar
Lebron's Birthday Shoes	lb bday
Lebron's Black and Crimson shoes	lb crimsonblack
Lebron's White and Gold shoes	lb whitegold
Navy Blue Uniform	cle 2nd
NBA 2K6 Team	NBA2K6
New Indiana Pacers Jerseys	31andonly
Nike Shoes	anklebreakers Uptempo
Red Pistons Uniform	det 2nd
Unlocks Chicago Bulls Throwback	chi retro
Unlocks Houston Rockets Throwback	hou retro
Unlocks L.A. Clippers Throwback	lac retro
Unlocks Memphis Grizzlies Throwback	mem retro
Unlocks Miami Heat Throwback	mia retro
Unlocks New Jersey Nets Throwback	nj retro
Unlocks New Orleans Hornets Throwback	no retro

NBA 2K6 (continued)

Unlockable	Password
Unlocks New York Knicks Throwback	ny retro
Unlocks Orlando Magic Throwback	orl retro
Unlocks Phoenix Suns Throwback	phx retro
Unlocks Seattle Sonics Throwback	sea retro
Unlocks Shawn Marions signature shoes "MTX"	crazylift
Unlocks Washington Wizards Throwback	was retro
Visual Concepts Team	vcteam

Enter these passwords at the Vending Machine located in "The Crib".

Unlockable	Password
+10 defensive awareness	lockdown
+10 offensive awareness	getaclue
No quick game fatigue	nrgmax
No quick game injuries	noinjury
Power bar tattoo in the create player mode	pbink

NBA 2K7

Enter these passwords in the Codes menu under Features.

Unlockable	Code
ABA Ball	payrespect
Defensive Awareness	getstops
Maximum Durability for One Game	ironman
Offensive Awareness	inthezone
Unlimited Stamina for One Game	norest
All-Star Uniforms	syt6cii
Bobcats Secondary	bcb8sta
Jazz Secondary	zjb3lau
Nets Secondary	nrd4esj
Wizards Secondary	zw9idla
St. Patrick Day uniforms	tpk7sgn
International All-Stars	tns9roi
NBA 2K Team	bestsim
Superstar Team	rta1spe
Topps 2K Sports All-Stars	topps2ksports
2007 All-Star Ball	ply8mia
2007 All-Star Uniforms	syt6cii
New Orleans Hornets Uniforms (Valentine's Day)	vdr5lya

NBA 2K8

Unlockables

Go to the Features menu and select the Codes section to enter the following codes.

Unlockable	How to Unlock
2008 All Star Jerseys	haeitgyebs
2K Sports Team	2ksports
ABA Ball	payrespect
Bobcats Racing Uniforms	agtaccsinr
Pacers' Secondary Road Uniforms	cpares

NBA 2K8 (continued)

Unlockable	How to Unlock
NBA Development Team	nba2k
St. Patrick's Day Uniforms	uclerehanp
Superstars Team	llmohffaae
Valentine's Day Uniforms	amcnreo
Visual Concepts team	vcteam

Achievements

Unlockable	How to Unlock
3 Online Ranked Streak (15)	Win three online ranked games in a row.
3-For-All (20)	Make at least 10 three-point FGs while shooting at least 45% from three-point range with any team.
3pt Shootout (25)	Win the three-point shootout.
5 Online Ranked Streak (20)	Win five online ranked games in a row.
5 Online Ranked Wins (15)	Win five online ranked games.
10 Online Ranked Wins (25)	Win 10 online ranked games.
15 Blocks (20)	Record 15 blocks or more with any team.
15 Steals (20)	Record 15 steals or more with any team.
15 Threes (15)	Make 15 three-pointers or more with any team.
20 Online Ranked Wins (35)	Win 20 online ranked games.
30 Assists (20)	Record 30 assists or more with any team.
2K Beats Playlist (10)	Create a 2K Beats playlist.
All-Heart (15)	Start the fourth period losing by 10 or more points and win the game with any team.
All-Hustle (15)	Record at least 10 offensive rebounds, five blocks, and five steals with any team.
Allen Iverson (25)	Record at least 30 points, 10 assists, and five steals with Allen Iverson.
Carmelo Anthony (25)	Record at least 40 points and eight rebounds with Carmelo Anthony.
Chris Bosh (25)	Record at least 30 points, 15 rebounds, and two blocks with Chris Bosh.
Chris Paul (25)	Record at least 25 points, 10 assists, and five steals with Chris Paul.
Create Player (10)	Use the Create Player feature.
Defensive FG% (15)	Hold the opposing team's FG% below 40% with any team.
Dwight Howard (25)	Record at least 20 points, 15 rebounds, and five blocks with Dwight Howard.
Dwyane Wade (25)	Record at least 30 points, nine rebounds, and nine assists with Dwyane Wade.
East vs. West (15)	User-controlled team must win this matchup on All-Star difficulty.
Gilbert Arenas (25)	Record at least 35 points, five steals, and five threes with Gilbert Arenas.
Good Hands (20)	Record 20 assists with no more than five turnovers with any team.
Ice Water (15)	FT% over 85% with at least 15 FTAs with any team.
Inside Domination (20)	Score at least 60 points in the paint with any team.

NBA 2K8 (continued)

Unlockable	How to Unlock
Kevin Garnett (25)	Record at least 25 points, 15 rebounds, and seven assists with Kevin Garnett.
Kobe Bryant (25)	Record at least 40 points, five rebounds, and five assists with Kobe Bryant.
Kobe Bryant Dunk-Off (35)	Defeat Kobe Bryant in a Dunk-Off.
Lakers vs. Clippers (15)	User-controlled team must win this matchup on All-Star difficulty.
LeBron James (25)	Record at least 35 points, seven rebounds, and seven assists with LeBron James.
Lights Out (15)	FG% over 55% for the game (minimum 40 FGAs) with any team.
Lockdown (20)	Record at least 10 blocks and 10 steals with any team.
Online Draft League (10)	Participate in an online draft.
Online League Game (15)	Complete an online league game.
Online Ranked Game (15)	Win one online ranked game.
Online Ranked NBA Blacktop Game (15)	Win one online ranked NBA Blacktop game.
Online Tournament Game (15)	Complete an online tournament game.
Pistons vs. Heat (15)	User-controlled team must win this matchup on All-Star difficulty.
Rebound Margin +7 (20)	Win the rebound battle by a margin of +7 with any team.
Second Unit (15)	Score at least 40 bench points with any team.
Sprite Slam Dunk (35)	Win the Sprite Slam Dunk Contest using LeBron James.
Spurs vs. Mavericks (15)	User-controlled team must win this matchup on All-Star difficulty.
Steve Nash (25)	Record at least 20 points and 15 assists with Steve Nash.
Suns vs. Lakers (15)	User-controlled team must win this matchup on All-Star difficulty.
Suns vs. Mavericks (15)	User-controlled team must win this matchup on All-Star difficulty.
Track Meet (15)	Score at least 15 fastbreak points with any team.
Trivia (35)	Answer 30 trivia questions correctly.
Yao Ming (25)	Record at least 30 points, 15 rebounds, and five blocks with Yao Ming.

NBA Ballers: Chosen One

Achievements

Unlockable	How to Unlock
3-Pointer (25)	Defeat Episode 3.
Achiever (25)	Perform a Level 3 Shut 'Em Down move in any Ranked Match.
Big Air (50)	Make a 3-pt. shot in a 2v2 Match beyond the half-court line in Single Player Game modes.
Can't Stop the Reign (100)	Unlock all Super Dunks.
Dedicated (100)	Win 25 Ranked Matches.
Double Double (100)	Defeat every Episode of Story mode twice.
Dynasty! (40)	Defeat Episode 4.
Free Throw (25)	Defeat Episode 1.
Getting Into It (25)	Win 5 Ranked Matches.

NBA Ballers: Chosen One (continued)

Unlockable	How to Unlock
Hall-of-Fame! (200)	Defeat Episode 6.
Jump Shot (25)	Defeat Episode 2.
Just Getting Started (20)	Complete your first chapter of Story mode.
Legend! (50)	Defeat Episode 5.
Own the Court (50)	Perform a 7-Move Combo String in Single Player game modes.
Pass the Rock! (20)	Complete an Alley-Oop from your Pass-To Buddy in a Single Player 1v1 or Xbox LIVE Match.
Show Off! (100)	Perform a Level 3 Shut 'Em Down move in a Single Match in Single Player game modes.
Show-n-Prove (25)	Perform a Shut 'Em Down move in a Ranked Match.
Takin' it Downtown (10)	Win Your First Ranked Match on Xbox LIVE.

NBA Street Homecourt

Enter these codes at the main menu.

Unlockable	Code
All Courts	Hold LB and RB and press ↑, →, ↓, ←
Virtual Ball	Hold LB and RB and press ↑, ↓, ←, →

NCAA Football 08

Achievements

Complete the following achievements to get the gamerscore.

Unlockable	How to Unlock
1-Star into 6-Star (50)	Turn a one-star prestige school into a six-star prestige school in single team Dynasty mode.
2 Sack Player (10)	Make two sacks in a Play Now or Dynasty mode game with the same player.
5-Star Legend Prospect (20)	Create a five-star legend prospect.
50 Yard Field Goal (25)	Kick a 50 or more yard field goal in a Play Now or Dynasty mode game.
50 Yard Punt (15)	Punt the ball 50 or more net yards in a Play Now or Dynasty mode game.
100 Yard Receiver (10)	Gain 100 or more receiving yards with a single player in a Play Now or Dynasty mode game.
100 Yard Rusher (10)	Rush for 100 or more yards with a single player in a Play Now or Dynasty mode game.
200 Total Rushing Yards (15)	Rush for 200 or more total yards in a Play Now or Dynasty mode game.
350 Total Passing Yards (15)	Pass for 350 or more total yards in a Play Now or Dynasty mode game.
Allow No Sacks (15)	Do not give up any sacks in a Play Now or Dynasty mode game.
BCS Conference Invite (25)	Get an invite to a BCS conference in single team Dynasty mode.
Block a Field Goal (25)	Block a field goal in a Play Now or Dynasty mode game.
Block a Punt (25)	Block a punt in a Play Now or Dynasty mode game.
Bowl Win (10)	Win a bowl game in single team Dynasty mode or Campus Legend mode.
Break a 30 Yard Run (10)	Break a run for 30 or more yards in a Play Now or Dynasty mode game.
Break a 60 Yard Run (20)	Break a run for 60 or more yards in a Play Now or Dynasty mode game.
Complete a 30 Yard Pass (10)	Complete a pass for 30 or more yards in a Play Now or Dynasty mode game.

NCAA Football 08 (continued)

Unlockable	How to Unlock
Complete a 60 Yard Pass (20)	Complete a pass for 60 or more yards in a Play Now or Dynasty mode game.
Conference Champs! (10)	Win a conference championship game in single team Dynasty mode or Campus Legend mode.
Develop New Pipeline State (25)	Develop a new pipeline state in single team Dynasty mode.
Fill Up Legend Meter (30)	Completely fill up the legend meter.
Heisman Memorial Trophy (25)	Win the Heisman Memorial Trophy in single team Dynasty mode or Campus Legend mode.
Held Under 100 Yards (25)	Hold the opposition to under 100 total yards in a Play Now or Dynasty mode game.
Held Under 200 Yards (10)	Hold the opposition to under 200 total yards in a Play Now or Dynasty mode game.
High Score—Option Dash (30)	Score 15,000 or more points in Option Dash.
Intercept 2 Passes (15)	Intercept two passes in a Play Now or Dynasty mode game.
Kickoff Return for TD (20)	Return a kickoff for a touchdown in a Play Now or Dynasty mode game.
Make 4 Sacks (20)	Sack the opposing quarterback four or more times in a Play Now or Dynasty mode game.
Make Promise to a Prospect (10)	Make a promise to a prospect in single team Dynasty mode.
Mr. February (30)	Have the number-one ranked recruiting class in a season in single team Dynasty mode.
National Champions! (30)	Lead your team to a BCS championship in single team Dynasty mode or Campus Legend mode.
No Interceptions in a Game (15)	Do not throw any interceptions in a Play Now or Dynasty mode game.
Old Spice Red Zone Perfection (15)	Complete a Play Now or Dynasty mode game with a Red Zone Efficiency rating of 100 percent.
Old Spice Red Zone Shutout (20)	Complete a Play Now or Dynasty mode game without giving up a touchdown while in the Red Zone.
Pass to 5 Different Receivers (10)	Complete a pass to five or more different receivers in a Play Now or Dynasty mode game.
Perfect Game (30)	Bowl a 300 game in a single player Bowling minigame.
Player Interception Record (25)	Break the game record for interceptions with one player (5) in a Play Now or Dynasty mode game.
Player Passing Record in a Game (25)	Break the game record for passing yards with one player (716) in a Play Now or Dynasty mode game.
Player Rushing Record in a Game (25)	Break the game record for rushing yards with one player (406) in a Play Now or Dynasty mode game.
Pontiac 4th Quarter Comeback (30)	Win a Play Now or Dynasty mode game when down by 14 to start the fourth quarter. (Min Difficulty: Varsity)
Punt Return for TD (15)	Return a punt for a touchdown in a Play Now or Dynasty mode game.
Ranked Game (10)	Play a ranked game.
Return Fumble for TD (20)	Score a touchdown after recovering a fumble on defense in a Play Now or Dynasty mode game.
Return Interception for a TD (20)	Return an interception for a touchdown on defense in a Play Now or Dynasty mode game.
Score 35 Points (15)	Score 35 points or more in a Play Now or Dynasty mode game.
Score a Safety (30)	Score a safety on defense in a Play Now or Dynasty mode game.
Shutout (30)	Prevent your opponent from scoring any points in a Play Now or Dynasty mode game.

NCAA Football 08 (continued)

Unlockable	How to Unlock
Throw 4 TD Passes in a Game (15)	Throw four touchdown passes in a single Play Now or Dynasty mode game.
Win by 21 (10)	Win a Play Now or Dynasty mode game by 21 points or more.
Win Tug-of-War (30)	Win the Tug-of-War minigame.

NCAA Football '09

Achievements

Unlockable	How to Unlock
A/V Club President (20)	Upload a Video or Photo Highlight.
BCS Conference Invite (25)	Get an invite to a BCS conference in single-team Dynasty mode.
Break the Ice (10)	Make a Field Goal when "Iced."
Breaker Breaker 4-9 (20)	Break a run for 49 or more yards in a Play Now or Dynasty mode game.
Conference Champs! (10)	Play and win a conference championship game in single-team Dynasty mode or Campus Legend mode.
Create Stadium Sound (20)	Create a custom Stadium Sound event.
Cue the Fat Lady (10)	Win a Play Now or Dynasty mode game by 21 points or more.
Don't Mess with Texas (10)	While playing as the Texas Longhorns, celebrate a touchdown by running to your mascot.
Get Creative (30)	On a non-option play, score a TD with at least one lateral.
Go Deep for 50+ (20)	Complete a pass for 50 or more yards in a Play Now or Dynasty mode game.
Got Gator Bait? (10)	While playing as the Florida Gators, celebrate a touchdown by running to your mascot.
Heisman Memorial Trophy® (25)	Win the Heisman Memorial Trophy® in single-team Dynasty mode or Campus Legend mode.
High School Hero (20)	Become a 5-star legend prospect.
HIT STUCK (10)	Jar the ball loose with a User-Controlled Hit Stick tackle.
I'm Special! (20)	Take a punt or kickoff back to the house for a touchdown. Valid only in Play Now or Dynasty mode.
Ice in Your Veins (20)	Be the hero and win a game by taking the lead as time expires.
Is That Even Legal? (20)	Return a missed field goal for a touchdown. Only valid in Play Now or Dynasty mode.
Join the Ranks (10)	Play a ranked game.
Let the Air Out (15)	As the away team, get into the end zone in the first 30 seconds of the game.
Mmmmm...Donut (30)	Pitch a shutout by holding your opponent to zero points. Valid only in Play Now or Dynasty mode.
Mr. February (30)	Have the #1 ranked recruiting class in a season in single-team Dynasty mode.
National Champions! (30)	Play and win a BCS championship in single-team Dynasty mode or Campus Legend mode.
Oil Tycoon (25)	Develop a new pipeline state in single-team Dynasty mode.
Old Spice Red Zone Perfection (15)	Complete a Play Now or Dynasty mode game with a Red Zone Efficiency rating of 100%.
Old Spice Red Zone Shutout (5)	Complete a Play Now or Dynasty mode game without allowing a touchdown from the red zone.

NCAA Football '09 (continued)

Unlockable	How to Unlock
On Lockdown (20)	Hold the opposition to under 100 total yards in a Play Now or Dynasty mode game.
Out on a High Note (10)	Play and win a bowl game in single-team Dynasty mode or Campus Legend mode.
Pick 6! (20)	Take an interception back to the house in a Play Now or Dynasty mode game.
Pick Two (15)	Intercept 2 passes in a Play Now or Dynasty mode game.
Pick-Free (15)	Do not throw any interceptions in a Play Now or Dynasty mode game.
Place at the Table! (10)	Become a starter in Campus Legend mode.
Play a Mascot Game (15)	Play a Mascot Game with any mascot teams.
Pontiac G8 4th Quarter Comeback (30)	Win a Play Now or Dynasty mode game when down by 14 to start the 4th qtr. (Min Difficulty: Varsity)
QB Quiz Success (10)	Successfully complete a quiz in the QB Challenge.
Reach Out and Crush Someone (30)	Join or host an Online Dynasty.
Record Breaker—Interceptions (25)	Break the game record for interceptions with one player (5) in a Play Now or Dynasty mode game.
Russell High School Champ (40)	Win the Russell High School Championship Game in any state.
Safety and Sound (30)	Force a safety in Play Now or Dynasty mode.
Scoop and Score! (20)	Scoop a fumble on defense and take it to the house in a Play Now or Dynasty mode game.
Sick 'Em Smokey (10)	While playing as the Tennessee Volunteers, celebrate a touchdown by running to your mascot.
Special Teams Challenge Winner (20)	Win the Special Teams Challenge mini-game.
Take Control in the Clutch (10)	Sack the QB with a user-controlled defender on 3rd down to force a punt situation.
That Just Happened! (25)	Score a rushing touchdown with your punter in a Play Now or Dynasty mode game.
The Legend of Campus Legend (100)	Earn more than 1,000 points in Campus Legend mode.
Tippy Toe! Lemon Tree! (30)	Score a touchdown with your receiver by performing a toe-drag animation.
Triple Threat (20)	Score a receiving, rushing, and passing touchdown with one player.
Up and Over (10)	Take it up the middle in a goal line situation and dive into the end zone.
What Were You Thinking?!?! (5)	Throw the ball away on 4th down. Nice one.
Win at H _ _ _ _ (20)	Win the H.O.R.S.E mini-game.

Need for Speed Carbon

Enter at the main menu.

Unlockable	Code
Infinite Crew Charge	↓, ↑, ↑, →, ←, ←, →, X
Infinite NOS	←, ↑, ←, ↓, ←, ↓, →, X
Infinite SpeedBreaker	↓, →, →, ←, →, ↑, ↓, X
Need For Speed Carbon Logo Vinyls Unlocked	→, ↑, ↓, ↑, ↓, ←, →, X
Need For Speed Carbon Special Logo Vinyls Unlocked	↑, ↑, ↓, ↓, ↓, ↓, ↑, X

Need for Speed Most Wanted

All codes should be entered at the Start screen.

Unlockable	Code
Unlocks Burger King Challenge Event (#69)	↑, ↓, ↓, ↓, ←, →, ←, →
Unlocks Free Engine Upgrade Bonus Marker (Can be used in the backroom of the customization shops)	↑, ↑, ↓, ↓, ←, →, ↑, ↓
Unlocks Special Edition Castrol Ford GT (Which is added to your bonus cars)	←, →, ←, →, ↑, ↓, ↑, ↓

Need for Speed ProStreet

Codes

Go to the "Enter Codes" section of the Career menu and enter the following codes.

Unlockable	How to Unlock
5 Repair Tokens	SAFETYNET
Extra $2,000	1MA9X99
Extra $4,000	W2iOLLO1
Extra $8,000	L1iS97A1
Extra $10,000	1Mi9K7E1
Extra $10,000	CASHMONEY
Extra $10,000 and Castrol Syntec Bonus Vinyl	CASTROLSYNTEC
Extra $10,000, unlocks Camaro concept, Mustang GT500, and r34 Skyline	REGGAME
Audi TT 3.2 Quattro (In Garage)	ITSABOUTYOU
Bonus Energizer Lithium Vinyl	ENERGIZERLITHIUM
K&N Bonus Vinyl	WORLDSLONGESTLASTING
Lancer Evo (In Garage)	MITSUBISHIGOFAR
Pre-tuned Grip Coke Zero Golf GTI (In Garage) and bonus Coke Zero Vinyl	ZEROZEROZERO
Re-Locks Everything Unlocked by "Unlockallthings"	LEIPZIG
Solstice GXP in Collectors Edition	collectorsed
Unlocks Acura Integra, NSX, Audi RS4, Lexus IS350, and Unlocks Engine Upgrades	HORSEPOWER
Unlocks Everything (maps, cars, parts)	UNLOCKALLTHINGS

King Cars

After you beat each of the five Kings, you get their car as the reward.

Unlockable	How to Unlock
06 Mustang GT (Karol Monroe)	Beat Drag King in Career mode.
08 Evo X (Ryo Watanabe)	Beat Showdown King in Career mode.
08 M3 E92 (Ray Krieger)	Beat Grip King in Career mode.
65 GTO (Nate Denver)	Beat Speed King in Career mode.
95 RX-7 (Aki Kimura)	Beat Drift King in Career mode.

Achievements

Unlockable	How to Unlock
8 Player Race (10)	Competed in an online multiplayer race against seven human opponents.
Beat Showdown 1 (25)	Awarded for beating Showdown 1 in Career.
Beat Showdown 2 (25)	Awarded for beating Showdown 2 in Career.

Need for Speed ProStreet (continued)

Unlockable	How to Unlock
Beat Showdown 3 (25)	Awarded for beating Showdown 3 in Career.
Best Blueprint (50)	Your Blueprint is used by a player in the Top 100 on any weekly Freestyle Race Day leaderboard.
Blueprint Apprentice (15)	Awarded when your Blueprint has been shared five times.
Blueprint Master (25)	Awarded when your Blueprint has been shared 25 times.
Career Domination (125)	Dominated Career. Awarded for dominating all Career Race Days.
Clutch (15)	Won five times in a Drag event using Clutch.
Co-op Victory (20)	Achieved when all eight players in a multiplayer Race Day score a total of 10,000 points.
Community Race Day 1 (15)	Awarded for participating in the Community Race Day 1. Visit *www.NeedforSpeed.com* for details.
Community Race Day 2 (15)	Awarded for participating in the Community Race Day 2. Visit *www.NeedforSpeed.com* for details
Domination (15)	Awarded for dominating a Career Race Day.
Drag King (25)	Defeat the Drag King. Awarded for beating the Drag King in Career.
Drag Master (15)	Awarded for unlocking the Rogue Speed Org in Career.
Drift King (25)	Defeat the Drift King. Awarded for beating the Drift King in Career.
Drift Master (15)	Awarded for unlocking the Noise Bomb Org in Career.
EA Moderator (25)	Beat an EA Moderator in a Ranked Online Multiplayer race.
First Big Crash (5)	Awarded for crashing and totaling a car. Brought to you by Progressive Insurance!
Friction Fever (10)	Catch Friction Fever by playing an Online Grip race with an infected player.
Gear Strain (10)	Catch the Gear Strain by playing an Online Drag race with an infected player.
Grip King (25)	Defeat the Grip King. Awarded for beating the Grip King in Career.
Grip Master (15)	Awarded for unlocking the GEffect Org in Career.
Horsepower Challenge (10)	Increase your car's HP by 25. Brought to you by K&N—THE Performance Air Filter.
Keep on Wheelin' (5)	Wheelie 50 or more feet in a Wheelie Competition.
Manual Transmission (10)	Won five times in a non-Drag event using Manual Transmission.
Paparazzi (15)	Awarded when you upload your car photo to *NeedforSpeed.com*
Perfect Tire Grip (10)	Awarded for having maximum tire grip in drag staging.
Performance Upgrade (10)	Modify a Tier 1 car into a Tier 3 car. Brought to you by K&N—The Original High-Flow Air Filter.
Race Day Coordinator (15)	Awarded when your Race Day has been shared five times.
Race Day Leader (15)	Rank first on the leaderboard for a shared Race Day. Leaderboard must have at least three players.
Race Day Organizer (25)	Awarded when your Race Day has been shared 25 times.
Race Day Victory (10)	Awarded for winning a Career Race Day.
Ryo's Record 1 (15)	Beat Ryo's Record within Battle Machine at Grip at Chicago Airfield in Career.

Need for Speed ProStreet (continued)

Unlockable	How to Unlock
Ryo's Record 2 (15)	Beat Ryo's Record within Battle Machine at Drift at Nevada Highway II in Career.
Ryo's Record 3 (15)	Beat Ryo's Record in Battle Machine at Half-Mile Drag at Portland International Raceway II in Career.
Ryo's Record 4 (15)	Beat Ryo's Record within React Team Sessions at Sector Shootout at Autopolis in Career.
Ryo's Record 5 (15)	Beat Ryo's Record within React Team Sessions at Drift at Tokyo Dockyard II in Career.
Ryo's Record 6 (15)	Beat Ryo's Record within React Team Sessions at Top Speed Run at Autobahnring II in Career.
Ryo's Record 7 (15)	Beat Ryo's Record within Super Promotion at Time Attack at Infineon II in Career.
Ryo's Record 8 (15)	Beat Ryo's Record within Super Promotion at Quarter-Mile Drag at Texas World Speedway in Career.
Ryo's Record 9 (15)	Beat Ryo's Record within Super Promotion at Wheelie Competition at Autobahnring II in Career.
Ryo's Record 10 (15)	Beat Ryo's Record within Super Promotion at Speed Challenge at Nevada Highway II in Career.
Safe Driver (50)	Finish five Career or Ranked Race Days with no car damage. Brought to you by Progressive Insurance!
Share a Blueprint (10)	Successfully share a Blueprint with another player.
Showdown King (75)	Defeat the Showdown King. Awarded for beating the Showdown King in Career.
Speed King (25)	Defeat the Speed King. Awarded for beating the Speed King in Career.
Speed Master (15)	Awarded for unlocking the Nitrocide Org in Career.

NHL 2K6

Enter this as a profile name. Case Sensitive.

Unlockable	Password
Unlock everything	Turco813

NHL 08

Gear

Enter the code in the RBK Edge Code option.

Unlockable	How to Unlock
RBK Edge Jerseys	h3oyxpwksf8ibcgt

All Jerseys

Under the Features menu, go to "Unlock 2007-2008 Uniforms" then enter the following case-sensitive password.

Unlockable	How to Unlock
All Jerseys	S6j83RMK01

Unlockable	How to Unlock
AHL Upset (25)	As the lead *NHL 08* Profile, beat an NHL team with an AHL team on Superstar mode.
Beating Tough Competition (100)	As the lead *NHL 08* Profile, beat an opponent ranked Online in the Top 50.
Create a Goalie (25)	As the lead *NHL 08* Profile, use a Created Goalie in a Play Now game.

NHL 08 (continued)	
Unlockable	**How to Unlock**
Create a Skater (25)	As the lead *NHL 08* Profile, use a Created Skater in a Play Now game.
Create a Team (25)	As the lead *NHL 08* Profile, use a Created Team in a Play Now game.
Elite League Upset (25)	As the lead *NHL 08* Profile, beat an NHL team with an Elite League team on Superstar mode.
Fun for All (25)	As the lead *NHL 08* Profile, be on the winning team in an Online Team Play game.
Goalie's Nightmare (50)	As the lead *NHL 08* Profile, score 70 goals with one player in Dynasty mode.
He Shoots, He Scores (25)	As the lead *NHL 08* Profile, score a goal with the Goalie on Superstar mode.
Last Minute of Play (25)	As the lead *NHL 08* Profile, score a goal in the last minute of play on Superstar mode.
On a Roll (50)	As the lead *NHL 08* Profile, win five games in a row in the Playoffs in Dynasty mode.
Online All the Time (75)	As the lead *NHL 08* Profile, play 50 Online Ranked Versus games.
OT Winner (25)	As the lead *NHL 08* Profile, win an Online Ranked Versus game in Overtime.
Penalty Kill Special (25)	As the lead *NHL 08* Profile, score a goal when two men down on Pro mode.
Penalty Shot Hero (25)	As the lead *NHL 08* Profile, score a goal on the penalty shot in Pro mode.
Players of the Game (25)	As the lead *NHL 08* Profile, earn all three stars in Superstar mode.
Playing as a Team (50)	As the lead *NHL 08* Profile, win an Online Ranked Versus game with a friend on the same Xbox 360 console.
Regular Season Best (50)	As the lead *NHL 08* Profile, have your team finish the regular season with the best overall record.
Seeing Lots of Rubber (50)	As the lead *NHL 08* Profile, record 40 shots or more on goal in an Online Ranked Versus game.
Shoot It! (50)	As the lead*NHL 08* Profile, record 25 shots in one period of play on Superstar mode.
Shootout King (25)	As the lead *NHL 08* Profile, play 25 Online Ranked S hootout games.
Shootout Mastery (50)	As the lead *NHL 08* Profile, win an Online Ranked Versus game in Shootout Overtime.
Shorthanded, No Problem (25)	As the lead *NHL 08* Profile, score a Shorthanded Goal in an Online Ranked Versus game.
Shutting the Door (50)	As the lead *NHL 08* Profile, record a shutout in an Online Ranked Versus game.
Stay Out of the Box (25)	As the lead *NHL 08* Profile, play an entire game in Superstar mode without getting a penalty.
Tournament Champs (50)	As the lead *NHL 08* Profile, win the EA Sports World Tournament.

DS
PSP
PS2
PS3
Wii
Xbox
Xbox 360
Index

Ninety-Nine Nights

Unlockables

Unlockable	How to Unlock
Character Profiles	Clear all of a character's missions to unlock his or her profile
Special Stage	Complete each character's story and then play Inphyy's last stage again and you will travel to fight the King of Nights
Character: Aspharr	Clear Fort Wyandeek with Inphyy
Character: Dwingvatt	Clear all of Inphyy, Aspharr, and Myifee's missions
Character: Klarrann	Clear all of Dwingvatt's missions
Character: Myifee	Clear the Pholya Flatlands with Inphyy
Character: Tyurru	Clear all of Dwingvatt's missions
Character: Vigk Vagk	Clear all of Tyurru and Klarrann's missions

Ninja Gaiden II

Achievements

Unlockable	How to Unlock
Completed Chapter 5 (10G)	Clear Chapter 5, The Aqua Capita.
Completed Chapter 7 (10G)	Clear Chapter 7, The Flying Fortress Daedalus.
Completed Chapter 9 (10G)	Clear Chapter 9, Heart of Darkness.
Diffused the Lightening (15G)	Defeat Alexei for the second time.
Dragon Sword Master (5)	Complete the game using only the Dragon Sword.
Dual Katana Master (5)	Complete the game using only the Dragons Claw and Tigers Fang.
Eclipse Scythe Master (5)	Complete the game using only the Eclipse Scythe.
Eight of White (15G)	Beat the eighth Test of Valor.
Ended the Infernal Reign (15G)	Defeat High Infernal Priest, Dagra Dai.
Extinguished the Flame (15G)	Defeat Zedonius for the second time.
Falcon's Talons Master (5)	Complete the game using only the Falcon's Talons.
Feat of a Hundred Slashes (20)	Achieve a 100-hit combo with any weapon.
Feat of a Thousand Obliterations (20)	Defeat 1,000 enemies using Obliteration Techniques.
Feat of Ultimate Destruction (20)	Defeat 1,000 enemies using Ultimate Techniques.
Finished Chapter 1 (10)	Finish Chapter 1, "Sky City Tokyo."
Finished Chapter 2 (10)	Finish Chapter 2, "The Castle of the Dragon."
Finished Chapter 3 (10)	Finish Chapter 3, "Thunderclap of Catastrophe."
Five of Yellow (15G)	Beat the fifth Test of Valor.
Four of Green (15G)	Beat the fourth Test of Valor.
Indomitable Spirit (5G)	Choose to continue the game 100 times.
Karma of the Master Ninja (20)	Obtain all of the Crystal Skulls.
Karma of the Mentor (20)	Obtain 20 Crystal Skulls.
Karma of the Warrior (20)	Obtain 10 Crystal Skulls.
Kusari-gama Master (5)	Complete the game using only the Kusari-gama.
Lunar Staff Master (5)	Complete the game using only the Lunar Staff.
Mastered Counter Attack (5)	Successfully perform the Counter Attack Technique.
Mastered Flying Bird Flip (5)	Successfully perform the Flying Bird Flip Technique.
Mastered Flying Swallow (5)	Successfully perform the Flying Swallow Technique.
Mastered Furious Wind (5)	Successfully perform the Furious Wind Technique.

Ninja Gaiden II (continued)	
Unlockable	**How to Unlock**
Mastered Invisible Path (5)	Successfully perform the Invisible Path Technique.
Mastered Obliteration Technique (5)	Successfully perform the Obliteration Technique.
Mastered Reverse Wind (5)	Successfully perform the Reverse Wind Technique.
Mastered Shadowless Footsteps (5)	Successfully perform the Shadowless Footsteps Technique.
Mastered Ultimate Guidance (5)	Successfully perform the Ultimate Guidance Technique.
Mastered Ultimate Technique (5)	Successfully perform the Ultimate Technique.
Mastered Unrivaled Soaring (5)	Successfully perform the Ultimate Soaring Technique.
Nine of Violet (15G)	Beat the last Test of Valor.
One of White (15)	Purify the site of the first Test of Valor.
Redeemed Genshin (15G)	Defeat Genshin for the last time.
Seven of Red (15G)	Beat the seventh Test of Valor.
Silenced the Storm (15G)	Defeat Volf for the second time.
Six of White (15G)	Beat the sixth Test of Valor.
Staunched the Blood (15G)	Defeat Elizébet for the second time.
The Art of Inferno (5)	Successfully perform the Art of the Inferno Ninpo.
The Art of the Flame Phoenix (5)	Successfully perform the Art of the Flame Phoenix Ninpo.
The Art of the Piercing Void (5)	Successfully perform the Art of the Piercing V oid Ninpo.
The Art of the Wind Blades (5)	Successfully perform the Art of the Wind Blades Ninpo.
Three of Blue (15G)	Beat the third Test of Valor.
Tonfa Master (5)	Complete the game using only the Tonfa.
Two of Black (15)	Purify the site of the second Test of Valor.
Vanquished Alexei (15)	Defeat Alexei in battle.
Vanquished Elizébet (15)	Defeat Elizébet in battle.
Vanquished Genshin (15)	Defeat Genshin in battle.
Vanquished Volf (15)	Defeat Volf in battle.
Vanquished Zedonius (15)	Defeat Zedonius in battle.
Vigoorian Flail Master (5)	Complete the game using only the Vigoorian Flail.
Way of the Acolyte (100)	Complete the game on the Path of the Acolyte.
Way of the Master Ninja (100)	Complete the game on the Path of the Master Ninja.
Way of the Mentor (100)	Complete the game on the Path of the Mentor.
Way of the Warrior (100)	Complete the game on the Path of the Warrior.

Mission Mode Achievements

Complete Mission mode with the following conditions met to unlock new Downloadable Content Achievements.

Unlockable	How to Unlock
Acolyte of Missions (20)	Complete all Karma Attack Missions on Path of the Acolyte.
All Bronze (30)	Obtain all Bronze Medallions in the Survival Missions.
All Gold (30)	Obtain all Gold Medallions in the Survival Missions.
All Silver (30)	Obtain all Silver Medallions in the Survival Missions.
Eight Missions Completed (30)	Complete 8 Missions.

Ninja Gaiden II (continued)

Unlockable	How to Unlock
First Medallion (20)	Obtain a Medallion in a Survival Mission.
Four Missions Completed (30)	Complete 4 Missions.
Master Ninja of Missions (20)	Complete all Karma Attack Missions on Path of the Master Ninja.
Mentor of Missions (20)	Complete all Karma Attack Missions on Path of the Mentor.
Warrior of Missions (20)	Complete all Karma Attack Missions on Path of the Warrior.

Unlockables

Unlockable	How to Unlock
Black Jaguar Costume	Complete Path of Mentor.
Camouflage Ninja Outfit	Complete the game on Warrior.
Gamerpic of Ryu	Complete the game on Path of the Master Ninja.
Gamerpic	Collect all 30 crystal skulls.
Golden Ninja Costume	Complete the game on Path of The Master Ninja.
Music Test	Clear the game on any difficulty.
New Game +	Complete the game and save after Credit Scroll.
Old Film Filter	Beat the game.
Path of the Master Ninja	Beat Path of the Mentor.
Path of the Mentor	Beat Path of the Warrior.
Red Ninja Outfit	Complete the game on Acolyte.

Easter Eggs: Hidden Silver Xbox

At the bottom of the Statue of Liberty diagonally across from where the save point there is a false wall. Inside of the breakable wall is a silver Xbox that will regenerate Ryu's health.

Peter Jackson's King Kong

At the Main menu screen, hold (LT)+(RT)+(RB)+(LB), and press (D-pad Down), (D-pad Up), (Y), (X), (D-pad Down), (D-pad Down), (Y), (Y). This opens the Cheat Menu. Now enter any of these case sensitive passwords.

Unlockable	Password
999 ammunition	KK 999 mun
Bonuses completed	KKmuseum
God mode	8wonder
Level select	KKst0ry
Machine gun	KKcapone
One-hit kills	GrosBras
Sniper rifle	KKsn1per
Unlimited spears	lance 1nf

Phantasy Star Universe: Ambition of the Illuminus

Achievements

Unlockable	How to Unlock
De Rol Le Slayer (40 points)	Defeat De Rol Le
Mother Brain Slayer (50 points)	Defeat Mother Brain
Slterazgohg Slayer (40 points)	Defeat Slterazgohg

DS PSP PS2 PS3 Wii Xbox Xbox 360 Index

Prince of Persia Classic

Passwords

Password	Effect	Password	Effect
73232535	Level 2	51139315	Level 9
96479232	Level 3	53246739	Level 10
53049212	Level 4	32015527	Level 11
51144526	Level 5	44153123	Level 12
18736748	Level 6	96635134	Level 13
42085223	Level 7	75423134	Level 14
98564243	Level 8	89012414	End

Pro Evolution Soccer 2008

Unlockables

Unlockable	How to Unlock
Classic Argentina	Win the World Cup with Argentina.
Classic Brazil	Win the World Cup with Brazil.
Classic England	Win the World Cup with England.
Classic France	Win the World Cup with France.
Classic Germany	Win the World Cup with Germany.
Classic Italy	Win the World Cup with Italy.
Classic Netherlands	Win the World Cup with Netherlands.
Classic Players 1	At the Master League, win the Division 1 League.
Classic Players 2	At the Master League, win the Division 1 Cup.
Classic Players 3	Win the European League.
Classic Players 4	At the Master League, win the European Cup.
Classic Players 5	Win the England League.
Classic Players 6	Win the France League.
Classic Players 7	Win the Italy League.
Classic Players 8	Win the Netherlands League.
Classic Players 9	Win the Spanish League.
Classic Players 10	Win the European Cup.
Classic Players 11	Win the African Cup.
Classic Players 12	Win the American Cup.
Classic Players 13	Win the Asia/Oceania Cup.

Achievements

Unlockable	How to Unlock
100 Matches (25)	Play 100 matches.
100 Wins (20)	Win 100 matches.
Ace Striker (30)	Score an average of two goals in the last five games. Can only be achieved after playing 20 games.
Attacking Midfielder (30)	Get your successive pass ratio to 85% in the last 10 matches. Can only be achieved after playing 100 games.
Brick Wall (30)	Keep 100 clean sheets.
England League Dominated (25)	Defeat all England League teams.
Eredivisie Dominated (25)	Defeat all Eredivisie teams.
First Glory (10)	Achieved with your first victory.

Pro Evolution Soccer 2008 (continued)

Unlockable	How to Unlock
FK Goal (50)	Score a direct free kick in a Xbox LIVE Ranked match.
Gentleman (25)	Get your foul per match ratio below 1 in the last 10 matches.
Goal Getter (25)	Score 100 goals.
Hat-trick Hunter (15)	Achieved after scoring five hat-tricks.
Hat-trick Hunter (Xbox LIVE) (50)	Score a hat-trick in an Xbox LIVE Ranked Match.
High Win Ratio (100)	Win 75% of your last 20 Xbox LIVE Ranked matches
Liga Espanola Dominated (25)	Defeat all Liga Espanola teams.
Ligue 1 Dominated (25)	Defeat all Ligue 1 teams.
Long Ranger (30)	Score from a distance greater than 35 meters.
National Teams Dominated (40)	Defeat all national teams.
Owner (25)	Ball possession must be above 60% in the last 10 matches.
PK Master (20)	Win at least 10 penalty shootouts following regulation time.
Serie A Dominated (25)	Defeat all Serie A teams.
Silver Service (25)	Make 100 assists.
Sniper (40)	Get your successive shot ratio to 70% in the last 10 matches. Can only be achieved after playing 100 games.
Super Striker (40)	Score an average of 2+ goals in the last five games. Can only be achieved after playing 100 games.
Ultimate Player (100)	Unlocked when you have played 500 matches, scored 1,000 goals, and won all leagues and cups.
Winning Streak (50)	Win 10 consecutive games.
Winning Streak (Xbox LIVE) (70)	Win five successive Ranked Matches on Xbox LIVE.
World Traveler (20)	Play a game in every stadium in the game.

Project Gotham Racing

From the simple to the complex, these badges are your rewards for what you can accomplish as a driver.

Race Craft Badges

Unlockable Badge	Objective
3 Back-to-Back Wins	Successfully complete three races in a row.
5 Back-to-Back Wins	Successfully complete five races in a row.
10 Back-to-Back Wins	Successfully complete ten races in a row.
10 Races with No Penalties	Keep it clean by completing 10 races in a row without hitting another car or the barrier.
20m Power Slide	Complete a 20 meter powerslide anywhere on the track.
30m Power Slide	Complete a 30 meter powerslide anywhere on the track.
50m Power Slide	Complete a 50 meter powerslide anywhere on the track.
All Kudos Maneuvers in Game	In a single race, complete every type of Kudos maneuver there is!
All Slide Types in Race	Perform every type of slide-based Kudo maneuver there is in a race.
Big Air	Hit an incline and stay in the air for two seconds or more.

Project Gotham Racing (continued)

Unlockable Badge	Objective
Millionaire Badge	Spend one million credits on cars.
My First Win	Finish in first place in any street race.
No Penalties	Successfully complete a race without smashing into either the barriers or another car.
X3 Combo	Complete three Kudos maneuvers in a row.
X5 Combo	Complete five Kudos maneuvers in a row.
X10 Combo	Perform 10 Kudos maneuvers in a row to earn this badge.

Career Badges focus on your victories in Gotham Career mode.

Career Badges

Unlockable Badge	Objective
All Bronze	Win every match in Gotham Career mode on Easy difficulty.
All Gold	Win every match in Gotham Career mode on Hard difficulty.
All Platinum	Win every match in Gotham Career mode on Hardcore difficulty.
All Silver	Win every match in Gotham Career mode on Medium difficulty.
All Steel	Win every match in Gotham Career mode on Novice difficulty.
Complete a Championship in Manual	Drive a stick for an entire tournament.
First Medal	Earn your first medal in Gotham Career mode.
First Platinum Medal	Earn one platinum medal.
First Platinum Trophy	Complete every race in a tournament on Hardcore difficulty.
First Trophy	Win your first championship in Career mode.
Own a Car from Each Group	Buy a car from each of the five car classes.
Own All Cars	Collect every car in the game.
Pro Racer	Complete any championship on Hardcore difficulty using only a car with a manual transmission.
Race King	Complete all the wheel-to-wheel championships.
Style King	Complete all the style-based championships.
Time King	Complete all the time-based championships.

Online badges are rewarded based on your performance in Online Career mode.

Online Badges

Unlockable Badge	Objective
Clean Racer	Complete a race in Online Career mode without hitting another car or a barrier.
Complete 25 Races	Complete 25 races in Online Career mode.
Complete 50 Races	Complete 50 races in Online Career mode.
Complete 100 Races	Complete 100 races in Online Career mode.
Earn 250 Kudos in One Race	Earn 250 Kudos in a single online race.
Earn 500 Kudos in One Race	Earn 500 Kudos in one race while in Online mode.
Earn 1,000 Kudos in One Race	Earn 1,000 Kudos in a single race in Online mode.

Project Gotham Racing (continued)

Unlockable Badge	Objective
Earn 10,000K Online	Gather more than 10,000 Kudos in the Online Career mode.
Earn 25,000K Online	Gather more than 25,000 Kudos in the Online Career mode.
Earn 100,000K Online	Gather more than 100,000 Kudos in the Online Career mode.
First Online Win	Win one race on Xbox Live.
Start Last, Finish First	Overcome your tragic handicap to win this badge.
Win in Each Online Scenario	Try all of the Online Career scenarios and win at least once each.
Winning Streak X3	Win three races in a row.
Winning Streak X5	Win five races in a row.
Winning Streak X10	Win ten races in a row.

Quake 4

To enter these codes, press the Back button while playing.

Unlockable	Code
Ammo Refill for All Weapons	B, A, X, Y, Left, Right, Left
Full Health Refill	B, A, B, A, Up, Up, Down, X

Ratatouille

Passwords

Password	Effect
SPEEDY	Unlimited running
MATTELME	Unlock all single player and multiplayer minigames

Rez HD

Beyond Mode Viewpoints

There are four extra unlockable "views" in Beyond mode. Unlock them by doing the following.

Unlockable	How to Unlock
Dynamic View	Get first place in four Areas in Score Attack mode.
Far View	Get first place in three Areas in Score Attack mode.
First Person View	Get first place in five Areas in Score Attack mode.
Near View	Get first place in two Areas in Score Attack mode.

Beyond Mode Forms

Successfully complete the following tasks to unlock the corresponding form.

Unlockable	How to Unlock
Fifth Form	Four areas 100 percent shot down (Play mode)/Play time more than eight hours.
Final Form	All areas 100 percent shot down (Play mode)/Play time more than nine hours.
Fourth Form	Three areas 100 percent shot down (Play mode)/Play time more than seven hours.
Morolian Form	All areas 100 percent shot down, 100 percent Support Item (Play mode)/Play time more than 10 hours.

Rez HD (continued)

Unlockable	How to Unlock
Third Form	Two areas 100 percent shot down (Play mode)/Play time more than six hours.
Zero Form/Second Form	One area 100 percent shot down (Play mode)/Play time more than five hours.

Achievements

Unlockable	How to Unlock
Eden (20)	Clear Play mode area 5.
Firewall Buster (15)	Get a local ranking of first in boss rush.
Laser Assassin (15)	Shot down over 95 percent in area 1-5.
Power Breaker (10)	Clear score attack over 30 times.
The EARTH (20)	Clear Play mode area 1.
The Forgotten (15)	Get a local raking of first in lost area.
The MARS (20)	Clear Play mode area 2.
The Rezident (15)	Achieve 100 percent shot down and support items in areas 1-5, or play for over 10 hours.
The URANUS (20)	Clear Play mode area 4.
The VENUS (20)	Clear Play mode area 3.
Trance Hacker (15)	Clear direct assault (trance).
Ultimate Cracker (15)	Get a local ranking of first in all five areas in score attack.

Beyond Options

Unlockable	How to Unlock
Overdrive Infinity	Rank first in boss rush.

Robert Ludlum's The Bourne Conspiracy

Codes

Insert the following codes from the main screen in the cheats section.

Effect	Code
Replace the Assault Shotgun with an Automatic Shotgun	ALWAYSANOBJECTIVE
Silenced Machine Gun	HATTHEYMAKEYOUGIVE

Achievements

Unlockable	How to Unlock
30 Million Dollar Weapon (50)	Finish off 200 opponents using hand-to-hand takedowns.
Adrenaline Junkie (15)	Use three full bars of Adrenaline while driving through the streets of Paris.
Assassinate Wombosi (15)	Complete Assassinate Wombosi.
Assassinate Wombosi Passports (10)	Collect all passports in Assassinate Wombosi.
Brawler (15)	Defeat 50 opponents in hand-to-hand without performing a takedown.
Bullet Master (50)	Finish off 200 opponents using shooting takedowns.
Castel Fight (15)	Complete Castel Fight.
Civic Menace (20)	Rampage through Paris: Destroy the cafe, china shop, and 200 props.
Collateral Damage (10)	Destroy 10 explodables.
Dangerous Beginning (15)	Complete Dangerous Beginning.
Dangerous Beginning Passports (10)	Collect all passports in Dangerous Beginning.

Robert Ludlum's The Bourne Conspiracy (continued)

Unlockable	How to Unlock
Deadeye (25)	Finish 3 missions with an accuracy of at least 90%.
Disarm Renard (15)	Complete Disarm Renard.
Disarm Renard Passports (10)	Collect all passports in Disarm Renard.
Eliminate Divandelen (15)	Complete Eliminate Divandelen.
Eliminate Divandelen Passports (10)	Collect all passports in Eliminate Divandelen.
Escape the Embassy (15)	Complete Escape the Embassy.
Escape the Embassy Passports (10)	Collect all passports in Escape the Embassy.
Eye on the Target (15)	Finish a mission with an accuracy of at least 90%.
Fancy Shooter (15)	Finish off 50 opponents using shooting takedowns.
Frequent Flyer (15)	Collect 30 passports.
Good Shot Clustering (10)	Finish a mission with an accuracy of at least 75%.
Hard Slog (5)	Finish a mission without using any hand-to-hand takedowns.
Heavyweight (50)	Defeat 200 opponents in hand-to-hand without performing a takedown.
Homebody (5)	Collect 5 passports.
Laser Aim (50)	Kill 150 enemies with headshots.
Living Weapon (25)	Finish off 50 opponents using hand-to-hand takedowns.
Lucky Shot! (10)	Kill 25 enemies with headshots.
Manual Shooter (5)	Finish a mission without using a shooting takedown.
Massive Collateral Damage (25)	Destroy 50 explodables.
Master of Environment (30)	Defeat 100 opponents with contextual takedowns.
Need Glasses (5)	Finish a mission with an accuracy below 10%.
One-Man Gang (5)	Take out multiple opponents with one takedown 3 times.
Paris Chase (15)	Complete Paris Chase.
Pugilist (25)	Defeat 100 opponents in hand-to-hand without performing a takedown.
Shipyard Infiltration (15)	Complete Shipyard Infiltration.
Shipyard Infiltration Passports (10)	Collect all passports in Shipyard Infiltration.
Silence Rurik (15)	Complete Silence Rurik.
Silence Rurik Passports (10)	Collect all passports in Silence Rurik.
Student of Surroundings (10)	Defeat 20 opponents with contextual takedowns.
Survive the Professor (15)	Complete Survive the Professor.
Survive the Professor Passports (10)	Collect all passports in Survive the Professor.
Treadstone Agent (60)	Complete all campaign missions on Agent or higher.
Treadstone Assassin (100)	Complete all campaign missions on Assassin.
Treadstone Safehouse (15)	Complete Treadstone Safehouse.
Treadstone Safehouse Passports (10)	Collect all passports in Treadstone Safehouse.
Treadstone Trainee (40)	Complete all campaign missions on Trainee or higher.
World Traveler (30)	Collect all passports.
Wrecking Machine (25)	Take out multiple opponents with one takedown 30 times.

Rock Band

Unlock All

Enter quickly at the "Rock Band" title screen (disables saving).

Code	Effect
Red, Yellow, Blue, Red, Red, Blue, Blue, Red, Yellow, Blue	Unlock All Songs

Rock Band 2

Codes

Go to the "Extras" option in the main menu. Choose "Modify Game," then input the following codes. All codes disable saving.

Effect	Code
Awesome Detection	Yellow, Blue, Orange, Yellow, Blue, Orange, Yellow, Blue, Orange
Stage Mode	Blue, Yellow, Red, Blue, Yellow, Red, Blue, Yellow, Red
Unlock All Songs	Red, Yellow, Blue, Red, Red, Blue, Blue, Red, Yellow, Blue
Venue Select: Unlock All Venues	Blue, Orange, Orange, Blue, Yellow, Blue, Orange, Orange, Blue, Yellow

Roogoo

Achievements

Unlockable	How to Unlock
Acc-ROO-acy (10)	Score 100% accuracy on any 10 levels.
Bat Attack (35)	Score 100% accuracy on Bat Attack.
Bonus Drop (10)	Score perfect on any bonus stage.
Comeback ROO (13)	Win a multiplayer match with only one shape to lose remaining.
Fly Butterfly (20)	Score 100% accuracy on Fly Butterfly.
Meemoo Headache (7)	Knock off 7 consecutive Meemoo on a platform.

Roogoo (cOntinued)

Unlockable	How to Unlock
Meemoo Savvy (10)	Don't miss any shapes after the first Meemoo attack.
One Track Mind (5)	Only rotate in one direction for any 5 levels.
ROO-Race (15)	Win a multiplayer match on Bursting EX.
ROO-Worthy (10)	Unlock the first 10 levels.
Roogoo Guru (50)	Achieve par time on all levels.
Tower of Moo (15)	Beat par time on Tower of Moo.

Rush 'n Attack

Codes

A meow confirms that the code was entered correctly.

Code	Effect
At the main menu, using the D-pad, press ↑/↑/↓/↓/←/→/←/→/Ⓑ/Ⓐ	Alternate Sound FX

DS
PSP
PS2
PS3
Wii
Xbox
Xbox 360
Index

Saints Row

Codes

Dial the following phone numbers in the phone book to get the corresponding effects.

Effect	Code
12 Gauge	#920
1,000 dollars	#cashmoneyz
.44 Cal	#921
Add Gang Notoriety	#35
Add Police Notoriety	#4
Annihilator RPG	#947
AR-200	#922
AR-50	#923
AR-50 with Grenade launcher	#924
AS14 Hammer	#925
Baseball Bat	#926
Car Mass Increased	#2
Chainsaw	#927
Clear Sky	#sunny
Crowbar	#955
Drunk Pedestrians	#15
Everybody Is Shrunk	#202
Evil Cars	#16
Fire Extinguisher	#928
Flame Thrower	#929
Flashbang	#930
Full Health	#1
GAL 43	#931
GDHC	#932
Get Horizon	#711
Get Snipes 57	#712
Get Tornado	#713
Get Wolverine	#714
Giant	#200
Grenade	#933
Gyro Daddy Added to Garage	#4976
Heaven Bound	#12
Itty Bitty	#201
KC	#935
Knife	#936
Kobra	#934
Lighting Strikes	#666
Low Gravity	#18
Machete	#937
McManus 2010	#938
Milk Bones	#3
Mini-Gun	#939
Molotov	#940
Never Die	#36
Nightstick	#941
No Cop Notoriety	#50
No Gang Notoriety	#51
NR4	#942
Pedestrian Wars	#19
Pepper Spray	#943
Pimp Slap	#969
Pimpcane	#944
Pipe Bomb	#945
Player Pratfalls	#5
Raining Pedestrians	#20
RPG	#946
Samurai Sword	#948
Satchel Charge	#949
Shock Paddles	#950
SKR-9	#951
Sledge Hammer	#952
Stun Gun	#953
Super Explosions	#7
Super Saints	#8
TK3	#954
Tombstone	#956
Unlimited Ammo	#11
Unlimited Clip	#9
Unlimited Sprint	#6
Unlock D-STROY UFO	#728237
Unlock Peewee Mini Bike	#7266837
Vice 9	#957
XS-2 Ultimax	#958

Saints Row (continued)

Unlockables

Unlockable	How to Unlock
75% Mechanic Discount	Complete all 5 Chop Shop lists
Bodyguards and Ninjas	Game Progression
Brotherhood Gang Cars	Complete Last Mission for the Brotherhood
Brotherhood Melee	Complete Brotherhood Mission 6
Buggy	Complete Truck Yard Chop Shop list
Chainsaw in Weapon Cache	Complete Crowd Control (Marina) Level 6
Clothing Store Discount	Crowd Control Level 3 (Suburbs)
Crib Customization Discount	Mayhem Level 3 (Red Light)
Demo Derby Vehicles	Complete Demo Derby Level 6
Donnie's Vehicle	Complete Brotherhood Mission 2
Explosion Damage -5%	Level 3, Trail Blazing (Downtown)
Gang Customization Cars	15% hoods conquered
Gang Customization Cars	45% hoods conquered
Health Regeneration 2x	Snatch Level 3 (Chinatown)
Health Regeneration 3x	Snatch Level 6 (Chinatown)
Infinite Respect	Raise your respect past level 99
Infinite SMG Ammo	Successfully complete Snatch Level 6 Downtown
Kobra (Pistol)	Fuzz Level 3 (Projects)
Legal Lee	Beat Stilwater Prison Fight Club Level 3
Mechanic Discount	Complete Demo Derby Level 3
One Follower	Complete Prologue Mission 4
Pepper Spray in Weapon Cache	Complete Crowd Control (Marina) Level 3
Police Notoriety Reduced	Complete FUZZ Level 3, Suburbs
Police Notoriety Reduced 2	Complete FUZZ Level 6, Suburbs
Pumped Up	Fight Club Level 6 (Arena)
Pumped Up	Fight Club Level 3 (Arena)
Red Light Apartment Crib	Complete Prologue Mission 2
Reduced Bullet Damage	Heli assault Level 3 (Bario)
Ronin Gang Cars	Complete Last Mission for the Ronin
Ronin Melee	Complete Ronin Mission 6
Ronin Notoriety Reduced	Drug Trafficking Level 3 (Hotel and Marina)
Saints Hideout	Complete Prologue Mission 3
Sons of Samedi Gang Cars	Complete Last Mission for Sons of Samedi
Sons of Samedi Melee	Complete Mission "Bad Trip"
Sons of Samedi Notoriety Reduced	Complete Escort Level 3, University
Sprint Increased	Insurance Fraud level 3 (Factories)
Sprint Increased (Unlimited)	Insurance Fraud Level 6 (Factories)
The News Helicopter	Complete Sons of Samedi Mission 3
Three Followers	50% hoods conquered
Tobias	Complete Sons of Samedi Mission 3
Troy	Beat Stilwater Prison Fight Club Level 6
Two Followers	25% hoods conquered

Saints Row (continued)

Unlockable	How to Unlock
Unlimited Pistol Ammo	Fuzz Level 6 (Projects)
Vehicle Delivery	Escort Level 3 (Red Light)
X2 Ultimax (Shotgun)	Drug Trafficking Level 3 (Airport)
Zombie Carlos	Call eye for an eye after you complete the brother hood story

Schizoid

Achievements

Unlockable	How to Unlock
21st Century Schizoid Man (15)	Complete level 21 ("Tyger Tyger") either in Local Co-Op, Xbox LIVE, or Uberschizoid.
Barber of Schizzville (20)	Shave the Orbiddles from 8 Astramoebas on a level, without destroying Astramoebas or losing a life.
Corpus Callosum Severed (20)	Complete level 119 ("Ragnarok") in Uberschizoid mode.
Flitt Breeder (10)	Get a gold medal on level 5 ("My Man Flitt") without destroying any Flitts.
Huevos Done Naked (20)	Gold level 47 ("Los Huevos") without activating any power-ups.
One Mind, Two Goals (20)	Earn 20 silver or gold medals in Uberschizoid mode.
Playing the Field (15)	Play a game in each mode: Xbox LIVE, Local Co-Op, Wingman Bot Training, and Uberschizoid.
Schiz Hunter (20)	Destroy 30 Schizzes on a single level, using power-ups and without losing any lives.
Schizoid Sensei (20)	Earn 10 medals (any combination of gold, silver, and bronze) over Xbox LIVE.
Seafood Buffet (20)	Destroy 2,500 Scorpios.
Sploderific (10)	Destroy all enemies on level 12 ("Smartbomb") with a single smartbomb.
Wired (10)	Destroy an enemy with a razorwire.

Shrek the Third

Gold

Code	Effect
Up B, Down, Up, Right, Left	Receive 10,000 gold coins

Skate

Best Buy Clothes

Code	Effect
Up, Down, Left, Right, X, RB, Y, LB	Unlock exclusive Best Buy clothes

Unlock Dem Bones Character

Unlockable	How to Unlock
Dem Bones	Break each bone in your body at least 3 times

The Simpsons Game

Unlockables

Go into the "Extras" section of the main menu and insert the following codes. If the code is accepted, you hear a sound effect.

Unlockable	How to Unlock
All Homer's Costumes and Trophies	⇨,⇦,Ⓧ,Ⓧ,Ⓨ,R1
All Lisa's Costumes and Trophies	⇦,⇨,Ⓨ,Ⓨ,Ⓧ,L1
All Marge's Costumes and Trophies	Ⓧ,Ⓨ,Ⓧ,Ⓧ,Ⓨ,L1
All Bart's Costumes and Trophies	Ⓨ,Ⓧ,Ⓨ,Ⓨ,Ⓧ,R1

Achievements

Unlockable	How to Unlock
A Passive Fish (15)	Finish The Day of the Dolphin.
Back to the Futurama (5)	Win time challenge for Five Characters in Search of an Author.
Burger Victory (10)	Finish Around the World in 80 Bites.
Burns Baby Burns (10)	Finish Lisa the Tree Hugger.
Challenger (50)	Win every time challenge.
Chocolate Heaven (5)	Win time challenge for The Land of Chocolate.
Chocolate Victory (10)	Finish The Land of Chocolate.
Cloud Nine (100)	Finish Game Over.
Clown Around (5)	Win time challenge for Shadow of the Colossal Donut.
Complete Package (150)	Finish every episode, find every collectible, and discover every Video Game Cliché Moment.
Doggie Dazed (25)	Finish Grand Theft Scratchy.
Doll Crazy (50)	Find all of Lisa's Malibu Stacy Seals.
Dragon Slayer (25)	Finish NeverQuest.
Dufftacular Finish (50)	Find all of Homer's Duff Bottle Caps.
Engine Fun (5)	Win time challenge for Enter the Cheatrix.
Fast Times (50)	Beat every episode target time.
Fight the Power (10)	Finish Mob Rules.
Goes to 11 (30)	Find all of the collectibles in Springfield.
Hairs to You (50)	Find all of Marge's Try-n-Save Coupons.
Heavenly Joy (5)	Win time challenge for Game Over.
Heavenly Score (20)	Get a perfect score on the final Boss battle.
Heist Hijinx (10)	Finish Bartman Begins.
Hot Coffee (5)	Win time challenge for Grand Theft Scratchy.
Maki Roll Mania (5)	Win time challenge for Big Super Happy Fun Fun Game.
Mall Rising (5)	Win time challenge for Invasion of the Yokel-Snatchers.
Mmm Donut (15)	Finish Shadow of the Colossal Donut.
My Precious (5)	Win time challenge for NeverQuest.
Nice Cans! (5)	Win time challenge for The Day of the Dolphin.
On the Matt (40)	Finish Five Characters in Search of an Author.
Poster Paster (50)	Find all of Bart's Krusty Kollectible Koupons.
Power Up! (15)	Finish Enter the Cheatrix.
Press START to Play (5)	Easiest achievement...ever.
Pwnd (0)	Dude, need help? You've died, like, 10 times...
Save the Simpsons (15)	Finish Bargain Bin.
Shooters Rejoice (5)	Win time challenge for Medal of Homer.

The Simpsons Game (continued)

Unlockable	How to Unlock
Sim Sandwich (5)	Win time challenge for Bargain Bin.
Sparkling Defeat (25)	Finish Big Super Happy Fun Fun Game.
Steady Mobbin' (5)	Win time challenge for Mob Rules.
Table Smasher 2000 (5)	Win time challenge for Around the World in 80 Bites.
The Alienator (15)	Finish Invasion of the Yokel-Snatchers.
Up and Atom (5)	Win time challenge for Bartman Begins.
Victory at Sea! (25)	Finish Medal of Homer.
Wood Chippin' (5)	Win time challenge for Lisa the Tree Hugger.
Worst Cliché Ever (50)	Find all of the Video Game Cliché Moments.

Small Arms

Unlockables

Unlockable	How to Unlock
Shooting Range Practice	Beat Mission mode
Billy Ray Logg	Beat him in Mission mode with any character
ISO-7982	Complete Mission mode
Mousey McNuts	Beat him in Mission mode with any character
Professor Von Brown	Beat him in Mission mode with any character

Smash TV

Invincibility

Code	Effect
Press Ⓐ+Ⓨ	Become invincible. This code must be entered in every room. You can move around and change the angle of your shooting. If you stop shooting, the code deactivates. Don't stop shooting unless you want to pick up a new weapon or prize.

Sonic the Hedgehog 2

Code	Effect
17	Play Invincibility Music
65	Plays a Shifting Sound
09	Plays Casino Night Zone 1-Player Music
19	Plays Sonic 2 Theme

Soulcalibur IV

Items/Weapons

Unlockable	How to Unlock
Advanced Equipment	Achieve 20 achievements.
All Weapons for a Character	Clear Story mode with that character.
Animal Head Equipment	Achieve 25 achievements.
Basic Equipment	Achieve 5 achievements.
Intermediate Equipment	Achieve 15 achievements.
Leviathan and Voodoo Equipment	Achieve 30 achievements.
More Equipment	Achieve 10 achievements.

Characters

Unlockable	How to Unlock
Algol	Beat Story mode with a character that faces him as the last boss (Mitsurugi, Taki, etc.).

Soulcalibur IV (continued)

Unlockable	How to Unlock
Amy	Purchase her in the Character Creation for 4,000 gold.
Angol Fear	Defeat her in Story mode.
Ashlotte	Defeat her in Story mode.
Cervantes	Purchase him in the Character Creation for 4,000 gold.
Hong Yun-seong	Purchase him in the Character Creation for 4,000 gold.
Kamikirimusi	Defeat her in Story mode.
Lizardman	Buy for 4,000 gold.
Rock	Purchase him in the Character Creation for 4,000 gold.
Scheherazade	Defeat her in Story mode.
Seong Mi Na	Highlight and purchase for 4,000 gold.
Setsuka	Highlight and purchase for 4,000 gold.
Shura	Defeat her in Story mode.
Sophitia	Purchase her in the Create a Soul mode for 4,000 Gold.
Talim	Buy her for 4,000 gold in Character Creation mode.
The Apprentice	Beat Arcade mode with Yoda.
Yoshimitsu	Highlight and purchase for 4000 gold.
Zasalamel	Buy him for 4,000 gold in Character Creation mode.

Tower of Lost Souls Hidden Items (Ascending)

Unlockable	How to Unlock
01f Soldier's Hat	Clear stage while taking no damage.
02f Warrior Trousers	Clear stage with no ring outs from either side.
03f Pauldron	Switch with ally more than 2 times.
04f Warlord's Belt	Perform 3 attack throws.
05f Clergy Clothes	Defeat an enemy with a ring out.
06f Wonder Jacket	Throw an opponent.
07f Warrior Trousers	Clear the stage without missing any attacks.
08f Armor Ring: Ice Mirror	Switch characters twice.
09f Scarlett Blossoms	Guard against the opponent's attack 3 times in a row.
10f Silver Boots	Guard the opponent's attack 10 times in a row.
11f Grim Horn	Defeat all enemies with a critical finish.
12f Magus Cloth	Defeat all enemies with ring outs.
13f Pegasus Sallet	Destroy all the walls.
14f Stage: Phantom Pavilion Seesaw	Perform guard impact more than 3 times.
15f Submissions Belt	Clear the stage using only the A and G buttons.
16f Warlord's Belt	Clear the stage with 0 time remaining.
17f Arm Bandages	Execute a 5+ combo.
18f Kouchu Kabuto	Stand on all corners of the stage.
19f Longhua Qippo	Switch with ally more than 5 times.
20f Life Gem: Sun	Clear the stage with a critical finish.
21f Longhua Qippo	Voluntarily ring yourself out.
22f Honor Boots	Perform more than 4 counter hits.
23F Frilled Skirt	Guard more than 3 times in a row.

DS
PSP
PS2
PS3
Wii
Xbox
Xbox 360
Index

Soulcalibur IV (continued)

Unlockable	How to Unlock
24f Protect Gem: Cardinal Directions	Perform a combo with more than 240 damage.
25f Zhuque Changpao	Throw more than 5 times.
26f Warthog Cuirass	Execute a 10+ combo.
27f Iron Gauntlets	Clear the stage with no damage taken.
28F Aculeus Suit	Opponent guards a guard break attack at least twice.
29f Menghu Boots	Switch with ally 5+ times.
30f Spirit Gem: Noniple Heads	Clear stage without guarding.
31f Longming Qippo	Perform 5+ Just Inputs.
32f Vane Mask	Perform a low throw.
33f Battle Dress	Perform 3 attack throws.
34f Power Gem: Warrior Princess	Perform guard impact 3+ times.
35f Warthog Pauldrons	Clear without switching.
36f Parlor Blouse	Clear stage with 0 time remaining.
37f Siren's Helm	Defeat all enemies with critical finishes.
38f Gorgon Fauld	Defeat all enemies with ring out.
39f Kingfisher Greaves	Clear the stage without changing position.
40f Deer Head	Execute a 5+ combo.
41f Minotaur	Perform 5+ Just Inputs.
42f Demonic Gloves	Clear the stage without letting opponents invoke a skill.
43f Repel Gem: Iron Shell	Perform an over the back throw.
44f War Cloak	No ring outs either side.
45f Tiger Lily Kabuto	Defeat enemies without using any skills.
46f Butterfly Salet	Defeat enemies without using any skills.
47f Succubus Boots	Throw 5 times.
48f Life Dem: Jade	Clear stage with a character equipped with the "invisible" skill.
49f Horns of Calamity	Clear stage with no attacks missing.
50f Tiger Lily Breastplates	Execute a 10+ combo.
51f Tiger Lily Fauld	Perform more than 4 counter hits.
52f Feathered Wings	Clear stage with a critical finish.
53f Blade Ring: Demon Lord	Defeat all enemies with a ring out.
54f Leviathan Pauldron	Destroy all the walls.
55f Priestess Kimono	Perform 3 attack throws.
56f Leviathan Burgonet	Perform a combo with more than 240 damage.
57f Voodoo Armlets	Voluntarily perform a ring out.
58f Tiger Pauldrons	Defeat all enemies without any skills equipped.
59f Voodoo Greaves	Guard an enemy's attack 10 times in a row.
60f Voodoo Breastplate	Clear the stage without switching character.

Tower of Lost Souls Reward Items (Descending)

Unlockable	How to Unlock
B05	Dark Knight's Cloak
B10	Blade Ring: Raging Thunder

Soulcalibur IV (continued)

Unlockable	How to Unlock
B15	Lapin Chapeau
B20	Repel Gem: Fox Demon
B25	Succubus Gauntlets
B30	Demonic Armor
B35	Demonic Pauldrons
B40	Voodoo Crown

Create-a-Soul Items/Weapons

Unlockable	How to Unlock
Advanced Equipment	Achieve 20 achievements.
All Weapons for a Character	Clear Story mode with that Character.
Animal Head Equipment	Achieve 25 achievements.
Basic Equipment	Achieve 5 achievements.
Intermediate Equipment	Achieve 15 achievements.
Leviathan and Voodoo Equipment	Achieve 30 achievements.
More Equipment	Achieve 10 achievements.

Easter Eggs

Unlockable	How to Unlock
Metallic Characters	At the Character Select screen, hold down ® and choose a character by pressing Ⓐ. When the battle begins, your character is metallic.

Achievements

Unlockable	How to Unlock
Apprentice (5)	Play 3 characters in any mode.
Art Connoisseur (5)	Explore the different areas in the museum.
Champion (25)	Beat Time Attack mode in under 4 minutes.
Close Call (15)	Defeat an opponent under adverse conditions.
Conqueror (25)	Beat 25 opponents in Extra Survival mode.
Edge Master (30)	Beat Arcade mode with all characters.
Guardian (15)	Perform 25 consecutive bursts with Freestyle set to Guard Impact in Practice mode.
Noble Soul (25)	Beat the game in Ultra Hard without losing a round.
Ring Out (15)	Finish Time Attack mode with all Ring Outs.
Summon Suffering (20)	Perform the move Summon Suffering with Ivy.
Warrior (10)	Complete Arcade mode.
Zen Warrior (10)	Play 3 characters in any mode.

Space Giraffe

Super Ox Mode

Do this after finishing the game once, when the game asks you to choose between tutorial or main game mode.

Code	Effect
Hold Ⓨ, then push Ⓐ	Play an extra 100 levels

DS
PSP
PS2
PS3
Wii
Xbox
Xbox 360
Index

Spider-Man: Friend or Foe

Codes

Venom and new Green Goblin (from the movie) can be unlocked by entering the following codes using the d-pad when standing in the Helicarrier in between levels. You hear a tone if you entered the code correctly, and they are then be selectable from the sidekick select console.

Code	Effect
↑, ↑, ↓, ↓, ←, →	Gain 5,000 upgrade points
←, ↓, →, →, ↓, ←	New Green Goblin
←, ←, →, ↑, ↓, ↓	Venom

Star Trek: Legacy

Unlockable	How to Unlock
Unlock the U.S.S. Legacy	To unlock the secret ship (and receive the achievement), beat the game once on any difficulty, then load your game. When you do, you should be on the ship buying screen right before the final mission. From there; sell and/or buy ships to make sure you have 3 Sovereign-class ships. The final ship you buy will be the U.S.S. Legacy.

Star Wars: The Force Unleashed

Codes

Input the following codes at the "Input Code" screen.

Effect	Code
All Databank Entries Unlocked	OSSUS
All Force Push Ranks Unlocked	EXARKUN
All Saber Throw Ranks Unlocked	ADEGAN
All Talents Unlocked	JOCASTA
Combo Unlock	RAGNOS
Incinerator Trooper	PHOENIX
Makes Levels Mirrored	MINDTRICK
New Combo	FREEDON
New Combo	LUMIYA
New Combo	MARAJADE
New Combo	MASSASSI
New Combo	SAZEN
New Combo	YADDLE
Proxy Skin Code	PROTOTYPE
Shadowtrooper Costume	BLACKHOLE
Snowtrooper	SNOWMAN
Stormtrooper Commander Costume	TK421BLUE
Unlock All Lightsaber Crystals	HURRIKANE
Unlock Emperor Costume	MASTERMIND
Unlocks All 32 Costumes	SOHNDANN
Unlocks All Force Combos	MOLDYCROW
Unlocks Bail Organa Costume	VICEROY
Unlocks Deadly Saber	LIGHTSABER
Unlocks Kashyyyk Trooper Costume	TK421GREEN
Unlocks Maximum Force Powers	KATARN

Star Wars: The Force Unleashed (continued)	
Unlocks Maximum Force Repulse Ranks	DATHOMIR
Unlocks Scout Trooper Costume	FERRAL
Unlocks Sith Master difficulty	SITHSPAWN
Unlocks Stormtrooper Costume	TK421WHITE
Unlocks the Aerial Ambush Combo	VENTRESS
Unlocks the Aerial Assault Combo	EETHKOTH
Unlocks the Ceremonial Jedi Robes	DANTOOINE
Unlocks the Devastating Lightsaber Impale	BRUTALSTAB
Unlocks the Drunken Kota Costume	HARDBOILED
Unlocks the Jedi Adventure Robes	HOLOCRON
Unlocks the Master Kento Costume "The Apprentice's Father"	WOOKIEE
Unlocks the Rahm Kota Costume	MANDALORE
Unlocks the Saber Slam Combo	PLOKOON
Unlocks the Saber Sling Combo	KITFISTO
Unlocks the Sith Slash Combo	DARAGON
Unlocks the Sith Stalker Armor	KORRIBAN

Stranglehold

Achievements

Unlockable	How to Unlock
Asplosion (20)	In multiplayer, kill an opponent with an explosive in Slums Downpour.
Barrage Specialist (10)	Use the Barrage special move with every weapon.
Be the Master (20)	Kill 100 opponents as John Woo in Multiplayer matches.
Boomtown (20)	In multiplayer, kill an opponent with an explosion in Slums Courtyard.
Bullet Ballet (20)	Kill 50 opponents while in Tequila Time in Multiplayer matches.
Bulletproof (40)	Win a multiplayer match without using a health pack.
Castaway (20)	In multiplayer, kill an opponent on the Heavy Machine Gun platform in Tai O Settlement.
Chicago History Museum Completed (20)	Complete the Chicago History Museum level on any difficulty setting.
Chow Would Be Proud (15)	Kill 10 enemies with a five-star kill rating.
Deadly World (25)	Kill 50 enemies by using the environment instead of guns.
Death by Swing (25)	Kill 50 enemies while hanging from a chandelier.
Death from Above (20)	In multiplayer, kill an opponent with a falling object in Kowloon Market.
Diplomatic Immunity (20)	In multiplayer, kill an opponent in the hull of the ship in Naval Exercise.
Fisticuffs (10)	In multiplayer, kill an opponent with a melee attack.
Freedom! (10)	Purchase all of the Multiplayer characters in the Unlock Shop.
Game Completed—Casual (40)	Complete the entire game on the Casual difficulty setting.
Game Completed—Hard (60)	Complete the entire game on the Hard difficulty setting.
Game Completed—Hard Boiled (70)	Complete the entire game on the Hard Boiled difficulty setting.
Game Completed—Normal (50)	Complete the entire game on the Normal difficulty setting.

Stranglehold (continued)

Unlockable	How to Unlock
Geronimo! (15)	Host and complete 10 multiplayer matches on the Totem Pole Gallery map.
God of Guns (40)	Win a multiplayer match without using a Tequila Bomb.
Hardboiled Killer (20)	Kill 307 opponents in Multiplayer matches.
Having a Blast (20)	In multiplayer, kill an opponent with an explosion in Fisherman's Cove.
Hong Kong Marketplace Completed (10)	Complete the Hong Kong Marketplace level on any difficulty setting.
I Don't Know How to Play Those (20)	In The Mega Restaurant level, complete the Casino or the Restaurant without using the Guitar Cases.
It's All Mine... (30)	Purchase every item in the Unlock Shop.
Jurassic Battle (15)	Host and complete 10 multiplayer matches on the Dinosaur Rotunda map.
Killing Spree (20)	Get five kills in a row without dying in a Multiplayer ranked match.
Lounge Lizard (15)	Host and complete 10 multiplayer matches on the Mega Lounge map.
Massive D (20)	Cause at least $75,000,000 of damage.
Master of Barrage (25)	Kill 100 enemies with the Barrage special move.
Master of Precision Aim (25)	Kill 50 enemies with the Precision Aim special move.
Master of Spin Attack (25)	Kill 100 enemies with the Spin Attack special move.
Meet John Woo (5)	Visit the Unlock Shop.
Mega Jackpot (15)	Host and complete 10 multiplayer matches on the Golden Dragon Casino map.
Movin' on Up (15)	Host and complete 10 multiplayer matches on the Chicago Penthouse map.
Nobody Has That Much Style... (60)	Acquire 5,000 total Style Points.
Old School (25)	On any difficulty setting, complete a level without using any of the Tequila Bomb special moves.
One Gun To Rule Them All (10)	Finish in first place in a Multiplayer ranked match.
Origami Master (35)	Collect 250 Origami Cranes.
Paleontologist (10)	In the Chicago History Museum level, completely destroy the Brachiosaurus or the T-Rex.
Rolling Death (25)	Kill 50 enemies while riding on a roll cart.
Ruthless (30)	Perform a 50 star Style Combo.
Sea Food (15)	Host and complete 10 multiplayer matches on the Tai O Drug Labs map.
Slums of Kowloon Completed (20)	Complete the Slums of Kowloon level on any difficulty setting.
Stay Dry (10)	In the Slums of Kowloon level, stay along the top pathway in the crumbling sewer area.
Tai O Completed (10)	Complete the Tai O level on any difficulty setting.
Tea Party (15)	Host and complete 10 multiplayer matches on the Kowloon Teahouse map.
Testikill (40)	In multiplayer, kill an opponent with a precision aim crotch shot.
The Killer (10)	Fire 10,000 times.

Stranglehold (continued)

Unlockable	How to Unlock
The Mega Restaurant Completed (15)	Complete The Mega Restaurant level on any difficulty setting.
Untouchable (10)	On any difficulty setting, complete a Standoff by defeating all enemies without taking any damage.
Winner Takes All (20)	Kill 50 opponents using Tequila Bombs in Multiplayer matches.
Wong's Estate Completed (25)	Complete the Wong's Estate level on any difficulty setting.
Zakarov's Penthouse Completed (15)	Complete the Zakarov's Penthouse level on any difficulty setting.

Stuntman Ignition

Passwords

Password	Effect
COOLPROP	3 props in Stunt Creator mode
NOBLEMAN	All items unlocked for Construction mode
GFXMODES	Several new camera effects and styles
Kungfoopete	Unlock all cheats
IceAge	Unlock Ice Wheels cheat
TheDuke	Unlock Nitro Addiction cheat
Imtarex	Unlock Touchable cheat
Wearefrozen	Unlock Vision Switcher cheat
fastride	Unlocks the MVX Spartan

Super Contra

Unlockable	How to Unlock
Unlimited Lives and Super Machine Gun	On the main menu, select Arcade Game, and then enter the following code: (using the D-Pad) ↑, ↑, ↓, ↓, ←, →, ←, →, Ⓑ, Ⓐ. If done correctly, the game will start up instead of backing out to the main menu. You will begin with 5 lives that never decrease when killed, and you will have a super machine gun weapon equipped at all times! Using this code disables all Achievements and you cannot upload scores to Xbox Live Leaderboards. The code remain active until you exit the game using the Exit Game option in the Pause menu.

Super Puzzle Fighter II Turbo HD Remix

Hidden Characters

Unlockable	How to Unlock
Akuma	Press ↓, while having Hsien-Ko highlighted on the Player Select screen
Anita	Press LB or RB on Donovan, then press Ⓐ
Bat	Press LB or RB on Morrigan then press Ⓐ
Dan Hibiki	Press ↓, while having Donovan highlighted on the Player Select screen

Alternate Finishing Moves

Devilot	Press ↓, while having Morrigan highlighted on the Player Select screen
Mei-Ling	Hold the LB or RB button on Hsien-Ko, then press Ⓐ

Unlockable	How to Unlock
Ken's Alternate Finishing Move	Hold LB or RB during selection of Ken
Ryu's Alternate Finishing Move	Hold LB or RB during selection of Ryu

Superman Returns

Cheat Codes

Anytime during gameplay after the Gladiator Battle first set, pause the game. Enter the following buttons to unlock the cheats. A chime confirms that the code has been entered correctly.

Unlockable	How to Unlock
Infinite Health (Metropolis)	Y, →, Y, →, ↑, ←, →, Y
Infinite Stamina	↑, ↑, ↓, ↓, ←, →, ←, →, Y, X
Unlock All Costumes, Trophies, and Theater Items	←, ↑, →, ↓, Y, X, Y, ↑, →, X
Unlock All Moves	←, Y, →, X, ↓, Y, ↑, ↓, X, Y, X

Unlockables

Unlockable	How to Unlock
Bizarro	↑,→,↓,→,↑,←,↓,→,↑ (Enter it when you load your game, at the menu that lets you choose Metropolis or Fortress of Solitude before you start the game you loaded.)
Golden Age Superman Suit	Save Metropolis from the tornadoes
Pod Suit	Beat Bizarro

Surf's Up

Passwords

Password	Effect
MYPRECIOUS	All Boards unlocked
GOINGDOWN	All Leaf Slide stages unlocked
WATCHAMOVIE	Unlocks all videos
TINYBUTSTRONG	Unlocks Arnold
THELEGEND	Unlocks Big Z
SURPRISEGUEST	Unlocks Elliot
SLOWANDSTEADY	Unlocks Geek
KOBAYASHI	Unlocks Kobayashi
IMTHEBEST	Unlocks Tank Evans

Thrillville: Off the Rails

In-Park Cheats

To enter cheats, quickly enter the following button presses while you're in any park. For most, you won't see any changes, but you will get results if you entered them correctly.

Effect	Code
$50,000	X,B,Y,X,B,Y,A
500 Thrill Points	B,X,Y,B,X,Y,X
Activate Mission Unlock	X,B,Y,X,B,Y,B
Unlock All Minigames in Party Play	X,B,Y,X,B,Y,→
Unlock All Parks	X,B,Y,X,B,Y,X
Unlock All Rides in Current Park	X,B,Y,X,B,Y,Y

Achievements

Complete each achievement to get the allotted gamerscore.

Unlockable	How to Unlock
Bandito Beater (20)	Complete Bandito Chinchilla.
Casanova (10)	Become sweethearts with 10 park guests.

Thrillville: Off the Rails (continued)	
Unlockable	How to Unlock
Challenge Champ (10)	Win 10 challenges with park guests on any minigames.
Chatter Box (10)	Fill your MyCrowd list.
Coaster Boaster (10)	Design a rollercoaster.
Coaster Dropper (10)	Build a coaster with a drop height of more than 300 ft.
Coaster Speedster (10)	Build a coaster with a top speed over 80 mph.
Crackshot (10)	Get a X5 combo multiplier in a shooting gallery.
Critics (30)	Complete the "Bribery 101!" mission in Thrillville Stunts.
Disc Jockey (10)	Collect all the Hypnodiscs.
Flippin' Great (10)	Perform a 720 backflip in Stunt Rider.
Fore! (10)	Complete a round of timed minigolf on Hard difficulty.
Games Master (40)	Complete all arcade games.
Hypnosis (30)	Complete the "Trance-Cendtal" mission in Thrillville Giant.
Karting Krazy (10)	Finish first in 20 races.
King of the Ring (15)	Win a match by knockout on Robo K.O. without losing any health.
Lunar Lunatic (15)	Complete Event Horizon 2 on Hard difficulty.
Money Maker (10)	Achieve a combined park value of $100,000.
Party Dude (10)	Play 20 party games with your friends.
Party Host (10)	Complete a four-player battle or co-op game in party play.
Perfect Clearance (15)	Pocket all the balls in one turn at the table.
Propaganda (10)	Collect all the anti-Thrillville propaganda boards.
Putt Putt Power (10)	Design a minigolf course.
Robots (30)	Complete the "Clearance Sale" mission in Thrillville Otherworlds.
Sabotage (30)	Complete the "Alien Antics" mission in Thrillville Explorer.
Sideshow Superstar (20)	Get a 5-star rating score on all sideshow games.
Smooth Move (10)	Get a 60-note combo in the entertainer minigame.
Sparkling Secret (10)	Discover all the secret areas on Sparkle Quest level 1.
Spoon Time (15)	Get 30,000 points in three moves on trampolines.
Sprint King (15)	Get a best lap time under 4'90" seconds on the first track on Autosprint 2.
Squadron Ace! (20)	Complete Squadron Ace.
Stunt Rider! (20)	Complete Stunt Rider.
Super Sparkler (20)	Complete Sparkle Quest.
Tank Commander (20)	Complete Tank Frenzy.
Teamwork (10)	Complete a minigame in co-op mode.
The Green (10)	Find all Mortimer's cash drops hidden in all parks.
The Rainbow (10)	Collect all the Nano Paint Sprayers.
Thrillville Explorer (40)	Unlock Thrillville Explorer.
Thrillville Giant (40)	Unlock Thrillville Giant.
Thrillville Holiday (50)	Unlock Thrillville Holiday.
Thrillville Otherworlds (40)	Unlock Thrillville Otherworlds.
Thrillville Phenomenon (60)	Reach park owner level 10.

Thrillville: Off the Rails (continued)

Unlockable	How to Unlock
Thrillville Sensation (40)	Reach park owner level 5.
Thrillville Superstar (50)	Rank in the top 10 on any online leaderboard for *Thrillville: Off the Rails.*
Thrillville Talent (20)	Reach park owner level 2.
Traitor (30)	Complete the "Traitors Arena" mission in Thrillville Holiday.
UFO Survivor (15)	Survive without being knocked out of the arena in Saucer Sumo on normal difficulty.
White Knuckle Ace (10)	Build all WHOA pieces.
Whoa (10)	Finish a coaster using a WHOA piece.
Winner! (20)	Successfully win 20 multiplayer battle games.

Tiger Woods PGA Tour 07

Enter this password in the Passwords menu under options.

Unlockable	Code
Crowd has big heads	tengallonhat

Tiger Woods PGA Tour 08

Passwords

Password	Effect
cream	Unlimited money
allstars	Unlock all golfers
playfifa08	Unlock Wayne Rooney
greensfees	Unlocks All Courses

TMNT

Codes

At the main menu screen, hold LB and enter the code, then release LB. You should hear a sound to confirm you entered the code right.

Code	Effect
AABA	Unlocks challenge map 2
BYAX	Unlocks Don's big head goodie

TNA iMPACT!

Arenas

Unlockable	How to Unlock
Armoury Arena	Defeat James Storm in Story mode
England Arena	Accumulate 420,000 Style Points
Freedom Center Arena	Become the X Division Champion in Story mode
Japanese Arena	Defeat the Motor City Machine Guns in Story mode
Mexican Arena	Win the Mexican Gauntlet Match in Story mode
Vegas Arena	Defeat Kurt Angle in Story mode

Unlockables

Unlockable	How to Unlock
Abyss	Win Abyss in Story mode Part 6
Benny the Clown (from Story mode, Chapter Two)	350,000 SP
Brother Ray	Beat Team 3D in Story mode
Don West	Earn 260,000 Style Points

DS PSP PS2 PS3 Wii Xbox Xbox 360 Index

TNA iMPACT! (continued)

Unlockable	How to Unlock
Eric Young	Win your tag match in Story mode
Jay Lethal	Beat Jay Lethal in Story mode
Jeff Jarrett	Win Jarrett in Story mode Part 6
Senshi	Earn 200,000 Style Points
Sonjay Dutt	Beat Sonjay Dutt in Story mode
Suicide	Complete Story mode, and Suicide is unlocked after the credits are finished
Tomko	Beat Tomko and AJ Styles in Story mode

Tom Clancy's Ghost Recon Advanced Warfighter

When the game is paused, enter these codes while holding (BACK), (LT), (RT).

Unlockable	Code
Full Life	(L1), (L1), (RB), (X), (RB), (Y)
Scott Mitchell Invincible	(Y), (Y), (X), (RB), (X), (L1)
Team Invincible	(X), (X), (Y), (RB), (Y), (L1)
Unlimited Ammo	(RB), (RB), (L1), (X), (L1), (Y)

Enter this code on the Mission Select screen while holding (BACK), (LT), (RT).

Unlockable	Code
All Levels	(Y), (RB), (Y), (RB), (X)

Tom Clancy's Ghost Recon Advanced Warfighter 2

Enter this password as a name.

Unlockable	Code
FAMAS in Quick Missions Only (works in Australian version only)	GRAW2QUICKFAMAS

Tom Clancy's Rainbow Six Vegas

Unlockable	How To
01 Private 2nd Class	All Starting Equipment
02 Private 1st Class	Headgears 1: Tactical Helm, Balaclava
03 Specialist	Rainbow Weapons: MP7A1, SIG552, USP40
04 Corporal	Camo 1: Desert, Urban, Russian, Guerrilla, Fall, Desert 2
05 Sergeant	Tactical Armor: Raven Recon Armor, Vulture Combat Armor, Falcon Assault Armor
06 Staff Sergeant	Headgears 2: 3 Hole Balaclava, Baseball Cap, Breathing Mask
07 Sergeant First Class	Camo 2: Flecktarn, Orange, Swedish, War2k5, Alpen, White
08 Master Sergeant	Freedom Fighter weapons: AK47, Raging Bull, SV98
09 First Sergeant	Headgears 3: Bonnie Hat, Beret, Tinted Goggles
10 Sergeant Major	Black Market Armor: Typhoon Recon Armor, Cyclone Combat Armor, Hurricane Assault Armor
11 2nd Lieutenant	Camo 3: Pink, Blue, Woodland, Wasp, Sand, Crimson
12 1st Lieutenant	Headgears 4: Half-Face Mask, Reinforced Helm, Tactical Goggles
13 Captain	Merc Weapons: MG36, SPAS12, Deagle
14 Major	Military Armor: Vier Recon Armor, Diamondback Combat Armor, Anaconda Assault Armor

Tom Clancy's Rainbow Six Vegas (continued)

Unlockable	How To
15 Lt. Colonel	Camo 4: Yellow Urban, Red Urban, Tiger, Rust, Urban 2, Grey
16 Colonel	Headgears 5: Ballistic Face Mask, Riot Helm, NVGs
17 Elite	Camo 5: Custom 1, Custom 2, Custom 3

Tom Clancy's Rainbow Six Vegas 2

Codes

During gameplay, pause the game, hold the right shoulder button, and enter the following codes.

Unlockable	How to Unlock
GI John Doe Mode	L1,L1,A,R1,R1,B,L1,L1,X,R1,R1,Y
Super Ragdoll	A,A,B,B,X,X,Y,Y,A,B,X,Y
Third Person Mode	X,B,X,B,L1,L1,Y,A,Y,A,R1,R1

Weapons

When you are customizing your character, hold down the right bumper and insert the following code.

Unlockable	How to Unlock
AR-21 Assault Rifle	↓,↓,↑,↑,X,B,X,B,Y,↑,↑,Y

Comcast Multiplayer Map

At the main menu, go to the Extras menu, select Comcast Gift, then enter the following password.

Password	Effect
Comcast faster	Comcast multiplayer map

Achievements

Unlockable	How to Unlock
Ace of Spades (15)	Perform five consecutive kills without dying in an adversarial match without respawns.
Bring It On! (10)	Complete a Terrorist Hunt mission at the hardest difficulty.
Cluster Bomb (10)	Kill three enemies at once using explosives with at least six players present.
Come Closer (20)	Kill 100 enemies using a shotgun with at least six players present.
Completed Convention Center (25)	Complete Convention Center in Story mode at any djfficulty.
Completed Estate (25)	Complete Estate in Story mode at any difficulty.
Completed Nevada Desert (25)	Complete Nevada Desert in Story mode at any difficulty.
Completed Old Vegas (25)	Complete Old Vegas in Story mode at any difficulty.
Completed Pic des Pyrénées (25)	Complete Pic des Pyrénées in Story mode at any difficulty.
Completed Recreational Center (25)	Complete Recreational Center in Story mode at any difficulty.
Completed Theater (25)	Complete Theater in Story mode at any difficulty.
Covert Ops Specialist (10)	Extract the intel item 10 times with at least six players present.
Demo Expert (10)	Defuse 10 bombs in Attack & Defend with at least six players present.

Tom Clancy's Rainbow Six Vegas 2 (continued)

Unlockable	How to Unlock
Don't Mess With Me (45)	Kill 1,000 enemies in multiplayer adversarial with at least six players present.
Double or Nothin' (10)	Win two ranked matches in a row.
Elite (50)	Achieve the rank of Elite.
Extreme Hunter (50)	Complete all Terrorist Hunt missions on Realistic difficulty.
Eye of the Sniper (30)	Kill 500 enemies in multiplayer adversarial with at least six players present.
Freedom Shall Prevail (75)	Complete the Story mode on Realistic difficulty.
Gimme a High Five! (10)	Complete five scenes as Bishop's teammate, Knight, in co-op Story mode at any difficulty.
Gun Shark (25)	Kill 300 enemies in multiplayer adversarial with at least six players present.
Haute Couture (10)	Create your own custom camouflage.
Here's for a Wicked Five! (20)	Complete 10 scenes as Bishop's teammate, Knight, in co-op Story mode at any difficulty.
I Like the Sound It Makes (25)	Kill 150 terrorists with a Shotgun.
Kamikaze (10)	Plant and detonate 10 bombs in Attack & Defend with at least six players present.
Machine Gunner (20)	Kill 100 enemies using a Light Machine Gun with at least six players present.
My Hero! (10)	Rescue both Hostages 10 times in Attack & Defend with at least six players present.
My Name Is Sam (25)	Neutralize five terrorists in a row by performing headshots using a Sound Suppressor.
Natural Leader (15)	Lead your team to Victory 20 times in Team Leader with at least six players present.
Novice Hunter (5)	Complete your first Terrorist Hunt mission at any difficulty.
Officer (30)	Achieve the rank of Officer.
One Shot, One Kill (30)	Kill 100 enemies using a Sniper Rifle with at least six players present.
Pointman (10)	Kill 50 enemies in multiplayer adversarial with at least six players present.
Private First Class (10)	Achieve the rank of Private First Class.
Rappel King (20)	Kill 25 enemies while suspended from a rope.
Royal Flush (30)	Win 100 adversarial matches with at least six players present.
Short Controlled Bursts (15)	Kill 100 enemies using an Assault Rifle with at least six players present.
Sidearm Frenzy (25)	Kill 100 enemies using a Pistol with at least six players present.
Spray and Pray (15)	Kill 100 enemies using a Sub-Machine Gun with at least six players present.
That Wasn't So Hard (5)	Complete a scene as Bishop's teammate, Knight, in co-op Story mode at any difficulty.
The Ace Always Wins (5)	Win your first ranked match online.
The House Always Wins (15)	Host and win 10 matches with at least six players present.
Three of a Kind (15)	Win three consecutive ranked matches in a row.

Tom Clancy's Rainbow Six Vegas 2 (continued)

Unlockable	How to Unlock
Triggerman (20)	Kill 150 enemies in multiplayer adversarial with at least six players present.
True Identity (20)	Use the Xbox Live Vision to create a character with your appearance.
Veteran Hunter (20)	Complete five Terrorist Hunt missions at any difficulty.
Weapon Collector (30)	Unlock every weapon in the game.

Tom Clancy's Splinter Cell Double Agent

Unlockables

Unlockable	How to Unlock
Spy—Second Skin	Achieve RECRUIT level (with a general average higher that 1%)
Spy—Third Skin	Achieve SPECIAL AGENT level (with a general average higher than 45%)
Uspilon Forces—Second Skin	Achieve FIELD AGENT level (with a general average higher than 20%)
Upsilon Forces—Third Skin	Achieve COMMANDER level (with a general average higher than 95%)
Unlock All Multiplayer maps	Win 6 games as a Spy, 6 games as a UPSILON Force member, and play 25 games overall.
Electric Lock Pick	Complete the primary objectives in JBA HQ 1
EMP Device—Enhanced	Complete the primary objectives in JBA HQ 1
EMP Grenade	Complete the secondary objectives in the Iceland Assignment
EMP Grenade Attachment	Complete the secondary objectives in the Cozumel Assignment
Explosive Sticky Camera Attachment	Complete the secondary objectives in the Iceland Assignment
Frag Grenade Attachment	Complete the primary objectives in JBA HQ 3
Gas Grenade	Complete the primary objectives in JBA HQ 1
Gas Grenade Attachment	Complete the secondary objectives in the Cozumel Assignment
Hacking Device—Force Hack Upgrade	Complete the primary objectives in JBA HQ 2
Hacking Device—Software Upgrade	Complete the secondary objectives in the Shanghai Assignment
Night Vision—Enhanced	Complete the primary objectives in JBA HQ 3
Shotgun Shell Attachment	Complete the secondary objectives in the Okhotsk Assignment
Smoke Grenade - Attachment	Complete the secondary objectives in the Shanghai Assignment
Sonic Grenade Attachment	Complete the primary objectives in JBA HQ 2
Ultrasonic Emitter	Complete the secondary objectives in the Ellsworth Assignment
Wall Mine—Flash	Complete the secondary objectives in the Okhotsk Assignment
Wall Mine—Stun	Complete the secondary objectives in the Ellsworth Assignment

Tom Clancy's Splinter Cell Double Agent (continued)

Unlockable	How to Unlock
Ending A: Good	NSA trust above 33%, and you managed to save at least two of the three targets.
Ending B: Normal	NSA trust below 33%, but you managed to save the three targets. Or destroy two of the three targets, and NSA trust above 33%.
Ending C: Bad	Destroy/Kill all three targets. Or Destroy/Kill two of the targets, and NSA trust below 33%.

Tomb Raider Legends

Enter these codes in game. Codes can not be used until they are unlocked.

Unlockable	Code
Bulletproof	Hold LT press A, RT, Y, RT, X, LB
Draw enemies' health	Hold LT press X, B, A, LB, RT, Y
Excalibur	Hold LB press Y, A, B, RT, Y, LT
Infinite Assault Ammo	Hold LB press A, B, A, LT, X, Y
Infinite Grenade Launcher Ammo	Hold LB press LT, Y, RT, B, LT, X
Infinite Shotgun Ammo	Hold LB press RT, B, X, LT, X, A
Infinite SMG Ammo	Hold LB press B, Y, LT, RT, A, B
One Shot Kills	Hold LT press Y, A, Y, X, LB, B
Soul Reaver	Hold BLK press A, RT, B, RT, LT, X
Textureless Mode	Hold LT press BLK, A, B, A, Y, RT

Tony Hawk's American Wasteland

In the Options menu, select the Cheats menu and enter these passwords. (Note: case sensitive)

Unlockable	Password
Matt Hoffman	the_condor
Perfect Grinds	grindXpert
Perfect Manuals	2wheels!

Tony Hawk's Project 8

Enter these passwords in the Cheats menu.

Unlockable	Password
All decks unlocked and free except for inkblot deck and Gamestop deck	needaride
All specials in shop	yougotitall
Travis Barker	plus44
Grim Reaper (Freeskate)	enterandwin
Jason Lee	notmono
Anchor Man	newshound
Big Realtor	shescaresme
Christian Hosoi	hohohosoi
Colonel and Security Guard	militarymen
Inkblot Deck	birdhouse
Kevin Staab	mixitup
Nerd	wearelosers
Photographer Girl and Filmer	themedia
Zombie	suckstobedead
Dad and Skater Jam Kid	strangefellows

DS
PSP
PS2
PS3
Wii
Xbox
Xbox 360
Index

Tony Hawk's Proving Ground

Cheats

Enter the codes in the Options menu of the main menu.

Unlockable	How to Unlock
100% Branch Completion (NTT)	FOREVERNAILED
Invisible Man	THEMISSING
Mini Skater	TINYTATER
No Bails	ANDAINTFALLIN
No Board	MAGICMAN
Perfect Manual	STILLAINTFALLIN
Perfect Rail	AINTFALLIN
Super Check	BOOYAH
Unlimited Focus	MYOPIC
Unlimited Slash Grind	SUPERSLASHIN
Unlock Judy Nails	LOVEROCKNROLL

Items

Unlockable	How to Unlock
50 Extra Skill Points	NEEDSHELP
All CAS Items	GIVEMESTUFF
All Decks	LETSGOSKATE

Skaters

All Fun Items	OVERTHETOP
All Game Movies	WATCHTHIS
All Lounge Bling Items	SWEETSTUFF
All Lounge Themes	LAIDBACKLOUNGE
All Rigger Pieces	IMGONNABUILD
All Special Tricks Available	LOTSOFTRICKS
All Video Editor Effects	TRIPPY
All Video Editor Overlays	PUTEMONTOP
Full Stats	BEEFEDUP

Levels

Unlockable	How to Unlock
Unlock Air and Space Museum	THEINDOORPARK
Unlock FDR	THEPREZPARK
Unlock Lansdowne	THELOCALPARK

Unlockable	How to Unlock
Boneman	CRAZYBONEMAN
Bosco	MOREMILK
Cam	NOTACAMERA
Cooper	THECOOP
Eddie X	SKETCHY
El Patinador	PILEDRIVER
Eric	FLYAWAY
Mad Dog	RABBIES
MCA	INTERGALACTIC

Tony Hawk's Proving Ground (continued)

Unlockable	How to Unlock
Mel	NOTADUDE
Rube	LOOKSSMELLY
Shayne	MOVERS
Spence	DAPPER
TV Producer	SHAKER

Achievements

Unlockable	How to Unlock
1,000 Online Games Played (20)	Accumulate 1,000 games played.
5 out of 5! Online Domination (20)	Win all five rounds in a match with at least four gamertags in the room.
Aggro Episode (10)	Mike V's Go Epic episode completed.
All Classic (10)	Complete all Classic goals at AM ranking or better.
All Film Goals (10)	Complete all Film goals at AM ranking or better.
All Gaps (50)	Find all the Gaps on the View Gaps list.
All Hawk-man (10)	Complete all Hawk-man goals at AM ranking or better.
All Line Goals (10)	Complete all Line goals at AM ranking or better.
All Photo Goals (10)	Complete all Photo goals at AM ranking or better.
All Pro (70)	Complete all goals at PRO ranking or better.
All Skater Items (20)	Purchase all Skater Gear including unlocked items.
All Skill Goals (10)	Complete all Skill Challenges at AM ranking or better.
All Skill Upgrades (10)	Upgrade all skater skills.
All Uber Goals (20)	Complete all Lifestyle Uber Goals.
AM All Goals (40)	Complete all goals at AM ranking or better.
Bowl Skating Episode (25)	Lance's Bowl Skating episode completed.
Build Your Team (10)	Achieved "Build Your Team" Game Milestone.
Cashtastic (40)	Find all cash spots.
Climbing Episode (15)	Bam's Climbing episode completed.
Complete All Hawk-man Goals Pro (15)	Complete all Hawk-man Goals at PRO ranking or better.
Deck Milestone (10)	Achieve "Get your own skate deck" Milestone.
High Score Video (10)	Make a video worth 20,000 points.
Join Team Milestone (30)	Achieved the "Join Team" Game Milestone.
Mod All Spots (35)	Modify all environment areas.
Mod the World (25)	Daewon and Rodney's Modify the World episode completed.
NTG Episode (15)	Bob's Nail the Grab episode completed.
NTM Episode (25)	Stevie's Nail the Manual episode completed.
NTT Episode (10)	Arto's Nail the Trick episode completed.
Pro All Classic (15)	Complete all Classic goals at PRO ranking or better.
Pro All Film Goals (15)	Complete all Film goals at PRO ranking or better.
Pro All Line Goals (15)	Complete all Line goals at PRO ranking or better.
Pro All Photo Goals (15)	Complete all Photo goals at PRO ranking or better.
Pro All Skill Goals (15)	Complete all Skill Challenges at PRO ranking or better.
Rigging Episode (10)	Jeff's Rigging episode completed.

Tony Hawk's Proving Ground (continued)

Unlockable	How to Unlock
Shoe Milestone (10)	Achieve "Get your own skate shoe" Game Milestone.
Sick All Classic (40)	Complete all Classic goals at SICK.
Sick All Film Goals (40)	Completed all Film Goals at SICK.
Sick All Hawk-man (40)	Complete all Hawk-man Goals at SICK.
Sick All Line Goals (40)	Complete all Line goals at SICK.
Sick All Photo Goals (40)	Complete all Photo goals at SICK.
Sick All Skill Goals (40)	Completed all Skill Challenges at SICK.
Skate Check Episode (15)	Dustin's Skate Checking episode completed.
Sponsored Milestone (15)	Achieve the "Sponsored" Game Milestone progress.
Team Built (20)	Achieved "Team Built" Game Milestone.
Thug Check Distance (5)	Knock Thug 150 feet.
Win $100,000 in Wagers Online (25)	Win enough wagers to accumulate $100,000 in winnings. Ranked matches only.

Transformers: The Game

Codes

Enter codes at the "Campaign/Bonus Features" main menu. Enter codes for each character during one of their missions. This changes the character's appearance to their Generation 1 skin. Note: Using these cheats prevents you from achieving gamerscore!

Code	Effect
Down, Left, Left, Down, Right, Right, Up	Generation 1 Skin Megatron
Up, Right, Left, Up, Down, Down, Left	Generation 1 Skin Prime
Left, Up, Down, Down, Left, Up, Right	Generation 1 Skin Jazz
Down, Down, Up, Up, Right, Right, Right	Generation 1 Skin Optimus Prime
Right, Down, Left, Left, Down, Up, Up	Generation 1 Skin Starscream
Left, Left, Up, Left, Right, Down, Right	Infinite Health—Invincible
Up, Down, Left, Right, Up, Up, Down	No Ammo Reload
Right, Left, Right, Left, Right, Left, Right	No Military or Police
Down, Up, Left, Right, Right, Right, Up, Down	Unlock All mission including 2 special mission
Right, Up, Up, Down, Right, Left, Left	Unlocks the two Cybertron missions.

Unlockables

Unlockable	How to Unlock
G1 Megatron	Collect all the Transformer Shields in the Decepticons Story mode
G1 Optimus Prime (Cartoon Model)	Find all the Autobot faction symbols during the Autobot campaign.
G1 Robo-vision Optimus	Finish the Autobot campaign.
Jazz G1 Repaint	Complete all of the "challenge" sub-missions in both Autobot and Decepticon campaigns.
Starscream G1 repaint	Complete Decepticon Story mode.

Turning Point: Fall of Liberty

Achievements

Unlockable	How to Unlock
Clingy (25)	Kill 15 enemies in a row by grappling them on any difficulty.
Combat Experience (10)	Kill 50 enemies in the campaign on any difficulty.
Combat Veteran (25)	Kill 250 enemies in the campaign on any difficulty.
Dead-eye (50)	Complete any mission with an accuracy of 80% or higher on Normal or higher difficulty.
Defender (20)	Help defend the barricade in New York on Normal or higher difficulty.
Dolly Madison Award (20)	Save the Constitution from being burned on Normal or higher difficulty.
Environmentalism (15)	Complete 40 environmental or grapple kills on any difficulty.
Exploding Monkey (20)	Kill at least four enemies with one explosion on any difficulty.
First Time for Everything (5)	Finish a multiplayer game.
Going Nuclear (30)	Rewire an Atom Bomb on Normal or Higher difficulty.
Gravity Is a Harsh Mistress (5)	Toss a paratrooper onto the streets below New York on any difficulty.
I Saved the General (20)	Rescue General Donnelly from the D.C. courthouse on Normal or higher difficulty.
Impeached (30)	Oust the false president from office on any difficulty.
Killer (20)	Get 100 ranked match kills in any mode.
Killer Instinct (30)	Get 500 ranked match kills in any mode.
Master Sniper (35)	Kill 10 enemies in a row with a headshot on any difficulty.
Maybe I Should Go Outside... (40)	Get 2,500 ranked match kills in any mode.
MVP (30)	Win an 8-player ranked or player match in Team Deathmatch mode with the highest score.
Need a Ride? (20)	Meet up with the rescue team in Washington, D.C. on Normal or higher difficulty.
Next Time Take the Stairs (5)	Fall to your death during a multiplayer game.
Oh, the Humanity! (30)	Destroy all the assault blimps at the Tower Bridge on any difficulty.
One in the Chamber (10)	Kill a player in a ranked match with the last bullet in a pistol clip.
One Man Army (45)	Kill 400 enemies in the campaign on any difficulty.
Presidential Citizens Medal (75)	Complete the campaign on Hard difficulty.
Presidential Medal for Merit (35)	Complete the campaign on Normal difficulty.
Presidential Medal of Freedom (100)	Complete the game on Insane Difficulty.
pwnt (15)	Finish an 8-player ranked or player match in Deathmatch mode with the highest number of kills.
Reservation for One (5)	Make your way down to Hotel Langteau on Normal or higher difficulty.
Run! (25)	Sprint for a total of 30 minutes throughout the campaign on any difficulty.
Save Yourself (25)	Escape from New York on any difficulty.

Turning Point: Fall of Liberty (continued)

Unlockable	How to Unlock
Sharpshooter (10)	Kill all the paratroopers as you make your way down the skyscraper on any difficulty.
Stayin' Alive (25)	Finish a ranked match in Deathmatch mode without dying.
Stowaway (30)	Sneak onto the zeppelin on Normal or higher difficulty.
Swirly Time! (5)	Drown a German in a toilet in the Tower of London on any difficulty.
Team Player (25)	Win 20 ranked matches in Team Deathmatch mode.
Turning Point (25)	Complete the campaign on any difficulty.
TV Repairs (5)	Smash an enemy's head through a TV in the White House on any difficulty.
Uberdork (25)	Win 5 ranked matches in Deathmatch mode.
World Tour (15)	Finish a multiplayer game on every map in every mode.

Bonus Codes

Unlockable	How to Unlock
Double Health Regeneration Rate	Complete the game on any difficulty.
Infinite Ammo	Complete the game on any difficulty.
Infinite Grenades	Complete the game on any difficulty.

Turok

Achievements

Unlockable	How to Unlock
5, 4, 3, 2, 1...BOOM! (15G)	Kill 3 soldiers with one Frag Grenade in the Story mode campaign.
Accuracy Award (20G)	Achieve an accuracy of 75 percent or greater with at least 20 shots fired in one ranked match.
All-Purpose Warrior (30G)	Win 10 public games of each team game option (Small Team, Large Team, Co-Op).
Angler Ribbon (20G)	Fishing anyone?
Arch-Nemesis (15G)	Kill the same player five times in a row without killing anyone else between during a public match.
Arsenal (20G)	Kill at least one enemy with every weapon in the game during public play.
Big Game Ribbon (20G)	You managed to survive Mama Scarface.
Boomstick (10G)	Destroy a dino with the stickygun during a public match.
Buddy Blowout (20G)	Play a full 8-on-8 private team game.
Co-Op 1 (30G)	Finish Co-op Map 1.
Co-Op 2 (30G)	Finish Co-op Map 2.
Co-Op 3 (30G)	Finish Co-op Map 3.
Crack Shot (15G)	Kill five opponents in a public game with headshots.
Dino Dominance (25G)	You skillfully knife-killed 50 creatures in the Story mode campaign.
Dino Hunter (15G)	Kill 20 dinos in one public game.
Exterminator (15G)	Kill 20 bugs in one public game.
Gamesman (15G)	Play a full round of each gametype in public or private matches.

Turok (continued)	
Unlockable	**How to Unlock**
Grab Bag (10G)	Kill at least one creature, one enemy, one teammate, and yourself in the same round of a public match. (Patched 1/08 to eliminate the teammate kill requirement.)
Great Round (15G)	Finish a public DM match with a Battle Rating of greater than 100.
Hometown Hero (25G)	Return five flags to your base in one public game.
Impaler Ribbon (10G)	Pin an enemy to the wall with an arrow in the Story mode campaign.
It's a Trap! (15G)	Get dinos to kill five soldiers by sticking them with the flare in the Story mode campaign.
Loud Love (15G)	Kill three soldiers with one ORO Copperhead Rocket Launcher shot in the Story mode campaign.
Man or Animal (30G)	Record 100 stealth kills of soldiers with the ORO P23 Combat Knife.
Massive Battle (10G)	Participate in a public 6-on-6 team game.
Medal of Citation (50G)	Achieve 100 player kills in ranked matches.
Multiplayer First-Class (35G)	Finish a ranked match with 100 percent accuracy and at least five kills.
Multiplayer Master-Class (40G)	Finish a ranked match with all headshots and at least five kills.
Pacifist (15G)	Play a public match with no shots fired or kills awarded, capturing the flag at least twice.
Pincushion (25G)	Pin 50 enemies with the bow in the Story mode campaign.
Practically Canadian (20G)	How aboot defending your flag, eh? And that's in ranked matches, sorry.
Primitive Weapons (15G)	Play a public match using only the bow or knife, earning at least 10 kills.
Resurrection (15G)	Finish a player match free-for-all game with at least 10 deaths and 10 kills.
Retribution (15G)	Knife-kill your rival in a public match.
Sell Your Shotguns (35G)	Just for fun, you completed "Mother Superior" without using the ORO Shotgun.
Sniper! (40G)	Head shot 10 enemies in a row during the Story mode campaign.
Thorn in Side (20G)	Kill the flag carrier five times in a ranked match.
Triple Kill (20G)	Kill three opponents within four seconds of each other in a ranked match.
Turok Campaign Ribbon (60G)	Complete the Story mode campaign on Inhuman difficulty.
Turok Defense Force (25G)	Successfully fight off 20 raptor mauls during the Story mode campaign.
Turok Service Ribbon (40G)	Complete the Story mode campaign and unlock Inhuman difficulty.
Unbreakable (30G)	Play through a ranked match without dying.

Inhuman Mode

Unlockable	How to Unlock
Inhuman Mode	Beat the game on Normal or Hard difficulty.

Two Worlds

Codes

Note that Bonus codes do NOT stop you from getting achievements. But all other codes DO. To open the code menu hold down LB + RB and hit A. A small text box appears. Now hit X to open up the keyboard menu. Remember, only codes that start with "Bonuscode" will not affect your achievements. All codes other than the Bonuscodes require you to put in "twoworldscheats 1" first before entering the code. This permanently disables achievements for this character.

Code	Effect
ec.dbg addskillpoints	Add skill points
AddGold XXXX	Adds gold, where XXXX is the amount of gold added
AddParamPoints	Adds Param Points, where X is the number of points added
AddSkillPoints X	Adds Skill Points, where X is the number of skill points added
AddExperiencePoints XXX	Adds XXX amounts of experience
Bonuscode 9728-1349-2105-2168	Armor of Darkness
BonusCode 9470-4690-1542-1152	Aziraal's Sword of Fire
Create Lockpick	Creates a lockpick
Create Personal_Teleport	Creates a Teleport Stone
Bonuscode 9470-6557-8820-9563	Great Shield of Yatolen
ec.dbg levelup	Level Up
ec.dbg skills	Makes all skills available
Create Teleport_Activator	Recover lost teleport activator
ResetFog	Reveal map
ec.dbg levels X	Sets you to level 'X'
Bonuscode 9144-3879-7593-9224	Spear of Destiny
Bonuscode 9447-1204-8639-0832	The Great Bow of Heaven's Fury
Jump2	Transports player to where mouse is pointing
PhysX.Door.RemoveAll 1	Walk through doors and walls

Ultimate Mortal Kombat 3

Codes

Enter codes at the VS screen.

Code	Effect
Player 1: LPx9, BLx8, LKx7; Player 2: LPx6, BLx6, LKx6	"Hold Flippers During Casino Run" Message
Player 1: LPx7, BLx1, LKx1; Player 2: LPx3, BLx1, LKx3	"Rain Can Be Found in the Graveyard" Message
Player 1: LPx1, BLx2, LKx3; Player 2: LPx9, BLx2, LKx6	"There Is No Knowledge That Is Not Power" Message
Player 1: LKx4; Player 2: LPx4	"Whatcha Gun Do?" Message
Player 1: BLx2; Player 2: BLx2	Blocking Disabled
Player 1: LPx6, BLx8, LKx8; Player 2: LPx6, BLx8, LKx8	Dark Kombat
Player 1: LPx1, BLx2, LKx2; Player 2: LPx2, BLx2, LKx1	Display "Skunky !!" Message
Player 1: LPx4, BLx4, LKx8; Player 2: LPx8, BLx4, LKx4	Don't Jump at Me

Ultimate Mortal Kombat 3 (continued)

Code	Effect
Player 1: LPx2, BLx2, LKx7; Player 2: LPx2, BLx2, LKx7	Explosive Combat (2 on 2 only)
Player 1: LPx6, BLx8, LKx8; Player 2: LPx4, BLx2, LKx2	Fast Uppercut Recovery Enabled
Player 1: BLx9, BLx1; Player 2: LPx1, BLx9	Kombat Zone: Bell Tower
Player 1: LPx3, BLx3; Player 2: BLx3, LKx3	Kombat Zone: Jade's Desert
Player 1: LKx4; Player 2: BLx7	Kombat Zone: Kahn's Kave
Player 1: LPx8, BLx8; Player 2: LPx2, BLx2	Kombat Zone: Kahn's Tower
Player 1: LPx6; Player 2: BLx4	Kombat Zone: Kombat Temple
Player 1: BLx5; Player 2: BLx5	Kombat Zone: Noob Saibot Dorfen
Player 1: LKx2; Player 2: LKx3	Kombat Zone: River Kombat
Player 1: LPx3, BLx4, LKx3; Player 2: LPx3, BLx4, LKx3	Kombat Zone: Rooftop
Player 1: LPx9, BLx3, LKx3	Kombat Zone: Scislac Busorez
Player 1: LPx6, BLx6, LKx6; Player 2: LPx4, BLx4, LKx4	Kombat Zone: Scorpion's Lair
Player 1: LPx1, BLx2, LKx3; Player 2: LPx9, LKx1	Kombat Zone: Soul Chamber
Player 1: BLx7, LKx9; Player 2: BLx3, LKx5	Kombat Zone: Street
Player 1: LPx8, BLx8; Player 2: BLx8, LKx8	Kombat Zone: Subway
Player 1: BLx7, LKx7; Player 2: BLx2, LKx2	Kombat Zone: The Bridge
Player 1: LPx6, BLx6, LKx6; Player 2: LPx3, BLx3, LKx3	Kombat Zone: The Graveyard
Player 1: LPx8, BLx2; Player 2: BLx2, LKx8	Kombat Zone: The Pit 3
Player 1: LPx2, BLx8, LKx2; Player 2: LPx2, BLx8, LKx2	No Fear = EB Button, Skydive, Max Countdown
Player 1: LPx9, BLx8, LKx7; Player 2: LPx1, BLx2, LKx3	No Powerbars
Player 1: BLx3, LKx3	Player 1 Half Power
Player 1: LPx7, LKx7	Player 1 Quarter Power
Player 2: BLx3, LKx3	Player 2 Half Power
Player 2: LPx7, LKx7	Player 2 Quarter Power
Player 1: LPx4, BLx4, LKx4; Player 2: LPx4, BLx4, LKx4	RandPer Kombat (Method 1)
Player 1: LPx4, BLx6; Player 2: LPx4, BLx6	RandPer Kombat (Method 2)
Player 1: LPx9, BLx9, LKx9; Player 2: LPx9, BLx9, LKx9	Revision
Player 1: LPx5, BLx5; Player 2: LPx5, BLx5	See the Mortal Kombat Live Tour !!
Player 1: LPx3; Player 2: LPx3	Silent Kombat
Player 1: LPx1; Player 2: LPx1	Throwing Disabled
Player 1: LPx6, BLx4, LKx2; Player 2: LPx4, BLx6, LKx8	Two-Player Minigame of Galaga
Player 1: BLx4, LKx4; Player 2: LPx4, BLx4	Unikoriv Referri: Sans Power
Player 1: LPx4, BLx6, LKx6 - Player 2: LPx4, BLx6, LKx6	Unlimited Run
Player 1: LPx9, BLx6, LKx9; Player 2: LPx1, BLx4, LKx1	Winner of this round battles Motaro
Player 1: BLx3, LKx3; Player 2: LPx5, BLx6, LKx4	Winner of this round battles Shao Kahn
Player 1: LPx2, LKx5; Player 2: LPx2, LKx5	Winner of this round battles Smoke
Player 1: LPx7, BLx6, LKx9; Player 2: LPx3, BLx4, LKx2	Winner of this round battles Noob Saibot

DS PSP PS2 PS3 Wii Xbox Xbox 360 Index

Ultimate Mortal Kombat 3 (continued)

Unlock and Save Hidden Characters

Choose Arcade mode, lose a match. Then let the timer run out. You have 10 seconds to enter the ultimate kombat code for the character, one at a time. After unlocking them in Arcade mode, get to the Character Select screen. Pause, then exit the game. You'll have them for the rest of that play session. Now, very important, when you start the game up the next time around, you need to first go to the Arcade mode. This loads the characters you unlocked. Just wait and get to the Character Select screen, then exit. Now you can play with the characters online. If you do not go to the Arcade mode first, you will erase the characters. Just load and exit, then play online.

Unreal Tournament 3

Achievements

Unlockable	How to Unlock
Ace (10)	Get the "Top Gun" award in 20 matches.
Armadillo (10)	Get the "Roadkill" award in 10 matches.
Around the World (20)	Win a multiplayer match on every map.
Bag of Bolts (30)	Complete Chapter 3 in Insane.
Being a Hero (10)	Return 100 Orbs in Warfare matches.
Big Game Hunter (10)	Get the "Big Game Hunter" award in 10 matches.
Brain Surgeon (10)	Get the "Head Hunter" award in 10 matches.
Connect the Dots (20)	Complete 100 Warfare matches played to at least 3 points.
Deathwish (10)	Get "Bullseye" (self-destruct to destroy an enemy) award in 20 matches.
Delivering the Hurt (10)	Have over 20 minutes of "UDamage Time."
Does Not Compute (30)	Complete Chapter 3.
Don't Taze Me Bro! (10)	Get the "Combo King" award in 10 matches.
Equal Opportunity Destroyer (20)	Win a Ranked match in every game type.
Fear the Reaper (60)	Defeat Akasha and complete the campaign in Insane.
Flag Waver (20)	Complete 100 CTF matches played to at least 3 captures.
Get a Life... (50)	Get 200 kills in multiplayer on 50 different days.
Goo God (10)	Get the "Biohazard" award in 10 matches.
Got Your back (20)	Complete 10 missions in co-op.
Hammerhead (10)	Get the "JackHammer" award in 10 matches.
Hat Trick (20)	Achieve a Hat Trick in 10 CTF or VCTF matches.
Have a Nice Day! (20)	Get the "Rocket Scientist" award in 10 matches and "Flak Master" award in 10 matches.
I Need Some Backup (10)	Complete 1 mission in co-op.
I See How It Is (10)	Complete an Instant Action match in every game mode.
I'm Not on a Holy War (60)	Defeat Akasha and complete the campaign.
Jack of All Trades (10)	Kill an enemy with every vehicle (except hoverboard).
Just Business (30)	Complete Chapter 2 in Insane.
Just Warming Up (10)	Finish playing a "Versus" Ranked match.
Killjoy (10)	End sprees in 20 matches.
Lets Get It On (20)	Complete a multiplayer match in every game type.
Like the Back of My Hand (40)	Collect every power-up on every map.
Lock and Load (10)	Complete Chapter 1.

Unreal Tournament 3 (continued)

Unlockable	How to Unlock
Never Saw It Coming (10)	Have over 20 minutes of "Invisibility Time."
Not in Kansas Anymore (30)	Complete Chapter 4.
Off to a Good Start (10)	Get the "First Blood" award in 40 matches.
Open War (30)	Complete Chapter 4 in Insane.
Paint the Town Red (20)	Complete 100 Deathmatch or Duel matches played to at least 20 kills.
Pistolero (10)	Get the "Gun Slinger" award in 10 matches.
Ranked Champion (50)	Win 500 Ranked matches.
Seeing Red (10)	Have over 20 minutes of "Berserk Time."
Serial Killer (20)	Get the "Killing Spree" award in 20 matches.
Shard-o-matic (10)	Get the "Blue Streak" award in 10 matches.
Sir Slays a Lot (20)	Get the "Monster Kill" award in 20 matches.
Soldier's Blood (30)	Complete Chapter 2.
Spice of Life (20)	Play a match with every mutator, using only 1 per match.
Strongest Link (10)	Get the "Shaft Master" award in 10 matches.
Survival of the Fittest (10)	Have over 10 minutes of "Invulnerable Time."
Thanks to All the Little People (40)	Complete a campaign in co-op.
Thirty Minutes or Less (20)	Complete 100 VCTF matches played to at least 3 captures.
Untouchable (20)	Reach 20 kills against a god-like bot in instant action without dying.
Winning Is the Only Thing (10)	Finish with the highest points in a Ranked match.

Virtua Tennis 3

Enter these codes at the main menu.

Unlockable	Code
Unlock All Courts	⇧, ⇧, ⇩, ⇩, ⇦, ⇨, ⇦, ⇨
Unlock King & Duke	⇧, ⇧, ⇩, ⇩, ⇦, ⇨, ⇦, ⇨
Unlock All Gear	⇦, ⇨, ⬇, ⇦, ⇨, ⬇, ⇧, ⇩
Test End Sequence (win one match to win tournament)	⬇, ⇦, ⬇, ⇨, ⬇, ⇧, ⬇, ⇩

Viva Piñata

Enter these passwords as names for your garden.

Unlockable	Password
Five Extra Accessories at the Pet Shop	chewnicorn
Items for Your Piñatas to Wear	goobaa nlock
Items for Your Piñatas to Wear	Bullseye
YMCA Gear	Kittyfloss

WALL-E

Cheats

Enter the following codes in the cheat section of the Bonus Features menu.

Effect	Code
All Bonus Features Unlocked	WALL-E, Auto, EVE, ZPM
All Game Contents Unlocked	M-O, Auto, ZPM, EVE
Costumes	ZPM, WALL-E, M-O, Auto

DS PSP PS2 PS3 Wii Xbox Xbox 360 Index

WALL-E (continued)

Effect	Code
Gives WALL-E Super Laser Blaster	WALL-E, Auto, EVE, Mo
Invincibility	WALL-E, M-O, Auto, M-O
Make Any Cube Any Time	Auto, M-O, Auto, M-O

Achievements

Unlockable	How to Unlock
500 Cubes (30)	Crush down 500 Cubes in the entire game.
All Concepts (30)	Get all Sketchbooks in the game.
All Echoes of EVE (30)	Find all EVE Radios.
All Echoes of WALL-E (30)	Find all WALL-E Radios.
Boosters Activity (10)	Complete the activity in the Directive level.
Crushing, Part 1 (25)	Crush down 100 Basic Cubes.
Crushing, Part 2 (25)	Crush down 100 Heavy Cubes.
Crushing, Part 3 (25)	Crush down 100 Charge Cubes.
EVE Suitcases (30)	Find all of EVE's costumes in the game.
I Am the Best! (60)	Beat the entire game.
Junk Buster Activity (10)	Complete the activity in the Directive level.
Knocking Over Humans (30)	It's possible that knocking over humans could be advantageous.
M-O Is Easily Distracted (15)	M-O will clean what is dropped on the floor in the Life on the Axiom level.
Making of the Game (5)	Watch the credits.
Panicking Protection Procedures (30)	Avoid taking damage from any humans in the Captain's Orders level.
Power to the Axiom (30)	Free all Reject Bots to enter a secret location in the Good Intentions level.
Power to the City (30)	Turn on all Power Pylons to enter a secret location in the Welcome to Earth level.
Ring Race Activity (10)	Complete the activity in the Time Together level.
Scan Racer Activity (10)	Complete the activity in the Directive level.
Short Storks (15)	Complete the Sandstorm level in 30 stork jumps or less.
Special Object, Part 1 (30)	Collect the Special Object in the Welcome to Earth level.

WALL-E (continued)	
Unlockable	**How to Unlock**
Special Object, Part 2 (30)	Collect the Special Object in the Directive level.
Special Object, Part 3 (30)	Collect the Special Object in the Sandstorm level.
Special Object, Part 4 (30)	Collect the Special Object in the Life on the Axiom level.
Special Object, Part 5 (30)	Collect the Special Object in the Good Intentions level.
Special Object, Part 6 (30)	Collect the Special Object in the Time Together level.
Special Object, Part 7 (30)	Collect the Special Object in the 100% Unsanitary level.
Special Object, Part 8 (30)	Collect the Special Object in the Captain's Orders level.
Special Object, Part 9 (30)	Collect the Special Object in the EVE Loves WALL-E level.
Super Quick Scanning (30)	Scan all WALL-E parts in less than 2 minutes in the EVE Loves WALL-E level.
Taking out the Trash Activity (10)	Complete the activity in the Time Together level.
The Cockroach (5)	Find the cockroach.
The Spoils of Steward (15)	Clear out the Stewards in the Good Intentions level.
Total Perseverance, Part 1 (15)	Beat the Welcome to Earth level without losing all health!
Total Perseverance, Part 2 (15)	Beat the Directive level without losing all health!
Total Perseverance, Part 3 (15)	Beat the Sandstorm level without losing all health!
Total Perseverance, Part 4 (15)	Beat the Life on the Axiom level without losing all health!
Total Perseverance, Part 5 (15)	Beat the Good Intentions level without losing all health!
Total Perseverance, Part 6 (15)	Beat the Time Together level without losing all health!
Total Perseverance, Part 7 (15)	Beat the 100% Unsanitary level without losing all health!
Total Perseverance, Part 8 (15)	Beat the Captain's Orders level without losing all health!
Tunnel Time Trials, Part 1 (15)	Complete all tunnels in the Directive level without running out of time.
Tunnel Time Trials, Part 2 (15)	Complete all tunnels in the Time Together level without running out of time.
WALL-E Away Activity (10)	Complete the activity in the Time Together level.
WALL-E Suitcases (30)	Find all of WALL-E's costumes in the game.

DS PSP PS2 PS3 Wii Xbox Xbox 360 Index

Index

DS PSP PS2 PS3 Wii Xbox Xbox 360 Index